D0203746

THE LETTERS OF WILLIAM AND DOROTHY WORDSWORTH

VII. *THE LATER YEARS*

PART IV

1840–1853

THE LETTERS OF WILLIAM AND DOROTHY WORDSWORTH

SECOND EDITION

VII

The Later Years

PART IV

1840–1853

REVISED, ARRANGED
AND EDITED BY

ALAN G. HILL

FROM THE FIRST EDITION
EDITED BY THE LATE
ERNEST DE SELINCOURT

CLARENDON PRESS · OXFORD

1988

Oxford University Press, Walton Street, Oxford OX2 6DP

Oxford New York Toronto
Delhi Bombay Calcutta Madras Karachi
Petaling Jaya Singapore Hong Kong Tokyo
Nairobi Dar es Salaam Cape Town
Melbourne Auckland

and associated companies in
Beirut Berlin Ibadan Nicosia

Oxford is a trade mark of Oxford University Press

Published in the United States
by Oxford University Press, New York

British Library Cataloguing in Publication Data

Wordsworth, William, 1770–1850
[Correspondence]. The Letters of William and Dorothy Wordsworth.—
2nd ed. 7 : The later years, Part IV 1840–1853
1. Wordsworth, William, 1770–1850—Biography 2. Poets, English—
19th century—Correspondence 3. Wordsworth, Dorothy—Biography
4. Authors, English—19th century—Biography I. Title
II. Wordsworth, Dorothy III. De Selincourt, Ernest
IV. Hill, Alan G. 821'.7 PR5881

ISBN 0–19–812606–9

Library of Congress Cataloging in Publication Data

Wordsworth, William, 1770–1850.
The letters of William and Dorothy Wordsworth.
Contents: 1. The early years, 1787–1805, revised by Chester L. Shaver.—2. The middle years: pt. I. 1806–1811, revised by Mary Moorman.—[etc.]—7. The later years: pt. 4. 1840–1853, revised, arranged, and edited by Alan G. Hill. 1. Wordsworth, William, 1770–1850—Correspondence. 2. Wordsworth, Dorothy, 1771–1855—Correspondence. 3. Poets, English—19th century—Correspondence. I. Wordsworth, Dorothy, 1771–1855. II. De Sélincourt, Ernest, 1870–1943, ed. III. Shaver, Chester L. IV. Title.

PR5881.A48 1967 821'.7 [B] 67–89058

ISBN 0–19–812606–9

Set by Hope Services, Abingdon
Printed in Great Britain
at the University Printing House, Oxford
by David Stanford
Printer to the University

CONTENTS

LIST OF ILLUSTRATIONS

ABBREVIATIONS

PERSONAL INITIALS

W. W., D. W., M. W., R. W., C. W.: William, Dorothy, Mary, Richard, and Christopher Wordsworth.

S. H.: Sara Hutchinson, E. Q.: Edward Quillinan. S. T. C.: Samuel Taylor Coleridge. C. C.: Catherine Clarkson. H. C. R.: Henry Crabb Robinson. I. F.: Isabella Fenwick.

SOURCES

Broughton	*Some Letters of the Wordsworth Family*, edited by L. N. Broughton, Cornell University Press, 1942.
Cornell	Department of Rare Books, Cornell University Library, Ithaca, N. Y.
Curry	*New Letters of Robert Southey*, edited by Kenneth Curry, 2 vols., Columbia University Press, 1965.
DWJ	*The Journals of Dorothy Wordsworth*, edited by Ernest de Selincourt, 2 vols., 1941.
EY	*The Letters of William and Dorothy Wordsworth*, edited by the late Ernest de Selincourt, second edition, I, *The Early Years*, 1787–1805, revised by Chester L. Shaver, Oxford, 1967.
Griggs	*Collected Letters of Samuel Taylor Coleridge*, edited by Earl Leslie Griggs, 6 vols., Oxford, 1956–71.
Grosart	*The Prose Works of William Wordsworth*, edited by Alexander B. Grosart, 3 vols., 1876.
Hamilton	*The Life of Sir William Rowan Hamilton*, by R. P. Graves, 3 vols., 1882–9.
Haydon	*Correspondence and Table Talk of Benjamin Robert Haydon*, edited by his son, F. W. Haydon, 1876.
HCR	*Henry Crabb Robinson on Books and their Writers*, edited by Edith J. Morley, 3 vols., 1938.
K	*Letters of the Wordsworth Family*, edited by William Knight, 3 vols., 1907.
LY	*The Letters of William and Dorothy Wordsworth, The Later Years*, edited by Ernest de Selincourt, 3 vols., Oxford, 1939.
Mem.	*Memoirs of William Wordsworth*, by Christopher Wordsworth, 2 vols., 1851.
MLN	*Modern Language Notes*.
MLR	*Modern Language Review*.

Morley	*Correspondence of Henry Crabb Robinson with the Wordsworth Circle*, edited by Edith J. Morley, 2 vols., Oxford, 1927.
MP	*Modern Philology.*
MW	*The Letters of Mary Wordsworth*, edited by Mary E. Burton, Oxford, 1958.
MY	*The Letters of William and Dorothy Wordsworth*, edited by the late Ernest de Selincourt, second edition. II: *The Middle Years*: Part I, 1806–11, revised by Mary Moorman, Part II, 1812–20, revised by Mary Moorman and Alan G. Hill, Oxford, 1969–70.
NQ	*Notes and Queries.*
Pearson	*Papers, Letters and Journals of William Pearson*, edited by his widow. Printed for private circulation, 1863.
PMLA	*Publications of the Modern Language Association of America.*
Prel.	*Wordsworth's Prelude*, edited by Ernest de Selincourt: second edition, revised by Helen Darbishire, Oxford, 1959.
Prose Works	*The Prose Works of William Wordsworth*, edited by W. J. B. Owen and Jane Worthington Smyser, 3 vols., Oxford, 1974.
PW	*The Poetical Works of William Wordsworth*, edited by Ernest de Selincourt and Helen Darbishire, 5 vols., Oxford, 1940–9, and revised issues, 1952–9.
RES	*The Review of English Studies.*
R.M. Cat.	*Catalogue of the Varied and Valuable Historical, Poetical, Theological, and Miscellaneous Library of the late venerated Poet-Laureate, William Wordsworth* . . . Preston, 1859; reprinted in *Transactions of the Wordsworth Society*, Edinburgh [1882–7], and in *Sale Catalogues of Libraries of Eminent Persons*, vol. ix, ed. Roy Park, 1974.
RMVB	*Rydal Mount Visitors Book*, Wordsworth Library, Grasmere.
Rogers	*Rogers and his Contemporaries*, edited by P. W. Clayden, 2 vols., 1889.
Sadler	*Diary, Reminiscences and Correspondence of Henry Crabb Robinson*, edited by Thomas Sadler, 3 vols., 1869.
Southey	*Life and Correspondence of Robert Southey*, edited by C. C. Southey, 6 vols., 1849–50.
TLS	*Times Literary Supplement.*
Warter	*A Selection from the Letters of Robert Southey*, edited by John Wood Warter, 4 vols., 1856.
WL	The Wordsworth Library, Grasmere.

LIST OF LETTERS

PART VII

1840

List of Letters

1841

List of Letters

List of Letters

List of Letters

List of Letters

1845

1846

List of Letters

1847

1848

List of Letters

1362. W. W. to C. W.

Address: The Rev^d the Master of Trinity, Lodge, Cambridge.
Postmark: 3 Jan. 1840.
Stamp: Ambleside.
Endorsed: My Brother.
MS. Mr. William Wordsworth.
Mem. (—). *Grosart* (—). *K* (—). *LY ii. 994* (—).

Friday 3^d Jan^ry [1840]

My very dear Brother,

It is in times of trouble and affliction that one feels most deeply the strength of the ties of family and nature. We all most affectionately condole with you, and those who are around you at this melancholy time.[1] The departed was beloved in this House as he deserved to be; but our sorrow, great as it is for our own sakes, is still heavier for yours and his Brothers'. He is a power gone out of our family and they will be perpetually reminded of it. But the best of all consolations will be with you, with them, with us, and all his numerous Relatives and Friends especially with Mrs Hoare, that his life had been as blameless as a man's could well be. He was a pure Spirit and through the goodness of God, is gone to his reward.

It was a happiness for us that we did not receive Susan's *hopeful* Letter to Isabella and forwarded by her till two hours after the receipt of yours. We were further favored by the kindness of Mrs Cookson of Ambleside who in consequence of a Letter from her Son Henry [2] had previously prepared us for the worst. I mention this to you, more on your niece's account than any one's else, for her health is such that shocks of sorrow she cannot bear as otherwise she would have been enabled to do. Her love for her Cousin was among the leading affections of her heart. I have not yet spoken of our poor Sister; her bodily health is upon the whole decidedly improved in a manner that surprizes every one. Though her mind is much weakened, she habitually recurrs in conversation with me to deceased Relations and

[1] C.W. had written on 31 Dec. to announce the death of his son John earlier that day. (*WL MSS.*) See also next letter. He was buried in Trinity College Chapel, where there is a monument to his memory by Henry Weekes.

[2] For Henry Cookson see pt. iii, L. 1175.

Friends, and I am prepared for her frequently recurring to the sad things of yesterday.—

You will learn with pleasure that Mary's health which was lately much deranged is restored though her strength not quite so. We all write in affectionate sympathy with you all. You do not mention your health; perhaps Susan or either of my Nephews will write to us and tell us how you are, and other things.

I remain your loving Brother
Wm Wordsworth

1363. W. W. to LADY FREDERICK BENTINCK

MS. untraced.
Mem. (—). Grosart (—). K (—). LY ii. 994.

Rydal Mount, Ambleside, Jan. 3, [1840]

My dear Lady Frederick,

Yesterday brought us melancholy news in a letter from my brother Dr Wordsworth, which announced the death of his eldest son. He died last Tuesday in Trinity College, of which he was a fellow, having been tenderly nursed by his father during rather a long illness. He was a most amiable man, and I have reason to believe was one of the best scholars in Europe.[1] We were all strongly attached to him; and, as his poor father writes, 'the loss is to me, and to my sorrowing sons, irreparable on this side of the grave. . . .'

W. W.

[1] John Wordsworth was working at the time of his death on an edition of Bentley's letters, which was completed and published by C.W. jnr. as *The Correspondence of Richard Bentley*, 2 vols., 1842. In the Preface to the first volume, he gives some account of his brother's Classical attainments and his projected edition of Aeschylus.

1364. W. W. to MARY GASKELL[1]

MS. St. John's College, Cambridge.
LY ii. 995.

Rydal Mount 9th Jan^ry 1840.

My dear Madam,

I must thank you for the pains you have taken, though unsuccessfully, for the Almery[2] which I cannot help still wishing might be turned over to me by the owner. The only means that seems open for procuring it under the circumstances, is the getting as good a piece of antient furniture which possibly might be accepted as a Substitute. With this view I shall make enquiries among my Friends. It is true that there is an account of this Relique in Mr Hunter's Book; wherein he mentions its Relation to our Family. He gives a Copy of the Latin Inscription corresponding with what Mrs Beaumont[3] reports. Nevertheless, as he confines himself to that without giving a sketch of it, were it not presuming too much upon your kindness I should be glad of a drawing of the thing, especially as it might enable me to judge what sort of a Work would be most likely to be taken in its place.—

I feel truly obliged to Mr De Wint[4] for the attention he is disposed to pay to Miss C. Marshall's[5] and my request in favor of your young Friend. We are all pretty well under this roof. Hoping that Mr Gaskell and yourself are the same, I remain with the Kindest wishes of the Season in which Mrs W. and my daughter unite, faithfully

dear Madam
your obliged
Wm Wordsworth

[1] See pt. iii, L. 1174.

[2] The Wordsworth family aumbry (see pt. ii, L. 648).

[3] Wife of Thomas Wentworth Beaumont (see pt. ii, L. 672), the present owner of the aumbry.

[4] Peter De Wint (1784–1849), landscape painter in water-colour. He had been staying at Lowther the previous October, where W. W. probably met him. On 23 Oct. 1839 he wrote declining W. W.'s invitation to Rydal Mount (*WL MSS.*).

[5] Cordelia Marshall.

1365. W. W. to THOMAS POWELL

Address: Tho[s] Powell Esq[re], 2 Leadenhall St., London.
Postmark: (1) 10 Jan. 1840 (2) 11 Jan. 1840.
Stamp: Ambleside.
MS. Cornell. Hitherto unpublished.

[*In M. W.'s hand*]

Rydal Mount
Jan[ry] 9th [1840]

My dear Mr Powell,

I rec[d] your's two or three hours ago—excuse my replying to it at present for I have not time, and shall *not* have perhaps, for two or three days—

I am much pleased with your attempt upon Chaucer[1]—which I return submitting to y[r] judgment a few verbal alterations—insignificant as they are, they have cost me more trouble than I could well spare—which I mention because I cannot promise hereafter to bestow any pains upon the endeavours of yourself and y[r] Associates, in this very promising Work. Remember I am nearly at the close of my 70th Year, and have neither time nor strength to spare. A few years back I should have delighted in the employment.

The first 8 lines of your Victoria Sonnet[2] are very pleasing—I wish I were better able to sympathize with the latter part. The 4 first of the other are hurtful to the ear—"line" and "time" making rhymes nearly. You are I take for granted aware that the image in the two last lines was used by Coleridge, whether for the first time by him, I cannot tell, not less than half a century ago—I go along with the sentiment in this Sonnet.

Ever faithfully yours
W[m] Wordsworth[3]

[1] Powell had written on 3 Jan. (*WL. MSS.*) to report progress on the Chaucer project (see pt. iii, L. 1361), and promising to send shortly his version of *The Flower and the Leaf*. This poem, modernized by Dryden, was still thought to be Chaucer's.

[2] A sonnet to Queen Victoria which he had enclosed.

[3] Not signed by W. W.

1366. W. W. to EDWARD MOXON

Address: Edward Moxon Esqre, 44 Dover St, London. *paid*
Postmark: (1) 19 Jan. 1840 (2) 20 Jan. 1840.
Stamp: Ambleside.
MS. Henry E. Huntington Library.
LY ii. 996.

Rydal 10th Jan^{y}—40

My dear Mr Moxon,

Having an opportunity of returning the three Volumes by the hand of Mr W. Westall,[1] who will be in Town by the end of next week (this is Saturday), I prefer sending this by him, to charging the Binder, negligent as he has been, with the Carriage.—Mr. W. has been a week with us taking a few sketches, with a view to the illustration of my Poems. The Weather and a bad cold had been much against him, but he has done pretty well. In particular he has made one very good drawing in perspective of the interior of our chief sitting-room.[2] It has a most picturesque appearance and I cannot but think would be acceptable to those who take an interest in me or my writings. He has done the outside of the House and the surrounding Landscape.—

I set my face *entirely* against the publication of Mr Field's Mss.[3] I ought to have written to him several weeks ago, but feeling as I did truly sensible of the interest he took in my character and writings and grateful to him for having bestowed so much of his valuable time, upon the subject, I could not bring myself to tell him what I have just with all frankness stated to you. I must however do so. Mr Field has been very little in England, I imagine, for above twenty years and consequently is not aware, that much the greatest part of his labour would only answer the purpose of reviving forgotten theories and exploded opinions. Besides, there are in his notions things that are personally *disagreeable* (not to use a harsher term) to myself and those about me. And if such an objection did not lie against the publication, it is enough that the thing is *superfluous*. In the present state of this Country in general, how could this kind

[1] William Westall (see *MY* ii. 362, 510), the artist.

[2] See Blanshard, *Portraits of Wordsworth*, pp. 88, 166. The engraving was published by Moxon later this year.

[3] See next letter.

natured Friend ever be deceived into the thought that criticism and particulars so minute could attract attention even from a few.

Hartley has positively affirmed to my Son, and another Gentleman that he considers his part of the Work[1] at an end. 'True', said he, 'I could go on for ever, but 60 Pages—20 more than Jonson—are surely enough.' I write this in consequence of your saying in your last 'The introduction to Massinger is still unfinished'. Perhaps all is right by this time.

I have not sent the Spectacles by Mr Westall, hoping that some person in the neighbourhood may set them right.

Murray used to say that advertizing always paid. So it might with him—but with old books like mine I sh^{d} imagine that ad^{ts} frequently repeated on the forthcoming of a new Ed: w^{d} never answer, and therefore I am myself against it rather—I leave the decision to your friendly judgment. If I have overlooked any thing in y^{r} [letter] requiring notice, tell me in y^{r} next. I enclose a slip of paper from my Clerk—the erratum noticed is important and I should there[fore] like to have it inserted in such Copies as are not put into circulation. faithfully y^{rs} with remembrance etc

Wm Wordsworth

Please pay to Longman on our acc^{t} the enclosed bill.

1367. W. W. to BARRON FIELD

MS. untraced.
K (—). *LY ii. 997.*

Rydal Mount, January 16, 1840.

My dear Mr Field,

I have at last brought myself to write to you. After maturely considering the subject, however painful it may be to me, I must regret that I am decidedly against the publication of your Critical Memoir;[2] your wish is, I know, to serve me, and I am grateful

[1] His biographical and critical introductions to Massinger and Ford.

[2] Barron Field (see pt. i, L. 334) had written from Gibraltar on 21 Nov. 1839 about his MS. Memoir of W. W., which he was about to offer to Moxon for publication, having added a history of the *Lyrical Ballads* from Cottle's *Early Recollections* and other controversial sources. 'As for my MS. it was not written for you, but for the public, if it will in any degree contribute to the diffusion of your poetry. . . . I have taken the liberty of introducing that very interesting

for the strength of this feeling in your excellent heart. I am also truly proud of the pains of which you have thought my writings worthy; but I am sure that your intention to benefit me in this way would not be fulfilled. The hostility which you combat so ably is in a great measure passed away, but might in some degree be revived by your recurrence to it, so that in this respect your work would, if published, be either superfluous or injurious, so far as concerns the main portion of it. I shall endeavour, during the short remainder of my life, to profit by it, both as an author and a man, in a private way; but the notices of me by many others which you have thought it worth while to insert are full of gross mistakes, both as to facts and opinions, and the sooner they are forgotten the better. Old as I am, I live in the hope of seeing you, and should in that event have no difficulty in reconciling you to the suppression of a great part of this work entirely, and of the whole of it in its present shape. . . . One last word in matter of authorship: it is far better not to admit people so much behind the scenes, as it has been lately fashionable to do. . . . Believe me to be,

Most faithfully, your much obliged
Wm Wordsworth

1368. W. W. to THOMAS POWELL

Address: Tho[s]. Powell Esq[re], 2 Leadenhall Street, London. *Paid.* [*In M. W.'s hand*]
Postmark: (1) 19 Jan. 1840 (2) 20 Jan. 1840.
Stamp: Ambleside.
MS. University of Virginia Library.
LY ii. 998.

Saturday, Noon—18th Jan[ry] [1840]

My dear Mr Powell,

Many thanks for your beautiful Milton,[1] and your Stilton which arrived safely yesterday.—I must now briefly advert to

letter which you wrote to me in Oct[r] 1828 on the subject of the alterations in your Poems.' But he added that 'if you object to the publication, there is an end of it.' (*WL MSS.*) Field was now back in England and called at Rydal Mount in March (*RMVB*). His Memoir was eventually published, ed. Geoffrey Little, 1975.

[1] See pt. iii, L. 1361.

certain points in your last Letter. You seem in too great a hurry to be in the *press* with Chaucer. He is a mighty Genius as you well know, and not lightly to be dealt with.—For my own part, I am not prepared to incur any responsibility in the execution of this project, which I much approve of, beyond furnishing my own little Quota; which I almost fear now must be confined to permission to reprint the Prioress's Tale, if thought worth while; and the Cuckoo and Nightingale which is ready; but with great diligence have Mrs Wordsworth and I looked in vain among my papers for the Mss which contains the Manciple's Tale, and if I am not mistaken a small portion of Troilus and Cressida—It contained also, by the bye, a Translation of two Books of Ariosto's Orlando,[1] and this and other of its contents, I should be sorry to lose altogether.—

My *approbation* of the Endeavo[u]r to tempt people to read Chaucer by making a part of him intelligible to the unlettered, and tuneable to modern ears, will be sufficiently apparent by my own little Contributions to the intended Volume. But *beyond this* I do not wish to do any thing; or rather it could not be right that I should. Little matters in Composition hang about and teaze me awkwardly, and at improper times when I ought to be taking my meals or asleep. On this account, however reluctantly, I must *decline* even *looking over* the Mss either of yourself or your Friends. I am sure I should find some thing which I should attempt to change, and probably after a good deal of pains make the passage no better, perhaps worse—This is my infirmity, I have employed scores of hours during the course of my life in retouching favorite passages of favorite Authors, of which labour not a trace remains nor ought to remain—

As my connection with the intended little work originated with you, and probably the work altogether, why should not you, with the consent of Coadjutors [?decide] the management of it, both as to Editorship and the choice of a publisher. You could prefix an advertisement expressing how the Attempt came to be made, and upon what principles it was conducted.—I hope I have now made myself sufficiently intelligible, and that Mr Horne[2] etc will not be hurt that I decline, for the reasons above

[1] The short passage printed in *PW* iv. 367–9 is all that seems to have survived of this translation. See also *EY*, p. 628.

[2] Richard Hengist Horne (1803–84), poet and miscellaneous writer, friend and correspondent of Elizabeth Barrett. His best-known works were an epic *Orion* (1843) which was sold at a farthing and went through six editions within

given, the pleas[ure] which it would otherwise be, of perusing his Mss.—I wish him and Mr Hunt,[1] to whom present my kind regards, success in their disinterested labours. My love and reverence for Chaucer are unbounded. Affectionately

Your much obliged
W. W.

Miss Gillies[2] returns to us today or tomorrow. She has been absent since Wednesday.

1369. W. W. to H. C. R.

Endorsed: 23ᵈ *Jan*: 1840. Mʳˢ Wordsworth.
MS. Dr. Williams's Library.
Morley, i. 395.

[*In M. W.'s hand*]

Ambleside. Thursday night—
[23 Jan. 1840]

My dear Friend

We have long been looking for a letter from you and I now am going to dictate to Mary a *short* one—as we are at Miss Fenwick's, come to meet Lady Monro[3] and liable to be interrupted. Dʳ W.[4] communicated to us, the sad tidings of the death of his Son in a letter very affecting and in the highest degree creditable to his heart and head; so that we trust he is bearing his loss, as so sincere a Christian ought to bear afflictions of this kind. J. W. had he lived, would have done not a little for classical literature—he was one of the most accurate Scholars living, and certainly beloved in proportion as he was known.—Mʳˢ Hoare, whom you know, mourns for him as a Mother.

the year, and his *New Spirit of the Age*, 2 vols., 1844. He was now at work on a version of the *Knight's Tale* for *Chaucer's Poems Modernized*, but it was not included in the final selection. See also L. 1784 below.

[1] Leigh Hunt was at present trying his hand on the *Prologues*. His contribution to the volume finally consisted of versions of *The Maunciple's Tale* (after W. W. had withdrawn his own), *The Friar's Tale*, and *The Squire's Tale*.

[2] Margaret Gillies, the artist. See pt. iii, L. 1345.

[3] The Dowager Lady Munro (d.1850), widow of Maj. Gen. Sir Thomas Munro, 1st Bart., (d.1827), Governor of Madras. She was Jane, daughter of Richard Campbell, of Craigie, Ayrshire.

[4] C. W.

I thoroughly sympathize with your indignation upon the conduct of the house of C. as to the question of Privilege.[1] I have never troubled myself to ascertain what side this Man, or that Man takes—or any portion of this or that Party take; and without entering into the merits of the case at all, but merely regarding it as Authority opposed to Authority, I should side with the Judges, Not being able to find a single motive that should tempt them to decide wrong—while I see a thousand that are likely to mislead a great portion of a popular Assembly—therefore, I sh[d] say at once, the odds are incalculable, that in cases of this kind, the Judges will be right. You cannot feel more strongly upon this subject than I do. I am glad to hear you speak in such terms of Sir R[t] Inglis—he is a Man who for his honesty and intelligence is entitled to universal esteem, and I question whether there is a Man in the house so much respected as he is.

Having so little sight to spare in our house and so few voices that can read aloud for any length of time, we have little acquaintance with the Oxford controversy[2]—I have only read one of their tracts.

The New Ed: contains nothing new but what is in the Ap[p]endix, and that is only the 13 Sonnets first published in the volume of Sonnets. I thought it would be dealing unfairly with the Purchasers of the former Ed: if I added anything to the new one not found in the former. A hundred copies of the Appendix

[1] The firm of Hansard, printers of the 'Parliamentary Debates', were the defendants in the famous action Stockdale v. Hansard, in which they were accused of libel for printing by order of the House of Commons a report of the inspectors of prisons. The case led to a direct collision between the Courts and the House of Commons towards the end of 1839 on the issue of Parliamentary privilege, and the difficulty was only resolved by legislation in 1840 protecting the printers of parliamentary papers.

[2] The controversy occasioned by the publication of the *Tracts for the Times*, which began to appear in 1833 from the hands of Newman, Keble, Pusey, and other Oxford high-churchmen. The debate had become particularly acrimonious after the appearance early in 1839 of Tract 80, *On Reserve in Communicating Religious Knowledge*, by Isaac Williams (1802–65), which lost him the election to the Chair of Poetry in 1842. To judge from a remark of H. C. R.'s (*HCR* ii. 576), this is almost certainly the tract which W. W. had read. In spite of his disavowal here of any real knowledge of the details of Tractarian controversy, he was well aware of the issues at stake, and had already met and conversed with several of the leaders of the movement, including Williams himself. See pt. iii, Ls. 1195 and 1330, and Ls. 1372 and 1424 below.

were struck off for such Purchasers of the former who might think it worth while to add them to their copies.

We have not heard from dear Mrs Clarkson upon the occasion of her Brother's death.[1] If you are in correspondence with her, pray present our best love and sincere condolences.

Our good friend Miss Fenwick intends going to London about the 11th of next month—and I am glad to tell you, that Dora is to be the Companion of her journey, and will be to be heard of at Mrs Hoare's—while Miss F. sees her London friends,—but no doubt she will write a note to appoint a meeting with you as soon as she finds herself settled. They mean after a few weeks to proceed into Somersetshire—whence Miss F. hopes to bring back with them, her Sister,[2] to see our beautiful Country in which she has found her health so much improved during residence of more than 18 months.

We are glad, especially for your sake, Miss F's and other friends, that the American Stock is improving. Dr Arnold has nothing in the U. S. States Bank—his money is lodged in different States for which the faith of the State is pledged, so that he is in no fear. I have myself, by the advice of Courtenay no less than £3,000 in the N. B. Bank,[3] and frankly own to you, that I do not like to be in this situation, not so much on acc^t^ of the am^t^ of the lodgement, as that I dislike the principle of these banks—the failures in them have been numerous and destructive and one is liable to the extent of all one's means, to be called upon for making up any deficiencies which either foolishness or dishonesty might cause.

I have been employed these 3 or 4 last days in revising some verses of Chaucer, which I modernized some years ago—intending them as a gift to Mr Powell a friend of mine, who in conjuction with some literary acquaintances, is engaged in doing other things of this Author upon my principle; as exemplified in the Prioresses Tale. My love and reverence for Chaucer are unbounded, and I should like for the sake of unlearned readers to see the greatest part of his works done in the same way. Dryden and Pope[4] have treated these originals admirably in a manner of their own, which tho' good in itself is not Chaucers.

[1] Earlier this year.

[2] Mrs. Popham (see pt. iii, L. 1301).

[3] W. W. means the National Provincial Bank.

[4] In his youth Pope had written 'imitations' of *The Merchant's Tale* and *The Wife of Bath's Prologue*.

John was with us last week, he is quite well, as is his family—his Mother and Aunt Joanna who is now at Rydal, purpose getting into the Mail on Saturday in order to pass a week at Brigham, previous to Dora's leaving home.

William I believe leaves Herefordshire for Carlisle this very day—Where he has been passing a few weeks with his Uncle[1]—he writes, that he finds his Uncle considerably improved —Yet he is still in a helpless state—William's own health you will be glad to hear is amended. Your Old friend our Sister too we think, in many respects improved—She would, did she know of our writing—send kind remembrances to you—As would Dora—The Arnolds leave Fox How next week—they have, as usual much enjoyed their residence there, spite of the very rainy season we have had during their sojourn. Of dear M[r] Southey we can only give a melancholy report—his family seem to think him sinking fast—He suffers no pain, which is a great blessing—but he is become pitiably helpless [but] he continues to be patient and uncomplaining—indeed from what we hear he scarcely seems sensible to the melancholy change that has taken place—His daughter Bertha, who now lives in Flemings[2] house at the foot of the hill, has just returned from Keswick, and her reports of her Fathers state is most affecting.—

We had a notice the other day (in a letter to a young lady of this neighbourhood from M[rs] Lutwidge's[3] Niece, Miss Taylor) from M[r] Kenyon then at Rome—with a promise that we should hear from him from that place—So we presume he is still in the Eternal City—*You* must think again before you make up your mind to run away without seeing your friends in West[d]. You know you engaged your next visit should be in summer, and alas! we know little what may happen before 1841! Our united love and best wishes that you may continue to enjoy your Continental travels—as well as to find comfort in your new home. (I, M W) am closing this joint letter before I sleep. W. is already in bed, and not finding an envelope in my room, I hope

[1] At Brinsop.

[2] Bertha and her husband, the Revd. Herbert Hill, were now living in John Fleming's cottage at Rydal (see pt. i, L. 83).

[3] Mary (1779–1859), wife of Capt. Thomas Henry Lutwidge, R.N. (see pt. i, L. 180), of Ambleside and Holmrook, nr. Ravenglass, who had fought under Jervis at Cape St. Vincent, and spent ten years as a prisoner of the French. She was the youngest daughter of John Taylor of Townhead, Lancs. I. F. had taken her house in Ambleside while she was away in Italy.

you will notice my contrivance and frugality in turning your's. God bless you. Affly your's

W. and M. W.

PS I had missed your PS. on a separate paper, and enclosed and directed my note before I saw it—Do you not defend St Tal's books[1] more warmly than my slight (not slighting) expression of opinion about some portions of them warrants? Quis vituperavit?—Yet in addition to my objection to certain trivialities, and too much of gin and porter, and the Cat and Salutation, and assenting as I do entirely to your conviction that the dreadful act of poor Miss Lamb (not Miss Lamb) and its effects on her brother must make him more loved than ever by all who loved him without knowing that history, I have my doubts whether the subject ought to have been received. I do not think that *he* would like it if he could be consulted.—[I had seen all those letters to the Wordsworths long ago.][2]

I am very sorry that you give so poor an account of the state of your Brother's health—or rather of the necessity of his abstinence from mental excitement, for that is not always possible with any of us.—

1370. W. W. to EDWARD MOXON

MS. Henry E. Huntington Library.
LY ii. 1000.

Rydal Mount
27 Jan^y –40

My dear Mr Moxon,

I sit down to thank you for the Beaumont and Fletcher,[3] which I see you have kindly dedicated to me. The others all except Hartley's and my Son's which is here, awaiting an opportunity, have been sent to their several destinations. I should have written sooner but I had nothing particular to say; nor have I at present.

You know the general state of my eyes to be such as that they allow me to read very very little. In consequence I am yet

[1] Sergeant Talfourd's *Life and Letters of Charles Lamb.*

[2] *Sentence added by H. C. R.*

[3] See *R.M. Cat.*, no. 463.

unacquainted with Mr Leigh Hunt's play,[1] and Mr Darley's Thomas a Becket,[2] for which I am sorry but it cannot be helped. Pray when you see either of these Gentlemen tell them this with many thanks for their obliging attentions.

I do not see much of poor Hartley C. but my opinion continues the same that though he writes much and very ably, he is not to be depended upon for unfinished work. I believe he is upon the whole more regular as to Drink than he used to be but the other day I was very much shocked to meet him quite tipsy in Ambleside Streets—poor Fellow.

The Sonnets upon Capital Punishment[3] which I read you, then no more I believe than 4, are now 11. I should not be sorry to put them into circulation on account of the importance of the subject if I knew how. I cannot print them in a Magazine for reasons you are aware of.

All here are pretty well as I hope you all are. My Son Wm is with us and sends his kind regards,

ever yours

W. Wordsworth

1371. W. W. to THOMAS POWELL

MS. St. John's College, Cambridge.
LY ii. 1001.

[early Feb. 1840][4]

. . . but you are quite welcome to the Prioress's Tale, Cuckoo and Nightingale, and the passage from the Troilus and Cressida. When you see Miss Gillies pray tell her that she is remembered in this house with much pleasure and great affection, and a

[1] *A Legend of Florence*, produced at Covent Garden on 7 Feb. 1840, was a brilliant success. According to Hunt's *Autobiography*, the Queen came to see it twice, and it was subsequently performed, by Royal Command, at Windsor Castle in 1852.

[2] For George Darley see pt. iii, L. 1017. He had undertaken the edition of Beaumont and Fletcher in place of Southey.

[3] The *Sonnets upon the Punishment of Death* (*PW* iv. 135–41), 14 in number, were eventually published by Henry Taylor in the *Quarterly Review* in Dec. 1841.

[4] Written, as de Selincourt notes, soon after L. 1368, when W. W. had found the mislaid passage from *Troilus and Cresida*, and after Miss Gillies had left Rydal.

hundred good wishes for her success. Her picture[1] just arrived, appears to be much approved; but of course as to the degree of likeness in each there is great diversity of opinion. How mortifying in this respect would be the Profession of a Portrait-Painter if the Artist did not rise above the common region of inexperienced judgement. Pray let me hear from you at your leisure. With best remembrances to Mrs Powell and yourself and kind regards to your Brother believe me faithfully yours

Wm Wordsworth

My eyes are in their better way, but alas they allow me to read very little. The general health of us all is good, thank God.

The non-arrival of Miss Roughsedge's portrait[2] was a great disappointment.

1372. W. W. to WALTER FARQUHAR HOOK

MS. untraced.
Stephens, Life and Letters of Walter Farquhar Hook, ii. 46.

Rydal Mount: February 5, 1840.

My dear Sir,

Though I have not regularly acknowledged the receipt of the several publications[3] you have sent me, I trust that you do not infer from that omission that I am indifferent to those marks of your regard, or insensible to their merits; I have perused them carefully, and with much pleasure and profit. The last I received is the excellent sermon upon the Novelties of Romanism.[4] I read it over again yesterday, and am happy to say that I concur with

[1] Probably Miss Gillies's miniature of W. W. and M. W., in which she combined the two separate portraits taken earlier. See L. 1376 below and Blanshard, *Portraits of Wordsworth*, p. 164.

[2] Probably a portrait by Miss Gillies of the daughter of W. W.'s neighbour and friend Mr. Roughsedge of Fox Ghyll.

[3] Since his appointment to Leeds, Dr. Hook had taken up a moderate position in regard to the Oxford Tracts. His recent publications included a sermon *Hear the Church*, 1838 (31st edn., 1841), preached before the Queen at the Chapel Royal, in which he upheld the Apostolic succession of the Church of England; and a pamphlet *Presbyterian Rights Asserted* [anon.], 1839, in which he criticised the assumption of arbitrary powers by many of the Bishops.

[4] *The Novelties of Romanism: or Popery Refuted by Tradition. A Sermon . . .*, 1839.

your views. But allow me to add one remark: you point to the additions the Romans have made to the ancient faith, which the Reformation endeavoured to restore, and which we hold. Now, much the greatest part of the particulars which you select are, in conversation at least, disclaimed by almost every Romanist of education, clergy or laymen, with whom it has been my fortune to converse. And this is one of the strongest objections I have to their religion. I accuse it boldly of having many faces, and two the direct opposites of each other: a face for the cultivated mind, and another, the reverse of that, for the great body of the ignorant. I have lived nearly four years of my life abroad, in countries where Popery was the established of prevailing religion; I have carefully observed its operation, and I have no hesitation in saying that the bulk of the people who belong to it, do believe, or act at least as if they believed, in those additions which you have enumerated. After all, I reckon the constrained celibacy of the clergy the monstrous root of the greatest part of the mischiefs of Popery. If that could be got rid of, most of the other evils would gradually melt away. If we would truly spiritualise men, we must take care that we do not begin by unhumanising them, which is the process in respect to all those who are brought up with a view to the making of that unnatural vow. The inevitable result of it upon the minds of the great body of the clergy is an inordinate desire to enlarge the power of their order, *per fas et nefas*, in other words, to enslave the minds of others for their own exaltation. Believe me, dear Sir, to remain faithfully,

Your much obliged,
W. Wordsworth

1373. W. W. to UNKNOWN CORRESPONDENT

MS. Massachusetts Historical Society.
David Bonnell Green, 'Two Wordsworth Letters', NQ ccx (Nov. 1965), 414–5.

[*In unidentified hand*]

Rydal Mount
Ambleside
Feb^{ry} 12th 1840

Sir,

Yesterday I received your letter, in which you do me the honour of requesting permission to dedicate a forthcoming

Volume of your Poems to me. I feel obliged to return the same answer upon this occasion that I have done upon other similar applications, it was to this effect, not having the honour of knowing you, and being unacquainted with your writings, I must refuse permission thus formerly asked for, though I acknowledge at the same time that every one is at liberty to dedicate his productions to whom he likes, provided that he makes no declaration, that this is done with the consent of the party to whom he has chosen to inscribe his work. I am pretty sure you will not be offended with this reply to your request, as the reasonableness of it must upon a little reflexion be quite obvious. I remain Sir

y^r obliged
[*signed*] Wm Wordsworth

1374. W. W. to THOMAS NOON TALFOURD

Address: Mr Sergeant Talfourd MP, Russel Square, London.
Postmark: (1) 17 Feb. 1840 (2) 18 Feb. 1840.
Stamp: Ambleside.
MS. Harvard University Library. Hitherto unpublished.

[*In M. W.'s hand*]

16th Feb. (1840]

My dear Sergeant Talfourd,

I have long owed you a letter, but having nothing very particular to say, I put it off from time to time; but as the Papers state that your Copy-right bill is to be read a second time next Wed:[1] I cannot forbear writing—Tegg[2] I see has lately circulated an acc^t of the great profits made by such Authors as Walter Scott, Bulwer etc etc—inferring no doubt, or meaning it to be inferred, that those large profits were a substantial reason why the term of Copy-right should not be extended. Now it must have struck you, that throwing aside considerations of justice, upon which after all the question ought to be determined, these large profits furnish, in some cases, the strongest reason why the term *should* be extended. The practice of reading, the number of

[1] There was a majority of 30 on the Second Reading of Talfourd's Copyright Bill on 19 Feb.; but progress with the measure was once again frustrated, and Talfourd wrote on 7 May to say that the Bill had been dropped (*Cornell MSS.*).

[2] The bookseller (see pt. iii, L. 1235).

readers, and the ability to purchase books have all so greatly increased of late years that the existing public is able to hold out temptations which few Authors have virtue enough to resist. Therefore, whether a Man be fond of praise or money he is more likely than ever to write below himself, if he be a man of ability, in order to suit the transient or corrupt taste of the day—therefore let the term be extended to counterbalance as far as it may this mischief. So that if an Author of small means endeavours to rise above his age, and aims at giving lasting pleasure, or producing lasting good, he may in conscience be reconciled to the foregoing of present advantage in money, for the benefit of Successors. The Public of the day is becoming *every* day a Patron more and more formidable to the production of solid literature —look at the pestilent influence of Encyclopedias in this respect—their Publishers can afford to give such prices as tempt Authors of first rate talents to work for them, and think of the disadvantages under which such work is performed, the several Authors being limited both as to space and time, and compelled to labor whatever be the State of their health, mind or circumstances. Contrast a work so produced with Gibbon's History of 20 years.—But something of this kind I have said to you before.

The only opposition you have to dread is that of Men who contend that books would become dearer, but this you have seen clearly is a delusion. Publishers like Tegg and Tilt[1] would in time cut each other's throats by competition—and as an Author's heirs would not have that to dread, they c^{d} venture upon larger Editions, and there is no reason to fear they would not do this, on acc^{t} of the increase of Readers; an increase likely ere long to take place among the humblest classes of Society—but enough, I hope there is no danger of your not making up a house. If y^{r} proposed Pamphlet[2] be printed be so good as to send a copy of it to 'Lieu^{t} Genl Sir Wm Gomm Jamaica'.

I rec^{d} thro' Moxon a Tragedy[3] under secresy—printed but not published—tho' I make but little use of my eyes for reading, I have gone through it carefully.—Some of the allusions to mountain scenery I could almost [have] imagined I had written myself.

Many thanks for your hospitable invitation—but I shall

[1] See pt. iii, L. 1251.

[2] Talfourd's *Three Speeches* (see pt. iii, L. 1248).

[3] *Glencoe; or, The Fate of the Macdonalds*, 1840.

scarcely be able to profit by it, having no intention of going to Town this Spring. A London Campaign *every* year is rather too hard. . . .

[*cetera desunt*]

1375. W. W. to EDWARD MOXON

MS. Henry E. Huntington Library.
K (—). LY ii. 1004.

[? 18 Feb. 1840][1]

My dear Mr Moxon,

Not being able to meet with H. C.[2] immediately on receipt of your Letter, I wrote him a note a couple of days after; and told him its Contents—I have since seen him, and done all I could.—And now let me give you in respect to him a piece of advice once for all, viz, that you *never* engage with him for any *unperformed* Work, where either time or quantity is of importance. Poor Fellow he has no resolution;—in fact nothing that can be called rational volition, or command of himself, as to what he will do or not do; of course I mean setting aside the *fundamental* obligations of morality. Yesterday I learnt that he had disappeared from his Lodgings, and that he had been seen at 8 o'clock that morning entering the Town of Kendal. He was at Ambleside the night before till 11 o'clock, so he must have [been] out [a] great part of the night.—I have lately begun to think, that he has given himself up so to his own notions, fancies reveries, abstractions, etc that he is scarcely in his right [mind] at all times. I admire his Genius and talents far more than I could find words to express, especially for writing prose, which I am inclined to think, as far as I have seen, is more masterly than his Verse. The *work*manship of the latter seems to me not infrequently too hasty, has indeed too much the air of Italian improvizatore production.—

Mr Powell, my Friend, has some thought of preparing for Publication some portions of Chaucer modernized so far and no farther than is done in my treatment of the Prioress's Tale. That will in fact be his model.—He will have Coadjutors, among

[1] Dated by reference to next letter which refers to Dora W. going to stay with Sara Coleridge on the 19th. This letter is dated to 21 Feb. in another hand, probably by reference to the postmark on the address sheet which is missing.

[2] Hartley Coleridge.

whom I believe will be Mr Leigh Hunt, a man as capable of doing the work well as any living Author. I have placed at my Friend Mr Powell's disposal, in addition to the Prioress's Tale, three other pieces which I did long ago, but revised the other day. They are the Manciple's Tale, The Cuckoo and the Nightingale, and 24 Stanzas of Troilus and Cressida. This I have done mainly out of my love and reverence for Chaucer, in hopes that whatever may be the merit of Mr Powell's attempt, the attention of other Writers may be drawn to the subject; and a work hereafter be produced by different pens which will place the treasures of one of the greatest of Poets within the reach of the multitude which now they are not. I mention all of this to you, because though I have not given Mr Powell the least encouragement to do so, he may sound you as to your disposition to undertake the Publication.—I have myself nothing further to do with it than I have stated. Had the thing been suggested to me by any number of competent Persons 20 years ago I would have undertaken the editorship, done much more myself, and endeavoured to improve the several Contributions where they seemed to require it. But that is now out of the question.—

I am glad to hear so favorable an account of the Sale of the new Edition. The penny-postage has let in an inundation of complimentary Letters upon me. Yesterday I had one that would amuse you by the language of awe, admiration, gratitude etc in which it abounds, and two or three days ago I had one from a little Boy eight years old! telling me how he had been charmed with the Idiot Boy etc etc. In several of these Letters there is one thing which gratifies, viz the frequent mention of the consolation which my Poems have afforded the Writer under affliction and the calmness and elevation etc which they have produced in him.

My Paper is quite full. I hope you will see my dear daughter from time to time. Tomorrow she goes to Number 10 Chester Place to her friends the Coleridges. Kind remembrances to Mrs Moxon and your Sister and Brother.

I am not inclined to go to London this Spring. Visiting, talking etc late dinners are too hard work for me

[*unsigned*]

1376. W. W. to CORDELIA MARSHALL

MS. Cornell.
LY ii. 1003.

Rydal Mount
Febry 19th 1840

My dear Cordelia,

If you had known how little my *promised* Letter was likely to contain[1] you would not have honoured it with a wish for its arrival—In fact when I told Mrs W. or Dora I should write to you myself, it was because I thought it became me to do so, in order to thank you for your Drawing from the far Terrace. I like it much, but sincerity compels me to say, not so well as the Sketch—The fault is in the management of the projecting firbough in its connection with the round Island. This you will easily correct when we have the pleasure of seeing you as I hope we shall, next summer.—

I shall be truly glad to receive the Drawing of the Cabinet[2] from the pencil of Mrs Gaskell—

Dora has been a week gone from home; this day, she takes up her Abode at her Friend Sarah Coleridge's 10 Chester place, near the Colyseum, Regent's park. She chuses to be there at this time for quiet's sake, in order to avoid the bustle of a Wedding at Mrs Hoare's Hampstead, the Bride who has been long resident with Mrs H— is Louisa Lloyd.[3] Dora describes herself as well, but we know her to be weak, and She was looking miserably thin when she left us. They had a most agreeable and unfatiguing journey by Railway from Preston.—Miss Fenwick is well and no doubt will contrive to see you as soon as you arrive in London. After this week she changes her Lodgings, so I cannot give you her address—

The Author of Ernest is Mr Loft son of the late Capel Loft near Bury St Edmunds, so you need not trouble yourself with further inquiries, as I know a good deal about him. He was a distinguished Scholar when at Trin: Coll. Cambridge—[4]

[1] *Written* contained.

[2] The Wordsworth family aumbry (see L. 1364 above).

[3] A connection of the Lloyds of Birmingham. She was the youngest daughter of C. Lloyd of Olton Green, Warwickshire, and married J. C. Powell, eldest son of James Powell of Clapton.

[4] See pt. iii, L. 1335. Capel Lofft jnr. was a Fellow of King's, not Trinity. His

I hope you will all enjoy yourselves in London; there is no likelihood of our going thither this Spring, in fact every other year in London is quite enough for my strength. I find it too hard service, though Mr Rogers 7 years my Senior does not.

I have no news for you—this neighbourhood being quite barren of any thing so precious. Miss Gillies's pictures we learn are much liked, especially one of Mrs Wordsworth and my self in the same Piece.[1] I shall be glad if you and all your family approve of them. Pray be so good as to let Mr Wyon[2] know that we are anxious to have back the two Medallions improved, as he promised. Dora could bring them with her, if he could finish them immediately.—Poor dear Mr Southey is no better; with affectionate remembrances to yourself, Father and Mother and Sisters and all your friends in which Mrs W joins

I remain ever yours
W W

1377. W. W. to HENRY ALFORD

Address: The Rev[d] Henry Alford, Wymeswold, near Loughborough, Leicestershire. [*In M. W.'s hand*]
Postmark: 21 Feb. 1840.
Stamp: Ambleside.
MS. The Robert H. Taylor Collection, Princeton, N.J.
Mem. (—). *Life, Journals, and Letters of Henry Alford, D.D., p. 115* (—). *K* (—). *LY ii. 1006* (—).

[*c.*20 Feb. 1840]

My dear Sir,

Pray excuse my having been some little time in your debt.[3] I

father, Capel Lofft snr. (1751–1824), inherited the family estates at Troston and Stanton, nr. Bury St. Edmunds, on the death of his uncle in 1781, and devoted himself to literary pursuits and radical causes. He was a staunch supporter of Napoleon. He edited *The Poems of Robert Bloomfield* (1803), and published poems, translations, and works on legal and political issues.

[1] See L. 1371 above. A replica of this joint portait is preserved at Dove Cottage.

[2] For E. W. Wyon and his medallion of W. W., see pt. iii, L. 1016. W. W. gave him another sitting at the Marshalls' house when he was down in London in June 1839 (see *HCR* ii. 572).

[3] Alford (see pt. iii, L. 927) had written on 2 Feb. (*WL MSS.*) recalling his

could plead many things in extenuation, the chief, that old one of the state of my eyes, which never leaves me at liberty either to read or write a tenth part as much as I could wish, and as otherwise I ought to do.

It cannot but be highly gratifying to me to learn that my writings are prized so highly by a Poet and Critic of your powers. The essay upon them which you have so kindly sent me, seems well qualified to promote your views in writing it. I was particularly pleased with your distinction between religion in Poetry and versified Religion. For my own part, I have been averse to frequent mention of the mysteries of Christian faith, not from a want of a due sense of their momentous nature; but the contrary. I felt it far too deeply to venture on handling the subject as familiarly as many scruple not to do. I am far from blaming them, but let them not blame me, nor turn from my companionship on that account. Besides general reasons for diffidence in treating subjects of holy writ I have some especial ones. I might err in points of faith; and I should not deem my

visit with his wife to Rydal Mount in July 1838 (see *RMVB*), and sending a recent article of his on W. W.'s poetry. This had just appeared in *Dearden's Miscellany*, iii (1840), 93–108, of which he was now editor, and included a notable discussion of W. W.'s poetry in relation to the Christian religion. W. W.'s poetry, he maintained, and particularly *The Excursion*, deals with the region where morbid feeling ends and healthy action and faith begin: 'Therefore it is, that enunciation of the lofty mysteries of our creed by their theological appellations would be for the most part out of place in his great poem, and in those lesser ones which depend on it and fill it up.' And he went on to distinguish between religious poetry and versified religion. 'The former ranges at a distance from the subject, and brings the mind and feelings into unconscious and hourly subjection, clearing the temple, as it were, of intruders, before the solemn music of spiritual truth bursts on the ear of the soul; the latter hitches into doggerel, better or worse, the deepest solemnities of our faith, talking in texts, and descants on doctrines; forbids the gentle and inquiring, disgusts the practised ear of taste, and furnishes laughing matter for the trifling.' In a letter to Mrs. Hemans of 16 Aug. 1834, R. P. Graves referred to a conversation he had had with W. W. on the same theme. 'In the course of it he expressed to me the feelings of reverence which prevented him from venturing to lay his hand on what he always thought a subject too high for him; and he accompanied this with the earnest protest that his works . . . should not be considered as developing all the influences which his own heart recognised, but rather those which he considered himself able as an artist to display to advantage, and which he thought most applicable to the wants, and admitted by the usages, of the world at large.' (*WL MSS.*)

mistakes less to be deprecated because they were expressed in metre. Even Milton, in my humble judgement, has erred and grievously; and what Poet could hope to atone for his apprehensions in the way in which that mighty mind has done?

I am not at all desirous that any one should write an elaborate critique on my Poetry—there is no call for it—if they be from above they will do their own work in course of time, if not, they will perish as they ought. But scarcely a week passes in which I do not receive grateful acknowledgments of the good they have done to the minds of the several writers. They speak of the relief they have received from them under affliction and in grief, and of the calmness and elevation of Spirit which the Poems either give, or assist them in attaining. As these benefits are not without a traceable bearing upon the good of the immortal soul, the sooner perhaps they are pointed out and illustrated in a work like yours the better.

Pray excuse my talking so much about myself; your Letter and critique called me to the subject, but I assure you it would have been more grateful to me to acknowledge the debt we owe you in this House, where we have read your Poems with no common pleasure. Your Abbot of Muchelnaye[1] also makes me curious to hear more of him.

But I must conclude, dinner being on the Table. I was truly sorry to have missed you when you and Mrs Alford called at Rydal.

Mrs W. unites with me in kind regards to you both, and believe me

my dear Sir
Faithfully your much obliged,
Wm Wordsworth

[1] Publ. 1841.

1378. W. W. to JOHN HILLS[1]

Address: John Hills Esq[re], c/o Whittaker and Co, Ave Maria Lane, London. *Prepaid*. [*readdressed to*] Hotel D'Angleterre, Caen, France.
Postmark: (1) 23 Feb. 1840 (2) 24 Feb. 1840 (3) 6 Mar. 1840 (4) 8 Mars 1840.
Stamp: (1) Ambleside (2) London (3) Caen.
MS. Yale University Library. Hitherto unpublished.

Rydal Mount
Feb[ry] 20th 1840

My dear Sir,

I have long been in your debt for the gift of your Translation of Faust; it appears to me admirably done, but I have no acquaintance with the original, therefore my commendation is of little Value. It was this conviction along with the fact of your being abroad, mentioned to me about the time I received your work, which caused me to defer my acknowledgement. The honorable mention which you make of me in your notes[2] calls for an expression of pleasure on my part. Be assured that I am not insensible of the honor conferred by the praise of one so accomplished in literature as you are—

My Son John was here soon after Christmas, and we often talked about you. You will be glad to hear that his health is now good, after a long and severe indisposition consequent upon an attack of typhus fever. He has lately, in a manner agreeable to himself and still more to me connected his name with mine, by publishing a few translations into Latin verse from my Poems. A few Copies have been struck off in an appendix to the 2nd Stereotype impression of my Works in six Volumes. If you will call at Moxon's with my Compts he will be glad to let you have the appendix on a separate sheet. You will find there also a dozen Sonnets of mine, not any of them in the Edition of 1837; but

[1] John Hills (1803–48), a schoolfriend of John W.'s at Sedbergh, went on to St. John's College, Cambridge, where he graduated in 1826, and was called to the Bar in 1830. Soon after his marriage in 1834, he went to live in Italy where he became the friend of Mazzini. His translation of *Faust* into English verse appeared in 1840.

[2] In a note, p. 385, Hills compared Goethe's denunciation of the analytical philosophy of the eighteenth century with W. W.'s, but maintained the latter's genius was 'far superior to that of Goethe . . . and destined ultimately to be of deeper and more abiding influence in his own nation than I believe will fall to the lot of his German contemporary.'

they were all previously printed in a Volume containing all the Sonnets, and nothing else.—

Pray present my kind remembrances in which Mrs W. joins, to Mrs Hills, and believe me with our united respects.

very sincerely
your much obliged
Wm Wordsworth

1379. W. W. to ISABELLA FENWICK

MS. WL.
LY ii. 1019.

[*c.* Feb. 1840]

I sit down to write to you my very dear Friend with nothing to say in the way of *news*, and so much in the way of feeling to which I can do no justice, and which it would be superfluous to express if I could, that I am not a little at a loss what to touch upon.—One particular however I must express, namely, that your absence has convinced me I never can be at ease, if you were in this country and not within hourly walking reach of us. It is an odd thing to say, but it is true, that I enjoy the thought of your separation from us now where you are, and are likely to be, among Friends to whom you are so dear, and who are so dear to you. But I could not endure your being long, at such a distance as Calgarth even, where you would be so much parted from us, without any compensation from the company of your other Friends, and your kindred. Besides, looking at the matter selfishly, I feel that I should be perpetually on the fret, having you so near, and seeing what would appear to myself, and all of us so *little* of you as unavoidably we should see. A few years ago, as I have often said to you, it would have been otherwise; a walk of 6 or 7 miles would have then been nothing, and I could have done it without loss of time, as my mind might have been employed in composition all the way. So much therefore is settled that we must have you *near* us. When I think of this I borrow hope from yourself and from Mary and Dora, otherwise I should despond. Mr Hill[1] is now fixed at Rydal, Mr Combe[2] at

[1] Herbert Hill, Southey's son-in-law.

[2] Probably the Mr. Combe who in 1841 built the Independent Chapel on the outskirts of Ambleside,—'Mr. Combe's Synagogue', as Hartley Coleridge called it.

Bellevue and we cannot expect a House to spring up out of the ground like a mushroom. Still I will try to hope, as I ought to do.—

I have been twice at Grasmere since you went away, all my other walks have been in the opposite direction, along the Rotha to the bridge, and several times round by Ambleside. Yesterday when I was crossing that Bridge, I saw to my great sorrow several of the trees that grow near it in the field by the waterside levelled with the ground. They were a great ornament, a few were still standing, Mr Cookson[1] the Proprietor was there and I entreated him earnestly to spare them but all in vain—Money, money, is the God of the old in that rank of life, almost in every case, whatever it may be elsewhere. Your few words upon London talk and Society are very depressing. If hopelessness were not a sin I should be without hope. We appear as a nation, at least the prominent portion of us, to be sinking deeper and deeper every month, in dishonesty and dishonor. Good men and sincere Patriots, ought to look upon this as a trial of their resignation to the decrees of Providence, yet at the same time, as a call upon them to do their utmost in every way towards counteracting the mischief.—

Pray tell Mr Villiers[2] that I am deeply sensible of his kind feelings towards my Son. Be his destiny what it may, it never will be mended by any writings of mine, this I feel and in some degree lament. But as long as such iniquit[y] as the heads of both Parties, Russel and Peel, are disposed to perpetrate in the matter of Copy-rights, how can it be expected that literary men will ever be dealt with as they ought to be. This injustice I shall never cease to resent; nor can I feel aught but contempt for the understanding of men who are unable to perceive that their opposition to this Bill is strictly *preposterous*; the worth of the article is upon their scheme sacrificed to presumed, and even falsely presumed, facilities for its circulation. Common sense points the other way; do what you can to assist in making books good in the first place,

[*cetera desunt*]

[1] James Cookson of Clappersgate.

[2] For Edward Villiers see pt. iii, L. 1326. See also L. 1387 below.

1380. W. W. to BASIL MONTAGU

Address: Basil Montagu Esqre, St. Albans.
Postmark: 23 Feb. 1840.
Stamp: Ambleside.
MS. WL. transcript. Hitherto unpublished.

[*c.*22 Feb. 1840]

My dear Montagu,

The common saying of "better late than never" scarcely seems to apply to correspondence by letter, and fearing that my acknowledgements for the expression of your sympathy might be deferred till they lost all their value I sit down to thank you at once; and also to tell you how happy I am in hearing so good an account of yourself.

The death of my nephew[1] has been a great affliction to his Father, and a source of much sorrow to his Brothers and indeed to us all. He was a man of the kindest affections and of blameless life. Had it pleased God that he should continue in this world, such was his industry and so exact and accurate his mind, that they who knew him best are assured he would have placed his name among the first Scholars in Europe. Merit of that kind is apt to be overlooked or despised in these busy days of scientific discovery, and useful invention, and on this account the few whose education has enabled them to perceive and *feel* what mankind owe to classical literature, and what they would lose by the neglect of it, are still more disposed now than they could have been in other times to respect Students who give themselves quietly up to these unambitious researches.

I am not surprized to learn that you are so fond of St Albans. Never shall I forget my sensations when having past from the magnificent and huge Cathedral or Conventical Church I opened the side-door of the humble Fabric[2] in which I knew Lord Bacon was laid. There was he sitting before me in alabaster, quite alone. I see him now, and shall do so from time to time as long as I live.

It pleases me to hear you have been so busily and so well employed, and that your health is so good. Mine thank God is the same, but I am not without symptoms of decay, which I trust will prove salutary. I say nothing about my eyes because I

[1] C. W.'s son John.

[2] St. Michael's Church.

believe it is universally known among my Friends how sadly they have cut me off from intercourse with Books, and how often the irritability and inflammation to which they are subject, made it injurious to labour even in my mind; but God's will be done!

Is not there a good Book of Godwyns upon Sepulture,[1] no doubt you have looked at Wever's Funeral Monuments[2]—the lines of mine you quote were never printed, therefore no wonder you looked for them in vain. They stand thus in my MS.

——there is
One great Society alone on earth
The noble living, and the noble dead.[3]

and so they have stood since I either read or repeated them to you.

I am anxious to learn from your Book[4] how you treat the pleasures of Wealth. *Wealth* is altogether a comparative thing. There is a young Lady in my neighbourhood whose elder Brother spent three thousand a year of inherited Estate and left himself without a sixpence—he is now gone to Vandiemen's land with 12 Children upon a subscription raised by his Friends. His Sister the Lady to whom I allude though brought up in affluence and luxury, lives, exclusive of her dress, upon 20 pounds per annum, and is contented, healthy, happy, chearful, and even gay, she is therefore richer than ever her Brother was, in his best day.—

Anything you are inclined to send me will always find its way hither through Moxon, though not instantly.

Pray give my kind remembrances to Mrs Montagu in which Mrs W. unites, and believe my my dear Montagu

faithfully yours
Wm Wordsworth

[1] William Godwin, *Essay on Sepulchres: or, a proposal for erecting some memorial of the illustrious dead in all ages on the spot where their remains have been interred*, 1809.

[2] Robert Weaver (1773–1852), Congregational minister: author of *Monumenta Antiqua, or the Stone Monuments of Antiquity yet remaining in the British Isles, particularly as illustrated by Scripture. Also a Dissertation on Stonehenge, together with a compendious account of the Druids. To which are added Conjectures on the origin and design of the Pyramids of Egypt and of the Round Towers of Ireland*, 1840.

[3] *The Prelude* (1805), x. 968–70.

[4] *The Funerals of the Quakers*, 1840.

Excuse bad writing, I am anxious to get my eyes off the paper. You speak of the last Edit. of my Poems—is it the 2nd Impression of the stereotype struck off a few weeks ago—if not, pray apply in my name to Moxon for an appendix which may be had separately—it contains 12 Sonnets, one of which beginning —Blest Statesman![1] I shall like you to read as a summary of my [ ] in Politics.

1381. W. W. to ISABELLA FENWICK

MS. WL. Hitherto unpublished.

[*In M. W.'s hand*]

[late Feb. 1840]

Dearest Friend,

This page is to be occupied by the *omissions* of yesterday. First of all the Cuckoo Clock was forgotten to be thanked for, and my attempt to pacify, by saying thanks would be in good time when the article arrived, did not satisfy, so I take the pen for my husband to tell you he has already heard it in fancy, and hopes to be present when you and little William[2] first hear it together.—Next do not (Wm now dictates) I beg put yourself to the expence of purchasing, or the trouble of sending the Edinburgh Review. I can get a sight of it I am sure in this neighbourhood—and except for the Article you mention[3] it would be so much money thrown away—for, if I may judge of the Spirit of that periodical from extracts I occasionally see in the Radical Papers, it is, as far as the Church of England is concerned in particular, as odious as ever: besides, tho' I dare scarcely mention this, I am becoming penurious in regard to your purse, as I have often told you I am in respect to my own. Then, there is that bad news from America which provokes me, even on your account more than it ought to do, but still more upon Mr Elliot's,[4] to whom it is of so much consequence. I ought also in my yesterday's letter (which was directed to the care of Mr Taylor at the Colonial, we

[1] *PW* iv. 129.

[2] W. W.'s grandson.

[3] Probably an article by David Brewster on 'The Life and Discoveries of James Watt', whom W. W. much admired (see pt. ii, L. 408), published in the issue for Jan. 1840.

[4] Probably Frederick Elliot (see pt. iii, L. 1048).

not knowing where you might be) to have expressed my regret that you and dear Dora are not here to enjoy the delightful weather we have had for some days. The Glass M. tells me is higher than she ever knew it, and the pure cerulean of the Sky gives to the Lakes a blue more beautiful than we recollect ever to have observed—and Mr Carr who cannot walk so as to keep himself warm when the weather is at all sharp, told me yesterday, that he sate 2 hours in the sunshine while the temperature was as mild as he found it at Sorento that day twelvemonth. My customary walk between 4 and 5 yesterday along the banks of the Rotha treated me with a most beautiful exhibition of the mountains in their sunset splendour. I must add my own affectionate remembrances to Laura Carr,[1] and say to her that I would give not a trifle were she here at this moment, for we would start for a three hours ramble over Loughrigg fell. The air is still, not a leaf moves, and the Laurels are so dazzling in the sunshine that I can scarcely bear the light tho' my eyes are quite well. The finger continues swoln and stiff, but I trust is going on right. But dear Miss F. how uncertain are health, life, and strength and what hair-breadth escapes are perpetually recurring. The evening before last, I was coming down the steps from the terrace, and in my care to get well thro' a heap of laurel boughs with which they were strewn, I did not notice that I was touching a large ball of hewn freestone that I had placed some years ago upon the flat-topped wall. Just as I set my foot upon the gravel, this ball fell within a few inches of it, and of course made a deep dint in the ground—had it fallen upon my foot, the least part of the mischief must have been, that I should have been a cripple for life. I mention this knowing my dear friend that you and Dora will share my gratitude to Almighty God—a feeling which has not often been out of my heart since. I have taken care that nobody shall incur a like risk. By the bye James had a still narrower escape from this same stone when it stood as an ornament upon the point of the gavel, of the little building upon your left as you come from the Gate to the front door. He was standing under it and a Peacock which had been frightened, flying from a distance knocked it down, and the stone fell within an inch or two of his head. Had it struck the scull, he must have

[1] Miss Laura Carr of London, youngest daughter of Thomas Carr of Frognal, Hampstead, called at Rydal Mount in Jan. and Oct. 1840 (*RMVB*). In 1845 she married H. C. R.'s friend Robert Monsey Rolfe, Lord Cranworth (see pt. i, L. 279).

inevitably been killed! Be so good as write to us as often as you can without inconvenience, I cannot subscribe my name without telling you how anxious I am about Dora's health—notwithstanding she tells us she is 'quite well', but allows that 'she coughs in a morning, and puffs and coughs in going up stairs, and that her medicines are taken in vain.' Pray thank Dr Fergusson[1] for his goodness and tell him that W^m whose bashfulness I cannot excuse for not having written himself, is very much better, indeed as he says in a letter of yesterday, *quite well*, which happy change he ascribes not a little to horse-exercise which he has had, since his return from Brinsop, without expence, and will have till the Spring is farther advanced. I have offered him £20 towards the purchase of a horse, and told him that what he cannot spare I will supply for the keeping of it. This I did some time since, nevertheless poor dear fellow so unselfish is he, that provender being so dear as it now is, he could not bring himself to incur the expence. But I shall insist upon it being done, when his invalid Friend, whose horse he now exercises can make use of it himself.

ever most affectionately and faithfully yours
[*signed*] Wm Wordsworth

I wish Dora would consult Mr Strickland Cookson about the Miss[iss]ippi Bonds—

[*M. W. writes*]

As no letter has yet arrived in reply, my dearest Friend to your last, I think it well to enclose that part of Mrs Lutwidge's[2] former one—so that you may re-peruse what she says about their movements, and judge if it be probable she should deem that to be a sufficient answer to the question you put of 'how long you might retain the house?'—And perhaps it would be well, at any rate to repeat by writing again to her—directing to Florence or Bologna—so that she may clearly understand you are not *their* Tenant, until you receive her sanction to be so for 6 months from the time of your receiving an answer to your letter forwarded the 26th Jan^ry. We hear that the manservant has written that they mean to leave Rome the 1st of March, and that they are all tired and want to be at home—but this is no authority for us.—

[1] See pt. iii, L. 1030.

[2] See L. 1369 above.

The Cover to this came by post to day from London I suppose—Seeing by its shape and being open at one end, that it was of no consequence I opened it, and tho' it bears no date and is imperfectly expressed we understand that it is a debt you can best discharge where you are. I send it—And truly my dear friend, as *we* see all Mr Roughsedge's Morn^g Post it is not right that you should go on paying for the St J's[1] during your absence.—Mrs Luff has just been here. She is about to creep into Owen's[2] lodgings after all. She begs her love to you and to Dora. We are very glad that you have seen Dr Southey—In vindication of Herbert[3] I must tell you that Bertha says, he was but one day in Town as he came down, and that day he dined with his Uncle, and but one day on his return, and on that day according to previous engagement he dined with the Coleridges in Chester Place, and had so many commission[s] to execute that she thinks he scarcely could have time to go to Harley St, but she does not know that he did not—Kate's[4] late letters have not spoken particularly of her Father's state, so we hope he is no worse—adieu we long for your return.

[*unsigned*]

1382. W. W. to THOMAS SOUTHWOOD SMITH[5]

MS. Cornell. Hitherto unpublished.

Rydal Mount
[late Feb. 1840]

Sir,

I am glad to learn that the Sanatorium prospers. Pray call at Mr Moxon's 44 Dover Street and present him the enclosed and he will pay you the amount of my Subscription.

I have the honor to be
truly yours
Wm Wordsworth

[1] *St. James's Chronicle.*

[2] Owen Lloyd.

[3] Herbert Hill.

[4] Kate Southey.

[5] Southwood Smith (see pt. iii, L. 1199) had been engaged for some time in collecting contributions for a sanatorium in London to treat patients from the

1383. W. W. to CHARLES WORDSWORTH

MS. Mr. Jonathan Wordsworth. Hitherto unpublished.

[Mar. 1840]

My dear Nephew,

I sent through Mrs Hoare a little time ago a message which perhaps you have received, it was of thanks for the Memorials of dear John which you and Christopher were so kind as to send me, on the Works of Nardini[1] and Nebbi.[2]—My sight is too much impaired, and my age too advanced to leave it probable that I shall be able to make satisfactory use of them; I shall nevertheless consult them I hope not infrequently, and at all events the mere sight of the Books which he possessed and probably read on the ground they refer to will make them valuable to me. Excuse me for saying that my Son W^{m} would have been gratified to possess a Remembrancer however small of his Cousin to whom he was strongly attached. They shed tears together after being joint-witnesses of the almost unprecedented respect paid to me at the Oxford Commemoration. last Summer. W^{m} is very modest, and probably has not imparted the feeling which I am confident he must have, and therefore I again beg you would excuse my mentioning it.—

We are glad to hear that your little Daughter is thriving so well, and we pray my dear Charles, that she may be preserved to be a blessing to you.—You know, no doubt, that Dora, is at Hampstead; and that while in London she caught a desperate and almost dangerous cold,—dangerous I mean for one who has so little strength to spare. Your poor Aunt Dorothy is a good deal improved both in health of body and mind. Your Aunt W. and I have both been well during the winter, and spring which has. . .

[*cetera desunt*]

middle classes of both sexes. Thomas Powell had referred to the project in his letter to W. W. of 3 Jan., and Southwood Smith himself sent W. W. a progress report on 24 Feb. (*WL MSS.*). The institution was founded on 6 Mar. 1840 at a public meeting headed by James Pattison, M.P. and Lord Robert Grosvenor (see pt. iii, L. 1338), and was opened on 6 Apr. 1842 at Devonshire House, York Gate, W. W.'s name appearing in the list of subscribers. Lord Ashley was Chairman; Charles Dickens took a deep interest in the undertaking as one of the committee members.

[1] Perhaps Leonardo Nardine, Italian literary scholar, editor of Ariosto, Tasso, Boccaccio, etc.

[2] Unidentified.

1384. W. W. and M. W. to ISABELLA FENWICK

MS. WL.
LY ii. 1001 (—). *MW, p. 238* (—).

[*c.* Mar. 1840]

. . . But whatever may be the execution of the portions done by Mr Powell and his Friends the attempt[1] cannot but excite some little attention to the subject, and in so far as it does will tend to a good purpose. Chaucer was one of the greatest poets the world has ever seen. He is certainly, at times, in his comic tales indecent, but he is never, as far as I know, insidiously or openly voluptuous, much less would a stronger term, which would apply to some popular writers of our own day apply to him. He had towards the female sex as exquisite and pure feelings as ever the heart of man was blessed with, and has expressed them as beautifully in the language of his age, as ever man did. But it is time that I should stop. I have noticed but few points in your Letter; but be assured every word of it was interesting to me. God bless you, my dear, dear Friend.

Wm Wordsworth

[*M. W. writes*]

My dear Friend,

Together with this letter, W sends you a packet which he thought while writing the enclosed, was in Mr Powell's hands—but which I detained from my own distaste, strengthened by the opinion expressed in your invaluable letter—and I rejoice to say that my dr Husband is glad I have detained it, to send to you. I wish the poems had been written upon better paper for the sake of your eyes, as well as those of Mr Taylor to whom with his Compts Mr W. hopes he will take the trouble to read them and say if he thinks the truth and beauty of the Manciple's Tale[2] does not more than counterbalance any objection that might be made to the subject. It appears from a letter recd yesterday that the projectors of the intended publication have changed their purpose of modernizing *all* Chaucer, but first of all mean to give a Selection 'by way of feeling the pulse of the public'—and this sample is to consist of Wm's Prioresses Tale

[1] *Chaucer's Poems Modernized* (see pt. iii, L. 1361).

[2] W. W.'s version of *The Manciple's Tale* was not in the end included, and remained unpublished in his lifetime. A version by Leigh Hunt was substituted instead (see L. 1405 below).

already published, the Cuckoo and Nightingale (now in Mr P's hands) and those before you, while the other coadjutors give one piece each, a much larger quantity perhaps—but will this be a fair Specimen of what they mean to send out afterwards without aught from the *Masters* hand! To me it seems plain what the motive is—they are in haste to appear in connection with a name of influence.—I hope you do not think there will be any thing dishonorable in Mr W. changing his purpose at this late hour. No letter from Mrs Lutwidge—God bless you dearest friend. Joanna's best love—

ever y[r]
M. W.

Mr W. begs you to keep the Mss till you hear from him again—after he hears your opinion about withdrawing his intention—I do trust it will be in accord with my own.

1385. W. W. to LORD MORPETH[1]

MS. untraced.
Mem. (—). *Grosart* (—). *K* (—). *LY ii. 1007.*

March 2, 1840.

. . . I never did seek or accept a pension from the present or any other administration, directly or indirectly. . . .

[1] Lord Morpeth (see pt. ii, L. 582) was at this time Chief Secretary of Ireland. On 27 Feb., during the Parliamentary debate on a pension for Sir John Newport, lately Chancellor of the Exchequer in Ireland, H. T. Liddell (see pt. iii, L. 875) had complained that W. W.'s name was not on the Civil List. Upon it being objected that W. W. held an office under the Crown, Liddell replied that it was true W. W. held a provincial office which afforded a tolerably respectable income, and that an offer had been made to transfer the appointment to his son and to place W. W.'s own name upon the pension list; but the proposed pension of £150 per annum was so much lower than that awarded to other persons of literary distinction that a just and commendable self-esteem induced him to decline it. Later in the debate Lord Morpeth, from the Government side, maintained that it was a bad principle to canvass the claims of individuals, however eminent, and that W. W.'s dignity and standing would not be well served by such a move. He rejoiced to see the names of distinguished men on the Civil List, but not as of right. This public discussion of a long-standing problem which W. W. had been unable to resolve the previous year during his visit to London, led him to write to Morpeth for a clarification of the Government's position, and to set the record right as to his own.

1386. W. W. to ISABELLA FENWICK

MS. Mr. Jonathan Wordsworth. Hitherto unpublished.

[Mar. 1840]

. . . go on with a series of these republications the next to be Spenser, but he[1] says this interruption has put him out of spirits with the project and the more so as he was much annoyed by H. C'^s[2] procrastination. This long story will have proved tedious; but I was uneasy under what appeared to me an undeserved censure, of the more importance as coming from so high-minded a Man as Mr Taylor.

Mary is gone to look after Mrs Fraggart's House at Clappersgate, that which was Mrs Freemans,[3] not without a hope should you approve of hiring it for four months for [ ] Mrs Luff had offered

[*Half a page missing*]

There are gentlemen among the humblest Peasants, O that this man and such as he could borrow something of their spirit.—We are sorry at the thought of losing Joanna.[4] She is an excellent person, with admirable sense for the concerns of hourly life, much more than I had given her credit for. She has a most tender heart and no one acts now habitually from the sense of duty. But I must conclude: say all that is proper to your dear Sister,[5] and every other friend we have in your present neighbourhood.

ever most affectionately yours
Wm Wordsworth

Our weather continues as glorious as ever.

[1] Edward Moxon.

[2] Hartley Coleridge's. He sent Moxon his notices of Massinger and Ford on 12 Mar. See *Letters of Hartley Coleridge* (ed. Griggs), pp. 235–6.

[3] See pt. iii, L. 1122.

[4] Joanna Hutchinson, now on a visit from the Isle of Man.

[5] Mrs. Popham (see L. 1369 above). I. F. was now staying with her in Somerset. Mr., Mrs. and Miss Popham paid her a return visit in Ambleside in May (see *RMVB*).

1387. W. W. to DORA W.

MS. WL.
LY ii. 1017 (—).

Wed. mor^{g} [Mar. 1840]

I sit down, my beloved Child, to write to you without the least prospect of anything being contained in my Letter to entertain you. But the account you give of your susceptibility of Changes in place or weather so troubles me that I cannot help entreating with my own pen that you would put yourself, as to exposure, moving about etc, upon the invalid list. I am anxious exceedingly about this hoarseness which seems by your last to have recurred as bad as ever. Let me beg that you would not think of going to Church nor enter an open carriage; and in short that you would keep yourself in a temperature as equable as possible.

But for anxiety about your health I should be quite pleased with your prolonging your stay in London and the neighbourhood; though I cannot help often wishing you were here to enjoy this enchanting weather that we have had now nearly five weeks. Sun and moon have lately vied and are still vying with each other which can do most to beautify this beautiful country. James,[1] you know, is not only a Painter, but a little of a Poet. While he was working in the garden the other evening and we were admiring together the things we saw he said—'And look at Wansfell what a *heat* that is', pointing to the deep copper reflection of the light from the western clouds, in which the mountain was steeped. 'Each had his *glowing* Mountain',[2] as you remember in the Excursion. We rejoice in the prospect for dear William—the woods and forests[3] are the very thing for him; fresh air and horse-exercise just what he wants. I am most grateful to our Friends whether they succeed or no. But what a strange Creature is your Br John. Not a word in his letter to you upon the point of insuring his life, which I pressed upon him so earnestly. It was indeed only to enable him to do this that I encountered all the disagreeables of writing a long letter to Mr

[1] W. W.'s gardener.

[2] *Exc.*, ix. 447.

[3] With the help of I.F.'s friends, the Villiers, W. W. was at this time looking into the possibility of obtaining a post for Willy in the department of Woods and Forests. See *MW*, pp. 239–40, and L. 1393 below.

Curwen[1] upon what I then understood to be *Henry's*[2] proposal that 100£ of the £200 annuity should be transferred to him. And what stuff about his playing the dinner-Patron to the poor curates in Brigham Parish! Let the Lay-rector[3] or any great Squire of the neighbourhood do this, if needful. *He* as Incumbent of Brigham was as much plundered by the Reformation and by monastic abuses preceding it, as any of the poorest among the Curates. They are fellow-sufferers. In all this I see kindness of feeling more hasty than wise, too much of the little vanity of great-manism (a queer word coined for the occasion) and that sad want of circumspection that is shewn in almost all his proceedings. This, I assure you, troubles me, notwithstanding all his good and amiable qualities, whenever I think of him.—

Tell Mr Quillinan, I think he has taken rather a *narrow* view of the spirit of the Manciple's Tale, especially as concerns its *morality*. The formal prosing at the end, and the selfishness that pervades it flows from the genius of Chaucer, mainly as characteristic of the Narrator whom he describes in the Prologue as eminent for shrewdness and clever worldly Prudence. The main lesson, and the most important one, is inculcated as a Poet ought chiefly to inculcate his lessons, not formally, but by implication; as when Phoebus in a transport of passion slays a wife whom he loved so dearly. How could the mischief of telling truth, merely because it *is* truth, be more feelingly exemplified. The Manciple himself is not, in his understanding, conscious of this; but his heart dictates what was natural to be felt and the moral, without being intended, forces itself more or less upon every Reader.—Then how vividly is impressed the mischief of jealous vigilance and how truly and touchingly in contrast with the world's judgments are the transgressions of a woman in a low rank of life and one in high estate placed on the same level, treated. But enough; continue dear Dora to write as often as you can.

There is a probability of Miss Fenwick's getting for the Summer Mrs Fraggat's house.

[1] John W.'s father-in-law.

[2] John W.'s brother-in-law, rector of Workington (see pt. ii, L. 482).

[3] The Earl of Lonsdale, the present patron and impropriator of the endowments, who paid the vicar a stipend. The church of this extensive parish had been unusually wealthy during the Middle Ages, but the foundation of a chantry had drawn off some of its income, and the endowments were further depleted after the Reformation by a succession of lay impropriations.

Love to the Marshalls, Mrs Hoare, Mrs Gee[1] etc etc etc.

Your most affectionate Father

[*M. W. writes*]

Father was pleased with y^r criticism on Calvert's[2] picture and when you meet he will talk to you about him. If you have not left Mrs Gee's I (Father) think your voice might have returned ere this—

1388. W. W. to DORA W.

MS. WL.
LY ii. 1008.

Monday [Mar.] 9th [1840]

My very dear Child,

I have been much troubled at this severe illness of yours, especially bearing in mind the old *habit* of your Body. If I could but learn that any progress had been made in correcting *that* it would make me happy indeed. I am therefore very anxious that you should see Dr Ferguson, and not for once merely, but with such intervals of time as would allow him to ascertain the effects of anything he might prescribe. On this account, and in order that the time of dear Miss Fenwick's departure may be delayed thereby as little as may be, I wish your visit at Hampstead to be shortened. The Marshalls will be most happy to receive you.[3]—Now for lighter matter! the weather here continues to be enchanting; sharp frost, I own, in the night, but in the day time the sun without a cloud is as warm as summer. Mr Carr exclaimed again the other day 'it is just as we had the air at Sorento last year at this time; I could almost think I was there again'.—We had Roby[4] here the other evening; he brought along with him young Mr Colman[5] of Brathay. They drank tea and the youth in his modesty made an offer of moving, but

[1] Dora W. was now staying with Mrs. Gee at Hendon.

[2] Charles Calvert (1785–1852), landscape painter, practising his art in Manchester and the Lake District. He died at Bowness.

[3] In Upper Grosvenor Street.

[4] i.e. Capt. Charles Robinson of Ambleside (see pt. i, L. 23).

[5] Old Brathay had been taken for the winter by Edward Colman (1818–42), of Trinity College, Cambridge (see *RMVB* for Feb. and Apr. 1840), who graduated in 1842, but died at Naples the same year.

Roby, to shew I suppose on what familiar terms he was here, said, 'no, no'. The attempt was repeated three times with the same result, and the poor youth was forced to remain till within a few minutes of nine. Your Mother in the course of the evening said, Miss Gillies' picture of Mrs Hopkinson[1] is much admired in London. Yes, replied he, I always thought it her *chief dōver*, you know he has undertaken to teach his Daughter *French*! ! ! ! We talked about a new ministry, which was said to be in contemplation. Lord J. Russel to be Premier, Lord Brougham etc to have office. Pshaw! said I, or some thing like it; and Mr R: gravely, yet with a smile, observed 'These ephemeral administrations never last.' When I told this to dear Aunty, she was delighted above measure.—

I have had a friendly answer from Lord Morpeth.[2] He tells me he *actually said* words to which I have no objection whatever, so moderate your wrath.—I was desirous that my Letter should as soon as possible be in Mr Powell's hands, otherwise I should have requested Miss F. to send it to you.—There was, and continues to be, an unpleasantness about John's having Plumbland[3] in which good Mr Curwen[4] had no part. It rises entirely out of Henry's[5] *cupidity*, and John's good nature, standing in the way of due reflection.

[*cetera desunt*]

[1] A local acquaintance.

[2] See L. 1385 above.

[3] John W. had accepted the living of Plumbland, which he proposed to hold along with nearby Brigham. It had previously been held by his wife's uncle, the late Edward Stanley (see pt. ii, L. 562); later on, Cuthbert Southey was John W.'s curate there.

[4] John W.'s father-in-law, patron of the living.

[5] Henry Curwen, John W.'s brother-in-law, rector of Workington.

1389. W. W. to EDWARD QUILLINAN

Address: Edward Quillinan Esq., 121 Crawford Street, London. [*In M. W.'s hand*]
Postmark: 10 Mar. 1840.
Stamp: Ambleside.
MS. British Library.
'Some Unpublished Letters of William Wordsworth', Cornhill Magazine, xx (1893), 257–76 (—). *K* (—). *LY ii. 1009* (—).

Rydal Mount March 9th '40

We have to thank you my dear Mr Quillinan for two long Letters both of which were very acceptable and interesting. I will first touch upon the points of business, by noticing the information you have procured about modelling which seems sufficient for fulfilment of my promise to the person at Keswick.—Upon consulting Mr Courtenay's Letter, I find he says: 'as the Bank is *chartered*, your risk would be less:' what do these words mean? is it that I should only be answerable to the amount I have subscribed or engaged for, or what else? I do not like the *principle* of these Banks; however well they be conducted for a time; you neither have nor can have security for like caution and judgement continuing: and therefore I intend, at present at least, to withdraw when the next statement of accounts is made (which will be shortly) if I can do so without material loss.—Mr Liddell[1] spoke from personal kindness to me, and the value he sets upon my writings. But he judged ill and I am sorry that he mentioned my name. I have written to Lord Morpeth and had, as Dora will tell you, a friendly and satisfactory answer.[2]

I do not acknowledge the force of the objections made to my publishing the specimens of Chaucer, nevertheless I have yielded to the judgments of others, and have not sent more than the Cuckoo and Nightingale. You noticed properly Talfourd's *blunder*, if it be not a misprint. Tegg[3] is what you say. He has written two long and stupid Letters to the Times, in one of which the Blockhead says, 'look at the profits, the enormous ones of such and such people'—Now that is so far from being an objection to the Bill, that it is one of the strongest reasons in favor of it. The large and increasing instant demand for literature

[1] H. T. Liddell. See pt. iii, L. 875.

[2] See L. 1385 above.

[3] The bookseller.

of a certain quality, holds out the strongest temptation to men, who could do better, writing below themselves, to suit the taste of the superficial Many. What we want is not books to catch purchasers, Readers not worth a moment's notice, not light but solid matter, not things treated in a broad and coarse, or at best a superficial way, but profound or refined works comprehensive of human interests through time as well as space. Kotzebue[1] was acted and read at once from Cadiz to Moscow; what is become of him now? But Tegg has the impudence to affirm, that another Paradise Lost, or a poem as good, would at once produce £10,000 from Mr Murray and others. 'Credat Judaeus Apella.' Paradise Lost is indeed bought because people for their own credit must now have it. But how few, how very few, read it; when it is read by the multitude, it is almost exclusively not as a poem, but a religious Book. But even were it true that substantial work would at once secure a wide circulation, justice would still be violated, by withholding from the Descendants or Heirs of a great Author the further advantage he is so strongly entitled to. The wretch Tegg says his 'line is to watch expiring Copyrights', and would be, no doubt, if he dared to murder the authors for the sake of getting sooner at his prey. But too much of this disgusting subject. We have here and have had for the last three weeks, through the whole day, celestial weather, and the stars by night brilliant almost as in the West Indies. For the two or three last days there has been a sort of steaming heat, as in summer, especially towards sunset, but it goes off and the nights are clear as I have described. I disturb myself with thinking that Dora *might* have escaped her terrible cold if she had remained here; but she has had what she deems a far more than sufficient set off, in her enjoyment of your company,[2] and that of her

[1] August Friedrich Ferdinand von Kotzebue (1761–1819), the highly prolific and successful German playright: author of *Lover's Vows*, performed at Covent Garden in 1798.

[2] Dora W. and E. Q. saw a good deal of each other in London at this time, and their friends assumed that this was a public acknowledgment of their engagement. But when he had left Rydal Mount the previous December, E. Q. had not been able to offer her much hope for the future. 'You must be happy and so will I . . . in the assurance of our mutual love', he wrote on 9 Dec. 'Something must turn up in our favor, the cards have been against us so long.' (*WL MSS.*) But in February he confessed to H. C. R. that his property was still encumbered with debt, and the latter concluded that 'everything remains in the same unsettled state in which it has so long been.' See *HCR* ii. 580.

other Friends. I cannot however altogether forgive dear Sara Coleridge being such a monopolist of your conversation in Dora's presence. It was to say the least indelicate; but blue-stockingism is sadly at enmity with true refinement of mind—John's new living[1] has been overstated by Isabella; it is £420 per ann: I have written a long Letter to Dora this morning, and my back aches, with stooping in the way which I am so little accustomed to. Mary is engaged with company or she would [have] added a few words. She sends her love and thanks—and believe me with love to your Daughter, my dear Friend,

faithfully yours
W. Wordsworth

[*M. W. adds*]

D^r^ friend—W. bids me add he fully accords with y^r^ opinion of Mr Westall's drawings—his landscapes—God bless you!

1390. W. W. to ROBERT PERCEVAL GRAVES

MS. Cornell.
Robert Graves, The Crowning Privilege, 1955, p. 53 (—).

[*In M. W.'s hand*]

Rydal M^t^. [? Spring 1840 or earlier]

Mr Graves will bear in mind what I said against the phrase of making a Tour in Switzerland, as generally understood to relate to Alpine Switzerland—the best thing to be done is to cross the Alps by as many passes as you conveniently can; descending into Italy and back again—to and fro.

Taking you up to Berne is in some respects inconvenient—as it leaves the Lakes of Zurich and Wallenstad, and the noble pass of the Via-Mala, and over the Splugen, and so down upon Chiavenna and the Lake of Como etc upon your left hand. But as you must start from Berne, it would probably be best as *we* did, in 1820, to go to Thun. At *T.* (if you have an hour to spare) is a pleasant walk in the grounds of [?][2] where is a small Tablet to the memory of Aloys Reding.[3] The views from the Ch:yd[4] and

[1] Plumbland. See previous letter.
[2] *Gap in MS.*
[3] The Swiss patriot. See pt. i, L. 95.
[4] Churchyard.

Castle are also very interesting. Up the Lake to Unterseen and Interlacken. The Lake of Brientz—the Fall etc near it which we did not visit—are worth seeing, if you have time, but we preferred going to Lauterbrunnen and over the Wengern Alp to Grindelwald—thence over the Schidec to Meyringham.[1] Observe on your descent upon M.—look for the celebrated fall of Reichenbach. From M. we gave a day to the Oberhasli Vale, and the famous falls of the Handec—whence we *might* have proceeded over the Grimsel Pass, to Urseren etc—but we preferred returning to M.—thence by side of the Lakes of Lungern and Sarnan, on to Lucerne.

From Lucerne to the top of the Riga;—thence by the Town of Switz, to Brunnen on the Uri branch of the Lake of the 4 Cantons. So on, by Boat, to Tell's Chapel and Fluellen. Then to *Altorf, Arnstag*, to the Valley of Urseren. Here let me observe you might cross over to Dissentis, on one of the branches of the Rhine, and thence up the Via Mala to Splugen and over to Chiavenna, and so down the Lake of Como. This I did 50 years ago only reversing it[2]—Or, from Urseren, as *we* did in 1820 over the St Gotard Pass down by *Airola, Bellingzona, Locarno*, where embark to *Luvina* thence by *Ponte Fresa* to Lugano. Here ascend San Salvador—for the views. Then take boat for *Porlezza*, and over the hill to Managgio—thence to *Cannabbia*, thence cross the Lake to the promontory of *Bellagio* and from the Alcove in the Duke's grounds you see parts of the 3 reaches of the Lake of Como—magnificent prospect. Here, if you find our names, pray refresh them. (Here you must determine whether you will go to Como and Milan—and so by Varesa, Bavana, the Borromean Islands, and over the Semplin back into Switzerland, —*or*, if time allows, on by the Lecco branch to Bergamo, a fine Situation,—the Town and Lake of *Issea*, to Louvera at its head, and by *Brescia*, where are Roman Antiquities, to the Lago di Garda, up to Riva at its head, where is magnificent scenery. Hence you might cross over into the Tyrol, but all this would carry you a long way from Switzerland.—So I will suppose you to go, by the Lake, from Cadenabbia to Como—thence if time allows to Milan for the sake of the Cathedral etc.—From Milan by Varesa to the Borromean Islands and over the Semplin. But I

[1] M. W.'s spelling of foreign names is often irregular. Thus Meyringham = Meiringen, Cannabbia = Candenabbia, Louvera = Lovere, Semplon, or Semplin = Simplon, Riva = Righi, etc.

[2] i.e. in 1790. See *EY*, pp. 32 ff.

regret much that we did not turn aside from Baveno so to take in the Lago di Orta in our way to Domo d'Ossola. Near Domo d'Ossola (as also near Varesa I believe,) is one of those shrines to which you ascend by different Stations, as they are called, which Chantrey told me was altogether very striking. From *Brig*, in the Vallais downwards, we turned up to the Baths of Leuk—so up the noble ascent of the Gemmi, returning, after we had looked down into the Vale which leads to Thun, to Leuk—thence by *Sion* to *Martigny*. From this place you might recross into Italy by the Grand St Bernard, and here you need directions which I cannot give, for coming back from behind M[t] Blanc, somewhere into Savoy or Switzerland. *We* went from Martigny over the Col de Balm into Chameny, from which you explore the Mere de Glas and as much of Mont Blanc as time and strength will allow. Thence down the Vallies to Geneva; in Geneva are steam boats, (as are also upon the Lago di Garda—and a public boat from Iseo to [?Lovere][1])—And now supposing you to bear the General direction in mind I have done, and will only observe that of the minor Passes, by which I mean from one part of Switzerland to another, that of the Gemmi, that of the Wengern Alp and that from Meyringham to Sarnan—are far the most interesting. See them all if possible.

I have only one comprehensive remark to add, that the respective Passes of the Alps into Italy, should be looked at thro' the whole length of their Avenues—from the plains of Switzerland to the Plains of Italy—as for example—the Lake of Geneva, the Vallais, the Semplon, and the parts of the Lago Maggiore included in the direct road to the plains of Lombardy. The pass of the St Gotard should be taken up in mind from the plain of Lucerne, and so on by its Lake, up the Reuss, and down by the Tecino and Lago Maggiore. Another Pass might start from Zurich including the Lake of Wallenstat, the Via Mala—Chiavenna, and so on by the Lake of Como, as before described. A glance over the Map will at once shew you the importance of this remark—as far as concerns scenery.

I send you the best possible guide and pray return a line to say that you have rec[d] these—from Kendal.

One word more by way of correction—Mr Robinson and I were encumbered with a Carriage,[2] so that we were obliged to go back from Louvera to the Town of Isea, whereas pedestrians

[1] Lovere *written above the line*: Riva *deleted*.

[2] During the Continental tour of 1837.

no doubt might cross from Louvera to Riva—and so save space and time. With the best of good wishes I remain faithfully

Yrs
W. W.

N.B. Every foot of ground spoken of that I have seen myself is interesting.

1391. W. W. to BENJAMIN ROBERT HAYDON

MS. untraced.
K. LY ii. 1011.

Rydal Mt Ambleside Mar. 12th—40

My dear Haydon,

Though I have nothing to say but merely words of congratulation,[1] hearty congratulation, I cannot forbear to thank you for your Letter. You write in high spirits, and I am glad of it; it is only fair, that having had so many difficulties to encounter, you should have a large share of triumph. Nevertheless, though I partake most cordially of your pleasure, I should have been still more delighted to learn, that your pencil, for that after all is the tool you were made for, met with the encouragement which it so well deserves.

I should have liked to be among your Auditors, particularly so, as I have seen, not long ago, so many first-rate pictures on the Continent; and to have heard you at Oxford would have added largely to my gratification. I love and honor that place for abundant reasons; nor can I ever forget the distinction bestowed upon myself last summer by that noble-minded University.

Allow me to mention one thing upon which, if I were

[1] Haydon had written on 4 Mar., 'At last I have accomplished one of the glorious daydreams of my earlier youth, viz. Lecturing on Art at the University. I have been received with distinction by the Vice-Chancellor and heads of Colleges, granted the Ashmolean Museum, and gave my first lecture yesterday which was brilliantly attended and positively hailed. There are four honors in my life: viz: First—the sonnet of Wordsworth—Second—the freedom of my native town of Plymouth—Third, the public dinner in Edinburgh, and Fourth—my reception at Oxford. The first and the last are the greatest—But the first is *the* first and will ever remain so, whilst a vibration of my heart continues to quiver.' (*WL MSS.*) See also *Diary of Benjamin Robert Haydon* (ed. Pope), iv. 608 ff.

qualified to lecture upon your Art, I should dwell with more attention than, as far as I know has been bestowed upon it; I mean perfection in each kind as far as it is attainable. This in widely different minds has been shewn, by the Italians by the Flemings and Dutch, the Spaniards, the Germans, and why should I exclude the English? Now as a masterly, or first rate Ode or Elegy, or piece of humour even, is better than a poorly or feebly executed epic Poem, so is the picture, tho' in point of subject the humblest that ever came from an easel better than a work after Michael Angelo or Raphael in choice of subject or aim of style if moderately performed. All styles down to the humblest are good, if there be thrown into the doing all that the subject is capable of, and this truth is a great honour, not only to painting, but in degree to every other fine art. Now it is well worth a Lecturer's while who sees the matter in this light first to point out through the whole scale of Art what stands highest, and then to shew what constitutes its appropriate perfection of all down to the lowest. Ever my dear Haydon

faithfully your's
Wm Wordsworth

1392. W. W. to H. C. R.

Address: Prepaid. H. C. Robinson Esq[re], 30 Russel Square, London. [*In M. W.'s hand*]

Postmark: 16 Mar. 1840.

Stamp: Ambleside.

Endorsed: 16 Mar: 1840. Wordsworth (Miss Mackenzie) Coleridge's imputed plagiarisms.

MS. Dr. Williams's Library.

K (—). *Morley, i. 400.*

March 16 [1840]

Poor dear Miss Mackenzie![1] I was sadly grieved with the unthought of event; and I assure you my dear Friend, it will be lamented by me for the remainder of my days. I have scarcely ever known a person for whom, after so limited an acquaintance, limited I mean as to time, for it was not so as to heart and mind,

[1] Miss Frances Mackenzie, whom W. W. had met in Rome (see pt. iii, L. 1137).

I felt so much esteem, or to whom I have been more sincerely attached. I had scarcely a pleasant remembrance connected with Rome in which her amiable qualities were not mixed, and now a shade is cast over them all. I had hoped, too, to see her here, and that M^rs^ W— Dora, and Miss Fenwick would all have taken to her as you and I did. If you should learn anything further about her, her last moments, and about the poor orphan Bepina,[1] pray do not fail to let me know. If that arrangement affecting me and William, which was rather unluckily talked of lately in the House of C—[2], could be brought about I certainly should think of visiting Italy once more, but with much less interest than if our lost Friend had still been at Rome to receive us. But I dwell too long upon this melancholy subject.

How comes it that you write to us so seldom, now that Postage[3] is nothing. Letters are sure to be impoverished by the change, and if they do not come oftener, the gain will be a *loss*, and a grievous one too.—

I have been much annoyed by a serious charge of Plagiarism brought against Coleridge in the last number of Blackwood.[4] I procured the number for the purpose of reading it—With the part concerning the imputation of the thefts from Schelling, having never read a word of German metaphysics, thank Heaven! though I doubt not they are good diet for some tastes I feel no disposition to meddle. But when in further disparagement of the object of his remarks he asserts that C. was indebted 'to Germans for the brightest gems of his poetic crown', I feel myself competent to say a few words upon that subject. The

[1] Miss Mackenzie's ward, who was later sent to Scotland to be brought up by her relatives there. See L. 1412 below.

[2] See L. 1385 above.

[3] The penny post had just been introduced by Sir Rowland Hill.

[4] 'The Plagiarisms of S. T. Coleridge', *Blackwood's Magazine*, xlvii (Mar. 1840), 287–99. The author was James Ferrier, Professor Wilson's son-in-law (see pt. ii, L. 568), later (1845–64) Professor of Moral Philosophy at St. Andrews. The charge had been made by De Quincey in *Tait's Magazine*, and rebutted by Julius Hare (see pt. ii, L. 844), but it was now brought forward again by a professional metaphysician with a formidable array of quotations from Schelling in particular. 'That Coleridge was tempted to this course by vanity, by the paltry desire of applause, or by direct intention to defraud others of their due, we do not believe; this never was believed, and never will be believed. But still he *was* seduced into it—God knows how—he *did* defraud others of their due, and therefore we have considered it necessary to expose his proceedings, and to vindicate the rights of his victims.'

Critic names Schiller and Stolberg[1] as, among others, strong instances in support of his assertion.—And what are the passages adduced, two Hexameter verses, and a hexameter and pentameter, word for word from Schiller, and passed off by Coleridge as his own. If it be true this was excessive folly on Coleridge's part, but it is beyond measure absurd to talk of this paltry stuff as the Magazinist has ventured to do. So far from such things being gems in his crown they would be much honoured by calling them farthings in his Pocket. But then C. produced the lines to shew that he was a great discoverer in metre, one who had for the first time found out and by these specimens exemplified in a modern language and that his own, the spirit of these several constructions of musical sound. But having admitted that it was silly if not worse in my Friend to claim what was not his own, I feel free to affirm that Coleridge had carefully studied and successfully practised English Hexameters before he knew a word of German. And I am astonished that he did not give specimens of his own, with which he had taken, in Hexameters, I know far more pains than anything of the sort is worth. These are the sole proofs of his robberies of Schiller, but if he had stolen ten times as freely, I could have added in explanation and partly in exculpation, that he gave to Schiller 50 times more than he took without thinking worth while to let the world know what he had done. C. translated the 2nd part of Wallenstein[2] under my roof at Grasmere from MSS.—about that time I saw the passages of the Astronomical Times and the antient Mythology, which, as treated in Coleridge's professed translation, were infinitely superior.—As to the passage from Stolberg,[3] it was begun, as I know, as a translation, and amplified. Coleridge took incredible pains with the execution, and has greatly excelled the original; but why he did not in this case also speak the plain truth I am quite at a loss to conceive—Compare Chiabrera's epitaph upon Ambrosio Salinero, which I have translated,[4] with Coleridge's tombless epitaph[5] upon one he calls Satyrane and you will have another

[1] Friedrich Leopold Stolberg (1750–1819), one of the founders of the Sturm und Drang School.

[2] In 1800.

[3] Coleridge's *On a Cataract*, first published in 1834, was cited by Ferrier as a prime example of plagiarism from Stolberg.

[4] See *PW* iv. 250.

[5] *A Tombless Epitaph* first published in *The Friend*, no. xiv, 23 Nov. 1809.

instance how unadvised was his way in these little matters. I used to beg he would take the trouble of noting his obligations, but half his time was passed in dreams, so that such hints were thrown away. I should not have thought it worth while to write so much, had not the unfairness with which the Blackwoodite treats the *Poet* C in this point led me to suspect that as a metaphysician he has been used somewhat in the same manner[1]

Ever affection
Yours
W. Wordsworth

1393. W. W. and M. W. to ISABELLA FENWICK

MS. WL.
MW, p. 239.

[*In M. W.'s hand*]

Tuesday night [24 Mar. 1840]

My dear Friend,

Immediately upon the receipt of your letter, (which anticipates an answer to our last) W^m^ started for Mrs Pedder's,[2] and all is settled—the house is yours, from the 1st or 10th of May as suits you best, for 4 months—at 4 Gs,[3] a week—inclusive of the Garden, and the use of a Servant, who is left in the house, and will be competent to act under Hannah.[4] Wm stipulated for the option of the 1st or 10th of May deeming it possible that you might not be able to get into Westd or your Sister come to you as soon as you wish—and mean time you can stay happily with us. This arrangement has taken a good deal of anxiety off our minds, and tho' W. likes Mrs Lutwidge's house so much, he is not sorry that her apparently ungentlewomanly behaviour

[1] Dora W., writing to Sara Coleridge about this time, quotes M. W. as saying, 'Yr Father is *quite* indignant that it shd be said that Coleridge owed the brightest gems of his poetry to the Germans—*this* he *can* confute and it is not said how much he *gave* to Schiller in his Wallenstein without noticing it, and doubtless he was as liberal in his Theology—' (*Victoria University Library MSS.*). For Hartley Coleridge's defence of his father, see *Letters of Hartley Coleridge* (ed. Griggs), pp. 241–2.

[2] A local acquaintance.

[3] Guineas.

[4] I. F.'s maid.

should not pass without some disappointment—but above all we secure 2 additional months. Mrs P mentioned that nothing would be locked which you could want, only she must retain one Press and one Wardrobe, for things of her own probably.

We repeat our best thanks both to yourself and the Villiers[1] for kind dispositions towards W^{m}. Mr Jesse[2] is a selfish man of the world—and as I told you, I think before, he was stirring some time ago for an appointment in that quarter, for his Son-in-law Mr Ed: Curwen. It would therefore we think not be eligible to apply to him for information—and we have now no connection to that department—formerly we had a close one. Our B^{r}[3] held the office of Solicitor to the Woods and Forests—having rec^{d} his appointment from his Cousin Mr Robinson[4] then at the head of it. It has struck W^{m} that *Cousin Roby*[5] may, thro' a surviving clerk of his Uncle, have, or be able to procure some knowledge. Lord Lowther, had he been at home could have given all the information required. And I will write tomorrow to Lady F. Bentinck enclosing a letter to be forwarded to her Brother.

We have had better accounts to day of Dora, both from herself and Mr Quillinan—but Mr Marshall, as you will have learnt from Dora, has had something of a relapse, and we cannot but fear for him. Pray press upon Dora (this from her Father) the necessity of keeping within doors. He was much grieved to learn that she was talking of going with C. Marshall[6] to day to Harrow, if it were fine. *With us* it has been the very worst day we have had since you went. Therefore I hope they have been deterred. But in fact she should bear in mind that there is no dependence from hour to hour once the weather is broken.—W^{m} is ashamed to tell you because you will be sorry to hear it, that he could find no better employment for this morn^{g}, than

[1] i.e. Henry Taylor's friends Mr. and Mrs. Edward Villiers. Their eldest brother was George William Villiers, 4th Earl of Clarendon (1800–70), who had just entered the Cabinet as Lord Privy Seal. He was Foreign Secretary, 1853–8, 1865–6, and 1868–70. His predecessor as Lord Privy Seal was Lord Duncannon, who retained the office of First Commissioner of Woods and Forests.

[2] Edward Jesse (see pt. ii, L. 748 and pt. iii, L. 1037), father-in-law of Edward Stanley Curwen, eldest brother of Isabella Wordsworth.

[3] i.e. R. W.

[4] John Robinson, M.P. for Harwich, was Surveyor-General of Woods and Forests from 1787. See *EY* p. 57.

[5] Capt. Charles Robinson (see L. 1388 above).

[6] Cordelia Marshall.

composing what I will now transcribe, and which he sends with his love—Joanna says *to* his love.

Stanzas

Hint to a simple-minded Lover of Nature and of Art.[1]

If thou be wont, when Sleep has taken flight,
To crave a voice that softliest will foreshew
How far off yet the gleams of morning light,
And whether wakefulness be wise or no,
Thou needst not covet a Repeater's stroke
That, answering to thy touch, will tell the hour;
Better provide thee with a Cuckoo-Clock,
For service hung beside thy chamber door,
And wait, in patience wait. The gentle Shock
The double note, as if with living power,
Will teach thee to be blithe as bird in bower.
List, Cuckoo, cuckoo! Tho' the tempest howl,
Or nipping frost remind thee trees are bare,
How cattle pine, and droop the shivering fowl,
Thy Spirits will seem to feed on balmy air;
I speak from knowledge. By that Sound beguiled
Oft will thou greet old memories as they throng
Into thy heart; and fancies running wild
Beside clear streams and budding groves among
Will make thee happy, happy as a child:
Of Sunshine will thou think, of Flowers and Song,
And breathe as in a world where nothing can go wrong.

Having several other letters to write, I interrupt W. who would have otherwise gone on confessing worse transgressions than the above.

God bless you dearest friend—Joanna sends her love, and believe us ever faithfully

yours
W. and M. Wordsworth.

[1] The first draft of the first two stanzas of *The Cuckoo-Clock* (*PW* ii. 315), completed on 7 Apr. See also L. 1396 below, and *MW*, p. 242.

1394. W. W. to MARY GASKELL

MS. St. John's College, Cambridge.
LY ii. 1012.

Rydal Mount March 25th –40

Dear Madam,

Pray accept my sincere thanks both for your obliging Letter and [? also] the trouble you have taken towards putting me in possession of a drawing of that interesting relique of my ancestral Name-sake.[1] May I beg also that you would make my acknowledgements to the Draughtsman who went without a dinner in the service of one unknown to him, and tell him I should be glad if he would give me an opportunity to straight[en] the account (if that were possible) at my own table. The view which Mr Brackenbridge[2] takes of my pretensions to become, through Mr and Mrs Beaumont's kind consideration, the owner of this memorial of my family, is flattering, and I should like him to know that it was gratifying to me. I still cherish a hope that Mr and Mrs Beaumont may be induced to look at my wish, simple as it may be deemed, in the same light.

My Daughter is now staying at Mr Marshall's in Grosvenor Street, and if the drawing could be directed to her there she would bring it down safely and I should have it in the course of a month.

It gives me sincere pleasure to be told that I have been in any degree influential for the improvement of Miss Brandreth[3] in the charming Art to which she has attached herself; and I am truly sensible of the honor Mr De Wint[4] has done me in this matter. Miss Brandreth with whom no doubt you are in communication, will oblige me by telling him so, with the expression of my regards to Himself and Mrs Dewint.[5]

Pray present my respects to Mr Gaskell and believe me with kind regards, in which Mrs Wordsworth unites: faithfully your much obliged

Wm Wordsworth

[1] The Wordsworth family aumbry. See L. 1364 above.

[2] John Brackenbridge, agent to Mr. Beaumont, the present owner of the aumbry.

[3] Mrs. Gaskell's sister.

[4] The artist (see L. 1364 above).

[5] Sister of William Hilton, R.A. (1786–1839), the historical painter.

1395. W. W. to JOSEPH COTTLE

Address: Joseph Cottle Esqre, Farfield House, Bristol.
Postmark: 27 Mar. 1840.
Stamp: Ambleside.
MS. Harvard University Library. Hitherto unpublished.

Rydal Mount
Ambleside
March 26th –40

My dear old Friend

I lose no time in thanking you for your affectionate remembrance of me. No one knows or ever will to what a degree I have been a Sufferer from disease in my eyes; I do not mean from pain in them, of which I have had little, nor from distress in the organ of which I have had much, but from the sad privations of which the disease has been the cause. It has not only prevented my reading frequently for many months together; but often compelled me to abstain from composition, and even as much as possible from thinking as an Act which aggravated the irritation. At present they are in their better way, and did I not find reading injurious to them I should have little to complain of. The malady has its origin in the lids, as I believe far the greatest part of the unhealthy action of the eye has. Though the inflammation has, as I have said, been attended with little pain it has more than once gone so far as to produce ulcers which have made one eye for a time totally blind. From that melancholy state I have been brought by the use of nitre of silver; and I have also drawn benefit for the lids from remedies such as the one you have so kindly sent; and which I will again try as soon as the occasion returns which no doubt it will.

Poor dear Southey lies in a state melancholy for his Friends to behold and especially when they bear in mind what he once and even not long ago was, and what we had no fear he would continue to be; He suffers no pain, thank God! Body and mind seem to be going out gently together; but the immortal Spirit, we know, cannot be touched.

Truly grieved was I not to find you and your sister at home when I called with Mr Peace.[1] If my life be prolonged till next spring it is not unlikely I shall see Bristol again; and we must contrive a Meeting whatever it costs. My poor Sister, though in

[1] In Apr. 1839. See pt. iii, L. 1313.

a melancholy State, is both in body and Mind a good deal better. She talks about you with great pleasure. Should you see Mr Wade and Mr Peace tell the former with my kind remembrances that I hope he will act upon my suggestion as to the destiny of his fine portrait of Coleridge,[1] and the latter that, I promise myself the pleasure of writing to him shortly.

My poor Sister and Mrs W. join with me in good wishes to yourself and Sister (my daughter is not at home) and believe me my dear Cottle

faithfully yours
Wm Wordsworth

1396. W. W. to ISABELLA FENWICK

Address: Miss Fenwick, 17 Brock Street, Bath. *prepaid*. [*In M. W.'s hand*]
Postmark: 27 Mar. 1840.
Stamp: Ambleside.
MS. WL.
LY ii. 1013.

[26 Mar. 1840]

After I had sent off my Cuckoo verses[2] I felt as if they wanted something of solidity, and am now tempted, my beloved Friend, to send you, in Joanna's writing, a copy slightly revised, with an additional stanza toiled at unsuccessfully yesterday evening, but thrown off in a few minutes this morning. We all like it and hope you and Dora will do the same. But it is too lately born for sound judgment, and I never sent to any one verses immediately after they were composed without some cause for regret I had been so hasty.

I called again upon Mrs Pedder[3] after the receipt of your Letter; all is settled though not exactly according to your wish. I found she could not *bind* herself to let you have the house any part of September; from what she said I felt myself not justified in pressing. She said however that though she could not ensure you the House for that month she would do all in her power to meet your wishes. She is desirous of new-painting two of the

[1] See pt. iii, L. 1341.
[2] See L. 1393 above. The final version of the poem had four stanzas.
[3] The owner of the house which I. F. was proposing to rent.

Bedrooms. I was rather afraid of that, and only consented to it upon condition that the work was begun *instantly*. She said it should be so, by tomorrow at the latest. This is a good time, for the workmen have little to do. As we are yet five weeks from the first of May I trust the smell of the paint will be quite gone—Pray remember us most kindly to your dear Sister, and though I particularize no one else, all your connections at Bath are in our thoughts,

most affectionately yours, W. W.

1397. W. W. to DORA W. and ISABELLA FENWICK

MS. British Library.
Mem. 'Some Unpublished Letters of William Wordsworth', Cornhill Magazine, xx (1893), 257–76. K. LY ii. 1014.

7th April, 1840.

My dearest Dora,

Though my left eye has been rather troublesome these two or three last days, I cannot forbear writing to you, and let the Letter serve for dear Miss Fenwick also, upon the morning of my seventieth birth-day. I am, thank almighty God! in excellent health, and so is your dear Mother, and though some of my thoughts, upon this occasion, are naturally serious, even to sadness, I am, upon the whole, in a chearful state of mind. The day is bright as sunshine can make it, and the air fraught with as much stir and animating noise as the wind can put into it.

Your mother finds her ancles weak from the shock and sprain of her fall and consequent confinement, or I should have tempted her out with me to walk on the terrace, from which I have had an entertaining view of the merriment of the servants, with help from Arthur Jackson[1] and his Brother, shaking the glittering dust out of the carpets.

Sister is very comfortable, and we are going on nicely, though wishing much for your return. Yesterday I dined with Mrs Luff, after calling at the house high up Loughrigg side where dwells the good woman who lost her two children in the flood last winter. The wind was high when I knocked at her door, and I heard a voice from within that I knew not what to make of, though it sounded something like the lullaby of a Mother to her

[1] A local tradesman.

Baby. After entering I found it came from a little sister of those drowned Children, that was singing to a bundle of clouts, rudely put together to look like a Doll, which she held in her arms.

I tell you this little story in order that, if it be perfectly convenient, but on no account else, you may purchase what may answer the purpose with something more of pride and pleasure to this youngling of a nurse. Such is your mother's wish, I should not have had the wit to think of it. No matter, she says, how common a sort of thing the doll is, only let it be a good big one.

Dear Miss Fenwick, Mrs Luff does not wish to part with her sofas, but they are quite at your service, and she would be pleased if you would use them till she has a house of her own. But that time is, she fears, distant, her American property is so unpromising that she has scruples about taking Old Brathay. Now, should she decline it, might it not, as the Owner is willing to make some improvement, accommodate you for a time? I don't much like the thought; but, as a 'pis aller', it might possibly do until Mr Hill may be tempted to give his Cottage up.

I find from a talk with Mrs Fleming[1] that they are disposed to make improvements, could they let it for a term; and a term, with liberty of course to underlet, is what you want. But all this we long to talk over with you, among a thousand reasons for wishing you back again.

It had escaped my recollection when we heard about the woods and forests, and the Villiers' kindness,[2] that I talked this matter over with Lord Lowther, when he was Surveyor of that department, and he told me there was scarcely a single office under him that was an object, at least *then* a come-at-able one.

Were he in England now I should be inclined to ask him if my recollection be correct. But I must leave, which I do, dearest Friends, with love to you both; and wishes for many happy returns of your own Birthdays.

Ever most affectionately yours,
Wm Wordsworth

[1] Of Spring Cottage.

[2] See L. 1387 above. Lord Lowther was First Commissioner of Woods and Forests, 1828–30.

Mrs Pedder[1] is putting up a new staircase in some part of the house for the convenience of her new Tenant. Dearest Dora, your mother tells me she shrinks from Copies being spread of those Sonnets;[2] she does not wish one, on any account, to be given to Miss Gillies, for that, without blame to Miss G., would be like advertising them. I assure you her modesty and humble-mindedness were so much shocked that I doubt if she had more pleasure than pain from these compositions, though I never poured out anything more truly from the heart.

1398. W. W. to EDWARD MOXON

Address: Prepaid. Edward Moxon Esqre, 44 Dover Street, London. [*In M. W.'s hand*]
Postmark: (1) 13 Apr. 1840 (2) 14 Apr. 1840.
Stamp: Ambleside.
MS. Henry E. Huntington Library.
LY ii. 1016.

[*c.* 12 Apr. 1840]

Mr dear Mr Moxon,

I have been looking for a Letter from you, as I wished to know how far you could meet my wishes in respect to the sum I have to advance for my Son John. If any thing be due to me, but only due, remember, as I stated pray send it in a Bank post Bill, as soon as convenient, or at all events let me know what you can do—But do not, I repeat put yourself out of your course, as I shall have some more money erelong.—

I should like to have a sight of Mr Christie's Pamphlet[3] upon perpetual copyright of which the Morning Post, giving an unanswerable Extract, speaks highly. I suppose it is not so large but that it might be sent through Post without much expense.

[1] Owner of the house which I. F. had taken from 1 May.

[2] The two sonnets on M. W.'s portrait, painted by Miss Gillies. See *PW* iii. 54–5. Dora W. wrote to I. F.: 'The Sonnets are most beautiful, most true, most affecting, and Father tells me they were composed almost extemporare.' (*WL MSS.*)

[3] *A Plea for Perpetual Copyright, in a letter to Lord Monteagle*, 1840. The author, William Dougal Christie (1816–74), diplomatist and man of letters, was M.P. for Weymouth, 1842–7.

Let it be *prepaid* and put down to me, if I am right as to the size of it.—

I am truly anxious that Sergeant Talfourd's, and Christie's pamphlet also, should be sent to Lieutenant General Sir William Gomm, Jamaica; but of course not by Post. You will be able to learn through what Channel things of this kind go to Persons in his station. He is Commander in Chief of the forces in the West Indies.

Dora is coming north about the 20th or a day or two after. You might send any thing by her. She will be found at Mrs Hoare's Hampstead Heath.

ever faithfully yours
Wm Wordsworth

1399. W. W. to EDWARD MOXON

MS. Henry E. Huntington Library.
LY ii. 1016.

Rydal Mount
12th April 1840.

Dear Mr Moxon,

I enclose an application just received, and for an answer I have referred the Gentleman to you, stating that if *you* do not object, I shall not withhold my consent.

My Son John and his Brother William are both at present staying under this roof. They are well, and were they present would send their kind remembrances.

ever faithfully yours
Wm Wordsworth

[*W. W. jnr. adds*]

Please send the Daily news here for ten days to come. I have given up all thoughts of going up to Town this Spring.

Yours most afftly

W. W. Jn.

1400. W. W. to SIR WILLIAM GOMM

Address: Prepaid. Lieu. Gen. Sir Wm Gomm Bt etc etc etc, Kingston, Jamaica. [*In M. W.'s hand*]
Postmark: [?Apr.] 1840.
Stamp: Ambleside.
Endorsed: Wordsworth Rydal April. 8th June /40. Answer to mine 26th Feby.
MS. Henry E. Huntington Library.
LY ii. 1021.

Rydal Mount
Ambleside
[mid-] April 1840

Mr dear Sir W^{m}

Your Letter dated 25th Feb^{ry} I had the pleasure of receiving a fortnight ago; I feel much obliged by it and return you my sincere thanks. It was very kind on your part to think of introducing my Nephew[1] to Sir Howard and Lady Douglas;[2] and he has already been written to, to inform him of your intention to do so. We have heard from him twice since his arrival in the Ionian Islands, the climate of which agrees perfectly with his health, and he is much pleased with his situation. He says, nevertheless, he would prefer being attached to a regiment stationed in that quarter, to being on the staff; for two reasons principally; he would not be subject to such sudden changes of place, and he should have more to do in the way of his profession.—

It gives me much pleasure to learn that your present Situation is so agreeable to yourself and Lady Gomm; and there seems to be no doubt of its continuing so if you do not suffer from the climate, which we who have never been in the Country have perhaps unreasonable dread of. Every one has heard of the glorious scenery and striking and beautiful exhibitions of nature and natural effects with which Jamaica, and those Islands in general, abound. And sure I am that you both have hearts and minds to enjoy them.—Your exertions among the mountains will I hope not tempt you to forget the lameness under which

[1] R. W.'s son John.

[2] Gen. Sir Howard Douglas, 3rd Bart. (1776–1861), Governor of New Brunswick 1823–8, and founder of the University of Fredericton; Lord High Commissioner of the Ionian Islands (1835–40), M.P. for Liverpool (1842–6), and author of several works on military affairs.

you suffered not long ago. Mischiefs of that kind, and indeed all others affecting the Body have long memories. Last spring I was at Bath for a few weeks; and being so inconsiderate as to take very long walks (immediately after coming out of the warm bath) up and down those steep hillsides, I sprained, with that exertion and a slip of my foot, one of my ancles; and though by pouring cold water upon it I effected apparently a complete cure, I find that I cannot walk on the mountains over rough ground, as I used to do, without recalling something of the injury.—

You enquire about the Copy right Bill—It has been asleep some time, but comes on on the 28th Instnt.[1] I am full of fears about the issue.—My Publisher, Mr Moxon has had orders to send you Sergeant Talfourd's pamphlet,[2] and another in favor of the measure, by Mr Christie.[3]—I have not lately been in communication with any one upon the subject so that I know nothing but what the Papers will tell you. Should there be any important publication upon it, I will take care it shall be forwarded to you.

Our Country is now in exquisite beauty, and we have had for the last ten weeks such a season as I cannot remember. No climate, all things considered, health and exercise included, could I think surpass ours as it has been for the time I have mentioned.

Mrs W— unites with me in kindest remembrances and a thousand good wishes to yourself and Lady Gomm, and believe me to be my dear Sir Wm

very faithfully your
much obliged
Wm Wordsworth

[1] The Bill was not brought forward on 28 Apr. after all.

[2] Talfourd's *Three Speeches.*

[3] See L. 1398 above.

1401. W. W. to W. F. WATSON[1]

Address: W. F. Watson Esq[re], 52 Princes Street, Edinburgh. [*In M. W.'s hand*]
Postmark: (1) 21 Apr. 1840 (2) 22 Apr. 1840.
Stamp: Ambleside.
MS. National Library of Scotland.
LY ii. 1022.

Rydal Mount
Ambleside
20th April –40.

Sir,

My Friends are not satisfied with any Engraving of me, and therefore I cannot point out any in particular. The worst in my own judgement is that prefixed to the two last Editions of my poems—[2]

I am, sir, your obed[nt] Ser[vnt]
W[m] Wordsworth

1402. M. W. and W. W. to WILLIAM WESTALL

Address: W[m] Westall Esq[re], 5 North Bank, Regent's Park, London. *Prepaid.*
Postmark: (1) 22 Apr. 1840 (2) 23 Apr. 1840.
Stamp: Ambleside.
MS. Cornell. Hitherto unpublished.

[*M. W. writes*]

Apr. 21st [1840]

My dear Mr Westall,

Thank you for your enclosure which I shall take care to forward to John—Mr W. and myself are most happy to hear that your two Sons are settled so much to your and their own satisfaction. Poor fellows I hope they will do well and prosper and prove a comfort to their Mother and yourself.

You are very kind to think of Dora in the disposal of your Academy Tickets, and I am sure it would be a great pleasure could she avail herself of the offer—which I almost fear is quite

[1] An Edinburgh bookseller.

[2] The engraving by W. H. Watt from Pickersgill's portrait at St. John's College, Cambridge.

out of the question as she must be, together with Miss Quillinan, at the Euston Sq^{re} Rail-way Station[1] at 9oC AM. on Friday morning—to start northward—they hope to meet Miss Fenwick at Birmingham, and all be at Rydal on Saturday evening—So that I fear her time till that moment, must be already appropriated. A note however will meantime find her at Mrs Hoares the Heath Hampstead, and if she *should* be in Town on the Thursday it is not quite impossible that she might contrive to meet you, if you could propose a place for that purpose.

I must now give you Mr W^{s} opinion as to your title—Writing *now* from his dictation. 'I am quite puzzled as to the Title, in consequence of your beginning with the interior of my house from which every body would infer that every other plate was to be subordinate to my poems and me—Now I cannot but think this, while it is not agreeable to my feelings, would promote your interest which I principally look at—tho' I am very unwilling to have thrust upon public notice in the first no any thing so private.[2] I hope this can be deferred, if it can a title like the following might do. "Select Views in the Lake Country, chiefly to illustrate the Poems of W Wordsworth—taken upon the Spot, and engraved by Wm Westall".'

You do not mention Mrs Westall from which we trust she is no worse at least.

With our united good wishes to her and yourself and family believe me to be dear Sir in great haste very sincerely

yours
M Wordsworth

[1] Opened in 1836.,

[2] See also L. 1389 above. Writing to Westall on 25 Apr., on her return home, Dora W. explained: 'I have repeated to my Father all that past between us at the Rail way Station yesterday morning and he begs me to say that under the circumstances he quite withdraws his objection to publishing that print of this room in the first number and therefore hopes you will go on with the work according to your own wishes.' (*New York Public Library MSS.*)

1403. W. W. to JOHN GIBSON LOCKHART

Address: J. G. Lockhart Esq., Sussex Place, Regent's Park, London.
Postmark: (1) 28 Apr. 1840 (2) 29 Apr. 1840.
Stamp: Ambleside.
MS. National Library of Scotland.
LY ii. 1023.

Rydal Mount [*c.*27] April 1840

My dear Mr Lockhart,

Having received some little time ago the last Volume of the Second Edition of your Memoir of Sir Walter, I sit down to thank you for the very valuable Present. The embellishments[1] give a great additional Value to the Edit: they are judiciously selected and well executed. The former copy, which I received from your kindness also, I have presented to my younger Son who prizes it as it deserves.

The state of my eyes, though at present in their better way, does not allow me to read much, so that I should not be able to compare the two editions and to look at the corrections and additions with the care which I know they must deserve, and be assured I regret much this inability.—

You will grieve to hear that poor dear Southey is gradually declining both in mind and body. I should apprehend from some disease of the brain, but his Keswick medical attendant cannot make this out, and calls it premature old age; in which conclusion he must, I think, be mistaken. The Patient was for all kinds of exercise quite a strong man two years ago; and his life has been most regular, and all his habits, those of study included, under his own command, and judiciously and temperately managed.

The Copyright Bill is to come on again on the 28th.[2] Has your relation to Sir W. Scott prevented your noticing this important subject in the Quarterly? I cannot but think that an able Article upon it in that journal would do more towards putting the question in the way of being carried than any thing else.

[1] Robert Cadell's Edinburgh edition of 1839, in ten volumes, was embellished with engravings after Turner and other artists.

[2] In fact, it was postponed.

I hope your dear Children are well. Believe me my dear Mr Lockhart

very faithfully
your much obliged
Wm Wordsworth

1404. W. W. to FRANCIS MEREWETHER

Address: The Revd Francis Merewether, Coleorton Rectory, Ashby de la Zouch, Leicestershire.
Postmark: 29 Apr. 1840.
Stamp: Ambleside.
MS. Cornell.
Broughton, p. 76.

[*In M. W.'s hand*]

Rydal Mount Apr 29th—40

My dear Sir

If you knew how few letters I write or *can* write you would not take it ill that I have omitted replying to your's till this day. I thank you for it sincerely—and your Son[1] for the Speech of the Bishop which he has sent me. I have read, and think it unanswerable—and having that opinion of it of course I admire it much. It rejoices us all to have so good an account of your Son, and I hope and pray that you may continue to receive equally favorable ones. We thank you and dear Mrs M. for other particulars of the rest of your family—we being deeply interested in the welfare of them all—but I need scarcely say, how sorry we are that you have so many causes for discomfort and dissatisfaction, at Coleorton. When I met your Brother,[2] the Sergeant, at Oxford, we talked about a change in your situation, as being desireable, and which I was glad to hear he seemed to think might be effected, without serious diminution of income. I should be glad to know that something of this kind were in progress.

It is not my intention to go from home during this summer

[1] Francis, now in Australia. The reference is to a speech by the Bishop of Australia, which was enclosed with this letter.

[2] Henry Alworth Merewether (see pt. iii, L. 1014) had received a D.C.L. at Oxford on 12 June 1839 at the same time as W. W.

and therefore I cannot encourage the hope of our meeting at Coleorton, notwithstanding the increasing facilities of travel.

If you continue to think my opinion of any importance, as to the Tablet intended to be put up in the Church of Yeldham,[1] I shall be glad to give it—My undertaking, dear Sir, to write my Brothers Memoir[2] is a thing impossible—such a work could not be in hands so likely to disappoint the public as mine. It would be expected I should have much to say of him, a knowledge of which could not have come to me, but as his Brother. Now as I grievously lament we have had very, very little personal intercourse. I am between 4 and 5 years his senior which separated us, as it could not but do, as Boys; we having lost our Parents when we were children. I left Col: before he came thither, and I saw nothing of him during the Vacations. Many years of my life were afterwards spent in rambling about the Continent, and in residences in different parts of England; so that we seldom met, and only for a very short time, during many years. When he was at Bocking,[3] as you know, I paid him a visit—and he has twice been in this Country—except what might be gained from these and our own short visits at Cambridge (during which however he was always so much occupied in his study or other avocations, that I had little communication with him there). I am unacquainted with his pursuits and mode of life—in short I have none of that knowledge which would be looked for in a Brother writing his life—Besides it must be borne in mind that I have entered my 71st year—and therefore in course of Nature he will outlive me. As Mr Watson who I know is acquainted with, and has sympathized in all his views and undertakings, for substantial reasons declines the office of his Biographer, it will naturally devolve upon one of his Sons—from whom I trust it may be expected. Materials furnished me by others, to which you

[1] Merewether was planning to erect a memorial tablet in Yeldham Church, Essex, to his wife's eldest brother, the Rev. Lewis Way (1788–1835), of Spencer Grange, Yeldham, and wished to submit the inscription for W. W.'s approval. See also L. 1887 below.

[2] In his letter of 13 Apr. Merewether had suggested that W. W. should become his brother's biographer, as Joshua Watson was no longer equal to the task. 'Your name would carry the circulation of the Book beyond our profession.' (*WL MSS.*)

[3] C. W. was Dean of Bocking, Essex, from 1808 to 1816. W. W. visited him there in 1812 (see *MY* ii. 21).

advert, could not supply these deficiencies, especially as they would relate to Professional engagement, studies, and proceedings which lie in a walk so far apart from my own. I could not enter into the spirit of those materials, as one of his cooperators and coadjutors. Enough has been said I trust to reconcile you, to forgo the expectation that such a labor of love, could advantageously come from me.

It gratifies me that you were so much pleased with John's Translations,[1] and that you liked the introductory Poem, it is rather singular that a Person who was not brought up at one of the great public schools, and who had little practice in latin composition as a Boy or Youth, should have such a command of the poetic language of the Romans. He must have taken great delight in the perusal of those Authors to be able to translate as he has done, several passages in which the style of thinking and feeling is but little modified by antiquity. You know how charmingly his house at Brigham is situated,—and that it is in a chearful part of the Country, I mean in the way of society—I am therefore glad that it is in his power to remain there; as it can be done without either Parish suffering by his holding the 2 livings[2]—but were he to give up Brigham, and go to Plumbland, it does not seem probable that the sacrifice of income would be more than £10 per ann:

Pray when you write to your Son Frank, in my name congratulate [him][3] upon his agreeable prospects—and give our united affectionate remembrances; and add that, wretched correspondent as I am, it would give me pleasure to hear from him. I will communicate your message to our neighbour Mr Graves—he is a very admirable young Man, zealous and efficient, both *in* the Church, and *out* of it, as a Pastor. Poor dear Mr Southey is declining gradually, but slowly, both in body and mind—his state is most affecting, and would be, were it not for religious consolation, afflicting for all his friends to think of.—His daughter Mrs Hill who is living at the foot of *our hill*—Mrs M. will be glad to hear, has a sweet little girl nearly 3 months old—Mr H. is now the Curate of our Chapel—And has a Son of the Archbishop of Dublin[4] as Pupil—and he is

[1] See pt. iii, L. 1351.

[2] See L. 1388 above.

[3] *Word dropped out.*

[4] Edward William Whateley (b. 1823) had been at Rugby since 1837. He went up to Christ Church, Oxford, in 1841, and became rector of Chillendon, Kent,

expecting two Sons of the late Chancellor,[1] Ld Monteagle. Our John still wishes to be employed in like manner, but how to start him *advantageously* in that line I do not know; it seems indelicate in a Father to recommend his own *Untried* Son for a trust of such great responsibility. I know him to be a good Man of amiable dispositions and an excellent classical scholar both in Latin and Greek—but much more is required, for which *I as his father*, who may be suspected of partiality, dare not vouch. William is now with us, for a short visit and pretty well—Dora returned only a few days [ago][2] from a 10 weeks absence in the South, during which time she was chiefly confined by a succession of severe colds—She is better, tho' not quite free from their effects.—Mrs W. who you perceive writes for me, with dear love to Mrs M., trusts that she wil accept this as a reply to *both* your kind letters, as her time just *now* is much occupied. Our dear Sister, is in her [? better] way—The heat of the weather, so unusual at this early season—relieves her somewhat. What a beautiful Spring we have had. With our united best wishes believe me dear Mr M. ever to remain

most truly yours
[*signed*] Wm Wordsworth

1405. W. W. to THOMAS POWELL

MS. University of Virginia Library.
LY ii. 1024.

Rydal Mount First of May /40[3]

My dear Mr Powell,

Your kind present arrived in due time and your welcome Letter after it. It gives me much pleasure to learn that your Brothers health is going on so well; he and all about you have

and later Chancellor of St. Patrick's Cathedral, Dublin (1862–72). His *Personal and Family Glimpses of Remarkable People*, 1889, contains reminiscences of the Lake Poets.

[1] The reference is probably to Lord Monteagle's two youngest sons, Aubrey (1822–97), later a clergyman in Dorset, and William (1823–80), later a barrister and Secretary of the Lunacy Commission.

[2] *Word dropped out.*

[3] Address and date in Dora W.'s hand.

our best wishes. Mrs W. and I have both been in good health during the spring which for beauty of weather has exceeded all that I remember. We have been eleven weeks almost without rain; and the east winds are so broken by our mountains and tempered, that being softened also by the warmth of the sun we have scarcely felt any annoyance from them. One beautiful feature of the season has been most remarkable,—the profusion and size and splendor of the wild flowers; I do not remember having seen in England any thing like it.—I have almost lived in the open air, with nothing to complain of but that my eyes will not stand reading. How sadly this has been the case you may judge by my not having yet ventured upon the perusal of Mr Leigh Hunt's play,[1] though I received it several weeks ago. Pray tell him this with my thanks. I could get some one to read it to me, but this I don't like; it being my misfortune never to have an adequate perception, or right feeling of any thing read to me by others; I mean any thing that is not mere matter of fact or plain reasoning. Say to Mr Hunt further, that I wait in hope of this pleasure from his work, but if I continue to be disappointed I must submit to bear it.—

Not long ago I made mention in a Letter to you of a certain Critic,[2] the only one whose strictures on my writings had ever

[1] *A Legend of Florence* (see L. 1370 above).

[2] Chauncy Hare Townshend (see pt. i. L. 4; pt. ii, Ls. 498, 503) had sent W. W. on 29 Feb. a long and elaborate recantation of his criticism of ten years before. 'The Lyrical Ballads are the first poetry which I remember to have awoke within my childish breast a poetical feeling. At that period I accepted them with the sincerity of a child—was pleased, captivated, melted . . . In after years a germ of sarcasm . . . sprang up within me, grew, and overshadowed many feelings which should have been loftier than itself. . . .The society within which I was most intimately blended at Cambridge, contributed much to the growth of this fault. I was unfortunately in a witty set. I heard lofty feelings sneered at—the beautiful examined and dissected, till it ceased to appear beauty . . . I learned to be critical—the death to lofty thought . . . I had enrolled myself Anti-Wordsworthian. It was then that the greater part of the Essays on the Writings of Wordsworth—which appeared in Blackwood—were written.' But age and experience had brought wisdom, and he had learnt to value W. W. at his true worth. 'No one can now estimate more highly than myself those productions, which I once knew not how to appreciate, and which, if taken from our literature, would leave a chasm that nothing could supply . . . In the work now forwarded [on Animal Magnetism], it will be seen what my present opinions are, and how deeply I am indebted to an author, whom I formerly presumed to criticise in the rashness of ignorance . . .' (*WL MSS.*) W. W. accepted his

given me concern worth speaking of. I was hurt and even wounded by his unworthy mode of proceeding. He has lately written to me a long Letter of penitential recantation to which I have replied as, I trust, it became me. I therefore wish that no traces of my displeasure should exist; and accordingly I *beg* of you that if that Letter be not destroyed which I should wish to be the case with all my others, to whomsoever addressed, you would immediately put it into the fire and also give me assurance that you had done so—

Are you sure that it would answer to modernize the *whole* of Chaucer? I fear much would prove *tedious* and other parts to be objectionable upon the other grounds which I have formerly adverted to. You are welcome to my Cuckoo and Nightingale [and] to [the] small part of the Troilus and Cressida I have, and were my own judgment only to be consult[ed] to the 'Manciples tale', but there is a delicacy in respect to this last among some of my Friends which though I cannot sympathize with it I am bound to respect. Therefore in regard to that piece you will consider my decision as at present suspended. I must now conclude, with kind remembrances to Mrs Powell and yourself in which Mrs W unites and ever[y] good wish for yourself and yours

ever faithfully your much
obliged Wm Wordsworth

1406. W. W. to THOMAS NOON TALFOURD

Address: Mr Sergeant Talfourd, Russel Square, London.
Postmark: 3 May 1840.
Stamp: Ambleside.
MS. Cornell. Hitherto unpublished.

Rydal
Ambleside
May 3^d^ [1840]

My dear Sergeant Talfourd,

I sit down for a moment merely to say that my thoughts have often been with you for some time past, and that I sympathize with you in the vexations which the poor Copy-right Bill, and

apology and he was again received on friendly terms at Rydal Mount, when he called in July (*RMVB*).

the apparent indifference in the House about it, must have caused you. Could you find a moment to let me know its present condition and what your hopes are;[1] but do not put yourself to inconvenience on this account.—

It mortifies me that I know not how to aid you in any way. It seems not likely to be of use to go on writing Letters requesting members to attend, though I do not let slip any occasion of doing this without seeming to be troublesome.

I know not that any thing new in the way of argument has struck me on the subject. Indeed after your speeches and the accompanying observations and petitions, I do not see what more need be said. I have read Christie's pamphlet,[2] if people would take the trouble of going over it the cause would be served. He has made a strange blunder, in his animadversions upon what you and I have said upon the justice of the case, or the *right* of authors to prolonged or rather perpetual Copyright.

I should like if an opportunity occurred, that an argument both of great importance in itself, and as one especially addressed to the Liberals, you should point out the *aristocratic* character of their opposition, as tending to throw the production of solid works requiring time and much labour, exclusively into the hands of rich men, or men at least of independent fortune. I think I before observed to you, that Boswell's Life of Johnson, and Gibbon's History could neither have been written but by men of considerable fortune; and these two Works were the best in their several kinds produced in Europe during the last Century. As to what Tegg has written, that the great sums now gained for works upon their first appearance, are a sufficient reason for denying extension of the term; I should plead that such prices are in fact a reason especially applying to the present time why the *term* should be *lengthened* inasmuch as they hold out temptations strengthening, and likely to strengthen, for the production of works that must by necessity be short-lived. But—enough—believe me with a thousand good wishes and a deep sense of the claim you have upon the gratitude of literary Men

ever faithfully yours
Wm Wordsworth

[1] Talfourd replied on 7 May that the Bill had been dropped again (*Cornell MSS.*).

[2] See L. 1398 above.

1407. W. W. to ELIZABETH FRANCES OGLE[1]

Address: Miss Ogle, Cholmondeley Cottage, Richmond, Surrey.
Postmark: (1) 22 May 1840 (2) 23 May 1840.
Stamp: Ambleside.
MS. WL. Hitherto unpublished.

[*In M. W.'s hand*]

Rydal Mount
May 20th 1840

Dear Madam,

As the fittest return that I can make for your letter, which could not but be grateful to me, expressing so feelingly as it does the salutary effect my writings have had upon your mind; I send you the verses which you will find on the next leaf. They are not, I trust, wholly unworthy of the subject, which you were right in supposing would *to me* be interesting, as I have followed closely, (scarcely attempting any thing more) the touching account your letter gives of the single incident.—The blessed effects of piety, and of religious impressions upon the hearts and minds of young children, call for being treated in a higher and more comprehensive strain than they usually inspire, but there was no necessity for an attempt of that kind upon this occasion—the story, if such it may be called, carries along with it all that is required; and if you should not be disappointed with its appearance as I have been content to deal with it, I shall be well rewarded for the very little trouble it cost me. The lines were composed yesterday, it is not my Custom to forward to any one verses quite fresh from the pen, but I could not resist doing so in the present case lest by deferring my acknowledgements, I should seem insensible of your communication and perhaps by a prolonged silence hurt your feelings.

[1] This letter is W. W.'s reply to a long and effusive letter from Miss Ogle (*WL MSS.*), paying tribute to his influence on the formation of her mind, and submitting for his consideration the story on which he based *The Norman Boy* (*PW* i. 252). The date of composition of the poem can now be definitely established for the first time. The text which follows is the only known MS. version: it was enlarged within a few days and resubmitted to Miss Ogle, who wrote on 28 May that 'the additional stanzas are indeed beautiful' (*WL MSS.*), and the poem was published in 1842. W. W. wrote a sequel, *The Poet's Dream* (*PW* i. 253), immediately afterwards. H. C. R. met Miss Ogle at Brighton the following year, 'a pretty young woman . . . and would be very agreeable if she were quite free from affectation.' (*HCR* ii. 601)

I am rather surprized that in singling out the poems you referred to, as having induced you to offer the Subject to me, you should not have mentioned the Goatherd boy,[1] described in the same Series—for that has I think a still closer connection with the circumstances, and with the train of feeling which recommend[s] to sympathy the young Christian you so fortunately met with.

I have only to request that you will not allow these verses to be copied.

I have the honor to be,
dear Madam sincerely yours
[*signed*] Wm Wordsworth

The state of my eyes, which are subject to inflammation, causes me to employ an Amanuensis which you will excuse as all the interlations which always become more or less necessary when one dictates. W. W.

High on a wide infertile tract of forest-skirted Down
Not kept by Nature to herself, nor made by Man his own,
From home and company remote and every playful joy,
Served, tending a few Sheep and goats, a ragged Norman boy.

Him never saw I, nor the Spot: but from an english Dame
Stranger to me and friend of mine, a simple notice came,
With suit that I would speak in verse, of this sequestered child,
Whom, one bleak winter's day, she met upon that dreary wild.

There was he where of branches rent and withered and decayed,
For Shelter from the keen north wind, his hands a hut had made;
A tiny tenement and frail, as needs the Thing must be
Of such materials there composed, by children such as He.

The hut was finished by his pains, nor seemingly lacked aught
That skill or means of his could add, but the Architect had wrought
Some limber twigs into a Cross (well shaped with fingers nice)
Which he was fixing on the top of that small Edifice;

A Cross which he was fixing there as the surest power and best
To make up for deficiencies and wants of his rude nest,
And of the melancholy Place where, by all seasons tried
The lonely Boy, from morn to night, did with his flock abide.

[1] *The Danish Boy* (*PW* ii. 156), among the *Poems of the Fancy*.

Now, Lady! as thy suit is met, let us before we part,
With this dear lonely Shepherd-boy, breathe a prayer of earnest heart,
That unto him, where'er shall lie his life's appointed way,
The Cross, fixed in his Soul, may prove an all-sufficing stay.

1408. W. W. to CHARLES HENRY PARRY

MS. Henry E. Huntington Library.
Mem. Grosart. K. LY ii. 1025.

Rydal Mount
Ambleside
May 21st 1840

My dear Sir

Pray impute to any thing but a want of due sympathy with you in your affliction my not having earlier given an answer to your Letter.[1] In truth I was so much moved by it that I had not at first sufficient resolution to bring my thoughts so very close to your trouble as must have been done had I taken up the pen immediately.—I have been myself distrest in the same way though my two children were taken from us at an earlier age, one in her fifth and the other in his seventh years, and within half a year of each other.—I can therefore enter into your sorrow more feelingly than for others is possible who have not suffered like losses. Your departed Daughter struck me as having one of the most intelligent and impressive Countenances I ever looked upon, and I spoke of her as such to Mrs Wordsworth, my Friend Miss Fenwick and to others. The indications which I saw in her of a somewhat alarming state of health I could not but mention to you, when you accompanied me a little way from your own door; you spoke some thing encouraging, but they continued to haunt me, so that your kind communication was less of a Shock than it would otherwise have been, though not less of a sorrow. How pathetic is your account of the piety with which the dear Creature supported herself under those severe trials of mind and

[1] Parry had written on 11 May (*Bodleian Library MSS.*) to announce the death at the age of eighteen of his daughter Ellen, whom W. W. had met during his visit to Summer Hill, Bath, on 28 Apr. 1839 (see pt. iii, L. 1314). W. W.'s reply was copied into Parry's MS. Memoir of his daughter, which he published in 1842.

body with which it pleased God to prepare her for a happier world. The consolation which Children and very young Persons who have been religiously brought up, draw from the holy Scripture ought to be habitually on the minds of adults of all ages for the benefit of their own Souls, and requires to be treated in a loftier and more comprehensive train of thought and feeling than by writers has usually been bestowed upon it. It does not therefore surprize me that you hinted at my own pen being employed upon the subject as brought before the mind in your lamented Daughter's most touching case. I wish I were equal to any thing so holy, but I feel that I am not. It is remarkable however that within these last few days the subject has been presented to my mind by two several persons both unknown to me, which is something of a proof how widely its importance is felt, and also that there is a feeling of my not being wholly unworthy of treating it. Your Letter my dear Sir, I value exceedingly, and shall take the liberty, as I have done more than once with fit reverence, of reading it in quarters where it is likely to do good, or rather where I know it *must* do good.

Wishing and praying that the Almighty may bestow upon yourself, the Partner in your bereavement, and upon all the fellow sufferers of your Household that consolation and support which can proceed only from his grace,

I remain my dear Dr Parry

Most faithfully your much obliged
Wm Wordsworth

1409. W. W. to JOHN BRACKENRIDGE[1]

MS. Cornell. Hitherto unpublished.

Rydal Mount
Ambleside
23^d^ May 1840

Dear Sir,

It gives me such pleasure to learn from your obliging Letter that Mr Beaumont has been so kind as to present to me the valuable Relic of the family from which I am descended; more valuable as bearing upon it the name which I happen to bear, and

[1] Agent to Mr. Beaumont of Bretton Park, owner of the Wordsworth family aumbry.

which is borne by one of my Sons and one of my Grandsons also. I should take it, as an additional proof of your own kind consideration, if you would let me know Mr Beaumont's address abroad so that I may be enabled to return my thanks to him and to his Lady. If in the mean time you should have occasion to write, would you be so good as to say to them both, how sensible I am of the favor.

My address is *Ambleside Kendal* and if you will let me know when the package is likely to arrive at Kendal, which is only 15 miles from Rydal Mount where in fact I live, I will charge the Kendal and Ambleside Carrier to bring it forward instantly. Any expense respecting the removal (which I thank you for being so careful about) you will be so good as to inform me of.

I cannot conclude without expressing my sense of the gratifying terms in which you speak of myself and with many good wishes.

I remain
dear Sir
Sincerely your much obliged
Wm Wordsworth

1410. W. W. to MARY GASKELL

MS. St. John's College, Cambridge.
LY ii. 1026.

Rydal Mount May 23 1840

My dear Madam,

I have the pleasure of letting you know, though perhaps this may be no news to you, that Mr Beaumont has kindly presented me with the Crypt[1] in which you were so good as to interest yourself on my account. I owe you many thanks and pray accept them as cordially as they are offered. Without your friendly influence I never should have obtained this Relic of my good old Ancestor.

Yesterday I received the Letter from Mr Brakenbridge[2] telling me that he had been directed to forward it to me; and as the conveyance is by water to Kendal, it will be easy and safe; and I

[1] The Wordsworth family aumbry.

[2] See previous letter.

shall direct our Carrier to call for it instantly so that in a few days it will be probably under my roof.—

We are all in good health. You and Mr Gaskell are I hope the same. Finding two successive seasons in London rather too exhausting I do not mean to go thither this spring.

With a thousand good wishes in which Mrs W. and Dora unite I remain my dear Madam

faithfully
your much obliged
Wm Wordsworth

1411. W. W. to HENRY REED

Address: Henry Reed Esqre, Philadelphia, United States.
Endorsed: Rec. Aug. 5.
Postmark: 29 May 1840.
Stamp: (1) Ambleside (2) Boston.
MS. Cornell.
Wordsworth and Reed, p. 22.

[*In M. W.'s hand*]

Rydal Mount May 26 — 40

My dear Sir

I have just received your 2^{d} letter,[1] by which on many accounts I feel much obliged, but in replying to it I must confine myself to one point; being desirous to send off this letter instantly, with a view to receiving from you, as speedily as possible, information respecting the American Banks, which you kindly offer to do your best towards procuring. Within this ½ hour I have had a conversation with a female Friend especially dear to me and all my family and I find that she has no less a sum in the Bank of Pen[n]sylvania than £10,000 and also a considerable sum in that of the United States. She has been advised by

[1] Reed had written on 18 Mar., pressing W. W. to visit the United States, and he repeated his invitation in a second letter on 7 Apr. 'There are great *moral* ties between the two nations, which you more than any man living could draw closer.' And he offered his services in procuring information about the 'monetary derangements' in America, which had affected W. W.'s family and friends. 'Heretofore, unfortunately there has been a fatal facility in lending on the one side mated to a fatal facility of borrowing on the other.' See *Wordsworth and Reed*, pp. 15–22.

her London friends to sell out immediately, for fear of greater loss in future.

I reminded her of your friendly offer, which I had before told her of, to send me such information as you could procure, and she seemed wishful to have it along with your opinion—tho' it is possible that the urgency of her London friends may induce her to sell out, before we can have the pleasure of your answer. Pray then my dear Sir be so good as to comply with this request and also if you can give us any information of the Miss[iss]ippi Concern in which my Daughter and other Relatives is interested I shall be further obliged—but do not wait for this.

Excuse this brief note, which I have the less scruple in troubling you with, as I hope to be able to write more at length hereafter. I cannot conclude however without thanking you and Mrs Reed again for your hospitable invitation, which, I regret to say it is scarcely within the compass of probability, I can profit by; tho' I am thankful to say I am in good health and strength for my years.

With a thousand good wishes, to yourself and Mrs Reed, I remain my dear Sir very faithfully your obliged

[*signed*] Wm Wordsworth

1412. W. W. to H. C. R.

Endorsed: Wordsworth. [This is written by M. W. except the name.]
MS. Dr. Williams's Library.
Morley, i. 408.

[*In M. W.'s hand*]

June 3rd 1840

My dear Friend

I have been shamefully long in writing to you—Having two letters to acknowledge; for this delay which has cost me a good deal of self-reproach, I have no excuse to make, but such a one as you offer for yourself, in your former letter, that you had in fact nothing to say that you could persuade yourself w^d be found interesting.

Your first letter turned upon the narrow-mindedness of Warburton,[1] in connexion with the London University—he is

[1] Henry Warburton (see pt. iii, L. 1214), one of the leading opponents of the Copyright Bill, had recently fallen foul of H. C. R. by proposing 'that the new

one of those wrong-headed Men (as will be shewn also this day, when the unfortunate Copy-right bill comes before the House) whose obstinacy faithfully keeps pace with his ignorance: I quite go along with your views of the University question—as I did of the privilege question[1]—but I cannot say the same of that you take of Lord Stanley's bill[2] as far as I am able to judge of its contents from what has been said thereupon, and upon the subject in general, in the Ho: of C.—I have carefully read the speeches of both of its Advocates and its Enemies—and am decidedly of opinion that it is a disgrace to the House, that the majority in favour of the Motion was not larger. As to the fear of a rising in Ireland that may happen, or may not—happily for those who have voted in favor of the Mover *they* stand upon higher and firmer ground than is to be found in apprehensions of this sort—and with this observation, tho' I could willingly say much more upon it, I dismiss the Subject.

Our life here is without incident, except now and then, as the other day, we hear of a Person drowned—mostly by some fault of his own, in one of our Lakes. You may judge of how little happens among us when I think it worth while to tell you—that yesterday, being desirous of hearing the result of the Cockermouth Election[3] I walked out to waylay the Coach—I heard it

Charter of the London University shall enable the Senate to confer degrees on any man who can have crammed himself sufficiently to pass an examination—without enquiring where or how he got his knowledge!' (Morley, i. 406–7) H. C. R. wished to uphold the original conception of the University as a board of examiners conferring degrees on students from colleges all over the country where studies hitherto confined to Oxford and Cambridge might be encouraged.

[1] See L. 1369 above.

[2] The Government's new educational proposals (see pt. iii, L. 1335) had run into serious difficulties the previous summer. In June 1839 Lord Stanley, later 14th Earl of Derby (1799–1869), the Victorian Prime Minister, at this time M.P. for N. Lancs., moved for an Address to Her Majesty to rescind the Order in Council setting up the Board of the Privy Council to supervise the educational grant, arguing against entrusting any scheme for the moral and religious education of the people to any committee which would be exclusively political in character and which was based on no defined or fixed principle of action. The Motion was lost on 24 June by only 2 votes. A similar motion proposed by W. W.'s friend Dr. Howley, the Archbishop of Canterbury, in the Lords was subsequently carried by a large majority, but the Queen refused to revoke the Order in Council.

[3] Edward Horsman (see pt. iii, L. 1237) had stood for re-election in Cockermouth on his appointment as a Lord of the Treasury and retained his seat,

coming at some little distance and being in the high-way between Keswick and Ambleside I ran on before to ask the guard, who I thought might have occasion to stop at the foot of our hill—upon my beckoning to him he alighted good-naturedly, shewed me the state of the Poll—and said, Mr Horsman was in front upon the top of the Coach—there were several Persons there, and Mr H. stretched out his pale oval face, and said, upon my greeting him—'we have had some correspondence together Mr Wordsworth' 'Yes' said I 'upon the poor unfortunate Copyright bill, which has been so scurvily treated—as you are returned, Mr H. I hope you will take care of it'—My views of politics did not allow me to congratulate him upon his return and the Coach drove on. I have not yet heard any particulars of the election—but tho' Gen. Wyndham[1] has some things much against him—especially his living with a woman, openly—that no one believes to be his wife—I am pretty confident, from what I know of the place in general, that if he will live there something more than he does, and be gracious in his manners, which a Gentleman who formerly saw much of him tells me he used *not* to be—he will then oust Mr H. upon the next occasion. H. is a clever Man and to him *personally* I have no objection, but sh^d be rather glad to see him in Parliament as some with his opinions will, and *perhaps ought* to be there.

Yesterday I heard a good deal about little Pappina[2]—Our lamented friend Miss M. had little to leave her—but Mrs Fletcher[3] who lives close by some of her family, who are her most intimate friends, says they have among [them] settled upon the child £2000—and they have the best intentions towards her;

H. A. Aglionby (see pt. ii, L. 701) being the other member. In a closely-fought contest on 1 June, Horsman defeated his opponent General Wyndham by a majority of 26 votes. Violence broke out on the hustings as the result was announced. Horsman had made himself unpopular in the Tory press, which treated him as an ambitious parvenu from outside the county, and the Whig cause was further overshadowed by Chartist agitations. See *Cumberland Pacquet* for 26 May and 2 June 1840.

[1] General Sir Henry Wyndham, K.C.B. (1790–1860), son of the 3rd Earl of Egremont (see pt. i, L. 124), a distinguished Napoleonic field commander: M.P. for Cockermouth, 1852–7, and for West Cumberland, 1857–60.

[2] Beppina, ward of Miss Mackenzie, whose recent death had left the child in straitened circumstances (see also L. 1392 above).

[3] Mrs. Fletcher had returned to Grasmere on 1 June, and was living at Thorney How, while her new house was being built at Lancrigg.

but they are apprehensive of much discomfort from her, as they know she is of a violent and perverse temper—and they are not mistaken from what I saw in part, and from what Miss M told me. She is to come to Scotland (together with Miss M's Niece, who was with her Aunt at the time of her death—whither she had gone, poor thing! on acc[t] of her own health) and is to be brought up under their eye, tho' not living in their house. M[rs] Fletcher represents these Relatives of your late friend to be most excellent People, so that the Child will have a better chance of growing up for happiness, notwithstanding the heat of her southern blood, which perhaps may be moderated by the cooler climate of Scotland—I shall make farther enquiries, and if I hear anything more about her, which is likely to interest you, I will let you know.

Why should you be so troubled about not remember[g] whether you had mentioned your recitation of the Sonnets[1] before? You had done so—but bless me! if that is to dishearten one what is to become of poor M[rs] W. and myself who are not quite 5 years older than you—I cannot at this moment determine, whether I have written to thank M[r] Dice,[2] from whom a little while ago, I rec[d] 5 solid volumes of Middleton the Dramatist's Works it seems to me as if I *had* written but Mary says *No*—Should you fall in with that excellent Man, pray tell him the dilemma I am in—he would think me quite gone, if he sh[d] receive another letter upon the same subject. The memory is no doubt the first of the faculties that age impairs—Dryden writing at 70 tells us that it failed in him when nothing else had, as he gave striking proof—his most poetical, if not his best things, being written about that age.[3]

Give up Germany and come to us—we can, I trust get you a nice lodging where you were before—or a still more agreeable one through the field—by the brookside in the way to D[r]

[1] At a recent meeting of his Nonconformist club, H. C. R. had recited W. W.'s sonnets on 'Latitudinarianism' and 'Clerical Integrity' from the *Ecclesiastical Sonnets* (*PW* iii. 386–7).

[2] Alexander Dyce had written on 2 Mar. (*Dyce MSS., Victoria and Albert Museum*), sending his edition of Middleton, which had just appeared.

[3] Among Dryden's last poems were his St. Cecilia's Day Ode *Alexander's Feast* (1697), the translation of Virgil published the same year, and his versions of Homer, Ovid, Chaucer, and Boccaccio which make up *The Fables* (1700), published just before his death in his seventieth year.

Arnold's—Hartley Coleridge is come much nearer us,[1] and probably you might see as much of him as you liked—Of Genius he has not a little, and talent enough for fifty. The Hardens are just returned from Paris, and I know would be delighted to see you at any time.

We hear of no favourable acc^{t} from Keswick,[2] but the decay is very slow—No tidings of Lovel.[3] Poor Owen Lloyd is in confinement—and our best hope is that he will not live long,[4] as he has lately had frequent shocks of epilepsy—that has made grievous havoc both in his bodily health, and faculties of mind.

We in this house are all pretty well—Miss F. has had rather a bad cold, but she is recovering. She will be stationary in this country till the end of Sepr and means to return to it after a visit to her Durham friends—She expects M^{r} and Mrs H. Taylor in a few weeks—With best wishes from all aff^{ly} yours

[*signed*] Wm Wordsworth

1413. W. W. to H. C. R.

Endorsed: 8th June 1840. Wordsworth. W and Clarkson controversy. Southey's Letters.
MS. Dr. Williams's Library.
Morley, i. 411.

June 8th [18]40

My dear Friend

I find no difficulty in answering your question. M^{r} C[5] if his

[1] Since the death of Mrs. Fleming in 1837, Hartley Coleridge had been living in Grasmere with the Richardsons. When they moved to The Nab, beside Rydal Water, in the spring of 1840, Hartley went with them, and The Nab remained his home for the rest of his life. The Wordsworths continued to oversee his financial arrangements. M. W. had written to Hartley's mother on 21 Nov. 1839: 'We cannot say, poor fellow, that his expences are great—but how well would it be for himself, if his great talents were applied as they ought to be to his entire maintenance.' (*Victoria University Library MSS.*)

[2] i.e. of Southey.

[3] Robert Lovell jnr., son of Southey's sister-in-law, had been apprenticed to a printer and worked for a time for Hansard. About 1836 he went abroad to Rome, and disappeared in mysterious circumstances which were never satisfactorily cleared up. See Curry, i. 526.

[4] Owen Lloyd died the following year.

[5] The controversy between the Wilberforces and Thomas Clarkson over his

state of health allows it ought to demand or rather insist upon a sight of the Letters, of if he be unable to stir in the matter himself, some Friend of his, better if a person known to Messieurs Wilberforce, should do it for him. It is intolerable that at Mr C's age such a threat should be hanging over him, and his relatives and Friends. Looking at the question *prudentially* only, and bearing in mind what I recollect naming to you during our Tour, a charge reported to me on pretty high authority as being made in conversation by Lord Grey against Mr C, I am decidedly of opinion that this course should be taken. The accusations, if any such there be, may be repelled and the aspersions I doubt not wiped out, by Mr C himself while living, and even supposing the worst that something to be regretted or lamented would still remain, as in the matter of Mr C's importunity about his Brother, yet still nothing can be so bad, as an insinuation and menace (for a menace is in it) of this character—

In respect to Mr Southey's Letters to the Wilberforces as quoted by them, there is nothing in the opinion there expressed derogatory to Mr Clarksons moral character, or to the constitution of his mind morally considered—There is no ground whatever for believing that Mr Southey imputed what he thought amiss in Mr C's Book[1] to personal vanity, much less to any deliberate wish to derogate from the deserts of others. And I am pretty sure that no one could be farther from thinking Mr Clarkson unjust to Mr Wilberforce in particular, in that Book than Mr Southey was. All Mr Clarksons friends in this part of the Country were of one opinion—that Mr C's Book would have been more generally interesting, and better constructed as a literary composition, and more useful if it had been confined to his own personal exertions in this cause, and to what he was mixed up with, or was an eye witness of. And that nothing further was required from him or expedient, than a *brief* prefatory summary of what had been done in the cause before he took it up, and the like by way of appendix if the writing of his book were deferred till the Trade was abolished. But this putting off we all lamented—By the words 'nothing of this sort would

role in the abolition of slavery (see pt. iii, L. 1243) was now renewed with the publication of *The Correspondence of William Wilberforce*. See also Ls. 1416, 1417 and 1423 below.

[1] Clarkson's *History of the Rise, Progress and Accomplishment of the Abolition of the African Slave-Trade by the British Parliament.*

have happened etc', of what sort? it should seem that it is meant to be insinuated no injustice to Mr Wilberforce—M^r^ S could I am convinced have to disposition to make any such charge—though he had cause to regret, as all M^r^ Cs Friends had that owing to M^r^ C's having (in consequence of his health being utterly ruined by his labours) withdrawn from exertion, and probably from the same cause not kept his *mind* upon it for a while, He as an historian did not do justice to Mr Stephen[1] and Mr Macaulay[2] and perhaps some others. But neither Did Mr Southey nor any other candid person ever impute these deficiencies, for such they were, in a book calling itself the History of the Abolition, to love of self or any cause more reprehensible than want of due inquiry and consideration.—

For my own part I have many times expressed my regret, before I ever interchanged a word with Mr S. on the subject, that M^r^ C's book was not what he M^r^ S recommended, and [? which] I have little doubt (though I cannot recall the time, seeing so much more of Mr Clarkson than M^r^ S did) that I pressed upon him myself.——

I have said nothing upon the pain which the course taken by Messrs W— has caused me. I cannot bear to think of it either in one case or the other. I differ however from you in one respect. Unfeeling as it is, dreadfully so if the W's know poor dear S's state of Mind and Body to have quoted from his Letters in that way, I do still think their conduct in respect to the hanging out the menace still more reprehensible.—

I think you have quite sufficient grounds for calling upon Sir Robert Inglis,—if you are shy about it, I will write to him should you desire it.—ever affectionately

and faithfully yours W Wordsworth

I have galloped through the *penning* of this Letter on account of the disturbed state of my eyes, though thank God they are very far from being at their worst.

[1] James Stephen (1758–1832), Master in Chancery, 1811–31: brother-in-law and supporter of Wilberforce; author of *The Slavery of the British West India Colonies Delineated*, 2 vols., 1824–30, and father of W. W.'s friend James Stephen, of the Colonial Office.

[2] Zachary Macaulay (1768–1838), philanthropist and abolitionist: father of Thomas Babbington Macaulay.

1414. W. W. to JOHN BRACKENRIDGE

Address: John Brackenridge Esqre, Bretton Park, Wakefield. [*In M. W.'s hand*]
Postmark: (1) 16 June 1840 (2) 17 June 1840.
Stamp: (1) Ambleside (2) Wakefield.
MS. Cornell. Hitherto unpublished.

Rydal Mount
Ambleside
15 June—1840

Dear Sir,

I have the pleasure to inform you that the Crypt arrived here two days ago without the least injury, and I feel much obliged to yourself, and to others by whom such good care has been taken in packing and forwarding it.—

My house is but small, and therefore it cannot be seen here to all the advantage it had before Mr Beaumont was so kind as to part with it in my favor, still as the best place we have for it is in a room in which we live a good part of the day, and the light falls well upon it, we have little cause to complain that entire justice is not done by its present position to so valuable a relic of antiquity.

It would give me much pleasure if your occasions should ever draw you hither, to shew you something of the beauties of our neighbourhood as a slight return for your attentions, and the gratifying manner in which you have expressed yourself to me upon this occasion

Believe me dear Sir,
sincerely your much obliged
Wm Wordsworth

PS I mean to write to Mr Beaumont immediately.—

1415. W. W. to MARY GASKELL

MS. St. John's College, Cambridge.
LY ii. 1027.

Rydal Mount
Ambleside
18th June –40

Dear Mrs Gaskell,

The Crypt is arrived and you must be thanked again for your effectual exertions to procure it for me. It is certainly one of the handsomest and most interesting Reliques of the kind I ever saw, and will be I trust duly valued[1] by my descendants after I am no more.—

I have written to thank Mr and Mrs Beaumont this very day, and now let me add that it would give us all no common pleasure to shew it to you in the humble room in which it stands. To be sure it is not seen to such advantage as in its late station; however there is much in feeling to make up for that, and every Friend of ours who has seen it has looked upon the memorial of past times, and of my good old Ancestor (for such we must suppose him to have been) with due interest.

Mrs W. and my Daughter[2] unite with me in kind remembrances, and good wishes for yourself. Mr Gaskell and your family, and believe my dear Madam faithfully

your much obliged
Wm Wordsworth

1416. W. W. to H. C. R.

Endorsed: 19th June 1840. Wordsworth. Autograph.
MS. Dr. Williams's Library.
Morley, i. 414.

Friday Morning [19 June 1840]

My dear Friend,

I arrived home from a visit so late last night and so much jaded in mind and somewhat in body by a long walk, that I could not write to any one. A Letter however has this morning been

[1] *Written* valuable.

[2] Dora W. had just returned from staying with the Curwens on Belle Isle.

prepared for Sir R. I[1]—and I have only time to tell you that it will go with this mornings post along with this note

ever faithfully yours
W. W.

[*M. W. writes*]

Dear friend—

W^m^ and I called at Mr Harden's[2] the other day where we learnt that you contemplated a visit to West^d^ next *Winter*—Why defer this so long—We thought that your next was to be made in summer—for y^r^ own sake it ought to be; and we should rejoice to see you—it seems to be thro' Charity to *us* that you come always in winter—Always welcome however—

M. W.

1417. W. W. to H. C. R.

Endorsed: 24th June 1840. Wordsworth. (C and W affair)
MS. Dr. Williams's Library.
Morley, i. 414.

Rydal Mt June 24th [1840]

My dear Friend

I have nothing to say for not replying to your first letter immediately, and suffering a day to pass without notice of your second, but that I have been engaged in work, which too often deprives me of mastery over my own time and thoughts—besides my eyes are too often uneasy—and Mrs W. is often engaged—who holds the pen for me—by little less than necessity at this moment.

I am glad for Sir R. I's[3] own sake that he has called upon you—As to publishing any words from M^r^ S's[4] letters, in his present state of mind and body, as he cannot be consulted, I think it ought not to be done. it is quite enough to say publickly

[1] Sir Robert Inglis. The Wilberforces had quoted from a letter of Southey to themselves in such a way as to imply that Southey could find no fault in their *Life* of their father or in their treatment of Clarkson. H. C. R. had letters from Southey to himself which implied the contrary, and he wished to show them to Inglis.

[2] Of Field Head.

[3] Sir Robert Inglis. See previous letter.

[4] Southey.

that you hold letters from him and that you are both ready and wish to shew them to any friend of the W's[1] whose interference might tend to set them, and such of the Public, as they may have missled, right upon that point.

I am still decidedly of opinion that while Mr C.[2] is yet living some one of his friends should insist upon a sight of those passages in M^r^ W's or Mr Clarkson's letters injurious to the latter—in order that he may have an opportunity of defending himself. I think this by far the most important part of the painful question. Mr Clarkson has already confessed, to his own honor, that he was wrong in pressing to the degree and in the way he did his Brother's professional advancement and it is possible that from his mind, so apt to be possessed with one idea, other improprieties somewhat of the same sort, may have come; if it be so, and a sufficient explanation cannot be given, it could not but be satisfactory, I should think, to himself and to every one who reveres his name, that he should express his regret or sorrow.

The sketch of the conversation which you proposed to hold with Sir R. I. appears to me quite unobjectionable—

Let me hear from you after the interview, and as often as you feel disposed, your letters are always acceptible to us all.

E^r^ most faithfully
Yours
Wm Wordsworth

1418. W. W. to CHARLES HENRY PARRY

MS. Yale University Library.
Ellen Parry, p. 240.

Rydal Mount
June 27th 1840.

My dear Sir,

The verses[3] which you were so kind as to send me upon the subject of your lamented Daughter pleased me much. They are piously written; and feelingly, nor are they at all faulty in the expression. It might simply be a question with some whether

[1] i.e. Robert and Samuel Wilberforce.

[2] Clarkson.

[3] Susan Shakerley's verses on the death of Ellen Parry (see L. 1408 above).

verses more regular, that is with fewer redundant syllables, in other words deviating less from the common Iambic movement, would not prove more agreeable. People's ears have however lately become accustomed to that freer movement, which I am not so likely to be reconciled to, as a younger Reader. But too much upon a point of so little consequence, upon so momentous a subject, and so affecting, to you and your's and all who knew the excellence of the departed.

I sincerely hope that you and Mrs Parry derived benefit from chance of place, under your depression, and earnestly pray that it may please God to restore to you that tranquillity of spirit which must have received a shock so grievous.

I am not without hope of seeing you next Spring if all goes well with my family and self, and our excellent Friend Miss Fenwick; for we talk a good deal about a visit to Bath, and to Mr and Mrs Popham.[1] With kind remembrances to yourself and Mrs Parry and best wishes to all your family

I remain my dear Sir
ever sincerely and faithfully yours
W[m] Wordsworth

1419. W. W. to HENRY WILLIAM PICKERSGILL

Address: H. W. Pickersgill Esq[re], Soho Square, London.
Postmark: (1) 30 June 1840 (2) 1 July 1840.
Stamp: Ambleside.
MS. St. John's College, Cambridge.
LY ii. 1028.

[*In M. W.'s hand*]

Rydal Mount 29th June [1840]

Dear Sir

I should have replied to your letter immediately but I wished to make some enquiry about a house fit for your purpose.[2] We have one close by us, which I think may suit, as it has tall windows with half shutters fronting every aspect: all that is wanting at present is, the permission of the Gentleman to whom

[1] I. F.'s sister and brother-in-law.

[2] Pickersgill had been commissioned by Sir Robert Peel to paint a new portrait of W. W. to hang in Drayton Manor. He came to Rydal early in September (see L. 1430 below).

it belongs—who is now absent—but will shortly be at home—indeed I believe in a few days, when I have no doubt of his being ready to accommodate us—and I can say for my own part, that I am at liberty, and shall be glad to gratify Sir R[t] Peel's wishes by sitting to you when it suits your convenience to visit Rydal—but I regret to add, that we have in this house at present, and shall have until the month of Sep[r] visitors,[1] which will prevent our accommodating you with a lodging under our own roof—which, if you could defer your journey till that month, would not be the case. Should it be more convenient to you to come immediately—or during the month of August, if you will inform me I shall be happy to secure a lodging for you as near to Rydal, if not *in* the village, as I can—so that you may join us at meal times—when we shall always be happy to see you—

Mrs W. and my daughter join me in Comp[ts] and believe me to be, dear Sir

faithfully yours
[*signed*] Wm Wordsworth

PS Pray dont start without letting me know two or three days before, that I may be sure to be at home.

W. W.

1420. W. W. to UNKNOWN CORRESPONDENT

MS. Bookfellow Foundation Collection. Knox College.
Hitherto unpublished.

London
June 30th 1840

Sir,

Your Letter has only just found its way to my hands, in consequence of my having been moving about for some time. I am sorry for this delay but have to regret it the less, as I am not acquainted with any Person, whom I could recommend as fit to undertake the office of giving Lectures before your Society upon the subject of Poetry. It is a task which few would be inclined to

[1] E. Q. arrived for a six-week stay at Rydal Mount on 1 July: his daughter Jemima had already arrived there, having returned north with Dora W. at the end of April. Other visitors this summer included Thomas and Ebba Hutchinson and Mary Monkhouse from Brinsop.

venture upon, and the reluctance would probably be pretty much in proportion to the fitness of the Individual for the office. If this observation should appear to you to have a good foundation you will be the less disappointed should not your application in other quarters prove in the issue satisfactory.

I remain Sir
Your obedient Ser^{vnt}
Wm Wordsworth

1421. W. W. to STANSFELD RAWSON[1]

MS. King Edward VI School, Southampton. Hitherto unpublished.

Rydal Mount, July 21,
1840 —

My dear Sir,

Upon our return home, we find that the Ring *is* missing, and my daughter does not doubt that it was lost by her on the road to Kendal.

I have written by this day's post to the police officer at Keswick begging him to retain it, without advertising it, till he sees or hears from you. Will you be so kind as to take such steps as you think proper for its being restored to us, and I shall be glad to take the earliest opportunity to repay any expense that has been incurred.[2]

We reached home yesterday evening after a pleasant tour,[3] though with some interruptions from bad weather. Among the agreeable remembrances which the ramble has left upon the minds of us all, none are more so than those connected with Wastdale and your own and Mrs Rawson's most kind hospitality.

I remain my dear [Sir][4]
faithfully yours
Wm Wordsworth

[1] Of Wastdale Hall: son of William and Mrs. Rawson.

[2] *Written* occurred.

[3] W. W. and M. W., with their summer visitors, had been away on a week's tour (14–20 July) to Buttermere, Wastdale, and the Duddon (see also L. 1425 below). E. Q.'s MS. Diary (*WL MSS.*) gives a full account of their itinerary. They were at Keswick on the first day for the opening of the new school: later they visited Cold Fell, where W. W.'s father lost his way in Dec. 1783, thereby bringing on the illness from which he died.

[4] *Word dropped out.*

1422. W. W. to NICHOLAS LEE TORRE[1]

Address: Nicholas L. Torre Esq[re], Leamington, Warwickshire.
MS. Folger Library, Washington.

Rydal Mount
21st July —40

Sir

Absence from home has prevented my replying sooner to your letter.

Be assured I am duly sensible of the honor done me by your request on the part of the Shakespeare Committee that my name may be included in the list of Contributors to the objects stated in your Letter. As one who venerates in common with the whole world the Genius of Shakespeare, I am pleased to see so many royal noble and distinguished Persons interested in the undertaking. But in truth Literature stands much less in need of monuments to the dead than of justice to the living. And while so little attention is paid by the Legislature and by the public also to the principles set forth in Sergeant Talfourd's Copy right Bill, I cannot do more, upon the present occasion, than offer respectfully to the Committee my good wishes—

I have the honor to be
Sincerely yours
W[m] Wordsworth

[1] Nicholas Lee Torre (1795–1868), of Snydale Hall, Yorks., Fellow of New College, Oxford, 1813–18, and author of *Translations of the Oxford and Cambridge Latin Prize Poems*, 1833, was Secretary of the newly-established Shakespeare Society, formed to promote the publication of works connected with, and illustrative of, the plays of Shakespeare and his contemporaries.

1422a. W. W. to WILLIAM GASKELL[1]

Address: To the Author of the Pamphlet entitled Temperance Rhymes, at Mr Forrest's, Manchester.
MS. John Rylands Library. Hitherto unpublished.

Rydal Mount
Ambleside
July 22nd 40.

Dear Sir,

I have read your Temperance Rhymes with much pleasure and cannot but think that they must do good.

You have judged well in adding those that present pictures of the good and virtuous, by way of contrast to the wretched whom you would deter from continuing in a course that must end in death, and if not repented of in misery unspeakable—

In this latter division of your Work I was especially pleased with the Verses founded on the beautiful old Welsh custom, with which you have first made me acquainted.

I remain dear Sir with prayers for the success of your humane endeavours

sincerely yours
Wm Wordsworth

1423. W. W. to H. C. R.

Endorsed: July 1840. Wordsworth (the book).
MS. Dr. Williams's Library.
Morley, i. 416.

[late July 1840]

My dear Friend

I see no objection on the ground of delicacy or any other to your printing what you have sent.[2] *But* as Mr S.[3] speaks of

[1] The Revd. William Gaskell (1805–84), Unitarian minister of Cross Street Chapel, Manchester, from 1828, married Elizabeth Cleghorn Gaskell the novelist in 1832, and became Professor of English History and Literature at Manchester New College (1846–53), and later a lecturer at Owens College. He edited the *Unitarian Herald*, 1861–75. His *Temperance Rhymes* had appeared in 1839. See also L. 2118 below.

[2] H. C. R. was about to publish his *Exposure of Misrepresentations contained in the preface to the Correspondence of William Wilberforce*, 1840.

[3] Southey.

himself as quite well, I strongly advise that the expression, in respect to his state of health should be softened. The word 'lamentible' in particular omitted; and the rest put as gently as you can to answer your purpose.

You surprize me by saying that Mrs Clarkson cares so little about the *threat* held over her husband and his memory. For under the boast lies obviously a *threat*. As I said in a former Letter, this appears to me far the ugliest part of the proceeding. As to you, you are comparatively young and vigorous and quite able to take care of yourself, but it is not so with that good old man—Ever faithfully yours

W. W.

Pickersgill has offered to come down and paint my picture for Sir Robert Peel's Gallery at his request——

Suppose instead of '*put it out of his power*' has put out of the question his writing, or you might hit upon something better

1424. W. W. to LADY FREDERICK BENTINCK

MS. untraced.
Mem. K (—). *LY ii. 1029.*

[30 July 1840][1]

I hope, dear Lady Frederick, that nothing will prevent my appearance at Lowther towards the end of next week. But I have for these last few years been visited always with a serious inflammation in my eyes about this season of the year, which causes me to have fears about the fulfilment of any engagement, however agreeable. Pray thank Lord Lonsdale, on my part, for his thinking of me upon this occasion.

On Monday morning, a little before nine, a beautiful and bright day, the Queen Dowager[2] and her sister[3] appeared at

[1] Dated by reference to E.Q.'s MS. Diary (*WL MSS.*) which records W. W.'s visit to Southey, mentioned below, on 28 July. W. W. left for Hallsteads and Lowther on 7 Aug.

[2] Queen Adelaide (1792–1849), eldest daughter of George, Duke of Saxe-Coburg Meiningen, and widow of William IV, had arrived at Bowness with her suite on Friday, 24 July. On the Saturday she visited Storrs. The visit to Rydal, of which Dora W. left an account (*WL MSS.*), took place on the 27th, and the names of the distinguished visitors were duly recorded in the *RMVB*. See also *Cumberland Pacquet* for 28 July 1840.

[3] The Duchess of Saxe-Weimar.

Rydal. I met them at the lower waterfall, with which her Majesty seemed much pleased. Upon hearing that it was not more than half a mile to the higher fall, she said, briskly, she would go; though Lord Denbigh[1] and Lord Howe[2] felt that they were pressed for time, having to go upon Keswick Lake, and thence to Paterdale. I walked by the Queen's side up to the higher waterfall, and she seemed to be struck much with the beauty of the scenery. Her step was exceedingly light; but I learned that her health is not good, or rather that she still suffers from the state of her constitution, which caused her to go abroad.

Upon quitting the park of Rydal, nearly opposite our own gate, the Queen was saluted with a pretty rural spectacle; nearly fifty children, drawn up in avenue, with bright garlands in their hands, three large flags flying, and a band of music. They had come from Ambleside, and the garlands were such as are annually prepared at this season for a ceremony called 'the Rush-bearing';[3] and the parish-clerk of Ambleside hit upon this way of showing at Rydal the same respect to the Queen which had been previously shown at Ambleside. I led the Queen to the principal points of view in our little domain, particularly to that, through the summer house, which shows the lake of Rydal to such advantage. The Queen talked more than once about having a cottage among the lakes, which of course was nothing more than a natural way of giving vent to the pleasure which she had in the country. You will think, I fear, that I have dwelt already too long upon the subject; and I shall therefore only add, that all went off satisfactorily, and that every one was delighted with her Majesty's demeanour. Lord and Lady Sheffield[4] were the

[1] William Basil Feilding, 7th Earl of Denbigh (1796–1865). He was accompanied by his daughter Lady Mary Feilding (d. 1896).

[2] Lord Howe (see pt. i, L. 308) was Queen Adelaide's Chamberlain, and his daughter Lady Georgiana Curzon (d. 1906), who married the 8th Duke of Beaufort in 1845, was also in her suite.

[3] This traditional ceremony had been taken up with enthusiasm by Frederick Faber (see pt. iii, Ls. 1195 and 1330), who preached the annual Rush-Bearing Sermon in Ambleside this year. He called at Rydal Mount in January and July (*RMVB*), and was now living in Benson Harrison's household as tutor to his eldest son. His *Cherwell Water-Lily, and other poems*, published this autumn, reflects the influence of W. W. and Faber's own love of Lakeland scenery and customs.

[4] George Augustus Holroyd, 2nd Earl of Sheffield (1802–76), of Sheffield

only persons of her suite whom I had seen before. Lord Howe was pleased with the sight of the pictures from his friend Sir George Beaumont's pencil, and showed them to the Queen, who, having sat some little time in the house, took her leave, cordially shaking Mrs Wordsworth by the hand, as a friend of her own rank might have done. She had also inquired for Dora, who was introduced to her. I hope she will come again into the country, and visit Lowther.

Pray excuse the above long story, which I should not have ventured upon, but that you expressed a wish upon the subject.

What enchanting weather! I hope, and do not doubt, that you all enjoy it, my dear Lady Frederick, as we are doing.

I ought not to forget, that two days ago I went over to see Mr Southey, or rather Mrs Southey, for he is past taking pleasure in the presence of any of his friends. He did not recognise me till he was told. Then his eyes flashed for a moment with their former brightness, but he sank into the state in which I had found him, patting with both hands his books affectionately, like a child. Having attempted in vain to interest him by a few observations, I took my leave, after five minutes or so. It was, for me, a mournful visit, and for his poor wife also. His health is good, and he may live many years; though the body is much enfeebled.

Ever affectionately yours,
Wm Wordsworth

We hope your lameness will soon leave you, that you may ramble about as usual.

1425. W. W. to C. W. JNR.

MS. untraced.
LY ii. 1030.

[*c.* 31 July 1840]

My dear Christopher,

I forward this Letter[1] sent to me by mistake; as there is no call

Park, nr. Uckfield, Sussex, married Lady Harriet (d. 1889), eldest daughter of the 2nd Earl of Harewood. His sister was Lady Stanley of Alderley (see pt. iii, L. 1027).

[1] Written at the end of a letter to C. W. jnr. from Dr. John von Horn of Saxony, dated 29 July, offering to translate his *Greece* into German, and sent to W. W. by mistake.

for my answering it, you will probably think right to take the trouble—

We were much shocked to hear of the death of Mrs Wagner,[1] it will be [a] sad blow for her Father, as for all his nearest friends, your Father in particular—

We hope that Susan and the Baby[2] continue to do well, and that you are in good health. Is this about the time of your vacation; if so, where do you purpose spending it?

I had a Letter from Charles the other day with a sermon[3] of his Composition, his first attempt he says—I am glad to see him so employed, and hope that his natural spirits are coming back. We are all pretty well here; rather overpowered just at this time with strangers.[4] But pray understand that we shall always at all times, be happy most happy to see you and yours.

You are probably aware that a Niece of our Friend Miss Fenwick is about to become a cousin of Susan's.—[5]

We have lately been a party of seven, on a Tour of seven days, Keswick, Buttermere, etc. Ennerdale, Calder Abbey, Wastdale, Eskdale, Duddon, Broughton, Furness Abbey, Coniston. We enjoyed ourselves much Mary, Dora, Miss Fenwick, a Niece of hers, Mr Quillinan and his elder Daughter, who were here on a Visit. At the end of next week I go to Lowther to meet the Judges and Lawyers.—The Queen Dowager paid us a visit for the sake, we must humbly suppose, of seeing the Waterfalls, and views from our ground, which I shewed her majesty. We were

[1] Joshua Watson's daughter Mary, who had married the Revd. Henry Mitchell Wagner (1792–1870), Fellow of King's College, Cambridge, 1815–24, and thereafter vicar of Brighton, had died on 19 July. See also L. 1441 below.

[2] C. W. jnr.'s eldest child Elizabeth (1840–1932), b. 22 June, first Principal of Lady Margaret Hall, Oxford, 1878–1909: author of the official biography of her father and her own *Glimpses of the Past*, 1912.

[3] A sermon on 1 John v. 8, preached in Winchester College Chapel. See *Annals of my Early Life*, pp. 246–7.

[4] Recent visitors included Henry Taylor and his wife, with whom the Wordsworths dined at I. F.'s on 30 July, according to E. Q.'s MS. Diary (*WL MSS.*). Henry Hallam the historian, and Dr. W. F. Hook called in August, and Blomfield, Bishop of London, in September (*RMVB*).

[5] On 3 Dec. 1840 Isabella, daughter of William Tudor, medical practitioner, of Kelston Knoll, Bath, and his wife Dorothy (née Fenwick), married George Edward Frere (1807–87), of Roydon Hall, Norfolk. The Wordsworths had visited the family in Bath in Apr. 1839 (see *MW*, pp. 221, 230), and Mrs. Tudor had called at Rydal Mount in the July (*RMVB*) while staying with I. F. in Ambleside.

all pleased with her manner; she shook your Aunt cordially by the hand, and begged to be introduced to Dora. All went off well, and she seemed highly gratified with the beauty of the Country in general, and her reception in it. With Love to Susan, and kisses to the Baby, in which Mary and Dora unite, ever

Your affectionate Uncle
Wm Wordsworth

1426. W. W. to H. C. R.

Endorsed: Aug[t] 1840. Wordsworth (the book).
MS. Dr. Williams's Library.
Morley, i. 371.

[*In M. W.'s hand*]

[early Aug. 1840]

My dear Friend

Thanks for your Pamphlet.[1] I have not had time to read more, wishing to save the Post, than what relates to M[r] Southey—which I thoroughly approve and need only say that you are quite at liberty to write to M[rs] Southey what you think proper.

Thank you also for your former letter. With best regards from all, most aff[ly] yours

[*signed*] W[m] Wordsworth

Will write again when I have read the book.

1427. W. W. to UNKNOWN CORRESPONDENT

MS. Henry E. Huntington Library.
LY ii. 1032.

Rydal Mount
17th August 40

Sir

Having been from home I could not reply earlier to your Letter—I have no such Poem as you require in Mss and therefore cannot meet your wishes and those of your Friend which I

[1] See L. 1423 above.

regret; and also that I could not give you this information earlier—

I remain
Sir
Sincerely yours
Wm Wordsworth

1428. W. W. to BENJAMIN ROBERT HAYDON

MS. untraced.
K (—). LY ii. 1033.

Rydal Septr 2nd 1840

My dear Haydon

We are all charmed with your Etching;[1] it is both poetically and pictorially conceived, and finely executed. I should have written immediately to thank you for it and for your Letter; and the enclosed one, which is interesting, but I wished to gratify you by writing a sonnet. I now send it, but with an earnest request that it may not be put into circulation for some little time, as it is warm from the brain, and may require, in consequence, some little retouching.[2] It has this at least remarkable attached to it, which will add to its value in your eyes, that it was actually composed while I was climbing Helvellyn last Monday. My daughter and Mr Quillinan were with me; and She, which I believe had scarcely if ever been done before, *rode* every inch of the way to the summit, and a magnificent day we had.

Poor dear Mrs Haydon! I am very sorry that she is so ill as you describe. God grant that she may soon recover her Health. We congratulate you heartily upon your flattering prospects and reputation which this last work cannot but encrease. You call it an Etching; I pres[ume] hence and from the face, that the engraving is not quite finished. Am I right? The outline of the

[1] The engraving by Thomas Lupton (1791–1873) of Haydon's picture of Wellington on the Field of Waterloo (see pt. iii, L. 1338).

[2] The sonnet in fact gave W. W. not a little trouble, as succeeding letters show. After numerous revisions it was eventually published in an unidentified newspaper, and then in the *United Service Journal* for Oct. 1840. See George J. Worth, 'A Troublesome Wordsworth Sonnet', *NQ* cciii (Nov. 1958), 466–8.

face we all think too faint—that is not sufficiently distinguished from the Paper. Ever faithfully

with best wishes, yours
Wm Wordsworth

[*Here follows* Sonnet suggested by Haydon's picture of the Duke of Wellington upon the Field of Waterloo 20 yrs after the action, *as in PW iii. 53, but for ll. 9–12 read*

In his calm presence. Since the mighty deed
Him years have brought far nearer the grave's rest,
As shows that face time-worn. But genuine seed
Has sowed—that bears, we trust, the fruit of fame]

Composed while ascending Helvellyn Monday Aug 31st 1840

Wm Wordsworth

1429. W. W. to E. R. MORAN[1]

Address: E. R. Moran Esqre, Globe Newspaper Office, London.
Postmark: 4 Sept. 1840.
Stamp: Ambleside.
MS. Henry E. Huntington Library.
LY ii. 1032.

[*In M. W.'s hand*]

Ambleside
Sep^{t} 2^{d} 1840

Dear Sir

I take your communication very kindly, and thank you for it—the thought that runs thro' the Sonnet gives it a great interest. I am writing where I have it not before me, or I should have taken the liberty of quoting one line towards the conclusion, in which the word *to* occurs twice causing an inelegance both of sound and construction which might be easily remedied.

Tho' not very anxious about making Proselites it is nevertheless natural that I should be pleased to hear of Converts, or *Convertites* as with the authority of Shakespear[2] and others you give the word. I can claim no merit in being a Member of the Camden Society as you are, owing as I do the position of my

[1] A journalist, otherwise unidentified.

[2] See *As You Like It*, v.4.190; *King John*, v.1.19.

name there, to the kindness of a friend[1]—who unknown to me placed me on the list; the Papers and Works selected are many of them valuable—My Brother's and my nephew's names, I am happy to see, are among the subscribers

I remain dear Sir
yours respectfully
[*signed*] Wm Wordsworth

1430. W. W. to HENRY WILLIAM PICKERSGILL

MS. Private Collection. Hitherto unpublished.

Rydal Mount
Sept^{br} 2nd 40

My dear Sir,

The sooner you come the better.[2] I do not hear from Mr Rogers with whom I have a conditional engagement to leave home; but that need not prevent you, as I am sure he would prolong his stay here till your work was done. I shall wait your convenience. —We shall all be truly glad to see you. I ought to say that if you should prefer a lodging at Rydal to an Inn at Ambleside there is one at the foot of our Hill now empty.— Your direction about the package shall be attended to.

ever my dear Sir
faithfully yours
W Wordsworth

[1] H. C. R. See pt. iii, L. 1334.

[2] Pickersgill arrived a few days later to paint W. W.'s portrait for Sir Robert Peel. According to E. Q.'s MS. Diary (*WL MSS.*), the sittings began on 8 Sept. at the Ivy Cottage, now enlarged by William Ball the Quaker (see pt. iii, L. 1048), and renamed Glen Rothay. See also Rogers, ii. 325.

1431. W. W. to HENRY REED

Address: Henry Reed Esqre, Philadelphia. Single.
Endorsed: Rec. Sept. 21. Ans. Sep. 28.
Postmark: (1) 2 Sept. 1840 (2) 18 Sept.
Stamp: (1) Ambleside (2) Boston.
MS. Cornell.
Wordsworth and Reed, p. 31.

Rydal Sep^{br} 2nd 40

My dear Mr Reed,

I am truly thankful for your valuable letter;[1] as is also my excellent Friend. She read it yesterday, but as she is confined to her bed by illness, she cannot answer so satisfactorily as she wishes, your Queries. The Lady's name is Isabella Fenwick, but whether the money stands in her own name or that of some one else, I have not yet had an opportunity of learning. She is not certain in which of the two[2] her investment is; she rather thinks in the *Loans*. The Gentleman who recommended this Investment, and I believe managed the matter for her, bears the name of *Wilson*, so perhaps the money may stand in that name. I prepare this letter to be sent to-day, if I learn from the post office, (which is a mile and a half from my residence) that time will be gained by its being dispatched immediately; otherwise it will be detained till I can procure fuller information of particulars. How mortifying my letter should have been so long on the road. I will write again shortly, should my letter be dispatched to-day. On the other page is all the information I possess upon the Missisippi Bonds[3]—Pray excuse this wretched scrawl, done so hastily to save the Post—

[*signature cut away*]

[1] Reed had written at length on 5 Aug. (*Wordsworth and Reed*, pp. 26–31) in reply to W. W.'s request (L. 1411 above) for information about the reliability of investment in the American banks.

[2] i.e. whether it was an investment in the Bank of Pennsylvania or in the Loans of the State of Pennsylvania. Reed had queried which it was, stating his conviction that both investments would be perfectly secure.

[3] Reed reported less favourably of these, and of the 'general distrust' that prevailed in the north in regard to the pecuniary affairs of the southern states.

[*In John Carter's hand*]

Mississipi Stock

"London 9 Feby 1835.
"Bot. 6/1000$ New Mississipi 6 pCt. with div[d] from 1 Sepbr 1834 @ 110½. 1491. 15. —"
"I Hutchinson & Son, Brokers."

"London 2 Apr. 1835.
"Bot. for Saturday 4/4
"$3000 Mississipi 6 pCt. @ 109½ 739. 2. 6"
"I Hutchinson & Son, Brokers."

[*In M. W.'s hand*]

I shall be truly glad if you can send me a satisfactory report of the above, for tho' the amount of the Stock is inconsiderable, it is of great consequence to the Parties concerned—and it is a Trust which has devolved upon my wife.[1]

1432. W. W. to HENRY WILLIAM PICKERSGILL

Address: H. W. Pickersgill Esq[re], Soho Square, London.
MS. St. John's College, Cambridge.
LY ii. 1034.

[*In M. W.'s hand*]

Rydal Mount Sep[r] 3[d] [1840]

My dear Sir

Mr Rogers has arrived this evening, and unfortunately I cannot prevail upon him to stay longer than till Monday morn[g]. When I wrote to you the other day, trusting that as I had not heard from him he would not be here so soon, or that if he did come it might have suited him to wait till you had finished with me, I wished you to come as soon as you could. Having been long engaged to accompany Mr R. to Lord Lonsdale's I am now under the necessity of requesting that your journey may be deferred for at least a fortnight. I am the less reluctant in making this request as your note does not speak positively of its being convenient to you to be here at this time, and you add that to suit my convenience you could defer your coming.

[1] See L. 1444 below.

I much lament this clashing of engagements, but I cannot blame myself for it.

Pray let me hear from you by return of Post.

very sincerely yours
[*signed*] W. Wordsworth

1433. W. W. to BENJAMIN ROBERT HAYDON

MS. untraced.
K. LY ii. 1034.

Friday 4th [Sept. 1840]

My dear Haydon

Correct thus the lines toward the close of the Sonnet:[1]

As shows that time-worn face. But he such seed
Hath sown, as yields, we trust, the fruit of fame
In Heaven etc—

You will see the reason of this alteration—it applies now to his life in general and not that particular act as before—You may print the Son. where and when you like, if you think it will serve you—only it may be as well that I should hear from you first, as you may have something to suggest, either as to the title, or the lines.

Yours etc in haste,
Wm Wordsworth

1434. W. W. to H. C. R.

Address: H. C. Robinson Esq., 30 Russel place, London.
Postmark: (1) 3 Sept. 1840 (2) 4 Sept. 1840.
Stamp: Ambleside.
Endorsed: 4th Septr 1840. Wordsworth. The book.
MS. Dr. Williams's Library.
Morley, i. 417.

Thursday 4th [3rd?] Sepbr [18]40.

My dear Friend

We are all rather sorry that you are about to leave England;[2] as we had some hopes that you might be induced to turn your steps

[1] See L. 1428 above. [2] H. C. R. was going to Frankfurt.

this way. I have just left my dear Sister, having told her I was going to write to you. She said give my love to him and say it would cheer my aged heart to see him. These were her very words. For this last six weeks, or two months, we have lived in a crowd, and shall not be sorry when the heat of the season is over. We have had several of our relations under our roof, and Mr Quillinan and his Daughter have been with us some time. They are I believe about to depart, and my Son John and his second Son W^m^ leave us tomorrow. The Boy is full as interesting as when you saw him. He charms us all by his sweet looks and ways, and his remarkable intelligence—We shall be truly grieved to part with him—

What you say of the W's[1] is little different from what might be expected. I lament that it should be so—Your Pamphlet[2] I read carefully over; and found only one passage which I could have wished otherwise put. It is that in which you place the supposed remissness of the Members of the Church in somewhat invidious contrast with the Dissenters in the matter of the slave-trade. Neither the clerical nor Lay members of an Establishment are naturally so much given to stirring as Sectarians of any denomination; but to my certain knowledge a great many of our Clergy took a deep interest in that question, And some as the World knows, a conspicuous part in it.—I have not seen poor Southeys Letter upon the death of his Son; the Book not having fallen in my way. He is decaying mind and body by slow but sure process; and his Brother[3] who saw him the other day, says that if his disease be as he suspects a *softening* of the brain he may be carried off by paralysis at any moment; if on the contrary a *hardening* of it, he may last some time. It is a sad case, with the alleviation however that he appears to suffer no pain.—The chest, or rather Crypt which you kindly allude to is arrived. It fully answered our expectations, being both curious, and, in the carving, beautifully; wholly uninjured and its age 315-years. It is much admired by everybody.—Haydon has just sent me a spirited Etching of his Portrait of the Duke of Wellington taken 20 years after the Battle of Waterloo, from the Life. He is represented upon the field; but no more of the Picture—take my Sonnet which it suggested the other day. The lines were composed while I was climbing Helvellyn. We had a glorious

[1] Wilberforces.

[2] See L. 1423 above.

[3] Dr. Henry Southey.

day, and Dora reached the top without ever dismounting. Mr Quillinan and I walked.—I wish you had been with us. I was seven hours on my feet without being at all tired; so that if we are to see Italy again together in tolerable time I am still capable of some exertion.—

Pickersgill is coming down to take my portrait for Sir Robert Peel, and we are daily looking for Rogers, with whom I am engaged to go to Lowther—We are all well—I must conclude, with a thousand good wishes to save the Post, or you will not get my Letter, tomorrow being a blank day. We are all well—With much love from every one,

your faithful friend W. Wordsworth

Don't give a copy of the Sonnet to any one, as I consider it wholly at Haydon's disposal.

farewell
Pray write to us from Germany.

1435. W. W. to BENJAMIN ROBERT HAYDON

MS. untraced.
K. LY ii. 1035.

Rydal Mount, Monday Sep^{t} 7th, 1840.

I am quite ashamed to trouble you again, but after considering and reconsidering, changing and rechanging, it has been resolved that the troublesome passage[1] shall stand thus

In his calm presence. Him the mighty deed
Elates not brought far nearer the grave's rest
As shows that time-worn face. But he such seed
Hath sown as yields, we trust, etc.

faithfully yours
W. W.

[1] See L. 1433 above.

1436. W. W. to SAMUEL ROGERS

MS. Cornell. Hitherto unpublished.

Monday Morn.
Rydal Mount
half past nine [? early Sept. 1840]

My dear Rogers,

The morning is at present very wet. I am however in hopes that it may clear up before noon; if so you will see me and my little Phaeton; if not, then pray come to us in a chaise, and the sooner the better.—Your gout, I hope is no worse—

affectionately yours
Wm Wordsworth

1437. W. W. to BENJAMIN ROBERT HAYDON

MS. untraced.
K. LY ii. 1035.

Rydal, Sept. 10th, [1840]

By is certainly a better word than *through*, but I fear it cannot be employed on account of the subsequent line, 'But, *by* the Chieftain's look'.

To me the two 'bys' clash both to the ear and understanding, and it was on that account I changed the word. I have also a slight objection to the alliteration 'By bold' occurring so soon. I am glad you like 'Elates not'; as the passage first stood, 'Since the mighty deed'—there was a transfer of the thought from the picture to the living Man, which divided the Sonnet into two parts—the presence of the Portrait is now carried thro', till the last line where the Man is taken up. To prevent the possibility of a mistake I will repeat the passage as last sent, and in which state I still consider it finished—and you will do what you like with it,

'Him the mighty deed
Elates not, brought far nearer the grave's rest,
As shews that time-worn face. But He such seed
Hath sown as yields,' etc.

I hope you are right in thinking this the best of the three. I forget whether I thanked you for your sketch of the Slave-trade picture.[1] Your friendship has misled you. I must on no account be introduced. I was not present at the meeting, as a matter of fact; and tho' from the first I look a lively interest in the Abolition of Slavery, except joining with those who petitioned Parliament, I was too little of a Man of business to have an active part in the Work—Besides, my place of Abode would have prevented it, had I been so inclined. The only public act of mine connected with the Event, was sending forth that Sonnet which I addressed to Mr. Clarkson,[2] upon the success of the undertaking.

Thank you for your last letter. I am this moment (while dictating this letter) sitting to Mr. Pickersgill, who has kindly come down to paint me at leisure, for Sir Rob[t] Peel, in whose gallery at Drayton the Portrait will probably be hung by that of my poor Friend Southey. I am, dear Haydon, faithfully yours

Wm Wordsworth

P. S.—Your suggestion about the Engraver is very candid, but the Verses taking so high a flight, and particularly in the line 'lies fixed for ages', it would be injurious to put forward the cold matter of fact, and the sense and spirit of the Sonnet both demand that it should be suggested at the sight of the *Picture*.

1438. W. W. to UNKNOWN CORRESPONDENT

MS. Cornell. Hitherto unpublished.

[*In M. W.'s hand*]

Rydal Mount
Sep[r] 10.th [1840]

Dear Sir

I lose no time in thanking you for your interesting little Work of Bethgellert and its neighbourhood—and the gratifying letter by which it is accompanied. More than 50 years have passed,

[1] Haydon's picture of the Anti-Slavery Society Convention, 1840, commissioned by the British and Foreign Slavery Society who wished for a permanent record of their meeting at the Freemason's Tavern, 12–23 June. The picture represents the Chairman, Thomas Clarkson, addressing the Convention, and portrays over one hundred members of it. Haydon began work on the portraits in June 1840 and the picture was completed the following April and exhibited at the Egyptian Hall. It is now in the National Portrait Gallery. See *Diary of Benjamin Robert Haydon* (ed. Pope), iv. 640 ff.

[2] See *PW* iii. 126.

since, in the course of a pedestrian tour with a lamented friend,[1] a native of North Wales, I first had a sight of Bethgellert, and the beautiful country around, and in the neighbourhood of the Village. From an Inn, a humble one it was at that time, I set off from the Village about 10 oc at night for Snowden and reached its summet under the most favorable circumstances: I have endeavoured to preserve the impression then made upon me in Verse[2]—which at some future day will see the light, I hope for the gratification of others, whether they have been similarly fortunate or not.

I remain dear Sir respectfully your obliged

[*signed*] Wm Wordsworth

I have been obliged to dictate this, while sitting for my Portrait to Mr Pickersgill.

W. W.

1439. W. W. to BENJAMIN ROBERT HAYDON

MS. untraced.
K (—). LY ii. 1036.

Rydal Mount, Sept. 11th, [1840]

My dear Haydon

Your remarks are just and had passed thro' Mrs W's mind and my own—nevertheless I could not otherwise get rid of the prosaic declaration of the matter of fact that the Hero was so much older. You will recollect that it at first stood

'Since the mighty deed
Him years,' etc.

I know not what to do with the passage, if it be not well corrected as follows

Him the mighty deed
Elates not: neither doth a cloud find rest
Upon that time-worn face; for he such seed
Hath sown etc.

[1] Robert Jones.

[2] See *Prel.*, pp. 478 ff. and L. 1450 below.

I sent the Sonnet as it was before corrected—to Mr Lowndes[1] as you desired.

When you print it if it be in the course of next week, pray send a copy to this house and another to me at Lowther Castle—whither I am going to-morrow

Very faithfully your's
W Wordsworth

The space for alteration in this troublesome passage, you will observe, was very confined, as it was necessary to advert to the Duke being much older, which is yet done in the words time-worn face—but not so strongly as before

W W

1440. W. W. to BENJAMIN ROBERT HAYDON

Address: B. R. Haydon Esq[re], London.
MS. untraced.
LY ii. 1037.

Friday [11 Sept. 1840]

Dear Haydon

I have just rec[d] your letter and am glad you are so well pleased with the Sonnet. This morn[g] I sent off an imperfect correction—and now have to beg you to read it thus.

'His life is brought far nearer the grave's rest,
As shews that time-worn face. But he, such seed
Hath sown, as yields etc—

Mr Rogers is arrived and speaks highly of your picture of Wellington and tells me you have done one of Buonaparte[2] for him.—Ever y[rs] etc.

W Wordsworth

I said in a former Letter, you were quite at liberty to *print* the Sonnet, when and where you liked. But perhaps it would be better to hold it back a little, as that would afford an opportunity

[1] Matthew D. Lowndes, a Liverpool attorney, who had purchased the picture. In 1837 he had commissioned Haydon's *Christ Blessing Little Children* for the Liverpool Blind Asylum.

[2] 'Napoleon Musing at St. Helena', purchased by Rogers for £31.10s.

of paying a Compliment here and there by sending it in Mss as you design to do to the Queen Dowager—

I am much pleased as we all are with the idea of your coming down, and painting me on my own ground poetically. Do not impute this to vanity; I do think you would make of it a fine Picture. But there is one, I fear insurmountable objection, you cannot afford to work without pay, nor can *I* afford to pay you. And I see not how you can expect from any quarter a pecuniary remuneration. Do ponder this before you commit yourself.[1]

I am sorry that your poor wife appears to be no better. I truly grieve for you and anxiously wish for her recovery. Let me hear from you again at your leisure.—

P.S. As the Sonnet first stood, there was a pleonasm in

Him Years have brought
and *time*-worn face.

By reading His Life—etc. that is avoided.

1441. W. W. to JOSHUA WATSON

Endorsed: Wm Wordsworth Esq. 10 Sep 1840.
MS. Amherst College Library.
Amherst Wordsworth Collection, p. 63 (—). *LY ii. 1002.*

Rydal Mount [? Sept.][2] 11th 1840

My dear Sir,

Yesterday I received the Enclosed; respecting which there must be some mistake.

On the 26th Febry last my Daughter called in Park Street; and, not finding you at home, She left with your *Housekeeper* the amount of the enclosed Demand, under cover directed to you. How it comes yet to be standing in my name on Mr Harrison's Books[3] I do not see how, under this circumstance, I can explain, without troubling you which I very much *regret*. Would you be

[1] W. W. eventually sat to Haydon in London for the famous *Wordsworth on Helvellyn* (1842).

[2] *Written* Febry; but the letter clearly refers to the death on 19 July 1840 of Watson's daughter Mary (see L. 1425 above), and the later date is confirmed by the endorsement.

[3] A puzzling reference, perhaps to a London tradesman.

so kind as either to write to me upon the subject, or directly, yourself, satisfy the applicants.

This occasion has emboldened me, to do what I could not venture upon before, that is, to assure you of my own sympathy and that of Mrs Wordsworth and my Daughter upon your afflicting and desolating loss. I do not presume to speak of consolation *that* your own mind, I know, has through prayer furnished you with, from the first feeling perhaps of the blow. But the assurance that Friends have in some degree our sorrow is always more or less grateful to the suffering mind, and that assurance I humbly offer from my heart; and we all join in this tribute. God bless you my dear Sir, and believe me with fervent prayers that you may be supported from above under this and every other affliction,

Faithfully and affectionately yours,
Wm Wordsworth

Pray present my respectful sympathy to Mr Wagner, along with the expression of a hope and prayer that the Little one may prove a blessing to you Both.

W. W.

1442. W. W. to DORA W.

Address: Miss Wordsworth, Stamp Office, Carlisle.
Postmark: 14 Sept. 1840.
Stamp: Penrith.
MS. Harvard University Library.
LY ii. 1038.

[Lowther Castle]
Monday Morning [14 Sept. 1840]

My dearest Dora

Thanks for your 2nd Letter. We must look out for another Horse—I never should be at ease with this.—

I now write to express some little *selfish* regret that your return is likely to be put off. This is *solely* as that will deprive me of the gratification of seeing Wm under this roof. Mr Rogers and I leave for Drumlanrigg[1] on Monday as I told you, and I had hoped that as you meant to quit Carlisle on Friday, Wm would

[1] Seat of the Duke of Buccleuch in Dumfriesshire (see next letter).

have come hither on that day. But I do not desire (far from it) that you should change your last intention, as I am sure you would enjoy yourselves at Carlisle; and I like the notion of your going to take a peep at Newcastle. Lady Frederick has just said to me how glad they would be to see Wm on Friday to stay longer than Monday if convenient. But he can come at some time when I am not here, for example, when he returns from Rydal.—

Take care, and let Ebba[1] do the same, that you do not catch cold by alternations of heat and exposure—Love to you all, and believe me your most affectionate Father

W Wordsworth

1443. W. W. to ISABELLA FENWICK

Address: Miss Fenwick, Ambleside.
Postmark: 14 Sept. 1840.
Stamp: Penrith.
MS. WL.
LY ii. 1039 (—).

Lowther, Monday Morn. [14 Sept. 1840]

A thousand thanks, my most dear Friend, for your letter, and the good news it contained. Pray God you may go on so well.

You know of my intended expedition with Mr Rogers to the Duke of Buccleugh's.[2] The Duchess's Letter to Lady F.[3] was in such a strain, and especially in the modest way in which she mentioned the Duke's wish to see me, that it would have been ungracious to refuse; but I cannot help grudging the time; particularly as dearest Mary will be so soon setting off for Herefordshire, and as it is *not certain* but that you may think yourself well enough to go into Durham; in which point you might be deceived, and I and Dora would lose your company for perhaps a month. You may think perhaps that I dwell too much

[1] Ebba Hutchinson.

[2] Walter Francis Montagu-Douglas-Scott, 5th Duke of Buccleuch and 7th Duke of Queensberry (1806–84): successively Lord Privy Seal and Lord President of the Council in Peel's second Cabinet. He married in 1829 Lady Charlotte Thynne (1811–95), youngest daughter of Thomas, 2nd Marquess of Bath.

[3] Lady Frederick Bentinck.

on these separations from beloved Friends, but the uncertainty of human life, particularly for people so far in years as Mary and I are, and accustomed to illness as you have been, is perpetually before me. You must therefore, my beloved Friend, excuse this infirmity, and so must Mary who I hope will read this.—Mr R. told me yesterday that a Friend of his went to Dr Bailey,[1] and said to him 'I am come to consult you about several complaints or diseases I am troubled with.' 'What age are you?' 'I am seventy.' 'O' replied the Doctor, 'that is disease enough for any thing'. And, would you believe it? the poor Man took this rather inconsiderate expression so much to heart, that it was supposed to have hastened his departure out of this world. It would not, I assure you, have done so with me, but when I think of any beloved Friend I cannot help having something of the Doctor's view of the case. And, I repeat, this must be my excuse with those I love best.

I have little to write about from this place. You would hear under what circumstances we crossed Kirkstone; and that I was above measure enchanted with the views from Mr Askew's walk.[2] I could scarcely tear myself away to the pair who were waiting in the Carriage.

The poor Horse has come down again, so that we must part with him. This is very mortifying. Love to Isabella;[3] as I perhaps may not write to Mary today she must content herself with this scrawl to you. Mr Haydon's note which she sent me has bothered me much, I mean about the alteration in the Sonnet, so that I know not how it will come out at last. Lady Frederick prefers

Elates not; neither doth a cloud find rest

Upon that time-worn face, For the etc, and so did Mary, and you, I believe.—If it were [not] for the subject I should care nothing about it. And now, dearest Friend, and dearest Mary, and poor dear Sister, farewell. Take care of yourselves, most affectionately yours W. Wordsworth

Wm is invited to meet me here on Friday; but as they[4] don't mean to leave Carlisle till Monday, I have written to beg their purpose may not be changed; I need not say had they kept to their first intention I should have been glad to see W^{m} under this roof.—W. W.

[1] A London physician.

[2] At Glenridding.

[3] I. F.'s niece (see L. 1425 above).

[4] i.e. Dora W. and Ebba Hutchinson.

1444. W. W. to HENRY REED

Address: Henry Reed Esqre, Philadelphia.
Endorsed: Rec. Oct. 19.
Postmark: (1) 29 Sept. 1840 (2) 17 Oct.
Stamp: (1) Ambleside (2) Boston.
MS. Cornell.
K (—). *Wordsworth and Reed, p. 35.*

[*In M. W.'s hand*]

Rydal Mount Sepr 14th 1840

This letter I have been obliged to keep. It cannot leave England as we are told to go direct till the 3d of October.—

My dear Sir

Following your good example I send you a Duplicate of our concern with the Mississippi Bonds:—

"I Hutchison & Son Brokers *London Feb^ry^ 9th 1835.*
Bought for Mr. Strickland Cookson
6/1000$ New Mississippi 6 pct. with div^d^ from 1st Sepr 1834 @ 110½ } 1491. 15. —"

From my other friend I am enabled now to give you the following statement, of her Transatlantic Stock

"Pennsylvania 5 P.ct Stock

Certificate No 442 dated Aug 1st 1833	10000 Dollars
443	5000
444	5000
445	5000
446	5000
447	5000
448	5000
together Dol	35000[1]

United States Bank Shares

Certificate No 4699 dated 13 May 1837—	50 Shares
4700	30
4701	20
together Sh.	100

I am much pleased by what you say in your letter of the 18th of

[1] This should be 40,000, as Reed points out in his reply.

May last, upon the tract of the Convention of Cintra,[1] and I think myself with some interest upon its being reprinted hereafter, along with my other writings. But the respect, which in common with all the rest of the rational parts of the world, I bear for the Duke of Wellington, will prevent my reprinting the Pamphlet during his life-time. It has not been in my power to read the Volumes of his Despatches[2] which I hear so highly spoken of, but I am convinced that nothing they contain could alter my opinion of the injurious tendency of that, or any other Convention, conducted upon such principles. It was I repeat gratifying to me that you should have spoken of that work as you do, and particularly that you should have considered it in relation to my Poems, somewhat in the same manner you had done in respect to my little Book upon the Lakes.[3]

I send you a Sonnet composed the other day while I was climbing our Mountain—Helvellyn.

Upon Haydon's Portrait of
The Duke of Wellington. Supposed to be on the field
of Waterloo 20 years after the Battle

[*The sonnet follows, as in PW iii. 53, except that in l. 1 read* Through Art's bold privilege, *and in l. 11* But he.]

The above was sent to Mr Haydon with liberty to print it when and where he liked; and accordingly it has been published in several Newspapers but with such[4] gross blunders that I have ventured to send you a corrected Copy. The Picture is of great

[1] In his letter of 18 Mar. Reed had written: 'I was not less surprised than delighted in finding so much more of permanent and universal interest than I had any reason to look for in a work professedly of an *occasional* character. . . . I was quite unprepared to find in it so little that was *fugitive*—in fact after the lapse of more than 30 years it may have even greater interest than at the date of its publication, for now it will be read with a view to *principles*—to its abiding truths, which may make a deeper impression, when abstracted from the special events to which they were originally applied.' (*Wordsworth and Reed*, p. 16).

[2] *The Despatches of the Duke of Wellington*, appeared in 13 volumes, 1834–9,

[3] In his earlier letter to W. W. of 3 Jan. 1839, acknowledging a copy of the *Guide to the Lakes*, Reed had written: 'It may not be uninteresting to you to learn that a volume so purely local in its nature should afford so much value to a distant reader as I have drawn from it. I have found it a guide to the mind in kindred scenes and that it cultivates a taste for landscape which finds its indulgence in the worthy admiration of regions that are accessible to us.' (*Wordsworth and Reed*, p. 6).

[4] such *written twice*.

merit, and is now engraving, so that perhaps an impression may find its way to America, and you see it.—

I am truly glad to find that the principal part of my Friends money is in the better quarter, indeed it should seem by your Letter that it is quite safe. The dividends upon the Mississippi [Bonds] have hitherto been paid. Truly glad should we be of any information you could give us relative to that subject. The money belonged to a sister of Mrs Wordsworth some time deceased and a portion of it has come to my daughter, the remainder is of a great consequence to a surviving sister of Mrs W.—With a thousand thanks I remain my dear Sir your much obliged Friend

[*signed*] Wm Wordsworth

1445. M. W. to HENRY WILLIAM PICKERSGILL

MS. Cornell.
Broughton, p. 80.

Tuesday
Sepr 15th [1840]

My dear Sir

I have the satisfaction and pleasure to inform you that the Picture[1] arrived safely at Rydal Mount this morning—and that it looks remarkably well where, for the present, I have found a station for it, above the fire-place in our general sitting room.—So that when the door between the rooms stands open the two Poets[2] look at each other. When our friends return a less obtrusive situation must be found for one of them—or strangers will be apt to say that the presence of the Master haunts them.

You will hear further of this Portrait, when she who is privileged kindly by you to call it her own, returns home. I trust that Mrs P. and you are safely landed in Soho Square. I have heard good tidings of all our Absentees—and you will be glad to

[1] Not, clearly, the portrait of W. W. which Pickersgill had just completed for Sir Robert Peel; but one of the copies of Pickersgill's earlier portrait of 1832, the one made for Dora W., as this letter makes clear later on. See Blanshard, *Portraits of Wordsworth*, pp. 158–9, and next letter.

[2] The other portrait M. W. refers to is Haydon's chalk drawing of the poet, which hung in the dining room (see pt. ii, L. 619).

hear that our friend Miss Fenwick is better. With respectful regards to Mrs Pickersgill believe me to be very sincerely yours

M. Wordsworth

1446. W. W. to ISABELLA FENWICK

Address: Miss Fenwick, Ambleside.
Postmark: 17 Sept. 1840.
Stamp: Penrith.
MS. WL.
LY ii. 1040.

[Lowther Castle]
Thursday Morning, 11 o'clock [17 Sept. 1840]

Your Letter my beloved Friend has delighted me, though after giving an account so perfectly satisfactory of Tuesday, you are obliged to add on Wednesday morning '*a very tolerable* night'. But if upon the whole you go on as well as you have done, what reason shall we all have to be thankful! Dont grieve about Mrs Pedder's resolve to return to her House; nor if you cannot get another to your mind—I shall not, nor will Mary, we shall be happy to have you under our roof—and for Dora, it will be the best medicine she can have!—Yesterday we had wretched weather, and to day it is little better, so Mr R.[1] [and I] must content ourselves with a two hours' walk as we had yesterday in the cloister here which commands a very pleasing view of trees and a visto of lawn; the trees having already got some thing of the autumnal tinge. This is a very beautiful region for persons resident. Strangers who merely come and go are likely to be disappointed. But the windings of the River among woods and rocks for those who have leisure to pursue them are truly charming; and if you follow the paths when they lead from the level ground up to commanding points, you have fine distances over plains now bright with ripe cornfields, and at all times interesting in connection with the far-off blue mountains, and distant as they are, these mountains, from many points of the grounds, seem to touch the unbroken domes of wood above which they rise, and when seen thus, with the river rolling and murmuring below, the effect is enchanting. Nevertheless, (and were the attractions here ten times as great it would be the same)

[1] Rogers.

I cannot [help] wishing, half the day through, that I were back again amongst you. Mary writes me that you think of going together to Halsteads about the 30th, and hopes that I will accompany you. Certainly I will, and that most readily.—

The verses Mary has sent me are much above the common run, and I shall be sure to take care of them. I have not seen the unfortunate sonnet printed; only think of 'forever,' being given instead of 'for ages'—thus turning the passage into down right nonsense. The liability to these errors is a very strong reason why poetry composed with care should never be first published in Newspapers, unless the author has an opportunity of correcting the press.

I am sorry that the old Picture[1] is so much inferior to the last. Mary says it has a lack-a-daysical look; and I can well believe it. How unlucky the Artist did not send it down by Mail—he might then have inspected it as he wished to do. If I go to London in the Spring, and my eyes should be in as good order as they are at present, the picture shall meet me there and I will get P. to retouch it. And now my dearest Friend with repeated thanks to dear Isabella,[2] I must bid you goodbye, ever most affectionately your grateful

Wm Wordsworth

1447. W. W. to BENJAMIN ROBERT HAYDON

MS. untraced.
Haydon. LY ii. 1042.

23rd September, 1840

My dear Haydon,

I received your Letter the Evening before I left Lowther, and reply to it on my first leisure.

[1] Presumably Dora W.'s copy of Pickersgill's first portrait of W. W., 1832 (see previous letter). The Wordsworths' unease about this portrait was shared by their friends. In a letter to I. F. of 25 May 1851, Sara Coleridge described it as 'insufferable'. '. . .velvet waistcoat—neat shiny boots—just the sort of dress he would not have worn if you could have hired him—and a sombre sentimentalism of countenance quite unlike his own look which was either elevated with high gladness or deep thought or at times simply and childishly gruff—but never tender after that fashion, so lackadaisical and mawkishly sentimental.' (*Memoir and Letters of Sara Coleridge, Edited by Her Daughter*, 2 vols., 1873, ii. 358).

[2] I. F.'s niece.

Believe me to be duly sensible of the respect you pay me by naming your last born after me.[1] My name being conjoined with that of Wilkie, will, I hope be of use on some future day to your Son, by attaching an interest to my writing, which may induce him to become better acquainted there than otherwise he might have been. Nevertheless I cannot but feel a wish that you had selected a Sponsor far short of my age and one whose station in society might have enabled him to serve his Godchild in a way which I can have no means of doing. But the impulse of feeling to which you have yielded[2] will at least prove to the Boy that there are other things of value in human life, according to your estimation, besides world advancement and prosperity. Pray present him with my best good wishes, which I offer trusting that he will not fail in the important duties which his profession[3] will lay upon him and that he will look up to the Father of us all for guidance and support upon every trying occasion of his life.—As you do not mention his Mother, I venture to hope that she is no worse, and if so improvement may be looked for which God grant—

I am glad your Lecture was so much applauded—

The unlucky Sonnet I have not yet seen in print—The reading—

> Elates not, brought far nearer the grave's rest
> As shows that time-worn face. But [? He]

is most liked by the best judges, especially by Mr Rogers who is now writing at the same table with me.—

Excuse more, as I find on my return home, many Letter[s] that require immediate Answer

ever my dear Haydon
truly yours
W Wordsworth

Pickersgill was gone so that Mrs W— could not turn your recommendation [to] account. She thanks you for your interesting

[1] Frederick Wordsworth Haydon (b. 1827) had been christened on 18 Sept. (*Diary*, ed. Pope, v. 4–5), W. W. standing as sponsor.

[2] *Written* yielding.

[3] Frederick Haydon was destined for the Navy.

Letter—The Portrait by P—[1] is liked by my friends, and I hope won't displease you—

1448. W. W. to THOMAS BOYLES MURRAY[2]

MS. untraced.
Mem. Grosart. LY ii. 1043.

Rydal Mount, Ambleside, Sep. 24, 1840.

Dear Sir,

Upon returning home after an absence of ten days, I have the pleasure of finding your obliging letter, and the number of the 'Ecclesiastical Gazette' containing the 'Ecclesiastical Duties and Revenues Act':[3] for both marks of attention I beg you to accept my sincere thanks. As soon as I can find leisure, I will carefully peruse the Act; at present I can only say that I look upon changes so extensive and searching with a degree of alarm proportionate to my love and affection for the Establishment with which they are connected.

As you have put me in possession of the 'Gazette,' I can scarcely feel justified in looking to the fulfilment of your promise to send me the Act, separately printed. Indeed, I feel that it would be giving yourself more trouble than there is occasion for.

It pleases me much to learn that Mrs Murray and you enjoyed your ramble among the lakes.

Believe me to be, dear Sir,
Faithfully,
Your obliged servant,
Wm Wordsworth

[1] Pickersgill's portrait was exhibited at the Royal Academy in 1841, and remained at Drayton Manor until it was sold, and thereafter it passed to Dove Cottage. An engraving by Joseph Skelton appeared in the *Mem.*

[2] The Revd. Thomas Boyles Murray (1798–1860), rector of St. Dunstan-in-the-east, 1837–60, and Prebendary of St. Paul's from 1843: author of *An Alphabet of Emblems* (1844), *Lays of Christmas* (1847), a Concordance to the Bible, and several historical works. He had visited W. W. towards the end of August with his bride, Helen, daughter of Sir William Douglas of Timpingdean, Roxburgh (*RMVB*).

[3] The Ecclesiastical Duties and Revenues Bill, which embodied proposals made several years earlier for reforming and redistributing cathedral endowments, had been given its Third Reading in July, amid fears that it marked (in the words of Sir Robert Inglis) 'the destruction of the Cathedral system.'

1449. W. W. to HENRY WILLIAM PICKERSGILL

Address: H. W. Pickersgill Esq[re], 18 Soho Square. *[In Dora W.'s hand]*
MS. St. John's College, Cambridge.
LY ii. 1043.

Sept[r] 24 [1840]

My dear Sir

The Bearer is Mr Blakesley[1] of Trin. Coll. Camb. a friend of mine; pray let him see my picture, and if anything else in your Gallery so much the better—

ever faithfully yours
Wm Wordsworth

1450. W. W. to UNKNOWN CORRESPONDENT[2]

MS. Princeton University Library. Hitherto unpublished.

Rydal Mount Ambleside
Sept[br] 24th [18]40

Dear Sir,

Upon returning home after an absence of ten days I have the pleasure of finding your letter, and the very interesting account

[1] J. W. Blakesley (see also pt. ii, L. 706), the Cambridge 'Apostle', Tennyson's 'clear-headed friend'; now Tutor of Trinity. Earlier this summer, in May and June, W. W. had received two other 'Apostles' at Rydal Mount: Henry Lushington (1812–55), Fellow of Trinity (1836), and Chief Secretary to the Government of Malta (1847); and his elder brother Edmund Lushington (1811–93), Professor of Greek at the University of Glasgow, 1838–75, who married Tennyson's sister Cecilia (*RMVB*).

[2] See also L. 1438 above. The addressee of these two letters was perhaps Angharad Llwyd, author of *A History of the Island of Mona or Anglesey . . . being the prize essay . . . at the Royal Beaumaris Eisteddfod held at Beaumaris . . . 1832*, Ruthin, 1833. W. W. had been sent a copy by Robert Jones (see pt. iii, L. 874). The shipwreck referred to in the letter was probably that of the *Rothesay Castle*, which was sunk in a storm after striking a sandbank between the Angelsey and the Caernarvonshire coast on 17 Aug. 1831. The steamer was bound with passengers from Liverpool to Beaumaris and there were few survivors. The wreck of the *Rothesay Castle* was chosen as the title for the prize poem at the Beaumaris Eisteddfod the following year, and there were nineteen competitors including some of the greatest Welsh poets of the century. Several of these

of the preservation from shipwreck upon the Carnarvon Coast. Pray accept my cordial thanks for both.—

You attach too much importance to what I said upon my ascent of Snowdon; though I believe that I expressed myself strongly upon the pleasure it gave me, and the vivid remembrance which I have of the scene. The Description is written in blank verse, and occurs towards the close of the long Poem written for the most part many years ago, upon my own poetical Education. From the personal character of this work its publication has been long deferred and is likely to be so till the end of my days.

Thanking you once more for your obliging intentions

I remain, dear Sir
with much respect
sincerely yours
Wm Wordsworth

Advanced in life as I am I can scarcely calculate upon revisiting your beautiful Country; were such [to be][1] my good fortune I should be truly happy to profit by the guidance you so kindly offer.

1451. W. W. to BENJAMIN DOCKRAY

MS. Cornell. Hitherto unpublished.

Rydal Sept^br^ 25th [1840][2]

Dear Sir,

I regret that an absence from home of some length has prevented my thanking you earlier for the continued mark of your attention in sending me the Third part of your Egeria.[3] The pleasure and instruction which I derived from the two former leave me little cause for doubt that I shall gain still more from the still larger collection of your valuable thoughts and observations, as soon as I shall have it in my power to peruse it.

poems were published and widely read, thus fortifying the powerful and sombre impression left on the Welsh mind by the disaster.

[1] *MS. obscure.*

[2] Year added by Dockray.

[3] See pt. ii, L. 755.

In the mean while pray accept my thanks, and believe me dear Sir

Very sincerely your obliged
W[m] Wordsworth

1452. W. W. to [?] RICHARD MONCKTON MILNES

MS. Yale University Library. Hitherto unpublished.

Rydal Mount
Ambleside
25th Sept[br] 1840

Dear Sir,

Your obliging Letter was entitled to a much earlier answer; but I have been from home for some time, and you must therefore be so kind as to excuse my silence. I have also to thank you for a number of the Shrewsbury Journal containing some spirited verses of yours,[1] which has during my absence been most unfortunately mislaid.—

Poor dear Mr Southey to whom you so naturally avert is in a sad state both as to mind and body; the former prematurely decayed and the latter giving way along with it. He is however thank almighty God free from pain. Dutiful affectionate, and anxious tenderness upon his deceased wife during her long and painful illness have been the cause of this afflicting malady, which has entirely put a[n] end to the usefulness of this great and good man, leaving to his Friends no hope but that of its termination in death.—

I have had the pleasure of passing an Evening with Mrs Sigourney[2] of whom you speak, under my own roof. I was not unacquainted with her writings which have great and varied

[1] These verses cannot be identified with certainty. The *Shrewsbury Journal*, or *Eddowes's Journal and General Advertiser for Shropshire* as it was originally called, was not started until 1843, and the reference here is probably to an earlier 'journal', the *Shrewsbury Chronicle*, founded in 1772. Monckton Milnes's verses *Rich and Poor* appeared in the issue for 3 Apr. 1840 and are perhaps the poem referred to here. Hence the tentative identification of the addressee of this letter. The poem had been printed in *Poems of Many Years*, 1838.

[2] Lydia Sigourney (see pt. iii, L. 1184), like so many others of W. W.'s American visitors, was introduced by Washington Allston (*WL MSS.*). For her recollections of this visit, see *Pleasant Memories of Pleasant Lands*, 1843, pp. 42–4.

merit; and her conversation I found also to be eminently interesting. It appears from her and her countrymen of whom I have seen many this Summer,[1] that my Poetry, though opposed in some quarters, which I ought to regard as a favorable symptom, is making its way into the American heart and mind—

Did you happen to see lately a Sonnet of mine in the Newspapers upon Haydon's picture of the Duke of Wellington at Waterloo. I mention it, because it is in some places printed with gross errors and with material ones in all—If you have seen it

Read

On ground *yet* strewn with *their* last battle's wreck and for 'lies fixed *for ever*', read 'fixed for *ages*' and for 'face timeworn', read less stiffly, 'time-worn face.'—Thank you again for your verses and Letter and believe [me] my dear Sir,

faithfully your obliged
Wm Wordsworth

You kindly inquire after my family, We are all well and sincerely hope that you and yours are the same.

1453. W. W. to LADY FREDERICK BENTINCK

MS. untraced.
Mem. Grosart. K. LY ii. 1044.

Rydal Mount, Sept. 26, 1840.

Dear Lady Frederick,

Mr Rogers and I had a very pleasant journey to Rydal the day we left all our kind friends at Lowther. We alighted at Lyulph's Tower, and saw the waterfall in great power after the night's rain, the sun shining full into the chasm and making a splendid rainbow of the spray. Afterwards, walking through Mr Askew's grounds, we saw the lake to the greatest possible advantage. Mr

[1] Among W. W.'s other American visitors this summer were: Charles Edwards Lester (1815–90), Presbyterian minister and abolitionist, author of *Chains and Freedom*, 1839; George Henry Calvert (1803–89), minor poet and liberal Christian; the Revd. Leonard Woods (1807–78), President of Bowdoin College from 1839; the Revd. William Adams (1807–80), later President of Union Theological Seminary; and Benjamin Tappan (1773–1857), the jurist and abolitionist. See *RMVB* and *WL MSS.*

R. left on Thursday, the morning most beautiful, though it rained afterwards. I know not how he could tear himself away from this lovely country at this charming season. I say charming, notwithstanding this is a dull day; but yesterday was most glorious. I hope our excellent friend does not mean to remain in London. . . . We have had no visits from strangers since my return, so that the press of the season seems to be over. The leaves are not changed here so much as at Lowther, and of course not yet so beautiful, nor are they ever quite so as with you, your trees being so much finer, and your woods so very much more extensive. We have a great deal of coppice, which makes but a poor show in autumn compared with timber trees.

Your son George[1] knows what he has to expect in the few sheets which I enclose for him.

With many thanks for the endless kind attentions which I received from you and others under your father's hospitable roof, and with my grateful respects to him, and a thousand good wishes for all, I remain, my wife and daughter joining in these feelings, my dear Lady Frederick, affectionately yours,

Wm Wordsworth

1454. W. W. to ELIZA HAMILTON

MS. Cornell. Hitherto unpublished.

[*In Dora W.'s hand*]

[Autumn 1840][2]

My dear Miss Hamilton,

I am truly sensible of y^{r} kind congrat^{s} and thankful for what you tell me of y^{r} brother's children.[3] I need not add that Lady Hamilton's deranged head gives me much concern—truly am I sorry also for w^{t} you say of y^{r} Cousin. I remember him very well and was much pleased with him, and am grieved to hear of this illness w^{h} has lain on him now for so long [a] time. I had a

[1] See pt. ii, L. 622.

[2] This letter was written shortly before the death of Hamilton's cousin Arthur (see pt. ii, L. 488) on 9 Dec. 1840. See *Hamilton*, ii. 331.

[3] Sir William Hamilton's third child, a daughter Helen, had been born on 11 Aug.

letter from y^{r} brother many months ago[1] w^{h} I s^{d} have thanked him for and the verses it contained but I continued to look out in vain for that friend of his whom his letter was written to introduce—pray let him know this with my kindest remembrances. Your funereal Verses I have read with much satisfaction. I am not prepared to compare them with y^{r} earlier performances w^{h} I have been in the habit of holding in great esteem. I send you the copy back with several alterations not wishing that any one of them should be adopted on my authority. Indeed I am well aware that many readers might think I had taken some of the poetic spirit out of your verses by a cold correctness of expression but with critics of this sort I have been for more than *40* years at variance. I shall only make one remark; for the sake of grammatical correctness I have altered tho' not to my own satisfaction the second verse where the word 'banner' occurs, but I would wish the confusion w^{h} exists thro' the whole of this Stanza between the *material* banner and helmet and the *Spiritual* ones should be got rid of altogether. Better not allude at all to the former than introduce the Images as here done. They are in my apprehension at war with each other. I have not time to write more. The pains w^{h} I have taken to correct y^{r} verses is what I would have done scarcely for any one else w^{h} must [? convey] to you without my saying more about them how highly I think of their merit. We were all most glad to hear of you—and with the love of Mrs W— and Dora and of my poor Sister who often speaks with aff^{te} interest of you I remain dear Miss Hamilton faithfully yours

[*signed*] Wm Wordsworth

Pray let us have another copy revised according to y^{r} new judgement.

[1] Hamilton had written on 21 May 1840 (*Cornell MSS.*), introducing Surgeon Wilde, author of a travel book about the Near East. William, later Sir William, Robert Wills Wilde (1815–76), qualified in Dublin in 1837 and thereafter took a long sea voyage in charge of a patient, which produced his *Narrative of a Voyage to Madeira, Teneriffe, and along the Shores of the Mediterranean, including a visit to Algiers, Egypt, Palestine . . . Cyprus and Greece. With observations on the present state and prospects of Egypt and Palestine, and on the character, internal history, antiquities, etc. of the countries visited*, 2 vols., Dublin, 1840. On his return he embarked on a highly successful career in Dublin, becoming the leading surgeon of his day and author of medical and antiquarian works. He was the father of Oscar Wilde.

1455. W. W. to THOMAS POWELL

Address: Thos Powell Esqre, 2 Leadenhall Street, London.
Postmark: (1) 16 Oct. 1840. (2) 17 Oct. 1840.
Stamp: Ambleside.
MS. University of Virginia Library.
LY ii. 1044.

[*In M. W.'s hand*]

Rydal Mount, Octr. 16th, 1840

My dear Mr. Powell,

I thought I *had* replied to your Letter, and I am the less surprized at my mistake because when I had read it, it did not strike me that I had any thing important to say upon the subject—You asked me indeed to point out any thing in Chaucer which in my judgment was best worthy of attention or most likely to please—Taking for granted that by every one indelicacy would be avoided; and also extreme lengthiness, to which Chaucer is sometimes prone, I felt that there was no call for my interference, and that it was best to leave every one to his own choice. On that letter therefore I have only to express my satisfaction that you are pleased with the contributions, especially with the Prologue which always appeared to me the most difficult thing to deal with.

Yesterday I received a letter from a Lady from which I transcribe the following. 'I have read in a Newspaper that you are about to publish Chaucer's Tales modernized'—and a friend also tells me that he has seen an advertizement of your Publication in which my name stands first in large letters.—Now dear Sir, you will remember that the condition upon which I placed these things at your disposal was, that for many reasons I should not be brought prominently forward in the Matter—but that my communications, given *solely* out of regard for you and reverence for Chaucer, should appear as unostentatiously as possible. I am therefore much concerned for what has been done, as it cannot be undone.[1]

[1] Powell replied on 23 Oct. (*WL MSS.*) enclosing the advertisement and explaining with profuse apologies the use to which W. W.'s name had been put: '. . . nothing would embitter my future life more than you should imagine I had used your honored and farfamed name for any private purpose . . .' In the offending advertisement W. W.'s name had been put at the head of the list of contributors, several of whom dropped out or were intending to contribute to a

To return to the Lady above mentioned, and it would be best to let her speak in her own words 'I have for my amusement modernized Chaucer's beautiful Tale of Constance,[1] and my friends (probably partial ones) have thought I had succeeded in preserving something of the Spirit and tone of the original, and perhaps under the same delusion I fancy that with your corrections and improvements it might be worthy of appearing in the Work advertized, and if you are not provided with a modernized Constance, I would send my attempt to you. I am engaged with Griselda.'[2]

This Lady I have seen once some years ago, but am altogether unable to judge of her competence.—Of course I declined to have any thing to do with corrections or improvements, but told her in my answer that if she had no objection to submit her production to your judgment I would introduce her by letter to you—so that she might learn all particulars regarding the publication, both as to what was done and what was intended, and I told her that the Newspaper had misled her as to my part in the Concern, adding what it really was—as I have above stated to you.

One word more, I hope you have stated that my versions had been lying by me many years.

We were sorry to learn you h[ad been][3] ill—I am thank God! in good health and have just returned home from a 10 days absence with Mrs W. who is also well—and joins me in regards to yourself and Mrs P, your Son and Br included—and believe me to be

faithfully yours
[*signed*] W Wordsworth

second volume that never materialised (Monckton Milnes, 'Barry Cornwall', and Lord Thurlow). The Preface was to be by R. H. Horne, and there was to be a Life of Chaucer by Professor Leonhard Schmitz (1807–90), the German-born Classical scholar and translator, later rector of the High School in Edinburgh.

[1] i.e. *The Man of Law's Tale.*

[2] i.e. *The Clerk's Tale.* Neither of these Tales were included, and the authoress is unidentified.

[3] *MS. torn.*

1456. W. W. to BASIL MONTAGU

MS. Bodleian Library.
LY ii. 1046.

Rydal Mount,
Ambleside,
Oct^{br} 17, 1840

My dear Montagu,

I have been shamefully long in acknowledging receipt of your Tract upon Quaker funerals,[1] and thanking you for it. My fault would have been greater but that I read it carefully upon its reaching me. It gives me pleasure to add that I approve of the spirit in which it is written. With kind regards to Mrs Montagu, and best wishes for her yourself and all yours, I remain dear Montagu, sincerely and faithfully your obliged Friend

Wm Wordsworth

1457. W. W. to BENJAMIN ROBERT HAYDON

Endorsed: 1840. BRH.
MS. Henry E. Huntington Library. Hitherto unpublished.

Sat: 24th [Oct. 1840]

My dear Haydon,

I have to thank you for the Lit. Gaz. containing the Sonnet. I wrote

On ground *yet* strewn,

and so read and repeat it, not

On ground *still* strewn,

as it stands. The twists are to my ear intolerable—And instead of

As shews that face, time worn,

read less stiffly

That time-worn face.

Thus altered, I hope the Lines are not altogether unworthy of the Subject or of the Painter.

[*Several sentences erased*][2] I need not say that I and mine would

[1] *The Funerals of the Quakers*, 1840.
[2] Apparently by Haydon.

be most happy to see you here next Summer, for the purpose.[1] There is no end to the number of scenes in this neighbourhood which would suit your purpose.

ever sincerely yours
Wm Wordsworth

1458. W. W. to H. C. R.

MS. Dr. Williams's Library.
Morley, i. 419.

Levens near Kendal
Oct^br^ 27th [1840]

My dear Friend,

Welcome to England—your long and kind letter was most acceptable, and afforded us much pleasure in every thing, but your annoyance and loss by the Hamnrley [?] Bank.[2] Surely there must have been much knavery in that concern—I now write merely to thank you for your Letter and to tell you that we all have been and are well. M^rs^ W— is here but tomorrow evening will put herself into the Railway at Lancaster, and expects by half past eleven to be at Birmingham so far on the way to Hereford and her Brother's House with whom, poor Man! she purposes staying at least a month; and whether I shall have resolution to go thither and after a weeks stay conduct her home, is still somewhat uncertain.—

Were I fourteen years younger, and could have gotten leave, I would have ventured, I think, upon the trip of which you give so tempting a sketch—but that is all over. I still howev[er][3] can not wholly suppress a wish to have a peep at Naples and do what the cholera prevented us doing.—

Have you seen the last Quarterly—There is a well-intended but very feeble notice of me in it, and an ignorant and injurious one of Coleridge—The Passage occurs at the beginning of an

[1] i.e. of painting W. W. on his own poetic ground, as Haydon had suggested (see L. 1440 above).

[2] *MS. obscure.*

[3] *MS. damaged.*

article upon Carlyle;[1] and it is said to be written by Sewell, a high Church[ma]n of Oxford.

The Sonnet upon the Duke's Picture[2] was printed very incorrectly, in all the newspapers in which I saw it. It was in one passage altered by myself after I sent it to you, thus.

In his calm presence. Him the mighty deed
Elates not, brought far nearer the grave's rest
As shews that time-worn face—

[1] 'Carlyle's Works', *Quarterly Review*, lxvi (Sept. 1840), 466–503. The opening passage briefly discussed Coleridge and Wordsworth as evidence of a healthier spirit at work in British philosophy. 'In this country the faint beginning of better things may be traced first in the works of Coleridge and Wordsworth. The former, a vigorous, self-formed, irregular, but penetrative mind, incapable of acquiescing in the meagre fare set before it by popular literature, was compelled to seek for something more substantial in the new world of German metaphysics. How largely he was indebted to these for the views, and even words, which he promulgated in England, we need not now inquire. But whatever he may have borrowed, he was a man of true native genius . . . We are very far from thinking Coleridge a safe or sound writer, but he has done good: he opened one eye of the sleeping intellect of this country—and the whole body is now beginning to show signs of animation.' But to Wordsworth the country owed a still greater debt of gratitude. 'Even he has only made a step to the restoration of better philosophy among us: but it is a great step, in a safer direction, and its influence will be felt far more extensively . . . Wordsworth, the kind, gentle, affectionate, Wordsworth, seems to have been almost paired with the acute, restless, deep-thinking Coleridge. And if God has a work to be done in this land, it is not strange that he should employ instruments to address both the head and the heart. It is in this latter work that Wordsworth has been most efficient. We can scarcely overrate the blessing to this country of recovering a school of poetry quiet, pure, and sober, and yet not superficial—which, even if it be at times, as it certainly is, artificial and affected, is affected in imitation of the better and simpler parts of nature . . .' The author of the article was William Sewell (1804–74), Fellow of Exeter College, Oxford (1827), and Whyte's Professor of Moral Philosophy (1836–41), an early supporter of the Tractarians who, however, withdrew from the movement after the publication of Newman's *Tract Ninety* in 1841. He contributed a volume on *Christian Morals* (1840) to the Tractarian series *The Englishman's Library*, and wrote a remarkable novel *Hawkstone* (1845), dedicated to Lord John Manners, which embodied the ideals of the Young England Movement. He founded St. Columba's College, nr. Dublin, and Radley (1847), and was the brother of Elizabeth Sewell, the novelist. See Lionel James, *A Forgotten Genius, Sewell of St. Columba's and Radley*, 1945, which reproduces (p. 296) Sewell's translation of the *Immortality Ode* into Latin elegiac couplets.

[2] 'On a Portrait of the Duke of Wellington Upon the Field of Waterloo, by Haydon'. See L. 1428 above.

Haydon tells me that it is Altered.—But too much of this. I return to Rydal on Friday, on Monday go to Carlisle and on Wednesday thence to Lord Lonsdales at Whitehaven. M^rs^ W— sends affectionate remembrances

ever yours,
W W.

1458a. W. W. to THOMAS POWELL

MS. untraced.
Bookseller's Catalogue.

[late Oct. 1840]

. . . . Now that I have seen it[1] I find no fault with it. My age considered, no one can find fault with my name being placed first. . . . [The purpose of the volume] which is namely to tempt the ordinary Reader to endeavour at mastering the original, and that the rule of the Contributors was merely to make their several Essays intelligible at once and to fit them for modern ears that have not been spoiled by monotonous versification. . . .I have avoided *identical* rhymes which sometimes occur in the original as many as three in a stanza, and are certainly objectionable in themselves. . . .

1459. W. W. to ISABELLA FENWICK

MS. WL.
LY ii. 1046.

[? Whitehaven]
Tuesday noon.—[3 Nov. 1840]

I wished my *dearest Friend* (observe I readily adopt your term) to write to you yesterday, but I could not bring myself to do so, without either holding back from you a fact which if told might cause you some uneasiness, or telling you the thing as it was, viz. that since Thursday I have been a good deal disordered in my body. I am now glad that I did not write, as I am decidedly better this day. Whether the diarhoea with which I have been affected has been caused by the atmosphere, or from something

[1] The proposed Advertisement to *Chaucer's Poems Modernized.*

that I have eaten or drunk which has disagreed with [me] I cannot say. But the Medical Man whom I consulted yesterday says that such attacks are common at this season and that he has little doubt that I shall be well in a couple of days; and I am inclined to be of his opinion, I am so much easier to day; and if you do not hear from me again by next post be assured all is going on satisfactorily.—

Your Letter, my beloved Friend, was most welcome; and especially as you say nothing but that you are well. How sad I was to part with you!—it seemed so easy to accompany you as far as Newcastle, and the weather was so inviting. But surely it would have been a little piece of extravagance, at least I thought so, for it would not have been treating Wm well to leave him behind. I should otherwise have indeed enjoyed seeing with you that beautiful Country over again which we travelled through together. Wm and I did not go into the Corby Grounds,[1] for it was not a public day, but we walked under the Grand viaduct,[2] and crossed the Ferry and visited the Church of Weatherall and strolled about the Village. Here survives one of those pleasant rural features, a village green. It was purchased by the Inhabitants when the Enclosure of Inglewood forest took place, and I was delighted to see the Children, Boys and Girls, playing upon it. Formerly there stood at a corner of the Green a Maypole, and the stone platform remains from which it rose, but there is no maypole—and why, think you? Some of the Inhabitants were for having it raised upon the same place, in the corner of the Green, and others contended that it should be in the middle, and so not being able to agree there is no Pole at all—Can we wonder at the disputes which vex the Great World, in politics and Religion etc—when these Rustics cannot agree about so indifferent a matter?

Our walk altogether was not less than eight miles—a little too much for Wm, I was not at all tired, and the day was indeed glorious, a *borrowed* day[3] as Mrs Carrick[4] called it, but she might have almost added borrowed from Heaven. As we were return-

[1] The grounds of Corby Castle, seat of Henry Howard (see pt. ii, L. 610), were noted for the river walks beside the Eden and the caves and grottoes hewn out of its rocky and precipitous banks.

[2] The railway viaduct over the Eden at Wetheral (1830–4).

[3] This expression, as de Selincourt notes, is still current in the district for a fine day in a rainy season.

[4] W. W. jnr.'s landlady.

ing towards Carlisle we were passed by a Lady driving her grown-up Daughter in a Pony chaise. They were both gaily dressed and exactly alike. The Mother's appearance seemed to say (for she was a widow) that she was looking out for another Husband. Her former one married her in India and left her by will half his fortune, naming her in the Instrument his wife and *Niece*, as in fact she was. I should have thought this incredible, but W. vouches for the fact. The Husband was an Army Surgeon.—In the evening I walked down to the River, and had from the Bridge a glorious view of the western sky with its reflection in the water. Next morning was wet and dismal, a more uninteresting ride than that from Carlisle to Allonby cannot well be imagined. From Allonby to Workington the road passes along the seashore or very near it; and that is always more or less impressive. Before 4 o'clock the Sun broke out and the sky was driven over by stormy Clouds beautifully tinged with golden and amber light, and endlessly diversified in Form. Next day came on my Indisposition, so that I have nothing to add but that we had on that evening a wondrous and for this place, a splendid Ball. How they mustered so many Gentlemen I cannot guess. Of the males all I remarked was that they were uncommonly tall. One *Lady* had exquisitely beautiful eyes, eyelashes, and brows, quite for a Picture—and there was a Miss Atwood[1] distinguished, though a girl, by a matronly or Minerva dignity and beauty which one does not often meet with. But though striking in appearance she is not a person to fall in love with.—

And now my dearest Friend it is time that I should respond to the affectionate language in which you speak of our prospects. I could fill pages with the subject but I dare not trust myself with it. All that you have said has an echo in our hearts, and mine rings with it. God almighty bless you, and make us worthy of the love which you cherish for us, and give us grace to profit to the utmost by your presence and conversation! O that you were back again and dearest Mary, too, and that we were all under one roof. Wm departs tomorrow; and so do I for Brigham if the day prove fine. He has been there already and gives a most favourable Report of the Children, but says that Isabella is far from well. I will probably return to Rydal on Tuesday—if not

[1] Probably a daughter or connection of Matthias Attwood, M.P. for Whitehaven (see pt. iii, L. 1224).

on Wednesday at the latest—pray write again and above all mention your health.

Do present my very kind remembrances to Mr and Mrs Taylor, and if you meet Archdeacon Thorp[1] say how glad I should be to see him at Rydal. With kindest love to Isabella and best remembrances in which Wm joins both to yourself and her, I remain my pretious Friend most gratefully and affectionately yours

W. Wordsworth

1460. W. W. to UNKNOWN CORRESPONDENT

MS. WL.[2] *Hitherto unpublished.*

[*In the hand of W. W. Jnr.*]

Rydal Mount
12 Novr 40.

Sir,

I write to you as Agent of the Company employing the Mail Coach that runs between Kendal and Whitehaven to state the particulars of an accident which occurred yesterday causing great danger and alarm to my son and myself, some slight personal injury, and much damage to our gig, which with the particulars connected with the misfortune will cause an expence for the repayment of which I consider the Company responsible, and beg you would lay before them the following statement.

Something more than three miles from Keswick on the road to Ambleside is a narrow bridge (over the Naddle) which stands nearly at the foot of a steep winding slope of about eighty paces long. With my Companion I was crossing this bridge when the Coach appeared at the top of the hill. The road becoming narrower as you ascend the slope my Companion very judiciously stopped his horse about five yards from the end of the bridge, drawing up within two inches of the wall on his left, in expectation that the Coachman, as soon as he came in sight of our carriage, would slacken his pace as he had ample time to do. But instead of that, he drove downwards at full speed; keeping so near the middle of the road as not to make any use of three

[1] Of Durham. See L. 1732 below.

[2] Apparently a copy of the letter actually sent, which W. W. kept by him for reference.

feet of road on his left, which with a reasonable degree of care and skill might have been done, notwithstanding the bridge, which narrows in the middle, was in front.

In consequence of this the Driver's apparently reckless inattention the wheels of the Coach struck those of our gig with great violence and forced the horse and gig backwards along the road, and through a gap in the wall into a plantation, a yard below the level of the road, the stones of the road tumbling about us.

We got clear of the carriage while the horse was struggling against the Bank, and broken wall to recover himself, which he did galloping off with the traces and shafts hanging about him, till he reached the toll-bar at Grasmere—seven miles. We sent by the Mail for a Chaise to convey us to Rydal, and hired a Cart to convey the gig to be repaired at Keswick.

A bill of all the expences incident to this unfortunate affair I shall send in to you, not doubting that a sense of justice will prevail with the Company so far that they will give orders for the discharge of the same.

To three reputable Individuals, who came up soon after, were pointed out the tracks of the wheels both of the Coach and of the gig, and they all concurred in opinion that no harm would have been done if the Coachman had availed himself of the space which, as described above, he had on his left.

Expecting your reply in due time

I am, Sir,

y^r^ obd^t^ S^t^

W. W.

1461. W. W. to ISABELLA FENWICK

Address: Miss Fenwick, Witton Hall, Bishop Auckland. [*readdressed to*] Rectory Stanhope.[1]
Postmark: 15 Nov. 1840.
Stamp: (1) Ambleside (2) Witton le Wear.
MS. WL.
LY ii. 1049 (—).

Rydal Mount Saturday Evening.—
14th [Nov. 1840]

I wished, my dearest Friend, to have written the day after I returned Home, but I was occupied all the morning, and have since been interrupted when I was sitting down for the purpose of writing. As I hoped my indisposition was going off I did not write from Whitehaven[2] which I left on Monday noon, John having driven over to fetch me. I found the children *all* well and looking well; but their poor Mother much otherwise. She is suffering from a kind of intermittent fever which has weakened her much. On Tuesday we should have gone to Plumblands, John's new Living,[3] but the morning was very unfavourable, so I was not sorry to keep in and about the House. Of dear Wm[4] I can say little more than that he seems scarcely altered; I could have judged something better of him if his person had not been so disguised in a kind of frock jacket. What progress he has made as to intelligence I could not tell, but his countenance is as attractive I think, perhaps, as ever. John, the next Boy, though backward in talking has also a very interesting countenance, is remarkably well grown, stout and lively, and the Baby[5] is all that a mother could wish. With the exception of Jane, the eldest, they are all fresh complexioned—she is a little sallow or rather dark, but quick as lightning. Henry is slow, but affectionate in his looks and ways. Pray, my dear Friend, excuse this minute account, as I had little else to write about from that place, unless I had dwelt, which would have been tedious, upon the beauty of the prospect up and down the fine River and Vale, as seen from the Window.

On Wednesday we left Brigham, John driving the Gig.

[1] In Weardale.
[2] W. W. had been staying with Lord Lonsdale in Whitehaven Castle.
[3] See L. 1388 above.
[4] i.e. W. W.'s grandson.
[5] Charles, born the previous year.

Nothing could be more striking than the view of Bassenthwaite Water as we proceeded under the woods of Wythop-brows with Skiddaw opposite, clad in sunbeams and vapory lights and solemn shadows. We did not call at Greta Hall, as we had learnt that Kate and Cuthbert were gone to Levens. Our drive continued most pleasant till we reached the bridge that stands, upon the Ambleside Road, three miles beyond Keswick. From this Bridge we spied the mail Coach, coming from Ambleside, on the top of the Hill which slopes rapidly towards the Bridge. Nothing could be done by John but to cross the Bridge and draw up close to the wall on our left: this he did: but the Coach came full speed towards us down the Hill, the Driver neither slackening his pace, nor taking the least care to keep clear of our wheels, though he had at least 70 paces to check his Horses in, and a yard of spare ground on his left, when his Wheels struck ours with extreme violence. And here let me tell you that through God's mercy we escaped personal injury; but the shock drove the horse and gig a few yards back, in the straight line of the road; a swerve was then made, and our Carriage was driven through a small gap in a wall into a plantation that lay a yard perpendicular below the level of the road. The Horse was driven along with the Carriage and we in it, the stones of the wall tumbling about us. The Horse plunged furiously: we partly got and were partly thrown out; the shafts of the carriage were broken off, the traces snapped. The Horse got back into the road and away he flew, desperate with fear, and gallopped 7 miles to the Grasmere turnpike gate, the shafts and traces sticking to him to the last. Providentially he met no Carriage in a narrow part of the road else great mischief might have been caused. We sent by the coach to Keswick for a chaise, and procured a Cart in a neighbouring Farm House to take the Gig to be repaired at Keswick. Enough of this ugly affair. I was a good deal shaken but I trust I am no worse—John was not at all hurt. I thought of you, Isabella,[1] and poor Hannah.[2] What would have been the situation of either of them on the Dickey of your carriage had it met with such a shock? I wish you were safe at home again, and dearest Mary[3] too. In the paper of today I have read of two railway accidents both causing loss of life. I ought to have mentioned that as the road narrows as you round the Hill, John was compelled to draw up where he did, the road being there

[1] I. F.'s niece. [2] I. F.'s maid.

[3] M. W. was away at Brinsop.

both level and broader than any where else. So that the Coachman cannot be too severely blamed for his recklessness.—John is gone home today upon his poor Horse, which though somewhat stiff and sore, I hope will have escaped without lasting injury.—

I found dear Sister very well for her, but Dora—voice gone with one of her worst colds: yesterday it was still worse, but today it seems loosening. Kate Southey and her Brother are returned from Levens and she sleeps here to night. She is now with her Sister.[1] I wish I could add that my indisposition was quite removed. I never had any thing of the kind that lasted more than a day or two before, but I am certainly much better than for the first three days.—Having been so much from home lately, and so much tossed about and unwell, I cannot muster courage to face the notion of going into Herefordshire, for (see last page of this sheet) in addition to, or rather the night previous to, the Gig accident, I had struck my head (while rising from stirring the fire at Brigham in the dark) violently against a projecting black mantelpiece, which I had forgotten, though I believe not a visitor or inmate was ever two days at the House without suffering from it; it projects so dangerously. But all is well with me, as far as I know. And now, though so late, let me say how happy I was to learn from your affectionate Letter to Dora that your own health is good. I know that you are not careless of it, and I believe that you are most judicious in managing yourself. How we long to see you again! My dear Mary will be sadly disappointed if I dont go to her—but unless I am quite well I could not possibly go, and I really do think that at this season it is a long journey to take for persons of her and my years, though I am truly pleased that she has seen her dear Brother. Kindest Love to you, my excellent Friend, in which Dora unites. Love to Isabella and best remembrances to your Host and hostess.[2]

ever yours W. W.

(Pray excuse the wretched confusion in the pages of this Scrawl).[3]

[1] Bertha, living in Rydal with her husband Herbert Hill.

[2] Mr. and Mrs. George Taylor.

[3] Dora W. adds a brief note: 'I know not what Father has said of himself but indeed there is no cause for anxiety: he is not yet *quite* right . . . Father and Katy are talking at such a rate, and sometimes to me, that I hardly know what I am writing. . .'

1462. W. W. to LADY FREDERICK BENTINCK

MS. untraced.
Mem. Grosart. K. LY ii. 1052.

Rydal Mount,
Monday Evening [16 Nov. 1840]

The accident after which you inquire, dear Lady Frederick, with so much feeling, might have been fatal, but through God's mercy we escaped without bodily injury, as far as I know, worth naming. These were the particulars: About three miles beyond Keswick, on the Ambleside road, is a small bridge, from the top of which we got sight of the mail-coach coming towards us, at about forty yards' distance, just before the road begins to descend a narrow, steep, and winding slope. Nothing was left for John, who drove the gig in which we were, but to cross the bridge, and, as the road narrowed up the slope that was in our front, to draw up as close to the wall on our left (our side of the road) as possible. This he did, both of us hoping that the coachman would slacken his pace down the hill, and pass us as far from our wheel as the road would allow. But he did neither. On the contrary, he drove furiously down the hill; and though, as we afterwards ascertained by the track of his wheels, he had a yard width of road to spare, he made no use of it. In consequence of this recklessness and his want of skill, the wheel of his coach struck our wheel most violently, drove back our horse and gig some yards, and then sent us all together through a small gap in the wall, with the stones of the wall tumbling about us, into a plantation that lay a yard perpendicular below the level of the road from which the horse and gig, with us in it, had been driven. The shafts were broken off close to the carriage, and we were partly thrown and partly leaped out. After breaking the traces, the horse leaped back into the road and galloped off, the shafts and traces sticking to him; nor did the poor creature stop till he reached the turnpike at Grasmere, seven miles from the spot where the mischief was done. We sent by the coach for a chaise to take us to Rydal, and hired a cart to take the broken gig to be mended at Keswick.

The mercy was that the violent shock from the coach did not tear off our wheel; for if this had been done, John, and probably I also, must have fallen under the hind wheels of the coach, and in all likelihood been killed. We have since learned that the coachman had only just come upon the road, which is in a great many places very dangerous, and that he was wholly unpractised in driving four-in-hand. Pray excuse this long and minute account. I should have written to you next day, but I waited, hoping to be able to add that my indisposition was gone, as I now trust it is. With respectful remembrances to Lord Lonsdale, and kindest regards to yourself and Miss Thompson I remain,

Dear Lady Frederick, affectionately yours,

Wm Wordsworth

1463. W. W. to AMELIA LOCOCK[1]

Address: Mrs Locock, Hanover Square, London.
Postmark: 24 Nov. 1840.
MS. Mr. W. Hugh Peal. Hitherto unpublished.

Rydal Mount
Ambleside
Nov^{br} 22nd —40.

My dear Madam,

I regret not being able to reply by return of Post to the congratulations on my late escape from extreme danger which you have so feelingly expressed. The main particulars of the accident were correctly given in the Newspapers. Our situation was truly frightful but through God's mercy neither my Son nor myself, as far as we know, were injured to a degree worth speaking of, though I was somewhat shaken among the stones of the wall as they fell round us, when we were driven through it into the plantation better than three feet below the level of the road along which we had been forced back, horse and carriage, several yards.—

It does not surprize me that you think with pleasure and some regret upon your Cottage and the beautiful Scenes around it; and

[1] Wife of Dr. Charles, later Sir Charles, Locock, F.R.S. (1799–1875), the leading London obstetrician. He had just attended Queen Victoria at the birth on 21 Nov. of her first child Victoria, the Princess Royal (1840–1901). He declined a baronetcy on this occasion, but accepted one in 1857, having attended the Queen at the birth of all her children. Dr. and Mrs. Locock, with their four sons, had spent the summer in a cottage at Grasmere. See *RMVB* for July and Aug. 1840, and L. 1466 below.

we cannot but hope that soon or later you will be tempted to revisit them. Almost immediately opposite your humble Cottage, on the other side of the Lake Mr Dawson is building what promises or shall I say threatens to be for size at least a Palace. Another large house is erecting at the head of the Lake, the work of a Gentleman of Maidstone; whether these additions to the landscape will be improvements is perhaps questionable.—

As you will infer I have very many Letters to write upon this occasion, so that I do not apologize for concluding abruptly. I cannot however forbear from saying that when Mrs Wordsworth (she is now in Herefordshire) and I visit London we shall have great pleasure in paying our respects to you and Dr Locock as new and prized Acquaintances whose friendship, advanced in life as we are, we should be happy to cultivate.

Pray make my acknowledgements to Dr Locock for his kind congratulations. It rejoiced me, and not a little on his and Dr Ferguson's[1] account, that our young Queen has been carried through her 'travail' happily, as appears. A Prince would no doubt have been more welcome; but we must be thankful for what God sends!

Believe me dear Madam
to remain faithfully
your much obliged
Wm Wordsworth

1464. W. W. to THOMAS POWELL

MS. Cornell. Hitherto unpublished.

22 Nov^br^ [1840]
Rydal

My dear Mr Powell,

You would perhaps hear of my late peril from the rash driving of a Coach. Through God's Mercy neither I nor my Son were as far as we know any worse. The particulars were faithfully given in the Newspapers except that it was not mentioned that the Horse and Carriage were driven several yeards back along the Road before [they][2] were forced through the stone Wall into the

[1] See pt. iii, L. 1030.

[2] *Word dropped out.*

ground of the Plantation which lay something more than three feet perpendicular below the Road.

I enclose a Letter from the Lady whom I spoke of some time ago. It explains itself. Mr H.[1] in his Prologue appears to have mistaken the sense in the passage in the Prioress's character where it is said, I cannot now consult the original, it pained her or she paind.[2] The expression means she took pains, I think. And in the Scholar[3] In Wyrd had he etc.,—means he had made great progress.—I have a score of Letters to write upon my late accident so pray excuse extreme haste. It would have been well if in the Life of Chaucer that [?most][4] characteristic prose passage of his[5] had been quoted where in his old age he condemns so feelingly so many of his poems as "souning into sin"—

Mrs Wordsworth is in Herefordshire.

ever faithfully yours
Wm Wordsworth

1465. W. W. to ISABELLA FENWICK

Address: Miss Fenwick, Thos Thorp's, Esqre, Alnwick. [*In Dora W.'s hand*]
Postmark: 24 Nov. 1840.
Stamp: Ambleside.
MS. WL.
LY ii. 1053 (—).

[*c.* 23 Nov. 1840]

Little more than another week my dearest Friend will bring you to us, so that I almost feel as if this Letter were a welcome to you at our door. Thanks many and grateful for your last, which happily gave us no reason to believe that your health was suffering. The weather has here been windy almost beyond experience and I have sometimes feared that the passages of this old House would in like weather of severe winter prove too cold for you. But we will take every possible care to prevent this, and

[1] R. H. Horne had now taken on the General Prologue to *The Canterbury Tales* for *Chaucer's Poems Modernized*.

[2] See l. 139.

[3] i.e. the Clerk—but Chaucer does not use these words of him.

[4] *MS. obscure.*

[5] In the retraction at the end of *The Canterbury Tales.*

Dora and I have already given repeated lessons to the Servants upon the really important point of keeping our many Doors shut, one and all. Her cold is certainly much better, though not so well to day as yesterday. This morning was wet, and yesterday fine. But her voice is come back, and I trust that the hard barking cough will be gone before your return. Last night she was kept up till past midnight and this did her harm. She had numerous Letters to write and so had I, many of them occasioned by the accident. You will not be displeased that the Queen Adelaide[1] has been so gracious as to give it a command to Earl Howe to express her 'sincere trust' that neither I nor my Son were injured, etc etc. Our answer to Royalty required some pains though not quite so much as the Durham Presentation Copy[2] which you will not easily forget. We hear pretty regularly from dearest Mary. She never mentions her health, therefore we hope it is at least as good as usual. Her last Letter, of yesterday, was almost entirely about me; as in justification of my not going to Brinsop, which she seemd hurt at on account of our Friends' disappointment, I had told her that I felt too much shaken in body, by my last accident, and, I scarcely knew how, too much depressed in spirits to go so far for so short a time. Dear Creature, she speaks of being with us by the end of next week.—

In compliance with the earnest request of Col. and Mrs Howard, and also of Lady Frederick Bentinck, I go on Wednesday to Levens to meet Lord Lonsdale, Lady F. etc. there. I shall make a point of returning on Friday, both because I have been far too much from home lately, and because I wish to be with dear Dora. Here enters Lady Cadogan, as she calls herself, my dear ruin of a Sister. She is for her wonderfully well, except for her malady of '*bizzing*' which is much encreased upon her. I hope she will drop it ere long. 'Who are you writing to?' she says. 'To Miss Fenwick.' 'Give my love to her.' I hope she will stay with us an hour this evening.—

Dora has told Anne[3] that she supposed were Anne in Carlisle by one of the three o'clock Saturday Coaches, that would do. Otherwise she must have gone to Carlisle on Friday.[4] She left us

[1] The Queen Dowager, who had visited Rydal Mount the previous July.

[2] Presumably W. W.'s letter of acceptance of his honorary degree from Durham University in 1838.

[3] One of I. F.'s maids.

[4] Dora W. adds: 'as there is no coach from Penrith earlier in the day.'

on Friday. If Saturday three o'clock be not soon enough, or we heard in the mean time of different arrangements made by you, Dora will let Anne know.—You will not I trust be likely to leave Keswick, as probably you will come that way, before the Mail Coach arrives. This I am most thankful for, as I cannot bear the thought of you meeting that dangerous vehicle. Kate Southey left us to day after a most melancholy visit, made so by Mrs Southey's conduct, and the manner in which she was supported in it by her Uncle.[1] Mrs S. is a strange Creature, putting herself upon the sternest abstractions of marriage rights and privileges, as established by Law, and this in a case where the Husband was incapable from failure of mind to fulfill the Contract in the sense which the Law requires. What a sad thing all this is. But there will be a way of mercy out of it for the poor Child, I trust, as for all sufferers.

And now my beloved Friend farewell, farewell and welcome in one breath. How rejoiced shall we be to see you, and what a happy week if God so pleases; for as I told you Mary will be with us also, before it ends. Dora sends her dear Love. Pray present the same from both of us to Isabella. Remember us also kindly to Mr and Mrs Thorp,[2] and believe me ever faithfully and tenderly yours

Wm Wordsworth

[*Dora W. writes*]

Father is really quite well—he reads a great deal in the morn^{g} and he has written this long letter and three short ones by candlelight. Yesterday in my mother's absence I replied to a very kind note of enquiry from Mrs Tudor.[3] Dearest Miss Fenwick, how thankful shall we be to welcome you—Poor darling Kate calculates upon seeing you for a few minutes *if* you pass thro' Keswick. I did my best to try to prevail upon her to be ready to return to Rydal with you, but no—'When Cuthbert is gone back to Oxford' was her reply, sobs choking her utterance. It is a cruel case. Really I do think Mrs S. is—no I wont write it. Gratefully and lovingly yours Dora Wordsworth.

Jemima[4] in a note I received yesterday begged me, had I an

[1] Dr. Henry Southey, who took Mrs. Southey's side in the family quarrel.

[2] Thomas Thorp (1805–54), of Doxford Hall, Ellingham, and of Alnwick, married Elizabeth (d. 1890), a niece of I. F.'s and daughter of William Tudor of Bath.

[3] I. F.'s sister (see L. 1425 above).

[4] Jemima Quillinan.

opportunity, to thank dear Isabella[1] for a delightful letter w^h w^d be answered in due time.

1466. W. W. to SIR JOHN TAYLOR COLERIDGE

Endorsed: 1840 Novr 28th. W. Wordsworth Rydal Mount.
MS. British Library.
K (—). *LY ii. 1056* (—).

[*In Dora W.'s hand*]

Rydal Mount
Nov. 28th [1840]

My dear Mr Justice Coleridge,

You must excuse my employing an Amanuensis and this you will do I know the more readily as it is my daughter who writes for me which neither she, nor anyone else, for some time, has been under the necessity of doing as my eyes upon the whole have been very much better; but they caught a small blight a day or two ago, the extreme beauty of the weather having tempted me to come on the outside of the coach from Kendal where by the bye, I had as a fellow traveller a gentleman who was born, and bred, and lived in the Orkneys. It pleased me much to see how the beauty of the country, thro' w^h we passed, enchanted him, the comfortable appearance of the dwellings, and the features of the Lake and Mountains; he told me that as to integrity and good character of the inhabitants there was a great difference in the several Islands and it seemed to depend much upon the Clergy; wherever the Minister was an upright, pious, and good man and zealous in the discharge of his duties, the behaviour of the people was for the most part good in proportion. I wish our Legislature w^d pay more attention to the facts tending to establish the same conclusion w^h our own country of England would supply—but it is high time to thank you and Lady Coleridge for taking so much thought about our late accident; it was not at all exaggerated in the Newspapers: the peril we incurred was greater than there reported but thro' God's mercy, except a little shake to myself, we were neither of us any worse: and happily we were the first to bring the intelligence to my daughter—and Mrs Wordsworth, who is in Herefordshire heard of it first from my own pen. This was surely a great

[1] I. F.'s niece.

blessing, for had it not been that the turnpike gate at Grasmere w^h is mostly open was closed the horse would have gallopped on to Rydal with the broken shafts and harness dangling about him.

It is a pity that the Lococks[1] could not realize their project of passing a few weeks in the year among us. The Spring had been dry to a degree unprecedented: we were 14 weeks without rain except one wet day and two or three showers and it seemed as if the elements were determined to straight the accounts, for the summer and great part of autumn the country as Mrs Locock experienced to her sorrow was drenched with rain—We were much pleased with what we had of their society and are truly glad that our engagements w^h you know are pretty numerous at that season did not materially interfere with our wishes in respect to them.

Mrs L. in particular we saw several times. I have had a very kind letter from her, but it was written before the Queen's Accouchement.[2] How rejoiced they must be at the happy course of the event.

Though I may without vanity reckon myself a pretty good judge in laying out grounds upon a large scale and have not neglected the minuter beauties of Flower gardens, yet I can scarcely be deem'd an authority in this department of taste: there are however here certain principles upon w^h my mind is made up—for example, whenever a house fronts a grand or sublime scene of mountains, I would not admit beds of flowers and shrubs imitating, with lawn interspersed, those diversities of shape w^h are so pleasing when we meet with them in wild Nature. I would either have no flowers, or an architectural garden with Terraces and formal beds after the manner of the French and Italians—but a scheme of this kind requires something of an antique air in the house to correspond with it. In such a site and with such a building, the garden w^d at once be referred to the house and w^h obviously depend upon it without having other pretensions, nevertheless we often see in such situations a disposition of flowers and shrubs and lawn w^h is neither art nor Nature, and accordingly it is to me displeasing to look upon. As to your own intended work[3] I c^d not presume to give any advice

[1] Dr. and Mrs. Charles Locock (see L. 1463 above).

[2] See L. 1463 above.

[3] Sir John Coleridge had recently come into possession of the family estate of Heath's Court, Ottery St. Mary, and was planning to enlarge the house and lay out the grounds.

but I think it possible to avoid the class of mistakes I have been alluding to. I c^{d} fancy to myself a scale, from the little cottage garden with its beds and borders up to a modern Villa, w^{h} w^{d} be far more agreeable than one mostly sees. Still however when the landscape has no grandeur but is merely soft and somewhat Arcadian a little Cyclades of exotic shrubs and flowers may be introduced in front of a Gentleman's house with good effect.

It gives me pleasure to hear so promising an account of y^{r} Son[1] and that we are likely to have him in our neighbourhood for a short time at Xmas. He will be as you well know with a most amiable family, active and cheerful within doors and without, one and all of them, to an enviable degree—he will not have much time to spare, but I hope we shall see him occasionally at the Mount. Your Report of the Palace and especially of the mode in w^{h} the Prince[2] passes a considerable portion of his time, was very gratifying and the more so because it reminds me of what in the year 1837 Prof. W. Schlegel, under whose care Prince Albert was, told me at Bomal[3] of his promising habits and dispositions, w^{h} he was prompted to do by the then already talked of probability that the Prince would become the Husband of our young Queen—Knowing how much you are engaged and upon what important business I must beg you to excuse my taking up so much of y^{r} time but the temptation y^{r} kindness held out in writing me so long a letter, would not easily have been resisted.

[1] John Duke Coleridge (1820–94), later Lord Chief Justice of England, had moved on the previous year from Eton to Balliol College, Oxford, where he had now been joined by Matthew Arnold. He had first visited Rydal when Sir John Coleridge brought his family to Fox How for a brief holiday in 1836 (see pt. iii, L. 1073). See *Life and Correspondence of John Duke Lord Coleridge*, ed. Ernest Hartley Coleridge, 2 vols., 1904, i. 45–6.

[2] Prince Albert (1819–61) had studied under A. W. Schlegel at Bonn in 1837. See C. Grey, *The Early Years of His Royal Highness The Prince Consort*, 1867, pp. 147 ff.

[3] W. W. had met Schlegel at Bonn during the Continental tour of 1828 (see pt. i, L. 346), and had corresponded with him in 1834 (see pt. ii, L. 813). There is no evidence, this letter apart, that they met again during W. W.'s Continental tour of 1837, and no such meeting is mentioned in H. C. R.'s Travel Diary (*Dr. Williams's Library MSS.*), either during their return home through Bonn on 30–31 July, or when they were in Brussels on 2 Aug. and could have visited Bomal. But the probability still remains that the meeting described in this letter actually took place.

With kindest regards to Lady Coleridge and yourself and good wishes for all your Family in w^{h} my daughter unites, as Mrs Wordsworth would have gladly done had she been here,

I remain my dear Mr Justice Coleridge

faithfully yours
[*signed*] Wm Wordsworth

1467. W. W. to ISABELLA FENWICK

MS. WL.
LY ii. 1055.

Monday Noon. [30 Nov. 1840]

I cannot refrain my dearest Friend from welcoming you to Keswick; but I have another reason for writing. Pray let Anne point out to you the spot where we incurred our peril; I am sure it will be gratifying to you to give thanks to God for our escape as you pass it.—It is very good in you to stop for the purpose of comforting the afflicted; but let me caution you to bear in mind that poor dear K.[1] is too apt to put unwarrantably an unfavorable construction upon some of Mrs. S.'s proceedings. This is very pardonable considering K.'s position, nevertheless one should be upon one's guard lest compassion and sympathy so justly due from her Friend should countenance that infirmity of mind.

May we not expect you about one, Wednesday at the latest. Should it not rain, so as to make me an improper Companion in your carriage, I will meet you. Dora's cold is better, in the chest and voice, much better, but the throat is a good deal disordered. She was the worse for a ride into Easedale which the beautiful weather tempted us to take—

I have seen Edward Wilson[2] about his house.

ever yours W. W.

[1] Kate Southey.

[2] Joiner, of Goody Bridge.

1468. W. W. to CHARLES REED[1]

Address: Charles Reed, 7 Portland Place, Leeds. [*In Dora W.'s hand*]
Postmark: 1 Dec. 1840.
Stamp: Ambleside.
Endorsed: William Wordsworth Rydal Mount. Enclosing a note to me in answer to one in which I request his Autograph. December 2nd 1840. CR.
MS. Cornell. Hitherto unpublished.

Rydal Mount
30th Novr. 1840.

Sir,

In compliance with your request I send you my Autograph.

yours truly
Wm Wordsworth

1469. W. W. to BENJAMIN ROBERT HAYDON

MS. Professor Willard Pope.
LY ii. 1056.

[late Nov. 1840]

My dear Haydon

All is well thank God at least as far as we know. Though the account given in the newspapers was in the main very accurate the peril incurred was even greater than there spoken of; the two joints of the little finger of my left hand are both sprained but I am aware of nothing worse than this small hurt. God bless you with kind remembrances to Mrs Haydon, believe me ever faithfully yours

Wm Wordsworth

[1] Charles, later Sir Charles, Reed (1819–81) the educationalist, had been apprenticed to a firm of woollen manufacturers in Leeds in 1836, and three years later started *The Leeds Repository*. In 1842 he moved to London and taking a partner, started the firm of Tyler and Reed, printers. He was an active member of the Sunday School Movement, took a prominent part in the government of the City of London, and represented Hackney as a liberal, 1868–74, taking a leading part in the debates on the Elementary Education Bill in 1870 and becoming Chairman of the London School Board in 1873.

Mrs Wordsworth who is in Herefordshire first heard of the accident from ourselves, and my Daughter, who is at home, knew nothing of it thank heaven till we told her ourselves. If the horse had not been stopped by a turnpike Gate he would have gallopped on to Rydal or Ambleside with the shafts hanging to his sides, as it was he ran a race of 8 miles.

1470. W. W. to WALTER FARQUHAR HOOK

MS. Colby College, Maine.
LY ii. 1057. Colby Library Quarterly, i. (Jan. 1944), 82.

Rydal Mount
Decr 7th —40

My dear Sir

Accept my thanks for your letter, and the enclosed verses, which were read in this House, by us all with pleasure; and I may say that as a composition they do the Author no little credit—I need scarcely add, that it cannot but be gratifying to me to learn that my endeavours have been felt in the way which you allude to, and especially among the class to which the person who has thus given vent to his feelings belongs.

You will be pleased to learn that I frequently receive testimonies from Individuals who live by the labour of their hands, that what I have written has not been a dead letter to them; and for this reason chiefly, I shall propose to my Publisher to print the Excursion in double column, so that it may circulate as cheaply as can be afforded.

The peril which my Son and I incurred was even more formidable than the account of the Newspapers represent.—thro' the mercy of God my Son escaped without injury, and I only slightly hurt.

With the united kind regards of Mrs W. and my Daughter to yourself and Mrs Hook

I remain, my dear Sir

faithfully your obliged
Wm Wordsworth

1471. W. W. to ROBERT BIGSBY[1]

Address: Robt Bigsby Esqre, Repton, N^{r} Derby. [*In M. W.'s hand*]
Postmark: (1) 15 Dec. 1840 (2) 16 Dec. 1840.
Stamp: Ambleside.
Endorsed: Wordsworth, Wm Esqr, Dec. 15, 1840. *Address*: Rydal Mount, Westmorland.
MS. Harvard University Library.
LY ii. 1057.

[14 *or* 15 Dec. 1840]

Sir,

Upon the point to which your obliging Letter refers me, I have really nothing to say. My Writings are like those of any other Author who has given his to the World are open to the praise or censure of every one who thinks them of sufficient consequence to be noticed. Wishing your intended publication the success which I have no doubt it will merit I remain Sir sincerely

your obliged Ser^{nt}
Wm Wordsworth

1472. W. W. to EDWARD MOXON

MS. Henry E. Huntington Library.
K (—). LY ii. 1058.

[*In M. W.'s hand*]

Decr. 17th —40

Dear Mr Moxon,

Your parcel has arrived to-day, containing however one book which must have been put in by mistake—viz. the 2^{d} vol of

[1] Robert Bigsby (1806–73), author of *Miscellaneous Poems and Essays*, 1842; *Historical and Topographical Description of Repton, in the County of Derby*, 1854, and other antiquarian works. He had written on 13 Dec., sending an extract from his poem 'Hours of Rural Solitude' for W. W.'s opinion, 'my anxious desire being to testify the deepest veneration for your genius, and to avoid putting on paper anything which may be considered inapplicable, or altogether unworthy of the subject.' (*WL MSS.*) The passage sent was an address to W. W., in which his genius was contrasted with Byron's.

Moore's Poems[1] now in course of publication, and intended, by the direction, for Mrs. Shelley.[2]—Mr Robinson[3] I am happy to say is coming down to us—and if no earlier opportunity than his return should occur, it may be sent back by him free of expence.

Thanks for the information you gave me, some time ago, about the expence of printing the Sonnets I wrote to you about—if I come to town in the Spring I may perhaps act upon it. You told me the Excursion was out of print. What do you say to reprinting it in double column stereotyped, all but the pages—so that the same plates might serve hereafter, the paging being altered for the concluding part of the vol when the whole shall be published in one? I have two motives for this, the one a desire to make the book acceptable to Mechanics and others who have little money to spare, and next to shew from so many instances with which this would concur that books are as likely to be sold as cheap as they can be afforded, should the term of copy-right be extended, and that in fact, they could in that case be sold cheaper, as there being no dread of competition, Editions might be larger—and would of course be sold at less price. Let me hear from you on this point at your earliest convenience.[4]

You mentioned when you were here that you were in the habit of supplying Parish Libraries with books. My Son John is about establishing one—his is a very poor neighbourhood, and he is not likely to receive much assistance from it—so that if you could lend a helping hand, any books you could furnish him with would be most acceptable—as were those you kindly sent to the Library at Ambleside.

I am glad the Hares arrived safe. Mrs W. hopes Mrs M. may find them good—and with her good wishes united to my own and my daughter's believe me

ever sincerely yours
[*signed*] Wm Wordsworth

[1] *The Poetical Works of Thomas Moore. Collected by Himself*, 10 vols., 1840–1.

[2] Mary Wollstonecraft Shelley (1797–1851) Godwin's daughter, the poet's second wife: author of *Frankenstein*, 1818, *The Last Man*, 1826, etc. In recent years she had contributed to Lardner's *Cabinet Cyclopaedia* and the annuals, and edited Shelley's *Poetical Works* (see pt. iii, L. 1348) and prose remains (see *HCR* ii. 587) for Moxon.

[3] H. C. R.

[4] See L. 1485 below.

1473. W. W. to H. C. R.

MS. Dr. Williams's Library.
Morley, i. 420.

[*In M. W.'s hand*]

Decr 17 [18]40

My dear Friend

Two or three words will suffice as we are to have the great pleasure of seeing you so soon—[1]

Your old lodgings are ready for you—you will not find Agnes there, but a very nice Person in her place and I doubt not but that you will find all things as comfortable as heretofore, and at the same rate—therefore come as speedily as you can—

You will be happy to learn that Miss Fenwick is under our roof—and that we are all pretty well—The Arnolds arrived at Fox how on Tuesday all well—and delighted to hear that we are to see you.

With our joint best regards ever aff^ly yours
[*signed*] W Wordsworth

1474. W. W. to MARY SPRING RICE[2]

MS. Cornell.
Broughton, p. 80.

Rydal Mount
28th Decb. 1840

Having, my dear Friend, through a long series of years had opportunities of coming to an intimate knowledge of the excellent character of Mr James Marshall, and having confidence in your own amiable qualities of head and heart I am impelled to offer my sincere congratulations upon your approaching union with a person for whom I entertain so high a respect. In giving way to this feeling I have the more pleasure, as I can speak from

[1] H. C. R. arrived at Rydal on the 24th and stayed until 22 Jan. He found D. W. 'amazingly improved': 'She can talk for a time rationally enough, but she has no command of herself . . .' (*HCR* ii. 588). He also considered W. W.'s tone of argument 'far more liberal than it used to be' (Morley, i. 422).

[2] Mary Spring Rice (see pt. ii, L. 743) married James Marshall (see pt. ii, L. 453) on 9 Feb. 1841.

the experience of nearly forty years of the happiness which the state of marriage can confer; and of benefits intellectual moral and spiritual, which must daily flow from it if the fault be not our own, and the choice has been made with due consideration.—

It cannot be necessary to say that we all look forward with great pleasure to the time when we shall count you among our neighbours. I reckon Coniston Water-head one of the most beautiful places in this beautiful neighbourhood, and I am sure you will be delighted with every thing about it.

With every good wish of the season and for your future happiness in which we all unite I remain my dear Friend

faithfully yours
Wm Wordsworth

1475. W. W. to JAMES SPEDDING[1]

Endorsed: 1840 Wm Wordsworth to James.
MS. Mr. J. H. F. Spedding. Hitherto unpublished.

[*In M. W.'s hand*]

Rydal Mount
Decr 28 —40

My dear Sir,

Hearing you are in the North and hoping that you have leisure upon your hands, Miss Fenwick, and Mrs Wordsworth join with me in expressing a wish that you would give us a few days of your Company at Rydal Mount during this fine Season. If it should not be convenient to you, or interfere with present engagements it would be most agreeable to us to see you here before next Tueday, the 5th—as one day we are expecting our Son and 2 Grandsons from Brigham, and as our younger Son is also with us, our small house, you might find, too much crowded and noisy for comfort.

With best wishes of the Season from us all here to the family at Mirehouse I remain dear Sir very Sincerely and faithfully yours

[*signed*] Wm Wordsworth

[1] Of the Colonial Office: the editor of Bacon. See pt. iii, L. 1003.

1476. W. W. to THE GOVERNORS OF REPTON SCHOOL

MS. Miriam Lutcher Stark Library, University of Texas. Hitherto unpublished.

Rydal Mount
Ambleside Dec^{br} 31st —40

To the hereditary Governors of the united Corporation of Etwall and Repton,[1]

Gentlemen,

Having learned from the Reverend Derwent Coleridge[2] that he is desirous to obtain the vacant Headmastership of Repton School and being informed that private testimony in behalf of Candidates will be duly considered in determining the election, I venture to state my belief that he is eminently fitted to fill an office of this kind.—I have known Mr Coleridge from his infancy—up to the period when he went to College most intimately; and though distance of place has prevented much personal intercourse between us since that period, I have had uninterrupted opportunities to hear of him and his course of life from his nearest Connections and Friends. Among these must be included Mr Southey, who, had his state of health permitted would (I am confident from what he said to me after passing some days under Mr Coleridge's roof at Helston School two[3] years ago) have been most ready and happy to add his testimony to the undoubted qualifications of our common Friend. In presuming to speak thus the Electors will understand that I am expressing a firm belief that both as concerns Scholarship,

[1] The Corporation set up in 1622 by royal charter to administer Sir John Port's Hospital at Etwall, Derbys., and the School at Repton, which he had founded in 1557.

[2] Derwent Coleridge had been master of Helston School since 1826, and had recently brought out his most considerable work, *The Scriptural Character of the English Church*, 1839 (*R.M.Cat.* no. 216). He was unsuccessful in this application, T. W. Peile (see pt. i, L. 180) securing the appointment; but the following year he was made first Principal of St. Mark's College, Chelsea, which had been recently established by the National Society. There he played an important part in shaping the course of elementary education in England, and turned the College chapel into a centre for the choral revival in the Church. Among his other testimonials for Repton, was one from Frederick Denison Maurice (*University of Texas MSS.*), who had been much impressed by his book.

[3] Actually *four* years before this, in Dec. 1836.

intellectual Powers, and the still higher considerations of moral rectitude and religious faith Mr Coleridge is a Gentleman under whose care and management Repton School would be likely to be conducted to the satisfaction of those in whom the important appointment to the Mastership rests.

I have the honor to be Gentlemen
most respectfully your obedient Servant
Wm Wordsworth

1477. W. W. to [?] ROBINSON WORDSWORTH[1]

MS. Professor Kenneth W. Cameron.
Emerson Society Quarterly, no. 13 (1958), 25.

[*In M. W.'s hand*]

[1840]

. . .cousin James'[2] death. I am truly sorry for the situation in w^{h} his widow is left but I have unfortunately no interest whatever in the quarter [ ]

[*signed*] Wm Wordsworth

[*W. W. adds*]

I hope you have good news from your Sons.

W. W.

[1] This fragment was probably addressed to W. W.'s cousin Robinson Wordsworth (see *EY* pp. 121, 184), youngest son of W. W.'s uncle Richard Wordsworth of Whitehaven, who had retired from the Collectorship of Customs at Harwich in 1834 and subsequently settled at Seer Green, Bucks. Robinson Wordsworth had eight sons and four daughters, including Caroline, who married Henry Miles Haviland of Denham, and Elizabeth (d. 1852), who married Charles William Wood, of the Inner Temple. See L. 2018 below. Robinson Wordsworth visited Rydal Mount in Nov. 1833 (*RMVB*).

[2] James Wordsworth (1757–1840), third son of Richard Wordsworth of Whitehaven. He married Elizabeth Fowler (1764–1847).

1478. W. W. to UNKNOWN CORRESPONDENT[1]

MS. untraced.
LY ii. 1059.

[late 1840?]

My dear Sir,

We all thank you for the trouble you have taken in making inquiries about the State of Credit in Pensylvania. I am happy to assure you Miss Fenwick's money is lodged not in the Pensylvania Bank as you apprehended, but in a State Loan[2]—so that other friends, as well as myself, think that under these circumstances[3] there is little ground for fear but that the interest will be paid—tho' no one can calculate as to the time. In this uncertainty she feels herself obliged to decline taking your house—and gives way, with satisfaction to our Neighbour Mr Hill,[4] who stands in need of more accommodation than is afforded by the house which he at present occupies. He himself will in all probability write to you to-morrow upon the subject.

In the course of next week, for I am very much engaged at present, I trust I shall be able to bestow due consideration up[on] the sketch of the Epitaph of your excellent Parents, which you have done me the honor to submit to my revisal. If it should not suit you to wait so long as till towards the latter end of the week, pray let me know and I will do the best that I can.

Thank you for the interest you express about my family at Brigham—you will be glad to hear that the last account, which was 3 days ago, was an improved one—and as we have heard nothing since we understand the Sufferer to be going on favourably,—and think the rest of the family are doing well.

I remain dear Sir, with kind remembrances from Miss F. and Mrs Wordsworth, faithfully

Your's
Wm Wordsworth

[1] This letter was perhaps addressed to William Ball the Quaker, of Glen Rothay (see pt. iii, L. 1048), whose main residence was at Bruce Grove, Tottenham.

[2] See L. 1431 above.

[3] *Written* commonstancies, as de Selincourt notes.

[4] Herbert Hill's first child had been born recently.

1479. W. W. to SAMUEL ROGERS

MS. Cornell. Hitherto unpublished.

[?1840][1]

. . . .the privilege of friendship—farewell—I hope you think somewhere of me and mine, and the beautiful scene which by God's mercy I am enabled to enjoy. Every body here sends kindest remembrances. I remain my dear Rogers

yours most faithfully
Wm Wordsworth

1480. M. W. to JAMES SPEDDING

MS. Smith College Library. Hitherto unpublished.

New years day [1841]

My dear Sir

I write to say to you that should you and your Friend (whom we shall be very glad to see at Rydal)[2] find my Son and his two boys in the Mail on their way hither, *on Monday*—that you are not to be deterred from coming forward from the fear of inconveniencing us;—as we can arrange to receive you all, by the aid of good neighbourhood, if one of the Party will not object going to sleep at the foot of *our* hill, where our friend Mr H. C. Robinson at present has a comfortable lodging.

We shall all be glad to see you, and hope it will not be inconvenient to you to remain with us over Tuesday, on which day we expect the pleasure of the Company of Dr and Mrs Arnold at dinner.[3]

Very sincerely dear Mr Spedding, your's

M. Wordsworth

[1] Apparently a late fragment—but the dating is purely conjectural.

[2] The visit of James Spedding and his friend Mr. Lawrence (who is unidentified) is recorded in *RMVB*.

[3] H. C. R. met Spedding at this party on the 5th, when they were fellow-guests along with the Arnolds and W. W.'s cousins, the Robinsons from Ambleside: '. . . a liberal thinker, in politics rather more than a Whig, for he advocates the ballot. He is not a brilliant and learned man, but clear-headed and judicious . . . He is seemingly free in his religious opinions, but religious in his tastes and feelings—he does not oppress by superiority but encourages by sympathy.' (*HCR* ii. 588).

1481. W. W. to SAMUEL CARTER HALL[1]

Address: Mr Hall, Lowther Street, Whitehaven.
MS. Cornell. Hitherto unpublished.

[*In M. W.'s hand*] Rydal Mount
Jan^ry 8th —41.

My dear Sir

I was pleased to hear that you and Mrs Hall had been employed in giving topographical accounts of your native Country.[2]

In answer to your's just rec'^d I must say, first that you are under a mistake in supposing that I ever gave it as my opinion, that the Lakes of Killarney were of superior interest to those of the District in which I live. All that I ever said upon this subject, was, that the three Lakes of Killarney considered as one, as they might naturally be, lying so close to each other, were together more important than any *one* of our Lakes: but I could not ever have taken so narrow a view of those of Cumb^d West^d and Lancashire as to assert what you have been led to believe. I have however more than once given it as my opinion, that if I might judge from what I saw of the County of Kerry, that County so nobly indented with bays of the Atlantic Ocean and possessing a climate so favourable for vegitation, along with its Mountains and inland Waters might, without injustice, be pronounced in point of scenery the finest portion of these Islands. So much indeed was I struck with it that I should have been happy when I saw it, about ten years ago,[3] to do what is now in better hands, viz to write a topographical description of it, in connection with some skillful Artist.

Thanking you for the interesting No: of your publication which you have sent me—and begging you to accept my kind remembrances—and to offer the same to Mrs Hall,

I remain dear Sir
faithfully your's
[*signed*] Wm Wordsworth

[1] Formerly editor of *The Amulet* and the *New Monthly Magazine* (see pt. i, L. 285): now editing the *Art Union Monthly Journal.*

[2] *Ireland: its Scenery, Character, etc.*, 3 vols., 1841–3. 'The charm of the book is the natural eloquence, as well as the generous affections of the Irish peasantry related in pathetic tales' (*HCR* ii. 601).

[3] Actually rather more than eleven years before, in the autumn of 1829.

1482. W. W. to JOHN WILSON[1]

MS. Cornell.
LY iii. 1061.

Rydal Mount
Jan^{ry} 11th —41.

Dear Mr Wilson,

I received the accompanying Vol:[2] from Mr Powell some little time ago to be forwarded to you, which would have been sooner done had not my Son W^{m}, who was to take it to Carlisle, been detained by the severe weather.

The attempt originated, I believe, in the Specimen I gave some years since,[3] of the Prioresses Tale, and has no other object but to tempt the mere modern Reader to recur to the original.

I hope that yourself and your family are well. My own, thank God are, and are all with me at present; and join me in kindest remembrances. We are sorry to hear that you think of parting with Elleray.[4] Ever

faithfully yours
Wm Wordsworth

1483. W. W. to HENRY REED

MS. Cornell.
Mem. (—). Grosart (—). K (—). Wordsworth and Reed, p. 41.

[*In M. W.'s hand*]

Rydal Mount Jan^{ry} 13th 1841

My dear Mr Reed

Your most obliging letter of Oct. 30th would have been earlier acknowledged if my friend Miss Fenwick had not been absent—from Her who begs to return her cordial thanks for the trouble you have taken on her account. I have learnt that the error[5] you mention was merely as you imagined, caused by a

[1] Professor John Wilson, 'Christopher North' of *Blackwood's*.

[2] *Chaucer's Poems Modernized*, 1841. See pt. iii, L. 1361.

[3] In 1820.

[4] Wilson's last visit to Elleray was in summer 1848.

[5] See L. 1444 above.

slip of the transcribers pen. And of course the Bankers books are accurate.

As your assurances have set us at ease in respect of the Pensylvania securities I have only to request on behalf of Miss F. and my daughter that you will be so kind as to keep your eye upon the United States bank, and upon the Missi[ssi]ppi bonds,—in respect to both of which we should be very thankful for such advice as your future experience may suggest.

It is gratifying to learn that thro' your means, Mr Alston[1] has been reminded of me. We became acquainted many years ago thro' our common Friend Mr Coleridge, who had seen much of Mr Allston when they were both living at Rome. Mr A. had he remained in London would have soon made his way to public approbation; his genius and style of painting were too much above the standard of taste, at that time prevalent, to be duly acknowledge[d] at once, by the Many; but so convinced am I that he would have succeeded in obtaining general admiration, that I have ever regretted his speedy return to his native Country, not so much that we have lost him (for that feeling would be more than counterbalanced by what America has gained) as because while living in Europe he would have continued to be more in the way of the works of the great Masters, which could not but have been beneficial to his own powers. Let me add that he sometimes favors me with an opportunity of hearing from, and of him, thro' his American friends whom he does me the honor of introducing to me.[2]

You mention the Sonnet I wrote upon Haydon's Picture of the Duke of Wellington. I have known Haydon and Wilkie[3] also, from their contemporaneous introduction to the world as

[1] Washington Allston, the American painter (see *MY* i. 516; ii. 504–5). The retrospective exhibition of his work at Boston in 1839 had made a powerful impression on the New England public and led to tributes from Margaret Fuller, Oliver Wendell Holmes, Elizabeth Peabody, and others. See E. P. Richardson, *Washington Allston, A Study of the Romantic Artist in America*, Chicago, 1948, Ch. xiii. Allston was now busy on his monumental *Belshazzar's Feast*, which was still uncompleted at his death.

[2] Allston's letters of introduction are preserved among the *WL MSS*. For full details, see Alan G. Hill, 'Wordsworth and his American Friends', *Bulletin of Research in the Humanities*, lxxxi (1978), 146–60.

[3] Reed had mentioned seeing Haydon's picture *Christ's Entry into Jerusalem* at the Philadelphia Academy of Fine Arts (*Wordsworth and Reed*, p. 39). For Sir David Wilkie, see pt. i, L. 134.

Artists: their powers were perceived and acknowledged by my lamented friend Sir George Beaumont, and patronized by him accordingly; and it was at his house where I first became acquainted with them both. Haydon is bent upon coming to Rydal next summer with a view to paint a likeness of me—not as a mere matter of fact Portrait, but one of a poetical character, in which he will endeavour to place his friend in some favorite scene of these mountains. I am rather afraid, I own, of any attempt of this kind, notwithstanding my high opinion of his ability—but if he keeps in his present mind, which I doubt, it would be in vain to oppose his inclination—He is a great enthusiast possessed also of a most active intellect—but he wants that submissive and steady good sense, which is absolutely necessary for the adequate development of power in that art to which he is attached. As I am on the subject of painting, it may be worth while to add that Pickersgill came down last summer to paint a Portrait of me for Sir R^t Peel's gallery at Drayton manor—it was generally thought here that this work was more successful as a likeness than the one he painted some years ago, for St. John's College, at the request of the Master and fellows.

There has recently been published in London a Volume of some of Chaucer's tales and Poems, modernized—this little specimen originated in what I attempted with the Prioresses Tale—and if the book should find its way to America you will see in it 2 further specimens[1] from myself—I had no further connection with the publication than by making a present of these to one of the Contributors.[2] Let me however recommend to your notice, the Prologue, and the Franklin's tale—they are both by Mr Horne,[3] a gentleman unknown to me but are, the latter in particular, very well done. Mr L. Hunt has not failed in the Manciple's tale which I myself modernized many years ago, but tho' I much admire the genius of Chaucer as displayed in this performance, I could not place my version at the disposal of the Editor, as I deemed the subject somewhat too indelicate for pure taste to be offered to the world at this time of day. Mr Horne has much hurt this publication by not abstaining from the Reeve's Tale—this, after making all allowance for the rude manners of Chaucer's age is intolerable, and by indispensable softening down the incidents he has killed the spirit of that humour, gross

[1] *The Cuckoo and the Nightingale* and a small part of *Troilus and Cresida*.

[2] Thomas Powell.

[3] Richard Hengist Horne (see L. 1368 above).

and farcical, that pervades the original. When the work was first mentioned to me, I protested as strongly as possible against admitting any coarseness or indelicacy—so that my conscience is clear of countenancing aught of that kind. So great is my admiration of Chaucer's genius, and so profound my reverence for him as an instrument in the hands of Providence for spreading the light of literature thro' his native land that notwithstanding the defects and faults in this Publication, I am glad of it, as a mean for making many acquainted with the original, who would otherwise be ignorant of every thing about him, but his name. I shall always d^r Sir be happy to hear from you, and believe me to be ever faithfully and gratefully your's

[*signed*] Wm Wordsworth

1484. W. W. to UNKNOWN CORRESPONDENT

MS. National Library of Scotland.
LY iii. 1061.

Rydal Mount Ambleside Jan^ry 16th 1841

Dear Sir,

I have been much disturbed at being obliged to defer writing to you from day to day, in the hope that your Letter which upon the receipt of the Parcel was accidentally mislaid, would be found. It has not been so, to my great concern, and nothing remains for me but to thank you for it, though unseen, and for the valuable Work which you have sent me. As far as I can judge your Addresses to Communicants and the sermons must have greatly benefited those to whom they were delivered and cannot fail to do the same wherever they are read.

I need scarcely add that I sympathize with your domestic afflictions which no doubt contributed to enable you to write so feelingly. Believe me to be with sincere respect

Your obliged
Wm Wordsworth

1485. W. W. to EDWARD MOXON

MS. Henry E. Huntington Library.
LY iii. 1062.

[Jan. 17, 1841][1]

My dear Mr Moxon,

As the prevention of overflowing lines would encrease the price, I am resolved to give it up.—Upon reviewing the question of publishing the Excursion separately in double Column, I am inclined to defer it till the 6 Volumes are brought out in one; and then but not before I think it would be well to give the Excursion separately. The reason which makes me think thus, is that many who had first purchased the Excursion, were it to come out separately, and might wish to have the whole of the other Poems when they also should appear in double column, would find they could not gain their wish without paying *twice* for the Excursion, which would be a hardship; for it would never answer to sell the miscellaneous Poems separately from the Excursion.

What strikes me as best to be done is as follows, but I should like to hear your opinion. 1st To begin as soon as you think proper with printing the whole in double column; but so managing the paging of the Excursion as I said in a former Letter, that the same stereotype in every other respect would answer both for it, to be sold as a separate work, and as the concluding part of the Volume containing all the Poems.

2ndly, I would strike off immediately a certain number of the Excursion[2] to continue to be sold in its present shape, which many readers would prefer though twice the price at which the double column could be offered; for you must allow that a thin Volume like Mr Rogers's or Mr Campbell's, and the Excursion would be no more than the Latter, is a very disagreeable pamphlet shape. It is too thin to bind, and won't stand easily upon a shelf—

I have now given you my notions and I should be glad to hear your own opinion upon them, at your early convenience.

ever faithfully yours
Wm Wordsworth

[1] Date added in another hand.

[2] A new edition of *The Excursion* appeared later this year.

My Son John was highly gratified with your present to his village Library. He left us yesterday.—

(Turn over)

I have been reading the above to my Daughter. She differs from me when I say that it would never answer to sell the miscellaneous Poems without the Excursion. What do you think of this change. Thus far you know the miscellaneous Poems have never been sold separate from the Excursion, though the Ex. has from them.

1486. W. W. to JOHN PEACE

MS. untraced.
Mem. (—). *Grosart* (—). *K* (—). *LY* iii. 1063 (—).

Rydal Mount, Jan. 19, 1841.

My dear Mr Peace,

It is an age since I heard from you, or of you. Probably I am a letter, or more than one, in your debt; but for many reasons I am a bad correspondent, as you know, and will, I doubt not, excuse. I have no special reason for writing at this moment of time, but I have long wished to thank *you* for the *Apology for Cathedrals*,[1] which I have learned is from your pen. The little work does you great credit; it is full of that wisdom which the heart and imagination alone could adequately supply for such a subject, and is, moreover, very pleasingly diversified by styles of treatment all good in their kind. I need add no more than that I entirely concur in the views you take; but what avails it? the mischief is done, and they who have been most prominent in setting it on foot will have to repent of their narrow comprehension, which, however, is no satisfaction to us, who from the first foresaw the evil tendency of the measure.

Though I can make but little use of my eyes in writing, or reading, I have lately been reading Cowper's 'Task' aloud, and in so doing was tempted to look over the parallelisms, for which

[1] Peace had published his *Apology for Cathedral Service* anonymously in 1839, with a dedication to W. W., whose poems were cited frequently in the body of the work. Deploring the utilitarian notions of the Ecclesiastical Commissioners in cutting down Cathedral establishments, Peace upheld the Cathedral service as 'one of the purest feasts to be enjoyed on earth.' See Bernarr Rainbow, *The Choral Revival in the Anglican Church, 1839–1872*, 1970, pp. 246 ff.

Mr Southey was, in his edition, indebted to you. Knowing how comprehensive your acquaintance with poetry is, I was rather surprised that you did not notice the identity of the thought, and accompanying illustrations of it, in a passage of Shenstone's 'Ode upon Rural Elegance', compared with one in 'The Task',[1] where Cowper speaks of the inextinguishable love of the country as manifested by the inhabitants of cities in their culture of plants and flowers, where the want of air, cleanliness, and light is so unfavourable to their growth and beauty. The germ of the main thought is to be found in Horace:

> Nempe inter varias nutritur sylva columnas,
> Laudaturque domus longos quae prospicit agros.
> Naturam expelles furca, tamen usque recurret.
>
> Lib. i, *epist.* 10, v. 22.

Pray write to me soon. . . . Ever, my dear Friend,

Faithfully, your obliged
Wm Wordsworth

1487. W. W. to H. C. R.

Address: H. C. Robinson Esq—
Endorsed: 28th Jan. 1841. Wordsworth, on the Southey family.
MS. Dr. Williams's Library.
Morley, i. 422.

[*In M. W.'s hand*]

Rydal Mount
Janry 26th 1841.

My dear Friend

As Mrs Wordsworth and Dora are making comments upon your Extracts from Mrs Southey's letter to Mrs Hughes,[2] the best thing I can do is to give you in writing a brief detail of such part as I have taken in this unhappy affair:[3] and pray understand that I

[1] Book iv, 'It is a flame,' etc. compared with Shenstone's *Ode to the Duchess of Somerset*, 'Her impulse nothing may restrain.' (note apparently by W. W., added to the MS.)

[2] Southey's friend (see pt. iii, L. 1235).

[3] H. C. R. had returned to London on the 22nd, his mind engrossed in the details of the Southey family quarrel (see pt. iii, L. 1350), which he had heard about from Dr. Henry Southey in London. He seems to have visited the Southeys just before he left Rydal (see Morley, i. 422).

do this, not in justification of myself, or to rebut the charges brought against me, but solely to furnish better means of determining the value of my judgement, a point in which I am mainly interested on account of the Connections of M[r] Southey who have been, and are suffering so much from the imputations cast on them.

And first—as every one must know, with whom I at any time conversed upon M[r] S's intended marriage, I thoroughly approved both of his marrying again, and of the choice he had made; which, as far as I knew, promised all that his friends could desire.

About the middle of Oct[r] 1838, the Miss Southeys (Bertha not being then married) chanced to be staying some time in this neighbourhood, and their Father's engagement with Miss Bowles was then communicated to them in a letter from himself. This intelligence was a shock to them—how could it be otherwise? They were wearing deep mourning for their Mother, who had not been buried 12 months; and whom they had watched day and night during the long and melancholy disease that preceded her dissolution. In addition to this, I observed that those consideration[s] and feelings which naturally indispose grown-up Daughters to look favorably upon their Father's second marriage, affected them more than was to be wished; and thinking that their notions upon second marriages in general, were not sufficiently enlarged, I took much pains to set them right on this subject, and I can safely say not without success.

This was my first step in the affair.

(In justice to Kate I must here add that she frequently said, that if her Father was to marry again, Miss B was of all Persons, from what she had heard, and seen of her in her writings, the one whom she should prefer.)

And now I proceed to give you a clear understanding of the next.

Not long after M[rs] S—'s arrival at Keswick I heard with great pain that there was no domestic harmony between the old and new Female Inmates of Greta Hall. Having opportunities of seeing Kate from time to time, I did all that I could to tranquillize her mind, urging her to bear the change, and all things consequent upon it that troubled her, with patience and resignation; and never did I shrink from endeavouring to rectify whatever appeared to me to be amiss in her own views, purposes and conduct; in this also I *know* I was in no small degree successful.

On the first Monday of July last, Mrs Wordsworth, in passing through Keswick, had an interview with Mrs Southey: I was in the Town at the same time, but an important engagement prevented my calling at Greta Hall, as I had anxiously wished to do; Mrs W. was deeply affected by the distress of mind with which Mrs S:, entering herself upon the subject, spoke of the discord in the house; and the earnestness with which she prayed to be judged charitably by her, and the family at Rydal Mount. The report of this strengthened greatly my desire to converse with Mrs S., and encouraged a hope that I might *possibly* be of some use in bringing about a reconcilement between her and Kate.

Accordingly I went over to Keswick on[1] purpose. I need not say how much the condition in which I found my poor friend, Southey, afflicted me. With Mrs S. I had a long conversation;—for truth's sake, and in order to prove that I was under no degree of partiality which would preclude a fair consideration of all she could urge in her own behalf, I did not conceal from Mrs S. what, as I thought, had been erroneous in Kate's judgement, and unwarrantable in her feelings; but I added, that before Mrs S's arrival at K: she had corrected and subdued all this—and to you I cannot but say my belief is, that had Mrs S: then taken a just view of Kate's feelings and claims as a Daughter; and of her own position in the family, and been as candidly and kindly disposed towards Kate as Kate was towards her, all things might have gone on as well as could be, under circumstances otherwise so afflicting.

To return to the interview I have pleasure in declaring that tho' Mrs S was extremely agitated, she took in good part every question I thought it necessary or expedient to put to her; and more than this—she entreated me to *cross*-question her, that was her very expression. In several points with which I had been dissatisfied, and *especially* in respect to her not having communicated to Mr Southey's daughters the state of body and mind in which their Father had been, during his residence in Miss Bowles's house before his marriage,[2]—and their protracted sojourn there after that event, she gave explanations to me that were most acceptable, as removing much of the blame I had previously attached to her conduct, (before her marriage) as evincing an error in judgement, if not a want of feeling. But

[1] on *written twice.*

[2] See pt. iii, L. 1281.

upon the whole the interview was sadly unpromising. The views she had taken of Kate's behaviour, the interpretations she had put upon her words and actions, and the notions *so different* from my own, which she obviously entertained of her general character, *extinguished*, when I bore in mind Kate's sentiments, whether right or wrong, towards Mrs S., the faint hope I had carried with me of being serviceable—I left the house however with a strong sympathy in M^rs^ S's suffering, and with an unqualified pity for her, as being exposed to trials which her constitution of body and mind, conjoined with her previous position, for so long a time, as a single Lady and sole Mistress of her house had made her unequal to.

Kate, tho' she was at K. at the time knew nothing of the conversation between Mrs S. and Mrs W. nor of my own with Mrs S. As I clearly foresaw that no good could come by communicating to her what had passed.

Succeeding weeks brought no alleviation of this unhappiness; but seeing Kate from [time][1] to time, I continued to do my best to calm, to soothe and support her in what, all circumstances considered, was assuredly a grievous lot.

As you know, the old, faithful and cherished Servant of Mr Southey was dismissed, and Kate, being at Rydal M^t^ when she heard of this from her Brother,[2] who came from K.[3] to tell her and M^r^ and Mrs Hill, what had occurred, I of course became acquainted with their plan of proceeding for the future. They mentioned two objects they were fixed upon; the one to have an arrangement for Kate living under their Father's roof, apart from intercourse, as much as possible, with Mrs S.; and the other that she might be allowed to see her Father once a day, alone at any convenient hour. I approved of both these proposals the one as the best means of preserving peace, and the other as being due to the rights and claims of filial affection.

And, as Cuthbert was about to write to his Uncle I authorized him, if he thought it would be of any service, to tell Dr Southey of that approval.

Here it may be proper to state that Cuthbert's letter making these same proposals to Mrs S., and dated by mistake 'Rydal *Mount*' instead of Rydal Lodge (Mr Hill's residence) I did *not* see, and therefore was in no way answerable for the terms in which it was expressed. Nor ought I here to omit, that I was not aware

[1] *Word dropped out.*

[2] Cuthbert. [3] Keswick.

that Cuth: had quitted his Father's roof, or that it was his intention to do so, till he had been two or three days in lodgings at Keswick. Had I been apprized of his purpose by himself, I should have spoken against it, in the belief that he might sufficiently have shewn to the Old Servant what was due to her long-tried merits and various claims, without going so far while he was dependent upon his Father;—but he, remembering what his Father had enjoined, and what his poor Mother and all her Children owed to this faithful Creature, thought otherwise,—and acted upon the dictates of his Conscience, as his own letter to Mr Myers[1] feelingly sets forth.

About this time I recommended to Kate to draw up a Narrative as impartially as she could, of all that had passed between Mrs S. and herself, and this I did chiefly in the hope that at some *future* day it might become an instrument for rectifying her Sister Warter's unkind and unjust notions respecting her character and conduct, and so assist in bringing about a reconciliation between them. But in consequence of Mrs S. having sent for and told her own story to Mr Myers, I thought it right (before he decided *against* Kate, that he should be made acquainted with *her* view of their common grievances) that the statement should be shewn to him, and this was done. Soon after this time M^r^ and Mrs Warter were about to visit Mrs S., upon which Dora wrote to them requesting from me that they would call at Rydal on their way to Keswick; for believing that their unfavourable impressions must have been taken from *one* quarter, I wished they should hear something of the other side, before they should meet the conflicting Parties—This proposal was rejected and drew from Mrs W. those unworthy reflections upon my conduct, so prominent in her's and her husbands letters.

And now there is only one point to touch upon, and that is of a negative character, and therefore not so palpable. Mr Myers (a clergyman of K. who had been *called* in by Mrs S. as a 'Defender'—her own word as gathered from your abstract) came over to Rydal to ask me to go to Keswick as a Mediator—this I declined for many reasons in which *both* Parties were considered; *two* only need be mentioned. I did not see how

[1] The Revd. Frederick Myers (1811–51), Fellow of Clare College, Cambridge, 1833–9, and perpetual curate of the new church of St. John's, Keswick, 1838–51: author of *Lectures on Great Men*, 1848. In 1842 he married as his second wife Susan Harriet (1811–78), youngest daughter of John Marshall of Hallsteads.

any benefit could arise from my presence, unless Mrs S. and Kate should be confronted, and point by point discussed between them, which I felt must be impossible, having witnessed their respective agitations when speaking of these matters *apart* from each other. And before things were pushed to such a painful extreme, a conviction was forced upon me, as I have told you above, that no reconciliation which might lead to *domestic* harmony, was practicable.

Kate is now at Rydal Mount and I need scarcely say, that during, and since Mrs Warter's unsisterly visit to this neighbourhood, I have continued, and shall continue to support, and do all in my power to comfort the Children of my afflicted Friend.

And now I have done, and have only to beg that you, my dear friend, Mr Kenyon, or any other friend of the Southey family, to whom you may shew this letter, would bear in mind what I have said in the beginning, of my motive for writing it.

I am glad that nothing untoward, beyond a little delay, on your journey occurred. We were all very sorry to part with you, and miss you much and shall be most happy to have you back again at any time. Let us hear from you ere long.

Ever most faithfully, Your's
[*signed*] Wm Wordsworth

Pray let M^{r} and Mrs H. N. Coleridge see this letter at your convenience—but do not allow it to be copied

[*In Dora W.'s hand*]

P.S. In two most important points the above letter is I feel deficient; it has not been stated that I was especially moved to give every possible consideration to this course of painful events by a knowledge of the very delicate state of health into which Kate had been thrown by the anxiety and fatigue she underwent during her dutiful attendance upon her Mother for the last three or four years of her life whilst she was labouring under a most afflicting malady—by a severe and dangerous sickness she was herself seized with—and subsequently by the ignorance in which she was kept as to the condition of her Father from the 12th of March when he left Keswick for Buckland till the last day of Augst when he returned home with Mrs Southey. This has been omitted—neither have I more than glanced at far the worst feature in these proceedings viz: M^{rs} S—s jealousy of the participation of M^{r} S—s daughter in the offices and attentions w^{h} his lamentable state required; this I believe to have been manifested far beyond what Kate's statement sets forth and M^rs^ S's reluctance to tolerate such participation has now been carried so far as to permit an interview between the Parent and daughter only once a week!!

I must not conclude without testifying that Kate, who has been at Rydal for the last six weeks during three of w^h^ she has been an Inmate of my house, has borne up under the most trying circumstances with admirable calmness and submitted patiently to the hard terms imposed upon her—has been dispassionate in her judgements of others and not in any way eager to justify herself.—

[*signed*] Wm Wordsworth

1488. DORA W. to H. C. R.

Endorsed: Feb. 2, 1841. Dora Wordsworth.
MS. Dr. Williams's Library.
Morley, i. 429 (—).

Tuesday night
Feby 2^d^ [1841]

Dear Sir,

Is that what you desire—I suppose so seeing your letter to me begins thus 'Dear Miss Wordsworth' well then Dear Sir—my Father bids me say it gives him much pleasure that his letter[1] was approved by you and Mr Kenyon and he further bids me say and there fore I must tho' I feel it to be an unnecessary caution that he does not wish the letter to be shewn except to those few friends who from the interest they take in this unhappy affair may be entitled to this mark of confidence. *If a convenient opportunity* should present itself my Father would wish the letter to be seen by Mr Taylor—[2] Miss Fenwick probably will be in town next month and you might prefer its being put into his hands by her rather than by yourself—but please yourself—we feel *very very* grateful to you for what you have already done—

[1] See previous letter.
[2] Henry Taylor.

Here is Edith's[1] sad letter pray make what use of it you judge best, for I know that will be the best.—

All unite with me in very affe^te regards and

Believe me *dear Sir*

faithfully yours
Dora Wordsworth

We regret with you that the apology made to Dr Southey, (who answered the note to Mrs Southey) for the *wording* of that note was not repeated in the second letter to Mrs Southey. Mrs Southey tho' doubtless knew such an apology had been made by [?Kate] but still it ought to have been made to her, and I am confident it was thro' mere oversight that it was not done.

Maybe I may accompany Miss Fenwick in her travels south—she kindly wishes me to do so and Father and Mother both seem to wish it too—

1489. W. W. to EDWARD MOXON

MS. Henry E. Huntington Library.
LY iii. 1064.

[*In M. W.'s hand*]

Feb^ry 4th [1841]

Dear Mr Moxon,

I put off replying to y^r last letter for a reason which I will now tell you—You know that I expressed in a series of Sonnets my thoughts upon the punishment of Death,[2] they amount to 13. I do not like to publish them in a newspaper, nor in any periodical publication, for with any of these I have carefully abstained from connecting myself. In consequence of this dislike it struck me, and feeling a strong objection to separate publication of these Sonnets, that it might answer to publish them in connection with a certain number of smaller pieces which I have in Mss.[3] These I have been correcting, and in a few days they will be fairly transcribed—but the whole would not amount to more than about 80 or 90 pages—and we think, and you will probably

[1] Edith Warter, Southey's daughter.

[2] See L. 1370 above. The sonnets were first published in the *Quarterly Review* for Dec. 1841, in an article by Henry Taylor. See Ls. 1554 and 1557 below.

[3] It is not clear which of the shorter poems are referred to here. But see L. 1496 below.

concur with us in opinion, that it would be injurious to the sale of the 6 Vols. to venture upon such a Publication—therefore I have given it up—and have merely told you this long story to account for my not having written to you before. For the present I have resolved to give up the double column—and in a few days I will write again, about commencing another impression of the 6 vols—but I wish to look them over first.

Be so good as discharge for me the enclosed bill at Longmans, at your convenience—with affec regards to Mrs and Miss M. from Mrs W. my daughter and myself

ever y^{rs}

W Wordsworth[1]

1490. W. W. to the SECRETARY OF THE WESTERN LITERARY CLUB

MS. Harvard University Library.
LY iii. 1065.

Rydal Mount Ambleside
Feb^{ry} 6th 1841.

Sir,

I must have seemed unworthy of the honor, in such flattering terms, proposed by the Western Literary Club, to my acceptance, if I had replied to your Letter instantly upon receipt of it.

After taking the subject into due consideration it appears that before coming to a decision I ought to know those particulars respecting the society with which you offer to make me acquainted, if I desire it. And may I ask, as the Society has already been in existence ten years if it be possessed of a Hall of Meeting and a Library, acquisitions which could not but tend to give it stability and ensure its permanence.

I have the honor to be
Sir
Your obedient Servant
Wm Wordsworth

To the Secretary of the Western literary Club.

[1] Not signed by W. W.

1491. W. W. to THOMAS NOON TALFOURD

MS. Berg Collection, New York Public Library. Hitherto unpublished.

[*In M. W.'s hand*]

Rydal Mount
Feb^{ry} 8th [1841]

My dear Sergeant Talfourd,

Tho' I have been silent you have been daily in my thoughts. Notwithstanding what I feel, I cannot bring myself to condole with you, upon the loss of the Copy-right bill, for this Session.[1] Indignation stifles every other emotion but gratitude towards you, for the noble and persevering exertions which you have made so long. I have seen nothing of the debate but a me[a]gre report in the St. James Chronicle that gives Macauley's[2] speech at some length, but alots to your notice of it,[3] only a few lines—Pray find a moment to tell me what had best be done in future—I would write and publish in my own name a letter addressed to you, in refutation of that trash advanced by Macauley if all that he has said had not been anticipated over and over by yourself and others. This same gentleman, if he has acted upon conscientious motives, without supposing him to be more stupid than I can think possible, ought to set about introducing a bill for the repeal of the law of Copyright as it now stands—in order to shorten its term, or rather abolish it altogether. But let me turn to another Subject. In your last letter

[1] The Copyright Bill had been dropped the previous July, but Talfourd reintroduced it on 27 Jan. 1841. In the resumed debate on the 29th, it was attacked by Warburton and Hume, but the First Reading was carried by 112 votes. The Second Reading came on 5th Feb., but further debate was adjourned for six months.

[2] Thomas Babington Macaulay, 1st Baron Macaulay (1800–59), had returned from India in 1838 and was now M.P. for Edinburgh and Secretary at War. His literary reputation was already well established by his contributions to the *Edinburgh Review*: his popular *Lays of Ancient Rome* followed in 1842, and his *History of England* began to appear in 1849. In the debate on 5 Feb. Macaulay had called the existing Copyright Law 'perfect', and argued against any further extension of the term: Copyright put an author in a monopoly position which should not be prolonged a day longer than was necessary for securing the good of literature.

[3] Speaking in defence of his own proposals, Talfourd had referred to the hardship of writers like Wordsworth, who found that just when his works were becoming profitable, the profit was snatched from him.

to me you held out a hope that we might have a glimpse of you at Rydal in the course of the Summer—the Summer passed away, and I looked for you in vain—I trust we may be more fortunate in the course of the next,—but before that comes, I hope to see you in London.

Ever faithfully
your very much obliged
[*signed*] Wm Wordsworth

1492. W. W. to UNKNOWN CORRESPONDENT

MS. Amherst College Library.
Amherst Wordsworth Collection, p. 64. LY iii. 1065.

Rydal Mount
Feb^{ry} 16th 1841

Dear Sir:

I have been indebted to you for several marks of attention of which I fear you will think from my silence that I have not been duly sensible. I have now to acknowledge your letter Feby 10th for which accept my thanks—also for the Newspapers which from time to time you have been so kind as to send me. The Copyright Bill was lost[1] for this session by the attractions of dinner, which proved stronger for its pledged supporters than its Enemies. The vote of thanks to the Forces in Syria[2] employed the House till seven, an ominous time for the Introduction of any but Party questions; so away flew our Friends, while the Warburtonian Phalanx,[3] men being generally firm and obstinate in proportion to their narrowness of mind and ignorance, remained at its Post.

You are quite at Liberty to make such use of my poems, as suits your present purpose, one which does you honor, and which I hope, if it does not promote the circulation of your paper, will I trust not tend to impede it. The Extracts which you

[1] On 5 Feb. See previous letter.

[2] On 5 Feb. Lord John Russell moved a Vote of Thanks in the House of Commons to Admiral Sir John Stopford, Sir Charles Napier, and others, for the successful outcome of the operations the previous autumn on the coast of Syria and at Acre against the Pasha of Egypt, whereby the Egyptian armies had been driven from the Lebanon.

[3] i.e. Henry Warburton and other opponents of the Copyright Bill.

have already given, both from Mr Rogers and myself, are well chosen.

Some time ago I received, I think from your neighborhood, a collection of Epitaphs upon Authors not long since dead—myself, by an odd mistake, included. The multitude of communications which reach me, especially since the reduction of postage to a trifle, is so great that I have neither time nor eyesight to acknowledge the greatest part of them. If you happen to know and to see the Gentleman who was so obliging as to send me that sheet of Epitaphs, pray thank him on my part. And now dear sir good bye, and excuse this scrawl which would have been better penned if my hand had not been made unsteady by an hour or two hard work in my garden from which I have just come.

Believe dear sir your obliged
Wm Wordsworth

1493. W. W. to C. W.

Address: To the Master, Trinity Lodge, Cambridge. [*In Dora W.'s hand*]
Postmark: (1) 17 Feb. 1841 (2) 19 Feb. 1841.
Stamp: (1) Ambleside (2) Cambridge.
MS. British Library.
Mem. (—). *LY iii. 1066* (—).

16 Feb [1841]

My dear Brother,

The good accounts which we receive from time to time of your progress towards perfect recovery from your late severe accident,[1] emboldens me to congratulate you in my own name and the whole of my family. We should have been dreadfully shocked had we been first made acquainted with your alarming state, as given in some of the Newspapers. But through the kindness of Christopher we were apprized of the melancholy event before. Susan has also been so good as to write several times, and to Charles and Mr Martin[2] also we have been indebted for their several reports.—

It remains now for us to join heartily, as we all do, in

[1] A letter from Dora W. to Susan Wordsworth of 2 Feb. (*British Library MSS.*) refers to the accident without making clear the details.

[2] Francis Martin (see pt. ii, L. 547).

expressing a wish that being convalescent you would not be tempted to over-exert yourself. I need scarcely add that we all unite with you and your Sons, with Susan, and your other relatives and all your friends in fervent thanks to almighty God for his goodness in preserving you. As a Brother I feel deeply, and regarding your life as most valuable to the community I the more rejoice in the prospect of your life being prolonged—

We are in pretty good health except Dora who is both weak and thin, I might almost say emaciated to a degree which it gives me pain to look upon; though thank God there does not appear to be any threatening of immediate danger. Mary and Dora unite in love to you and believe me

my dear Brother
most affectionately yours
Wm Wordsworth

1494. W. W. to WILLIAM PEARSON

MS. untraced.
Pearson.

[Spring 1841]

. . .At Mayence turn from the Rhine to Frankfort—Darmstadt—Heidelberg—by Carlsruhe to Baden Baden—Strasburg—then by Hornberg or Freyburg to Schaffhausen, see Falls of the Rhine—then to Zurich—Wallenstadt Lake—up the Valley of Glarus—Altorf—Schwytz—Mt. Righi—Lucerne—Lake of Four Cantons—up the Banks of the Reuss—over Mt. St. Gothard to Lake Maggiore, Boromean Islands, Lake Lugano, thence to Lake Como, which see perfectly—Varese—Lake Orta—Domo d'Ossola, see religious stations and cells—over the mountain to Bryg in the Valais—turn off to Gemmi Pass—to Kanda Grund[1] and Lakes of Thun and Brienz—up the Valley of Oberhasli, see Falls of the Handec at Meyringen—thence to Lungern Zee—Sarnen—to Berne and Geneva by any way most promising—make the Tour round the Lake of Geneva—see Chamouny—see as many of the Passes as you can. . .

[*cetera desunt*]

[1] On the Kander river, which flows into the lake of Thun.

1495. W. W. to THE SECRETARY OF THE WESTERN LITERARY CLUB

MS. National Library of Scotland. Hitherto unpublished.

Rydal Mount
Ambleside
1st March 1841.

Dear Sir,

Nothing but incessant engagements and frequent interruptions interfering with my daily intention, could have prevented my answering your second Letter so early as would have precluded the necessity of writing the one of enquiry received yesterday. I have now to thank you for that and your second Letter in reply to the questions I had asked,[1] and for the satisfactory statements and information which you have kindly given.—There is one important point, however, remaining to which I must be permitted now to advert. Your Extracts from the minutes of the Society showed that it has resolved to stand clear, as it hitherto has done, from disputes in matters of political doctrine and party-politics. Am I at liberty to infer that the same judicious and becoming caution has been and will be applied to religious opinions and concerns?—I am myself an attached Member of the Church of England; and it would gratify me to be assured that a decided majority at least of your Body not only cannot be justly charged with infidelity and Scepticism, but is in like manner in communion with the Kirk of Scotland, the Episcopal Church or some sound and durable society of Christians. If the answer to this enquiry which I feel to be justified by its importance prove such as I wish; and the office of Patron would really bring with it as you intimate no Duties that would make demands upon time of which at my age I have little to spare, I shall be well pleased to accept the honor proposed to me by the Western Literary Club.

I remain dear Sir,
respectfully yours
Wm Wordsworth

[1] See L. 1490 above.

1496. W. W. to EDWARD MOXON

MS. Henry E. Huntington Library.
K (—). LY iii. 1086.

March 4th [1841]

My dear Mr Moxon,

We were much grieved to hear of your affliction,[1] which Mrs W. and I can more especially sympathize with, from having ourselves lost two most promising children, the elder little more than six years of age. We hope, as we wish and pray, that both the Mother and yourself may through God's mercy be enabled to bear the heavy loss with the resignation which is required of Christians. Mrs Wordsworth unites with me in sincere condolence—We hope that your other little ones are well.—

Miss Fenwick and my Daughter left us this morning together, for London, but Dora proceeds from the Station to Mrs Gee's Hendon, and has two other visits to pay in that neighbourhood, first to Dr Wordsworth at Harrow, and then to Mrs Hoare. Before Miss Fenwick and she leave London at the beginning of next month, Dora will be a few days, no doubt, in London, and will then make a point of calling upon you and Mrs Moxon. In the mean while if you should be inclined to take a ride you will find her at Hendon in the course of the next week, afterwards at Harrow. Miss Fenwick is for a fortnight at Mr Taylor's, 16 Blandford Square London, and when you have a few minutes to spare, it might perhaps be agreeable to you to call upon her. She has been staying with us three months—

I have entrusted the looking over the six volumes to Mr Carter, who is much more able than myself to detect errors. He has been hindered by excessive pressure of office business, that has come upon us: by the bye, without remuneration from the reduction of duty and changes in the post off. But he will have his papers to send off in a couple of days, and then the printing[2] may commence.

By way of *secret* I must let you know, that I have just been copying out about 2000 Lines of miscellaneous Poems, from Mss, some of which date so far back [as] 1793;[3] and others from

[1] The death of Moxon's eldest son Edward on 2 Mar.

[2] Of the *Poetical Works*, 6 vols., 1841.

[3] W. W. was now beginning to put together *Poems, Chiefly of Early and Late Years*, 1842, including *Guilt and Sorrow*, and *The Borderers*. See L. 1498 below.

that time, at various periods, to the present day. If I could muster a 1000 lines more, there would be enough for another volume, to match pretty well in size with the rest, but this not being the case I am rather averse to publication. You will hear more of this hereafter. Mrs W and I will not be in Town till the middle of May at the earliest.—And now with many and sincere good wishes farewell.

ever faithfully yours
Wm Wordsworth

1497. W. W. to BENJAMIN ROBERT HAYDON

MS. Professor Willard Pope.
LY iii. 1069.

Rydal Mount
March 4th 1841

My dear Haydon,

I can now say *positively* that I shall not be in London till the third week of May at the earliest.—

I am much concerned by your sad account of poor Mrs Haydon. Pray God she may be better—ever faithfully

yours
Wm Wordsworth

1498. W. W. to THOMAS POWELL

Address: Thos Powell Esqre, 2 Leadenhall Street, London.
MS. University of Virginia Library.
LY iii. 1070.

Monday morning, 10 o'clock (Mar. 1841]

My dear Mr Powell,

It is not without considerable uneasiness that I have so long put off writing to you, but all my friends, and many strangers have been used in the same way, unavoidably so, on account of pressing engagements, and numerous interruptions. In fact I am preparing for an absence from home which probably will last three months, and I thought it right previous to my departure to revise several Mss[1] written at different periods of my life; and which would have been utterly lost but for the attention I have been bestowing upon them. Besides, I am so pestered in consequence of the deluge of Letters and small pamphlets in prose and verse, and Mss, which the reduced postage has poured in upon me, that if I were to attend to one half of them I should really have no time for myself. Let me now say that I am glad to learn the Chaucer is doing so well[2]—I have scarcely had time to read more than one half of it, but I am much pleased with the execution in general. Mr Horne[3] is particularly successful; but in my opinion he ought not to have meddled with the Reve's Tale; it is far too gross for the present age, and in consequence of the necessity of softening it down, the humour, such as it is, has evaporated. The Franklin's tale is as well done as need or can be.—I must tell you frankly, I have not found time yet to read your Nun's Priest's Tale[4]—and here I must explain. The lengthening days now allow me some time to spare for reading, but before I had scarcely any; for, as perhaps you are aware, I have not eyes for reading at all by Candlelight; and as I never walk less than two hours a day, the short days have been by necessity very unproductive of reading to me. You will excuse the length at which I have gone into this subject, and pray make my apologies to Dr Smith for not having replied to the Letter he kindly addressed to me long ago.[5] In the printed verses you sent

[1] These probably included *Guilt and Sorrow*, in preparation for the 1842 volume. See L. 1578 below.

[2] *Chaucer's Poems Modernized* had a mixed reception. In the *Athenaeum*, 6 Feb. 1841, Henry Chorley had commended most of the contributors, including W. W. himself; but he condemned Horne for diluting Chaucer 'to the level of Cockney comprehensions', and castigated the carelessness of the editors in attributing a passage of Drayton on the title-page to W. W.

[3] In addition to his versions of the General Prologue, *The Reeve's Tale*, and *The Franklin's Tale*, Horne provided an introduction discussing Chaucer's strengths as a poet and the difficulty of rendering him into modern English. He maintained that W. W. and S. T. C (and Keats and Shelley) in their style of versification were working in the tradition of Chaucer and Milton. See also Ann Blainey, *The Farthing Poet, A Biography of Richard Hengist Horne . . .*, 1968, pp. 114–15, 268.

[4] W. W. is confused here. *The Nun's Priest's Tale* was not included in the volume. Powell's contributions consisted of three stories from *The Legend of Good Women* and the *Flower and the Leaf*.

[5] Southwood Smith had written on 14 Dec. 1840 (*WL MSS.*), about his sanatorium (see L. 1382 above), and his efforts on a Parliamentary commission

me some time ago are several stanzas that pleased me much—I have this moment glanced my eye over them but of two that particularly touched me, I can only find one, it is

> Know! those who find no peace on earth will find none in the grave—

Mr Chapman's[1] Verses give indications of a very poetical mind. He must much be deplored by all who knew him—are you aware that there are several lines word for word or nearly so from Verses of mine—the Author being probably altogether unconscious of it. This gave me pleasure as a p[roo]f how familiar this interesting young M[an] must have been with my Poems. I am obliged to conclude, having to go fr[om] home for the day, to my great inconvenience

ever faithfully yours
Wm Wordsworth

1499. W. W. to ISABELLA FENWICK

MS. WL.
LY iii. 1071 (—).

Friday Even^{g} [Mar. 1841]

My dearest Friend,

I have just seen Donaldson who behaved very well (as he always does) about your Carriage. He said he would take it upon your terms, and make what he could of it; and added that with Mr Brown the Coachmaker of Kendal he had had considerable dealings, and he would try to make him take it, and if he could get more for it than you are prepared to accept so much the better, and the addition should be taken in to your account. He will send for the Carriage to Lancaster, so you may be quite easy about it. When I consider how useful the Carriage has been to you, and how many happy hours you and I have spent in it

of inquiry to benefit working children who were not protected by the recent Factory Act: 'I have engaged in it chiefly in the hope of being enabled by it to help on the great cause of National Education. The extent to which the minds and morals of large classes of the community are neglected is truly deplorable and my trust is that when the real magnitude of this evil is made known it will lead to some practical measure not only for improving the physical but also the intellectual and moral condition of these neglected classes.'

[1] See pt. iii, L. 1199.

together, I am sorry that it is not going into the hands of some one, who I could be sure would use it well, or I was going to say, at least treat it with respect.

A thousand thanks for your affectionate Letters. We are fearful that either you or Dearest Dora or both of you may catch that ugly influenza. We hope that the contents of the Letter forwarded from Paris are more favorable. The Marshalls of Coniston[1] called at Rydal, I mean at the bottom of the hill (we did not see them), to look after Aubrey[2] who has been unwell, and still is so. The weather here has been most glorious, as warm almost as June; yet two or three nights ago Windermere was skinned over with ice which could not have been but for the breathless calmness. Dearest Mary looks and is much better than when you left us, for myself I feel nervous and a good deal exhausted, because I cannot keep my poor brain quiet. I could sleep like a top all the afternoon, but in the night or rather morning after 4 o'clock I make poor work of it.—Mary has transcribed all the Poems except the Sonnets and my work of correction is over. But I have not yet had courage to look at the tragedy.[3]—I composed a Sonnet on my walk home after I left you, and I have since written upwards of 100 Lines in blank Verse, the scene Italy;[4] about 50 more will I hope finish the Poem. Do my very very dear Friend take care of yourself; and urge Dora to do the same. I seem to think that I have said too much about my own nerves; what I feel is, a certain numbness, about my wrist and finger especially. Over exertion of mind is I know the cause; but I trust it will go off when my time of absolute Holiday arrives. This is the second letter I have written this evening and I have another to be written, so with a thousand good wishes and kindest remembrances, I remain my most dear Friend

faithfully yours
Wm Wordsworth

[1] John Marshall's third son, James, and his bride Mary Spring Rice (see L. 1474 above), daughter of Lord Monteagle.

[2] Aubrey de Vere (see pt. ii, L. 739), Mary Spring Rice's cousin, was now making his first visit to the Lakes. See *Recollections of Aubrey de Vere*, 1897, pp. 120–2. He saw more of W. W. in London in the summer (see L. 1517 below).

[3] *The Borderers*.

[4] *Musings near Aquapendente* (*PW* iii. 202 ff.).

Friday evening
9 oclock—

The news of threatened war with America[1] troubles me much: do mention this subject when you write, as far at least as concerns your own property.

[*M. W. writes*]

I was sorry to find that the James Marshalls had been here without our seeing them. There was no need that their horses should have come up the hill, but had a Servant come up to say they were we should gladly have gone down to say good bye to them. But there was no message. I hope they are not hurt that we did not go to see them at C.[2] which we should, especially as the weather has been so lovely, have been most happy to have done—but we had the idea (I trust not a mistaken one) that they meant to be quite left to themselves on this occasion. If d^{r} friend you find that it was otherwise pray explain this misunderstanding—

My Sister Joanna is at Liverpool—she may be here tomorrow —but I rather think not till Monday. We go to Brigham with dear Joanna if weather continues favorable, next week.—God bless you dearest Friend—M. W.

1500. W. W. to UNKNOWN CORRESPONDENT

MS. Cornell. Hitherto unpublished.

Rydal Mount
March 18th —41

Madam,

Your Letter was unfortunately put aside and the occasion of it slipped out of my memory. I now sit down with pleasure to comply with your request

I remain,
Madam
sincerely yours
Wm Wordsworth

[1] The main point in dispute was the question of the north-east boundary, discussed in the U.S. Senate on 1 Mar.

[2] Coniston.

1501. W. W. to ROBERT MONTGOMERY[1]

Address: R. Montgomery Esq., 12 Leigh Street, Red Lion Square.
Postmark: 24 Mar. 18[ ].
Stamp: Charing Cross.
MS. Cornell. Hitherto unpublished.

[*c.* 23 Mar. ? 1841]

My dear Sir,

If you think my name would be of any use in the list you propose it is quite at your service.

It will give me pleasure to receive your forthcoming Poem both as a mark of your esteem, and for the gratification which I do not doubt the perusal of it will afford me.

It may be sent by your Publisher to Whitakers Ave Mary Lane to be forwarded in their first parcel through Mr Richardson of Kendal, directed to Mr Troughton Bookseller Ambleside for Mr Wordsworth Rydal Mount.

I remain Sir
Very sincerely
Your obliged
Wm Wordsworth

1502. W. W. to H. C. R.

Endorsed: 18th April 1841. Wordsworth.
MS. Dr. Williams's Library.
Morley, i. 431.

12 North Parade
Bath
April 18th [1841]

My dear Friend,

It will be a fortnight, what a blunder? *three* weeks next Wednesday since Mrs W and I left home, for Brinsop, where after stopping a day at Birmingham we remained ten days. Thence we came along the Wye the banks of which noble river I

[1] See pt. iii, L. 868. This letter cannot be dated with certainty, nor can the poem it refers to be identified among Montgomery's numerous publications. But it perhaps refers to the new edition of *Satan, A Poem* (1830), which appeared in 1841.

was truly glad to revisit—to Tintern Abbey where last Tuesday we had the great pleasure of meeting Miss Fenwick and Dora. We slept at Chepstow, thence by steam to Bristol, and to Bath immediately by rail, just by the Watch 23 minutes!——It is now high time to thank you my dear Friend for the valuable, and what will be to us the most useful present, of Tegg's (you see I can bring my Pen upon this occasion to write the name) *Teggs* Cyclopedia.[1] It is a sort of Book which all my life I have wanted, but on account of expense never thought it right to buy. In fact I had too many other drafts upon my means.—The Books reached Rydal since we left home.—This day I have attended, along with Mary, Widcomb Church, where as I have heard from you, your Mother's Remains lie.[2] I was there also the day before yesterday, and the place is so beautiful especially at this season of verdure, and blossoms, that it will be my favourite walk while I remain here, and I hope you will join us and take this ramble with me. We shall remain here till the 11th of May but the sooner you come the better.—

Some time before Mary and I left home we inscribed your name upon a Batch of Italian Memorials, which you must allow me to dedicate to you when the day of Publication shall come.[3] One of these pieces suggested at Acqua Pendente extends to 360 Lines[4] blank verse.—Pray let me hear from you at your early convenience. Miss Fenwick is not so well by any means as she was in Westmorland; and Dora's looks are not at all improved since she left home but this is not be wondered at considering the plunge she is going to make—[5]

All unite in kindest remembrances.

Ever your affectionate Friend
Wm Wordsworth

[1] *The London Encyclopaedia of Science, Art, Literature, and Practical Mechanics*, 22 vols., 1825–9, published by Thomas Tegg (see L. 1374 above).

[2] See pt. iii, L. 1312.

[3] *The Memorials of a Tour in Italy, 1837* were inscribed to H. C. R. in a dedicatory poem dated 14 Feb. 1842, and included in the *Poems, Chiefly of Early and Late Years.*

[4] Actually 372 lines.

[5] Her impending marriage to E. Q. at Bath on 11 May. As Dora W. explained to Susan Wordsworth on 25 Apr.: 'When I told you at Harrow that I should not return with my Father and Mother to London but must go to look after old Aunty I only told you what was the fact then as is now, tho' then I did not expect I should travel north with so dear a companion as God willing I am now likely to

1503. W. W. to LORD MONTEAGLE

Endorsed: W. Wordsworth 20 April 41 Congratulations.
MS. untraced.
LY iii. 1074.

Bath 12 North Parade [19 Apr. 1841]

My dear Lord,

Nearly a week has elapsed since your marriage, and I have often in mind congratulated you and my dear Friend Mary Anne, upon your Union.[1]—I now sit down to express to you both my sincere good wishes, and the firm assurance which my long knowledge of Lady Monteagle's excellent character gives me that there is every prospect of your being happy together to your hearts desire—

As it is probable that I shall in a few weeks be in Town with Mrs W— who joins with me in all that I feel upon this occasion,—I need say no more, than that it will give us both great pleasure, should [we][2] be fortunate enough to meet you there.

I have the honor to be,
with kindest remembrances
sincerely and faithfully
your much obliged
Wm Wordsworth

P.S. We left Aubrey[3] improving decidedly, three weeks ago—

do. It was in that time determined we should marry in the course of the summer but I did not expect the awful event would take place till July—since then however minor difficulties have been removed thro' Miss Fenwick's kindness and I am thankful, very thankful, not to have so many weeks as I expected to look forward to a point in one's life w^h^ when quite resolved upon the sooner it is got over the better for body and mind.' (*British Library MSS.*)

[1] Lord Monteagle had married Mary Anne Marshall on 13 Apr. He replied on 22 Apr. (*WL MSS.*), thanking W. W. for his congratulations. 'You know the full value of her who has ventured to confide her happiness to me . . .'

[2] *Word dropped out.*

[3] Aubrey de Vere (see L. 1499 above). In his *Recollections*, p. 109, he records a breakfast party later on in London with Whewell, Thirlwall, F. D. Maurice, and W. W. This was probably the party at the Marshalls' on 8 June, noted by H. C. R. (*HCR* ii. 595). Frederick Denison Maurice (1805–72), author of *The Kingdom of Christ*, 1838, was this year elected Professor of English Literature and History at King's College, London. An 'Apostle' at Cambridge and friend of J. C. Hare, he had known W. W. since at least 1836. (See *The Life of Frederick Denison Maurice*, ed. Frederick Maurice, 2 vols., 1884, i. 199.)

1504. W. W. to EDWARD MOXON

Address: Edward Moxon Esqre, 44 Dover Street, London. [*In M. W.'s hand*]
Postmark: (1) 20 Apr. 1841 (2) 21 Apr. 1841.
Stamp: Bath.
MS. Henry E. Huntington Library.
LY iii. 1073.

12 North Parade
Bath
19th April [1841]

My dear Mr Moxon,

Mr Robinson has just arrived here; from what passed between him and you, and also between Dora and you, concerning the delay in bringing out the new Edition of my Poems, I am fearful of some thing having gone wrong.—It cannot be less than six weeks since Mr Carter sent off the few corrections which he found to be necessary, with a request from me that the edition should be struck off as speedily as possible.—The Letter was addressed directly to Mr Bradbury.[1] I hope it reached him duly, for I am certain it was sent off regularly. Should he unfortunately not have received it, pray let Mr Carter be written to instantly at Rydal, and I hope he will be able to furnish the Corrections. If they were duly received by Mr Bradbury, and he has not gone to work immediately and regularly proceeded, he must have been greatly in fault. At all events be so good, as to do all in your power to make up for lost time,

ever faithfully yours
Wm Wordsworth

1505. W. W. to JOHN PEACE

MS. untraced.
Mem. (—). *K* (—). LY iii. 1073.

12 North Parade, Bath, April 19, 1841.

My dear Mr Peace,

Here I am and have been since last Wednesday evening. I came down the Wye and passed through Bristol, but arriving there at

[1] The printer.

the moment the railway train was about to set off, and being in the company of four ladies (Miss Fenwick, Mrs Wordsworth, and my daughter, and niece[1]), I had not a moment to spare, so could not call on you, my good friend, which I truly regretted. Pray spare an hour or two to come here, and then we can fix a day when, along with my daughter, I can visit Bristol, see you, Mr Cottle, and Mr Wade.[2] . . . All unite in kindest regards.

Ever yours
Wm Wordsworth

1506. W. W. to ROBERT SHELTON MACKENZIE

MS. Cornell.
The Autographic Mirror, 1865, p. 210.

Bath 19th April
—41

My dear Sir,

Your kind Letter has followed me to this place. The Newspaper was not sent after me, but it is of less consequence, for having been lately in the neighbourhood where the horrible event occurred I had both an opportunity of seeing the provincial Papers, and hearing many particulars about it, and the Man who had done the deed. It grieves me much to see that a false and short-sighted harmony induced so many well-meaning persons to plead for remission of punishment. A blacker offense cannot be conceived.

I remain dear Sir
Your much obliged
Wm Wordsworth

I shall not return to Rydal till the middle of June—

[1] Ebba Hutchinson from Brinsop.

[2] For Josiah Wade, see pt. iii, L. 1341. W. W. also saw Kenelm Digby (see pt. i, L. 376), during this visit to Bath. 'Mr. D. is looking very well and very handsome', Dora W. wrote to Susan Wordsworth on the 25th, 'but not to my eye not half so interesting as when I knew him as the pale faced knight of the Cam.' (*British Library MSS.*).

1507. W. W. to MRS ANNE HARE[1]

Address: Mrs Hare, Firfield, Bristol. [*In Dora W.'s hand*]
Endorsed: Note from Wordsworth.
MS. Cornell. Hitherto unpublished.

Bath
12 North parade
Thursday 29th [April][2] 41

Dear Madam,

It will give Mrs Wordsworth, myself, and the rest of our Party, three Ladies, including my Daughter,[3] much pleasure to accept of your invitation to dinner, just received through Mr Robinson.[4] To morrow by half past five at the latest, we shall be with you, unless of which there is no probability, the weather shall change to bad.—

Pray present our kind remembrances to your Brother, whom I trust we shall have the pleasure of seeing, (indeed that is one of my leading objects in going to Bristol)

and believe me
dear Madam
sincerely yours
Wm Wordsworth

1508. W. W. to EDWARD MOXON[5]

MS. untraced.
K (—).

12 North Parade, Bath.
[late Apr. 1841]

. . . The great objection to such a book at such a price seems to

[1] Joseph Cottle's sister (see pt. i, L. 347).

[2] Month added in another hand.

[3] The other two being I. F. and Ebba Hutchison.

[4] H. C. R., who had arrived in Bath on 19 Apr. See *HCR* ii. 592–4.

[5] According to K, Robert G. Clarke, of St. George's, Norwich, wrote to W. W. on 24 Apr. to enquire whether he held the copyright of Hine's *Selections from the Poems of William Wordsworth*, which Moxon had published in 1831 (see pt. ii, L. 617), and to ask if there was any chance of its being republished in a still cheaper form for more extensive use in schools and families than hitherto.

be the difficulty of making its existence known to those who would be most likely to become purchasers. . . .

1509. W. W. to C. W.

MS. WL. Hitherto unpublished.[1]

[Bath]
[3 *or* 4 May 1841]

My dear Brother,

Your affectionate and generous kindness to your, I trust, deserving Niece, has quite overpowered me and her Mother, to whom I could not forbear communicating the Contents of your Letter.[2]—

I see no occasion for any remark from me on the Deed; I have made one which a reperusal of the deed makes me think superfluous. I have only to put one Question. Supposing she should die leaving one child that should attain the age of 21, should you wish that child immediately to have the disposal of that money by Will or otherwise; or supposing two or three living children, should the child who had reached the majority have one half or one third immediately at its disposal, according to the number, the others being minors. It seems reasonable that these points should be settled, or would you prefer the whole 1000£ to remain undivided till the youngest attained the age of 21. I merely suggest these things, not requiring any observations from you, but that they may be determined as you think best.

I have not thought it necessary to wait for their arrival to [?

'Though all masters must value it and know it is well worth its price as *the best book ever published for young persons*, yet they do not like to furnish more than the higher classes with the book at 5s. I think that an edition of 2s. 6d. is highly desirable and would be a great boon to the public.' W. W. replied on the back of this letter to Moxon that he had answered this correspondent by saying that he 'found the expense of advertising such a book, to be sold at half a crown, would swallow up all the profits,' but that he would send his letter to the publisher for his decision.

[1] The first sentence was published in *Mem.* and *LY.* iii. 1074.

[2] C. W. had written on 1 May (*WL. MSS.*) proposing to set up a trust for Dora W., now that family objections to her marriage to E. Q. were at an end. £1000 was to be settled on her, the interest to be hers for life, and thereafter for her issue; otherwise it was to be divided equally between John and Willy W. He wrote again on 6 May: hence the dating of W. W.'s letter.

adopt] your proposal to make three Trustees, being assured that they will be happy to undertake the charge, and be duly sensible of your contingent arrangement for their benefit.

We expect John this evening or tomorrow, and W^{m} towards the end of the week. Dora's marriage is to take place on the 11th.

I am truly sensible of the delicacy which induced you, my dear Brother, to abstain entirely from taking any steps connected with this marriage previous to *my opposition* (for it was in truth my *opposition* that held out long after the poor mother's) was[1] withdrawn. And it is my duty *now* to mention to you, that, Mr Quillinan having *no* property of his own, and no present means of Support for himself and his two Daughters so long as *their* maternal uncle should live, but what are dependent upon his Brother and thc services he. . . .

[*cetera desunt*]

1510. M. W. to H. C. R.

Endorsed: May 1841. Mrs Wordsworth.
MS. Dr. Williams's Library.
Morley, i. 432.

Sunday Ev^{g} [9 May 1841]

My very dear Friend

I have but a few moments to tell you of our plans, since they were fixed—but I must first thank you for yur communication,[2] which was most welcome—and thankful were we for the *measure* of good which your note contained. We were glad that you were spared further attendance upon y^{r} poor Nephew[3] and Niece *for the present*—for truly you yourself needed rest.

Tuesday is to be the important day[4]—and in the afternoon the pair will take their way *towards* Alfoxden (you know that was

[1] *Written thus.*

[2] H. C. R. had left Bath on 4 May to return to London.

[3] Tom Robinson was dying of consumption, and H. C. R. had visited him at Clifton while staying at Bath.

[4] For Dora W.'s marriage to E. Q. On 6 May, I. F. wrote to Henry Taylor from Bath: 'Our marriage still stands for the 11th, and I do sincerely trust nothing will interfere with its taking place on that day, for all parties seem prepared for it. Mr. Wordsworth behaves beautifully.' (*Autobiography of Henry Taylor*, i. 337).

W^m^ and his Sisters residence) and Nether Stowey—Meaning to reach Wells that night—Next day, We all depart—(somewhat sorry to leave our pleasant abode here) Miss F. W^m^ and myself taking the same route, intending to overtake them, and pick them up, before we reach the object of this journey.—Whence we all return to Bridgewater on Thursday Evening and there separate, Q. and his Wife to proceed to Glo[u]cester to join the Rail way, for West^d^ and we to Miss F's Sisters, near Taunton—John and W., the younger, bend their course direct North on the day we depart.—And no more can I say for I must send directly to the Post—

Only d^r^ friend let us hear of y^r^ Brother and of yourself—directed to

Pophams Esq[1]
Begborough
n^r^ Taunton

to tell us of your B^r^[2] and yourself—we shall perhaps remain there one week—but you shall thence hear of our future movements meanwhile God bless you—the 2 W^s^ and John are at Bristol to day. Q. arrived last night

ever aff^dy^ y^rs^
M. W

1511. W. W. to JOHN PEACE

MS. untraced.
Mem. (—). Grosart (—). K (—). LY iii. 1074.

Bath May 11, 1841

My dear Mr Peace,

This morning my dear daughter was married[3] at St James's in this place. . . .

[1] I. F.'s brother-in-law Francis Popham (see pt. iii, L. 1301).

[2] Thomas Robinson.

[3] The ceremony was performed by John W. in the presence of E. Q.'s brother John, and Dora W. was given away by her brother Willy. Ebba Hutchinson and Isabella Fenwick, I.F.'s niece, were the bridesmaids. E. Q. subsequently sent long accounts to his two daughters Rotha and Jemima on 12 May and 21 May respectively (*WL MSS.*), in which he stressed that W. W. had only been prevented from attending by a sudden outburst of feeling at the last moment,

Tomorrow we leave Bath for Wells, and thence to the old haunts of Mr Coleridge and myself and dear sister, about Alfoxden.[1] Adieu

W. W.

1512. W. W. to HENRY REED

Address: Henry Reed Esqre, Philadelphia. Via Boston.
Postmark: 19 May 1841.
Stamp: Taunton.
Endorsed: Rec. June 24.
MS. Cornell.
K (—). *Wordsworth and Reed, p. 49.*

[Bagborough]
May 15th 1841

My dear Mr Reed,

I am now on a visit along with Mrs Wordsworth and our Friend Miss Fenwick to Miss F's Brother in law Mr Popham

when he and Dora were left alone together. 'Nothing indeed could be kinder than he and *all* have been', he wrote to Rotha. And M. W. voiced her sense of happiness and relief a few days later to Susan Wordsworth: '. . . when I tell you that I had the satisfaction of making Dora happy, by attending her to the Altar, and witnessing the calmness with which she went thro' the affecting and awful ceremony—and that, in all other respects, the day went off beyond, far far beyond my expectations—and that she felt herself blessed in having *us* all around her—(tho' her poor Father could not go to Church, and I think *she* could not have supported herself had he been able to do so—as he was *willing*), you must now excuse my saying more . . .' (*MW*, p. 245).

[1] 'We had two perfect days for our visit to Wells, Alfoxden, etc.,' I. F. wrote to Henry Taylor on 20 May. 'They were worthy of a page or two in the poet's life. Forty-two years, perhaps, never passed over any human head with more gain and less loss than over his. There he was again, after that long period, in the full vigour of his intellect, and with all the fervent feelings which have accompanied him through life; his bodily strength little impaired, but grey-headed, with an old wife and not a young daughter. The thought of what his sister, who had been his companion here, was then and now is, seemed the only painful feeling that moved in his mind. He was delighted to see again those scenes . . . where he had been so happy—where he had felt and thought so much. He pointed out the spots where he had written many of his early poems, and told us how they had been suggested.' (*Autobiography of Henry Taylor*, i. 338).

who lives in the rich and beautiful Vale of Taunton in Somersetshire. It is six weeks since we left home and your Letter of the 14th of April was duly forwarded to me at Bath where we have been residing for about a month.

The documents to which you allude I have not yet seen; but shall find them on my return home. For them and your two Letters[1] I most sincerely and cordially thank you. Upon their contents beyond the expression of mere thanks I have little to say, but that Miss Fenwick is determined to await the probability of a rise in the value of her Pensylvanian securities. With regard to the United States Bank she has reconciled her mind to the loss, and is quite prepared for the worst. In respect to the larger investment she trusts that there will be found integrity in the state sufficient to redeem its character, and if that be not wanting she trusts she and the other creditors may yet come out of the concern without much loss. She will await the issue in tranquillity. It is however her wish to place the money she still has in America, upon European Securities as soon as it can be done without a loss greater than it is probable she would have to incur were she to wait some time. Upon this point we should all be glad of your opinion, and if any preparatory steps could be taken to facilitate the transfer by Power of Attny or other Representative, so that the sale might take place at the most promising opportunity she would be glad to be instructed how to proceed for that purpose—

As to the Mississippi Bonds I have little hope about them. The Remittances for payment of interest have, I am told now failed, and I fear that the reputation for integrity in those southern States is very low indeed. This feature I feel the more on account of its coming to our knowledge a day or two before my only daughter was married, so that nearly one half of her little fortune is swallowed up; and what I feel still more is for Mrs Wordsworth['s] sister[2] who having many years ago lost 1500£ by Columbian Bonds has now in her old age to suffer this 2nd loss, along with a Brother who is in narrow circumstances. The money was trusted to the Missisippi, by a deceased Sister. Pray forgive this mere business Letter, when I hear from you again I

[1] Reed had written on 25 Feb. and 14 Apr. with further advice on I. F.'s American investments in the light of the 'disastrous condition' of the Bank of the United States, and enclosing an official report on the Pennsylvanian State debt. (See *Wordsworth and Reed*, pp. 43–9).

[2] Joanna Hutchinson.

will write upon miscellaneous and more agreeable matters. I hope Mrs Reeds health is reestablished.

ever faithfully your most obliged ever faithfully our most obliged Friend[1]

Wm Wordsworth

1513. M. W. to H. C. R.

Endorsed: 22d May 1841. Mrs Wordsw.
MS. Dr. Williams's Library.
Morley, i. 434.

Exeter May 22d [1841]
Sat: Evening

My dear Friend

So far have we arrived on our pleasant Tour, and that we may not miss the satisfaction of hearing from you I lose no time in telling you, that, if you write on the receipt of this, your letter may reach us directed to 'Elliott's Royal Hotel Devenport'—We stay here over tomorrow and on Monday proceed to that place—where I understand we shall be detained, by the interests thereof, for three days. Thence we proceed Coastwise towards Lyme—and soon after part from our dear friend[2]—who will return to Bagboro' and Wm and I to Town via Salisbury and Winchester.—It will be towards the end of the week after next before you hear of our arrival there.

We have had a pleasant drive[3] to day, the weather, after a week of cold and broken,—including 2 complete rainy days, has favoured us, and the country being quite new to us both, we have much enjoyed it—I wish you had been of our Party—

[1] W. W. repeats the words in order to include I. F. in the leave-taking.

[2] I. F.

[3] Probably the visit to Ottery St. Mary recorded by Arthur Duke Coleridge (1830–1913) in his *Reminiscences*, 1921, p. 15. W. W. had tea in the Manor House with his father Francis George Coleridge (1794–1854), S. T. C.'s nephew and brother of Sir John Taylor Coleridge, Henry Nelson Coleridge, and Edward Coleridge of Eton.

We have had good accts from Rydal[1]—*all* having had prosperous journeys—and found my sister well—Willy only parted with Dora and her husband at Kendal, and his business will take him to them again tomorrow—So that I doubt not they will be a happy household—and our absence will be scarcely felt among them.

We are anxious of news from Bury[2]—and to hear my dear friend that you are better—aff[ly] yours with good wishes from Miss F and William

M. Wordsworth

1514. M. W. to H. C. R.

Endorsed: 31 May 1841. M[rs] Wordsworth.
MS. Dr. Williams's Library.
Morley, i. 436.

Lyme Monday night May 31 [1841]

My dear Friend

Tomorrow M[g] we shall part with our dear friend[3] at Charmouth and trust ourselves to the Public Conveyances by which we hope to get on to Salisbury—were we are under engagement to pass 2 nights[4]—and the like space with our nephew[5] at Winchester—whence, on Saturday we trust the Railway will speed us to London—We shall be at first with our Friends the Marshalls 41 Grosvenor—and if on our arrival there we find that it should suit them and you, we can fit as early a day as you like, say Monday, to dine with you. But I cannot speak more *decidedly*, as they may have made some engagements in connection with us, that we could not break.

We have had a most delightful tour—been favourd by weather and every thing else—but feel very sad just now at the thought

[1] H. C. R. would already have received Dora Q.'s letter of 19 May (Morley, i. 433), thanking him for his wedding present and announcing the safe arrival of all the travellers: 'We find dear old Aunty very comfortable and delighted to see us and it is most affecting to me to observe the childlike *fun* and pleasure she makes for herself in addressing me by my new name—'

[2] i.e. news of Thomas Robinson.

[3] I. F.

[4] With Canon William Fisher and his wife Elizabeth, W. W.'s cousin.

[5] Charles Wordsworth.

of parting with our dear friend. I hope we shall find your ears in better plight and that you have comfortable news from Bury

I must not say more
ever faithfully yrs
M Wordsworth

1515. W. W. to ISABELLA FENWICK

MS. WL.
LY iii. 1075.

[Winchester]
[4 *or* 5 June 1841]

My dearest Friend

I meant to write you a few lines at all events this morning, and I shall do it still more gladly now, as Mary having already written six Letters naturally is desirous of being a little while this morning with the sweet little 'toddling' orphan[1] that we find under this scholastic and venerable roof.—Mary has not told you that Mr and Mrs Fisher[2] took us to old Sarum with which we were much delighted; and also with Wilton[3] inside and out. But of these things in detail when we meet. The great interest to us at Salisbury was our Cousin's family. They are all in appearance and manner more or less striking, the younger Daughter beautiful, and Emmie[4] would be very well looking if not handsome, were it not for her mouth and teeth which are ill set. She has, as you would expect, a fine capacious skull; her figure, however, like her Mother's, in inclined to be dumpy. But nothing can surpass her modest, her obedient, her affectionate and beautiful demeanour to everyone. You will be delighted to hear that her Parents have almost determined, as they strongly wish, that she should go with us from London to the North. The Father and Daughter of course both are set upon the visit taking place now, but the Mother would rather defer it to

[1] Charles Wordsworth's baby daughter. See pt. iii, Ls. 1320 and 1323.

[2] W. W.'s cousin. See previous letter.

[3] Wilton House, seat of the Earls of Pembroke, designed in part by Inigo Jones. A notable feature of the grounds is the Palladian bridge over the Nadder.

[4] The poetess (see pt. iii, L. 1185). See also Ls. 1547 and 1570 below.

another year for considerations which more naturally suggest themselves to a female. The inspired creature, for so I must call her in a sense which *you* will thoroughly understand, is in perfect health and looks, more than usually strong, and is agile in her movements notwithstanding her figure. We had some more of her smaller Poems read, which are really wonderful, so that I will repeat what I have often said in your hearing, that she is the greatest Prodigy I ever read or heard of. If she goes to the North with us how bitterly shall we lament your absence and grieve if she is not allowed to stay till you join us.

This morning I have been a long walk round Winchester with Charles and as the Sun was burning hot, I am doubly pleased with rest and coolness while writing to you.—Will you approve of my having thrown off both my breast plate and Leather waistcoat this morning; I hope no mischief will follow. Though I am perfectly well in health, I suffer so much inconvenience from a kind of eruption in my back and sides, brought on, I imagine, by the heat of the weather and so much stirring about that I hope to relieve myself by this change in my apparel, which I have long wished to effect. I did not however venture upon it without the precaution of putting on a second shirt, a light one, and this care I will take for a few days; and when I get to London I will ask Dr Ferguson about my diet. I could not withhold these little circumstances from you my most dear Friend, and I mention them without scruple as I am perfectly *well* and very strong, sleeping and eating as usual.

We have not yet seen the inside of Winchester Cathedral, when that is done I shall have made myself acquainted with every Cathedral Church in South Britain except Llandaff and St Davids.

I cannot conclude without a word upon our delightful tour together, and an expression of thanks and gratitude for all the happiness we have had in your dear Society. God grant us a happy meeting again. With love to your sister and kindest remembrances to Mr Popham, not forgetting your niece, I remain, dear Miss Fenwick your devoted Friend

Wm Wordsworth

1516. W. W. to D. McCORKINDALE[1]

MS. Harvard University Library.
LY iii. 1076.

London 7 June 1841
41 Upper Grosvenor Street

Sir

This moment I have received your Letter, and in reply to it feel compelled to say, that neither my situation in life, nor advanced age allow me to accept the high honor you offer me of being proposed in case of a Dissolution,[2] to represent the Ayr District of Burghs in Parliament.

Regretting as I do this inability I cannot forbear to add that I shall ever retain a deep sense of the distinction conferred by your wishes and that of other Gentlemen to confide in me, for the reasons assigned in your Letter, a trust, at all times and especially at the present, so important.

I have the honor to be
respectfully yours
Wm Wordsworth

1517. W. W. to THOMAS POWELL

MS. untraced.
E. S. Haynes, The Lawyer. A Conversation Piece, 1951, p. 81.

Friday [? 11 June 1841]

My dear Mr. Powell,

Here I am, 41 Upper Grosvenor Street, but so much tossed about in this vast city that I scarcely know where and when to

[1] D. McCorkindale, of 50 Gordon Street, Glasgow, had written on 5 June (*WL MSS.*) asking W. W. to stand as Conservative candidate for the Ayr Burghs in the event of a dissolution of Parliament. The retiring member was Lord Patrick Crichton Stuart (1794–1859), younger brother of the 2nd Marquess of Bute.

[2] On 27 May Peel put the motion that Lord Melbourne's ministry had lost the confidence of the House of Commons. The debate was concluded on 4 June, the motion being carried by a single vote. Parliament was dissolved on 22 June, the new Parliament met in August, and Peel replaced Melbourne as Prime Minister.

appoint a meeting. To-morrow I go to Windsor.[1] Sunday I am engaged, and so on. Could you call (one) day here between five and six and wait if I should not be in?

Ever yours faithfully,
Wm Wordsworth

1518. W. W. to CHARLES JAMES BLOMFIELD

MS. Pierpont Morgan Library. Hitherto unpublished.

37 Lower Brook Street
Tuesday morn. [15 June 1841]

My dear Lord Bishop,

Last Sunday afternoon knowing you were to preach at St. James's M[rs] W. and I went to the service, and not without a hope that we might exchange a few words with you on coming out of Church, but we were so unlucky as to miss you.

In answer to your kind note I have to say that we kept in mind our engagement to visit you and M[rs] Blomfield at Fulham, and should have called in St James's in the course of the last week, had we been able to fix the time when we should be at liberty—I can now say that if it be convenient to receive us at Fulham we have much pleasure in being with you on Monday the 28th and staying over the next day, previous to our departure from London.

Could I have spared a couple of days, I should have run down

[1] Probably the visit to Windsor and St. George's Chapel with Aubrey de Vere, who describes it in a letter to his sister on 25 June (see Wilfred Ward, *Aubrey de Vere, A Memoir*, 1904, pp. 64–6), and gives an interesting account of W. W.'s conversational habits: 'In his discourse I was at first principally struck by the extraordinary purity of his language, and the absolute perfection of his sentences; but by degrees I came to find a great charm in observing the exquisite balance of his mind, and the train of associations in which his thoughts followed each other. He does not put forward thoughts like those of Coleridge which astonished his hearers by their depth or vastness, but you gradually discover that there is a sort of inspiration in the mode in which his thoughts flow out of each other, and connect themselves with outward things. He is the voice and Nature the instrument; and they always keep in perfect tune.' W. W. is also quoted in the same letter as saying 'that the Recluse has never been written except a few passages—and probably never will', and 'that the poem on the Individual Mind consists of fifteen books, having been lately added to and quite perfected.'

to Oxford today where I should have had the pleasure of seeing you and many other Friends.

I remain
my dear Lord Bishop
with M^rs W's best respects to yourself and Mrs Blomfield
faithfully yours
Wm Wordsworth

1519. W. W. to JULIUS CHARLES HARE[1]

MS. Cornell. Hitherto unpublished.

37 Lower Brooke Street
Tuesday 15th June [1841]

My dear Mr Hare,

How sorry I was, not to have arrived in Town early enough to meet you! It was a great mortification both to Mrs W. and myself.

I have to thank you for many tokens of your kind regard; 1st for your collection of Metrical Translations of the Psalms[2] received long ago and also your Sermons on Faith[3]—most excellent—and latterly for your Charge[4] and Vol. of Parochial Sermons.[5] Both these will be on their way to Rydal tomorrow, I hope. The Charge I have already perused with much interest; the Sermons must wait my leisure; for as you may well believe, here I am almost run off my feet.

It will be full three weeks before we shall set off on our way northwards, our plans are thus arranged. We are now at Lord Monteagle's where we remain till thursday next, then we shall be at Miss Rogers' 5 Hanover terrace Regents park till the end of the following week, then 2 days at Fulham with the Bp of

[1] See pt. i, L. 123.

[2] *Portions of the Psalms, in English Verse*, 1839.

[3] *The Victory of Faith, and Other Sermons*, 1840.

[4] Hare's first Charge as Archdeacon of Lewes on *The Better Prospects of the Church*, 1840, in which he had praised the new ecclesiology pioneered by the Cambridge Camden Society (see pt. ii, L. 593 and L. 1849 below), while emphasising the importance of education and the role of the laity in building up vital religion.

[5] *Sermons Preacht in Herstmonceux Church*, 1841. A second volume was published in 1849.

London, then a few days at my Nephews Harrow, and at Mrs Hoare's Hamptead. I have troubled you with these details from a hope that at some of the places we may have the pleasure of seeing you.

ever faithfully yours
Wm Wordsworth

1520. W. W. to SIR ROBERT PEEL

MS. Cornell. Hitherto unpublished.

37 Lower Brook Street
June 16th
[18]41

Dear Sir Robert,

I regret much that I was not in the house, when you did me the honor of calling yesterday—

Allow me to thank you for this Attention, and for the note in which you so kindly express the considerations which made you wish to add my Portrait to a Collection so distinguished.[1]

Mr Pickersgill, it is generally thought, has been successful; and I was pleased to hear Mr Haydon, in particular, speak most favorably of the Work.

I have the honor to be
dear Sir Robert
with high respect
sincerely yours
Wm Wordsworth

1521. W. W. to HANNAH HOARE

MS. Cornell. Hitherto unpublished.

Sergeant Talfourd's
56 Russell Square
where I shall remain, till Tuesday—
Sat. 25th June[2] [1841]

My dear Mrs Hoare,

Would it be convenient to you to receive me next Tuesday

[1] See L. 1419 above.

[2] Saturday was the 26th.

afternoon for two or three days. It would give me much pleasure if you could.

ever sincerely and affectionately
yours
Wm Wordsworth

1522. M. W. to H. C. R.

Endorsed: 28th June 1841 Mrs Wordsworth.
MS. Dr. Williams's Library.
Morley, i. 438.

Monday Mg June 28th [1841]
5 Hanover Terrace[1]

My dear Friend

If you should be returned to town on Wednesday, and could call here about 4 oc A.M. we might have the satisfaction of a brief meeting on our transit between Fulham and Hampstead—Mrs Hoare's Carriage is to take us up at 5 oc—Dora and Q being already *in* the Carriage. Should this fail from your not having returned, or other cause, I trust you will come to us at Hampstead, where I am sure you will be a welcome Guest—for it will be a sad end to our sojourn among our good friends, if we have to depart altogether without again seeing you. Mr Q. will be going backwards and forwards I believe—his wife will remain with us while *we* remain.

Wm is, and has been at the Sergts[2] since this Saturday's dinner hour—but I saw him yesterday, he called in upon us during our Desert in Torrington Sq:[3] There too I was disappointed not having our host with us—he was suddenly called from home—so that with all my contrivance to catch him on a *Sunday*, by giving up the Talfourds etc I shall depart without once setting my eyes upon our old friend Strickland Cookson. Such a busy Wilderness this London is! Pray get out of it for a few weeks and come to Rydal—Emmie Fisher goes down with us—and Miss Rogers will come to us in the Autumn—so that we shall not be very solitary, tho' our Treasure is gone!

Ever faithfully your's
M. Wordsworth

[1] The Wordsworths had now moved on to stay with Miss Rogers.
[2] Sergeant Talfourd's.
[3] Home of Strickland Cookson.

I trust you leave your Brother and his Daughter in a measure reconciled to their bereavement,[1] so that you have left them with comfort to yourself?

1523. W. W. to ISABELLA FENWICK

MS. WL.
LY iii. 1078 (—).

Fulham Palace 29th June 41.

Your former Letter, my beloved Friend, was lost most unluckily, for it never reached us, and we could not but be anxious about you, though during your supposed silence we had a word or two of tidings about you from Mr Taylor.—We hope you have shaken off the ill effects of the change of weather; which since we came to London has however been very unpleasant. Excessive cold set in almost immediately upon our arrival, and since it has been very wet, so that a great deal of the Hay hereabouts is spoiled. Neither Mary nor I however have taken any harm; and the eruption upon my skin is quite gone. I may indeed say with a grateful heart that we are both quite well. I do not think that Dora looks any better, but she makes no complaint. Before her hurried and fatiguing departure from Rydal, Mr Q says she was very much improved in looks and strength, but I trust when she is settled she will mend again. Poor Rotha is dreadfully disfigured by her Rash, Mr Q. has something of the same appearance in his face, but he is well and seems very happy in his possession.—Anna Ricketts[2] whom we saw two or three days ago is looking wonderfully well. We had a hope that she would have obtained her Mother's consent to go with us to Rydal; but the obstacles proved insurmountable. I have seen very little of the Taylors. Through Mr T.'s kindness we procured tickets to attend the Ship Launch,[3] which delighted Mary very much. I was rather disappointed in the impression made by the mere Launch, but the spectacle of the vast crowd upon Land and Water was very striking. Of the persons whom

[1] The death of H. C. R.'s nephew Tom Robinson.

[2] See pt. iii, Ls. 1276 and 1350.

[3] H.M.S. Trafalgar was launched at Woolwich on 21 June 1841, in the presence of the Queen, Prince Albert, and some 30,000 spectators. (Morley's note).

we have seen in society I can give you no account, as I should not know where to begin or end. What would interest you most in this matter would, I think, be to tell you of the many acknowledgments of gratitude which I have received from your sex, and especially from the Young, of all ranks. As to places you probably know that we have been at Windsor;[1] Mr Rogers and I also went to Hampton Court one day, but were unlucky, as it was the day of the week upon which the Palace is closed, so that we were not admissible. The garden, however, is fine in its kind, and I was much gratified by seeing it again. The last time I visited the same place was in company with Walter Scott, Mrs Lockhart etc. etc.[2] Rogers was of the party, but Father and Daughter though so much younger are gone! Sadness and enjoyment, how they are mixed up in this mortal life of ours! Every day and every hour of the day my dear Friend do I think of you, and talk of you whenever and with whomsoever I can and dare. You must if possible be with us by the last week of September, that we may have you while the beauty of the Autumn is only beginning. The Fishers[3] have determined that Emmie shall go with us, and I hope she will not depart before you come.—This is a wretchedly dull Letter; but I really know not what to touch upon, among the multiplicity of topics; and what would it avail to tell you that at a large dinner table, or in such and such a throng I have seen or had a few minutes with such a Person or Personage. But O, my dear Friend, the hollowness of London society—but what an abuse of the term, and not only the hollowness but the tediousness especially among Dabblers in Literature—to me their talk, and their flattery above all, is insupportable. Heaven bless you, I do not say think of us, for that I know you do, but write to us as often as you can without tiring or hurting yourself. Tomorrow we go to Hampstead. The Bishop[4] and his family seem much pleased to see us. A young Lawyer Mrs B's Son by her former Husband[5] is a great *Admirer* of mine, and is here on purpose to be with me.

[1] See L. 1517 above.

[2] In 1828. See pt. i, L. 341.

[3] i.e. Canon and Mrs. Fisher of Salisbury.

[4] Blomfield, Bishop of London.

[5] Blomfield had married as his second wife (1819) Dorothy, widow of Thomas Kent, a barrister. Her son by her first marriage was Thomas Kent (b. 1817), who graduated at Balliol College, Oxford, in 1839, and entered Lincoln's Inn three years later.

29 June 1841

As I have written several Letters this morning I must bid you farewell with love to your dear Sister and kindest regards to Mr Popham, and your niece, ever and ever yours

W. W.

[*M. W. writes*]

You may have heard dearest friend from Dora, or if you have not you will be pleased to hear from me how successful have been our applications in behalf of our nieces.[1] Dear Cordelia[2] has arranged that the two elder Girls are to go to Brighton and to be admitted into Mr Elliott's Establishment,[3] here to be employed as Teachers if fit for that office *in* that Place. If not, to remain there for improvement while suitable situations are found to send them to, and such are daily sought for. Nothing I think can be more desirable than this prospect, with such good People if the Girls do but conduct themselves so as to deserve Mr Elliott's countenance. Kind Mr M.[4] thro' his daughter's hands gave Dora[5] money to defray the expences of the long journey. I think the Boy[6] must go to Derwent C's Est.[7] in the Autumn. We visited the embrio Col: yesterday and D. gave us hope that John should be admitted tho' under age. D. bears a lively and pleasant impression of my Br George's Kindness to him when he was a child, and says he would like to have his Boy.

W. gave me this sheet to try if I could not make the letter better worth reading, and here I have merely spoken of my own concerns, which will dearest friend *interest* you tho' they will not

[1] The six daughters of M. W.'s brother George Hutchinson of Brinsop. The letter goes on to refer to the two elder girls, Margaret and Dora.

[2] Cordelia Marshall.

[3] The Revd. Henry Venn Elliott (see pt. i, L. 70), had opened a school in Brighton in 1836 for the training of governesses. See Josiah Bateman, *The Life of the Rev. Henry Venn Elliott*, 1858, pp. 148 ff.

[4] Mr. Marshall.

[5] i.e. Dora Hutchinson.

[6] George Hutchinson's son John (see pt. iii, L. 1199), later Librarian at the Middle Temple.

[7] Establishment. i.e. Stanley Grove, later St. Mark's College, Chelsea, of which Derwent Coleridge had now been appointed Principal. John Hutchinson was admitted shortly afterwards (see *MW*, p. 256). It was the first national training college to be opened by the Church of England in response to Dr. James Kay's non-denominational training institution at Battersea (see also pt. iii, L. 1335 and L. 1412 above), and became noted for its daily choral service in Chapel, a feature which increasingly identified it with the high-church party.

entertain which was W's object. But I have other letters to cobble—So you will forgive me. God bless you—

[*unsigned*]

Our united love to yr Sister—and all who enquire after us when you reach Mrs Tudor's[1] etc—

1524. W. W. to W. MILLIKEN[2]

MS. Harvard University Library.
LY iii. 1079.

Hampstead Heath
July 5th 1841

Sir

I beg to give you notice that I do accept the no. of new shares offered me in the Australasian Bank. Being now resident for a few days at Hampstead I cannot fill up the above blank so as to specify the number of shares, but I take the whole number allowed me, according to what I hold.—

Wm Wordsworth

1525. W. W. to UNKNOWN CORRESPONDENT

Endorsed: Willm Wordsworth Esq. 5 July 1841. Mr Quillinan.
MS. Cornell. Hitherto unpublished.

Hampstead Heath
July 5th 1841

My dear Sir,

I sit down to write to you upon a matter of business, and to request a favor in connection with it. My Daughter, as perhaps you are aware, is, after a long attachment married to a Gentleman, whose means are lamentably short of what wor[l]dly prudence looks to, and almost requires. But a respectable though small income seems within his reach, as acting by commission for his Brother (who resides in Portugal) and is engaged in the wine trade. The Father also resided in Portugal,

[1] At Bath.

[2] Described on the MS. as Secretary of the Bank of Australia.

and was succeeded by his Son who was induced to attend less to the wine-business by another concern, in which he has been disappointed, but he is now desirous of extending the wine trade, on his own account and his Brother's. Now what I have to ask is whether you could not give my Son-in-Law some advice from your experience in this matter. He has already both in connection with his Father and Brother, himself had a good deal of experience, but he might in all probability profit from suggestions of yours. I have further to request that if you could recommend him to any Wine-Merchants, as a person of high respectability, you would on my account, and that of my Daughter, be so kind as to lend him a helping hand.

From your long experienced kindness I have ventured thus to address you, without apology. Be assured that Mrs W and I regret much that we have not seen you on our late visit to London. The Dr[1] who is here is much better than we expected or rather feared we should find him. Mr and Mrs Quillinan are here also, and we all adjourn to Harrow, on Wednesday, and separate on the Monday following when Mrs W. and I after an absence of great length return to Westmorland.—

My Son in Law's address after the 12th will be, Canterbury; Edward Quillinan Esq.—

Mrs and Miss Hoare are both well.

With Kindest remembrances in which Mrs W. and my Daughter unite, I remain my dear Sir,

faithfully
Your obliged
Wm Wordsworth

1526. W. W. to ISABELLA FENWICK

MS. WL.
LY iii. 1080.

Harrow 10th July 41

I steal a moment, my beloved Friend, to write you a few words, and tell you in part how I have been employed. On Wednesday last we came here from Hampstead. Sir Robert Peel attended the Speeches that day, and saw two prizes for Latin prose and Verse

[1] i.e. C. W.

adjudged to his Son.[1] I took that opportunity to request an interview with him upon the Copyright Bill, and accordingly it took place yesterday at his own House, Whitehall. I could not induce him to look favorably upon the Bill; in fact he was obviously afraid of being charged with favouring *monopoly*, if he gave it his support. He assigned some reasons for thinking that undeserving authors would profit by the privilege to the injury of the community. He acknowledged however both the justice and expediency of giving the privilege to particular Persons, and expressed a hope that Parliament would aid in such a measure.—I urged many and I think cogent objections to this scheme; combated his notion that any injury to the public would accrue from the quarters to which he had adverted, and gave many reasons for the belief that the literature of the Country would derive great benefit from the extension of the term, and that, though the number of Authors who might profit from it by means of works now existing was deplorably small, still we had just reasons for believing that the number would be encreased to the benefit and honor of the nation and in the service of mankind at large. I made, however, little or no impression, none indeed to encourage hope that he would support that or a similar measure. My day's labour was not, however, thrown away, for I called on Mr Lockhart, reported to him what had passed, and succeeded in persuading him to write an Article for the

[1] Sir Robert Peel, 3rd Bart. (1822–95), went on to Christ Church, Oxford, later this year, succeeded his father as M.P. for Tamworth (1850–80), and served as a Lord of the Admiralty (1855–7) and Chief Secretary for Ireland (1861–5). H. C. R. who accompanied W. W. to Harrow sent his brother an account of the proceedings: '. . . I heard an interesting speech from Sir Rob[t] Peal whose son ran off with all the glory. In it he introduced a very high compliment to Wordsworth which was echoed by the Master—W's nephew, who gave his health. W: co[d] not make himself heard in returning thanks. . . .An American Bishop, the Bp of Peterborough, Sir Rob[t] Inglis, Mr Cunningham (rector of Harrow], Wordsworth, and the Master of Trinity sat enthroned in stalls. W: was quite reverenced and shared the notice of the large party with Sir Rob[t] . . .' (Morley, i. 439–40). While at Harrow, W. W. seems to have just missed seeing Sir John Stoddart, now returned from Malta, who wrote on 17 July: 'I have resolved to make an attempt to see you once more—since as you feelingly say, after the death of our old and valued friends Lamb and Coleridge and Scott, we know not "who next may drop and disappear." . . . I shall be anxious to talk over with you the old Grasmere recollections, and to learn how you have borne the trials which a lengthened life must always bring.' (*WL MSS.*)

Quarterly, in support of the cause.[1] Today I go to London, to dine with Mr Robinson,[2] sleep at Mr Cookson's and return tomorrow. On Tuesday we depart for Coleorton. Emmie Fisher, it is at last determined, is to go with us for a longer stay than the Mother could at first bring herself to allow. Perhaps you have been told that we declined having her for so short a time as was before stipulated.—

It is high time now my dear Friend to express a fear that you cannot read either this or any other of my scrawls. Pray tell me sincerely how this is. Dora however is going [to][3] write, and from her you will learn particulars much better than from me.—Only I must add, what I am sure you will be able to make out, that we talk about you perpetually notwithstanding the hurry in which we live, and for myself I can say from the bottom of my heart, that I long to receive you at our own door, and again let me say do come in the last week of September if you can, or at the very latest before the first of October is over; but the sooner the better. And now farewell, and every blessing attend you, my beloved Friend, and heart-sister, ever yours

Wm Wordsworth

Kind remembrances to all about you.—

[1] See L. 1558 below.

[2] The guests included William Harness (see pt. iii, L. 1013), Copley Fielding, the water-colourist (see *HCR* ii. 459 and pt. iii. L. 1048), Dr. John Carlyle, Strickland Cookson, and James Booth, a Unitarian friend of H. C. R.'s. '. . . all my party consisted of religious people tho' in different ways—C: Fielding the capital water colour painter is even a Puseyite, Harness a very liberal belletrist Clergyman but a theoretical favorer of Oxford doctrines, and Dr Carlyle follows in the steps of his brother the philosopher. We kept it up till 12 OClock tho' the party broke into groups. Kenyon and Fellows [Sir Charles Fellows, the traveller and archaeologist] came in after dinner.' (Morley, i. 440). 'Wordsworth talked chiefly *tête à tête*, but he seemed to be in a good mood. On the whole he is improved as a companion since his last being in London. He is not triumphant at Tory success.' (*HCR* ii. 597).

[3] *Word dropped out.*

1527. W. W. to HENRY WEEKES[1]

MS. Cornell. Hitherto unpublished.

Coleorton
Hall
Leicestershire
20th July —1841

Sir

As requested by My Brother Dr Wordsworth, I write to beg that you would forward the Bust of my Nephew, which you have executed to my residence "Rydal near Ambleside Westtnd." I am in the habit of receiving Boxes of Books from my Publisher, Mr Moxon 44 Dover street, and at his Shop might be learned through what Conveyance. I am not sure however but that the Bust in question might prove too heavy for the Mode of carriage which he prefers, in which case may I beg that you would use your own discretion as to the best Mode of sending it; and if the carriage throughout can be paid beforehand the Bill might be sent in to Dr Wordsworth as it is his wish to defray the expense.—

I cannot conclude without adding that I admire the Bust very much as a Work of Art, and that the likeness is as good as circumstances could allow.

Pray remember me very kindly to Sir Francis and Lady Chantrey, and be so good as to say to Mr C.[2] that I directed Mr Moxon to send him the last Edition of my Poems.

I remain Sir
Yours very truly
Wm Wordsworth

If you should have occasion to write my address is Rydal Mount Ambleside

[1] Henry Weekes, R.A. (1807–78), the sculptor, entered the schools of the Royal Academy in 1823, and later engaged himself as an assistant to Sir Francis Chantrey, with whom he remained until Chantrey died, succeeding to many of his commissions, and occupying his studio till his own death. His bust of Queen Victoria was the first to be taken after her accession to the throne. He also executed figures for the Martyrs' Memorial at Oxford and for the Albert Memorial in Hyde Park. He had just completed his bust of John Wordsworth, C. W.'s son, which was to be placed in Trinity College Chapel, and he was sending W. W. a replica.

[2] Allan Cunningham.

1528. W. W. to ISABELLA FENWICK

MS. WL.
LY iii. 1081 (—).

Rydal Mount
Sat. 24th [July 1841]

Once more, dearest Friend, we have the pleasure of thinking of you, and wishing for you, at this sweet place, which we reached at two o'clock on Thursday morn. in our own little Phaeton, having sent Jane on by the Coach. We left Coleorton and Ashby de la Zouche on Wednesday at noon, proceeded in a double fly to Stafford which we reached at 7, and after a tedious waiting of 8 hours (none of us went to bed) we proceeded to Lancaster. All went well with every one but poor me, who had contrived last Sunday to pick up either a sprain of the hip, or something of Sciatic Rheumatism. I am better this morning, but I cannot stoop yet to put on my stockings. We found here Mrs Hutchinson and her daughter Sarah, both well; and my dear Sister and Joanna looking better than when we left them. Our stay at Coleorton, where we received your welcome Letter, was very agreeable. Nothing could surpass the kindness of our friends. We have brought away two pleasing pictures given us by Sir George B.[1] which look very well in our little drawing room mixed with the others which we have from the same pencil. Sir G. B. was so good as to say to me, that in case of my dying before Mrs. W., the annuity of 100£, as long as he lived, should be paid to her.

The place is beautiful. How I should like you to see it. The winter garden however has not been treated altogether as I wished.[2] An aviary has been introduced by the late Lady Beaumont, which takes up room that could not be spared, shuts out of view the ornamental masonry of the high terrace wall, and is altogether out of character with the place. The evergreens also have been far too much thinned.—One of the days when we were staying with the Merewethers we drove to a part of Charnwood forest where they are erecting a monastery for

[1] i.e. the present baronet. The pictures were presumably by W. W.'s patron, the late Sir George Beaumont.

[2] W. W. had himself supervised the planning of the winter garden during his stay at Coleorton in the winter of 1806–7. See *MY* i. 112 ff.

Trappists.[1] The situation is chosen with admirable judgement, a plain almost surrounded with wild rocks, not lofty with irregularly broken, and in one quarter is an opening to a most exensive prospect of cultivated country. The building is austere and massy, and when the whole shall be completed, the chapel is not yet begun, the effect will be most striking in the midst of that solitude. Several monks were at work in the adjoining Hayfields, working most industriously in their grey woollen gowns, one with his cowl up, and others, Lay brethren I believe, clothed in black. Some were mowing most lustily, and others as busy raking. The whole of this place and the sloping hillsides will erelong be reclaimed by these laborius creatures. We learned that Lord Shrewsbury[2] takes great interest in this society, and, as well as other Romanist Grandees, has visited several times, and no doubt they all have given it the support of their money. Where are these things to stop, is a question which any one who has reflected upon the constitution of the Romish Church will naturally put to himself with such objects before him, and not without some apprehensions of mischief. Perhaps alarm may be needless, but surely it is too late in the day for such Institutions to be of much service, in England at least. the whole appearance had in my eyes something of the nature of a dream, and it has often haunted me since—I wish you had been with us.

I have been so often interrupted by Callers[3] that I must be obliged to cut this Letter short. The enclosed paper is sent merely on account of the latter part which is marked. It has

[1] Mount St. Bernard's Abbey, the first Cistercian monastery in Britain since the Reformation, was founded in 1835 by Ambrose Phillipps de Lisle (1809–78) of Garendon Park and Grace Dieu Manor, Whitwick, a Roman Catholic convert and pioneer of the Catholic revival in England. The late Lady Beaumont had been friendly with his family and had written to D. W. about his conversion in July 1830: 'He appears intelligent but sadly out of health and spirits, and I should think had been in a great measure converted by his feelings.' (*WL MSS.*) De Lisle enlisted the support of the Earl of Shrewsbury for his plan and the abbey buildings were completed in 1844 to the designs of Augustus Welby Northmore Pugin (1812–52), the Gothic revival architect, who included them in his visionary frontispiece to *An Apology for the Revival of Christian Architecture in England*, 1843, dedicated to Lord Shrewsbury. See E. S. Purcell, *Life and Letters of Ambrose Phillipps de Lisle*, 2 vols., 1900, i. 66 ff.; Michael Trappes-Lomax, *Pugin, A Medieval Victorian*, 1932, pp. 123 ff. See also L. 1628 below.

[2] See pt. iii, L. 1037.

[3] Recent visitors had included the Arnolds from Fox How, and Bunsen. (RMVB).

struck me that possibly you might have a few Books to spare for so good a purpose. When you have read it pray direct it to the Rev[d] Francis Merewether, Coleorton Rectory, Ashby de la Zouche. Mrs Wilson,[1] as we learn from the Hamiltons[2] this afternoon, has given up her house near Bowness.—The Belles[3] are not here—Mrs Roughsedge has been poorly indeed and looks miserably, I am told, for I have not yet seen her. To save the Post I must here conclude, with a thousand affectionate good wishes, ever my beloved Friend most faithfully yours

Wm Wordsworth

I have not time to read over this scrawl, so you must make the best you can of it, miserable thing as it is.

[*M. W. adds*]

Dear Friend, The enclosed bill I ventured to look at, thinking from its appearance I might settle it without troubling you, but as neither Ann[4] nor myself can understand it, I think it better to send it first for your inspection. God bless you dearest Miss Fenwick—M. W.

When I am a little settled I will write at leisure—but I am bewildered by arrangements—visitors—writing etc—and interruptions without end. We have beautiful weather. Love to all our kind Bath friends.

1529. W. W. to CHARLES ALEXANDER JOHNS[5]

MS. Mitchell Library, Sydney.
G. L. Little, 'Two Unpublished Wordsworth Letters', NQ ccvii (May 1962), 178–9.

Rydal Mount
July 29th —41

Dear Sir,

Upon reaching home after a long absence, I have the pleasure of finding your agreeable Present of your Flora Sacra, which I

[1] Unidentified: possibly a temporary resident known to I. F.

[2] Capt. Thomas Hamilton and his wife, formerly Lady Farquhar.

[3] Probably the nickname for some local young ladies, otherwise unidentified.

[4] A maid.

[5] The Revd. Charles Alexander Johns (1811–74) served under Derwent Coleridge at Helston School (where Charles Kingsley was one of his pupils), and later opened his own school at Winchester. He wrote many popular scientific and

have examined with no small gratification. For this little Volume, and also for your interesting Letter, in the sentiments of which I entirely [agree],[1] let me offer you my sincere thanks. Much as I have enjoyed already your Book, I feel with regret how much more competent I should have been to appreciate it had I known more of Botany, but though not many Persons have found more delight in noticing plants and flowers, my pleasure has been too exclusively of a poetical kind; I have neglected more than I ought the minutiae or rather rudiments of the knowledge; into which neglect I was partly seduced by having in the early parts of my life, my Sister almost always at my side in my wanderings, and she for our native Plants was an excellent Botanist—

It gratifies me to know that what I have written upon the works of nature, and the vegetable creation in particular, has interested you. There is a little plant the small common Geranium, called with us "Poor Robin", that is an especial favorite with me, so much so that I was tempted last March to describe its characteristics in verse[2] and to moralize upon it in a way which perhaps will give you pleasure, when the Verses see the light, which they will probably next Spring.

Believe [me] dear Sir
your much obliged
W Wordsworth

1530. W. W. to ISABELLA FENWICK

MS. WL.
LY iii. 1083 (—).

[5 Aug. 1841]

I was interrupted in my last Letter, and now, my beloved

educational books, including *Flora Sacra; or, the knowledge of the works of Nature conducive to the knowledge of the God of Nature*, 1840, a work which illustrates his profound debt to W. W. Johns sent a copy of this letter some years later to Adam White (1817–79), the Scottish naturalist, who at the time of his decline was compiling *Weeds and Wild Flowers Loved by Wordsworth*, noting that 'It is valuable as containing an expression of Wordsworth's own feelings on the study of Botany'; and this copy is preserved in Adam White's album in the National Library of Scotland.

[1] *Word dropped out.*

[2] See *PW* iv. 158, and the I. F. note pp. 437–8.

Friend, I sit down with pleasure to talk to you for a short time. And first let me tell you that two large *packages* (do I spell right) arrived for you yesterday; and were most welcome as anything is which looks like an additional tie to us and this place, or neighbourhood. They are deposited in the granary, which is both dry and secure. But let me ask how your foot is; I have been anxious about it, for I was hurt formerly in the same way, some years ago. The nail of my great Toe blackened, and came off in consequence, and the fresh nail as it pushed off the old one grew into the side of the Toe, and for want of taking care an inflammation ensued which was troublesome and disabled me for some weeks. If anything of this kind should occur in your case the only way of proceeding is to pare the nail very thin, and put cotton in so as to raise it above the irritated flesh. By carefully managing this I got well; but I hope that by this time the effects of your injury may either have disappeared or been abated. Pray let us know.—

It was neither rheumatism nor sciatica with which I was troubled, but only the effect of a straining of the muscles from too much exercise, and imprudently climbing styles and gates, without due consideration of my age, and only looking at my natural lightness of body and activity. The pain, which, when I stooped or rose inconsiderately from my chair etc, was very acute, gradually went away and has for some days wholly disappeared. But it has taught me that I must yield to the invisible changes which Time makes in one's constitution.—

You probably know that Sarah Crackanthorpe[1] came over to Rydal upon Emmie Fisher's account. Today which by the bye is very wet she takes her over Kirkstone to Mr. Askew's,[2] at Patterdale, whence they proceed to Newbiggen. E. will not I think return till ten days are over; she grieves a good deal at this, having been so happy here; but I have no doubt of her enjoying herself with her kind relations on the other side of the Hills. She is of a sweet temper and loving disposition, as is apparent to every one, even the servants. I have endeavoured to recommend and inculcate the merging of the Genius in the Woman, as much as she can. It is obvious that though most amiably disposed to love the qualities of heart and mind that are loveable in others, she attaches, as is natural for one so gifted, too much importance to intellect and literature, and leans too much towards those

[1] W. W.'s cousin. See pt. iii, L. 1185.

[2] See pt. ii, L. 463.

who, she thinks, are distinguished in that way.—In knowledge of the world she is a mere child of 5 years, her mother having kept her so exclusively to herself and family. She is moreover utterly helpless in all that relates to dressing herself or taking care of her things. This is very foolish on the part of her Mother. The Girl's spirit, diligence, and enthusiasm in any thing that she undertakes are most striking, but so active is her imagination, and so prompt are her sensibilities, that one cannot but be apprehensive about her future welfare. In the first place we are sure that she would be apt to fall in love with any youth who could talk to her about Poetry etc. with the appearance of sympathy. Her own Imagination would at once invest him with all that was necessary to make the very thing she wished for, out of but an ordinary Person. But I am called off, as they are going to an early dinner before setting off. We also are to make this afternoon for Mr Hamilton's[1] where we shall pass the night—farewell dearest Friend, heaven bless you again and again, ever yours

W. Wordsworth

[*M. W. writes*]

Augt 5th. Kindest love to all the dear friends by whom you are surrounded. You will have heard that poor Dora has had one of her bad feverish colds—but it is better. God bless you dearest friend.

1531. W. W. to EDWARD MOXON

MS. Henry E. Huntington Library.
LY iii. 1085.

Rydal Mount
Ambleside
August 5th 1841.

My dear Mr Moxon,

I have directed Mr Champion a blind Poet of Chichester to apply to you, for the payment for a small Vol: of his Poems[2] to

[1] Capt. Thomas Hamilton's.

[2] *The Triumph of Music, with other Poems*, by The Blind Bard of Cicestria, Chichester, 1841. W. W.'s name is printed at the end among the subscribers, and his copy, with his autograph, is in the British Library: most of the pages are still uncut (de Selincourt's note). See *R.M.Cat.*, no. 621.

which I am a Subscriber; this I have taken the liberty of doing as the best or rather the only way I could hit upon for getting out of his Debt. Be so good as to place the amount in my Bill.—(turn over)

I was a good deal disappointed in finding that in the Parcel of Poems[1] sent down before me, there were no separate copies of the Excursion.[2] It has been a good deal called for at Ambleside, but none were to be had. Be so good as to send down a dozen Excursions, and eight copies of the Six Volumes which also, I find, are in demand here. As the Season is now pretty far advanced, you will be so good as to despatch the parcel immediately, directed to Mrs Nicholson, Bookseller, Ambleside—

We are all well, hoping the same of you. I remain with kindest regards to Mrs M. and your Sister and Brother

my dear Mr Moxon
faithfully yours
W Wordsworth

Are we to see you in West[d]?

1532. W. W. to T. G. BURTON[3]

MS. Cornell. Hitherto unpublished.

[*In M. W.'s hand*]

Rydal Mount
Aug 8th [? 1841][4]

Mr Wordsworth begs to say in answer to Mr T. G. Burton's enquiry—that no such Person as Josiah Simpson was ever employed by him, nor is the name known to his Family—

Probably Mr B. may have made a mistake in the name of J. S's Referee.

[1] i.e. of the new edition of the *Poetical Works* in six volumes.

[2] There was also a new edition of *The Excursion* in 1841.

[3] Unidentified.

[4] A later letter,—but the dating here is purely conjectural.

1533. W. W. to MARY FISHER[1]

MS. University Library, Davis, California. Hitherto unpublished.

Rydal Mount Ambleside
[*c.* 10] August [1841]

My dear Cousin,

We were glad to hear from you, and much interested in learning news of your Daughter, melancholy as it was. May God support you both and all your family through this anxious and distressful trial, whatever may be the event.

I need not say that we should have been happy to pay attention to Mr Symmons[2] both upon his own account and yours, but we have not seen him. He wrote in the earlier part of last week enclosing your Letters and saying he would be at Rydal on Thursday or Friday. His Letter was dated Whitehaven, and informed us that he was upon a tour of inspection of Mines—I did not answer his Letter both because I am not in the habit of doing so upon like occasions; and because I inferred he did not look for an answer neither having requested it nor given me his address, either at the post office or any where else. Mrs. W. whose Relative, though distant he is, and I should both be much concerned if we have missed seeing him here, by any punctilio of delicacy upon his part, arising from his Letter not having been answered and pray tell him so if you shall have an opportunity.

Emmie Fisher went to Newbiggen last Friday with our Cousin Sarah Crakenthorpe who had come over to see her. Her visit will be about ten days, and I hope her parents will permit her to prolong her stay with us till about the middle of next month when she will have an opportunity of returning as far as Worcestershire with a Sister-in Law of Mrs W.—Mrs Hutchinson who is now staying with us.

We are delighted with Emmie, her sweetness of disposition being scarcely less remarkable than her surprizing Genius and talents. She is of course greatly delighted with this charming Country, and as is natural, has been most happy under our roof.

Be assured my dear Cousin that we remember with deep

[1] W. W.'s cousin (see pt. iii, Ls. 1185 and 1323), whom W. W. and M. W. had recently visited at Southampton (see *MW*, p. 246).

[2] A distant relative of M. W.'s, as W.W. goes on to explain. But nothing more is known about him than is recorded here.

interest our short, too short, visit to you. Pray accept our very kind love and offer the same to your suffering Daughter if her state of health allow her to receive such notices from Friends who feel for her and you as we do.

ever affectionately and faithfully yours
Wm Wordsworth

1534. W. W. to C. W.

MS. British Library.
K (—). LY iii. 1086.

Rydal Aug 11th [1841]

My dear Brother,

I send you with the last corrections an Epitaph which I have just written for poor Owen Lloyd.[1] His brother Edward forwarded for my perusal some verses which he had composed with a view to that object; but he expressed a wish that I would compose something, myself. Not approving Edward's lines altogether, though the sentiments were sufficiently appropriate, I sent him what I now forward to you or rather the substance of it, for something has been added, and some change of expression introduced. I hope you will approve of it. I find no fault with it myself, the circumstances considered, except that it is too long for an Epitaph, but this was inevitable if the Memorial was to be as comprehensive as the subject required, at least according to the light in which it offered itself to my mind.

Yesterday I had a very interesting visit from a person you must once have known well, Mr Le Grice.[2] He spoke with much

[1] The late curate of Langdale. For the *Epitaph in the Chapel-Yard of Langdale, Westmoreland*, see *PW* iv. 255, and I. F. note p. 450. Owen Lloyd had four brothers.

[2] For Charles Valentine Le Grice, see *MY* i. 155. At Christ's Hospital he was a class-fellow of Coleridge and Lamb and senior 'Grecian'. In 'Christ's Hospital Five and Thirty Years Ago' in *Essays of Elia*, Lamb alludes to the combats of wit between Coleridge and Le Grice, Coleridge being a 'Spanish Galleon' and Le Grice 'an English man-of-war.' He afterwards went on to Trinity College, Cambridge, where he won the chief declamation prize, C. W. taking second place. He took orders and became rector of St. Mary's, Penzance, and perpetual curate of Madron, 1806–31, living after 1821 at Trereife, the family estate he inherited through his wife. He published *An Imitation of Horace's First Epistle*,

feeling of you, and much modesty and humility unaffected, of his own Academic course and Character, in contrast with yours. He left us, enclosed in a little pamphlet a speech of his, upon Cottage Gardens, three or four copies of a sonnet of his own writing, of which you are the subject. As you may not have seen the Verses I send them. We were agreeably surprized by the sight of them after he was gone, for when he put the little Pamphlet into my hands he had made no mention of them. He sate nine years in the same class with Coleridge and by his side, having with Coleridge the joint use of certain dictionaries and books of reference according to the custom of the school, by which these accommodations were assigned to the Scholars in pairs. He told us several anecdotes of Coleridge, of whose life, since they appeared together at Christ's Hospital, till Coleridge left College abruptly, he must have known more than any one else possibly could.

I have heard Coleridge speak of him hundreds and hundreds of times. Le Grice told me had had just been to visit Satterthwaite's[1] grave, and he would have gone 50 miles out of his way for that purpose. I was much pleased with this burst of feelings, as evinced by one who, according to his own account of himself, had in youth abandoned himself far too much to careless levity, and this coincides with what Coleridge used to say of him. He is now and perhaps has long been, of a serious and thoughtful conversation, and I assure you I have not for a long time had a visitor in whom I was so much interested.[2]

Le Grice told us also many particulars of Charles Lamb's boyhood. He remembered also having once heard you deliver a charge[3] before a religious society to certain missionaries, which impressed him more, both by the matter and manner, than any

1793; *An Analysis of Paley's Principles of Moral and Political Philosophy*, 1799, etc.; a translation of *Daphnis and Chloe*, 1803; and *College Reminiscences of Coleridge*, 1842 (reprinted from the *Gentleman's Magazine*, to which he was a lifelong contributor). On his return to Cornwall he wrote to W. W. on 21 Dec. 1841, sending Coleridge's *Monody on the Death of Chatterton* (first published in 1893), and introducing his son (*WL MSS.*). See also Morley, i. 441–2.

[1] C. W.'s friend, Dr. Satterthwaite, rector of Lowther, who had died in 1827 (see pt. i, L. 308).

[2] The MS. ends at this point. The rest of the letter is added from *K*.

[3] *A Charge, delivered at a special meeting of the Society for promoting Christian Knowledge . . . to the Rev. Lawrence Peter Haubroe and the Rev. David Rosen, previous to their departure as the Society's missionaries in India*, 1819.

charge that he had ever heard delivered. I suppose it was spoken before the Society for promoting Christian Knowledge. . . .

Your most affectionate brother,
Wm Wordsworth

1535. W. W. to ISABELLA FENWICK

MS. WL.
LY iii. 1087 (—).

[mid-August 1841]

We are most sorry dearest Friend to hear of your serious illness, and earnestly wish that you were again with us; though our household is at present in poor plight. Mrs Hutchinson[1] is but very little better; and poor Jane[2] is bent double almost with the rheumatism. Sarah[3] however is decidedly better, and Jane we trust will soon be quite well. My poor sister has been made very uneasy by the hot weather added to that huge fire which she insists upon keeping. Mary and I are quite well except occasionally when we are tired out with the company which at this season flocks in upon us.

Your news of Mrs Villiers[4] was very acceptable and pray offer to her our cordial congratulations and best wishes.

You say you hope you shall see us at Coniston before you go to Rydal. I did not like that sentence at all—after so long an absence I cannot bear the thought of seeing you for the first time in this Country in any house but ours, unless you had one of your own to come to. How do you propose to go to Coniston, I mean by what road, that we are not to see you first. Pray tell me this. I have another rather delicate point to touch. We fear Anna Ricketts[5] would be dull in our house as we shall have no companion for her but our antient selves—Mrs H. will probably be gone. We, therefore, would prefer her staying with you at Coniston if it could be managed. Had Emmie Fisher been here it would be very different. I am writing by candle light so I must bid my dear friend, Farewell

W. Wordsworth

[1] Mary Hutchinson, visiting Rydal Mount from Brinsop.

[2] Servant at Rydal Mount.

[3] Mrs. Hutchinson's youngest daughter.

[4] See pt. iii, L. 1326.

[5] See L. 1523 above.

[*M. W. adds*]

By the bye dearest friend W has not put the matter of Anna Ricketts quite *ingenuously*. It was not altogether in consideration of *her being dull* with us when he mentioned the subject *to me* this morning, but that he as well as myself would rather not have her to entertain being alone, dearly as we love and wish to see her here—but as it would make him uneasy not to walk with her, and after so fatiguing a season he would like a little quiet rest that he might be fresh my dearest friend to receive *you*, and the dear Girl with you.

1536. W. W. to GEORGE WASHINGTON DOANE[1]

MS. untraced.

The Englishman's Magazine, Aug. 1842, p. 178.[2] *William Croswell Doane, The Life and Writings of George Washington Doane, 4 vols., 1860, i. 299* (—).

Rydal Mount, Ambleside,
Aug. 16. 1841

I am not without hope that in some favourable moment I may be enabled to touch the union of the two Churches, through that venerable man,[3] in a manner not wholly unworthy of an event so important for the spread of Gospel truth and Christian charity. At all events, I trust the tribute may be sent after you; and pray let me have your address, which, not for this purpose only, I should like to be possessed of. Much do I regret that your short stay amongst us did not allow of my shewing you and your companion[4] more of this pastoral and poetical country. I could have liked especially to conduct you to the valley in which repose the remains of the excellent person[5] whose epitaph I send

[1] George Washington Doane (1799–1859), Bishop of New Jersey from 1832, and a warm supporter of the Oxford Movement (see E. Clowes Chorley, *Men and Movements in the American Episcopal Church*, New York, 1946, pp. 234–7). W. W. had met him recently in London. He called at Rydal Mount on 5 Aug. with his chaplain (*RMVB*), and went on to Leeds to preach on 2 Sept. at the consecration of the new Parish Church built by W. F. Hook. This letter, acknowledging the receipt of Doane's funeral sermon on Bishop White, was received by him at Leeds before his return to America.

[2] Reprinted from the *New York Churchman.*

[3] William White, first Bishop of Pennsylvania. See next letter.

[4] Doane's chaplain, the Revd. Benjamin Isaacs Haight (1809–79).

[5] Owen Lloyd. See L. 1534 above.

you, as an appropriate offering to yourself in your personal and official character. With a thousand good wishes, in which Mrs Wordsworth and the rest of my family unite, I remain, my dear bishop, thankful for having seen you, your affectionate friend,

Wm Wordsworth

1537. W. W. to HENRY REED

Address: Henry Reed Esqre, Philadelphia. [*In M. W.'s hand*]
Endorsed: Rec. Sep. 3.
Postmark: (1) 16 Aug. 1841 (2) 2 Sept.
Stamp: (1) Ambleside (2) Boston.
MS. Cornell.
Wordsworth and Reed, p. 56.

Rydal Mount
Ambleside
August 16th 41

My dear Mr Reed,

I have just received your last very obliging letter, and not to lose the Pacquet which leaves Liverpool in a day or two I write to thank you for it at once. It is already on its way to my Friend.[1] Mrs W. and I rejoice in the good news more than she will. She is so charitable and benevolent a creature that every one who knows her would grieve at her means being curtailed. Notwithstanding the resumption of payment I much wish that she had her money on this side of the Atlantic; for it appears to me next to impossible that peace can long be preserved in your Country. Your government I fear is too feeble; nor will your tumultuous democracy, I apprehend, be reconciled to subordination, till war either foreign or civil or perhaps both has taught them the necessity of it—God grant it may be otherwise, but such are my fears.

I have lately had the pleasure of seeing both in London and at my own Home the Bp of New Jersey.[2] He is a man of no ordinary powers of mind and attainments, of warm feeling, and sincere piety. Indeed I never saw a person of your Country, which is remarkable for cordiality, whose manner was so thoroughly cordial. He had been greatly delighted with his

[1] I. F.

[2] Dr. Doane. See previous letter.

reception in England and what he had seen of it both in Art and Nature. By the bye, I heard him preach an excellent sermon in London, I believe this privilege is of modern date. The B'p has furnished me with his funeral sermon upon Bp White,[1] to assist me in fulfilling a request which you first made to me, viz, that I would add a Sonnet to my ecclesiastical series, upon the union of the two episcopal churches of England and America.[2] I will endeavour to do so, when I have more leisure than at present, this being the season when our beautiful region attracts many strangers, who take up much of my time.—

Do you know Miss Peabody[3] of Boston? She has just sent me

[1] William White (1748–1836), the first Bishop of Pennyslvania, consecrated (with Samuel Provoost, first Bishop of New York) at Lambeth Palace on 4 Feb. 1787 by the Archbishops of Canterbury and York, and the Bishops of Bath and Wells and Peterborough. It was, as Broughton notes, chiefly through Bishop White that the American Church received the episcopal succession from the Church of England, for before his death he had taken part in the consecration of numerous American bishops. As Seabury's successor as Presiding Bishop, he was largely responsible for the original constitution of the Protestant Episcopal Church in America and for the American revision of the Prayer Book. Mrs. Henry Reed was his granddaughter.

[2] See *PW* iii. 390, 570. In fact, W. W. added three sonnets, on 'Aspects of Christianity in America'. See L. 1587 below. In his letter of 28 Apr. Reed had suggested as a theme for an addition to the *Ecclesiastical Sonnets* 'the transmission of the spiritual functions of the Church of England to the daughter Church in this Western Continent by *the consecration of the American Bishops*', recalling Bishop White's 'deep and reverential affection for Old England'. 'It was a great thing for England to give—and a great thing for America to receive—and how holy a temper seems to have prevailed in the whole transaction—how tranquillizing to contemplate the conduct of the saintly men who shared in it . . .' (*Wordsworth and Reed*, pp. 51–2.)

[3] Elizabeth Peabody (see pt. i, L. 312; pt. iii, L. 991), had written in Feb. 1838 sending Emerson's *Nature* and two other pamphlets (one of which was probably *The American Scholar*), and also a volume of Hawthorne's tales, to represent the ethos of the new America. In a subsequent letter on 20 Apr. 1839, she described Hawthorne's life at the Boston customs house: 'When I asked him what he did he said he was from sunrise to sunset quarrelling with Sea Captains and owners . . . and then he went home to his room and read *Wordsworth*.' She had written again on 29 Mar. 1841 sending more of Emerson's essays: 'I know no piety more awful than Mr. Emerson's—and yet it is one with joy—his creed might be the *Ode to Duty*.' (*WL MSS.*) The friendship of Ralph Waldo Emerson (1803–82) with Thomas Carlyle dates from his first visit to England in 1833, when he also called on W. W. (*RMVB*). Emerson's correspondence with Carlyle began the following year. See *English Traits*, 1856, Ch. i.

with the highest eulogy certain Essays of Mr Emerson. Our Carlyle and he appear to be what French used to call Esprits forts, though the French Idols shewed their spirit after a somewhat different Fashion. Our two present Philosophers, who have taken a language which they suppose to be English for their vehicle, are verily "Par nobile Fratrum," and it is a pity that the weakness of our age has not left them exclusively to the appropriate reward, mutual admiration. Where is the thing which now passes for philosophy at Boston to stop?[1]

I shall be very glad to hear from you at any time, being truly grateful for all your kindness, and sensible I trust of the claims you have upon my sincere esteem.

Ever faithfully yours
Wm Wordsworth

1538. W. W. to THOMAS POWELL

MS. Lilly Library, Indiana University.
Russell Noyes, 'Two Unpublished Wordsworth Letters', NQ ccix (Jan. 1964), 17–18.

Rydal Mount
August 19th—41

My dear Mr Powell,

I deferred writing to you till I could learn the price of the carriage upon the Portraits[2] that were sent down for my signature. It is 5/8 which be so good as to pay Mr Quillinan when you may happen to see him.—

The likeness seems much approved in this neighbourhood and the Engraving is certainly excellent. I cannot suggest any thing for its improvement. Our medical attendant is about to send for an impression, which he means to lend to a Bookseller in Ambleside to be exposed at his Shop-window, for a while—and this may induce others to apply for Copies. There is not much enthusiasm in this neighbourhood, so that I could scarcely venture to recommend sending Copies upon trial to Kendal, or Keswick in particular. At Kendal the Booksellers I employ, who

[1] Reed replied on 29 Nov.: 'It has assumed all the various phases of Socinianism, and with the restlessness of that heresy, it seems to be travelling to infidelity and pantheism and such, perhaps its natural, conclusions.' (*Wordsworth and Reed*, p. 60.)

[2] The engravings mentioned in L. 1541 below.

publish my little Vol: upon the Lakes, are named Hudson and Nicholson. They are responsible people, and perhaps a few Copies might be disposed of there by them. I will mention the subject to my Son Wm who lives at Carlisle, and he will be able to ascertain whether there is likely to be any demand there. There is a shop there, kept by Mr Turnham[1] who had prints sent down from London to dispose of upon commission but with what success I know not; but I do not know that there is little interest taken in literature or works of art in these two Counties; and for myself I do honestly believe that there is not a part of Great Britain in which I am less thought of than in Cumberland and Wes^{tnd} if you except my immediate neighbourhood.

Pray thank Mr Moon[2] on my part for his obliging intention of sending me a few Copies of the print. They will be much valued by my Connections.

Many thanks for the package of Cheeses.—and believe me my dear Mr Powell

faithfully yours Wm Wordsworth

1539. W. W. to MARY FRANCES HOWLEY[3]

MS. Lilly Library, Indiana University.
Russell Noyes, 'Wordsworth and Sir George Beaumont's Family', TLS, 10 Aug. 1962.

Rydal Mount
August 23^{d} 41

Dear Mrs Howley,

Engagements, which at this season of the year are incessant in this place, have prevented my earlier acknowledgement of your obliging Letter. When I was at Oxford more than two years ago, Mr. Sergeant Merewether[4] asked for my opinion about the desireableness of his Brother's removal from Coleorton, if that could be effected by exchange. The Sergeant was himself very anxious that it should be done, and the feeling which I then shared with him was strengthened by all that fell under my notice during my late residence at Coleorton. Accordingly I did not scruple to forward Mr. Merewether's Letter to Sir George,

[1] Charles Thurnham, of English Street.

[2] The publisher of the engraving.

[3] Wife of the Archbishop of Canterbury.

[4] Brother of Francis Merewether, rector of Coleorton (see pt. iii, L. 1014).

without waiting for the Writers permission; though I was aware that many reasons might prevent Mr. Merewether's wish being gratified. It only remains for those who are interested in the matter to hope that some more favorable opportunity may occur. There is however a depressing consideration attending the affair which one cannot get rid of; viz, the too great probability that wherever Mr. Merewether may be placed, there is something in his character, arising from bodily constitution I think, which will stand in the way of his ever being at peace with all those with whom he may have to act. This has occasioned some of his most judicious neighbours to say of him that he is fond of being in hot water,—I should rather say, that he cannot keep out of it.—It would be most unjust to him were I not to express my firm belief that his intentions are good and that he is most anxious to do his duty, while he fails sadly as a practical Man.

Our residence under dear Sir George's roof was most agreeable. A kinder or better man no where exists. You know how deeply I am interested in his welfare on his own account, and for the sake of those that are departed. Perhaps you and the Archbishop may think, I was interfering beyond what I was called upon or even had a right to do, when I tell you that looking at his solitary situation, I could not help expressing to him a regret that he had not married again, having been left a Widower so young.[1] With much feeling and in a tone that did his heart the highest honor, he replied "that having been blessed as he had been in the Wife he had lost, how was he to hope to meet with a second in whom he might not be grievously disappointed". I felt and acknowledged the force of this expression of his affections; but still I cannot forbear mentioning to you the impression on my mind that the circumstance in which he is placed would be less hazardous for his happiness if he could meet with a female Companion of suitable age, of good judgement, and temper and amiable manners. His life, except when his boys are with him, is for the most part very lonely. I was truly glad to hear that Mrs Kingsmill[2] and Constance[3] were about to visit him, and much regretted that I had not the pleasure of seeing them all together.—

[1] Lady Beaumont, Mrs Howley's daughter, had died in 1834.

[2] Mrs. Howley's second daughter Anne (see pt. iii, L. 1123).

[3] Sir George's daughter.

The grounds are beautifully kept and managed.—I suggested some improvement in the treatment of the shrubs upon the lawn in front, which were heavy in the appearance of the several plots.—I also thought but this I did not like to mention that the little nook in the winter garden where the pool is was too much dressed with shells and other pretty ornaments. Perhaps at some time you could hint that. There is a want of evergreens in place[s] of the winter garden which have been too freely cut. This I mentioned and Sir George seems quite willing to admit and supply the defect.

With most respectful remembrances to the Archbishop in which Mrs. Wordsworth unites and every good wish for both him and yourself believe me

dear Mrs Howley
faithfully yours
Wm Wordsworth

1540. W. W. and M. W. to ISABELLA FENWICK

MS. WL.
LY iii. 1088 (—).

Monday 30th [Aug. 1841]

I sit down to write you a few words, my beloved Friend, Mary being very much and somewhat painfully engaged. In the first place Jane,[1] of whose attack of fever you have probably heard, and which has kept her in bed a fortnight and 3 days is still in a state that requires perpetual attention; and next, little Sara[2] is in the midst of a much worse access of the same complaint from which she was suffering when you saw her at Tintern. Her poor Mother is afflicted beyond measure, and has prepared her mind to part with her; though I do not myself apprehend her death at present. Her Mother however says that she is held just in the same way, and more threateningly, than for some time her departed Sister[3] was. Nothing can be more admirable than the Mother's behaviour—she is a Woman of ten thousand. I wish you could witness her fortitude, her resignation, her activity and resolution, and the air even of chearfulness which she often

[1] The maid.
[2] Sarah Hutchinson.
[3] Mary Hutchinson (d. 1837).

keeps up for all our sakes. God bless her! She has been sorely tried for many a long year.—Poor little Sara is much worse this morning—otherwise my Mary and her Mother[1] would have gone to Ambleside.[2]

But enough—How fortunate it is that we have Anne[3] with us—and that my poor dear Sister is no worse, so that as we only see a little Tea-company the family, and our little establishment are equal to their duties. Emmie[4] grows upon us. She is a sweet affectionate Creature—she is learning to knit, which she takes to with admirable perseverance. I have said little or nothing to her about literature, being so much more anxious to impress her with the paramount importance of womanly virtues, and acquiring those Domestic habits which may make [her?] useful in a station however humble. Her mother, I fear, has more worldly ambition than I wish her Daughter to partake; who is, I believe, at present entirely free from it. She has attached herself much to Mrs Hutchinson, who has every thing which Emmie would be most likely to want hereafter.—Do you know that Jane Arnold is engaged to Mr Cotton,[5] one of the masters of Rugby School. He may be a very good young man and a clever one, but a more unattractive youth (but he is not like a youth) I never saw. He has a look about his eyes which is really formidable, his complection is that almost of a Mulatto, and he has two half [? brothers] whose hue is absolutely such. Well, Love sees everything through his own eyes and you know that love grows out of opportunity, in my mind indeed more than out of anything else.—I wish I could send you any pleasant news, but it is scarce; in small matters I must tell you that we hear that the Wishing Gate is destroyed, which put me upon

[1] i.e. Mrs. Hutchinson.

[2] At this point a whole paragraph was erased by M. W. who wrote in: 'Dearest Miss F. I have crossed this out not being willing that it should occupy your thoughts, it was of no consequence to you being absent.'

[3] A maid.

[4] Emmie Fisher.

[5] The Revd. George Edward Lynch Cotton, D.D. (1813–66), educated at Westminster and Trinity College, Cambridge, Assistant Master at Rugby, 1837–52, Headmaster of Marlborough, 1852–8, and Bishop of Calcutta, 1858–66, where he set up many schools on Arnold's principles. He met his death by accidental drowning in the Ganges. See *Memoir of George Edward Lynch Cotton, D.D.*, ed. Mrs. Cotton, 1871. He broke off his engagement to Jane Arnold the following year, and married his cousin in 1845. Jane Arnold married W. E. Forster in 1850.

writing a Poem[1] which will go to Dora tomorrow with a request that a transcript may be made of it for you—then, what is far worse, John Green, son of our late Butcher, is building a huge tall box of a House (right in the centre of the vale of Grasmere as you cross it) to the utter destruction of the primitive rustic beauty of the whole, as touchingly described by the Poet Gray in his journal written 70 years ago. This has hurt me more than, considering what human life is, ought to have done. Pray remember us most kindly to Mrs Master[2]—you know what a favorite she is with us.—I say nothing about public affairs. Mary is very anxious that my office[3] should be procured for Wm, an anxiety which I share to a certain extent, and for the same cause—a fear that from the state of his health, and a want of versatility in his mind, and of quickness, he would not be fit for the only employment which might be offered to him if any is to be offered, or is procurable. I have said nothing about my longing desire to have you under our roof—which I trust will be as near the end of the month as possible—ever yours most faithfully and affectionately

Wm Wordsworth

[*M. W. writes*]

Dearest friend, I cannot put up so much blank paper to you, and I am cheared this afternoon by seeing Jane somewhat revived. Mr Fell[4] has allowed us to give a little wine which is an encouraging symptom—but indeed we have been very fearful about her. As to little Sarah, she is truly in a melancholy state. I think W. has not mentioned Keswick, but there is nothing new to be said of them—During Bertha's visit, she saw her Father occasionally, but he knew her not. Mrs Lovell and Kate I hope go on comfortably with Cuth:[5] in their cottage—they visited all the People while the Hills[6] were there. Mr Myers[7] was at Fox-how the other day, he did not call here, which I did not regret.—The James Marshalls[8] have Capt and Mrs Temple[9]

[1] *The Wishing-Gate Destroyed* (*PW* ii. 301). This letter establishes the date of the poem.

[2] See pt. ii, L. 575.

[3] The Distributorship.

[4] The Ambleside surgeon.

[5] Cuthbert Southey.

[6] i.e. Bertha and Herbert Hill.

[7] The Revd. Frederick Myers (see L. 1487 above).

[8] James Marshall of Coniston and his wife, formerly Mary Spring Rice.

[9] James Marshall's sister and brother-in-law (see pt. ii, L. 463).

and their children with them at Conistone this week—on Friday they are to dine and sleep at Fox-how, and go to Keswick on Sat—whether, on their way to Hallsteads, to make way for the Bride and Bridegroom[1] whom Mary M. expects will pass the honeymoon at Coniston, and to attend the wedding I do not know.—She expects her Father at that time and Lady M[2] being at Hallsteads the family assemblage looks as if it was about to take place. Mary is very *large* and very happy.

You know that the Arnolds are detained here by the continuance of fever at Rugby. The D^{r} and Mr Cotton have their classes and the neighbourhood is more like that of a University than of the idle Lakes. Students with their books under their arms meet you at every turn—and all the beds are filled. Mrs Sted, Mary Huck—every house receives lodgers. All these will have departed before we see you dear friend. The Arnolds hope to go the next week—We shall also lose dear Emmie in the course of it. A favorable opportunity has occurred, for her to travel with Mr Ball's[3] sister Mrs Waring of Bristol who will leave her with her Father, whom we shall appoint to meet her at Glocester. This is a great relief to W. who feared he might have had to conduct her as far, at any rate as Liverpool, as he engaged to see her into safe *custody*, even to take her home if no proper escort was to be met with.—Poor Isabella[4] goes to town (via steam boat to Liverpool) on Thursday, to be under the Dentist—in all probability she will be in Town when you are. I think she will take the Q'^{s}[5] lodgings. Dorothy[6] and the Baby are to be her companions. She hopes to bring the *three motherless* Cousins from India home with her—poor things what is to become of them all!—They have got a new Governess which Isa: says promises well—and school is resumed at Brigham. Henry[7] left us last Tuesday. Tomorrow Mrs Curwen and Jane[8] are to breakfast with us, on their way from the Island where they have been staying a few weeks. Dearest Willy's sprained wrist I hope is better, as he tells of

[1] Cordelia Marshall was engaged to William Whewell (see pt. i, L. 382), who was about to succeed C. W. as Master of Trinity. See L. 1552 below.

[2] Lady Monteagle, formerly Mary Anne Marshall (see L. 1503 above).

[3] William Ball, owner of Glen Rothay (see pt. iii, L. 1048).

[4] John W.'s wife.

[5] Quillinans'.

[6] i.e. Mrs. Benson Harrison.

[7] M. W.'s grandson.

[8] Mrs. Curwen's fifth daughter, who died unmarried.

going into Roxboro'shire to shoot for 2 or 3 days—I hope these Coms:[1] may make a transfer in his favor—were I his Father I would make no stipulations for myself. We are in small room, and our days few, so that we are quite rich enough. By the bye, but this is secret, Dr W. means to give up T. C.[2] as soon as he can hope to have a chance for a worthy Successor—without stipulating for any thing. Wm blames him. In his own case I should not—Dearest friend you know not how much we long to have you at home. God bless you, write and tell me about your foot—With dear love from all, and affec regards to Miss Master—By the bye young Whately[3] who is returned for a short time saw much of the H. Taylors in Germany—they were well, and happy, Adieu

ever faithfully yrs
M. Wordsworth

The Qs go to Canterbury tomorrow. Are you not glad that they are to quit that place and will be among our own friends for the next 6 months—Dear Father takes true pains to push the wine trade for them.

1541. W. W. to [?] F. G. MOON[4]

MS. WL. Hitherto unpublished.

[late Aug. 1841]

Dear Sir,

I have duly received a Portfolio containing six Impressions of my Portrait, from the pencil [of] Miss Gillies, and engraved in a very superior style indeed. I trust that it will be liked by my Friends though as you must well know it is impossible entirely to please every body. Mr Powell begged me to make any remarks that might strike me when the Proof was sent some time ago. I did not see at that time any cause, but Mrs Wordsworth has since pointed out that in one important

[1] The Commissioners of Stamps.

[2] Trinity College.

[3] Edward Whateley (see L. 1404 above).

[4] The publisher who commissioned Miss Gillies's portrait of W. W. (see pt. ii, L. 1345), to be engraved. The engraving by Edward McInnes was published in London by Moon on 6 Aug. 1841.

particular Miss Gillies has failed in the likeness. If you take the trouble to look at the wretched portrait prefixed to my poems,[1] you will see that it differs much from Miss Gillies, in the shape of the upper part of the head. Miss G. has given a skull rising much too high above the ear, and not sufficiently bulged out at the sides, so that in this respect the peculiarity is better preserved in a performance otherwise contemptible.—I am afraid that it is too late to make in your Engraving any improvement in this point. Pray let me know if . . .

[*cetera desunt*]

1542. W. W. to DR. GOODFELLOW[2]

MS. WL. Hitherto unpublished.

Rydal Mount
Aug[t] 31st —41

Mr Wordsworth very much regrets that such an opposition should have been raised to D[r] Goodfellow's appointment to the office of Physician to the Infirmary of Carlisle,[3] and the more so because under existing circumstances Mr Wordsworth finds himself unable to acceed to D[r] Goodfellow's proposal.—

[1] W. H. Watt's engraving of Pickersgill's first portrait of W. W., published by Moxon in the *Poetical Works*, 1836.

[2] Perhaps Robert Goodfellow (b. 1805), the son of a Cumberland farmer, who was educated at Carlisle Grammar School, and entered Trinity College, Dublin, in 1826 but thereafter disappears from the records. No physician of this name is recorded at Carlisle in this period.

[3] The foundation stone of the County Infirmary, near the canal basin, was laid by Sir James Graham in 1830, but owing to some misunderstanding between the committee of management and the contractor, the building, to the design of Robert Tattersall of Manchester, was not opened until eleven years later, in Aug. 1841. The election of two physicians and two surgeons for the new institution was held on 11 Aug. amid expression of disquiet from the medical practitioners of the city. See *Carlisle Patriot* for 31 July, and 7, 14, and 28 Aug. 1841. The governors' choice as superintendent of the infirmary finally fell on Henry Lonsdale, M.D., author of *The Worthies of Cumberland*.

1543. W. W. to EDWARD and DORA QUILLINAN

MS. WL.
LY iii. 1090.

Sunday Morn, [late Aug. *or* early Sept. 1841]

My dear Mr Quillinan,

Many thanks for your Extract; but Miss Hoare must have forgotten one half of my request, which was that she would transcribe the passage from the same Book, where Sir Isaac[1] is reported to have expressed his wonder that the Lord Pembroke[2] of that day could have spent so much time money and pains in collecting Stone-dolls, the great Philosopher meaning the celebrated collection of statues and other marbles which are [at] Wilton House. This coupled with his evasion of the question about Poetry, and putting the answer into the mouth of Barrow[3] makes it very probable that he would have been no very competent judge in any department of imaginative literature. Those very words of his I still desire to possess if they could be found without much trouble.

We are going on but poorly in this House; Jane is still very unwell—this morning she has had an attack of Bile, has thrown up her medicine and is hot with an increase of fever. So that her illness must be long and tedious in the most favorable view that can be taken of [it.] We have not yet seen Mr Fell to-day—but his report will [be] given you before this letter goes to the Post. Then poor Sara,[4] is, dear Dora, just as she was when you saw her at Tintern Abbey, weeping or sleeping three parts of the day. Her mother says, I am glad to tell you, that she is better this morning. Her illness has to do with deranged Bile; and I own when I look at her slender form, and think of her departed sister, I am much alarmed, I do not mean for the immediate result, but for [the] further malady which may carry her off. Her Mother's behaviour under these trials is most beautiful and she is in truth a Woman, as her Brother[5] is a Man, of ten thousand.—I am not

[1] Sir Isaac Newton (1642–1727), the celebrated mathematician.

[2] Thomas Herbert, 8th Earl of Pembroke (1656–1733), politician and courtier: President of the Royal Society, 1689–90.

[3] Isaac Barrow (1630–77), theologian and mathematician, Newton's predecessor as Lucasian Professor of Mathematics at Cambridge, and Master of Trinity from 1673.

[4] Sarah Hutchinson.

[5] John Monkhouse of the Stow.

much daunted by that ugly extract from the American paper; but still I fear that the Mississippis are a bad concern. An American gentleman[1] who was here the other day told me that he had read much upon that subject, and had found it asserted that if taxes were imposed by the Mississippi Legislature for the payment of the interest on these Bonds, many of the people composing the State would fly off into some other. What infatuation to trust money to the good faith of such communities. Poor dear Aunt Sara,[2] I often think of what would have been her state of mind with her little fortune in such a condition. There is a little tract of Dr Channing's[3] reprinted at Bristol and sold for two pence; it might perhaps interest you on account of the manner in which your father is spoken of in it. It is entitled 'The Present Age'.—I quite agree with you about Miss Sedgewick's[4]

[1] Probably Dr. Gray of Boston (*RMVB*). [2] i.e. the late S. H.

[3] In *The Present Age: An Address Delivered before the Mercantile Library Company of Philadelphia, May 11, 1841*, W. E. Channing (see pt. i, L. 337; pt. iii, L. 991) spoke of the 'spirit of universal sympathy' evinced by the literature of the age, and went on to refer to W. W. as follows: 'The great poet of our times, Wordsworth, one of the few who are to live, has gone to common life, to the feelings of our universal nature, to the obscure and neglected portions of society, for beautiful and touching themes. Nor ought it to be said, that he has shed over these the charms of his genius; as if in themselves they had nothing grand or lovely. Genius is not a creator, in the sense of fancying or feigning what does not exist. Its distinction is, to discern more of truth than common minds. It sees, under disguises and humble forms, everlasting beauty. This it is the prerogative of Wordsworth to discern and reveal in the ordinary walks of life, in the common human heart. He has revealed the loveliness of the primitive feelings, of the universal affections of the human soul. The grand truth which pervades his poetry is, that the beautiful is not confined to the rare, the new, the distant, to scenery and modes of life open only to the few; but that it is poured forth profusely on the common earth and sky, that it gleams from the loneliest flower, that it lights up the humblest sphere, that the sweetest affections lodge in lowly hearts, that there is a sacredness, dignity, and loveliness, in lives which few eyes rest on, that even in the absence of all intellectual culture, the domestic relations can quietly nourish that disinterestedness which is the element of all greatness, and without which intellectual power is a splendid deformity. Wordsworth is the poet of humanity; he teaches reverence for our universal nature; he breaks down the factitious barriers between human hearts.' (*Works*, 6 vols., 1840–4, vi. 187–8).

[4] Catharine Maria Sedgwick (1789–1867), popular American novelist, whose celebrations of the American domestic scene won the praise of Bryant and Hawthorne. The reference here is either to her *Letters from Abroad to Kindred at Home*, published by Moxon in two vols. in 1841, or to the *Poetical Remains of the*

Book—such productions add to my dislike of Literary Ladies—indeed make me almost detest the name. By the bye—we have in our possession an odd thing—the sheet of that same publication which Mr Kenyon caused to be cancelled on account of the manner in which he is flattered therein. We shall keep it as a curiosity. I don't think it quite correct in the Moxons circulating those things as they do, as waste Paper. Our's came with a parcel of Excursions we had from their shop. Mr Fell has just been here—he says that we must go on cautiously, and resume the suspended medicine—Mr Fell is going and this letter with him. I will write again to-morrow and send the poem.[1]

W. W.

1544. W. W. to JOHN PEACE

MS. untraced.
Mem. Grosart (—). *K* (—). *LY iii. 1091* (—).

Rydal Mount, Sept. 4, 1841.

My dear Peace,

. . . Mrs W. is quite well. We were three months and as many weeks absent before we reached our own home again. We made a very agreeable tour in Devonshire, going by Exeter to Plymouth, and returning along the coast by Salisbury and Winchester to London. In London and its neighbourhood we stayed not quite a month. During this tour we visited my old haunts, at and about Alfoxden and Nether Stowey, and at Coleorton, where we stayed several days. These were farewell visits for life, and, of course, not a little interesting. . . .

Ever faithfully yours,
W. Wordsworth

late Lucretia Maria Davidson, Philadelphia, 1841, to which she contributed a memoir (see also pt. ii, L. 654).

[1] The epitaph on Owen Lloyd. See L. 1534 above.

1545. W. W. to MR. HORSFIELD

MS. untraced.
LY iii. 1091.

Rydal Sept^{br} 27th 1841

Sir

The applications made to me for Autographs have long been so numerous as to compel my declining to answer them, and this must be my excuse for not having before complied with your request

I remain

with thanks for the verses you sent though regretting you should have cause to write in so sad a strain

Yours truly
Wm Wordsworth

1546. W. W. to BENJAMIN ROBERT HAYDON

Address: B. R. Haydon Esq, Burwood-place, Connaught-Street, London.
Postmark: 28 Sept. 1841.
Stamp: Penrith.
MS. Profesor Willard Pope.
Haydon. LY iii. 1092.

Lowther,
Sept^{br} 28, '41.

My dear Haydon[1]

Your Letter of the 11th was duly received, and ought to have had an earlier [answer], especially on account of the notice of your Son, and the request that I would give him a Letter [of][2] advice. To tell you the truth I knew not how to set about it, any farther than concerned the expression of the interest I take in him, and my sincere and earnest wishes for his welfare. Upon an occasion like this it seems so difficult to say any thing which would not look like preaching, particularly is it difficult to a Son

[1] *Written* Letter.

[2] *Word dropped out*. Haydon had written on 11 Sept. from Devonport whither he had taken his son Frederick, W. W.'s godson, to join his ship, adding in a postscript, 'a letter of advice to Frederick might do good to a dear boy.' (*WL MSS.*)

of yours, who I know must have been religiously brought up, and duly impressed with moral principles. His thoughts also must have been directed by you to his profession[al] obligations, and those sentiments must have been fostered in him which will be likely to lead to his being an honour to his profession.—I will not however dismiss the subject from my thoughts, though I feel at present without courage to undertake what you propose.

I was at Devonport for three days last summer, along with Mrs Wordsworth and a dear Friend of ours. I wish our visit had happened at the same time as yours. We were much pleased with the surrounding objects of Art and Nature, and passed a delightful afternoon at Mount Edgecumb.[1] The three Towns,[2] the Surrounding hills, the shipping, Forts and the water combine beautifully. There is however one great want, a cathedral, or at least a majestic Church, which ought to be planted upon some rising ground, so as to preside over the whole, and thus remind the Beholder of the dependence of all human Power, whether by sea or land, upon Divine Providence. We were also at Exeter, and made a careful tour along the coast as far as Charmouth, thence to Salisbury, Southampton, and Winchester which last place I had never seen before.

Your account of your feelings upon revisiting your native place[3] was extremely interesting, and I thank you for the details you give of your early studies in the art to which your works have done much honor. With the best wishes for your future welfare and prosperity, I remain my dear Haydon, faithfully yours

Wm Wordsworth

You do not mention Mrs Haydon; may I venture to hope that her health is something better.—

[1] The Elizabethan mansion of the Edgecumbe family on the west side of Plymouth Sound. It was burnt out during the second world war.

[2] i.e. Plymouth, Devonport and Stonehouse.

[3] Haydon was a native of Plymouth. In his letter he had written: 'I went with my dear Boy, to a Farm I lodged at 50 years ago—two generations of Farmers were passed, it is called little Saltram—no modern improvement had reached it—there is the same lane the same meadows, the same rookery, the same date (1633 over the door), the same pure air, . . . the same dank and muddy path from the same lovely view, the same green fields. The world has rolled over it, with its wars, and its intrigues, and its slaveries, and its vices, as if unwilling to disturb its beauty, its tranquillity, its unearthly happiness! My Father and Mother and Friends are passed, but there stands the cottage, as if its silence and stability were eternal!'

1547. W. W. to ELIZABETH FISHER

MS. Cornell.
Fortnightly Review, xciv (Nov. 1910), 882–3.

[? Autumn 1841]

. . .I do not like to address conversation for guidance, or instruction to young persons *directly*, more than I find necessary. But I have thought it proper both directly and indirectly to impress Emmie's mind with a conviction that talents and Genius, and intellectual acquirements, are of little worth, compared with the right management of the affections, and sound judgement in the conduct of life; that what she may become as a Woman, is of infinitely more importance than what she may grow into as a person of splendid intellect, or an Authoress in any department of Literature. All this I have urged not merely for her own tranquility and happiness, but for much higher considerations of domestic and social duty, and religious obligation.

I have with pleasure observed what I was prepared for, that her heart was open to perceive all that was amiable in the manners and conduct of those around, though they were persons with little or no pretensions to intellectual distinction. Nevertheless I cannot conceal from you, that I have had opportunities of observing that, as is most natural for one so gifted, she attaches undue importance to powers of mind, not in any way to her discredit, but yet so as to call for counteracting influences, which must come mainly for some time, from the right-mindedness, or wisdom of those with whom she lives. But I am writing an enormously long letter, which might be lengthened still more unreasonably were I to give way to the temptations which the subject strongly suggests. I will only add, that I am decidedly against the publication just now of her Poems, and this from considerations wholly independent of their high merits, and which I will state, at least the chief of them, at some future time.

At present farewell
Ever faithfully your affectionate cousin and friend,
W. Wordsworth

1548. W. W. to EDWARD MOXON

MS. Henry E. Huntington Library.
K (—). LY iii. 1093.

[*In M. W.'s hand*]

Rydal M^t 2 Oct^r [1841]

Dear Mr Moxon,

It is quite impossible that the 8 Sonnets of which Lady Blessington[1] speaks, can be of my writing—the subject is one that I have not touched for many years. I am however truly glad to learn that such Sonnets are in course of production, and promise myself much pleasure in reading them, as I hope, and am pretty sure they will fall in my way. I *did* send to Mr Robinson a few Sonnets in M.S. in which I gave vent to my feelings upon the servitude under which Italy was languishing,[2] and these he told me he had lost—so that they may possibly see the light at some time or other without my consent.

As I am upon the matter of Sonnets, let me recur to the 13 or 14 which I wrote some time ago, upon the subject of Capital Punishment.[3] What would be the expence of printing, say 100 Copies? to be dispersed among my friends, or Persons of Consideration in Par^t or elsewhere. This question is asked because I am afraid of printing any thing that is composed with care, in Newspapers. To gratify Haydon I wrote lately a sonnet upon his Picture of Wellington etc., and placed it at his disposal, either to publish when and where he liked, or to circulate in M.S. It *was* published accordingly, but with so many gross typografical blunders that I am resolved nothing of mine shall make its first appearance in that way again. By the bye have you any copies of the Excursion as sold separately. It has been a good deal enquired after, and Mr Troughton the bookseller here recommends that they should be put up in a more tasty manner somewhat like the Poems—particularly as the book is sold for a shilling more than the others.

I have no more to say at present, but the expression of regret

[1] See pt. iii, L. 1023.

[2] See *Memorials of a Tour in Italy, 1837*, nos. vii, xi, xxv–vi (*PW* iii. 215, 217, 228).

[3] See L. 1370 above and Ls. 1554 and 1557 below.

that we have not seen you here—On Monday next Mrs W. and I leave home for 10 days, therefore if you still intend to favor us you must defer your visit till after that time.

Very sincerely d^r Mr Moxon
Yours
[*signed*] Wm Wordsworth

1549. W. W. to EDWARD QUILLINAN

Address: Mr Quillinan. [*In M. W.'s hand*]
Endorsed: Mr Wordsworth Rydal Mount Rec^d at Canterbury October 9, 1841.
MS. WL.
K (—). *Cornhill* (—). *LY iii. 1107* (—).

[*c.* 7 Oct. 1841]

My dear Mr Quillinan,

We have read your verses[1] with much pleasure; they want neither eye nor feeling, and are upon the whole—which is saying a great deal—worthy of the subject. But the expression is here and there faulty, as I am pretty sure you must be yourself aware.

'Piles' ought to be *pile*, but 'aisles', a necessary word, has caused a sacrifice to rhyme. 'Ecstatic' is a word not too strong perhaps, though referring to stone, considered apart from the human heart; but coupled with it thus, it strikes me as being so.

To 'conscious pillars' I should have preferred an epithet addressed to the sight, and appropriate to architecture. I should like *chequered* better than 'mottled', which is a word almost always used in an unfavorable or mean sense, as 'mottled with measles', 'mottled soap', etc.

'By her *sculpture*' seems too strong a word for the touch of the moon; and 'flecked', as far as I am acquainted with the word, applies to spots on the surface having reference to shade or colour, and not to incision.

[*In M. W.'s hand*]

The primary sense—that most frequently used—of the word 'anatomy', being the art or act of dissection, causes some

[1] *Interior of Canterbury Cathedral, as seen by Moonlight, September 30, 1841.* The text was evidently altered in the light of W. W.'s suggestions here and eventually published in E. Q.'s *Poems*, 1853.

obscurity or confusion when joined with the phrase of what he was; which might be avoided—though perhaps with some loss of force—if it was not for the confusion, by altering the passage thus:—

His grim anatomy,
So fall the rays *shed by the moon*,
That in their silent strife,

or *from the clear moon*.

A better epithet might be found than '*swelling* with richness bland'. You must be well aware that this is the worst line in the poem. All the rest is beautiful in feeling, as it is faultless in expression. . . .

[*cetera desunt*]

1550. W. W. to PHILIP COURTENAY

MS. British Library. Hitherto unpublished.

[? early Oct. 1841][1]

. . . the loss. I should be very glad of your judgement, and I hope if any thing promising should occur, you, with your usual kindness, would bear me in mind.—

I was glad to learn from Sir Gregory Lewin,[2] whom I had the pleasure of meeting the other day at Lowther, that you do not think of going abroad this Autumn, and also, he assured me, to my great satisfaction, that yourself and family were well.—

We are all in good health.

Believe me to be
dear Mr Courtenay
faithfully your
much obliged
Wm Wordsworth

return Mr Cooksons[3] note if you please.

[1] Perhaps to be dated by reference to next letter, where M. W. mentions that W. W. has instructed Courtenay, his financial adviser, to sell his National Provincial stock.

[2] Sir Gregory Allnutt Lewin (1801–45), barrister on the northern circuit, Recorder of Doncaster, 1842–5. W. W. had known him for some years. (See *RMVB* for 1832).

[3] Strickland Cookson.

1551. M. W. to H. C. R.

Endorsed: 14th Octr 1841. Mrs Wordsworth.
MS. Dr. Williams's Library.
Morley, i. 443.

Rydal Mount
Octr 14th [1841]

My dear Friend

The party assembled here, consisting of dear Miss Fenwick, our little friend, whom she brought with her 10 days ago, Anna Ricketts; Miss Rogers, my Sister Mary Hutchinson and her daughter (whom we found at Rydal after our return from our Spring wanderings) my husband and myself were overjoyed by the sight of your letter—having lost sight of you so long—We had frequently talked of you, wondering what you were about—and I could not help reading pro bono publico your very entertaining detail as we sate round the dinner table—before I sent it up to our poor dear Sister, to whom, like yourself, you so considerately addressed it—and your affectionate attention had its desired effect—for she was delighted—and assured me, as she generally does on such occasions, that she would answer it *tomorrow*.'—

Miss Rogers, who returned to us on Monday to *finish* a visit which *in part* she paid us on her way into Scotland, a month ago, leaves us tomorrow, and my Sister etc next day. Our little friend remains 2 or 3 weeks longer—before that time we look for Dr Wordsworth—when no doubt our Sons will contrive to meet their Uncle—after which, except perhaps for a visit from Kate Southey,—our dear friend Miss F. and we shall be closed-in for the Winter—and shall look forward to a Month of *Whist* by our Christmas fire a great pleasure dear friend which we claim from you as a *right*—and which you must on no consideration deprive us of.

Your letter is very interesting especially as we travelled over so much of the same ground ourselves—and shall have so much to say about it when we meet—You are right in your conjecture about Lyswyn farm[1]—but you do not mention Alfoxden—surely

[1] See *Anecdote for Fathers* (*PW* i. 241), ll. 30 ff. In his letter of 11 Oct. (see Morley, i. 443), H. C. R. had enquired whether the Lyswyn farm of the poem was in fact John Thelwall's farm in Wales where H. C. R. had visited him in 1799.

you did not miss seeing that place, *famous* above all the Poet's haunts—except perhaps Racedown, where with him and his Sister Mary Hutchinson (as she then was) passed a long winter and spring[1]—and to which our dear friend took us the day before our separation—We parted at Charmouth, we by Coach to Salisbury Winchester, etc, as you know to London when you were upon that melancholy occasion at Bury[2]—She to her Brother in Law's in Somersetshire

We hear little from Greta Hall—no change in dear S. except that we understand he is occasionally very much more irritable, sometimes violent. Poor Kate's visits are, as stipulated, merely for a few minutes once a week—Bertha, who was at Keswick with her Sister for a few weeks a short time since, occasionally, poor thing! went to look at her Father, who alas! was scarcely ever conscious of her presence. She never saw Mrs Southey. Since her return home she has given birth to a Son, who was christened last Sunday by the name of Herbert Southey.

The Arnolds only left Fox how at the end of last Month—having been confined here, in consequence of a fever which was prevalent, and in some instances fatal at Rugby—After the vacation some of the upper Classes joined them here, and you would have been surprized to have heard the humming sound of Latin and Greek that used, as we passed, to issue from the window of your sitting-room—where was located one of the Masters—by the bye one, who is to be married to that nice creature Jane Arnold[3] who in less than a year is to be converted into the *Matron* of a *boarding house*! The connection seems to be highly appro^{d} by the family—but we think it a pity so early that her youthful freedom should be interrupted—but this is not for us to determine.

I rejoice that Dora is about to draw nearer her old friends—I shall feel our separation to be much less painful than had they remained at Canterbury—tho' she seems to have liked the place, and certainly has been very happy there.

As W^{m} has not been in correspondence with you, since your magnificent present of books arrived, he begs me to tell you, with his best thanks how well they look upon the shelf on which Willy in our absence proudly placed them—And I am also to tell you, that, for the quiet of his mind he has given Courtenay

[1] In 1797.

[2] The death of his nephew.

[3] See L. 1540 above.

positive directions to sell out of the N.P.B.[1]—reconciling himself to any loss that may fall upon him.

And now, dear friend I will release you with the affec. remembrances fr all here, and in the earnest hope that we shall see you at the appointed time, viz to eat your Christmas day dinner with us, I remain most sincerely yours

M. Wordsworth

1552. W. W. to C. W.

MS. British Library. Hitherto unpublished.

Rydal Mount
15th Oct. 1841.

My dear Brother,

I hope the business of your resignation will be managed to your satisfaction, particularly as regards the appointment of your Successor.[2]

Before we received your Letter we had seen your intention announced in the Newspapers.—

We shall rejoice to see you and the longer you can stay the better.

We received a kind invitation to the wedding which we were obliged to decline for many reasons.[3]—

[1] National Provincial Bank. See previous letter and L. 1553 below.

[2] William Whewell (see also L. 1540 above) and Cordelia Marshall were married at Watermillock Church on 12 Oct. On the day of the marriage C. W. had written to W. W. to announce his resignation of the Mastership of Trinity (*WL MSS.*), and he wrote the same day to Whewell, 'I can truly say that I retained the office so long as I have done under one Administration, and have lost so little time in seeking to part with it under another, in the earnest *desire, hope* and *trust*, that you *may* be, and *will* be, my successor.' On 17 Oct. Peel wrote to Whewell announcing the Queen's approval of his appointment. See Mrs. Stair Douglas, *The Life and Selections from the Correspondence of William Whewell, D.D.*, 1881, pp. 225 ff.

[3] W. W. and M. W. subsequently spent two days at Monk Coniston with the Whewells, and they visited Rydal Mount early in November, while C. W. was there (*RMVB*). In his letter of invitation on 14 Oct. Whewell had written: 'One of the main objects in the remainder of my life will be [to] pursue such moral speculations as I have already entered upon; and in these if there be any thing good, I am persuaded that I have been led to it in no small degree by the lessons which in former times I learnt from your writings, to which I always ascribe a

We have this morning parted with Mrs Hutchinson and her younger Daughter who have been with us above three months.—

Miss Fenwick is under our roof and will remain for the winter. We have also Miss Anna Ricketts, who I hope will not be gone before you come.

Our dear Sister is often distressed by uncomfortable bodily feelings but she is on the whole much better than she used to be. It will delight her to see you.—

We have received a Vol. of Christopher's School Sermons[1] which we like much as far as we have read of it.—

Pray bring along with you that Edition of the Paradise lost in which you shewed me so many errors of the Press.—

With love from Mary and our dear Sister, I remain

your affectionate Brother
Wm Wordsworth

1553. W. W. to H. C. R.

Endorsed: Octr 1841. Wordsworth (investments).
MS. Dr. Williams's Library.
Morley, i. 447.

[late Oct. 1841]

I hold the pen for my Husband M. W.

My dear friend

I was determined by nothing that Mr Courtenay had said or insinuated. Only as far as he was concerned sanguine expectations, which he has often expressed to me upon the N. P. B.[2] having not been realized, but quite the contrary—I have had less confidence in his judgement both here, and in general.

My resolution was come to in consequence of a growing conviction that there is something very unsound in the constitution of these Banks however well any one or more of them may happen to be managed for any given length of time: and with regard to this particular one, the low and falling price of the Shares in the market proved the want of confidence of the Public in it. Furthermore I learnt from a Quarter entitled to much

considerable portion of the formation or reformation of my intellectual character.' (*WL MSS.*)

[1] Christopher Wordsworth, *Sermons Preached at Harrow School*, 1841.

[2] National Provincial Bank.

respect, that the N. P. had been commenced under the influence and direction of a Person[1] not remarkable for judgement—so that the plan of proceeding was obliged to be changed; I was further informed, that if Sir R^{t} Peel acted as he had hinted in Parliament respecting the law as it ought to stand with regard to these Banks, a great shock would be given to them all.

What mainly influenced me however was the consideration of my advanced age and the state and poor prospects of Dora and William—not overlooking John's numerous family without any prospect of increased means—I wished what I had to leave behind me, to be, for their sakes, as much upon a certainty as possible tho' at considerable loss—amounting to, in what has been sold to a little more than 1, 5th—I am very sorry indeed that you should have been so deep in it—having purchased so high.

I will conclude simply with observing that I saw no cause for fear that the Bank might break, and I or my heirs be called upon to make up deficiencies, but I apprehended that the Shares might prove so low that if there arose a *necessity* for selling that might be practicable only at very heavy loss.

Pray promise to come down for a month at Christmas! Miss F. consents to play whist, after her fashion every evening—so do Mary and I.

ever aff^{ly} your's
[*signed*] Wm Wordsworth

1554. W. W. to HENRY TAYLOR[2]

Endorsed: 3^{d} Novr. 1841.
MS. Bodleian Library.
K (—). *LY iii. 1094.*

Wednesday [3 Nov. 1841]

My dear Mr Taylor,

Would you be so kind as to substitute for the 3^{d} line of the Sonnet beginning

[1] Thomas Joplin (1790–1847), author of *The General Principles and Present Practice of Banking, in England and Scotland*, 1822, in which he advocated the extension of joint-stock banking and the Scottish system of branch banking to England. He founded the National Provincial Bank in 1833, and was the author of a number of other pamphlets on currency reform.

[2] W. W. had recently sent his *Sonnets upon the Punishment of Death* (*PW* iv.

3 November 1841

Not to the object specially designed[1]

this verse

(Bear this previous truth in constant memory)

reading for 'Good to promote or curb depravity'—

This alteration arises out of a wish to avoid repetition, which to a *certain degree* was inevitable in treating the subject as I have done, with a desire that each sonnet should be without *absolute* or a great dependance on the one preceding it.—

Thanks for your statistical paper; but allow me to say that Statistics both in this and almost every other truly important subject, are much less respected by me than they appear to be in your judgement. Here is a paper showing that Capital punishments are much diminished but not throwing (as how could it?) a single ray of light on the Causes.—May not that be mainly, not that there is less occasion for them but that notions of feeble and narrow-minded humanity, and spurious Christianity have spread

135), composed in 1839–40 (see L. 1370 above), to Henry Taylor, who was proposing to publish them in a forthcoming review of *The Sonnets of William Wordsworth*, 1838, in the *Quarterly Review*, lxix (Dec. 1841), 1–51. In his article Taylor prefaced his discussion of the penal sonnets with a brief survey of recent discussions in Parliament and elsewhere on the death penalty. In 1836 a report by the Commissioners on Criminal Law had been laid before Parliament with the result that in the following year Acts were passed abolishing the death penalty from about 200 offences (for most of which it was already in practice obsolete), leaving it applicable only to high treason, murder and attempted murder, rape, arson with danger to life, piracies, burglaries, and robberies when aggravated by cruelty and violence. But some members of the House, who had considerable support in the country, had conscientious objections to the death penalty for any crime, and as a move towards total abolition brought in a Bill to remove it from all offences exept treason and murder; as a compromise the offence of rape was also omitted from the list. 'Thus the broad question which is left for the country to look at, in respect to the punishment by death, is in effect its *abolition*. It is to this question that Mr. Wordsworth's Sonnets refer; and the general drift of the sentiments which they express is that there is a deeper charity and a more enlarged view of religious oligations than that which would dictate such a measure in this country in the present state of society.' The matter, Taylor maintained, 'being a subject for deep feelings, large views, and high argumentation, is essentially a subject for poetry, and especially so in the hands of one who has been accustomed . . . to consider the sentiments and judgments which he utters in poetry with as deep a solicitude as to their justness as if they were delivered from the bench or the pulpit.' The article was reprinted in *The Works of Sir Henry Taylor*, 5 vols., 1877–8, pp. 53 ff.

[1] The fifth sonnet in the series.

so as to prevent prosecutions, or have so influenced Judges in their charges; for instance Judge Maule[1] in more cases than one and juries in their verdicts.—

ever faithfully yours
W. Wordsworth

1555. W. W. to EDWARD MOXON

MS. Henry E. Huntington Library.
K (—). *LY iii. 1095* (—).

[Nov. 5th 1841][2]

My dear Mr Moxon,

It is long since I heard from you. I hope you and yours are all well—Since now, in consequence of hearing from Harty Coleridge, that owing to the wretched state of the Book trade, you decline publishing a Vol: of Poems of his which he has ready for the Press.—Perhaps the same consideration might disincline you to publish one of my own, smaller as to Contents a good deal than any of the six but which in the printing might be spread out so as to shelf with them in size. If you are afraid of meddling with it, or think it better to wait, pray let me know. Tell me also what progress you are making with the Sale of the last Edition.[3] I learn from several quarters, that we have given ground for Complaint by suppressing in the last Edition the Sonnets in the Appendix.[4] I am sorry we did it; as I purposed to print those Sonnets (which had not been widely circulated) in the proposed new Vol, I thought there would be no harm in their being kept back till these came out.

Mr Aubrey de Vere[5] is very much interested in the Publication of a Selection from my poems, but materially different in the

[1] Sir Willian Henry Maule (1788–1858), barrister, and Judge (from 1839), famed for his ironical humour; formerly (1811) Fellow of Trinity College, Cambridge.

[2] Dated added in another hand.

[3] i.e. the edition of 1840.

[4] See pt. iii, Ls. 1248 and 1351.

[5] Aubrey de Vere, who had visited Rydal Mount in early August (*RMVB*), wrote on 3 Sept., sending a list of poems for a proposed selection from W. W. which they had discussed; and on 7 Sept. he wrote again to thank W. W. for his hospitality: 'I shall ever look back to your hospitable kindness as one of the highest honours as well as greatest pleasures of my life.' (*WL MSS.*)

choice from Mr Hines.[1] What do you say to that,—dare you venture upon it. He has furnished me with a list according to his own choice.—

Mr Robinson is coming down to us at Christmas. Could you contrive to join us during some part of the month that he will stay?

Mrs W. unites with me in kind regards to yourself, Mrs M. and your Sister,

ever faithfully yours
Wm Wordworth

1556. W. W. to C. W. JNR.

MS. British Library.
Mem. (—). *Grosart* (—). *K* (—). *LY iii. 1096* (—).

Nov[br] 5th 1841
Rydal

My dear Christopher,

Your father left us yesterday, having been just a week under our roof. The weather was favorable, and he seemed to enjoy himself much. His muscular strength, as proved by the walks we took together, is great. One day were were nearly 4 hours on foot without resting, and he did not appear in the least fatigued. But I learned that his Frame is very susceptible of rheumatic pains, from the atmosphere, or exposure to damp air. He suffered much, one or two nights from this cause, though he never told us about it at the time. This liability to attack has reconciled me to his resigning his office of Master.[2] Not that I think any change of situation will protect him altogether from such injuries; but he will recover much more easily as his official anxieties are diminished. We all thought him looking well; and his mind appears as active as ever.—It was a great delight to us to see him here. I have long anxiously wished that he should be

[1] For Joseph Hine's *Selections* (1831), see pt. ii, L. 617. De Vere's proposed selection was directed at poorer readers. 'The principle on which I went was that of providing a continual ascent for the mind of the poor man, by beginning with subjects of peculiar interest, advancing to those of more various and excursive interest, and concluding with those of a higher and more directly spiritual interest.'

[2] See L. 1552 above.

able to judge, by his own observation, of the condition of our poor Sister, who was delight[ed] to have sight of him once more. We wished he could have prolonged his visit; but he was anxious to see Charles of whose health he had received such a poor account. He will reach Winchester this afternoon, I hope without injury.—

I have to thank you for a Vol: of sermons preached to the Harrow Boys. I like it much and trust it will do the good you hope for in writing it.

I send you a Copy of poor Owen's Epitaph, struck off at Kendal, upon the suggestion of Thomas Troughton, the Ambleside Chapel Clerk, and Bookseller. The letter and notes are I suspect of his own writing. They ought [ ][1]

John meant to come but was prevented by a severe cold which confined him to his bed. W^m left us yesterday.

Mary and your Aunt send Kindest love to you and Susan to which I add my own hoping that you both and the little one[2] are well. We were to have gone this day with Miss Fenwick to Halsteads for a few days visit to the Marshalls', but they are in great trouble, fearing that every post will bring them the sad news of Mrs Elliot's[3] death, consequent upon her recent confinement.

ever my dear Chris[4]

1557. W. W. to HENRY TAYLOR

MS. Bodleian Library.
Correspondence of Sir Henry Taylor, p. 129. K. LY iii. 1096.

[*In M. W.'s hand*]

Rydal Mt: Novr 8th [1841].

My dear Mr Taylor,

You and Mr Lockhart have been very kind in taking so much trouble about the Sonnets.[5] I have altered them as well as I could to meet your wishes and trust that you will find them improved,

[1] *MS. cut away.*

[2] Elizabeth.

[3] Formerly Julia Marshall (see pt. ii, L. 790). She died on 3 Nov. of scarlet fever, supervening on childbirth.

[4] *Signature cut away.*

[5] The *Sonnets upon the Punishment of Death.* See L. 1554 above.

as I am sure they are where I have adopted your own words.

As to double rhymes, I quite agree with Mr L that in the case disapproved by him, their effect is weak, and I believe will generally prove so in a Couplet at the close of a Sonnet. But having written so many I do not scruple, but rather like to employ them occasionally, tho' I have done it much less in proportion than my great Masters, especially Milton, who has two out of his 18 with double rhymes.

I am sure it will be a great advantage to these Pieces to be presented to the Public with your comments in the Quarterly Review, as you propose[1]—but I must return to your suggestions. Where I have a large amount of Sonnets in series I have not been unwilling to start sometimes with a logical connection of a 'Yet' or a 'But'. Here, however, as the series is not long, I wished that each Sonnet should stand independent of such formal tie; and therefore, tho' with some loss, I have not followed your alteration, '*Yet* not alone, nor chiefly'. Besides, and this by-the-by, 'Not alone' is less neat than 'solely', or 'only' rather.

Mr Elliott,[2] even if he should be disturbed by the clamour of the public Press against him—will find abundant compensation in your zealous and judicious opposition to it—and I have little doubt that his explanation will justify the most favourable of your presumptions in his behalf—he must rejoice in your kindness, and that of his other friends and his relatives.

You and Mrs Taylor will be grieved to hear that dear Miss Fenwick is suffering from one of her severe colds—not unlike that which she had in London. She has kept her room to-day and

[1] Taylor had written on 3 Nov.: 'We will take some time about the penal Sonnets and do whatever is done, very deliberately. . . .I introduced them into my article with connecting comments chiefly expository,—such as I thought w[d] lead review readers to a more ready apprehension of their drift, and also by giving them a *prose* setting, relieve them of some disadvantages which I believe to be incidental to the reading of sonnets consecutively. . . .The intervening prose relaxes the mind and prepares it for another effort.' (*WL MSS.*)

[2] Admiral Sir Charles Elliot (see pt. iii, L. 1048), Minister Plenipotentiary in China, had taken Hongkong, invested Canton, and was about to proceed to Pekin, when he was recalled for disobedience to instructions and superseded by Sir Henry Pottinger. He was violently attacked in the House of Commons and in the Press, especially in *John Bull*. Henry Taylor prepared a digest of his despatches with connecting comments, which brought over the Duke of Wellington and many others to the view that the Government owed him a great debt of gratitude. Henry Taylor later celebrated him in an ode entitled *Heroism in the Shade*. See *Autobiography of Sir Henry Taylor*, i. 295–305.

we have cause to hope she may be better tomorrow. We attribute this mischief, tho she will scarcely allow it, to her going in an open carriage with Anna Ricketts to Kendal—on a sunny bright day, which closed with a frosty dampness before she reached home. We regret exceedingly that she has parted with her own carriage.

We hope soon to hear thro' Mrs Taylor of our afflicted friends at Brighton.[1] We think it better for us not yet to break in upon them.

With our united kindest remembrances,

ever faithfully yours,
[*signed*] Wm Wordsworth

1558. W. W. to JOHN GIBSON LOCKHART

MS. National Library of Scotland.
LY iii. 1099.

Lowther, Penrith [early Nov. 1841]

My dear Mr Lockhart,

Your Letter reached me just as I was setting off for this place so that I cannot reply to it as I wish and mean to do hereafter. I rejoice to hear that you purpose to treat the Question of the Copyright Bill in the Quarterly.[2] My hopes are sanguine that your Article will be eminently serviceable to the cause. Your knowledge ability zeal and the vehicle you have at command,

[1] i.e. Henry Venn Elliott's family.

[2] 'The Copyright Question', *Quarterly Review*, lxix (Dec. 1841), 186–227, a discussion of eight items on Copyright, including Talfourd's *Three Speeches* and Macaulay's speech of 5 Feb. 1841 (see L. 1491 above). Lockhart's article owes something to W. W.'s suggestions in this letter, and as the best means of confuting Macaulay's arguments, he included in an appendix W. W.'s anonymous letter to the *Kendal Mercury* of 12 Apr. 1838 (see pt. iii, L. 1229 and *Prose Works*, iii. 309), in a text corrected by W. W. himself. 'Had he [Macaulay] made the fit preparation for entering on such a debate, in the doubly authoritative character of a cabinet minister and a distinguished literator, he would have given attention also to a certain document, which, though published anonymously in a provincial newspaper, at once affiliated itself on a most illustrious pen, and was of course a subject of conversation in most literary circles throughout the country. In this dignified and modest paper Mr. Macaulay, had he condescended to have read it, would have found every argument of his speech anticipated—we think conclusively answered.'

will I am strongly persuaded, bring over many who have either paid little attention to the subject, or entertained inconsiderate prejudices upon it.—

Till I return home I cannot meet your wishes in respect to books and tracts, and in truth I possess only Talfourd's Pamphlet containing his speeches, or detail of the proceedings, and several of the Petitions that were presented to Parliament praying for Extension, that pamphlet and one in favour of perpetual Copyright and another entitled Areopagitica, I believe by my Nephew, the Master of Harrow.[1] There is to be in print a report of legal Argument upon both sides of the question of the Bible Monopoly, which was contested in the Courts. I have never read it, but it was mentioned to me the other day and I think it would be well worth your while to procure it. Upon this point in fact of monopoly the whole question turns.[2] I could perceive that it was this which frightened Sir Robert Peel, notwithstanding he had read that able comment upon Macaulay's Speech in the Examiner;[3] which see by all means, as well as the Speech itself, shallow as it is and even absurd.—I am afraid I have not any MSS. of value upon the subject—indeed I am pretty sure I have not.—

Could you convince your Readers, which I trust you will be able to do, that the objections to monopoly in general do not apply in this case, but on the contrary that the privilege would and must make Books be sold cheaper the Battle would be gained, our opponents would fly. And as to the danger of Books being suppressed, upon which Macaulay dwelt at length, that argument is easily disposed of, and the instances that he gives, particularly the case of Richardson,[4] it might be shewn, have no force in them. At all events if you desire it I could procure accurately all that relates to Richardson's Heirs etc. But perhaps it is not worth while to enter into such details, as the obligations on that score would be met at once, by a clause in the Bill being

[1] See pt. iii, L. 1284.

[2] Macaulay had argued very strongly against copyright as a form of monopoly.

[3] See *The Examiner*, 28 Feb. 1841. Parts of the article were cited by Lockhart.

[4] Macaulay had argued that if the law of copyright in Richardson's day had stood as Talfourd and his associates wished it to be, his novels would have been suppressed after his death by his grandson, an ultra-religious clergyman who disapproved of works of fiction. Lockhart dismissed the suggestion in his article as based on misinformation.

so carefully drawn up as to make suppression for any length of time impossible.

Though I have nothing perhaps to say upon the general subject which has not been better said already by others, I will write again when I go home. In the meanwhile with many thanks for your very kind Letter

I remain my dear Sir, with high respect, faithfully yours

W Wordsworth

1559. D. W. and W. W. to DORA QUILLINAN

MS. WL.
LY iii. 1100.

[mid-Nov. 1841]

[*D. W. writes*]

My dearest Dora I know not what to write—Here I am in the room where dear Aunt Sara died. Strangely I have struggled; but now am better. I hope to see your Father from Lowther today. God bless you and your Husband and dear Mother

Your affect^{e}
D. W.

(Turn over)

[*W. W. writes*]

Moxon tells me that only 250 Copies of my last thousand have been sold, including those sent to Rydal. This is poor encouragement to print the Vol: I have been about making ready. M. has declined printing Hartley's[1] Vol: of Poems on account of the wretched state of the Book Trade, and the heavy stock he has on hand.—One of the causes I think of bad sale is the inundation of low priced Editions of old Publications. In these there must be much Fraud for I see Bruce's Travels,[2] a Book in many large Volumes, advertized at six-pence. This of course must be mutilated but the advertisement does not say a word of abridgement.

My Sonnets on Capital punishment 14 in number are about to

[1] Hartley Coleridge's.

[2] *Travels to Discover the Sources of the Nile in the Years 1768, 1769, 1770, 1771, 1772, and 1773*, 5 vols., 1790. The author was James Bruce (1730–94), the African explorer.

be printed in the Quarterly Review by Mr Taylor,[1] along with a general reviewal of my Poems in that form. Perhaps this may give some stimulus to the six Volumes which as Moxon says they sadly want.

Miss Fenwick seems a good deal better this evening and hopes to be down stairs tomorrow. Your Mother bids me ask whether you cannot take good Mutton Broth—do try that and every other nourishing thing but first in very small quantities. You remember what our Guide at Spa told us how he had saved his life, on their Retreat from Russia, by abstaining altogether from solid food for 17 days. I am not recommending anything like this to you, but it points out that you are right in treating in degree your weak stomach after the same fashion.—

Miss F. had a Letter today from Mrs Taylor, giving as comfortable account of the Brighton family[2] as could be expected. Cordelia[3] and Mary Anne,[4] Mrs Taylor says, are looking well in London. Your mother has written to Mrs Pollard,[5] to no-one else. It would be well taken if you were to write to Susan[6] by this time we suppose at Brighton. Again farewell your loving Father

W. W.

1560. W. W. to HENRY TAYLOR

Address: H. Taylor Esq, 16 Blandford Square, Dorset Square. [*In M. W.'s hand*]
Postmark: 19 Nov. 1841.
Endorsed: Wordsworth respecting Sonnets on Punishment of Death 1841.
MS. Bodleian Library.
K. LY iii. 1098.

Rydal. Friday morning in haste for the Post.
[19 Nov. 1841]

My dear Mr Taylor,

Nothing but the importance of the Subject can, I feel, justify

[1] See L. 1554 above.

[2] The family of Henry Venn Elliott, who had recently lost his wife (see L. 1556 above).

[3] Cordelia Marshall, now Mrs. Whewell.

[4] Lady Monteagle.

[5] Mrs. Jane Marshall's sister.

[6] Susan Marshall, who later married the Revd. Frederick Myers.

me in troubling you again. The additional Sonnet[1] sent the other day had only just been written. It is wrongly placed and would stand much better immediately after the third. I could wish it also to be altered thus towards the conclusion.

The strife
of individual will, to elevate
The grovelling mind, the craving to recall
And fortify etc.

Read in what could stand as the 9th[2]

Fit retribution by the moral code
Determined, lies beyond the State's embrace
Yet, as she may, for each peculiar case
She plants etc.

I am strongly inclined to think that for many reasons it would be better to leave these Sonnets untouched in your Review, but I leave the matter to your own judgement.

ever faithfully yours,
Wm Wordsworth

1561. W. W. to C. W.

MS. Mr. Jonathan Wordsworth. Hitherto unpublished.

Rydal Mount
[late] Novr 1841[3]

My dear Brother,

We were truly glad to hear from you. Your letter ought perhaps to have been acknowledged immediately, but having nothing particular to say is a temptation for putting off the discharge of these duties. The expedition with which your journey to Winchester was performed seems almost marvellous. Thankful we all were that you suffered little from the fatigue or exposure of it. I need scarcely say how much Mary and I were concerned at learning there is no prospect of dear Charles having his labour lightened or a larger portion of his time at his own disposal. As this cannot be, will it not end in his being obliged to quit the Post where he is so eminently useful? My regret will

[1] Sonnet ix in the final order.

[2] Sonnet viii in the final order.

[3] Address and date added by C. W.

indeed be great if this be so, as will that of all his intimate Friends.

Yesterday we received a Cambridge Newspaper, giving an account of the present Masters[1] installation in his high off: Due respect appears to have been paid to your conduct while under that great responsibility; and your act of resignation and the motives of it were properly appreciated. Christopher in all probability I should have thought did not err in his mention of Bentley[2] and the proposal he made for having a monument erected which should be more just to his memory. But judging only from his speech as reported, I had rather that the matter had been reserved for another occasion. There is so much in my mind that was tyranical and morally wrong in Bentley's character and behaviour as Master, that it seemed scarcely fair to bring him forward upon an occasion when the contrast between him and the late Master would be felt a thing not to be desired by all who wish that Bentley's integrity and temper had been worthy of his great abilities and wonderful learning.—Besides the proposal seemed to break in upon the simplicity of the main object of that meeting. But in all this my judgement, I am well aware, may be quite erroneous.

You will be glad to hear that Dora is much better since her change of Residence. Her stomach had been dreadfully disordered while she was at Canterbury. Pray let us hear from you from time to time. Love from Mary and Sisters and kind remembrances from Miss Fenwick ever your affectionate Brother

W. Wordsworth

[1] Whewell, who had just succeeded C. W. as Master of Trinity.

[2] Richard Bentley was Master of Trinity for 42 years (1700–42), despite the attempts of the Fellows of the college to eject him for his infringement of the statutes. In 1734 at the age of 72, he was actually sentenced to be deprived, but remained in office because the Vice-Master Richard Walker, who alone could carry out the sentence, was his friend.

1562. W. W. to H. C. R.

MS. Dr. Williams's Library.
Morley, i. 448.

(Private) [late Nov. 1841]

My dear Friend

We shall soon be looking out for your visit; and you must excuse me if I put you to a little trouble before you Leave London. I was thinking of publishing a Vol. of poems this winter and have given some little of our late leisure to prepare it for the Press; but I am checked by the fear which has been expressed to me 'that Moxon may Crash'; could you in a quiet way collect for me any information upon this point. I know that the publishing trade is in general in a most agitated state And I know no reason for thinking that his concerns are an exception but send for a contrary opinion. I should be glad if I could get some light from you—

Some time since I request[ed] Courtenay to sell out of the provincial Bank for me if he could procure an average of 34£ a share. I have heard nothing from him for several weeks—I know you do not like to communicate with him; and I am loth to annoy him with Letter after Letter, but if you could learn for me whether the shares have actually fallen below that average, I should conclude that this is the reason why I do not hear from him. It would then be my duty to consider whether I ought not to fix upon a still lower average for sale, or wait till the half years dividend.—Courtenay did sell out about six hundred pounds for me at rather *better than* 34£.

Now for a commission which you may execute with much less trouble by calling at Dwerry, and Bells, I think that is the name,—A watchmakers shop, on the left hand as you pass into Mount Street from Berkley Square.—Tell them that M[r] Wordsworth paid upward of thirty shillings to them last summer for repairing his watch; but he found it would not go and therefore he sent it by Miss Rogers to be set right. That no doubt must be done long before this time—Pray bring the watch down with you. I expect them to make no charge as though I . . .
[*sheet missing*]
The Quillinans are now in London.

1563. W. W. to DORA QUILLINAN

MS. WL. Hitherto unpublished.

Wednesday Evening
10 oclock [? Nov. *or* Dec. 1841]

My dearest Dora,

Your letter, giving so unfavorable an account of the state of your stomach has distressed us much. I shall not say too much if I add that it *alarmed me*: How I can be otherwise than afraid when I recall to mind what a condition you were in before Dr Davy's medicine brought you round: He is expected soon in England[1] and I am very anxious that you should see him. In the meanwhile let me earnestly entreat that you would call on Dr Fergusson, telling him that it is at my anxious desire that you have done so. I do hope that he may be able to benefit you; how I wish that Hendon had been close to Hampstead so that you might have had the advantage of frequent drives in Mrs Hoare's carriage. Where you are I fear you will be cut off from every thing of that kind, and you must not walk but a very little. And pray avoid bodily and mental fatigue of every kind. This appears to be destroying your Cousin Charles; and from your Uncle's Letter. . . [*sheet missing*]

your most affectionate Father
W Wordsworth

1564. W. W. to ISABELLA FENWICK

Address: Miss Fenwick, Rydal Mount, Ambleside.
Postmark: (1) 2 Dec. 1841 (2) 3 Dec. 1841.
Stamp: (1) Penrith (2) Ambleside.
MS. WL.
LY iii. 1101.

[Lowther]
[2 Dec. 1841]

My very very dear Friend,

You will have heard of my movements from dearest Mary, to whom I wrote a short note. I was detained three hours at

[1] Dr. John Davy had been in Constantinople since the previous year, at the request of Lord Palmerston, to initiate reforms in the medical department of the

Keswick, two and half of which I spent walking by the Lake side to and from Friar's Crag with magnificent views towards Lodore, which however I could not see for mist, and into Borrowdale. The luminous and dark vapours which were ever changing their shapes and their consistency round Castle crag and the other pointed hills thereabouts were most impressive in their appearance. So that I enjoyed myself wishing very much for my dearest Friends to partake of my pleasure. During that walk I added a Stanza to the Vallombrosa Poem[1] which I send you, hoping that you may puzzle out the words which I penned in my bedroom this morning, and which were shockingly blotted by the first penful of ink taken for the writing of this Letter. Pray excuse its ugly appearance which I know you would much rather see than think that I should have taken the trouble to write it twice over.

Lord Lonsdale is wonderfully recruited—wonderfully for a man of 84 years, after a pulse of 120 for ten days.—

I am most anxious to hear how you are and also I should be delighted if I could be told that my poor dear Sister were somewhat easier. Give my love to her and accept also an abundance yourself. It was my strong wish to be home on Saturday; but as Lord Lonsdale's health was going on so well Lady Frederick expressed an earnest wish that I should remain till Monday. On that day you may expect me, and on the same James must meet me at Patterdale if the horse be not otherwise engaged, and well enough for the journey. Be so kind as to let Mr Carter know how long I propose staying here so that he will be able to calculate up to what time Letters may be forwarded hither.—

I must say a word to you, my dear Friend, about my Grandchildren; they are really a fine cluster. Your Willy,[2] for so I will call him notwithstanding his ill behaviour when last among us at Rydal, has a character and expression in his face which is quite touching. I think he grows handsomer, and there is both intellect and sentiment in his features and countenance to

Turkish army. He returned in Jan. 1842. See *Autobiography of Mrs. Fletcher*, pp. 248–50.

[1] W. W. sent four stanzas of the poem, the first, second, fourth, and fifth: it is impossible to say which stanza was now added. The third stanza must have been written within a few days, before the next version of the poem was sent in the next letter.

[2] I. F.'s godchild.

which no one could be indifferent.—Jane is much more pleasing and handsomer also, except for her teeth, than she was. Indeed, except for her carriage she is I think the most improved in appearance of any of them, and was towards me very affectionate. I came away[1] you will be sure with great regret. John drove me over to Plumbland where I saw that excellent man Mr Bush,[2] his wife and several of his children. They seemed to like the place much and I hope will stay there. Mr B. was in his Cassock having been doing the duty—it was a Saints day, St Andrew's, and he always has service on those days which is not ill attended. The place in summer must be rather pretty, there being some groves of [?Trees], some good Land, an old Church in the interior of which is an Arch of exceeding beauty, so much so that a print of it ought to have a place in the County History.—It is old, I think, but I am not learned in these matters, as the Conquest[3]—perhaps prior to it—But enough of this. The best news I have of myself is my having done I trust with that most troublesome prefatory Poem;[4] never was I so hampered with anything, the chief difficulty rising out of the simultaneous actions of both the Bird and the Poet being engaged in singing, and the word 'while' not being manageable for both—that having done this to my own mind and Mary's and having improved, I cannot but think, the little I now send, I trust I shall not write another line while I am here. And if I have strength of mind to keep to this resolution you will, I hope, my dearest Friend, see me return in an amended state of body, for this continual teasing and minute Labour has hurt my side or heart a good deal. Luncheon is coming in, so I must break off with a thousand wishes. Dearest Mary, I hope you will be with Miss Fenwick on Saturday. Farewell ever yours

Wm Wordsworth

[*There follows, in W. W.'s hand, the first two and the last two stanzas*

[1] From Brigham.

[2] John W.'s curate at Plumbland, the Revd. James Bush, formerly of Keswick: according to Southey, 'a blessing to any parish' (Warter, iv. 422). See also L. 1591 below.

[3] Plumbland church was rebuilt in 1870, but the fine chancel arch of the mid-12th century has survived.

[4] *Prelude Prefixed to the Volume Entitled "Poems Chiefly of Early and Late Years"* (*PW* iv. 176). But W. W. had not 'done with it', if we can trust the date 26 Mar. 1842, which he appended to it on publication.

of At Vallombrosa, *as in PW iii. 223, but read in l. 6 House for* Cell, *l. 14* might *for* would, *l. 38* disdaining false pleasures, *and l. 40* To the Source from which]

1565. W. W. to DORA QUILLINAN

MS. WL.
LY iii. 1103.

Tuesday. Dec 7th [1841] Lowther Castle.

My dear Dora,

I start at 12 o'clock for Patterdale, where I hope James has been waiting since yesterday with the Carriage. My intention was to have left this place yesterday, but it rained till 12 o'clock and with a high wind, and I did not like to expose Lord L's Horses and Servant to such severe weather, besides they were very urgent that I should stay. I wrote yesterday to Wm begging him to come over if he could so as to be here before 12—the time of my departure—I left the Letter for the Coachman at Hackthorp[1] to receive a shilling if he delivered it that night at Carlisle, either but I fear he has not done so, or Wm has been out of the way, for it is now more than half past 12 and he is not arrived.

I have been think[ing] of you almost constantly since we left home yesterday week; with much anxiety, to learn that you have a return of your distressing and, as to its tendency, alarming complaint. Therefore do take, my dear Child, every possible care and act up to every wise resolution. I was much grieved to have only one day for Brigham, but it was my duty to come here as invited. Lord Lonsdale, I am happy to say, is gathering strength daily; and I hope will be able to set off for the South next week, which we are all anxious about, least severe weather should set in. The Autumn has been delightfully mind; in fact most charming weather. To-day it is most beautiful; and through a veil of tall leafless trees I have a prospect of silver and sunny clouds as pleasing as one could wish to look at. I am anxious to be at home for many reasons, one that I wish for quiet and repose, as I have exhausted myself a good deal of late, in disentangling a composition or two in which I have been engaged from awkwardnesses that annoyed me much. On the

[1] A village near Lowther, on the main road from Kendal to Carlisle.

other side, if I have time, I will transcribe a piece[1] of which two Stanzas were composed since I left home. I hope it will please you. Give my love to Mr Quillinan and the Girls and kind remembrances to Mrs Gee.[2]

Ever my dear child, your most affectionate Father

W. W.

1566. W. W. to C. W.

Address: The Rev^{d}. C. Wordsworth D.D., Buxted Rectory, Uckfield, Sussex.
Postmark: (1) 10 Dec. 1841 (2) 11 Dec. 1841.
Stamp: Ambleside.
MS. British Library and Mr. Jonathan Wordsworth. Hitherto unpublished.

Decr 10. 1841[3]

My dear Brother,

Our Letters must have crossed upon the Road. We were truly glad to hear of your arrival at Buxted and hope that by this time, things being settled for you, you find yourself comfortable—We much regret that there is no prospect of dear Charles's labour at Winchester being lightened; and I cannot, therefore, wholly divest myself of the fear that the Duties of the office, as he will perform them, will prove too much for his health, and strength—

Chris: has written to me at some length in consequence of the observations I made upon his speech, in my Letter to You.[4] I feel sensible of his kindness in so doing, but occupied as he is, I regret that I was the means of putting him to so much trouble.

I had no objection to something being done to testify that whatever resentment the College might once have felt towards the Memory of Dr Bentley it had passed away, on the contrary I entirely approve of such a proposal being made. *But* I regretted that it should have occurred at that time. It seemed to me to break in upon the unity of the object of the Meeting, and to

[1] There follows *At Vallombrosa*, but read 'might' for 'would' in l. 19, and 'would' for 'did' in l. 22. The first three stanzas were copied by W. W., the last two by M. W. The second and fifth stanzas have been cut away.

[2] Of Hendon.

[3] Dated added by C. W.

[4] See L. 1561 above.

distract attention from it. Besides, allow me to say that I thought it rather hard upon Dr Bentley's character, to have it brought forward under circumstances that *might* place it in contrast with yours; for many reasons it will not bear that process. All this was said or hinted in my Letter, with due diffidence I trust; But still I cannot but regret that the day of this Meeting was the Centenary of his death, otherwise probably the subject might not have been introduced.

Mary and I have just been at Brigham, where we saw John; his Wife and family all well. They are a crowd of very fine Children, and W^m in particular has a sweetness and beauty of expression in his Countenance which is most promising; but alas his frame is very delicate, much the most so apparently of any of them. I returned by Lowther were I stayed six days, and found to my great delight as to that of every one, that Lord Lonsdale was recovering and strengthening after his late severe illness in a manner wonderful for a Person of his age, 84.

Have you noticed the Dissentions at Oxford, in connection with the Poetry Professorship as a test of religious opinion?[1] It is altogether a sad business.

Did I mention to you before that W^m has had some reason lately to think that Sir R. Peel will remember him. I wish it may be so poor fellow; His life has thus far been a life of disappointments.

The name of the author[2] of the Apology for Cathedrals is

[1] John Keble was about to vacate the Professorship of Poetry at Oxford, and in the highly-charged atmosphere which followed the controversy over Newman's *Tract Ninety*, the election of a successor was bound to be a party issue between the Tractarians and their opponents. The candidate with an established reputation was Isaac Williams (see L. 1369 above) of Trinity, author of *The Cathedral* (1838) and *The Baptistery* (1842). But he was known as the author of the notorious *Tract Eighty* 'On Reserve' and the friend of Newman and Pusey, and he was therefore unacceptable to the Evangelicals. Their candidate was James Garbett (1802–79), of Brasenose, later Archdeacon of Chichester, a man of 'safe' theological views but no literary distinction. The contest was settled in Jan. 1842, when it became clear that Garbett had a majority of three to two votes over Williams, and the latter accordingly withdrew. Garbett's Bampton Lectures for 1842 were a sustained repudiation of Tractarian principles. See *The Autobiography of Isaac Williams*, 1892, pp. 137 ff.; R. W. Church, *The Oxford Movement, Twelve Years, 1833–1845*, 1891, 273–6.

[2] From this point on, the MS. is in the collection of Mr. Jonathan Wordsworth.

Peace.[1] He is Librarian of the City Library of Bristol. Some time or other I will let him know that you were pleased with his Book.—

Mary and your Sister, who is in her better way send their kindest Love; Miss Fenwick also begs to be kindly remembered to you. As you now will have some leisure pray be so good as to write to us now and then, if it were only to tell us how you are.

I remain
your affectionate Brother
Wm Wordsworth

We have good accounts of Dora's health, though she does not mention the subject half so often as I could wish. Be so good as forward this Letter to Chas. which I hope he will accept in return for his, as my eyes are not equal to much penmanship. Mary's thanks to Susan for her note enclosed.

[*M. W. adds*]

Our Cousin Mrs Combe, Nanny Wordsworth,[2] is just dead—the last of our Uncle's family except Robinson.[3]

1567. W. W. to THOMAS POWELL

MS. University of Virginia Library.
LY iii. 1104.

Rydal Mount. Decr 11th [1841]

My dear Mr Powell

I should have sent Back the sheet by return of Post, but I wanted to acknowledge the receipt of the Books and Stilton which you kindly announce, but the package has not yet come to hand.—

I have also for the like reason deferred thanking you for the Number of the Monthly Chronicle,[4] sent I presume on account

[1] See L. 1486 above.

[2] Ann (1771–1841), eighth child of Richard Wordsworth of Whitehaven. She married three times: (1) The Revd. Charles Favell (1739–1807), (2) The Revd. James Ireland (1772–1822), and (3) Bernard Coombe. She had no children from any of these marriages.

[3] For Robinson Wordsworth, the youngest of the family, see L. 1477 above.

[4] *The Monthly Chronicle; a national journal of politics, literature, science, and art,* ran from 1838 until 1841.

of the Poems it contains from your pen, especially the one you have done me the honor of addressing to me. They all have the characteristic merits of your writing; but I should like to have an opportunity of noting vivâ voce some of the faults, as I take them to be, of style.

Your account of your Brother gives me great concern indeed. I hope your fears may be more than the case would suggest to one less interested or who have less love for the invalid than you and Mrs Powell must have—

I made a remark or two on Mr Horne because of the Prologue.[1] I have since looked at the text and am confirmed in the opinion I expressed. I forget whether I mentioned my objection to the line in the description of the Sergeant at Law.

Who too oft had gossipp'd long in the Church Porch[2]—

The sense is here quite mistaken—the meaning is he had been frequent at consultations in the Parvis, the name of the places often in Churches, where Lawyers met for such purposes—ever faithfully

Yours
W. W.

1568. W. W. to THOMAS GRAHAM[3]

Address: Thos Graham Esq., Natl Provl Bank of Engd, 112 Bishopsgate Street, London.
Postmark: 17 Dec. 1841.
Stamp: Ambleside.
MS. Mrs. M. De Meza. Hitherto unpublished.

[*In John Carter's hand*]

Rydal Mount, Ambleside,
16 Decr. 1841

Dear Sir,

Believe me to be duly sensible of the delicate consideration with which you have communicated to me through my Son the sad and painful intelligence of the death of Mr Courtenay. We had been connected by a warm and sincere friendship of more

[1] Chaucer's *Prologue to the Canterbury Tales*, which R. H. Horne had modernized (see L. 1498 above).

[2] l. 310: That often hadde been at the parvys.

[3] See next letter.

than twentyfive years standing, during which time his active kindness conferred upon me many obligations, especially in respect to the management of my little property, which he undertook knowing that I was not myself a man of business, and for which services I could make little or no return beyond a grateful sense of them, and occasional verbal acknowledgements which he was always most unwilling to hear of.

Not having had any account of my Friend's death from his own Family I cannot venture to break in upon them with a Letter of Condolence and I will thank you to communicate to me, at your earliest convenience, any particulars of his decease which may have come to your knowledge since you last wrote to my Son, and also respecting his Family, how they bear this most severe loss, and where they are.

Sincerely do I thank you for your offer of service towards the fulfilment of the directions you received from Mr Courtenay as to the sale of my National Prov[l] Bank of England Shares.

First let me say that I directed Mr Courtenay with respect to my own shares lately sold out by him, as did also my Son and his Co-Trustee (for my Daughter) to pay the proceeds in London, mine was to be paid to Mr Cookson my Solicitor, Lincoln's Inn, and the other to Glyn and Co. Bankers. This has not been done, and of course I know not how to proceed in that part of the Business, and should be thankful for any instructions you could give me upon it.

Advanced in life and circumstances as I am, I requested Mr Courtenay to sell the whole of my shares on as favorable terms as he could, naming 34½ as the minimum price to which I could then bring my mind to accede. The shares I fear must have fallen since, but even in that event, I am still desirous of being freed from the anxiety which attaches in my mind to such engagements, and which are so remote from my pursuits. Mr Courtenay was aware that from my first connection with this Bank, as that connection took place in consequence of his earnestly pressing it upon me as likely to prove of great advantage, so also I was resolved to separate from it under any terms, in case of [his] ceasing to be a Director either by death or otherwise. My confidence rested upon him entirely, for I was not acquainted with any one who took an active share in the Bank but himself.

Being thus suddenly deprived of his valuable services, I cannot but wish to benefit by your most kind offer so far as to entreat you will give me such information for my future guidance in determining at what price to sell out, as is consistent with your duty as an officer of the Bank, which I presume you to be.

Hoping you will excuse my having troubled you at such length,

I remain, Dear Sir,
Your much obliged
[*signed*] Wm Wordsworth

1569. M. W. to H. C. R.

MS. Cornell.
Broughton, p. 81.

Decr 16th [1841]

My dear Friend

I readily answer your call for a *letter*, but not one of chat—for indeed I have not just now time to look beyond my near concerns, and as we trust to see you so very soon—(next week) we must defer chat till we meet.

Poor Courtenay![1] Since we read your letter, we too have seen the detailed report from Liverpool *in the Times*—Grieved are we for his loss, and in such a manner!—and alas for the distress of his Family. The death was announced to us from a gent. in the N. P. B.[2] who wrote to *Willy* in consequence of communication from him regarding the transfer of the Proceeds from the sale of Doras stock—which had been sold by Mr C some weeks since (about the time we had correspondence with you on that subject) and which Mr C deferred to remit as had been desired—both in the case of Dora's and what had been rec^d^ for her Father;—and letters from both the W^ms^ were in Town awaiting his return from Ireland—enquiring about this delay.

I hope you may get to Hendon on Sunday—and, if, as I trust you will remain all night, Dora will be able to answer any enquiries you may make about us—for I send *her* a scrawl in the midst of my busiest hours, very often.

Your lodgings shall be ready for you, I wish you had mentioned your day. The Arnolds will be at Fox-how the

[1] Philip Courtenay, W. W.'s man of business, had died on 10 Dec. at the Adelphi Hotel, Liverpool, of an overdose of morphia.

[2] National Provincial Bank.

middle of next week. Your hostess is most happy in the expectation of . . .

[*cetera desunt*]

1570. W. W. to ELIZABETH FISHER

MS. Cornell.
Fortnightly Review, xciv (Nov. 1910), 883–4.

[*In M. W.'s hand*]

Rydal Mount. Dec[r] 22[d]
[1841]

My dear Cousin,

I rejoice exceedingly that your resolution is fixed not to publish Emmie's Poems[1] and I lose not a moment to tell you so. As a general rule there cannot be a question that the writings of Children should not be sent into the world. If their merit should be overrated, as will mostly be the case by those who undertake such a responsibility, it is obvious at once that the effect cannot be good. In the case of your daughter, there is no fear of the poems being extolled beyond their *merits* in my judgement, for you must allow me to repeat, they are the most wonderful productions, for so young a Creature, that I ever saw or heard of. But observe, on *that very* account she would be pointed at wherever she went, as a Prodigy; and tho' it may be reasonably supposed that the superiority of her intellect, as hath been proved in the instances of all men of first-rate genius, would place her above that dependence upon praise and admiration, which minds of inferior order cling to, yet in her case we have no examples to guide us: and as no one would presume to affirm [?][2] *would not* in respect to the delicacy, purity, and humility of her mind be injured, the safe way, surely, is not to expose her to the trial. In fact, as I have said in my letter to S. C.[3] I do not think we have a *right* to do so. But without attempting to dive into the depths of the human heart, and explore our way thro' its labyrinths, what inconveniences, discomforts, and awkwardnesses of position would the dear child be subjected to! How difficult would it become for her to demean herself in the midst

[1] See L. 1547 above.

[2] *MS. damaged.*

[3] Sara Coleridge. The letter is untraced.

of a world of young, middle-aged, and old, anxious to show their sense of her powers—to express their gratitude and in fact do her domage! To say the least of it, her precious time, do what you would to keep her apart, would be encroached upon by these unpardonable . . .

[*cetera desunt*]

1571. W. W. to EDWARD MOXON

Address: Edward Moxon Esqr, 44 Dover St.
MS. Henry E. Huntington Library.
K (—). *LY iii.* 1105.

[*In M. W.'s hand*]

Decr 24th [1841]

My dear Mr Moxon,

The first words I have to say must be an expression of indignation at learning that you were charged the enormous sum of £83 for corrections in carrying the 6 vols thro' the Press. I know not what check Publishers have upon Printers, and what is the course of practise as to charging for alterations. But sure I am, that, in common justice, things ought not to go on in the way you have been treated; for I affirm, upon the strength of my own memory, and upon a much better authority, that of Mr Carter, my Clerk, thro' whose hands passed every sheet of the 6 vols, excepting a very few of the *first* vol:—that of the alterations, very very much the greatest part were caused by the inattention of the Printers to *directions precisely given*, or to their gross blunders. It was I own a case that required particular attention, because the whole vol of the 'Yarrow Revisited' was interwoven with the poems previously collected, and the arrangement was for good reasons in several instances, altered; but the directions given by Mr C. and myself were precise and distinct accordingly, and it is the first duty of a Printer to *attend* to such directions. I am sorry to say there was a like carelessness shewn in carrying the Vol: of Sonnets through the Press. The mention of this vol reminds me of a little difficulty in respect to the proposed Ed in *one* volume which I will here state. The Vol: of Sonnets contains 13 Son: that were then first added.[1] I should not like to have them reprinted in the proposed new Ed: as it

[1] i.e. in 1838. See L. 1555 above.

would give that Ed: an advantage over the one in 6 vols, which might be injurious to its Sale; and if the Sonnets were not reprinted it could not be said that either one or other were a complete Ed: of my Works. I will here add, by the bye, that, being prompted to take leave of Italy in verse, I wrote lately six Sonnets upon that suggestion,[1] and have added 11 others, that partly rose out of the farewell.—I should like these 30 sonnets some time or other to be printed in the *same* class, as they were all composed during the current year.

We must now come to the main point. From the experience which I have personally had of your liberality and what I know to the honor of your character, I have not the least doubt that the terms which you offer are the best that you can afford—the state of the Public mind being what it is in respect to poetical literature—but then it becomes me seriously to consider whether the pecuniary advantage to myself, would at all compensate the certain check which such an Ed: would give to the Sale of the previous one—and whether it might not altogether put a stop to it—in which case, the Stereotype would be entirely lost, and very much trouble incurred without any recompence. If you are decidedly of a contrary opinion, pray write to me and specify your reasons. If those should not prove satisfactory to me, we will defer any further consideration of the subject till I come to London, which, if all goes well, I propose to do by the 1st of May at the latest.

Ever faithfully yours
[*signed*] Wm Wordsworth

1572. W. W. to CHAUNCY HARE TOWNSHEND

MS. Mirian Lutcher Stark Library, University of Texas. Hitherto unpublished.

Rydal Mount
Decbr 27th [1841][2]

Dear Mr Townsend,

Thank you for your Christmas Cards, which I shall distribute, as I have already done in part, among my neighbours—

[1] See L. 1548 above.

[2] This letter cannot be dated with any certainty, nor can the references in it be fully explained. It clearly belongs to the period after W. W.'s reconciliation with Chauncy Hare Townshend (see L. 1405 above), and before the death of Henry

I wrote to the Earl of Lonsdale immediately on receiving Mr. H. C.'s[1] Letter; his Lordship's answer was that the place was at the disposal of Sir Robert Peel, and had it not been so, he could not have applied in your behalf as his interest would have gone in favour of another Gentleman whom he named.

These particulars I mentioned to Mr H. N. C.[2] immediately and am rather surprized that he did not acquaint you with the result—

Believe [me] to remain with much respect
sincerely yours
Wm Wordsworth

1573. W. W. to [?] DORA QUILLINAN

MS. WL. Hitherto unpublished.

[? late 1841]

. . .merits of dear Miss Fenwick's plan in general—but still I should rejoice that you could bear a little portion of animal food however little say a mouthful chopped and minced with your knife and kept in your mouth till it was quite soft and pulpy. . .

[*cetera desunt*]

1574. W. W. to WILLIAM JACKSON[3]

MS. Cornell. Hitherto unpublished.

[*In Elizabeth Cookson's hand*]

Rydal Mount
14th January 1842

My dear Dr Jackson,

Mr R. Jameson whom I have appointed my Subdistributor at Penrith has named as his Sureties his Brother John Jameson,[4]

Nelson Coleridge in Jan. 1843. It would also appear to refer to Peel's second administration, for W. W. and Townshend were estranged during his first brief term of office in 1834–5. Hence the suggested dating.

[1] Hartley Coleridge's. W. W. later renewed his application to Lord Lonsdale on Townshend's behalf at the request of Sara Coleridge, who acknowledged his help on 20 Dec. 1844. (*Victoria University Library MSS.*). See L. 1853 below.

[2] Henry Nelson Coleridge.

[3] Rector of Lowther (see pt. i, L. 9).

[4] A solicitor long established at Penrith, who became county treasurer. Richard Jameson was magistrates' clerk.

Sol^{r}, and Wm Hullock of Carleton near Penrith Yeoman. Will you be so kind as to let me know whether you are acquainted with the character and circumstances of these parties and if you think, from what you either do know, or could without much trouble learn for me, that they are fit persons to be received by me as Joint Sureties to the amount of £1,200.

Dora is here as well as William—both are well but they leave us in two or three days—John, who came over to see his sister, has just left us for Brigham. Ten of his family are either in or just out of the Scarlet-tina and we are much afraid that he may catch it, as their Governess did the other day immediately on her return from visiting her friends.

I am glad to say your Brother[1] seems recovered from his late severe attack of illness, he has been several times at Rydal lately. Mrs Jackson and your two Nieces called here last week and gave a good report of M^{r} and Mrs Partridge[2] who are about to leave Brighton for Hastings.

Mrs Wordsworth Dora and William unite in kindest regards to yourself and Mrs Jackson

I am my dear Dr Jackson
Yours faithfully
[*signed*] Wm Wordsworth

Mrs Wordsworth and Dora will be particularly obliged to Mrs Jackson to remember them affectionately when writing to her friends in Ireland. To Sophia[3] Dora begs her especial love.

1575. W. W. to JOSHUA STANGER

MS. WL (Moorsom Papers).
K (—). LY iii. 1108.

[*In Dora Q.'s hand*]

Jany 16th, 1842.

My dear Sir,

I take it very kindly that you should have thought of me and my family in y^{r} distress and am especially obliged as y^{r} letter

[1] Thomas Jackson of Waterhead.

[2] Probably Mr. and Mrs. Robert Partridge, formerly of Ambleside.

[3] Mrs. William Jackson's sister (see pt. i, L. 85).

gave us the first intimation of the decease of y^r lamented brother[1] w^h we should otherwise have abruptly learned from a newspaper of the same day.

We also feel indebted to you for having entered into those painful details of the long-continued malady w^h in spite of medical efforts and the affectionate attentions of his beloved Sister and yourself carried him in the noon-tide of life to his grave. This removal has naturally thrown my mind back as far as to Dr Calvert's Grandfather[2] and his Father[3] and Sister,[4] the former of whom was as you know among my intimate friends and his Uncle Raisley[5] whom I have so much cause to remember with gratitude for his testamentary remembrance of me, when the greatest part of our patrimony was kept back from us by injustice. It may be satisfactory to y^r wife for me to declare upon this melancholy occasion that my Friend's bequest enabled me to devote myself to literary pursuits, independent of any necessity to look at pecuniary emoluments, so that my talents, such as they might be, were free to take their natural course. Your brothers[6] Raisley and William were both so well known to me and I have so many reasons to respect them that I cannot forbear saying that my sympathy with this last bereavement is deepened by the remembrance that they both have been taken from you.

Let it not be supposed, however, that either myself or any of my family are insensible to the source of consolation to which you so affectingly point, a consolation which we know and feel will thro' the goodness of God, embrace them all. Accept our thanks for the lines by Mr Sterling[7] to be inscribed upon y^r

[1] Dr. John Calvert (see pt. ii, L. 403), Stanger's brother-in-law, had led a wandering life in search of health, finally settling in Falmouth early in 1840, where he joined the circle of Caroline Fox (see L. 1623 below), John Sterling, J. S. Mill, etc. His condition had worsened in summer 1841, and he died on the following 9 Jan. at the age of 39. Joshua Stanger and his wife had been at Falmouth for some time looking after him.

[2] Raisley Calvert, senior (see *EY*, p. 97).

[3] William Calvert (see *EY*, p. 97 and pt. ii, L. 403).

[4] i.e. William Calvert's sister Ann (see *EY* p. 127).

[5] See *EY*, pp. 126–7, 130 ff.

[6] i.e. his brothers-in-law, the Revd. Raisley Calvert and William Calvert, jnr. (see pt. i, L. 116). The former had died at his parish in Derbyshire in Jan. 1838, the latter in India in Aug. 1841.

[7] John Sterling (1806–44), an 'Apostle' and friend of F. D. Maurice and Trench at Trinity College, Cambridge, had left the University without taking a degree, becoming a contributor to *The Athenaeum*, and disciple of S. T. C. After

brother's tombstone. They are a very appropriate tribute, and the last couplet is excellent.[1]

Owing to a return of inflammation in the eyes caused by imprudently walking in the cold frosty air two hours after sunset I have been obliged to employ my daughter's pen. She has been passing her Christmas with us, and we shall lose her on Tuesday if the snow w^{h} is here lying very heavy permit her to go. William is also here and both well, and John left us on Friday not without anxiety on our part as the Scarletina is in his house and 7 out of their 9 children[2] have had it. Two of the servants and a governess just returned from a visit to Liverpool have taken the infection. All but Jane seem to have got through it well. With her it has left a tendency to low nervous fever.

Every one including my dear Sister join me in heart felt condolence and wishes and prayers that you may both support this affliction as becomes true Christians, faithfull under all trials.

I remain, my dear Sir,

Sincerely and affectionately y^{s},

[*signed*] Wm Wordsworth

studying in Germany, he was ordained (1834) and became Julius Hare's curate at Herstmonceaux for a few months, but gradually withdrew from the Church under the influence of Thomas Carlyle and wrote for *Blackwood's* and the *Westminster Review*. He published a novel *Arthur Coningsby* (1833), his *Poems* (1839), *The Election* (1841), and *Strafford: A Tragedy* (1843), dedicated to Emerson. In 1837 he wintered with Dr. Calvert in Madeira, and two years later joined the Fox circle at Falmouth. Sterling's *Essays and Tales* were published posthumously in two volumes in 1848 with a memoir by Julius Hare, which Carlyle found so unsatisfactory that he wrote his own *Life of John Sterling* (1851), in which he treated Sterling as an emblem of the intellectual and religious confusion of the age. Sterling had met W. W. in London in May 1828: '. . . his manner and conversation are full of the pleasant, playful sincerity and kindness which are so observable in his works. The utter absence of pretension in all he says and looks is very striking. . . . Coleridge is the philosopher in conversation by being all philosopher, and Wordsworth by not affecting to be it at all.' (See Richard Chenevix Trench, *Letters and Memorials*, 2 vols., 1888, i. 8–9.) W. W. was much impressed by his character and poetic ability: see *WL MSS.* and *Memories of Old Friends, Being Extracts from the Journals and Letters of Caroline Fox*, ed. Horance N. Pym, 2 vols., 1881, ii. 39.

[1] Reason thy Lamp, and Faith thy star while here;
Now both one brightness in the Light of God.
(ibid. i. 286)

[2] John W. had six children, but recently 'three little cousins from India' had come to stay with his family (see L. 1580 below).

1576. W. W. to JOHN GIBSON LOCKHART

MS. National Library of Scotland.
LY iii. 1110.

[*In M. W.'s hand*]

Rydal Mount Jan^{ry} 17th [1842]

My dear Mr Lockhart

I have been a long time in your debt which you will be so kind as to excuse—for I have had a return of inflammation in my eyes brought on by an imprudent walk on a frosty night, and I am still obliged to employ Mrs W.'s pen. We condole with you most sincerely upon the death of Mr Charles Scott,[1] who must be regretted by all his friends, and whose loss will be long and deeply felt by yourself and your Children. When we read of his death in the Newspapers we also thought much of the Misses Alexander[2] who had taken, as we witnessed, so lively an interest about him immediately previous to his departure.

Many thanks for your Article in the Review,[3] which was kindly sent me by Mr Murray. It treats several points of the subject to perfection, and I do trust it will benefit the cause—tho' if you had not been interfered with some deficiencies might have been supplied. The matter I hope will be again brought before Parliament the ensuing Session,[4] tho' to my no little surprize I have heard that Serg^{t} Talfourd thinks it had better be deferred. If you can point out any way in which I can be useful, command me.

Sir R. Inglis tells me, thro' a letter to Mr H. C. Robinson, who has been spending his Christmas at Rydal[5]—that he will tell

[1] Scott's younger son had died at Tehran on 29 Oct. 1841.

[2] Lockhart's London neighbours in Sussex Place, Regent's Park. See Andrew Lang, *Life and Letters of John Gibson Lockhart*, 2 vols., 1897, ii. 82.

[3] His article on Copyright in the *Quarterly* (see L. 1558 above). According to H. C. R., Lockhart had complained in a letter to W. W. that John Murray was 'on the other side, and insisted on certain things being left out.' (*HCR* ii. 607).

[4] See L. 1585 below.

[5] H. C. R. had arrived at Rydal on 24 Dec. in the company of the Quillinans and remained until 18 Jan., seeing much of the Arnolds at Fox How, and also Frederick Faber (see pt. iii, Ls. 1195 and 1330), who had accompanied Benson Harrison's son on a tour to the Near East and was now staying with the family at Green Bank. See *HCR* ii. 603–11. H. C. R. found W. W. 'more companionable, being more tolerant than he used to be.' (Morley i. 451).

me when any thing shall be settled—from which I infer there is no intention of its being dropped this Session.

I cannot conclude without thanking you also for Mr Taylor's Article upon my Sonnets[1] and shall be glad to think that the original ones which you have admitted have done no discredit to the Review.

Your children would be interested I hope in being told that we often think of them with the best of good wishes.

Believe me to be my dear Mr Lockhart

faithfully yours
[*signed*] Wm Wordsworth

1577. W. W. to HENRY TAYLOR

MS. University Library, Davis, California. Hitherto unpublished.

[*In M. W.'s hand*]

Rydal Mount
Jan^{ry} 17th, —42

My dear Mr Taylor

You probably have heard from Miss Fenwick how constantly I have been engaged, so as that I found it expedient to put off writing all letters—and for the last week, my old complaint, inflammation of the eyes, tho' not very bad, has prevented me from both reading and writing—except by proxy—which I still submit to.

Your Article upon the Sonnets is thoughtfully written, and will I trust materially promote the object you had in view. It has given us all very great pleasure both as a proof of the value you set upon my writings, and as carrying with it an assurance that by the ability with which it is executed the knowledge of them may be extended to many others, who may, for various reasons, have been disinclined to look into them.

Our dear friend bears the severe weather stoutly, tho' it has confined her to the house, except for a day or two. The rest of us are well, and unite in kind remembrance to yourself and Mrs. Taylor,

and believe me ever
faithfully yours
[*signed*] W. Wordsworth

[1] See L. 1554 above, and next letter.

I ought to have mentioned that your Article and my penal Sonnets and your observations upon them have excited the wrath of any anonymous quarrelsome Admirer of mine—who has inflicted upon me no less than 19 of his—in refutation, and abuse of us both. I have not read a tenth part of them—if you have any curiosity upon the subject, they shall be sent to you.

1578. W. W. to EDWARD MOXON

MS. Harvard University Library.
K (—). *LY iii. 1111.*

[*In M. W.'s hand*]

18th Janry 42

My dear Mr Moxon,

Your account of the depressed state of the book trade makes me almost indifferent about publishing the volume which I was preparing.[1] I nevertheless went on making corrections, and getting it transcribed by my kind friends and inmates. It is now quite ready for the Press,—and I'll give you a slight Sketch of its Contents. 1st a Poem of 75 Spenserian Stanzas,[2] 23 of which have already been published, in the former Edn, under the title of 'the Female Vagrant'. The whole Poem was written in the years 1793–4; but the yet unpublished Parts have been carefully revised. Next come 3 or 4 Elegiac Poems, 2 of them upon visiting the Grave of Burns[3]—next a[n] Epistle of 340 lines addressed to Sir G. Beaumont in 1811[4]—then other Miscellaneous Poems written about and after that Period. Several others of much more recent date, down to the present time (that is, since the 'Yarrow Red'). The 12 Sonnets of the Appendix[5] to be reprinted, with other miscellaneous ones—with the penal[6] 14.—Nearly 800 lines of 'Memorials of my Italian Tour'—the 2 versions of Chaucer, printed by Mr Powell[7]—and lastly a

[1] *Poems, Chiefly of Early and Late Years.*

[2] *Guilt and Sorrow.* See also pt. iii, L. 1261.

[3] *At the Grave of Burns, 1803. Seven Years After His Death,* and *Thoughts Suggested the Day Following, on the Banks of Nith, Near the Poet's Residence* (*PW* iii. 65, 67).

[4] See *PW* iv. 142.

[5] See L. 1555 above.

[6] The *Sonnets upon the Punishment of Death.*

[7] See pt. iii, L. 1361.

Tragedy[1] written in my 25th and 26th year, and which has lain by me till now. The whole will, if printed, one Son: in a page, and only 2 Spenserian stanzas—and at that rate, will make a volume fully as thick, I think, as the thickest of the six.

And now for the mode of proceeding. I must tell you at once, I would not *on any account* print less than two thousand, and am extremely averse to striking off less than *3* thousand—because I do not think it advisable to stereotype, these Poems being designed to be interspersed in some future Ed. of the whole—perhaps in double column. Your allusion to the 'Yarrow Revisited'—which, as you say, was only 1500 copies—does not bear upon the case, as you will instantly perceive, when you recollect how many thousand copies of my Poems have been sold since that publication—and also turn your thoughts to the consequent probability that a proportionate number of those Persons who possess the 6 Volumes will complete their set by purchasing this intended volume. In future Editions 'The Female Vagrant' will of course be omitted as a separate piece—but the re-printing it here is indispensible.

Let me hear from you at your early convenience upon what terms you will undertake the work—bearing in mind that I am in no wise anxious about it, now that my own labour is brought to an end.

You will be seeing Mr Robinson in a few days,[2] he and Mr Quillinan left us this $morn^{g}$. With our united good wishes to Mrs M, your Sister and yourself, believe me

ever yours
[*signed*] Wm Wordsworth

[1] *The Borderers* (*PW* i. 128 ff.), written 1796–7. See also pt. iii, L. 1085. For a full account of the textual history, see *The Borderers* (*The Cornell Wordsworth*), ed. Robert Osborn, 1982.

[2] H. C. R. met Moxon at Talfourd's on the 27th. Mary Lamb was also there, 'very flighty in her talk'. (*HCR* ii. 611).

1579. W. W. to JOHN S. BLIGH[1]

Address: Mr John S. Bligh, 4 Stebon Terrace, Philpot St, Commercial Road East, London. [*In unidentified hand*]
Postmark: 24 Jan. 1842.
Stamp: Ambleside.
MS. Cornell. Hitherto unpublished.

[*In M. W.'s hand*]

[*c.* 23 Jan. 1842]

Dear Sir

I have made two or three slight annotations, which is all that I have time for. It is a horrible story. I have not seen the original—

I am much pleased by the delicate way in which [you] have expressed your request that I would cast my eye over your lines. I have not read Mr Buxton's book[2]—but as you appear to attach an interest to sending it to me as a token of your gratitude—allow me to say that if you forward the volume to Mr Moxon 44 Dover St I could ere long receive it—and shall value the gift on your account.

I remain dear Sir
sincerely yours
[*signed*] W[m] Wordsworth

[1] Unidentified.

[2] Probably *The African Slave Trade and its Remedy*, 2nd edn. 1840. See *R.M. Cat.* no. 13. Thomas Fowell Buxton (see pt. i, L. 116), the emancipationist, had married Hannah Gurney of Earlham, younger sister of Elizabeth Fry, and became one of the leading abolitionists in Parliament while M.P. for Weymouth (1818–37). In 1839 he put forward far-reaching proposals for opening up central Africa to civilisation and commerce and thereby finally putting an end to the slave trade. His plan included an expedition up the Niger, which proved a costly failure at first, though it was productive of long-term benefits. See *Memoirs of Sir Thomas Fowell Buxton, Baronet*, ed. Charles Buxton, 1848, pp. 436–40. W. W. appears to be unaware that Buxton had been created a baronet in 1840.

1580. W. W. to C. W.

MS. Cornell. Hitherto unpublished.

[*In M. W.'s hand*]

Rydal Mount
Jan^{ry} 26th 1842

My dear Brother,

I have for many years been much interested in the Matter to which the enclosed letter from the Revd Henry Lowther[1] refers: and I believe that I spoke of it to you and Mr Watson[2] several years ago. It is the deplorable want of Church accommodation as this letter truly details it, in the poor, I might almost say beggarly, Town of Distington. My thoughts turn to you with some hope that you may be able to put us in the way of getting a New Church, for the patching up the Old is not to be desired, it would do so little! Lord Lonsdale, perhaps you may be aware, has just charged his Estates with the payment of £100 per ann: for the Maintenance of an evening Lecturer in our Native Town. The People when the late Earl of Egremont offered them a considerable sum for the benefit of the Town, as they might think it best provided, preferred a New Market place[3] to a Church—they had their wish and find, I am not sorry to say, that their Market house is rather an injury than an Advantage.

You will be sorry to hear that for the last Month the Vicarage at Brigham has been suffering from Scarlet fever. 7 out of 9 Children (perhaps you are not aware that Isabella has taken charge of 3 little Cousins from India, in addition to her own 6)—the Nurse and House Maid, are convalescent—but I grieve to say this dire disease has fallen heavily upon the Governess—a most respectable young Person, who has been of their household for only about 4 or 5 months—and last of all poor John has taken it. Isabella (who is, as you may suppose, almost worn out by fatigue) tells us that hitherto her husband, who sickened only

[1] Rector of Distington (see pt. i, L. 230), the mining town between Whitehaven and Workington. The Wesleyans had been particularly active there during the previous decade. The medieval parish church was not rebuilt until 1886.

[2] Joshua Watson.

[3] The new market house in Cockermouth was erected in 1837, with the support of the 3rd Earl of Egremont.

last Sunday evening, is mildly held. But she naturally dreads the after effects upon him who suffered so long from the Typhus fever.

Dora left us along with our friend Mr Robinson last week—She was with us 3 weeks and had the satisfaction of meeting both her Brothers.

I hope you are quite well—as we all are—notwithstanding this very severe weather. We shall be most happy to hear that you have escaped injury from it—and from your change of residence.

With our united love believe me ever your

affec Brother
[*signed*] Wm Wordsworth

1581. W. W. to MAURICE HARCOURT[1]

MS. untraced.
Maurice Harcourt, 'Windermere and Wordsworth', Bradshaw's Magazine, iv (Dec. 1842), 5.

[early 1842]

. . . Mr Prince's[2] verses do him great credit, and have not at all disappointed me. They shew sensibility, and observation of nature in no common degree, and are expressed with freshness, harmony, and vigour . . .

1582. W. W. to EDWARD MOXON

MS. Henry E. Huntington Library.
LY iii. 1112.

[*In M. W.'s hand*]

Feb^ry^ 3^d^ [1842]

My dear Mr Moxon,

I am very sorry indeed to learn that your connection with me, at least considered in its direct bearings has been so unprofitable

[1] A journalist who visited W. W. in Dec. 1841.
[2] For John Critchley Prince see L. 1707 below.

to you.[1] On your statement I have only one remark to make, which is, that, if my memory does not fail me, I should only have suffered *negatively* by the 2[d] Ed: of the Yarrow[2] not meeting with a sale. Of course I would not have broken my connection with the Longmans without relieving them of that Ed: but if another Copy had not been sold the terms of my agreement were such that I should have suffered no positive *loss*. Your trade at present seems a very bad one for you, and for myself I can with truth say, that the labour which from [the] first I have bestowed on the forth-coming volume is not likely to earn for me the wages of 2/- a day. Take that ye Men of the Trade, and make the best of it. I wish you may be right in charging the book so high—but I submit—regretting only, as I sincerely do, that I ever took the trouble I have done in preparing the book for the Press at this time.

More Mss will be sent to the Printer by this day's post and he shall regularly be supplied before-hand—so that he shall have no pretext for delay from that Quar[ter][3] and I beg you would strenuously urge him to be as quick as possible so that we may not lose, as we did last year to my great disappointment, the whole of the Spring season, and no small part of the Summer.

Believe me to be with our joint regards to Mrs M and your Sister

faithfully yours
[*signed*] W[m] Wordsworth

1583. W. W. to C. W.

MS. Mr. Jonathan Wordsworth. Hitherto unpublished.

Rydal
9th Feb[ry] 42

My dear Brother,

Mr Lowther[4] was highly gratified by the interest you took in his Project; and has probably thanked you himself before this

[1] Moxon strenuously denied this rumour in his reply of 5 Feb.: 'I am not I assure you, whatever you may have heard from other quarters, in the habit of saying that I lose by you, for such is not now the case . . .' (*WL MSS.*)

[2] Publ. 1836.

[3] *Edge of MS. worn away.*

[4] The Revd. Henry Lowther of Distington (see L. 1580 above).

time. I now write merely to advert to your connection with the State of Pennsylvania.[1] I have had no *private* intelligence since I saw you; but the accounts which appear in the Newspapers are most promising. The Governors and the Legislature of the State have in the strongest possible terms reprobated the abominable doctrine of repudiation, and the People are cautioned to reject every proposition of this kind, with the scorn and indignation which such a proposal cannot but excite where the least feeling of common honesty exists.—Now with regard to this State and every other it is at the bottom a mere question of *honesty*. Undoubtedly several of the States, that of Pennsylvania included, are much embarrassed, by having given way to temptation which they ought to have resisted, as the undertaking so much exceeded their means. Public works, such as Railways, Roads, etc, etc, have been commenced and carried on through all parts more or less of the Continent, and heavy debts incurred for that purpose; it will therefore happen that their Projects will be abandoned in many instances, and as the Works are of a slighter kind than things of the same sort in England, they will fall into decay, before money can be raised to complete them, and so a great deal of Capital, inevitably lost. But the resources of the States are inexhaustible, the activity and spirit of the people indefatigable, so that could we but give them credit for decent honesty, there is no doubt that the worst of them would erelong be able to discharge all their obligations. Thinking as I do that Pennsylvania is sound at heart, notwithstanding the infamous swindling of the United States nat [?] Bank,[2] I should have little fear of your money being lost. Dear Miss Fenwick has no less than ten thousand pounds in Pennsylvania stock, I hold the same language to her, which I am now using to you.—The Missisippi State has behaved so infamously that I cannot encourage hope as to that quarter. And as you know, through their dishonesty, Dora and the Hutchinson family are suffering. I must conclude, ever affectionately Yours—John's family are all recovering except the Governess who is in great danger—

W. W.

14 out of 16 have gone thro this sad disease.

[1] i.e. C. W.'s investments.

[2] *MS. obscure*. For the failure of the U.S. Bank, see pt. iii, L. 1353.

1584. W. W. to JOHN PEACE

MS. untraced.
Mem. (—). *K* (—). *LY iii.* 1113 (—).

Rydal Mount, Feb. 23rd, 1842

My dear Sir,

I was truly pleased with the receipt of the letter which you were put upon writing by the perusal of my *Penal Sonnets* in the 'Quarterly Review'.[1] Being much engaged at present, I might have deferred making my acknowledgments for this and other favors (particularly your 'Descant') if I had not had a special occasion for addressing you at this moment. A Bristol lady has kindly undertaken to be the bearer of the walking stick which I spoke to you of some time since. It was cut from a holly-tree planted in our garden by my own hand. . . .

Your *Descant*[2] amused me, but I must protest against your system, which would discard punctuation to the extent you propose. It would, I think, destroy the harmony of blank verse when skillfully written. What would become of the pauses at the third syllable, followed by an *and*, or any such word, without the rest which a comma, when consistent with the sense, calls upon the reader to make, and which being made, he starts with the weak syllable that follows, as from the begining of a verse? I am sure Milton would have supported me in this opinion. Thomson wrote his blank verse before his ear was formed as it was when he wrote the 'Castle of Indolence', and some of his short rhyme poems. It was, therefore, rather hard in you to select him as an instance of punctuation abused.

I am glad that you concur in my view on the *Punishment of Death*. An outcry, as I expected, has been raised against me by weak-minded humanitarians. What do you think of one person having opened a battery of nineteen fourteen-pounders upon me, i.e. nineteen sonnets, in which he gives himself credit for having blown me and my system to atoms? Another sonneteer has had a solitary shot at me from Ireland.

Ever faithfully yours,
W. Wordsworth

[1] See L. 1554 above.
[2] *A Descant on the Penny Postage*, [Anon.], 1841.

1585. W. W. to VISCOUNT MAHON

MS. Stanhope MSS., Chevening. Hitherto unpublished.

[*In M. W.'s hand*]

Rydal Mount. Feb 28th —42.

My dear Lord Mahon,

It gives me great pleasure to learn that a bill for the extention of Copy-right is about to be brought into the House under your management.[1] This I first learned from Sir Robt Inglis, but I am not therefore the less obliged by the letter which you yourself have written to me upon the Subject.

From Sir Robt Inglis I understand that you mean to stop short of the measure adopted in Prussia, and rather take that of France for your model.—You have been compelled I suppose to chuse this course in fear that the more liberal one might be rejected.

In my present ignorance of the particulars of your intended bill, I have nothing to suggest; only let me express a hope that due consideration will be paid in it to Posthumous publications: and to those which are given to the world late in the Author's life. In the poetical department of literature, it is remarkable that there is scarcely a writer of eminence of whom it may not be said, either that he died early, as Spenser, and Shakespear (for he may be named) Beaumont the Dramatist; and in our own times Burns, Shelley, Byron, and before these Chatterton, Collins, Goldsmith, Thompson and Akenside,—or that his principal works were written when he was old. This was the case with Chaucer, Milton, Dryden, Cowper and Crabbe—and I believe with the Author of the Night Thoughts.[2]

This being so, allow me to ask whether your bill will contain provision for the benefit, thro their heirs or successors, of writers so circumstanced, beyond what is done by the Law as it now stands? I should indeed be sorry if our Countrymen are indisposed to give any great writer credit for feeling and

[1] Talfourd was not a member of the new Parliament, and the management of the Copyright Bill now passed to Lord Mahon (see pt. iii, L. 1047). He reduced Talfourd's original proposal that the term of copyright should be 60 years from the date of publication to 25 years from the author's death, and he also inserted a new clause to prevent the suppression of valuable works by the representatives of a deceased author. In this new form the Bill was introduced on 3 Mar., and given a Second Reading on the 16th, after a conciliatory speech from Macaulay.

[2] Edward Young (1683–1765), who published his *Night Thoughts* in 1742.

pecuniary interest beyond the term of his own life. We are not likely to see another Milton, but if such a Man should rise up among us, or any one approaching him, who could bear to think that, without any fault of their own, his Grandchildren should stand in need of Alms while Booksellers were making thousands by his works?

Again, Burns published by much the most valuable part of his Poems when he was only 26 years of age[1]—had the term of Copy-right been in his time extended as it is now, his Widow and Children, would, even in that case as he died ten years after the publication, have had no more than 16 years pecuniary emolument from his Works, tho' it is said they have gone thro 100 Editions. Is that just, or can it be profitable to the Country?

Excuse me, my dear Lord, for saying this much—and allow me to congratulate the Country upon your having undertaken the Bills

I have the honor to be
faithfully, your much obliged
[*signed*] Wm Wordsworth

I find I have written upon two sheets of paper pray be so good as excuse the oversight.

1586. W. W. to EDWARD QUILLINAN

Address: Edward Quillinan Esqre.
MS. WL.
LY iii. 1114.

[*In M. W.'s hand*]

March 1st 1842

I hold the pen for my husband

My dear Quillinan,

Your letter to Miss Fenwick moved me much on many accounts. But my motive for writing this short letter is merely to assure you of our sympathy in your vexations and distresses, and still more, very much more, to assure you that you need have no anxiety respecting judgment which we are likely to form of your character on these sad proceedings. We have all an entire confidence in your integrity from the first to the last, in

[1] Actually 27. The Kilmarnock volume appeared in 1786.

your connection with the Brydges family,[1] and the Barrett property, and furthermore are but too well aware of the generous sacrifices which you have made for them who have proved to be so unworthy of them. The confidence you reposed in them, however chargeable it may be with want of discretion, affords itself a strong presumption of your being incapable of joining in any dishonourable transaction. As I have confidence that you will regulate your mind as becomes you, I have nothing to add but the expression of a wish that the business may be speedily brought to a close, with as little injustice as is possible under the untoward circumstances which the wicked arts of the adverse party have produced.

Believe me my dear Q affectionately yours
[*signed*] Wm Wordsworth

[1] In 1826 E. Q. had become entangled in the shady business concerns of the Brydges family, and through careless confidence had taken part in a fraudulent transaction by which they cleared some £15,000. (See Mary K. Woodworth, *The Literary Career of Sir Egerton Brydges*, Oxford, 1935). The matter was not cleared up until 1842, and W. W. wrote this letter just before E. Q. came up for trial on 11 Mar. 'There can be no doubt', H. C. R. noted, 'that he acted most incautiously and weakly in signing deeds, and being an assenting party to transactions which were of a most iniquitous character; but still I am perfectly convinced of his honour and integrity . . . but it is, after all a melancholy mode of escaping from an imputation on one's honour by allowing that the fault must be transferred to the head.' (*HCR* ii. 613). But the following month he was able to record the Vice-Chancellor's verdict that E. Q. had been free of all intention to commit fraud, though 'he is liable with some four or five others to make up the difference between £22,000 and £7,000, besides costs, which will be a sad dead weight lying on him, and prevent him doing anything for his wife.' (*HCR* ii. 614). It was, as de Selincourt notes, E. Q.'s financial straits, and the fact that this trial was hanging over him, that had been W. W.'s chief reason for opposing his marriage with Dora.

1587. W. W. to HENRY READ

Address: Henry Reed Esq[re], Philadelphia.
Postmark: (1) 2 Mar. 1842 (2) 28 Mar.
Stamp: (1) Ambleside (2) Boston Ship.
Endorsed: Rec. March 29. Ans[d] March 30.
MS. Cornell.
K (—). *Wordsworth and Reed, p. 62.*

[*In M. W.'s hand*]

Rydal Mount March 1st 42

My dear Sir

I had purposed to write a long letter in answer to your last, of Nov[r] 29th which I have deferred doing in pretty confident expectation of hearing again from you—and particularly since the consternation which the failure of the Banks of Philadelphia, and the stoppage of the payment of dividends in the State debt, have occasioned in England; and which one of my nearest connections and Miss Fenwick, of whom I have spoken so often, will feel deeply—My Brother the late Master of Trin: Coll: Cambridge, was induced by the aspect of things at home, to confide the whole of his savings during rather a long life, to what he thought the superior stability of Pensylvania credit. I now write earnestly to beg, that you would lose no time in letting me know what yourself and your most judicious friends think about the resumption of payment of the dividends, if it be expected to take place and when; and also upon the stability of the monetary system of the Pensylvanian State, its resources, and above all, upon the question of its *integrity*. I am very anxious for this on Miss F's account who is now sitting by me; and whose moral and domestic engagements are such, as rather than be disqualified from fulfilling them, she would willingly and gladly sacrifice one ½ of the money, she has entrusted to your State, for a certainty of recovering the other. I incur the great responsibility of endeavouring daily to dissuade this excellent Lady from acting upon such a disposition. For my own part, I cannot but hope, that notwithstanding the evil example of other States, and the bad, or rather no principles of the dregs of your democracy, all will yet come round with you. As to Mississippi and some other States, I think they are abandoned to utter profl[ig]acy and in the course of a righteous Providence will be doomed to suffer for their iniquity.

I have sent you 3 Sonnets[1] upon certain "Aspects of Religion in America" having as you will see a reference to the subject upon which you wished me to write. I wish they had been more worthy of the subject; I hope however you will not disapprove of the connection, which I have thought myself warranted in tracing, between the Puritan fugitives and Episcopacy. The Sonnets are already printed, and will be published, I hope, before I can receive an answer to this letter, in a New Volume of Poems which I am carrying thro' the Press. They are miscellaneous—but will contain the Tragedy[2] of which you have heard something. It was written so far back, as 1795–6.

By the same Packet I shall send a copy of those Sonnets to Bp: Doane[3]—tho' having mislaid his particular address, I can only forward them to the Bp: of New Jersey—as the letter may not reach him,—will you be kind enough to have the Sonnets transcribed, and forward them to him.

The motto you enquire after in the modernized Chaucer, is by Drayton;[4] it was in the MS. which I sent without noticing from what author it was taken.

I wrote a letter to Mr Gray—long since deceased, upon Dr Currie's Life of Burns[5]—it was never reprinted but I shall be glad to send you, as I have some copies by me, one of them if you will be so good as to point out ho[w][6] it may reach you safely.

[1] W. W. enclosed copies of his three sonnets on *Aspects of Christianity in America*, as in *PW* iii. 390–1, except that the second sonnet is entitled *Return to the Church in England.* In his letter of 29 Nov. 1841 (*Wordsworth and Reed*, pp. 57–61), Reed had reiterated his conviction that the consecration of the American Bishops 'might almost be considered as one of the greatest missions of your Church. . . .Surely no measure in the history of the Church of England has been calculated to spread her principles over a larger section of Christendom. . . .In the lower region of mere worldly concerns—diplomacy, and commerce, and money—there may, most unhappily be frequently arising occasions of dissatisfaction and estrangement. The more need therefore is there to cherish those feelings in which we are alike.'

[2] *The Borderers.*

[3] See next letter.

[4] Drayton's tribute to Chaucer from his lines *To my most dearely-loved friend Henery Reynolds Esquire, of Poets and Poesie*, was incorrectly attributed to W. W. on the title-page of *Chaucer's Poems Modernized.*

[5] See *MY* ii. 287 and *Prose Works*, iii. 111 ff.

[6] *MS. torn.*

I am glad you are so much pleased with Mr Hare's Works,[1] he is an old and valued friend of mine.

I would have written at greater length, but I have many letters in arrears—in consequence of being over-taxed in correcting my volume of Poems and carrying it thro' the Press. So I must conclude with many good wishes. Y^r much obliged

[*signed*] Wm Wordsworth

Is the *State* pledged, or only the Pensylvania *Bank*?

1588. W. W. to GEORGE WASHINGTON DOANE

MS. untraced.
William Croswell Doane, The Life and Writings of George Washington Doane. . . , 1860, i. 299n (—).

[*c.* 1 Mar. 1842]

My dear Bishop,

At last I am able to beg your acceptance of these Sonnets; the latter half of the second, and the third, upon the subject of the English Church in America.[2] I wish they had been more worthy of the matter, and of your perusal; but I have done my best. In commemorating Bishop White, you will observe that I am indebted to your admirable delineation of his character; in the course of the thought, and, partly, of the expression.

I hope your voyage has proved a favourable one; and that no painful change had taken place, among your family, friends, and flock, during your absence, beyond what the instability of our human condition prepares every thinking person to expect.

A few days ago, I received from dear Sir Robert Inglis, an impression of his portrait,[3] to supply the place of the one you so kindly accepted from me. It is declared by different friends, who have seen it, to be one of the best portraits ever taken; and you and I can both speak of the fidelity of the likeness. I mean to have

[1] Reed had been reading *Guesses at Truth* by A. W. and J. C. Hare (see pt. iii, L. 1249). 'What a delightful book it is . . . showing so much of those influences he has so gratefully acknowledged to you . . .' He also praised Julius Hare's sermons on *The Victory of Faith* (see L. 1519 above).

[2] See Ls. 1536 and 1537 above, and previous letter.

[3] Probably the portrait by George Richmond, R.A. (1809–96), engraved by J. Jenkins, published in 1837 in *Portraits of Eminent Conservatives and Statesmen*, a collection compiled by Henry Thomas Ryall (1811–67), the engraver.

fixed upon the back of mine, an account of the circumstances under which it came into my possession; with a hope of its being preserved, for more than one generation, as a sort of heir-loom in my family.

And now, my dear Bishop, let me bid you farewell, with store of good wishes. The event which brought you to England,[1] did yourself and the Church in which you fill so eminent a station, high credit. May the religious union established between our Churches, continue from age to age; and spread, till every corner of the world be a partaker of its benefits.

[*cetera desunt*]

1589. W. W. to VISCOUNT MAHON

MS. Stanhope MSS., Chevening.[2]
K (—). *LY iii. 1067* (—).

[*In M. W.'s hand*]

Rydal Mount. March 4th —42.

My dear Lord Mahon

Many thanks for your 2d letter, and the Extract which it contained, from Lord John Russel to you.[3]

Public opinion having the power which it has at present, and is likely to have, I think with you that it is utterly improbable that any attempt will be made to hold back from republication any valuable work whatever. Besides Sert Talfourd's bill provided against that in a clause, which if there had been any defect in its construction, might without difficulty have been improved.

I replied briefly to the 3 objections which you will find in the enclosed Ext from the only letter I received from Sir R. Peel (which he was so obliging as to write to me) upon the subject; but in an interview with which he honored me last Summer, we had a pretty long conversation upon it. It is remarkable that then

[1] The consecration of the new parish church at Leeds.

[2] A draft of this letter in M. W.'s hand, with corrections by W. W., is among the Cornell MSS.

[3] Mahon had sent on an extract from Lord John Russell's letter of 20 Feb., in which he stated that he would not oppose the Second Reading of Mahon's Bill, but that if it was similar to Talfourd's, he would wish to see it much altered in Committee. He considered 25 years a long enough term. (*WL MSS.*)

he did not recur to any of those objections, but dwelt in general terms upon the evils of monopoly and in particular he deprecated the mischief which might arise from confining the circulation of improved processes in Science, (he instanced arithmetic) to the books thro' which they had been first made known. I must own I thought this rather an out of the way apprehension. For how would it be done? I certainly must acknowledge that I left Sir R. Peel with no grounds for believing that he was more favorable to Extension of Term than when the conversation began. He dwelt a good deal upon a discretionary power to be lodged in a Section of the Privy Council to reward, in the shape of Pensions, meritorious Authors, or to confer a privilege upon particular works supposed to be entitled to it.

I objected strongly to this, as putting the approved Authors in an invidious position, and as submitting the claims of Literature to a decision liable and likely to be influenced by partialities or dislikes, person[al] or political.

Nor did I scruple to add, that men in high office could not, if they did their duty to their Country, be supposed to have time duly to consider the merits of any profound or laborious work, or the claims which it might have upon the gratitude of succeeding times.

I should never had thought it worth while to move as I have done in this question, but for a wish to raise the Literature, as far as might be above a temptation to degrade itself by courting the Taste of the Public at any particular time. And I am quite unable to perceive what would be gained by taking refuge from this evil in a Section of the Privy Council, an Academy, or any other body of men.

It is supposed by some, that tho' there might not be much cause for fear from an injurious monopoly in the Descendents of Authors, yet where Copyright passed into the hands of Booksellers it would be sure of taking place. This I think would not happen. Education and a taste for reading having spread so widely, and its being certain that they will spread more and more, no combination of booksellers could be ignorant that their interest would be better promoted by selling at a low price to multitudes, rather than at a high one to a few. And there is in this consideration a sufficient answer to all the vague things that have been dinned into our ears upon Monopoly.

The observation you have made upon your present aim not

precluding future improvements reconciles me to what I cannot but think, tho' a prudent, an inadequate measure.[1]

In regard to Posthumous works, which are often kept back that their Author may bestow more labour upon them, and are therefore, if they be good, entitled to especial regard, I may be allowed to say that a boon of 2 years (if that be granted) in addition to the 28 which the present law secures, is not an acquisition worth thinking about. Let us however be thankful for what we can get; and be assured, my dear Lord Mahon that I am duly sensible of the obligations Literature is under to you, for undertaking a Bill which is sure to meet with vexatious opposition from many Persons unworthy of the Seat they hold in the house of Commons, and but a lax support from many others, who may have no objection either to the principles or detail of your Measure.

I have the honor to be
faithfully your Lordship's
obliged
[*signed*] Wm Wordsworth

Extract—Sir R. Peele to M^r W.

"If the right of the Author to such extended Protection" (as proposed by Sergent Talfourd) "be admitted, can we refuse it in the case of Patents and every other discovery mainly owing to the ingenuity and skill of the discoverer? There, arises the difficulties of determining what constitutes an original work, as distinguishable from plagiarism, difficulties incident indeed to every degree of protection—but increasing, with the protraction of it. And there are too the difficulties of effectually preventing piracy in Countries not subject to our Jurisdiction"

[1] Lord Mahon's Bill, as a compromise measure, proposed a shorter term of copyright than that embodied in Talfourd's original Bill. See L. 1585 above.

1590. W. W. to SIR WILLIAM GOMM

Endorsed: Wordsworth 10th March/42. Rec^{d}. [?] Ans^{d}. 26th.
MS. Henry E. Huntington Library.
LY iii. 1115.

Rydal Mount
March 10th —42.

My dear Sir William,

Your very kind Letter of August 22nd is now lying before me. The intelligence it conveyed was mournful,[1] and made me very anxious on your own and Lady Gomm's[2] account; I should of course have replied to it immediately but the Newspapers at that time announced your instant return to England; and I thought my Letter would be sure of reaching you earlier if I waited till your arrival. Accordingly I did so; but most unfortunately whatever might have been said upon this subject afterwards never came to my knowledge; nor had I the means of knowing till two or three days ago where you actually were. To account for this I must tell you that the state of my eyes, which however, thank God, is not worse than usual, prevents me from ever looking into the Newspapers by Candlelight, and I can seldom turn to them in winter time by day. But enough of this, as I am confident that you must have imputed my Silence to any thing rather than a due sense of your kind attention, or of the importance of the matter upon which your Letter mainly turned. Let me now, late as it is, perhaps, congratulate you and Lady Gomm having escaped the disease by which so many of your friends, and some of such high Character, as well as such numbers of the Men under your care, have been laid low: Mrs W joins me in the expression of this congratulation, and in a hope that Lady Gomm and you have returned in unimpaired health. We have both weathered the winter stoutly, though latterly a good deal over exerted in preparing and carrying through the Press a new Vol of Miscellaneous Poems of which some were written so far back as 1793, and several others within these last 4 or 5 years, up almost to yesterday.—

I hope that you were able to succeed in your humane, and

[1] Gomm (see pt. ii, L. 816) had written from Jamaica on 22 Aug. 1841 about his work there, and the 'melancholy tidings of mortality among our poor troops' in a fever epidemic. (*WL MSS.*)

[2] *Written* Gordon (see pt. iii, L. 1347).

other-wise laudable endeavour to induce Government to sanction the establishment which you had set on foot for a mountain station for the Troops. Your character of your Friend Colonel Ellis interested me greatly and no one could have read it without deploring his loss.[1]

I condole with you upon the dismal news which we have just receive[d] from India.[2] Such a disastrous event could scarcely have happened without great error in judgement, somewhere; and perhaps other faults meriting severe blame. It is however no use to make such remarks now, unless as far as public expression of such an opinion may be of avail if justly founded, to prevent the like in future. The determination to die rather than submit to dishonour is noble and such as we have a right to expect from the British Soldier. May you my dear Sir Wm, and those under your command, never be reduced to the alternative that these poor Men appear to have been subject to, I mean under such circumstances; for all Soldiers worthy of the name must ever have the principle before their eyes.

Believe me with the kindest remembrances to yourself and Lady Gomm in which Mrs Wordsworth cordially unites

faithfully yours
Wm Wordsworth

[1] 'Your own "Happy Warrior", my dear Sir,' Gomm had written, 'will be picture to you, what Colonel Ellis was to his Corps, to myself, to his Family, and to Society at large,—in a word—to his Country. Mightier prototypes might have sat for the unrivalled Portrait:—far greater opportunities for filling it in, in the life, might have been presented and taken advantage of:—but a more graceful Representative, or one combining, in his own person, more of the milder and more engaging Elements of that complete Picture, it never had, than in the presence of him, over whose Bier we have not yet ceased sorrowing.'

[2] In the last months of 1841 there had been a general revolt in Afghanistan, a British force was annihilated in the Khyber Pass, and Sir William Macnaghten, Governor of Bombay, was treacherously murdered at Kabul whilst treating for peace. Gomm discussed the melancholy news from India in his reply, dated Chester, 26 Mar. (*WL MSS.*)

1591. W. W. to JAMES BUSH[1]

MS. University Library, Davis, California. Hitherto unpublished.

Rydal Mount
March 11th 1842

My dear Sir,

My Son having come over on Horseback to Rydal some time ago, was only able to bring over one copy of your little Book;[2] for which Miss Fenwick returns you her sincere thanks. That intended for me did not reach me till two or three days ago, owing to our having communications with Brigham till then, only by Letter. Pray accept my cordial acknowledgments for this token of your kindness. My Son would tell you that we read the Book with much pleasure.

When you commun[icate] with Mr Bailey[3] be so good as to mention my sense of the honor he has done me, and convey to him my thanks for his favorable opinion so well expressed.

With kind regards to yurself and Mrs Bush, in which Miss Fenwick and Mrs Wordsworth unite, with me, I remain my dear Sir

faithfully
your obliged
Wm Wordsworth

1592. W. W. to JOHN HUDSON

MS. WL. Hitherto unpublished.

Rydal
13th March 42

Dear Sir,

As I told you at Rydal I meant to entrust Mr Nicholson's Glossary[4] to Mr Coleridge[5] in the hope of his improving it. I did

[1] John W.'s curate at Plumbland. See also L. 1564 above.

[2] *The Choice; or, Lines on the Beatitudes*, 1841.

[3] Archdeacon Benjamin Bailey (see pt. ii, L. 638), now in Ceylon. Bush evidently sent this letter out to him, as it is preserved in Bailey's copy of W. W.'s *Poems*.

[4] Hudson's partner, Cornelius Nicholson (see pt. iii, L. 935), was compiling a glossary of local names for the new expanded *Complete Guide to the Lakes* (see L. 1596 below), which Hudson and Nicholson published later this year.

[5] Hartley Coleridge.

so on that very day, but on my return from Carlisle, whither I went the Monday after I had seen you, I find that Mr C. has not been at his lodgings, nor do I know where he is, perhaps he may be at Kendal, and has the M.S. with him—or may have given it to you or Mr N. Pray let me know if you have seen any thing of him, or of the Papers, which I barely glanced my eye over.

I am still of opinion that it is very desirable they should be looked over by Mr de Quincey if he could be got at but on no account whatever let them be sent to him without previously taking a correct copy, otherwise it is great odds Mr N'^s M.S. would be lost.

I am pretty sure that Mr de Q at one time of his life paid much attention to the subject,[1] and is likely to be competent greatly to improve the Glossary. I sent you your book from Carlisle and hope it was duly rec^d.

I remain d^r Sir
Sincerely y^rs
Wm Wordsworth

P. S. I repeat what I said to you at Rydal that if application be made to Mr de Q. my name must on no account be used in the business.[2] Mr N. must take it upon himself, which most likely he will not object to do, as you said he was well acquainted with Mr. de Q.

[1] In 1819–20, during and immediately after his editorship of the *Westmorland Gazette* (see *MY* ii. 478), De Quincey had published four articles on language and the dialects of the Lake District in the paper, and the main portion of these were reprinted as 'Danish Origin of the Lake-Country Dialect' in Charles Pollitt's *De Quincey's Editorship of the Westmorland Gazette*, Kendal, 1890. See De Quincey's *Works* (ed. Masson), xiii. 373–83.

[2] W. W.'s estrangement from de Quincey had only been deepened by his *Lake Reminiscences* in *Tait's* in 1839–40, in which he had accused the poet of ingratitude towards himself in early days when de Quincey had been among the few to recognise his genius. W. W. refused to read the articles or even to hear about them. De Quincey had moved his family to Lasswade, outside Edinburgh, in 1840, but debts and ill-health had now driven him to Glasgow. See H. A. Eaton, *Thomas de Quincey, A Biography*, Oxford, 1936, Ch. xix.

1593. W. W. to VISCOUNT MAHON

MS. Stanhope MSS., Chevening. Hitherto unpublished.

[*In M. W.'s hand*]

Rydal M^{t} 15 Mar [1842]

Dear Lord Mahon,

You have much obliged me by sending me a Copy of your Bill.[1] Upon its object I thankfully say, est quodam pro dire tenus,[2] and for the ultra we must trust to a more enlightened age.

I have no scruple in using these words, being confident that the circulation of books would rather be promoted than hindered by the privilege being extended. Books however good in themselves if not in much demand, cannot be printed, but to be sold at a high price—if they be in demand, they are sure of being accessible at a low one. And with regard to the former class, it is undeniable that they are more likely to be re-produced where there is no competition to be dreaded. Upon these points I think the Advocates of extention ought mainly to dwell; because in the mind, where these truths can be established any opposition that is at all formidable would vanish. As to Macaulay's suggestion that good Books would be suppressed, from the prejudices and narrow-minded scruples of those into whose hands the legal right of publishing might fall, it is a downright absurdity.

If I had the pleasure of an interview with you I could say much upon the general question—but nothing has suggested itself to my mind upon the particular Clauses of your bill, worthy of being mentioned.

To one consideration in favour of Extension of Copyright after the decease of the Author the House will pay little attention—I allude to the greater probability of correct Editions being secured by it. This is not of much moment to the fame of writers whose works have for ages been in every body's hands, tho it is to the readers of corrupt impressions—but to Authors who have their name to make it is of incalculable importance. Gray I think has said, that good writing requires the finest parts in their finest exercise;—if that be so, what are we to say of the crasse blunders with which almost every page of the cheap editions vomitted forth by Tilt and Tegg and others is disfigured. For my own productions, if I may be allowed to

[1] The new Copyright Bill. See L. 1585 above. [2] See Horace, *Epist.*, I. i. 32.

allude to them, I scarcely ever see a quotation in a newspaper or in one of these publications I have just stigmatized, that is not in this way grossly injurious—an instance met my eyes yesterday only.

Believe me my d[r] Lord Mahon with best, good wishes

faithfully yours
[*signed*] W[m] Wordsworth

1594. W. W. to EDWARD MOXON

MS. Henry E. Huntington Library.
K (—). LY iii. 1117.

March 23, 1842[1]

Dear Mr Moxon,

The task of Printing will be over instantly—tomorrow I expect the last of it—and heartily glad am I to be done. If I had foreseen the minute Labour which I have had to undergo in correcting these Poems, I never should have gone to Press with them at all. I actually detest Publication, and all that belongs to it; and if these Poems do not benefit some minds here and there, I shall reproach myself for playing the Fool at my time of life in such a way.

I have had much to commend in[2] the care and attention of Mess[rs] Bradbury and Evans; and pray tell them so from me if you should happen to see them.

The Book will upon the whole be found, I trust, correctly printed. But owing to some neglect of mine, perhaps originating in the bad state of my eyes, there are no less than four errors in three successive Pages. They occur,

In the beginning of the first of the Italian Poems[3] as follows
Page 97 'lowering' for 'towering'
98 page—from such comforts as are 'there' read 'thine'
Page 99th—with watchful eyes could *spare* or wish to *spare it*
—*read in both cases share*

Now I very much wish that in every copy these errors as they stand so near each other should be corrected in *printed* Letters with a Pen. It would be little trouble, and they are errors of an

[1] Date added in another hand.

[2] *Written* by.

[3] See *Musings Near Aquapendente* (*PW* iii. 202), ll. 8, 21, 55, 56.

odious kind for they leave something like sense. Tell me whether this had better be done before or after the Books are put up in boards. At all events done it must be.—

I will send you in a post or two the names of the Persons in and about London, to whom I wish Copies to be sent from myself. But I have particularly to request that no Copies be sent to any Reviewer or Editor of Magazines or Periodicals whatever. I shall send one myself to Mr Lockhart as a token of private Friendship, but not as editor of the Quarterly Review. I make no exception in this matter.

yours ever faithfully
Wm Wordsworth

Kind regards to Mrs M. and your Sister, in which Mrs W. joins.

1595. W. W. to EDWARD MOXON

MS. Henry E. Huntington Library.
K (—). LY iii. 1118.

[*In M. W.'s hand*]

Rydal Mount [March 27, 1842][1]

My dear Mr Moxon,

I have nothing now to do with the book but to correct the press of one additional note, which I expect today, and I write this merely to beg that you would give me an assurance that the 4 errors of the Press, pointed out in the 3 first Pages of the first of the Poems upon Italy have been or will be corrected according to the directions given in my former letters.[2] A slip of Errata would not answer, because those things, when found in the book, are scarcely ever attended to, but in fact the paper is seldom bound up with the volume, and I cannot bear the idea that these Poems should start with 4 bits of nonsense—the worse because not one in twenty would find it out—but the twenty-first who did find it out would say, 'What stuff does Mr Wordsworth write!' You will perhaps have thought that I was splenetic in insisting upon this volume not being sent to the Reviews—it is a thing which I exceedingly dislike, as done, seemingly, to propitiate. If any work comes from an Author of distinction, they will be sure to

[1] Date added in another hand. [2] See previous letter.

get hold of it, if they think it would serve their publication to do so; and if they be inclined to speak well of it, either from its own merits or their good opinion of the Author in general, sending the book is superfluous; and if they are hostile, it would only gratify the Editor's or Reviewer's vanity, and set an edge upon his malice. These are secrets of human nature which my turn for dramatic writing (early put aside) taught me—or rather that turn took its rise from the knowledge of this kind with which observation had furnished me.

Mrs W. protests against all this, and says if I am to write in such a strain I had better take the pen in to my own hand.

Good-bye faithfully yours
[*signed*] Wm Wordsworth

1596. W. W. to ADAM SEDGWICK[1]

MS. untraced.
Life and Letters of the Revd. Adam Sedgwick, ii. 40–1.

[late Mar. 1842]

My dear Sir,

You have much obliged me by the promptitude with which you have met the request made through an Acquaintance or Friend of my Publishers;[2] and I should be very happy to be the Medium of conveying to the public your view of the Geology of this interesting District, however concisely given. First, however, I

[1] The geologist (see pt. i, L. 382; pt. ii, L. 818).

[2] On 27 Sept. 1838, Hudson and Nicholson, the Kendal publishers of W. W.'s *Guide through the District of the Lakes* (see pt. iii, L. 915), had first mooted the idea of a new expanded edition of the work with more information for the tourist (*WL MSS.*), and with W. W.'s agreement, they had now approached Sedgwick through a mutual acquaintance, F. C. Danby, for a contribution. In his letter to W. W. on 26 Mar. (*WL MSS.*) to which this is a reply, Sedgwick had agreed to furnish short essays 'on the muscular integuments, ribs and bones of your mountains', and the new expanded work appeared later this year as *A Complete Guide to the Lakes, Comprising Minute Directions for the Tourist, With Mr. Wordsworth's Description of the Scenery of the Country, etc. And Three Letters on the Geology of the Lake District, by the Rev. Professor Sedgwick*, Edited by the Publisher. A fourth letter was added in 1846, and a fifth in 1853. See *Prose Works*, ii. 134 and L. 1617 below.

must tell you exactly how the matter stands between me and the Publishers. The last edition of my little work being nearly out I undertook about a twelvemonth since to furnish some new Matter in the way of a more minute Guide for the *Body* of the Tourist, as I found that the Guide Books which attended mainly to this were preferred much, by the generality of Tourists, to mine, which, though in fact containing as much of this sort of matter as could be of any real use, appeared to be wanting in this respect. The employment to which I had by a sort of promise committed myself I found upon further consideration to be very troublesome and *infra dig.*: and as I was still desirous that my Book should be circulated, not for any pecuniary emolument, for that was quite trifling, but for the principles of Taste which it recommended, I turned all that I had written over to Mr Hudson the Publisher, stipulating only that all that related to *mind*, should in my book be printed entire and separated from other matter, and so it now stands. Every thing of mine will be reprinted, but the *guide matter* of mine will be interwoven with what Mr Hudson has undertaken to write or compile, the whole however before struck off to be submitted to my approbation. Mr Gough[1] of Kendal, a Son of the celebrated blind man of that place, will, Mr Hudson expects, promote the Botany, and if you would condescend to act upon your promise made to me long ago under somewhat different circumstances, I think a Book would be produced answering every purpose that could be desired.

I am truly sorry, my dear Sir, to hear that your health is so much deranged. I believe that the bottom of it all is, your intense ardour of mind, and activity both of mind and body. In fact you have been living too fast; pray slacken your pace, and depend upon it you will not only, in a little time, be more comfortable in yourself, but the world will in the end get more out of the very great deal that you have to give it. We are pretty well and unite in kindest remembrances and good wishes.

Ever faithfully, My dear Mr Sedgwick,
Your much obliged,
W. Wordsworth

Pray give me a letter, however short.

[1] Thomas Gough, naturalist, son of John Gough (see *MY* ii. 115): author of *Personal Reminiscences of the Habits of Animals*, Kendal, 1872, and *Observations on the Heron and the Heronry at Dallam Tower, Westmorland*, Kendal, 1880.

1597. W. W. to SIR AUBREY DE VERE[1]

MS. Cornell. Hitherto unpublished.

Rydal Mount
31st March [18] 42

My dear Sir Aubrey,

You have gratified Me far beyond my deserts, Defaulter as I am both in respect to yourself, and my most valued Friend, your Son, by sending me your inaugural Address to the Society at Limerick.[2] After a very careful perusal of it I can say that it is worthy of yourself, and the important occasion upon which it was pronounced. The concluding notices of the paramount importance of sound religious knowledge, and of spiritual matters, were the more welcome, as one is not prepared for the treatment of these points in addresses to Bodies merely literary, in their appellation at least. The evidence you have given upon this occasion of the value you set upon my writings[3] could not but be highly acceptable to me; and I will enter no further into particulars than to notice that the passage where you speak of the self-complacency with which a certain class of Writers exercise their faculties, in drawing from the material Universe instances of divine ingenuity, fell in exactly with my own views.[4] And if I am not mistaken, I said something to this effect in my various conversations with your Son; at least it is from its importance in my estimation, a favorite topic of discourse with all Persons whose character and conversation interest me.

Pray be so kind as to thank Mr De Vere for the pains he took in printing out pieces from my Poems which he thought most

[1] See pt. ii, L. 464.

[2] *Inaugural Address delivered on the evening of the eighth of February, 1842, at the house of the Limerick Philosophical and Literary Society*, Dublin, 1842.

[3] In discussing the building up of a library, Sir Aubrey de Vere had said: 'Of living poets, novelists and political writers, I am disposed to advise that no purchases should be made, with one noble exception; for the works of Wordsworth must go down to posterity, the fairest offspring of the genius of our time.' (pp. 18–19).

[4] Sir Aubrey had warned against the prevalent utilitarianism of the age and the 'march of intellect', emphasising that 'true knowledge leads to humility and *faith*.' 'The habit of investigating nature minutely, in order to trace out the design of the Great Artificer, through every process, may turn our thoughts not so much to the wisdom of God, as to a certain divine ingenuity: not unattended by a complacent sense of our own cleverness in detecting it.' (p. 40).

adapted for selection in a Volume of Extracts from my Works to be circulated at a low price.[1] I should have thanked him long ago for this trouble he took so kindly in this matter, and would have been glad to profit still further by his judicious advice, but I find upon inquiry the State of the Book-Trade so hopeless, that I gave up the scheme altogether, as having no probability about it that it would pay its own expenses. The existence of such a Book could not be known without a cost in advertisements alone, which it would not bear.

I am sorry not to hear either of the publication of your own Vol. or your Son's.[2]

Most reluctantly and merely to save trouble to my Successors, have I encountered the labour of carrying through the Press or rather of preparing for it, a Miscellaneous Vol:[3] of my own, about the fate of which except for a faint hope that it may give some pleasure for good purposes I am sadly indifferent. I never cared much for what is called reputation or even for that rather more solid acquisition, fame, but as a presumption that one is doing some good in one's generation. This thought has in fact been the only support on which I have ever leaned or wished to lean, and it is not always in one's power to gain as much support of that kind as is needful.

M^r De Vere knows how impatient I am under the act of writing, and how averse to enter upon it, and I hope he will make allowance and forgive me for having left his Letter so long unnoticed.

I should have more leisure and less disinclination to take up a pen by candlelight but the tendency of my eyes to inflammation does not allow it; and so I lose for this purpose and the precious one of reading also, all the long Winter evenings. But it is high time to release you. With the kindest remembrances to Yourself and M^r De Vere in which Mrs W. unites I remain my dear Sir

faithfully your
Much obliged
Wm Wordsworth

[1] See L. 1555 above.

[2] Aubrey de Vere's first volume of verse *The Waldenses, or the Fall of Rora: a lyrical sketch, with other poems*, appeared later this year, dedicated to Sir William Rowan Hamilton. Sir Aubrey de Vere's *Song of Faith, Devout Exercises, and Sonnets*, was also published this year.

[3] *Poems, Chiefly of Early and Late Years.*

A week hence I enter upon my seventy-third year, an awful thought! *Eheu fugaces*!

1598. M. W. and W. W. to EDWARD MOXON

MS. Henry E. Huntington Library.
LY iii. 1119.

[April 1st 1842][1]

My dear Mr Moxon

Mr W. requests you will desire the Printers to send down the sheets, following upon those we have, which reach to the 224th page, as they are struck off—to complete the Copy, which will serve us to make notes upon, instead of using a fresh one.

Be kind enough to add Mr Boxall's[2] name to the list to whom the Author wishes a Copy to be sent. And pray, if dear Miss Lamb is in a state to receive pleasure from the attention do not let her be forgotten. Mr W. bids me add that he regrets you have nothing more favorable to hold out than that the book is likely to have a 'very *fair* sale—cold comfort he says for him who has wasted so much health and strength in minute correction which nobody will either thank him for, nor care any thing about, and which wasted health and strength (I now write from his dictation *observe*) might in part have been recovered if the profits of this volume would have left him free in conscience to take a recreative trip to Paris or elsewhere! such stuff my good husband compels me to write—

(Again from his dictation to the end)

There is a wretched Author of the name of Cornish who has published a 'National Poem, The Thames',[3] and he has been dunning me for praise of it—2 copies of it are probably in your possession to be sent down—a third he has sent me direct thro' the post, and in it I find my name down as a Sub: for 2 Copies. If

[1] Date added in another hand.

[2] The artist (see pt. ii, L. 603), one of a 'knot of true and sincere worshippers' of W. W., according to his letter of 29 Aug. 1836 (*WL MSS.*). 'Not a tree or a leaf or cloud but seems living with some thought or fancy . . . which finds utterance in your words . . . I cannot tell you how truly and sincerely they love you and I really believe there is no book but the Bible so full of inspiration.'

[3] *The Thames; a descriptive poem*, 1842. The author was Thomas Hartree Cornish (b. 1799), a barrister, of New Inn Hall, Oxford, who also published *British Melodies*, 1831, and *The Juryman's Legal Handbook*, 1843.

money for these be demanded, pray refuse payment—for, when he broached the matter to me he asked *my 'acceptance'* of two copies and for which in common civility I was obliged to thank him, tho' I would much rather have been without the favour. Now, if such Copies *are* in your possession, if you can, without rudeness, return them, pray do, with a message, saying that as Mr W. has received *one copy*, he cannot feel himself justified in retaining the other two.

Pray tell me what you think is the main cause of the great falling off in the Sale of books?—The young men in the Universities cannot be supposed to be straitened much in their allowance, yet I find that scarcely any books are sold them. Dr Arnold told me that his lads seemed to care for nothing but Bozzy's next No.[1] and the Classics suffered accordingly—Can that Man's pub[lic][2] and others of the like kind materially affect the Question—I am quite in the dark

Y^rs^ etc
[*signed*] Wm Wordsworth

1599. W. W. to UNKNOWN CORRESPONDENT

MS. Mr. J. H. Spedding. Hitherto unpublished.

Rydal
1st April, 42

Dear Sir,

The circumstances under which your Letter and Tract have been forwarded to me, could not but give them both a value

[1] Charles Dickens (1812–70), had published *Sketches by Boz* in 1836, followed by *Pickwick Papers*, *Oliver Twist*, *Nicholas Nickleby*, *The Old Curiosity Shop*, and *Barnaby Rudge*, in instalments. His triumphant visit to America in early 1842 formed the subject of his *American Notes*, which were now appearing. Though W. W. and Dickens had several friends in common, including Talfourd and Kenyon, it cannot be established that the two ever met. In a letter to Mrs. Ricketts of 14 Oct. 1839, however, Wilkie recalled Dickens expressing 'very great admiration' for W. W.'s genius, 'of which he thought the little poem *We are seven* was one of the most striking examples. What he seemed to like in this was divesting death of its horror by treating it as a separation and not an extinction.' (*MS. Bookseller's Catalogue*). Later, in *Household Words*, 25 May 1850 (i. 210–13), he paid posthumous tribute to W. W.'s courageous stand against the factory system in *The Excursion*, and his progressive views on education.

[2] *MS. faded.*

independent of their general contents, and far exceeding what otherwise any testimony of approbation could have had. There is no recompense for literary Labour in the slightest degree compared to the assurance you give me that the pain and uneasiness attendant upon an incurable complaint have been lightened and beguiled by a work of mine. I have written through life with a hope of pleasing for a much higher purpose than mere pleasure, and the [?][1] like yours, afford satisfactory evidence that this hope has not been a delusion; in other words that my time and labour and my health and strength, for these have occasionally suffered from over exertion, have not been thrown away.—

I am never in the practise of thinking myself in comparison with other Authors, and therefore I shall say nothing in respect to my relation to Lord Byron. Posterity will put us both in our places, but be assured I find no fault with those who like yourself have endeavoured to forward that decision. If in your Estimate you have *under*rated Lord Byron other Criticks may be as apt to overrate him and so in the end the balance is[2] fairly struck.

Will you forgive me if on your own account, (I sincerely assure you) it is not on mine I recommend the 2nd Book of the Excursion, to your reperusal. The description of the Author's *morning* Walk with the Wanderer, the freshness and cheerfulness of it, and the view from the Eminence with the picture of the Recess in which the Solitary dwells, the funeral and the lines concluding

> O blest are they who live and die like these,
> Loved with such love and with such sorrow mourned[3]

are surely not inferior to any thing in the Poem.

Praying that consolation and support from their highest source may not be wanting till you are removed from this troublesome world,

I remain,
faithfully your obliged
Wm Wordsworth

This day week I enter God willing, my 73rd year, an awful thought!

[1] *MS. obscure.*

[2] *Written* be.

[3] Lines 591–2.

1600. W. W. to THOMAS POWELL

MS. Amherst College Library.
LY iii. 1120.

Rydal Sat. 2nd April —42.

My dear Mr Powell,

I deferred noticing your Vol: of Poems[1] till I could find time, with daylight, to read it. I have now done so, and can sincerely say with great pleasure. The thoughts and sentiments I find myself in sympathy with, every where I think, except page 315. Napoleon,[2] or Buonaparte as I being an old man am accustomed to call him, was throughout the whole course of his life, and not less so when at St Helena, a false creature faithless in every object as long as he had power to the opportunity which the course of things under divine providence, gave him for doing good to mankind. He was essentially a mean spirit to the last.[3] I think I mentioned to you long ago that I found your workmanship as a Poet not equal to the beauty and grandeur of your thoughts and feelings. I still am of the same opinion notwithstanding the pleasure the perusal of your Vol. has given me; and how here to assist you I do not know. I can only then reflect that your Book has gratified me much. The divine History of the Earth, The invocation to the Earth etc etc are all in a high strain of thought and feeling, and other pieces are noticeable for appropriate tenderness.

I have directed Mr Moxon to send a copy of my forthcoming Vol. to you. I am heartily glad to get it off my hands; for being desirous to get it through the press before easter, I worked intemperately at the correction of such lines as I thought required [rewriting?][4] and did my health a good deal of harm by

[1] *Poems*, 1842.

[2] Powell's Byronic sonnet on Napoleon eulogized him as 'a giant, cast in Titan mould.'

[3] Napoleon had died in exile on St. Helena on 5 May, 1821. In 1840 an expedition was sent to bring his body back to France for interment in Les Invalides, and another poem 'Napoleon at Rest', p. 139, refers obliquely to these events. His nephew Prince Louis Napoleon (the future Napoleon III) was now promoting the Bonapartist cause from his prison at Ham in Picardy, where he had been sent after his abortive *coup* at Boulogne. For W. W.'s continuing interest in French politics in the 1840s, see James T. Fields, *Yesterdays with Authors*, 1872, pp. 254–5 (referring to his visit to the poet in 1847).

[4] *MS. obscure.*

an unnatural condensing of labour which if it had been spread over a longer time might not have hurt me. I hope you may find something that will interest you. With kindest remembrance in which Mrs Wordsworth unites and sincere regards for Mrs Powell.

W. Wordsworth

1601. W. W. to JOHN HUDSON

MS. WL. Hitherto unpublished.

[early Apr. 1842]

Dear Sir,

I am sorry to say that your letter and proof arrived together with several other communications and putting yours aside I entirely forgot it till this morning. I wrote to Prof. Sedgwick[1] in answer to a Letter from him, pressing him to prepare the essay as soon as he could; which I have no doubt he will do.—Any thing I have to say, had better be reserved for a brief advertisement. I am truly sorry to have disdained your proof as mentioned; but will take care the like shall not occur in future. The introduction[2] is well planned and I wish you success in the [?onerous][3] undertaking.

ever yours
W Wordsworth

Mr Hill my neighbour tells me that the Botany in Otley[4] is not arranged scientifically. Would Mr Gough[5] be so kind as to

[1] See L. 1596 above.

[2] Hudson's introduction to the new expanded *Complete Guide to the Lakes* discussed the best time of year for visiting the Lake country and the frame of mind in which the tourist should set out.

[3] *MS. obscure.*

[4] Jonathan Otley (1766–1856) the geologist, was born at Loughrigg, but moved to Keswick in 1797 and settled nearby at Brow Top, earning his living as a watchmaker, surveyor and guide. He was buried in Crosthwaite churchyard. His first map of the Lakes appeared in 1818, his popular *Guide* in 1823 (7th edn. 1842). See David Leitch, *A Memoir of Jonathan Otley*, written (1857) as a preface to the posthumous edition of the *Guide* and reprinted (1882) in Leitch's memory by his daughter.

[5] See L. 1596 above.

do it for us; pray ask him, joining my request with your own. It would be a decided advantage to have this done.—

W W.

1602. W. W. to EDWARD MOXON

MS. Carl H. Pforzheimer Library.
K (—). *LY iii.* 1121 (—).

April 3, 1842.

My dear Mr Moxon,

I see no reason for changing my mind about sending to the Reviews.[1] My friend and present neighbour, Mr Faber, who has just published a Vol: Price 16 Shillings, 'Sights and Thoughts',[2] with Rivington, tells me that he has not sent his work to the Reviewers, nor is in the habit of doing so, though well aware that a favorable review—in the *Quarterly*, for instance—helps sale very considerably. I cannot tolerate this idea of courting the favour, or seeming to do so, of any critical tribunal in this country, the House of Commons not excepted. It ought to have put down in an instant Wakley's Buffoonery,[3] as impertinent and utterly irrelevant to the Question. I suppose by this time my Vol:[4] is out. You need not fear its being noticed enough, whether for praise or censure.

Ever sincerely yours,
Wm Wordsworth

[1] See Ls. 1594 and 1595 above.

[2] Frederick Faber's *Sights and Thoughts in Foreign Churches and among Foreign Peoples*, 1842, which described his recent travels in Greece and the Balkans, was dedicated to W. W. 'in affectionate remembrance of much personal kindness, and many thoughtful conversations on the rites, prerogatives, and doctrines of the Holy Church.'

[3] i.e. his outspoken opposition to the Copyright Bill (see also pt. iii, L. 1201). See L. 1606 below.

[4] *Poems, Chiefly of Early and Late Years.*

1603. W. W. to DORA QUILLINAN

MS. WL.
K (—). Cornhill. LY iii. 1121.

April 7, 1842.

My dear Daughter,

I cannot suffer the morning of my Birth-day to pass without telling you that my heart is full of you and all that concerns you. Yesterday was lovely, and this morning is not less so. God grant that we may all have like sunshine in our hearts so long as we remain in this transient world.

It is about half-past nine; two hours hence we go to pay a condoling visit to poor Fanny.[1] Mr Carter, James, and I all attended the funeral on Monday,—it was a beautiful afternoon, the light of the declining sun glowing upon Fairfield, as described in the *Excursion*, at Dawson's funeral.[2] The Psalm sung before raising the Coffin from its station before the door, and afterwards as the procession moved between the trees, was most touching. Mr Greenwood[3] was there and told me the name (which I forget) of the Composer, who lived 200 years ago. The music was worthy of the occasion and admirably given, the School-master, a very respectable man, leading the four or five voices; upon the occasions the Women do not sing, and I think that is well judged, the sound being more grand and solemn, whatever it may lose in sweetness by the want of female tones.—After the funeral we walked to Mrs Fletchers[4]—the place very tempting—they are expected on Saturday.

I am pretty well, but far from having recovered the strength which I lost through several sleepless nights, the consequence of over and ill-timed exertion, to get the Volume out before Easter in which attempt I failed.—I am glad you like the tragedy.[5] I was myself surprized to find the interest so kept up in the 4th and fifth Acts. Of the third I never doubted, and quite agree with you that Herbert's speech is much the finest thing in the drama; I mean the most moving, or rather, the most in that style of the pathetic which one loves to dwell upon; though I acknowledge it is not so intensely dramatic as some parts of the 5th act especially. As to

[1] A bereaved neighbour.

[2] See *MY* i. 158 and *Exc.* vii. 875 ff.

[3] James Greenwood of The Wyke.

[4] At Lancrigg.

[5] *The Borderers.*

the first, my only fear was that the *action* was too *far* advanced in it. I think the scene where the Vagrant tells her false story has great merit—it is thoroughly natural and yet not commonplace nature. Some of the sentiments which the development of Oswald's character required will, I fear, be complained of as too depraved for anything but biographical writing.

With affectionate remembrances to your Husband and the Girls

ever yours
W. W.

1604. W. W. to BENJAMIN ROBERT HAYDON

MS. Professor Willard Pope.
LY iii. 1123.

Rydal Mount Ambleside
8th April '42
Yesterday I entered my 73d year.

My dear Haydon

Thank you for your Address.[1] It is a spirited thing, and judicious. I read it with much pleasure.—I particularly approve

[1] Haydon's lecture at the Royal Institution on 4 Mar., *Thoughts on the Relative Value of Fresco and Oil Painting as Applied to the Architectural Decorations of the Houses of Parliament*, which he claimed 'made a great hit' (*Diary*, ed. Pope, v, 134). The previous year Peel had set up the Fine Arts Commission, under the chairmanship of the Prince Consort, to determine the best ways to encourage British art with special reference to the decoration of the Houses of Parliament, now rebuilt to the designs of Barry and Pugin; and Haydon, who had once advocated the adornment of the old House of Lords with murals, had thrown himself enthusiastically into the scheme in spite of rebuffs, and was now campaigning for a revival of the art of fresco. In his letter to W. W. on 14 Jan. he had discussed the issue at length, maintaining that 'the object of Fresco is to restore a power of drawing which no longer exists' (*WL MSS.*); and he had written again more optimistically on 19 Mar., 'I think my *great object* is advancing.' (See Haydon, ii, 51–4). But his proposals set him at odds with the Royal Academy, which was opposed to any development that might diminish the prestige of oil painting, and with Charles Eastlake (see pt. iii, L. 1151), Haydon's former pupil, secretary of the Commission, and his cartoons were rejected following a public exhibition in Westminster Hall in June 1843. The debate, and the deliberations of the Commission, dragged on for more than 20 years amid much muddle and frustration, and the outcome bore little

of what you say of Modern German Art. It was in course of Nature that in long-past times Men should paint as they painted whom the Germans of this day take for Models, affectedly, as I think, and in proportion feebly. Nevertheless, I must say that I think there is a touching and austere simplicity and beauty, with a corresponded depth of expression, in many of the faces and persons of single figures in the Scripture pieces of Pietro Perugino and other painters both Italian and German of the elder Schools which Raphael with all his marvellous power failed to attain, or rather did not attempt, being inclined by classical influences to aim at some thing else.—

As to the comparative durability of Fresco and oil one thing is clear that in some situations, Fresco seems very perishable in others almost immortal. The deservedly celebrated Auroras of Guido,[1] at Rome, seemed to my eye as fresh as yesterday; while other things in the same City had faded almost to perishing.

I wish heartily the project in which creditably to yourself [you] have taken so lively an interest, and in which you are fit by talents and labour to take a prominent part may succeed—

I have desired Moxon to send a Copy of my new Vol. to you. Ever faithfully yours

my dear Haydon
Wm Wordsworth

1605. W. W. to JULIUS CHARLES HARE

MS. Cornell. Hitherto unpublished.

[11 Apr. 1842]

My dear Mr Hare,

Sincerely do I condole with you upon the death of your Brother Francis.[2] It comes upon me quite by surprize; he was a most amiable man, and will be deeply regretted wherever he was known. I had never heard a word of his illness so that your

resemblance to Haydon's original scheme. See Eric George, *The Life and Death of Benjamin Robert Haydon*, 2nd. edn. 1967, pp. 251 ff.

[1] Guido Reni (1575–1642). His two frescoes of Aurora, in the Casino Rospigliosi and the Casino Ludovisi respectively, belong to the years 1613–14, when he was working in Rome and away from his native Bologna.

[2] Hare had written on 8 Apr. (*WL MSS.*) to announce the death of his brother Francis at Palermo on 11 Jan.

Letter shocked me much.—When I saw him at Rome,[1] however, before his severe illness in which I left him at Florence, he had to me the appearance of a man wearing himself out by too much sensation, and energy of mind.

Thanks for your Charge,[2] in addition to the many valuable things I have received from your hands and your pen. By and bye, an American Editor of my Works,[3] tells me that your Sermons upon Faith are the best he ever read. I have not had time to look into your Charge, which came yesterday—but I shall read it probably this evening. You perhaps will be surprized at receiving my last Vol:[4] with *Mrs* Wordsworth's respects; in fact I did not like to send it myself to any one, especially to one so conversant with Literature as your self. Modesty, and humblemindedness whether true or false were really the cause; and I take this opportunity of explaining the matter.

Believe me, with Mrs Wordsworth's very kind regards ever faithfully

your most obliged
Wm Wordsworth

11th April—I have just entered my 73^d^ year. Eheu fugaces!

1606. W. W. to VISCOUNT MAHON

MS. Stanhope MSS., Chevening. Hitherto unpublished.

Rydal Mount
April 11th 42.

Dear Lord Mahon,

Let me begin with thanking you cordially for your Letter, but above all for your zealous exertions on behalf of the Literature of

[1] In 1837. See pt. iii, L. 1137.

[2] *Privileges Imply Duties*, 1841, Hare's second Charge as Archdeacon of Lewes, expressed his first misgivings about the Tractarian Movement at Oxford, and argued for a proper role for the laity within the Church, the revival of moral discipline, and the setting up of a national system of education to counteract the evil effects of the factory system.

[3] Henry Reed. See L. 1587 above.

[4] *Poems, Chiefly of Early and Late Years.* Hare had spoken in his letter of looking forward to seeing *The Borderers* and *Guilt and Sorrow* which he had heard S. T. C. praise.

the Country. The result[1] is lamentably short of what it must have been, if the House (I mean the majority of it) could have seen the matter in its true light, either as a question of justice, of feeling, or of policy. One point however is gained and that a very important one. The *principle* of postobit remuneration will be established if Sir Robert Peel's amendment become[s] Law. Seven years are indeed only a beggarly allowance; why did not Sir R. propose at least *nine*? and then there would have been a year for each of the Nine Muses, Urania included!!! Mr Macaulay by his oppositon to Sir R's amendment has taken no enviable position; in fact he had made himself an object of scorn to every highminded Man of Letters in the Country. Could any thing be more indecent than the reflection which he cast upon that class, as addicted to extravagance and apt to be without prudence or forethought. Grant that few are so; it is surely improbable that men who aim at the production of *solid* works will be of that number; and it is for *their* satisfaction that postobit recompense is sought; and is there either sense or feeling in depriving such Men of that support and consolation under their labours, because a few of their reckless Bretheren might, by bare possibility be tempted into unjustifiable expense by a prolonged privilege? Were one inclined to be personal, it might be observed that such proceedings are especially obnoxious in a man like Mr Macaulay who, as is well known, was *jobbed* out to India for the mere purpose of putting money into his pocket, by the profit of an office for the duties of which he had no experience, nor could possibly acquire *any*.[2] Pray excuse my making these allusions,

[1] After Macaulay's conciliatory speech on the Second Reading of the new Copyright Bill, it was clear that the House was at last moving towards a consensus on the issue. There was widespread agreement that the term of copyright should be extended: but for how long? This was the only remaining area of dispute during the Committee stage on 6 Apr., and the Bill which was finally sent to the Lords embodied a compromise. Macaulay's amendment, which called for a term of 42 years from the date of publication, or for the lifetime of the author, whichever was the longer, was carried; but so also was Peel's amendment, which granted further protection for a period of seven years after the author's death.

[2] In 1833 Macaulay was appointed a member of the Supreme Council of India at a salary of £10,000 per annum. His four years in India, during which he drew up a criminal code and a system of education were, according to Sir George Trevelyan, 'in many important respects . . . the most honourable chapter of his life.' But see also *The Letters of Thomas Babington Macaulay*, ed. Thomas Pinney, ii (1974), 299.

but his disingenuousness and want of feeling and judgement in the whole of this business have excited in my mind the strongest indignation—How came it that he alluded neither to Mr Southey or any living author?

Mr M. made a great parade of his biographical knowledge in Literature. It is true, as I observed in my former Letter to you upon the subject,[1] that many of the best works in Poetry were produced when their respective authors were far advanced in life. But in several cases he is mistaken, and particularly in Spenser and Pope. The most poetical works of the Latter, namely the Winsor Forest, and especially the Rape of the Lock and the Epistle of Eloisa to Abelard were composed about his 25th and 26th year, and Spenser died at little more than 40.[2] Tasso's Jerusalem delivered was finished in his 30th year. The best, far the best of Burns Poems, with the exception of Tam o Shanter were published when he was only 26. Shelley and Byron died young, the former under 30. The [ ][3] in your plan was forced upon you, by your knowledge of the ungenerous and unjust disposition of the House, as the utmost it was at all likely would be granted. But Mr Macaulay with perfect satisfaction lays down his 42 years as the limit within which all pecuniary emolument for the Author is to be confined, unless (I suppose) he should survive that period, or am I mistaken in the notion that he would allow the privilege to last for the whole of the Author's life?—But I have detained you too long. It is discreditable that the House did not at once put down Mr Wakeleys buffoonery[4] as having nothing to do with the question. Again repeating my thanks I remain dear Lord Mahon

faithfully yours
Wm Wordsworth

[1] See L. 1585 above. Macaulay had argued that no great works of imagination had been produced before the age of 30 or 35.

[2] Spenser was 47 when he died.

[3] *MS. obscure.*

[4] The only dissenting voice in the debate had been Thomas Wakley's (see L. 1602 above), who argued that the Bill was a form of 'aggrandizement' by living authors. Writers should not be treated differently from scientists like Jenner, who had never sought protection for discoveries which benefited mankind. Wakley had read out W. W.'s poems *Louisa, To a Butterfly*, and his lines on the Stock-Dove, and asked, 'Who could not string such lines together by the bushel?'

1607. W. W. to UNKNOWN CORRESPONDENT[1]

MS. Yale University Library. Hitherto unpublished.

[*In M. W.'s hand*]

Rydal Mount
April 16th —42

Dear Sir,

It quite shocks me that your elegant volume, dedicated to me should, with the accompanying letter, dated 26th August, 1841, have remained so long unacknowledged. In fact I only received it within the last 5 hours—with a number of other books from Mr Moxon. As I have had more than once parcels from Dover St since that time, and likewise other communication with him, I conclude that your Book must have been accidentally mislaid: be assured I regret this very much, and the more so because it has exposed me to censure on your part as being ungentlemanlike uncourteous and unfeeling. I am really so uneasy under this impression that I lose not a moment in telling you so.

Believe me to remain
Sincerely your much obliged
[*signed*] Wm Wordsworth

1608. W. W. to THOMAS NOON TALFOURD

MS. Berg Collection, New York Public Library.
K (—). *LY iii. 1123* (—).

17th Apr [1842]

My dear Sergeant Talfourd,

You pay me far too great a Compliment by the importance you attach to my being at home as an indispensable condition of your passing your vacation among our Lakes. My inclination last year was, and continues in this also, to visit Switzerland in the Autumn, and to pass thence on to Italy with a view to completing my notice of that country which the Cholera prevented, when I was at Rome with Mr Robinson. But there are still so many hindrances in the way that I cannot encourage

[1] Perhaps Francis Bennoch (1812–90), silk dealer in Cheapside and friend of Haydon: author of *The Storm, and Other Poems*, 1841, dedicated to W. W. See *R.M.Cat.*, no. 469.

the expectation of being able to get over them; so that I am at liberty to say, that for aught I can foresee, I shall be at Rydal the greatest part of the time you would have at your command. Nevertheless I cannot *bind* myself in the matter; I am dependent upon others in many ways, nor can I answer for what sort of inclinations might spring up in me, or what necessities I might be under. Be assured however, your being in the Country would be a strong inducement for my not yielding to a temptation to go from home. And this is all that I can say in answer to your question.[1]

I should have written to the above effect by return of post; but I thought it best to make previous enquiries about houses, and accomodation. Two are, I find likely to be at liberty at the time you mention. One in the Town, or rather village part of the Town of Ambleside, and which is now occupied by my Daughter and her Husband, and his two Daughters. It stands high near the Chapel which you may recollect, with a pleasing view of the Lake and Country. Terms three guineas a week, attendance and Kitchen fire included. The rooms are small rather, but in summer time that is not so much consequence. These are for a Lodging House, unusually well and neatly furnished. The two Sisters who keep the House are truly respectable and conscientious Persons. The other house stands a third of a mile out of the Town, upon the Hawkshead road upon a Bank a little above the river, and about two fields length from the Lake. This is let as a furnished House, without attendance. There are two very pleasant sitting rooms (the bed rooms low as well as small), with fine views, but not of the lake though so near. Here of course you would have either to hire Servants or bring your own. The terms are two guineas and a half per week. If you wish for either of these houses, which are the only ones at liberty that would suit you, pray speak at once; as they may be both snapped up at any time. Do not think of bringing your Carriage or Coachman, there is no stabling to either place, besides your Coachman and Carriage would actually be an incumbrance here. Vehicles of all sorts are to be hired when wanted; and the latter would be the finest attraction—

I have now only to add that you might deem yourself fortunate if you resolve to come, for I think you could not be disappointed in this beautiful Country, whether I and my family

[1] In fact, Talfourd spent the summer revisiting the Alps. See his *Vacation Rambles and Thoughts*, 2 vols., 1845.

were here or not; the probability as I have said is, that we shall be so, at least the greatest part of the time; but you will excuse my repeating the Caution that I cannot *bind* myself. With kind regards to Mrs Talfourd, in which Mrs W. begs to unite, I remain

very sincerely, and with great esteem
your much obliged
Wm Wordsworth

1609. W. W. to VISCOUNT MAHON

MS. Stanhope MSS., Chevening. Hitherto unpublished.

Rydal Mount
19th April, 42

Dear Lord Mahon,

Many thanks for the Copy of your Speech, which I have read with much pleasure.[1] There is only one point in which I differ from you, where you say, "Readers in truth were then only of *two* Classes. Books of devotion, Sermons, and Theology were assuredly eagerly sought after by no small part of the nation, notwithstanding the light and profligate habits which aversion to puritanism brought out and encouraged. But this is of no moment to the question which you have calmly and comprehensively and feelingly argued.—Did you happen to observe the confident and majestical manner, in which the Times delivered its opinion, declaring that the Author had no pretensions to a *right* in his works after publication; but it was expected that the Law should extend *some* protection as an inducement to the production of great literature; the measure, however, of that protection was to be the *Minimum* under which the Works were likely to be, or could be, produced. Now who is to be the judge of that? why, that selfish unfeeling abstraction, the Public; the very party who would have the Works, for nothing, if it could get them. This reminds me of a neighbour of mine, a common

[1] During the Committee stage of the Copyright Bill on 6 Apr. (see L. 1606 above). Mahon had set out to conciliate Macaulay and counter the objections he had raised, while trying to manoeuvre the House into granting some extension of the term. He left it to Sir Robert Inglis to put in a plea for protection for 'three illustrious living authors' (W. W., Campbell, and Southey).

Carrier, who when he was reproached for hungering his Horses, replied that "Whips were cheaper than corn and Hay"—

Pray let the Clause in your Bill respecting Piracy be as efficient as possible. A few years back I went into a Booksellers shop, Picadilly, where I was unknown and asked if I could have a copy of Gagliniani's Edit: of Wordsworth's Poems.[1]—Yes—Could I have five?—yes—ten?—yes—100? yes, and so on till 500, with the same answer, adding as to the latter numbers, "give me only time."—

Let me repeat my thanks to you and your Coadjutors, small as the gain is, and believe me

dear Lord Mahon
faithfully yours
Wm Wordsworth

1610. W. W. to MRS. A. MONTAGU WOODFORD

Address: Mrs A. M. Woodford, Cary Parade, Torquay. [*In M. W.'s hand*]
Postmark: 20 Apr. 1842.
Stamp: Torquay.
MS. Harvard University Library.
LY iii. 1124.

Rydal Mount
Ambleside
April 19th '42.

Dear Madam,

I have just received The Elegant Vol: of the Book of Sonnets,[2] and beg you would accept my thanks for it, and my acknowledgement of the honor you have done me in dedicating it to me. As far as I am able to judge, the selection seems such as will do you credit for taste and discrimination.

Believe me to remain
dear Madam
sincerely your
obliged
Wm Wordsworth

[1] i.e. Galignani's edition of 1828.

[2] *The Book of Sonnets*, edited by A. Montagu Woodford, 1841.

1611. W. W. to C. W.

MS. Mr. Jonathan Wordsworth. Hitherto unpublished.

Sunday Morn.
[?24 Apr. 1842]

My dear Brother,

The enclosed I have just received from Mr Read of Philadelphia.[1] He does not advert to one important point; the eagerness which obviously there is in a large portion of the American people to quarrel and go to war with England; in which case what would become of the English Coalition? and in case of the continuance of peace, if the American Democracies will not submit to the Taxation necessary to discharge the interest upon the Bonds, but that is to be paid by fresh Loans, it is clear that the Repudiation system has so shaken American credit, that no European nation will lend them money, and the Bubble must soon burst. Things being what they are, that is, the price so low, I think it would be folly to sell at such immense loss. I would very much rather trust to what there is of honesty among the people of Pennsylvania. Thank you for the Bentleys[2] which I have just received from Moxon. Not knowing how to send my new Vol: to you, We directed Dora to manage how it was to reach you, as also a Copy for Charles, and one for Chris.—

Some time ago after I received your last I wrote to Mr Watson upon the subject of Mr Lowther's Letter,[3] addressing Mr W. as you directed. But as eleven several weeks after that Letter might perhaps not find him at Mrs Watsons;[4] but I hope it would be forwarded—I have had no answer.

We start for London on the third of next month. My object is to endeavour to serve poor W^{m} who is languishing, poor Fellow! sadly at Carlisle.

I write in extreme haste to save the Post—

ever your affectionate Br
Wm Wordsworth

[1] The main part of Henry Reed's letter of late March was sent to C. W. and has not survived. The postcript, dated 30 Mar. 1842 is printed in *Wordsworth and Reed*, p. 65.

[2] C. W. jnr.'s edition of *The Correspondence of Richard Bentley*, 2 vols., 1842.

[3] See L. 1580 above.

[4] W. W.'s syntax is confused at this point. Joshua Watson's wife had died in 1831. The reference here is to his sister-in-law, the widow of his brother John James Watson (see pt. iii, L. 1048).

1612. W. W. to C. W.

MS. Mr. Jonathan Wordsworth. Hitherto unpublished.

no 7. Upper
Spring Street
Baker St London[1]
May 6th [1842]

My dear Brother,

Here we are, with Mr Quillinan and Dora; Having arrived; Mary, W^{m}, and I, on Wednesday evening; all well, except that I am hampered in my movements upon the pavement of these streets by a lameness in one of my knees, the consequence of a slight sprain acting upon the frame of a Man in his 73^{d} year. Dora is looking very thin, and suffers much from her Stomach, not having any faith in Medicine which has so often failed to do her good. We left our dear Sister in her usual way, and Miss Fenwick also pretty well; She brought us as far as Milnthorp, and is so kind as to act as Housekeeper in our absence.

Our *main* inducement to this journey, was the hope of serving Wm, it having been intimated to Me, that applications to Government are of no use, unless one can point out some particular employment, vacant or likely to be so, which the Party one sues for is Competent to undertake. I shall proceed in the matter with the advice of Lord Lowther.[2] Yesterday I dined with Lord Lonsdale, but I am advised not to mention my object to him on account of his advanced age and infirmities. Should we succeed in our object, our stay in London would be very short, as it is, we should remain as long as we can hope to do any good in the matter.

[1] This line of the address written in by Dora Q.

[2] Lord Lowther, Postmaster General in the new Tory Government, wrote to W. W. the following day, arranging to see him at Carlton Terrace on the 9th. He recalled that the previous Tory government of Peel had offered W. W. a pension, but had gone out before arrangements could be completed. 'It seems to me, that the simplest way would be to accept the pension and place your son in the office you now hold.' Following their meeting, he wrote again on the 14th that if W. W. was prepared to set out in detail what he would like to see done, Lord Lonsdale would ensure that it was forwarded with a covering letter to Peel. 'Your character is so well known to him, and as I believe, he is well disposed to you, that I should hope, it will be attended with a favorable result.' (*WL MSS.*)

Be so good as to return Mr Reed's Letter[1] to me at this place; I wish to shew it to one or two London Friends.

I hope you have received my new Vol, it has been forwarded from the Publisher, but how I dont exactly know.

William begs me to say that he is hurt, by finding that Captn Stuart[2] has intruded on you on the strength of being at the same House in the Charter-House when he was there. And W^{m} much regrets that this Gentleman should have turned to such an account, his former slight acquaintance with him. But distress is too apt to force Persons to make unwarrantable applications. I remain, with best love from all, ever your affectionate Br

Wm Wordsworth

1613. W. W. to ISABELLA FENWICK

MS. WL.
LY iii. 1125 (—).

[7 May 1842]

My dearest Friend

At the request of Mary I forward this note to you that you may see what high company I keep.[3]—Of our proceedings here Mary has told you up to this minute almost.—At Breakfast I have just seen Mr and Mrs Taylor,[4] both apparently very well. Mrs James,[5] not at Breakfast, but a minute or two before, looking rather well, and then Captn Elliot, but not his brother Frederic[6] whose wife is something better, Sir Francis Doyle,[7]

[1] See previous letter.

[2] Probably Henry Stuart (1808–1880), of Montford, Isle of Bute, nephew of the 1st Marquess of Bute, who entered Charterhouse in 1821, the year before W. W. jnr. left.

[3] This letter begins on a sheet of paper containing an invitation to W. W. from Octavian Blewitt (1810–84), Secretary of the Royal Literary Fund, to their anniversary dinner, Prince Albert in the Chair. Other guests included Hallam, Washington Irving, Lockhart, and Moore (see his *Memoirs*, vii. 319–20).

[4] The date of this letter is established by Taylor's reference to this party (*Correspondence of Henry Taylor*, p. 133).

[5] Probably Lord Monteagle's daughter Mary, Mrs. Taylor's sister, now Mrs. James Marshall.

[6] Sir Frederick Elliot (1808–80), later Under-Secretary of State for the Colonies (see also pt. iii, L. 1048). He married Jane Perry (d. 1859), in 1833.

[7] Gladstone's friend (see pt. iii, L. 1014), the lawyer and poet. See his *Reminiscences and Opinions*, 1886, pp. 164–5.

and Mr Everet the American Minister;[1] and lastly, for your information dear Miss Fenwick, Lady Harriet Baring.[2] Upon my return to my great joy appeared Dr Ferguson, who had been most kindly sent by Mr Taylor. Mr Taylor told me this fact. A Son of Mr Perceval, the Prime Minister, applied to Sir R. Peel and was answered. That he, Sir R, could hold out no hopes. He had been 8 months in office, and had only one place above 100 per annum at his disposal, which he had given to his Brother in law.[3] I do not therefore think I have any thing to hope for beyond surrendering my Off: in favour of Wm in case they will transfer it to him; and trusting to their doing something for me in the way of pension. Mrs Taylor invited me to stay sometime during her own absence with her Husband. Mr Taylor joined in the request; but being so near, I can easily see Mr Taylor without being his guest, and giving up the society of Mrs Hoare.—

Mary's heart as well as mine is much lightened by having seen Dr Ferguson; she is delighted by his excellent countenance and kind manner. Dr F will see Dora again on Tuesday when he will breakfast with us.—

Do not think my Head will be turned, when I tell you, that in addition to the invitation mentioned above I have had one from the President of the *Royal Society*, the Marquis of Northampton, to attend his Soirées—all very pretty, but I [would] give the whole and fifty times as much, to be free from the anoyance, and disability, which my knee causes me. But dearest Miss F. I will live in hope notwithstanding 72 years and one month, and all they may urge against it.

At the Exhibition I saw several things that pleased me, but there is a sad mediocrity upon the whole and nothing of *first* rate merit in all particulars.

[1] Edward Everett (1794–1865), American Minister at the Court of St. James's, 1841–5, President of Harvard from 1846, and Secretary of State, 1852–3.

[2] Lady Harriet Baring (d. 1857), the noted wit, eldest daughter of the 6th Earl of Sandwich, married William Bingham Baring, 2nd Baron Ashburton (1799–1864), M.P. for N. Staffs. and Secretary of the Board of Control (1841–5). See *Autobiography of Sir Henry Taylor*, i. 309–11.

[3] The Right Hon. George Robert Dawson (d. 1856), of Moyola Park, Co. Derry, formerly Peel's private secretary, and now Commissioner of the Customs, had married Peel's sister Mary (1785–1848) in 1816.

I cannot conclude dearest Miss Fenwick without thanks for your Letter which gave so agreeable an account of you both[1]

ever most affectionately yours
Wm Wordsworth

[*M. W. writes*]

Mr Grave[2] has called and now the Poet has been setting forth his several accidents, and sufferings therefrom which he would not care about 'but as an indication of breaking up'—yet cannot give up going with Mr G. to some Pictures—tho' we have to dine at Mr Rogers.[3] Dora thinks it prudent, and we think so too, that she had best stay at home and be quiet.

M. W.

1614. W. W. to VISCOUNT MAHON

Endorsed: May 8. 1842.
MS. Stanhope MSS., Chevening. Hitherto unpublished.

[7 Upper Spring Street]
[8 May 1842]

Dear Lord Mahon,

I am very sorry that I am engaged to breakfast on Wednesday morning[4]—

I have just been calling upon Lord Brougham about the Copyright Bill.[5] Even in conversation I could only give you a faint notion of all that he said and in this note it would be absurd

[1] I. F. was at Rydal Mount looking after D. W.

[2] Probably John Thomas Graves (see pt. iii, L. 1221).

[3] 'The Poet,' M. W. wrote to I. F. on the 9th, 'after dining with the Archbishop and Bishop of London and their Ladies, Mr W. Gladstone, and I know not what other important Personages at Mr Rogers—appeared . . . among the Stars, at the Marquis of Lansdowne' soirée on Sat. evening, and walked home with Lockhart at 12 oc.' (*MW*, p. 247).

[4] It is not clear whether W. W. was at Miss Rogers's breakfast party on Wednesday, 11th (*HCR* ii. 615) with Washington Irving (see pt. i, L. 201); but he certainly joined Rogers, H. C. R., and Irving afterwards on a visit to Leslie's studio (see pt. i, L. 139; pt. iii, L. 1166; and C. R. Leslie, *Autobiographical Recollections*, 2 vols., 1860, i. 240).

[5] See next letter.

for me to enter upon the subject. I wish I could see you before Tuesday for which day the Bill stands.[1]

ever faithfully
your Lordships
Wm Wordsworth

1615. W. W. to THOMAS NOON TALFOURD

MS. Rush Rhees Library, Rochester University.
LY iii. 1077.

Sunday noon [8 May 1842][2]
7 Upper Spring Street Baker Street

My dear Sergeant Talfourd,

Here have I been since Wednesday night; and should have called on you before this time, but for a weakness left in a sprained knee.

You have probably heard that Lord Mahon is alarmed by Lord Brougham's intended opposition to the Copy right Bill in the House of Lords,[3] which oppositon Lord Mahon apprehends will have strong support. This is most vexatious. I hope you will be able to influence Lord Denman,[4] and other Law Lords, to attend and support the interests of Literature upon this occasion.

[1] The Second Reading of the Copyright Bill in the Lords was in fact taken a day earlier, on Monday, 9 May.

[2] Incorrectly dated by de Selincourt to June 1841. W. W. had just returned from Westminster Abbey; later he visited the Zoological Gardens, and dined with the Lockharts (*MW*, p. 247).

[3] Brougham had long been known as an opponent of the Copyright Bill, preferring his own proposal that a discretionary power should be vested in the Judicial Committee of the Privy Council to extend the term in particular deserving cases (see pt. iii, L. 1270); and he had therefore to be conciliated, if possible, before the Committee stage of the Bill in the Lords was reached on 26 May. In a lengthy speech on that day he spoke in favour of those parts of the Bill which sought to protect authors from continental piracy, but attacked the compromise arrived at during the Committee stage in the Commons (see L. 1606 above).

[4] Lord Chief Justice (see pt. ii, L. 608). On the 10th W. W. visited the House of Lords to lobby Lord Monteagle and Lord Clarendon, brother of Taylor's friends Hyde and Edward Villiers (*Correspondence of Henry Taylor*, p. 134). He also sought out Lord Aberdeen (1784–1860), the Foreign Secretary, later Prime Minister (see *MW*, pp. 250–1).

Tomorrow morning I breakfast with Mr Robinson,[1] and will try to call before you stir out. ever faithfully

Your most obliged
Wm Wordsworth

Since the above was written I have seen Lord Brougham, upon the Copy right Bill—and am anxious to see you, could you call on me at Mr Robinson's where I breakfast.

1616. W. W. to EDWARD MOXON

Address: Mr Moxon, 44, Dover Street, from Mr Wordsworth, *immediate*.
Stamp: York St.
MS. Cornell. Hitherto unpublished.

7 Up. Spring St May 11. 1842

Dear Mr Moxon,

Pray send this[2] off to Mr Rio[3] *without the delay of a single post*

Yours truly
Wm Wordsworth

*I do not know his address
W. W.

[1] See *HCR* ii. 615, and Morley, i. 460.

[2] *The Eagle and the Dove* (*PW* iv. 390), 'tinkered' with the help of E. Q. (*MW*, p. 250).

[3] Alexis Francois Rio (1797–1874), French art historian and Catholic apologist: author of *De la Poésie Chrétienne*, 1836, (*R.M.Cat.*, no. 635), and *De l'Art Chrétien*, 1851. Rio studied at Cambridge, married an English Catholic, and lived in English society, 1837–41, mixing with most of the leading writers of the day. He met W. W. at Rogers's on 7 June 1841 (*HCR* ii. 595). 'His face is rough and red, particularly the nose which is of considerable dimensions and juts out like a promontory. His forehead is unusually low . . . but there is a wonderful symmetry in the outlines, and the eyes are remarkably commanding and more expressive of loftiness of thought than of softness of feeling. His deep-toned and melting voice is the most striking thing about him, and the sweetness of his expansive smile forms a contrast with the coarseness of his expression. . . . We spoke of French and English literature, of the intellectual tone in both countries, of the French Revolution and of the Peninsular War which gave me a capital opportunity of slipping in a word about Brittany. He confessed his utter ignorance of all the events I was alluding to, and declared that if he had known them, he would have paid his tribute to that country as he had done to Spain and the Tyrol.' (Mary C. Bowe, *Francois Rio, Sa Place dans le Renouveau Catholique en*

1617. W. W. to ADAM SEDGWICK

MS. untraced.
Life and Letters of the Revd. Adam Sedgwick, ii. 41.

Wednesday
[?11 May 1842][1]

My dear Sir,

I snatch a moment from the hurry of this place to thank you for the first of the Series of Letters on the Geology of the Lake district which you have done me the honor of addressing to me. I received it yesterday from Mr Danby, liked it very much, and am impatient for the rest. It will give the Kendal lake Book[2] so decided a superiority over every other, that the Publishers have good reason to rejoice. I am happy to think that my endeavours to illustrate the beautiful Region may be thought not unworthy of accompanying your scientific researches. I address this to you at random, but hope it will be forwarded should you be no longer at Cambridge.

You perhaps don't remember that the Pocket Hammerers were complained of not by me in my own person, but in the character of a splenetic Recluse;[3] I will, however, frankly own

Europe, Paris, 1938, pp. 136–7). Rio had now written on 11 and 20 Mar. 1842 reminding W. W. of his promise to write a poem about the Breton resistance to Napoleon for a volume to be published by Moxon. 'Of all the poetical geniuses who declared war on him, you are the only survivor. . . . Now, to have the last representative of that School in Europe, the greatest poet of the age, to express his sympathy for the struggle of an ill-appreciated population against the despotism of those days, appeared to me to be such a glorious reward for my countrymen, and I spoke so much of you when I was last among them, and they enjoyed so very much the idea of being praised by you, that I should be as much ashamed of publishing my book without your poem as of confessing that I had told them a lie.' (*WL MSS.*) In his poem W. W. celebrated the revolt of the schoolboys of the college of Vannes in 1815 against the soldiers of the French republic, a theme which Rio had suggested in his first letter, and the stanzas were duly published in *La Petite Chouannerie, ou, Histoire d'un Collège Breton sous l'Empire*, 1842, pp. 64–5, after a discussion (pp. 53–5) of W. W. as 'le plus hardi dans ses prophéties, le plus inépuisable en consolations et en encouragements pour les vaincus'. Other poems were contributed by Caroline Norton, Landor and Monckton Milnes.

[1] Sedgwick's First Letter (see L. 1596 above) is dated 2 May 1842.

[2] The new expanded *Complete Guide to the Lakes*.

[3] See *Exc.* iii. 178.

that to a certain extent I *sympathised* with my imaginary personage, but I am sure I need not define for you how far, but no farther, I went along with him. Geology and *Mineralogy* are very different things.

Ever, my dear Mr Sedgwick,
Faithfully yours,
Wm Wordsworth

I hope your health is improved.

1618. W. W. to D. W. and ISABELLA FENWICK

MS. WL. Hitherto unpublished.

[24 May 1842]

My beloved Friend,

I ought to have written to you much and often; but I have been harassed and run off my feet from morning to night; and latterly my eyes have given way, so that I am truly anxious to get into the Country.—Much do I rejoice that you have had such fine weather to set off the beauty around you, and that your health permits you to draw so much enjoyment from it, and the course of your peaceful life. And my Sister! I perpetually think of you both, and too often, notwithstanding Dear Dora, wish we were back again with you—Except two or three interviews with Mr Taylor, Mr Rogers,[1] his Sister and one or two more, and above all Mr Ferguson's great kindness in visiting Dora and also my occasional sight of my good Friends, Lord Lonsdale and others of that family, I have had to do with little that interests me. Every thing here is lost in hurry and distraction. Yesterday I dined at the Whig Lord Stanley's;[2] and there I met Mr Carlysle,[3] who inquired kindly after you. To day I dine at the B^p^ of London's; and thence go to the grand affair at the Dutchess of

[1] W. W. had breakfasted at Henry Hallam's on 21 May with Rogers, Campbell, and Moore (see *Rogers*, ii. 216; Moore's *Memoirs*, vii. 322).

[2] Lord Stanley, later 14th Earl of Derby (see L. 1412 above), a moderate Whig, had been approximating more and more to the policies of Peel, and had accepted office as Colonial Secretary the previous year. In 1844 he was called to the House of Lords.

[3] Thomas Carlyle, now a well known figure in London society since his lectures *On Heroes and Hero-Worship* in 1840.

Sutherland's[1] whereof the Post of the Morning tells us 800 of the haut Ton including several branches of the royal family will be assembled. Tomorrow I dine at the Marquis of Lansdown's.[2] Thursday at Home, and go to the House of Lords, it is the Copy right day[3]—But I find Mary has told you all this. Let me say a word about dear Dora, I wish it could be a more hopeful one. I cannot but think that she looks worse and worse. What she wants is absolute *tranquillity* and rest of body and mind. Both her temperament and her situation are against her having either one or the other; nor do I see how they are to be attained, so that I cannot but despond as to the issue. Fresh air she has none, exercise she has only had since we came yesterday, when Miss Rogers took her out kindly for an airing. But we have the happiness of seeing you again, you shall have all particulars.—The transfer of the office[4] I shall know more about in a day or two, whether it will be effected and if so, upon what terms. Nothing can exceed Lord Lonsdale's kindness, or that of all the members of his family. No doubt if the Transfer does take place, it will be under circumstances that will cause a great reduction of the income, W^{m} and I have together drawn from it, so that unless a pension follows in a reasonable time, we shall be much straitened and stand in need of the most rigid economy; and *that* will not be hard for us to practice—And now dearest of dear Friends I must bid farewell to you both, I mean you my Sister, though I have written little to you in particular, the whole is intended for Miss Fenwick and you jointly. God bless you both for ever and ever. ever faithfully yours—

Wm Wordsworth

[*M. W. writes*]

Dearest Friend—your tender friend is at this moment under the hands of Mr Stultz[5]—This does not look like economizing to which I see he has alluded—but they have persuaded him that to

[1] Harriet Elizabeth Georgiana Howard (d. 1868), third daughter of the 6th Earl of Carlisle (see also pt. ii, L. 582), married (1823) George Granville, 2nd Duke of Sutherland (see pt. iii, L. 1131). She became Mistress of the Robes to Queen Victoria.

[2] The Whig statesman (see pt. iii, L. 895), out of office since 1841, but again Lord President of the Council in Lord John Russell's first Cabinet (1846).

[3] The important Committee stage of the Copyright Bill on the 26th.

[4] W. W.'s Distributorship. See also L. 1612 above.

[5] The tailor in Clifford Street.

pay £5-5—is more frugal than to pay £4!—I have painful letters to write ab[t] Margaret[1] and am somewhat perplexed. God bless you ever lovingly my dearest friend—yours M. Wordsworth

I must send you Mr Reed's nice letter—You had so much to do with the Pilgrim Fathers[2] that you ought d[r] f[d] to have been among the first to learn the impression they had made among the Good, in a Bad country. You see what he says also about the Copyright.[3] Ld Mahon's bill comes on in the Ho: of Lords on Thursday.

I forgot to bring a copy of The 'Letter to Mr Gray', upon Burns, to send to Mr Reed, as he previously requested—will you desire Mr Carter to forward one to us, he will be able to get one out of one of the large boxes in the Garret where they are kept—if he cannot meet with a copy with much less trouble in the Cript[4] in the Hall, where I believe he will find one I had laid out with the intention of bringing with me. Ere this you probably have rec[d] Mr Reed's other letter which came by the same Mail, on the subject of the funds,[5] it was given to H. T.[6] who was to forward it to you—to be returned to us before D[r] W. comes to Town.

[1] M. W.'s niece (see L. 1523 above), who had been ill at Mr. Elliott's school at Brighton. See *MW*, p. 253.

[2] i.e. W. W.'s sonnet (see L. 1587 above). Henry Reed had written on 29 Apr. (*Wordsworth and Reed*, pp. 65–70) of the 'grander scope' that W. W. had brought to the subject he had suggested by connecting it with the Pilgrim Fathers. '. . .I have been much struck with the display of imagination (in one of its most important modes of action) in the *unity* that is given in them [the sonnets] to the events, running thro' more than a century and a half—from the migration of the Puritans to the Western World down to the return of the American divines seeking consecration from the Church of England.'

[3] Reed had encouraging news about discussions of internal copyright in the American Congress, though there was still no immediate prospect of legislation.

[4] i.e. the Wordsworth family aumbry.

[5] Reed enclosed a second letter also dated 29 Apr. (*Wordsworth and Reed*, pp. 70–2), in which he advised I. F. and C. W. to retain their Pennsylvanian stock rather than sell at a loss.

[6] Henry Taylor.

1619. W. W. to [?] ALLAN CUNNINGHAM

MS. Cornell. Hitherto unpublished.

[? late May 1842]

My dear Friend,

Pray thank Lady Chantrey and Mr Weiks[1] for their readiness in meeting the wishes of those of my friends who have expressed a desire to possess a Cast of My Bust.[2] I will mention the matter to some of them and they must look to it if they continue to wish the thing to be done. In that case I shall apply to Sir George Beaumont for his consent.

This morning when I called upon Mr Lough[3] the Sculptor he mentioned that the selection of a Sculptor to execute two funeral Monuments for persons whom he named was referred to you; and he begged me to speak a word in his favor so far as to say that I should be gratified if he were chosen. This I can say in sincerity, but not expecting that such a statement will sway with you except where other things are equal. In that case I hope a wish of mine would have some weight!

Ever faithfully y^rs
Wm Wordsworth

In great haste—

1620. W. W. to GEORGE WASHINGTON DOANE[4]

MS. untraced.
The Dial, iii (July 1842), 135. LY iii. 1133.

[*c.* May 1842]

. . . The proceedings of some of the States in your country, in money concerns, and the shock which is given to the credit of

[1] Henry Weekes. See L. 1527 above.

[2] The Chantrey bust (see *MY* ii. 615).

[3] John Graham Lough (see L. 1622 below) had written to W. W. on 31 May to thank the poet for approaching Allan Cunningham on his behalf in connection with a proposed monument to the Earl of Eldon in New College, Oxford (*WL MSS.*). Hence the suggested dating and recipient for this letter.

[4] Bishop of New Jersey. This letter was printed under 'literary intelligence' in the Boston periodical *The Dial*, after a brief notice of W. W.'s latest volume. The editor was Margaret Fuller (see L. 2000 below), who was later succeeded by

the State of Pennsylvania, have caused much trouble under our roof, by the injury done to some of my most valuable connexions and friends. I am not personally and directly a sufferer; but my brother, if the State of Pennsylvania should fail to fulfil its engagements, would lose almost all the little savings of his long and generous life. My daughter, through the perfidy of the State of Mississippi, has forfeited a sum, though but small in itself, large for her means; a great portion of my most valued friends have to lament their misplaced confidence. Topics of this kind are not pleasant to dwell upon, but the more extensively the injury is made known, the more likely is it, that where any remains of integrity, honor, or even common humanity exist, efforts will be made to set and keep things right. . . .

1621. W. W. to UNKNOWN CORRESPONDENT

MS. Cornell. Hitherto unpublished.

Hampstead
June 3^{d} [1842][1]

My dear Madam,

Innumerable and incessant engagements, will, I much regret, prevent my having the pleasure of profiting by your kind invitation during our proposed very short stay in London. Mrs Wordsworth has declined all visits since she came to Town, on account of her Daughter's deranged health.

With kindest remembrances to yourself and Mrs Savory,[2] in which Mrs W. unites, I remain dear Madam

Most sincerely yours
Wm Wordsworth

Emerson. Doane incurred the censure of the Rydal Mount household later this summer by publishing an account of his interviews with W. W. in an American newspaper 'in as indelicate a way as the veryest Yankee could have done', as M. W. remarked to I. F. (see *MW*, p. 262 and Morley, i. 468).

[1] W. W. and M. W., together with Willy W. and the Quillinans, had moved to Mrs. Hoare's on 1 June, where they were joined by C. W. On 29 May W. W. had breakfasted with Haydon (*Diary*, ed. Pope, v. 162–3), called at Chester Place, where H. N. Coleridge was now dangerously ill, and talked with F. D. Maurice (*Memories of Old Friends*, i. 299). On the 30th he visited Strickland Cookson, and on 31st dined at Talfourd's with Haydon (*Diary*, ed. Pope, v. 164).

[2] Probably Mrs. Mary Savory, daughter of Isaac Braithwaite, the Kendal

1622. W. W. to H. C. R.

MS. Mr. W. Hugh Peal. Hitherto unpublished.

Sat. Noon [4 June 1842]
Hampstead Heath

My dear Friend,

On Wednesday week, we shall leave London for the north if possible, and every hour of my time, till *Monday* week is pre-engaged, on that day or Tuesday I will do all in my power to give at your request a couple of hours to Mrs Aders[1] for whom we are all truly sorry.—Judge of my condition as to this operation of sitting. On Thursday, friday and Saturday next, beside several important calls that I have to make, I have to sit both to Pickersgill[2] and Haydon,[3] having already refused Mr Lough, the Sculptor.[4] We grieve to hear of your cold and

Quaker, and Anna Lloyd, fourth daughter of Charles Lloyd, snr. of Birmingham (see pt. i, L. 159; pt. ii, L. 531). She was a niece of Priscilla Wordsworth, C. W.'s wife, and married Joseph Savory (d. 1879) of Buckhurst Park, nr. Ascot. The addressee of this letter is possibly her mother.

[1] H. C. R. had written on 3 June (Morley, i. 464) that his old friend Mrs. Aders (see pt. i, L. 342) had been deserted by her husband and was 'utterly without means of support except what her pencil affords her'. She had taken up portrait painting and it had been put to him by Basil Montagu that if W. W. were to sit for her 'it might make her fortune.' The sittings actually began somewhat earlier than the date W. W. suggests here, on 10 June, after Moxon's breakfast party for W. W., Campbell, Monckton Milnes, and Sir John Hanmer the writer and politician, and were continued on the 15th. H. C. R. had misgivings about the likeness from the start, and the completed portrait did not satisfy Dora Q. 'She was struck, as I was, with a want of truth in the eye, which does not suit a profile . . .' (*HCR* ii. 618). H. C. R. bought one of the two copies made (see Blanshard, *Portraits of Wordsworth*, p. 92), but neither has apparently survived.

[2] Not a fresh portrait: almost certainly a retouching operation, or the taking of one of the copies of the St. John's College portrait which are discussed by Blanshard, p. 159.

[3] The sittings for *Wordsworth on Helvellyn* (see Blanshard, pp. 89–91), got off to a slow start on 14 June when W. W. fell asleep in the heat, but they were completed two days later when, Haydon recorded, 'We had a good set to . . . His knowledge of Art is extraordinary in technical knowledge'. (*Diary* ed. Pope, v. 168).

[4] John Graham Lough (1806–76), was born at Hexham and worked at Newcastle before coming down to London and exhibiting at the Royal Academy (from 1826). Haydon helped him to procure commissions, and he worked in Rome, 1834–8. He specialised in portrait statues and busts, and was responsible for the Southey monument in Crosthwaite Church.

lameness. On Tuesday afternoon we return to Spring Street, the next day W^{m} and I go to Clapham[1] for the night.

Pray remember me kindly to your brother. Today we go to Harrow.

ever affectionately yours
W W

Could you breakfast with us on Wednesday Morning—whatever hours I have to spare from that time must be given to an endeavour to procure some employment in Book making for Mr Carter,[2] with a hope that he will consent to occupy himself in that way—

1623. W. W. to CHARLES WILLIAM PASLEY

MS. E. L. McAdam, Jnr. Hitherto unpublished.

Wednesday
7 Upper Spring Street
[8 June 1842]

Dear Gen[l] Pasley,

Yesterday I returned from Hampstead, after a residence there of six days,[3] and being apprehensive that from pressure of business I may not be able to return your call as soon as I wish, I write to express my thanks for this valuable walking stick which you have presented to me. "Though yet my steady steps the Staff sustains",[4] I shall prize [?it none][5] the less as a memorial of

[1] i.e. to Sir Robert Inglis's, at Battersea Rise.

[2] W. W.'s clerk John Carter was likely to be under-employed if the proposed transfer of W. W.'s Distributorship to his son went through.

[3] On 4 June, during his stay at Mrs. Hoare's, W. W. saw Caroline Fox (1819–71), the diarist. See also L. 1575 above. She was second daughter of Robert Were Fox, F.R.S. (1789–1877), Quaker merchant and man of science, of Falmouth and Penjerrick, Cornwall, and niece of W. W.'s friend Mrs. Charles Fox (see pt. ii, L. 576). For an account of their conversation see *Memories of Old Friends*, i. 302–7. 'He evidently loves the monologue style of conversation, but shows great candour in giving due consideration to any remarks which others may make. His manner is simple, his general appearance that of the abstract thinker, whom his subject gradually warms into poetry.' W. W. had first met her during the family visit to Rydal Mount in Sept. 1837 (*RMVB*). See also her elder brother's account of the meeting at Mrs. Hoare's, *Barclay Fox's Journal*, ed. R. L. Brett, 1979, pp. 270–1.

[4] See Samuel Johnson, *London*, l. 41.

[5] *Words dropped out.*

your friendship, and particularly for the material's sake as a portion of that unfortunate Vessel, whose timbers, after so long a submersion have been raised by your Science,[1] and skill under your direction.

Believe me to remain with sincere regard
faithfully yours
Wm Wordsworth

We leave London as early next week as we possibly can[2]

1624. W. W. to WILLIAM EWART GLADSTONE

MS. British Library.
K (—). LY iii. 1127.

[*In M. W.'s hand*]

Rydal Mount, June 28th [1842]

My dear Mr Gladstone,

I left London for the North last Thursday week, and have been waiting for something definitive before I could with propriety write to you. Upon quitting you after our last interview[3] I called upon Lord Lonsdale, and put Ld Monteagle's Paper into his hands; his Lordship was then inclined to forward it to Sir R^t Peel as soon as he should receive from me certain notices with which I wished it to be accompanied; these I could not accurately give till I came home. When I was about to forward them to Ld L., I was informed from his Lordship that he had particular reasons for not moving in the matter for some little time, and expressed a hope that I should be satisfied with this decision. To this I replied that I submitted willingly to his judgment, and repeated what I had said to him in conversation,

[1] General Pasley had been busy for several years clearing the wreck of the Royal George from the anchorage at Spithead.

[2] M. W.'s letters to I. F. (*MW*, pp. 247–60) fill in all the details of W. W.'s activities during this busy visit to London, including his meetings with Whewell, Boxall, Aubrey de Vere, Sir William Gomm, Mary Lamb, Mr. Justice Coleridge, Lord Adare, William Harness, John Kenyon, Sedgwick, and many other friends.

[3] W. W. had called on Gladstone on 14 June to discuss the proposed transfer of his Distributorship to Willy W., which had still not been finally settled. (*The Gladstone Diaries*, ed. M. D. R. Foot and H. C. G. Matthew, vol. iii (1974), p. 207).

that I never wished Sir R. P. should be formally solicited to grant me a Gover^{t} Pension, but merely that he should early be made acquainted with the fact, that the annual sacrifice which I had made, upon his kind compliance with my desire that the Office I held should be transferred to my Son, amounted to upwards of £400, being more than half of my Income.[1] I was rather anxious that Sir R^{t} should know this as early as could be done with propriety, because the sum appropriated for the recompense of Persons thought deserving is limited, and might altogether be forestalled—further, as I have reached my 73^{d} year, there is not much time to lose, if I am thought worthy of being benefited.

Under these circumstances, dear Sir, I leave it to your judgment how to proceed, being fully assured that nothing will be done by you without the most delicate, well-weighed consideration of Persons and circumstances.

Pray give me a moment to say whether you would wish to have Ld Monteagle's paper, which has been returned to me by Ld L.[2]

A distressing inflammation in one of my eyes compels me to employ Mrs Wordsworth's pen which you will excuse. Pray present my compts to Mrs Gladstone, and believe me my dear Sir, faithfully to be,

your much obliged
[*signed*] Wm Wordsworth

[1] Gladstone noted on this letter, 'Mr. W. is in his 73rd year. His present available income is not more than £300 a year, including the annuity of £100 left him by the late Sir G. Beaumont.'

[2] Gladstone replied to W. W. on the 29th that he was willing to intervene on his behalf if it was necessary, but that Lord Lonsdale was already pressing Peel to complete the transfer (*WL MSS.*).

1625. W. W. to LADY MONTEAGLE

MS. WL.
LY iii. 1126.

[*In M. W.'s hand*]

I hold the pen for my Husband

Rydal June 28th [1842]

Dear Lady Monteagle,

I feel much obliged to you for your letter, and also to Lord M. for the Copy-right bill as amended.[1] I am rather slow and doubtful in ascertaining the language of Acts of Parliament, but say to Ld M. that as far as I am able to see into the matter, the main clause, viz the 4th, seems to secure what was desirable, and upon the whole, the proposed Law will be a decided benefit to Authors; but I am sure that the time will come, and is not far distant, when the Legislature will be convinced, and act upon the conviction, that they who are so gifted as to produce works whether in Prose or Verse of lasting interest, shd in their family and posterity be lastingly rewarded, out of the sale of their labours. For the sake of those who for such worthy motives have taken an interest in this tedious matter, I heartily wish that it may come to a speedy conclusion.

An inflammation in one of my eyes, which began in London, and was aggravated by my journey home, has compelled me to employ my Wife's pen which you will excuse. The attack will excite your sympathy as it has prevented me from enjoying the comfort and beauty of our Home to the degree that I should otherwise have done—but long and frequent trials of this kind have produced their natural and necessary effect—patience and resignation.

Mary and I have seen Mrs Arnold and others of her family. The afflicted Widow[2] is able to talk about her Husband—it is a great comfort, and one might almost say a pleasure, as she now weeps abundantly, a relief that did not come at first. We trust that, if we are spared, our society will be of much benefit to her,

[1] The Copyright Bill, as amended in the Commons (see L. 1606 above), received its Third Reading in the Lords on 24 June and the Royal Assent on 1 July.

[2] Thomas Arnold had died suddenly at Rugby on 12 June on the eve of his departure to Fox How for the summer holidays. The Wordsworths had heard the news in London (*HCR* ii. 618).

and I have already set her mind at ease about the management of her grounds, which I shall have the greatest pleasure to undertake. Her poor Daughter,[1] with whose heavy disappointment you are no doubt acquainted, supports herself as firmly, as under such trials could be expected—and all the children have but one wish, to comfort their Mother. Her own Sister is staying with her—and a widowed Sister of Dr Arnold, Mrs Ward,[2] with her family who have lately resided at Rugby, are about to follow her Brother's Widow and his children with the intention of settling near them.

I regret to say we are to lose Miss Fenwick on Monday or Tuesday next. Anna Ricketts,[3] who came down with us, we hope will remain a few weeks longer.

Your report is the last we have heard of your Father Mother and Aunts.[4] We have got into a vein of West weather, tho' often bright and beautiful, which we hope may improve before our Friends arrive on the other side of Kirkstone.

With our united regards and respects to Ld Monteagle and love to yourself, believe me aff^{dy} to be,

faithfully yours
[*signed*] Wm Wordsworth

Thanks many and great, for your kindness to Dora.

1626. W. W. to VISCOUNT MAHON

MS. Stanhope MSS., Chevening. Hitherto unpublished.

[*In M. W.'s hand*]

[late June 1842]

My dear Lord Mahon,

I congratulate you sincerely upon the end of the trouble which so honourably to yourself you have taken with respect to the

[1] Jane, whose engagement had recently been broken off (see L. 1540 above and *MW*, p. 253).

[2] Thomas Arnold's sister Martha, or 'Patty' (b. 1783), married John Ward, her father's deputy and successor as Collector of Customs for the Isle of Wight. After his death, she moved to Rugby in 1838.

[3] The Wordsworths had renewed their friendship with Mrs. Ricketts and her daughters during their recent visit to London.

[4] John and Jane Marshall and the Misses Pollard.

Copy-right Bill[1]—which tho' far short in its provisions of what you, and other enlightened friends of literature wished; will prove nevertheless no inconsiderable benefit.

Your copy of the proposed Amendment and the obliging letter with which it was accompanied were put into my hands just as I was setting off for the North, and I took the liberty of deferring my acknowledgements of this mark of y^r^ attention, until the Bill was fairly passed.

Since I left Town a meeting has taken place, at which Mr Longman presided, for the purpose of considering what is best to be done for preventing foreign piracies, by which English Authors suffer so much; had I been in Town I should certainly have attended; to allow me to express a wish and a hope that whenever this measure comes before Parliament, it may have your able support. Could this injustice be stopped, or even materially checked, in Europe, and the same effected in America, Men of letters would take that position in society, in connection with Property which they are entitled to. Of course I mean such as have real merit.

I remain, ever my dear Lord, faithfully yours

[*signed*] Wm Wordsworth

An inflammation in my eyes has compelled me to employ Mrs W.'s pen which you will be so kind as to excuse.

1627. W. W. to ROBERT FERGUSON

Address: [Dr] Ferguson, Queen Street, May Fair, London.
Postmark: (1) 5 July 1842 (2) 6 July 1842.
Stamp: Ambleside.
MS. Cornell. Hitherto unpublished.

[*In M. W.'s hand*]

Rydal Mount
July 4th 42

My dear Dr Ferguson

Having now been nearly three weeks returned to our quiet home I feel it right time to thank you for all your Kindness to Mrs W. myself and above all to our dear Daughter. The benefit which she has derived from your advice is great, and, she tells us, as she had told you, that she is "quite well"—perhaps stating

[1] See previous letter.

this too strongly to you, feeling that it was a great sacrifice on your part to visit her as often as you have done. I am not prepared to deny this: as far as relates to *pain* she is not in her own sense "*quite* well"—but in her last letters she thus expresses herself, "but truly I am good for nothing, and what's worse I see no prospect of *ever* being stronger, for I am perfectly well and eat well and sleep well, *doing nothing*, but then when I try myself in the least, I ever find myself wanting." We think it due to the affectionate concern you have taken in her health, that you should be frankly told this, which she might keep back from you, or at least not put it so strongly for the reason above mentioned. If you think as we are strongly inclined to do, that sea-air, and bathing which have heretofore been serviceable to her would be so now, perhaps you would recommend the trial to her Husband. We have a project for her and Rotha to come to Newcastle by steam, whence there is the rail-way which would convey them to Allonby where they might have an opportunity of joining her friends the Daughters of Mr Southey. It seems however doubtful whether a voyage of 36 hours would not too much exhaust her, else this would be the cheapest way, and a very convenient one, for her getting to us. Mrs W. and I feel how much we presume upon your goodness in taxing you in this manner, but we trust you will take it as an additional proof of the value we set upon your friendship.

Since my return I have been oppressed by an inflammation in one of my eyes, which I cannot yet employ either for writing or reading—this has kept me from Mr Taylor's Tragedy.[1] Miss Fenwick has read it with much delight, so has my Daughter; and we hear favorable reports of it from other quarters. The only objection seems to be some want of unity of interest which it is thought will make it somewhat less felt than its predecessor.[2] Every one says that it is rich in thought and beauty. The first use of any importance that I make of my eyes, will be to read this work.

As far as I can collect from the Parliamentary debates that have been read to me, in a broken way, I am not satisfied with the ministerial view of the Poor law amendment Bill.[3]—It does not

[1] *Edwin the Fair*, publ. June 1842.

[2] *Philip van Artevelde*.

[3] The Poor Law Amendment Act, which substituted the notorious workhouse system for older methods of outdoor relief, was passed in 1834, and had already occupied W. W.'s attention in the *Postscript, 1835* (see pt. iii, L. 863 and *Prose Works*,

appear to pay sufficient respect to principles which, in most determined opposition to the system of Ld Brougham,[1] I deem fundamental. No one wishes that an able-bodied man, who cannot procure wages enough to support him in his regular employment, should be maintained by the Public unless he be willing to work; but then the work assigned to him, should not be such as his previous employments have entirely disqualified him for, and whatever it may be, it should be required of him only under circumstances consistent with the dictates of humanity. Now there is obviously pervading this Bill, and actuating the minds of its supporters, a strong disposition to strain the application of the work-house test, to a degree which no machinery will render practicable, and in that impracticability lies sufficient proof, that the thing aimed at is unwise. A Man's being in want of opportunities to labour, not from any fault of his own, but owing to circumstances over which he has had no control, ought not to be made by legislative operations an example to deter others from such improvidence as he might, perhaps not unjustly, in some periods of his life, have been charged with. The bill appears to go too much upon the principle of punishing the existing generation by a begging of the question, that it will be for the benefit of the generation to come—Nay more, they are to be punished also for the faults of preceding ones.

Unfortunately for us dear Miss Fenwick leaves us tomorrow for the county of Durham, whence she goes into the [?][2] We have however the consolatory prospect of her return to us before the winter, if she is spared an attack of the illness, when the cold weather shall be coming on. She is hoping, on her progress, to meet Mr and Mrs Tayler at Malvern.

iii. 240 ff.). On 11 May 1842 Sir James Graham, the Home Secretary, brought in a Bill to continue the Poor Law Commission for another five years and further to amend the laws relating to the poor, and the subsequent debates in Parliament the following month reopened the whole contentious issue. See Sir Llewellyn Woodward, *The Age of Reform, 1815–1870*, 1962, pp. 449 ff.

[1] Brougham had been Lord Chancellor when the original Benthamite recommendations of the Poor Law Commission were announced early in 1834, and he had moved the Second Reading of the Poor Law Amendment Act in the Lords on 21 July (*Speeches of Henry Brougham*, 4 vols., 1838, iv. 475 ff.). He had subsequently spoken in defence of the system in 1838 (*Speeches*, iv. 529 ff.).

[2] *Word dropped out*. I. F. was bound for the south of England and her relations in Somerset.

Miss F. unites with Mrs W. and myself in kindest remembrances, and believe me to be

my dear, D[r] Ferguson
very faithfully, y[r] much obg[d]
[*signed*] W[m] Wordsworth

P. S. You may perhaps have seen the paragraph in the newspapers, that I had retired from the Stamp Off. *upon a Pension*—this is erroneous—but let us hope that this may prove *prophetic.*

1628. W. W. to GEORGE BURDER[1]

Address: Rev[d] George Burder, Nab Cottage (*delivered by hand*].
MS. Cornell. Hitherto unpublished.

[early July 1842]

My dear Sir,

I rejoice in the determination you have made. My Wife and I will be happy to attend as witnesses at any day and hour which may suit.

We have two or three friends to drink with us this evening at

[1] The Revd. George Burder (1814–81), second son of Henry Forster Burder, D.D. (1783–1864), of Hackney, and grandson of George Burder, D.D. (1752–1832), a prominent Congregationalist minister in Coventry and Islington, had entered Magdalen Hall, Oxford, in 1835, graduated B.A. in 1840, and was now curate to the Revd. James Duke Coleridge (1789–1857), S. T. C.'s nephew, at Thorverton, nr. Exeter. According to Morley, he was also remotely related to Mrs. Clarkson. In a letter dated Nab Cottage, Tuesday morning, he explained to W. W. his doubts about the validity of his baptism, his parents having been Dissenters, and asked W. W. and M. W. to stand as sponsors in a ceremony of conditional baptism, which was the only way of settling his doubts. 'What delight I shd have, if you grant (the request], it would be *impossible* for me to say—I am already, as to my Intellectual and Moral Being, a child of yours—how deep and pure would be the joy of feeling bound to you by still stronger and holier ties!' (*WL MSS.*) To W. W.'s regret, Burder followed Newman into the Roman Catholic Church in 1846 (see *HCR* ii. 657), joining the Cistercians at Mount St. Bernard's Abbey (see L. 1528 above), where he was Abbot, 1853–8. He told Aubrey de Vere that his first inclination towards the monastic life had arisen from reading the lines in *The Excursion* (iii. 400 ff.) about 'The life where hope and memory are as one'. (Ward, *Aubrey de Vere*, pp. 224–5). The date of this letter is established by reference to *RMVB*, which records Burder's place of residence as Babbacombe, Devon. See also L. 1633 below.

six. Will you be so kind as to join the party; if you come an hour before so much the better.

Ever my dear Sir faithfully yours

Wm Wordsworth

1629. W. W. to WILLIAM EWART GLADSTONE

Endorsed: July 11. Mr Wordsworth. Mem^um sent to Sir R. P. Aug 18.
MS. British Library.
K (—). *LY iii. 1128.*

[*In M. W.'s hand*]

Rydal Mount, July 11th —42.

My dear Mr. Gladstone

With many thanks for your kind letter I now enclose Lord Monteagle's statement, which I deferred doing in the hope, a faint one, I confess, that I might hear thro' Lord Lonsdale, or otherwise, something relative to the matter in which you have been so good as to take an interest.[1]

It is apparent from the newspapers that the sum appropriated to that class of Pensions has been exhausted during the course of last year, so that there is no surplus for the year ensuing; and this is, coupled with my advanced age, a strong reason why time should not be lost in reminding Sir R^t Peel of me. Nevertheless, after what has passed between Lord Lonsdale and myself, and which you are acquainted with, I do not like to resume the subject with his Lordship. If, therefore, an occasion sh^d occur which you think favorable, I leave it to your judgment to do as you think best; trusting that I shall stand free of any charge of indelicacy to Lord L., if I wish also to profit by your friendly dispositions and such opportunities, as might be more likely to fall in your way from your relation to the present Govern^t.[2]

The movements of the Stamp Off: have been rather slow in respect to the transfer of the Stamps under my charge, so that I cannot yet regard my Son as standing exactly in my late position; as soon as the Head Off: has authorized me to do this, I

[1] The transfer of W. W.'s Distributorship to Willy W. was now going through satisfactorily, but the question of a pension for W. W. to compensate him for the loss of income, was still very much in the air.

[2] Gladstone had accepted office under Peel as vice-president of the Board of Trade.

shall think it my duty to thank Sir R. P. for his compliance with my request, I having as yet only left a card at his house when in Town.

The inflammation in my eye is a good deal abated, but I still am obliged to employ Mrs W's pen. She joins me in kind respects to yourself and Mrs Gladstone; and believe me, my dear Sir,

faithfully, your much obliged
[*signed*] Wm Wordsworth

1630. W. W. to SAMUEL WILKINSON[1]

MS. Harvard University Library.
LY iii. 1129.

[*In M. W.'s hand*]

Rydal Mount
July 11. —42

Dear Sir

I feel no difficulty in saying that you are at liberty to make such extracts from my writings as are suitable to the publication of which you have sent me a specimen from the works of Mr Coleridge; tho' I think your proposal reasonable that I should see a copy before your selections appear.

As your work seems to consist much of Selection I think it proper to state to you, that you are mistaken in supposing you or any one has a '*legal right*' to publish at any length the works of any living Author, however long they may have been before the world (unless by express contracts with him to that effect). The Bill which has now the sanction of Parliament extends the term of the Author's right, under *all* circumstances, from 28 to 42 years—and allows (should the Author survive the 42 years) the term to continue to the end of his Life, and for 7 years after his demise.

It may not be amiss to mention that in a volume of my Poems,

[1] An associate of W. F. Hook, and editor of *The Christian's Miscellany*, Leeds, 1841–2, a high-church periodical which had just published a piece entitled 'Contributions of S. T. Coleridge to the Revival of Catholic Truth'. Wilkinson was anxious to make a similar selection from the poetry of W. W. See L. 1642 below.

making the 7th, are three Sonnets entitled 'Aspects of Christianity in America' that are not unlikely to suit your purpose.[1]

I am, Sir, respectfully
Yours
W. Wordsworth[2]

1631. W. W. to HENRY REED

MS. Cornell.
K (—). *Wordsworth and Reed, p. 74.*

[*In M. W.'s hand*]

Rydal Mount July 18th 1842

My dear Sir

Yesterday I received your kind letter dated June 30th, and thank you sincerely for it, as well as for two others which have remained till now unacknowledged.[3] That of yesterday is already on its way to Miss Fenwick, who will forward it to my Brother; as it seemed highly desireable that as soon as possible they should be prepared for their probable disappointment, which your former letters, however, must have rendered less than it otherwise would have been. As to the other parts of my family and connections who are in much greater need, I have given up all hopes of justice ever being done to them by the dishonest State of Mississippi. These injuries have been widely felt thro' England, we have at this moment staying in our house, a young Lady,[4] one of several Sisters whose mother has lost not less than £600 per ann. by entrusting her money to some of the new states—this is the more to be regretted as she was almost forced to invest her Property in that quarter, by the unwarrantable confidence of friends and connections.

In regard to the State of Pensylvania, the question resolves itself ultimately into one of honesty among the lower classes of democracy, whose votes may outweigh those of the respectable part of the community; and so deeply do I feel this mischief, that nothing would tempt me to trust any portion of my little Property to an unqualified Democracy; tho' I quite concur with

[1] See L. 1587 above.
[2] Not signed by W. W.
[3] See *Wordsworth and Reed*, pp. 65–74, and L. 1611 above.
[4] Anna Ricketts.

you, that had I been connected with the State of Pensylvania, I would leave my money in its place, trusting to the honesty of the People, rather than sell out at the heavy loss which could not at present be avoided.

As I am talking of Money matters, the interest you take in my concerns prompts me to let you know, that I have just resigned the office, which to my own great convenience and advantage I have held for nearly 30 years, in favour of my Younger Son—who has acted under me for more than 11 years. By this step my small Income has been reduced more than one half—for there is no truth in what you may have seen in the Newspapers that "I had retired upon a Pension."

I lately received from Mr Dickens a printed circular letter, in which he states there has been[1] presented thro' Mr Clay[2] a petition to Congress signed by the whole body of American Authors praying for the establish[men]t of an International Law of Copyright—

To counteract this petition, as the Circular states, a meeting was held at Boston—at which a memorial against any change in the existing state of things was agreed to, with but one dissentient voice: this document which was received deliberately stated, that if English Authors were invested with any control over the re-publication of their own books, it would be no longer possible for American editors to alter and adapt them (as they do now) to the American taste.

Thus for the circular. And I ask you if it be possible that any person of the lowest degree of respectability in Boston could sign a document in its spirit so monstrous, and so injurious in its tendency?

It gives me much pleasure to learn from your last, that you encourage the hope of crossing the Atlantic—notwithstanding the cloud under which the American good name, including that of the ancient State of Pensylvania, lies. Be assured that neither this nor any other dishonours which might fall upon the Transatlantic People, would prevent Mrs Wordsworth and myself giving a hearty welcome to you, and Mrs Reed, provided her domestic engagements would allow her to accompany you. And may I beg you to bear in mind that our advanced age

[1] *Written* states, that having.

[2] Henry Clay (1777–1852), Secretary of State under John Quincy Adams, 1824–8, and now leader of the Whigs in Congress. He unsuccessfully stood for the Presidency in 1844.

presses upon us the desireableness of your visit, if we are to profit by it, not being long deferred.

I returned to Rydal a month ago, after having been nearly six weeks in London; while there, I forwarded, to the address you gave me, a copy of my Letter upon the character of Burns, which you had expressed a desire to see. The Book Trade is in a most depressed state—nothing but such books as have a connection with Theology, and the religious ferment that originated in Oxford, seeming to have the power of inducing People to part with their money for Literature's sake. Nor is this much to be wondered at, for all ranks and classes are compelled, by difficulties in the state of things, to reduce their expenditure.

I brought back with me from London an inflammation in my eyes, from which I am recovering, but I am still obliged to employ Mrs W's pen. Who unites with me in kind remembrances to yourself and [Mrs Reed.]

[Your much obliged friend,]
Wm Wordsworth[1]

1632. W. W. to SIR ROBERT PEEL

Address: *Private*. The Right Honble Sir R^{t} Peel, Bart, etc etc etc [*In M. W.'s hand*]
Endorsed: 25 July Mr Wordsworth re: his Son's app^{t} to succeed him as Distributor of Stamps.
MS. British Library. Hitherto unpublished.

Private/

Rydal Mount
25 July 1842.

Dear Sir Robert,

The regulations under which my Son is to hold the Office of Distributor of Stamps, as my Successor, being now completed, and his appointement having arrived yesterday, I beg leave to return my grateful acknowledgements for your compliance with the request which, supported by my Friend and honored Patron the Earl of Lonsdale I ventured to make.[2]

[1] Closing words and signature cut away: conjecturally restored by Broughton.

[2] Peel replied on 7 Aug.: 'Allow me to assure you that I had the greatest personal satisfaction in promoting the arrangement to which you refer. It is some compensation for the severe toil and Anxieties of public life to have occasionally

As my Son has acted under me for eleven years at Carlisle, and is consequently acquainted with every department of the business, I firmly trust, from the knowledge which I have of his steadiness and punctuality, that the Duties of his Office will be performed in a manner with which the Public will be satisfied.

I have had much pleasure in seeing your Son, to whom I was introduced at Harrow,[1] and Mr Humphrey,[2] and have had two pretty long walks in their company, with the view of introducing them to some scenes in this neighbourhood which lie out of the beaten way of Tourists; and I look for a recurrence of a similar gratification.

I have the honor to be, dear Sir Robert, with sincere gratitude

your much obliged
Wm Wordsworth

1633. M. W. and W. W. to ISABELLA FENWICK

MS. WL.
LY iii. 1130 (—).

July 28th [1842]

My most dear Friend,

It seems an age since I wrote to you, and strange does it appear that this should have been so, feeling as I do, that you have never been absent from our thoughts—Your presence has been pressed upon us by the exquisite beauty and bountifulness of the season—the lovely moonlight nights, and that one especial brilliant star that dear Annie[3] and Willy have watched with so much anxiety to know more about it, craving for your help in their researches. Indeed, dear friend, unreasonable tho' it may have been we have grudged that you were not with us thro' this delightful time, instead of being as W^m says 'tossed about from place to place in those trains or otherwise different from your former mode of travel'. But enough we much look forward to a happy meeting and a quiet fireside, and this will fully satisfy us—and well it may for the thought *is* a blessed one.

the opportunity of serving or gratifying those who are an Honour to their Country.' (*WL MSS.*)

[1] See L. 1526 above.

[2] Young Peel's tutor.

[3] Anna Ricketts.

Dear Anna is still with us, no *Female* Escort offers itself, and as W^{m} (from the fear of a relapse in his eyes, which you will rejoice to hear are now well) dare not conduct her to $Birm^{g}$ Mrs Ricketts, much as she desires to see her before the Highland journey is taken, feels obliged to give her up till their return—So that the plan is for her to meet Major and Mrs Campbell[1] at Fleetwood, whence they are to take the Steamer to Glasgow. This will be in the course of next week I suppose. It is an ill wind that blows nobody good—Yet I regret that dear Mrs Rickett's disappointment is a consequence of the great pleasure the prolonged stay of darling Anna is to us. Our love of her encreases every day—and I cannot but feel she has been thoroughly happy with us—Then she is such a useful little thing! She is ready to help with her pen, her dear voice, and in every way. God bless her! She has had a share in winding up the Stamp Office affairs, by writing Circulars etc—so that in all substantial ways we have profitted by her, and sad shall we be to part with her as we must do, soon after all this is over, which will only last for a very few days longer. For Willy received his appointment last Sunday, for which they have been waiting some time before his Father had authority to resign the Stamps. On that day Willy had to go to Appleby to attend the Assizes, being subpoened upon an affair of damages to be awarded to a Person injured by the overthrow of a Coach—Willy's business was to prove who were the Proprietors—he having granted their licence—He returned on Tuesday, and now the preparations for his and Mr Carter's departure are going on.[2] This then is our present position—But to tell you dear friend of all the incidental occurrences, and daily and hourly visitants that we have had, and seemed to be in the midst of, is beyond my patience to write

[1] Her sister and brother-in-law (see *MW*, p. 259).

[2] The removal of the Stamp Office to Carlisle in August marked the end of an era, as M. W. recognised in a later letter to I. F.: 'You will easily believe we felt sad when we were first left—The removal of the *stamps* seemed a sort of breaking up, for seeing the last of what has been a nearly 30 years interest, could not but be seriously felt by us, at our age—and it *was* felt, but with thankfulness that what had been so great a benefit to us (in educating our children, and enabling us to live for so many years in the sort of hospitality we liked best), had passed into the hands of our beloved son . . . It was like a funeral going out of the house, when after so much bustle and pulling down in the Office, they had all passed away. I however next day set about *building* up again and we are now comfortably reconciled to our loneliness. . .' (*MW*, pp. 261–2).

and would tire you to read—All the comments upon the Rush-bearing carried on under Mr Faber's zeal for the Old Church, and Mr Harrison's[1] generosity in supporting it in a grand scale—great wedding at Grasmere, and [*W. W. writes*] Miss Orrel[2] the Bride, whose Brother is a mighty rich manufacturer, and she herself wondrous rich also, the Bridegroom a Banker. The whole Vale of Grasmere has been thinking of nothing but this Gala for many days. Every Girl had a new Frock and every boy a new Hat bound with blue ribbon, and you may judge of the feasting when you are told that Omnibuses, one of them with four Horses, came charged with panniers full of meats and drinks from Lancaster or beyond; two French Cooks superintended and the sound of Cannon heard at different times of the day and at the close of the evening until midnight proclaimed far and wide the rejoicing. How soon may this be turned into mourning for the principals and for no small Portion of those who partook the festivity! Have you my very dear Friend found out where Wm Wordsworth the Husband of Mary took up the Pen? She has told you that my eyes are well so far as relates to inflammation, it is so, but the eyelid has not fallen to its natural size, and the eye continues much weaker than is to be wished. You report Mr Taylor's opinion of light. Light and air are no doubt indispensable for the well being of the eyes, but then how difficult is it, nay it is impossible, to avoid mischief in courting the benefit. With regard [to this] I had an instance yester evening the effects of which I feel at this moment. Is it worth while to tell you that yesterday we had the two Archdeacons Wilberforce, their younger Br Henry I believe, Robert's wife and two other Ladies to tea.[3] It would have been an odd rencontre if they had

[1] Benson Harrison.

[2] Jane Elizabeth, only daughter of Mr. Orrell of Grasmere, had married William Brooks of Manchester, eldest son of Samuel Brooks, banker, on 27 July.

[3] W. W. had met the three Wilberforce brothers in 1818 when they stayed in Rydal with their father and mother (see *MY* ii. 482). Since then they had all gone on to Oriel College, Oxford, during the Tractarian Movement. Robert had been Archdeacon of the East Riding, in succession to Francis Wrangham, since 1841. He made a notable contribution to Tractarian theology in *The Doctrine of the Incarnation of Our Lord Jesus Christ* (1848), *The Doctrine of Holy Baptism* (1849), and *The Doctrine of the Holy Eucharist* (1853), but in 1854 he followed Manning into the Roman Catholic Church. He married Wrangham's daughter Agnes in 1832, and on her death her cousin Jane Legard, who is referred to here. Samuel became Archdeacon of Surrey (1839), rector of Alverstoke, Hants. (1840) and chaplain to Prince Albert (1841), and thereafter preferment followed quickly, to

appeared when Mr Robinson[1] was under our roof. [*M. W. adds*: who only left us a few days ago—he dined twice with us, once with Mrs Fletcher and had been with Miss Martineau at Tynemouth. If all be well he will play whist with us at Xtmas.]

A clergyman[2] has been with us twice, a most ardent admirer of mine who lives at Babbacomb, and has come so far principally to see me. He spoke much of his mortification upon learning from the B^p of Exeter that I had been in front of his cottage[3] of which he has left me a drawing done by a friend—as a work of art it is of no value, but interesting to me as a memorial of the place and of the worthy Man who gave it. Mr Englehart[4] (was he at Rydal before you left us) has given me a very good Drawing of the view from the Door of the Summer House which I should like one day to have engraved, it is from the same point as Cordelia Marshall's but much better done; he had been once an Artist by profession. This morning I conducted dear Anna to the point opposite the higher division of the high waterfall of Rydal, of which you must have heard me speak. I left her there drawing. She has done some very pretty things in and about our Village which will be delightful Memorials to take away with her. Her visit has I sincerely believe been a most happy one. We have only to regret that the bright weather and being so much out of doors drawing has been over trying for her eyes—the lids of which are a little affected exactly in the same way as mine, the space beneath the under lid being swoln and feeling weak and somewhat painful, just as mine did and is apt to do.—I wish we were as susceptible of the pleasure she gives by her music as by her pencil, though that we enjoy not a little. Mr

the Deanery of Westminster and the Bishopric of Oxford (1845). Henry held two livings in Kent, but became a Roman Catholic in 1850, editing the *Catholic Standard*, 1854–63. The visit of the three brothers to Rydal Mount (*RMVB*) was presumably intended to calm the controversy stirred up by the *Life of William Wilberforce*, in which both W. W. and H. C. R. had been involved (see pt. iii, L. 1243).

[1] H. C. R. had spent a few days at Tynemouth with Harriet Martineau (see pt. iii, L. 1190) early in July, and arrived at Ambleside on the 20th, remaining there for three days (see *HCR* ii. 619–22).

[2] George Burder (see L. 1628 above).

[3] During W. W.'s visit to Devon the previous summer. The reference would seem to imply that W. W. had seen something of Phillpotts, Bishop of Exeter, who resided at Torquay (see pt. ii, L. 722), and invited him to stay (*WL MSS.*).

[4] Apparently an amateur artist. His attractive drawing is now in the collection of Professor Paul Betz.

Faber has been here several times, he is writing poetry at an immense rate, meaning to have a Volume[1] out before his departure in Jan^{ry} for the Continent. Mrs Fletcher[2] appears to be doing as well as can be expected and Mrs Arnold feeds with delight upon the memory of her Husband. The Roughsedges have been on a sea coast Tour for some days at Rampside, Broughton etc. He continues very nervous and disturbed in his Head so that I, who am as you know too well in matters of health not a little of an alarmist, cannot help being uneasy about him, and I think his wife is the same.—

Mr Reed's Letter is ominous, but Mr Jefferay[3] a mercantile Friend of Mr Robinson's, in whose judgement he has the greatest confidence, and who has lived much in America says that if he had money at liberty he would lodge it with the State of Pennsylvania, not having a doubt that in no long course of time they will make good their engagements; because, says he, the Americans are a shrewd people and will soon learn that credit is power, and with Power comes Wealth, and that without keeping engagements credit cannot be maintained; so that you see leaving honesty out of the question he is nevertheless confident of a good result.—

And now my dear Friend I should like to let loose my heart upon this scrap of Paper—but it is folly to think of it. Mary has already told you how deeply we love you and how ardently we long for your return, though for my own part I must say that encreasing years are I feel making me less and less of an interesting companion. Nothing however said or done to me for some time has in relation to myself given me so much pleasure as a casual word of Anna's that the expression of my face was ever varying. I had begun to fear that it had lately been much otherwise. Take care of yourself

ever faithfully and fervently yours

Wm Wordsworth

[1] *The Styrian Lake and other poems*, 1842. Before taking up the living of Elton, Hunts., which was offered to him this autumn, Faber spent some months in France and Italy studying the parochial system in Catholic countries.

[2] Of Lancrigg (see *MW*, p. 263).

[3] See pt. iii, L. 1353.

1634. W. W. to DORA QUILLINAN

MS. WL.
LY iii. 1133.

Wednesday Noon 17th Augt. 42

My dear Child,

I drank your health along with Mother's yesterday in remembrance of your birthdays. And I now send you a thousand good wishes for happy returns of the same. I also send you three sonnets written for the Ecclesiastical series, where they are wanted. Two of them, viz those upon the marriage ceremony and the funeral service were suggested as necessary by Mr Reed[1] of Philadelphia, the other upon visiting the Sick, I added of my own accord.—

Your dear Mother and I pair very well, and get on most happily together; it only grieves me some times to see after a pretty long walk how she suffers in her Back; not that in fact she does walks which a few years ago we should have called much. Since my eye has improved I seem to myself to be strengthening slowly; I can take so much more exercise, and it does not seem at all to hurt me. Yesterday I worked from half past eight in the morning till nearly one at watering some Hollies which we have transplanted, and in the hayfield—our second crop. This morning also I have been very busy strewing out along with James, the Cook, and Jane.—I much like your project of going to the Isle of Man; if you can effect it; of course you will return by Rydal. Pray dont let Mr Quillinan print his Article upon the Vannes insurrection[2] without being paid for it.—Mr Taylor got for his upon my Sonnets etc as much at least as paid for his Continental trip with his Wife. Your Mother will have told you of the Company we have had; we have ceased to ask any Body to dinner; but we have a great deal of '*teaing*'; Mr Humphrey, Sir Robert Peel's Son's Tutor and the pupil, along with another

[1] See *PW* iii. 397–9. In his letter of 29 Apr. (*Wordsworth and Reed*, p. 68), Reed had written, 'Are not these (the former in its beautiful introductory address, and the latter throughout) among the most excellent of the liturgical ceremonies, and do they not—more perhaps than any other—appeal to that common human-heartedness, which is the very element in which your poetry moves and has its being?'

[2] Presumably inspired by Rio's *La Petite Chouannerie* and the poem which W. W. contributed to it (see L. 1616 above); but the article is untraced (if it was ever published).

three times. I am truly glad to hear that your health is so much improved and trust that strength will come hereafter; though one cannot confide much in that hope, till you are placed where you can have some exercise and *much* fresh air out of doors. May that day not be distant! Your Mother and I had on Thursday a delightful drive to Lord Bradford's[1] (St Catherines) and up to Captain Wilson's,[2] and around by Troutbeck Chapel. Your dear Mother was charmed, so was I; but the scene was newer to her than to me.—I do not disapprove of John's trip;[3] but I do deplore that he cannot put more energy into himself without such excitement. He has not fulfilled his promise to write to us from Southampton, nor have we heard at all from him except a short note dropped in passing. Will you be so kind as to forward the Sonnets to Miss Fenwick. I have heard again a third letter from that good man Mr Reed;[4] the contents more hopeful somewhat than I looked for. Some taxes are imposed with a view to discharge the State obligations, but the August interest will certainly be suspended. Remember me affectionately to Mr Quillinan and also to the Girls with the best of good wishes for poor Rotha. Your most affectionate Father

W. Wordsworth

1635. W. W. to THOMAS POWELL

MS. University of Virginia Library.
LY iii. 1135.

[*c*. Aug. 1842]

My dear Mr Powell,

Your fine Chedder Cheese and the six volumes of your Poems arrived punctually, and I thank you kindly for these tokens of your regard.—One of the Volumes I have already presented to an esteemed female Friend who will prize it as it deserves, and the chief part of the others I shall dispose of from time to time as

[1] George Augustus Bridgeman, 2nd Earl of Bradford (1789–1865), of Weston Park, Shifnal, had a small estate on the south shore of Windermere. He visited Rydal Mount with his friends several times, 1841–3 (*RMVB*).

[2] Capt. John Wilson of The Howe (see pt. i, L. 229).

[3] John W. had gone to London with a view to accompanying Moxon on a 'pedestrian tour' through Brittany (see *MW*, p. 263).

[4] See *Wordsworth and Reed*, p. 77.

a fitting occasion may offer.—I am truly sorry that the considerations you mention prevented you calling upon me; I rather thought that I was denied the pleasure of seeing you from your sense of your own engagements in business, otherwise I should have pressed you to come with us with much more earnestness. I regret the more that we [saw] so little of you, because I feel that I am too advanced in years to be free to encourage hope of renewing my visits to London. If that is to be, my plan must be entirely changed, for the late hours of dinner so different from what I am accustomed to, and the long-protracted exertions of the day, brought on an inflammation in one of my eyes from which I have not yet entirely recovered.

I was induced to go to Town, wholly upon business the last time, in which however I succeeded. One of my objects was to procure the transfer of the office I have held for 29 years and a quarter to my youngest Son. This has been effected through the kindness of Sir Robert Peel much to my satisfaction, though my income is reduced thereby more than one half. The pension spoken of in the Newspapers, was a fiction of their own—

My sitting to Mr Lough[1] was quite out of

[*cetera desunt*]

1636. W. W. to HENRY REED

MS. Cornell.
K (—). Wordsworth and Reed, p. 81.

Rydal Mount Ambleside
Sept^{br} 4th 1842.

My dear Mr Reed,

Having an opportunity of sending this note by a gentleman[2] going directly to America, I write to thank you for your last Letter, and for all the attention which your regard for me has induced you to bestow upon the money concerns of my family and Friends in America. It gives me pleasure that you still are in heart about the final result of things in Pennsylvania.[3] Neverthe-

[1] The sculptor (see L. 1622 above). [2] See next letter.

[3] In his letter of 29 July Reed wrote: 'I feel in better spirits respecting the prospects of the finances of the State than I have for some times past. . . .I have much less hesitation in saying (deeply as I feel the responsibility of my words) by [no] means let your friends be induced to sacrifice their investments.' (*Wordsworth and Reed*, p. 79).

less I cannot but incline to despond. Is it true that a stay-law has been passed, no taxes being imposed to pay the debt beyond a sum but sufficient to pay much more than a third of the interest due to the *native* creditor; and is it also true that the sum raised is to be exclusively appropriated to those classes? if so, I must own I cannot but blush for the State of Pennsylvania, and my hopes of justice sink in spite of all that you have, though with much caution and delicacy, said to keep them up. At present there is no remedy but patience, and that will not be wanting among those of my Friends who have suffered.

A few days ago after a very long interval I returned to poetical composition; and my first employment was to write a couple of sonnets upon subjects recommended by you[1] to take place in the Ecclesiastical Series. They are upon the marriage ceremony, and the funeral sermon. I have also at the same time, added two others,[2] one upon visiting the sick, and the other upon the thanksgiving of women after childbirth, both subjects taken from the services of our Liturgy. To the second part of the same series I have also added two,[3] in order to do more justice to the Papal Church for the services which she did actually render to Christianity and humanity in the middle ages. By the bye, the Sonnet beginning Men of the western world[4] etc was slightly altered after I sent it to you, not in the hope of substituting a better verse, but merely to avoid the repetition of the word, "brook" which occurs as a Rhyme in the "Pilgrim Fathers."[5] Those three sonnets I learn from several quarters have been well received by those of your Countrymen whom they most concern. Pray excuse this barren scrawl and believe me with high respect and very gratefully your's

Wm Wordsworth

[1] See L. 1634 above.

[2] See *PW* iii. 398.

[3] See *PW* iii. 362, 365.

[4] Written 1839. See *PW* iv. 131, 431–2. Reed had expressed his gratitude for 'the kind and forebearing' note which W. W. had added to this sonnet in the 1842 volume: 'The fit rebuke of the breach of faith by some of our States ought to be more keenly felt because of the charitable hope you have accompanied it with—that your brethren of the West will wipe off this stain from their name and nation. Indeed it would sadly grieve me—and doubtless many more, if any thing done here should occasion a departure from your wonted magnanimous hopefulness.' (*Wordsworth and Reed*, p. 80).

[5] i.e. the three sonnets on *Aspects on Christianity in America.*

1637. W. W. to JAMES SAVAGE[1]

MS. Henry E. Huntington Library.
LY ii. 1136.

[*In M. W.'s hand*]

Rydal Mount
Sepr. 6th —42

Dear Sir

The accompanying note addressed to Mr Thornton,[2] will I trust put you in the way of seeing those letters of Charles 1st which I spoke of—he lives at Clapham, but is almost sure of being found at the Stamp Office every day between the hours of 11 and 3. So that you had best call there.

Since I had the pleasure of seeing you I have been called upon by an American Gentleman[3] who embarks for his own Country, he was kind enough to take charge of two letters, which I had intended to trouble you with. If you have not already written to Mr Tickner upon the matter of the Boston petition,[4] pray spare yourself that trouble—for what passed between us upon that subject, having been confirmed by this Gentleman, I am fully persuaded, that the petition was got up by Publishers and others of inferior consideration—so that the City of Boston cannot be fairly considered as dishonored by it.

I cannot forbear telling you that Mrs Hill, the daughter of Mr Southey whom you saw at my house looking so well and chearful—gave birth to a fine stout boy before 6 oC next mor^{g}. Both the Mother and Child are doing well.

Allow me to say that I regret our interview was so short—and

[1] James Savage (1784–1873), of Boston, historian and state Senator for Massachusetts: author of *The History of New England from 1630 to 1649*, 2 vols., 1825–6, and *Genealogical Dictionary of the First Settlers of New England*, 4 vols., 1860–2. He was introduced by Washington Allston and George Ticknor (*WL MSS.*), and his visit in early Sept. is recorded in *RMVB*.

[2] See pt. ii, L. 780.

[3] The Revd. George Lewis Prentiss (1816–1903), of Boston, Congregationalist minister and author (*RMVB*): disciple of Tholuck and S. T. C., and Professor of Pastoral Theology at Union Theological Seminary from 1873. See also Ls. 1679 and 1988 below.

[4] See L. 1631 above.

believe me dear Sir, with best wishes for your safe return to your native land,[1] in which Mrs W. joins, sincerely yours

[*signed*] Wm Wordsworth

1638. W. W. to LYDIA HUNTLEY SIGOURNEY[2]

MS. Massachusetts Historical Society.
David Bonnell Green. 'William Wordsworth and Lydia Huntley Sigourney', New England Quarterly, xxxvii (1964), 527–31.

Rydal Mount
6th Sep^{r}—42

Dear Madam

During the bustle inseparable from a visit to London, I had the honor of receiving a Letter from you in which was enclosed a copy of verses upon my Birthday by your Daughter.[3] I owe you an apology for not making an earlier acknowledgement both to yourself and the young Lady for the Compliment; be assured however that I was duly sensible of it. While in the Metropolis I was actually engaged from morning to night; and since my return hence I have suffered from an old complaint inflammation in the eyes which has kept me almost entirely from the use of the pen; and this I am sure you will deem a sufficient excuse for my apparent inattention. With the best wishes for yourself and all your family especially the young Lady who was inclined to give vent to her feelings in a strain so creditable to her heart, I am ever

dear Madam
Sincerely your's
Wm Wordsworth

[1] Other American callers this summer (*RMVB*) included George Sumner, brother of Charles Sumner the jurist (the latter a visitor in 1838), and Bronson Alcott (1799–1888), the Transcendentalist, who delivered a letter from Elizabeth Peabody (*WL MSS.*).

[2] The American poetess (see pt. iii, L. 1184 and L. 1452 above).

[3] Mary Sigourney (1827–89), who later married the Revd. Francis Thayer Russell, Professor of Elocution at the General Theological Seminary, New York. In fact, the verses were not by her, but by Mrs. Sigourney herself, as she noted in the third edition of her *Pleasant Memories of Pleasant Lands*.

1639. W. W. to [?] CHARLES JAMES BLOMFIELD[1]

MS. Mr. Mark Reed. Hitherto unpublished.

Rydal Mount
Septr 8th 42.

. . .upon my Brother's acc[?ount] [ ] extract of my letter was published, in which I mentioned *him*. He has occupied a most important and eminent Station in England that of Master of the first of our Colleges, and therefore might be exposed to injurious comments in some [? quarters] as having looked out [? for preferment] . . .

I remain my dear Bishop
faithfully yours
Wm Wordsworth

1640. W. W. to THE GOVERNORS OF WARWICK SCHOOL[2]

MS. McGill University Library. Hitherto unpublished.

Rydal Mount
15th Septr 1842.

The Revd Herbert Hill[3] having intimated to me that he is a Candidate for the vacant mastership of Warwick School, I deem myself fortunate in being enabled from personal knowledge to speak to the character of one so estimable as a Clergyman, a Scholar and a Gentleman. Mr Hill has been my near neighbour for the last three years, during two and a half of which he has served the Chapel of Rydal with fervent piety, guided by sound judgement.

Mr Hill is practised in tuition, having been for some time private Tutor in the family of the late Dr Arnold, who has frequently in my hearing spoken of his abilities and conduct as a teacher with admiration, and the most affectionate regard. Since he resided in Rydal Mr Hill has had several pupils under his care;

[1] This damaged fragment seems to refer to the offer of the Deanery of Peterborough to C. W. (see L. 1653 below).

[2] The Royal Grammar School, Warwick, an ancient foundation said to pre-date the Norman Conquest.

[3] Southey's son-in-law. The appointment was vested in the Lord Chancellor.

and from my own daily observation I can testify that he was most attentive to his duty; and was, I believe, highly approved of by the Parents who entrusted him with the education of their Sons: I may venture to say in conclusion that Mr Hill appears to me well qualified to fill the office for which he is a Candidate.

Wm Wordsworth

1641. W. W. to CORNELIUS NICHOLSON[1]

Address: Mr C. Nicholson, Kendal.
MS. untraced.
Cornelia Nicholson, A Well-Spent Life. Memoir of Cornelius Nicholson, Kendal, 1890.

[*In M. W.'s hand*]

Septr 17, 1842.

Dear Sir,

I know nothing of the derivation of the name Hutchin—My Wife's family name is Hutchinson. The present head of the family George Hutchinson Esqr[2] resides at Whitton near Stockton upon Tees where his Family have been long settled and I am inclined to think he could give you some information upon that subject and would I believe have pleasure in doing so.

Col Hutchinson[3] one of the Persons who signed the Death warrant of Ch: the 1st was a Gentleman of fortune and consideration and lived in one of the Midland Counties, probably Nottinghamshire. Perhaps his genealogy may be found in the Memoirs of his celebrated wife Lucy[4]—It might be well also to consult the recent account of the Gentry of England by a writer whose name I forget but it begins with a B[5]—

[1] The Kendal publisher and antiquarian (see pt. iii, L. 935).

[2] George Thomas Hutchinson (b. 1794), of Whitton, a second cousin of M. W. He married Elizabeth, daughter of Capt. John Mercer in 1826.

[3] Col. John Hutchinson (1615–64), the parliamentarian, of Owthorpe, Notts. The family originally came from Yorkshire.

[4] Lucy (b. 1620), daughter of Sir Allen Apsley, Lieutenant-Governor of the Tower, married Col. Hutchinson in 1638. For her *Memoirs* of her husband, see *MY* i. 133, 140.

[5] John Burke (1787–1848), the genealogist, first issued his *Peerage and Baronetage* in 1826, and his *Genealogical and Heraldic History of the Commoners of Great Britain and Ireland* appeared between 1833 and 1838. In subsequent editions the work was given the name by which it is known today, *A Dictionary of the Landed Gentry*.

I would take this opportunity thro you of suggesting that more than one person has expressed a wish to me to have a Glossary of local designations attached to his Book of the Lakes, and an explanation of such terminations as thwaite and others that frequently occur. The late Mr Thompson[1] of Kendal published several Papers upon this subject, and it would be useful to refer to them.

I remain d^r Sir
Sincerely yours
Wm Wordsworth

1642. W. W. to SAMUEL WILKINSON

MS. Harvard University Library.
LY iii. 1137.

Rydal Mount Sepr 21st [1842]

Dear Sir

Many thanks for your communication and the accompanying Letter. Your purpose seems judiciously fulfilled;[2] only I have ventured upon the other leaf of this sheet to submit one or two remarks to your consideration which you will be so kind as to excuse. The whole I willingly leave to yourself.

Be assured that I deeply sympathize with you in what you have said upon the persecution which the Oxford Divines are undergoing;[3] but happily little of it reached my ears among these

[1] See *MY* ii. 442. Cornelius Nicholson acknowledged John Thompson's help with etymologies in the Preface to his *Annals of Kendal*, 1832.

[2] Wilkinson (see L. 1630 above) had now submitted to W. W. his proposed article on 'Contributions of W. Wordsworth to the Revival of Catholic Truth'. He argued that the tone of W. W.'s writings had done more to restore a sounder state of feeling on religious matters than any direct allusions to Catholic doctrines; but he went on to quote a number of passages from *The Excursion* and subsequent volumes to show that the Tractarian doctrines which were now being branded as Popish had quite recently been part of the creed of those whose zeal for the Anglican Church was irreproachable, and he concluded by quoting W. W.'s tribute to the Oxford Movement in a note appended to *Musings Near Aquapendente*, in *Poems, Chiefly of Early and Late Years* (see *PW* iii. 493). H. C. R., however, was incensed by this Tractarian attempt to claim W. W. as *their* poet. '. . . they have published a selection from his works, with a dishonest preface from wch one might infer he went all lengths with them—' (Morley, i. 472).

[3] W. W. is probably thinking of the treatment of Isaac Williams over the Poetry Professorship at the beginning of this year (see L. 1566 above).

mountains. I scarcely ever look into a periodical work except it be a daily newspaper. And Pamphlets I never see except such as are now and then sent me by their Authors. With none of the Tractarians have I a personal acquaintance, except Mr Keble[1] be one; he is I am sure as meek and humble minded a christian as is anywhere to be found—Differing in one particular from you I rather think that I should better serve the cause we have in common, were I to abstain from what you recommend. It would seem to enroll me as a partisan; and the support which I might otherwise give to Catholic truth would, I fear, in numerous quarters, be impaired accordingly.—Highly approving your object, I most heartily wish your publication success. Believe me dear Sir with high respect

sincerely yours
Wm Wordsworth

P.S. I have just added 4 sonnets to the ecclesiastical Series, upon the marriage ceremony, upon thanksgiving after childbirth, upon the visitation of the sick, and upon the funeral service. These were wanting to complete the notice of the English Liturgy. I have interwoven also, three others,[2] tending to qualify or mitigate the condemnation which by conscience I am compelled to pass upon the abuses of the Roman See.—

[*In M. W.'s hand*]

Errata and Corrections

See the article headed Childhood—

'And part far from them sweetest melodies'[3] dele and

Towards the close of the Ex. from the Abbey of S[t] Bees, is a line with which I have always been dissatisfied—

'She in her own would merge the Eternal will'[4]

I should like it to be corrected thus

[1] John Keble and his wife had called on W. W. towards the end of July (*RMVB*), in the course of a tour of the Lakes. Other high-church visitors this summer included Roundell Palmer, later 1st Earl of Selborne (1812–95), who came with Faber, and Robert Aston Coffin (1819–85), who followed Newman into the Roman Catholic Church (*RMVB*).

[2] Nos. ii, ix, and x in the Second Part (*PW* iii. 362, 365–6).

[3] *Personal Talk* (*PW* iv. 73), l. 25.

[4] *Stanzas Suggested in a Steamboat Off St. Bees' Heads* (*PW* iv. 25), l. 159. W. W. did not finally adopt the alternative reading suggested here.

She sinks, Idolatress of formal skill,
In her own systems Gods eternal will

The Ex: that follows seems scarcely intelligible, so much being omitted and not having a more definite title than Imaginative Regrets—What do you say to substituting the lines towards the bottom of the 297 Page in the 8th Book of the Excursion.

'of old

Our Ancestors etc[1]

Spiritual Attendance

The Soul~~s~~ to purer worlds'[2] dele s

Bruges

'A deeper peace than in the desert~~s~~ found'[3]

This line stands than *that* in deserts found

Than *that*, I feel to be prosaic, perhaps you have altered it on that account. In this case dele the s in deserts

Musings near Aquapendente

As she survives in union — — dele. r. ruin[4]
and below, for '*suffer* religious faith' read suffer*s*
I am loth to object to any mode of circulating the Cumberland Beggar, as I believe that Poem has done much good. But your general object being what it is, does not seem sufficiently appropriate—there is little I hope in my poetry that does not breathe more or less in a religious atmosphere; as these verses certainly do, but if you were to take as wide a range as this Ex: leads to, one scarcely sees why it should be selected in preference to many others. Would you object to substitute for it the beginning of the 6th Book of the Excursion—or an Ex: from the close of the preceding one, as having a more strict connection with your Title.

[1] *Exc.* viii. 185–6 (*PW* v. 271).
[2] *Apology* (*PW* iii. 350), l. 12.
[3] *Bruges* (*PW* iii. 165), l. 14.
[4] i.e. *read* ruin, l. 293. See *PW* iii. 210.

1643. W. W. to MARY FRANCES HOWLEY

MS. Lambeth Palace Library. Hitherto unpublished.

Rydal Mount
Sept^{br}[1] 1842

Dear Mrs Howley,

I abstained from breaking in upon you during the time of your sad anxiety; but I trust that it is now in a great measure over and that Mrs Wordsworth and I may with little apprehension present our joint congratulations upon the Archbishop's restoration to health. You may be sure that we thought of you as it became us to do, while the newspapers gave so unfavorable a report from day to day, and much was our joy when better tidings were announced. God grant that there may be no occasion for a different report. This is our earnest prayer both for private and public considerations.

May I beg that you would offer our respectful congratulations to his Grace; and believe me dear Madam, with every good wish in which Mrs Wordsworth unites,

faithfully yours
Wm Wordsworth

We hope that Sir George[2] and the children were well. My Son W^{m} was charmed with the conversation and manners of Constance[3] when he saw her at Lambeth.

1644. W. W. to WILLIAM EWART GLADSTONE

MS. British Library.
LY iii. 1139.

Rydal Mount Septr 29th 42

My dear Mr Gladstone,

I do not write to thank for your kind services,[4] though duly sensible of them, but in fulfilment of an intention put off from

[1] W. W. omitted the day of the month.

[2] Sir George Beaumont. [3] Sir George's daughter.

[4] W. W.'s friends were continuing to explore the possibility of a Government pension to compensate for the loss of income from his Distributorship, and Lord Monteagle had sent in a memorandum of support (see L. 1624 above), which Gladstone forwarded to Peel with a covering letter. 'I say little,' he wrote to

an unwillingness to obtrude my regret upon you at a time when so many inquiries would be made, and so much concern expressed upon the occasion of your late severe accident,[1] so I call it, depending upon the authority of the Newspapers—I may now congratulate you I hope upon all *danger* at least being passed away, and that such inconvenience as you have to suffer, will neither cause you pain, nor interfere with your usefulness. God grant that it may be so!

Believe me, with kind regards to Mrs Gladstone
faithfully your much obliged
Wm Wordsworth

1645. W. W. to SIR AUBREY DE VERE

MS. untraced.
S. M. P. Reilly, Aubrey de Vere, Victorian Observer, 1956, p. 37.

[30 Sept. 1842]

. . .I am confident that unless the critique[2] has been mispresented to me the time is not distant when my young friend Aubrey de Vere, if he *be* the author, will sincerely repent of having been so far misled as to write in such a strain. . .

[*cetera desunt*]

W. W. on the 28th, 'because it would have been presumptuous in me, and injurious to you and to him, if I had entered into anything like pleadings on your behalf.' (*WL MSS.*) See also L. 1649 below.

[1] On 18 Sept., when Gladstone was out shooting, the second barrel of his gun went off while he was reloading, and shattered the forefinger of his left hand.

[2] A review of Tennyson in the *Quarterly*, (see L. 1659 below), which W. W. mistakenly supposed was the work of Aubrey de Vere, who had recently stayed at Rydal Mount.

1646. W. W. to SAMUEL WILKINSON

Address: The Editor of the Christian's Miscellany, Leeds.
MS. Harvard University Library.
LY iii. 1139.

Rydal Mount, Oct^{br} 1st [1842]

Dear Sir,

As October is come, I fear I am too late in directing your attention to an important error of the Press which I have this moment discovered in looking over your Extracts from my Poems.[1] The Extract is headed

Antient Literature

The error 'shun' for 'skim'[2]

Upon looking over the Extract from the Cumberland Beggar, I regret having stated any objection to it, as it was already in type. I find it is more in the Spirit of several of the things selected than I was aware of. Pray excuse my over-haste in passing the former judgement.

Yesterday I looked over your Extracts from my friend Mr Coleridge. They cannot but do good. Is the Circulation of your Miscellany extensive?

I remain, my dear Sir, with great respect
sincerely yours
Wm Wordsworth

P.S. This Letter must be sent off immediately if I would save the Post, and unfortunately I cannot lay my hand upon your Letter, so that I am obliged to direct at random.

To S. Wilkinson.

[1] See L. 1642 above.

[2] *Exc.* iii. 135.

1647. W. W. to MARTIN FARQUHAR TUPPER[1]

MS. Illinois University Library.
Derek Hudson, Martin Tupper, His Rise and Fall, 1949, p. 35.

[early Oct. 1842]

Dear Sir,

Truly will it gratify me to add a 2nd vol: of your Proverbial Philosophy to that which I owe to your kindness and from which I have derived much both of profit and pleasure.

If your Book be sent under cover to my Publisher Mr Moxon 44 Dover Street, though I shall not probably receive it quite as early as I could wish, it will be sure of reaching me. Mrs Wordsworth to whom I have just read this, suggests that it had better be sent to Mrs Quillinan (my daughter). . . .

[*cetera desunt*]

1648. W. W. to FULKE GREVILLE HOWARD[2]

MS. Cornell. Hitherto unpublished.

[mid-Oct. 1842]

My dear Colonel Howard,

Absence from home, and a contingent engagement to visit my Son at Carlisle have prevented my giving an earlier answer to your acceptable invitation.

I am now at liberty to say that it will give Mrs Wordsworth and myself much pleasure to profit by your proposal of sending your Carriage to meet us at Bowness on Monday the 17th. We shall be there by half past two. It will add much to our pleasure to meet Mr and Mrs Newton[3] whom I well recollect as your

[1] Martin Farquhar Tupper (1810–89), author of *Proverbial Philosophy*, a work which achieved only moderate success on its first appearance in 1838, but which in its expanded form (4 series, 1839–76), became a Victorian best-seller. At least five thousand copies were sold annually for 25 years, and it is said that a million copies were sold in America. Tupper also published novels, plays and ballads, but none of them achieved anything like the phenomenal popularity of his first work, and after a meteoric rise to fame as a purveyor of homespun philosophy he died in comparative obscurity. See also L. 1663 below.

[2] See pt. i, Ls. 203 and 302. W. W. had met Col. Howard again during his visit to London in May (*MW*, p. 252).

[3] Unidentified.

visitors some years ago. With kindest remembrances to Mrs Howard and yourself, in which Mrs Wordsworth unites, I remain

my dear Colonel
very faithfully yours
Wm Wordsworth

1649. W. W. to WILLIAM EWART GLADSTONE

MS. British Library.
K (—). *LY iii. 1140.*

Oct^br 13th —42.

My dear Mr Gladstone,

Allow me to thank you for your last communication.[1] With your and Sir R. Peel's view of Lord Monteagle's proceeding I concur so far as that any wish to benefit me must have prevailed little in his mind compared with the desire of making room for himself by drawing so largely upon that fund for Sir John Newport.[2]

If I should not succeed in obtaining what you have so kindly endeavoured to assist in procuring for me, I must be content; and should the pension come, it would be most welcome both as a mark of public approbation and as preventing for the future the necessity of my looking more nearly to my expenditure than I have been accustomed to do.

[1] Gladstone had written on 11 Oct. (*WL MSS.*) to report on Peel's reaction to Lord Monteagle's memorandum (see L. 1644 above), which Peel (in his letter to Gladstone on the 10th) had described as 'a shabby act'. 'He and his friends did nothing for Mr. Wordsworth. They granted seven or eight hundred per annum last year to the music masters and Dancing masters who had attended the Queen in her youth, and now Lord Monteagle wants to get himself the credit of being instrumental in procuring a Pension for Mr Wordsworth.' To Peel's request for more information about W. W.'s financial circumstances, Gladstone replied on the 11th—the same day as his letter to W. W.—that his means were much curtailed, adding 'I deem it a great honour to take part, in any manner, in giving effect to ideas so strictly just as these appear to be, upon which you propose to proceed: even were the subject of consideration a person of less merit than Mr Wordsworth.' And he sent more details of W. W.'s income on the 13th, after consulting Moxon (*British Library MSS.*). See also next letters.

[2] Sir John Newport (1756–1843), Irish Whig politician: comptroller-general of the exchequer, 1834–9.

At all events I shall ever retain a grateful and most pleasing remembrance of your exertions to serve me upon this occasion; nor can I fail to be much gratified by the recollection of Sir R. Peel's favorable Opinion of my claims.

I wish you had mentioned whether you suffer pain from your late accident and whether it causes you much inconvenience.—I hope not.

Believe me, my dear Mr Gladstone,

faithfully, your much obliged
Wm Wordsworth

1650. W. W. to SIR ROBERT PEEL[1]

MS. British Library.
Sir Robert Peel from his Private Papers, iii. 438 (—).

Rydal Mount
Octr 17th 1842

Dear Sir Robert,

The provision that has been offered me as a mark of favor from the Crown consequent upon your recommendation I accept with entire satisfaction. It will prove a substantial addition to my comforts for the remainder of my life; and coming as the reward of literary merit from One so eminent in every respect as yourself the gratification is above measure enhanced. Let me add, that the considerate delicacy with which you have stated in your letter every thing bearing upon this Grant,[2] and the terms in which you express yourself towards me personally, have affected me more than I could find words to utter, had I courage to seek for them.

Fervently wishing you long continuance of health and

[1] Peel had written to Gladstone on 14 Oct., on hearing from him about W. W.'s straitened circumstances, that 'The whole Sum which I have available that is free from engagements is £600 and I shall feel perfectly justified considering the eminence of Mr Wordsworth, and above all considering the character of his works, in allotting one half of this Sum to him as a pension for life.' The following day he wrote to W. W. in these terms. (*British Library MSS.*)

[2] 'I need scarcely add', Peel had written, 'that the acceptance by you of this mark of favour from the Crown, considering the grounds on which it is proposed, will impose no Restraint upon your perfect Independence, and involve no obligation of a personal nature.'

Strength to preside over the government of our Country and to direct the public Measures, I remain dear Sir Robert, for this and other tokens of your esteem, with sincere gratitude

your much obliged
Wm Wordsworth

1651. W. W. to WILLIAM EWART GLADSTONE

Endorsed: *O*[1] 17/42 Mr Wordsworth.
MS. British Library.
K. LY iii. 1141.

Rydal Mount, Oct 17th 42.

My dear Mr Gladstone,

I do not lose a moment in letting you know that Sir Robert Peel has made me an offer of a Pension of £300 per ann: for my life, and in terms which have above measure enhanced the satisfaction I feel upon the occasion.

I will not run the risk of offending you by a renewal of thanks for your good offices in bringing this about, but will content myself with breathing sincere and fervent good wishes for your welfare.[2] Believe me, my dear Mr Gladstone,

faithfully yours
Wm Wordsworth

[1] i.e. October.

[2] Gladstone replied on 18 Oct. that he had just learnt of the offer made to W. W.: 'The whole transaction, as I feel, is scarcely more honourable to you, than to Sir Robert Peel and to the Country.' (*WL MSS.*) The award of the pension also gave pleasure to W. W.'s other supporters. 'I assure you', Peel wrote to Lord Lonsdale on 20 Oct., 'with perfect sincerity that if any thing could have added to the satisfaction which I derived from the opportunity of encreasing the ease and comfort of the declining years of Mr Wordsworth, it was the knowledge that *you* fully estimated his worth and his claims on public gratitude.' (*British Library MSS.*)

1652. W. W. to H. C. R.

MS. WL transcript.[1]

[17 Oct. 1842]

. . . And now for a piece of good news relating to myself. Yesterday I received a letter from Sir Robert Peel offering me a grant of £300 per ann: from the civil list for my life, and nothing could surpass in considerate delicacy the language in which the offer was made . . . .

[*cetera desunt*]

1653. W. W. to C. W.

MS. WL.
LY iii. 1141.

Rydal 17th Octbr [1842][2]

My dear Brother,

Sir Robert Peel in the most handsome terms has just made me an offer of a grant from the Civil List of 300£ per ann—for my life. You will be glad to hear this, above all as it leaves both Wm and me at ease respecting any insufficiency of my income.

I should have written more at length but we are just setting out upon a visit to Colonel and Mrs Howard[3] at Levens, and I do not like to lose a Post. The Bishop of London told me that the Deanery of Peterborough was offered to you,[4] was it so? I wish that dear Christopher might have the Regius Professorship of Divinity offered to him,[5] as it would suit his health much better

[1] Quoted in a letter of W. Strickland Cookson to W. W. jnr., Hampstead, 5 Dec. 1868.

[2] Year added by C. W.

[3] See L. 1648 above.

[4] See also L. 1639 above.

[5] 'The object itself is *the* one which, as far as anything human can be, has been the aim of my life, as that for which I most wished to live, and to spend my life upon', C. W. jnr. wrote to Joshua Watson on 6 Oct. (*Christopher Wordsworth, Bishop of Lincoln*, p. 101), and his failure to secure the appointment was, according to his daughter, 'perhaps *the* great disappointment' of his life. The successful candidate was the Revd. Alfred Ollivant, D.D., (1798–1882), another Trinity man, who occupied the Chair until 1849, when he was appointed Bishop of Llandaff.

than does his present situation. Pray do you hear about the state of his health, we are anxious but do not like to enquire either of himself or his wife. Mary is well, dearest Sister continues much the same.

In great haste
ever affectionately yours
Wm Wordsworth

Pray correct in one of the Sonnets sent you, the one upon thanks after childbirth, thus, 'a glance of Mind cast upon this observance may renew'[1]

1654. W. W. to EDWARD QUILLINAN

MS. British Library.
LY iii. 1142 (—).

Levens 18th Oct^r—42.

My dear Mr Quillinan

Mrs Wordsworth, not unauthorized, having mentioned that I proposed to write you a few lines after I had read Mr Taylor's play,[2] I sit down with that intention. And first let me say that I did not look into your reviewal of it till I had read the two acts to which such observations of yours, as we have seen, refer. In all that you condemn I entirely concur, and approve of the reverence with which your disapprobation is expressed; as I am pretty sure that it arose out of your personal relations to the author, and from an unwillingness to hurt Miss Fenwick's feelings. Of the impression which the whole play has made upon my mind, with much pain, I must tell you, that I regret that it was ever written. It shews great command of language, however, and in the versification there is much skill, though, owing to the want of trochaic endings in the lines, it is very often rather fit for didactic or epic poetry than the dramatic. [In] the play also are some particular passages that are very happy, but they are rather incidental than a part of the action, and

[1] See *PW* iii. 397. C. W. had written about the new sonnets on 6 Sept.: 'We read them, in common assembly, with very great pleasure; and I do not doubt, when they attain their own Station among the Ecclesiastical Sonnets, they will add greatly to the benefits which, age after age, will continue to be derived from that invaluable Series.' (*WL MSS.*)

[2] *Edwin the Fair.*

throughout the whole there are striking manifestations of talent; but alas it is talent prostrated or thrown away. The subject is most unfortunately chosen, and it is still more unfortunately treated, in fact, it has betrayed the Author. Religion he has truly said in his preface is a source which will naturally be looked to by one who would deal with the profound feelings of the human heart and the worthiest aspirations of the Soul. Something to this effect he has said; but it is not such religion as this play is conversant with. A dispute between Regulars and Seculars if conducted with ten times Mr Taylor's knowledge of the question would but little affect the Reader or Spectator in these days, and as it is managed by him it is wholly uninteresting. You care for neither side; you have neither wish nor anxiety about them. And as to Dunstan the hero he is a piece of incongruity, nay of impossibility throughout. His mode of proceeding as you mention is taken from reports of dealings ascribed to him by his enemies; and these wretched tricks and devices are wholly incompatible with that compass and even grandeur of mind with which Mr Taylor has endeavoured to endow him; I say endeavoured for nothing can be more vague and obscure than the speeches put into Dunstan's mouth where he gives vent to his notions of a spiritual and everlasting Church. On my judgement such meanness as he works by cannot coexist with elevation of mind; or if it be possible, we may confidently affirm that the character is utterly unfit for dramatic exhibition. That scene of the mimic cross is unendurably profane in itself, and still more if possible is the Author to be condemned, for making the Almighty a party to his own dishonour by representing him (Dunstan does it) as sanctioning such mechanical expedients by his own practice. In all these feelings Mrs Wordsworth more than shares; and again I say that I deeply lament that Mr Taylor should have produced such a work. Of other faults there is abundance; the love-concerns are mere excrescences; and there are far too many of them, though Lyulf's account of his own passion is the gem of the Play. Wolstan and his Daughter, a wanton Lyar and Impostor (Miss Byers)[1] are both excrescences, though Wolstan's speech about the voice of the wind is very pretty, and in fact the most poetical thing in the play; but enough. How Mr Taylor could think that with a story so uninteresting, people would take the trouble of learning who

[1] Presumably W. W. is quoting the view of a mutual acquaintance of theirs.

was who, in such a mob of dramatis Personae, I should be at a loss to conceive were I not aware that Shakespeare has seduced him into the practice—but alas, alas!

You would be delighted with the news of my Pension—the Letter[1] of Sir Robert was a masterpiece, you shall see it some time or other. Dearest Dora, this Letter if you think worth while to read it is for you also.

What a blessing was your escape from that horrible fire. Love to all. ever faithfully yours

W Wordsworth

1655. W. W. to ELLEN RICKETTS[2]

MS. Berg Collection, New York Public Library.
LY iii. 1144 (—).

Rydal Mount
Oct[b] 22[d] —42

Thanks, dear Miss Ricketts, in the name of Mrs W. and myself, for your kind consideration of us upon the approaching winter season. Your neckcloth will be put to proof on Monday; for on that day we shall cross Kirkstone on our road to Mr Marshall's and to Carlisle in an open carriage. How lucky should we be as to propose staying a week with our Son in Carlisle, if Anna should pass through during our stay there, though we might only have a peep at her for a moment.

Let us also avail ourselves of this Letter to thank Mrs Ricketts for her elegant Present of the marble Inkstand, which from the value attached to it as a memorial of her friendship we shall find not unworthy of making a companion to others which we prize for the Donor's sake, and one I expect, viz—a fac simile in Italian marble of Ariosto's Inkstand—

Dear Miss Fenwick reached Rydal in good health,—which continues; though she seems to think herself not quite so strong for walking as she was when she left this place.

Mrs W. is now at work with the 4th Vol. of Madame D'Arblay[3]—I had read a good deal of it before and liked it better

[1] See L. 1650 above.

[2] Sister of Anna Ricketts.

[3] *Diary and Letters of Madame d'Arblay (1778–1840)*. Edited by her niece, 7 vols., 1842–6.

than the preceding ones. Her vanity is provoking, but when one has got over that, there is a great deal of interest to be found in it.

With kind and affectionate regards to your mother and yourself and Miss Fenwick I remain dear Ellen, for so I will call you

faithfully your much obliged
W Wordsworth

1656. W. W. to ELIZABETH BARRETT

Address: Miss Barrett, 50 Wimpole Street, London. [*In M. W.'s hand*]
MS. Berg Collection, New York Public Library.
K. LY iii. 1144 (—).

Rydal Mount
Oct^br 26th—42

Dear Miss Barrett,

Through our common friend Mr Haydon I have received a Sonnet[1] which his portrait of me suggested; I should have thanked you sooner for this effusion of a feeling towards myself, with which I am much gratified, but I have been absent from home and much occupied.

The conception of your Sonnet is in full accordance with the Painter's intended work, and the expression vigorous; yet the word 'ebb' though I do not myself object to it, nor wish to have it altered, will I fear prove obscure to nine readers out of ten.

'A vision free
And noble, Haydon, hath thine Art released,'[2]

[1] Miss Barrett's sonnet, inspired by Haydon's *Wordsworth on Helvellyn* (see L. 1622 above), was published in the *Athenaeum* on 29 Oct. 'You have brought me Wordsworth and Helvellyn into this dark and solitary room!', she wrote gratefully to the artist when he sent the picture for her to see; and she wrote again to Haydon after receiving this letter from W. W.: 'I am obliged to you—obliged to your picture!—and the superabundance of my good humour expends itself even on my sonnet because that caught the light of the poet's countenance "as it *fell*".' See Iris Origo, 'Additions to the Keats Collection', *TLS*, 23 Apr. 1970.

[2] The published version of the sonnet ends as follows:

A noble vision free
Our Haydon's hand has flung out from the mist!
No portrait this with academic air!
This is the poet and his poetry.

Owing to the want of inflections in our language the construction here is obscure. Would it not be a little [? better] thus?—I was going to write a small change in the order of the words, but I find it would not remove the objection. The verse as I take it, would be somewhat clearer thus, if you could tolerate the redundant syllable

By a vision free
And noble, Haydon, is thine Art released—

I had the gratification of receiving a good while ago, two copies of a volume of your writing,[1] which I have read with much pleasure, and beg that the thanks which I charged a Friend to offer may be repeated through you.

It grieved me much to hear from Mr Kenyon, and now also from Mr Haydon that your health is so much deranged. But for that cause I should have presumed to call upon you when I was in London last Spring.

With every good wish I remain dear Miss Barrett

Your much obliged
Wm Wordsworth

1657. W. W. to UNKNOWN CORRESPONDENT[2]

MS. Trinity College, Cambridge. Hitherto unpublished.

Carlisle—Oct[br] 31st 1842.

My dear Sir,

Your kind Letter of congratulation has followed me to this place, where I am on a visit to my Son. Though you are well aware that persons in high official Situations find it an easy task to write complimentary Letters to those to whom they have done favors, yet I am sure you will be gratified by hearing that the terms on which Sir Robert conveyed to me the intelligence of what he had recommended on my behalf were distinguished

[1] Either *The Seraphim, and other poems* (see pt. iii, L. 1273), or her translation of the *Prometheus Bound* (*R.M.Cat.*, no. 623).

[2] Perhaps A. P. Stanley (see pt. iii, Ls. 1027 and 1328), now Fellow of University College, Oxford, who had been appointed biographer of Dr. Arnold and spent August at Ambleside with his friend W. C. Lake, advising the Fox How family and visiting W. W. (*RMVB*).

by the most considerate delicacy and greatly enhanced in my estimation the value of the benefit.—

Be assured that I deemed myself fortunate in seeing so much of you as I did during your residence among us last Summer; and that I shall rejoice in any opportunity that may occur for cultivating your kind regards.

Believe me my dear Sir
faithfully yours
Wm Wordsworth

1658. W. W. to SIR JOHN TAYLOR COLERIDGE

Endorsed: 1842 Novr 11th W. Wordsworth Rydal Mt.
MS. British Library.
K (—). *LY iii. 1146* (—).

Rydal Mount
11th Novr 1842

My dear Mr Justice Coleridge,

The interest you take in the provision[1] which Sir R. Peel has recommended to the Crown—to grant me for the remainder of my life, is highly gratifying. This surrender of income which I had thought it right to make on behalf of my Son, reduced my means so much, that without this accession, he would have been haunted by apprehensions that his Parents were straitened on his account. That fear is now removed, and he will feel as we do that for the remainder of our days we are quite at ease. I need scarcely say that the Intelligence of this mark of royal favor was conveyed to me in the most handsome terms possible by Sir Robert Peel, which greatly enhanced its value, and I may add that I have abundant reason for believing that the country is well satisfied with what has been done on my behalf.

I was prepared by my Daughter Mrs Quillinan who is now with us, for the sad tidings your Letter conveys. Your Brother[2] will be a great loss, to his Profession, to the World, and to his relatives and friends and above all to his dear and excellent Wife. In this Hour we all feel most deeply for her, and indeed for you and his other near connections. Towards Sarah I have much of

[1] See L. 1650 above.

[2] Henry Nelson Coleridge was now dying of spinal paralysis. See also L. 1668 below.

the tenderness of a Father, having had her so near to us and so long under our eye, while she was growing up and afterwards when circumstances brought her by necessity habitually to our thoughts. God will support her, for a more excellent Creature is not to be found.

Your poor Brother! I grieve indeed for his bodily sufferings, and pray that his patience may be equal to the bearing of them, and that he may be empowered sometimes to thank the Supreme Disposer of events for the suffering he has inflicted.

This Dr Arnold was enabled to do but his trial was very short, though most severe while it lasted; Henry's is awfully prolonged. If it would be right to communicate to him our sympathy, and to say that he is in our prayers, let it be done, either through yourself my dear Friend, or in any other way you think best.

We have at present a sick house. Mrs Wordsworth is under that tedious complaint the jaundice, my Daughter is suffering from one of her severest colds, and one of our most valued servants[1] is confined to her bed, but we look cheerfully to the recovery of them all. With many thanks for your affectionate Letter, and kindest regards to yourself and Lady Coleridge, I remain my dear Sir, most faithfully your obliged Friend,

Wm Wordsworth

I see Mrs Arnold and her family very often, she bears up wonderfully under her affliction. Her parental duties, and the love she has for the place[2] and the interest she takes in it, furnish her with constant employment, and the revered memory of her Husband is through God's grace a perpetual support to her.

1659. W. W. to AUBREY DE VERE

MS. untraced.
Recollections of Aubrey de Vere, pp. 126–9. LY iii. 1385.

Rydal Mount, Nov. 16, 1842

My dear Mr de Vere,—Every day since I received your kind letter, I wished to write to you, and most days have resolved to do so; but in vain, so inveterate is the habit of procrastination with me in these matters. I have only, therefore, to throw myself upon your indulgence, as I am so often obliged to do

[1] Jane, the housemaid. See Morley, i. 470. [2] Fox How.

with all my other friends. First, let me express my pleasure in learning that I had been misinformed concerning the article in 'The Quarterly'.[1] The thing I have not read, nor probably ever shall read; but it grieved me to think, from what I heard of it, that it should be written by any friend of mine, for whom I have so much regard, and whom I esteem as highly as yourself. And I was the more concerned upon these occasions because the only disparaging notices which I have ever cared the least for, unfortunately have ever come from persons with whom I have lived in close intimacy. And this occurred in several remarkable instances. Now, though I am far from supposing that everyone who likes me shall think well of my poetry, yet I do think that openness of dealing is necessary before a friend undertakes to decry one's writings to the world at large. But too much of this. Not till a couple of days ago did I hear of the volume of your poems[2] which you designed for myself, lying at Mr Taylor's for several months. But Mr Quillinan will be down here in a week or ten days, to join his wife, who is here with us, and will bring the book with him. Miss Fenwick, who is now under our roof

[1] 'Poems by Alfred Tennyson', *Quarterly Review*, lxx (Sept. 1842), 385–416. W. W. had mistakenly supposed that the author was Aubrey de Vere (see L. 1645 above), but he had denied the authorship in a letter to W. W. of 4 Oct. (*WL MSS.*) The article was in fact by John Sterling (see L. 1575 above). In pleading for a poetry equal to the demands of the new age, he praised Byron's *Don Juan* as 'a splendid attempt at a creative survey of modern life', but maintained that W. W., for all his grandeur, was too absorbed in his own meditations to convey what lay in the world outside. 'The present movements of human life, nay its varied and spontaneous joys, to him are little, save so far as they afford a text for a mind, in which fixed will, and stern speculation, and a heart austere and measured even in its pity, are far more obvious powers than fancy, emotion, or keen and versatile sympathy. He discourses indeed with divine wisdom of life and nature, and all their sweet and various impulses; but the impression of his own great calm judicial soul is always far too mighty for any all-powerful feeling of the objects he presents to us.' He contrasted Tennyson's idylls with *Michael* and the tale of Margaret, where 'The feelings are described, rather than shared; the tragic passions summoned up, only to be rebuked by a more solemn conjuration than their own; the free enjoyment of life and nature approved only within the bounds of unrelaxing caution; and love . . . a grave ritual sound, spoken over the still waters drawn from the well of Truth, for a penitential baptism.' (*Essays and Tales*, i. 422–62). In his letter to W. W., de Vere had commended Tennyson's latest poems, 'which I think you would approve of much more than you did of his earlier works.'

[2] *The Waldenses and other poems.*

for the winter, has read the volume with much pleasure, especially the Hymns. Upon her coming here she lent it to Mr Faber, as we have all been paying visits up and down as far as Halsteads and Carlisle. But then we are settling down in quiet for the winter, and your poems will be among the first I shall peruse. But, alas, the state of my eyes curtails my reading hours very much in these short days. Your father's 'Sonnets',[1] and Mr Taylor's 'Tragedy',[2] are the only verse I have read for many months. If the expression, especially in point of truthfulness, were equal in your father's poems to the sanctity and weight of the thoughts, they would be all that one could desire in that style of writing. But in respect to your father's poems, your own, and all other new productions in verse, whether of my friends or of strangers, I ought frankly to avow that the time is past with me for bestowing that sympathy to which they are entitled. For many reasons connected with advanced life, I read but little of new works either in prose or verse. Rogers says of me, partly in joke and partly in earnest, as he says of himself and others as frankly, and has avowed in one of his letters written when he was an old man, 'I read no poetry now but my own'. In respect to myself, my good old friend ought to have added that if I do read my own, it is mainly, if not entirely, to make it better. But certain it is that old men's literary pleasures lie chiefly among the books they were familiar with in their youth; and this is still more pointedly true of men who have practised composition themselves. They have fixed notions of style and of versification and their thoughts have moved on in a settled train so long that novelty in each or all of these, so far from being a recommendation, is distasteful to them, even though, if hard put to it, they might be brought to confess that the novelty was all improvement. You must be perfectly aware of all that I have said, as characteristic of human nature to a degree which scarcely allows of exceptions, though rigidity or obtuseness will prevail more in some minds than in others. For myself, however, I have many times, when called upon to give an opinion on works sent, felt obliged to recommend younger critics as more to be relied upon, and that for the reason I have mentioned. It is in vain to regret these changes which Time brings with it; one might as well sigh over one's grey hairs. Let me, with Mason, the poet, say:

[1] *A Song of Faith, Devotional Exercises, and Sonnets.*

[2] *Edwin the Fair.*

'As my winter, like the year's, is mild,
Give thanks to Him from whom all blessings flow.'[1]

You enquire after my MS. poem on my own life. It is lying, and in all probability will lie, where my 'Tragedy', and other 'Poems' lay ambushed for more than a generation of years. Publication was ever to me most irksome; so that if I had been rich, I question whether I should ever have published at all, though I believe I should have written. I am pleased that you find some things to like in my last volume.[2] It has called out a good deal of sorry criticism, as in truth happens to all my publications in succession and will do so as long as anything of mine comes forth. With respect to my last volume I feel no interest but that those who deem it worth while to *study* anything I write would read the contents of that volume, as the prelude hints, in connection with its predecessors.

Throwing myself upon your kind indulgence for having deferred this letter so long, I remain, with high regard,

Faithfully yours,
William Wordsworth

[1] William Mason's Sonnet vii, *Anniversary*, written on his 72nd birthday, 23 Feb. 1796 (misquoted).

[2] Aubrey de Vere had written, 'I have found that many of its finer harmonies had escaped me in the din of town and that the greater quietude of a country life is necessary in order fully to enjoy many parts of your poetry.' He singled out for praise *The Cuckoo at Laverna* and the versions of Chaucer: 'In the midst of your poems those two of Chaucer look to me like two vernal branches white with blossom blown by some casual wind into the gold and crimson boughs of an autumnal tree. . . . It seems to me that in your poetry more than of most poets we gain from the *number* of poems given to us. We are thus presented with your thoughts in many phases: and it is only thus, that we can learn to think of your works as constituting in fact one great work inspired by one spirit ebbing and flowing through it.'

1660. W. W. to EDWARD MOXON

MS. Henry E. Huntington Library.
LY iii. 1147.

[*In Dora Q.'s hand*]

Monday m^g,
Nov. 21st [1842]

My dear Mr Moxon,

Thanks for your check for £100 w^h was well timed as the same post brought me a demand of £18 — something, for fees and stamps incident to my Pension. I have not abandoned all thought of a 2 vol^d Ed^n but suspended the project till the 7 vols: now before the public are so near being sold out as to make it probable they would be so before the one vol. Ed^n would be published. I cant make up my mind to losing what would be lost to us by the cessation of sale of the 7 vols. w^h would take place upon issuing the one.

When you have sufficient reason for thinking that all the copies on hand would be disposed of in regular course of sale before the one vol: could be carried thro' the press pray let me know telling me at the same time the number of copies on hand both of the 6 vols and the one last published.

Your fellow Traveller's[1] health was much improved by his excursion. We expect him here in a few days—his family are all now in pretty good health.

With kind remembrances to yourself, Mrs Moxon and your Sister in w^h Mrs Wordsworth and Mrs Quillinan unite

I remain my dear Mr Moxon
faithfully yours
[*signed*] Wm Wordsworth

I wish you had mentioned y^r children about whom we are all much interested.

Pray remember us all very affec^ly to Miss Lamb when you see her.

[1] John W.

1661. W. W. to UNKNOWN CORRESPONDENT

MS. National Library of Scotland. Hitherto unpublished.

[*In Dora Q.'s hand*]

Rydal Mount
Dec. 1st 1842

Sir,

I am sorry to be under the necessity of confirming the unfavorable report of Mr. Southey's health—His disease in the opinion of his Physicians is a softening of the brain thro' which the mind has failed and the body along with it so that for neither is there the least hope of recovery—His friends under these distressing circumstances are comforted by a belief that he suffers little or no pain

I am Sir
yr obet Servant
[*signed*] Wm Wordsworth

1662. W. W. to THOMAS POWELL[1]

MS. untraced.
Bookseller's Catalogue.

Rydal 9 Dec [?1842]

. . . which I have read, and think it written with spirit and feeling manifested by many happy touches of expression which do the Author no little credit . . . I am much too advanced in life to be a proper recipient of the Verses of Authors so far my juniors. An old Man has great difficulty in accomodating himself to novelties of versification and style, and cannot therefore be a fair judge of the merits of performances which in these respects differ widely from what his ear and his taste have been accustomed to . . .

[1] Thanking him for *The Count de Foix*, 1842.

1663. W. W. to MARTIN FARQUHAR TUPPER

Address: Martin Farquhar Tupper Esq., Milton House, Brighton. [*readdressed to*] New Burlington St., London.
Postmark: (1) 11 Dec. 1842 (2) 13 Dec. 1842 (3) 14 Dec. 1842.
Stamp: (1) Ambleside (2) Brighton.
MS. Cornell.
Broughton, p. 82.

Rydal Mount
Decr 10th—42

Dear Sir

Having received your second Series of Proverbial Philosophy[1] I sit down with pleasure to thank you for it. As far as I am able to judge it seems worthy to take its place by the former, for which also y[ou][2] will accept the renewal of my acknowledgements made through a Third Person not long after I received the Book, as I well remember.

Owing to many causes, I am not an expeditious Reader, and your Maxims moreover to be read with profit must be read slowly and patiently, for which reason especially, I cannot speak yet as a competent judge of the whole; but I trust I shall in succession, duly become acquainted with all the subjects you have treated. In the meanwhile pray accept my thanks for the pleasure and instruction which already I owe to you,

and believe me dear Sir
with great respect
yours sincerely
Wm Wordsworth

1664. W. W. to JOHN PEACE

MS. WL transcript.
Mem. (—). *Grosart* (—). *K* (—). *LY iii. 1148* (—).

Rydal Mount, Dec. 12, 1842.

My dear Mr Peace,

. . . Poor Mr Wade![3] From his own modest merits, his long connection with Mr Coleridge, and my early Bristol remem-

[1] Publ. 1842. See L. 1647 above.
[2] *MS. blurred.*
[3] S. T. C.'s Bristol friend Josiah Wade, had just died.

brances, he was to me an interesting person. His desire to have my address must have risen, I think, from a wish to communicate with me upon the subject of Mr Alston's valuable portrait of Coleridge.[1] Pray tell me what has, or is likely to, become of it. I care comparatively little about the matter, provided due care has been taken for its preservation, and in his native country. It would be a sad pity if the late owner's intention of sending it to America be fulfilled. It is the only likeness of the great original that ever gave me the least pleasure; and it is, in fact, most happily executed, as every one who has a distinct remembrance of what C. was at that time must with delight acknowledge, and would be glad to certify.

Your health, I hope, continues good. We are all now well, but Mrs Wordsworth has lately suffered from a sharp fit of the jaundice;[2] which unaccountably has lately attacked many persons in this country. A few days ago I saw at Keswick Mr Southey's medical attendant. He tells me he never knew any one whose faculties were *entirely* gone like his. The bodily health is nevertheless good, and he looks better in the face than he has done for some years. . .

Ever faithfully your Friend
W. Wordsworth

1665. W. W. to FULKE GREVILLE HOWARD

MS. Cornell. Hitherto unpublished.

Rydal Mount
17th Dec^r^ —42.

My dear Colonel,

My Servant having occasion to pass by Levens tomorrow, I have directed him to call and inquire after the health of Mrs

[1] See pt. iii, L. 1341.

[2] M. W. was also feeling the increased burden of letter-writing and copying that had fallen exclusively to her with the departure of Dora Q. from the family circle. As she wrote to Julia Meakin (*née* Myers) on 15 Jan. 1843: 'The same employments, *now* that I have lost her, and that as you know, my husband requires almost all the time I have to spare from household concerns, are likely to continue to me as long as I am able to turn a pen—So that you must never think, if I fail to respond to your kindness, that it is for want of affection or interest in you.' (*MS. the late Mrs. Jane Myers*).

Howard and yourself, in the hope that you may still be there. This morning we received a brace of fine Pheasants, for which pray accept our thanks.—

Since our very agreeable visit to Levens, Mrs Wordsworth has had a severe attack of jaundice, which was beginning when we left you. Thank God she is now quite well, better than she was before the malady, which has been very prevalent in this neighbourhood; owing it is supposed, to the unusually warm summer. It would give us much pleasure to learn that you and Mrs Howard have both continued in good health during this mild season.—

A few days ago I was at Keswick, where I made inquiries of Mr Southey's medical Attendant how he was in body and mind. His bodily health, I was told is good, and he looks much better than he did some time since, but his mind is utterly gone. The Doctor assured me he had never attended a Person whose understanding and memory and perceptions had so deplorably failed. Is not this very affecting?

With most cordial good wishes, and kindest remembrances to Mrs Howard and yourself, in which Mrs W sincerely joins,

I remain
my dear Colonel
faithfully your much obliged
Wm Wordsworth

I have not heard from Lady Frederic for some time, and infer from this silence that there is little change in Lord Lonsdale's state of health.

1666. W. W. to GEORGE TICKNOR

MS. Baker Library, Dartmouth College.
Judson Stanley Lyon, 'Wordsworth and Ticknor', PMLA lxvi (1951), 432–40.

[Dec. 1842]

My dear Mr Ticknor,

Mrs Wordsworth's Letter to Mrs Ticknor I cannot suffer to depart without a word or two from my own pen addressed to yourself. Be assured it gives me great pleasure to receive such an account as Mrs T. gives of your health, and happiness in being restored to your own country, and settled in it after so long an absence and such wandering.—[1] How much will you all have to think of to talk of, and to describe and relate to others. It is this ghost or surviving Spirit of travelling which is often preferable to the substance. One enjoys objects while they are present but they are never truly endeared till they have been lodged some time in the memory. Intervening space must also have something of the same effect and partly in proportion to its length, as, notwithstanding the facilities given by steam you must have felt.

Mrs Ticknor enquires particularly after Mr Southey. The state in which he is, I grieve to say affords no ground for hope of improvements. His disease is thought by his Physicians to be a softening of the brain, from which the mind has suffered even still more than the Body. It has been slow; and though almost imperceptible in its progress, it has been advancing since its first appearance, evidenced by confusion in his head, and failing recollection of things, places, and persons. You may be sure his condition is a great trouble to all his Friends, (not to speak of his family) and to this Household in particular. Mr. S's second Daughter is married to Mr. Hill a clergyman our officiating Minister at present. We see much of her as they live at the foot of our Hill. His youngest Daughter[2] is at Keswick, but from circumstance too delicate to enter into,—and too complex to explain, there is alas! no harmony between her and her Step-mother.

I have dwelt more upon this Subject than I intended when I first touched upon it, but I could not turn my thoughts to any thing more agreeable, while writing to one who I know must respect highly and steadily this excellent man in whose life and situation so melancholy a change has, under the dispensations of Providence, taken place.—

As we have not infrequent opportunities of seeing American Travellers we have heard of you and your's, to our great satisfaction. Wishing that the same most acceptable answers may continue to be made to our inquiries, I remain with kindest remembrances to Mrs Ticknor, and your Daughter,[3] faithfully yours,

Wm Wordsworth

[1] W. W. had last seen the Ticknors in May 1838, just before their return to America (see pt. iii, L. 1243).

[2] Kate.

[3] Anna Eliot Ticknor, who helped compile her father's *Life, Letters, and Journals*.

1667. W. W. to W. W. JNR.

MS. WL.
LY iii. 1148.

Rydal Mount Monday morn [? late 1842 *or* early 1843]

My dear Wm

By no means let that fright of a Picture[1] be exhibited. You know the circumstances under which it was done, viz. good-natured compliance with the understood wishes of Mrs Curwen.[2] We expect the Quillinans by Wednesday morning coach

Your affectionate Father
Wm Wordsworth

[*M. W. adds*]

I hope I may get Isa: off to P. on Monday 6th. I shall go with her—so it will suit for your returning with James and me—I will wait for you at Plumbland. M. W.

1668. W. W. to SIR JOHN TAYLOR COLERIDGE

Endorsed: 1843 Janry 30th W. Wordsworth.
MS. British Library. Hitherto unpublished.

Rydal Mount
29th Jany 18[43]

My dear Mr Justice Coleridge,

It was very good in you to think of us, I was going to say in your distress, and might have said so without impropriety; but surely it is a blessed release for your Brother,[3] and a happy one for you all after he had so long endured such severe suffering—

Your account of his Departure is all that could be desire, may our end, and that of all we love be like his!

Immediately upon the Receipt of your Letter I stepped down to Mrs Hill, who had not heard of the event, and I went also

[1] Perhaps the portrait of W. W. by Miss McInnes, discussed by Blanshard, *Portraits of Wordsworth*, pp. 92–3, 168, and only surviving now in an engraved version of 1846 at Dove Cottage.

[2] Isabella W.'s mother.

[3] Henry Nelson Coleridge had died on 26 Jan.

directly to Mrs Arnold. Hartley had a Letter from Mr James Coleridge[1] by the same Post which brought me yours—

Dear Sara, we think much of her, and not without anxiety notwithstanding what you say of the calm state of her mind at present. May God support her; She is much beloved in this House, as she must be wherever she is half as well known as we know her. The Hills, to our great regret leave us, next Wednesday.[2] They will be much missed in our village, and Mr Hill exceedingly both on his own account, and because there will no doubt be a great falling off in his Successor.

Mrs Wordsworth unites with me in kind remembrances to yourself and Lady Coleridge, and believe

very faithfully your
much obliged
Wm Wordsworth

1669. W. W. to [?] JOHN HUDSON

Endorsed: Mr Wordsworth's handwriting in Feby 1843. J. H.
MS. WL. Hitherto unpublished.

[Feb. 1843]

. . .I was told by Mr Redmayne[3] that this is a church, but Mr Faber told me it is not so, nor could be without the Rector or Vicar of Hawkshead's consent, which he refuses. . .

[1] H. N. Coleridge's eldest brother (see L. 1628 above).

[2] Herbert Hill had been successful in his application for the headmastership of Warwick School (see L. 1640 above).

[3] Giles Redmayne (see pt. ii, L. 758) had built Brathay Church in 1836 as a chapel of ease to Hawkshead (see pt. iii, L. 984). In 1837, he had returned to London and lived thereafter on Highgate Hill. Hudson had presumably raised some query about the church in connection with the new expanded *Complete Guide to the Lakes.*

1670. W. W. to JOHN HUDSON

Address: Mr Hudson, Bookseller, Kendal.
MS. WL.
LY iii. 1150.

Ash Wednesday, [1 Mar. 1843]
Stamp Off. Carlisle

Dear Sir

I am sorry that unexpected engagements prevented me from keeping my promise of sending the Book on Tuesday. I am now at Carlisle but have brought the Book with me and have already looked over one half of it so that I do not think you will again be disappointed if I say that you may look for it in the course of three days at the latest. My principal difficulty is in making out your pencil writing; and every one in this House (Mrs Wordsworth included) is too busy to help me.

sincerely yours
Wm Wordsworth

I remain here till Tuesday next, I expect to be at Rydal before the end of next week.

1671. W. W. to JAMES WILSON[1]

MS. untraced.
James Hamilton, Memoirs of the Life of James Wilson, Esq. . .of Woodville, 1859, p. 220.

Rydal Mount,
14th March '43.

My dear Mr Wilson,

You will almost be at a loss to think what has become of me, I have been so tardy in acknowledging the kind present of your 'Voyage.'[2] If I am not mistaken, I told you that the book would

[1] James Wilson (1795–1856), Professor Wilson's youngest brother, naturalist and sportsman: contributor to *Blackwood's*, and author of numerous works, including *Illustrations of Zoology*, 1831. He was W. W.'s friend and admirer for more than twenty years, since they first met at Elleray *c.* 1825, and once referred to the poet as 'my mind's father'. Wilson had called at Rydal Mount the previous autumn, and visited the Wordsworths again in Oct. 1849. This letter was sent with a copy of *Grace Darling* (see next letter).

[2] *A Voyage Round the Coasts of Scotland and the Isles*, 2 vols., 1842.

remain at Carlisle till my son William had read it. He was then upon the point of going to Herefordshire, ...and various causes have kept him from Carlisle seven weeks, so that I have not long had your book in my possession. But I am now enabled to say, that though I have not read every part of it, it has given me very great pleasure, both on account of the interesting and rarely visited regions you passed through, but also by the manner in which you have described what you saw. Your pages abound with lively pictures, and not unfrequently occurs a very happy and original expression, such as "the small pure *breathing places* through the deep blue sky,' in your animated picture of the Loch Corruiskin.

When there is so much to admire, I feel little scruple in expressing an opinion that here and there your descriptions might advantageously have been pruned down a little, a fault which has arisen entirely from your not being practised in writing for the press. Had I been a man of fifty years, or even sixty (and not of seventy-three, as I shall be if I live to the 7th of next April), I should have wished heartily to be your fellow-voyager. Thanking you again for the pleasure you have afforded me, I remain, my dear Mr Wilson, sincerely your much obliged,

Wm Wordsworth

1672. W. W. to RICHARD PARKINSON[1]

Address: The Revd R. Parkinson, Broughton Cliff, Near Manchester. [*In M. W.'s hand*]

MS. National Library of Scotland. Hitherto unpublished.

Rydal Mount 17th March [1843]

My dear Sir

You are quite a[t] liberty to print my little Memoir of Robert Walker[2] in any way you think most likely to make it serviceable to piety and goodness.

Thank you for your communications. We have read your Old Church Clock with no little interest, and think it will please and

[1] Of St. Bees College. See pt. ii, L. 729.

[2] W. W.'s *Memoir of the Rev. Robert Walker*, originally attached as a note to *The River Duddon* sonnets (*PW* iii. 510 ff.), was republished as a preface to Parkinson's *The Old Church Clock*, which appeared later this year.

instruct those particularly well among whom you chiefly wish it to circulate—We shall be glad to see the whole when finished.

I send you a little piece[1] written two or three weeks ago, but not published as you will see. I hope you may not think it unworthy of the subject. I was impelled to write it by the miserable shipwrecks which the storms of the late winter have caused and thought it well to present a contrast to the cruelty with which the sufferers were treated upon the French coast.

believe me dear Sir,
respectfully and sincerely
Yours
Wm Wordsworth

1673. W. W. to CHARLES WORDSWORTH

MS. Mr. W. Hugh Peal. Hitherto unpublished.

[*c.* 19 Mar. 1843]

My dear Charles,

We are much indebted to you for your three sermons upon Communion in prayer,[2] which reached us by Post, probably in consequence of your direction. Mrs Wordsworth, our Friend Miss Fenwick and I have all read them carefully and are of one opinion that they cannot but do much [? good][3] as far as they are read.—

I sent you a message of thanks also upon the receipt of your Easter Sermon, and now repeat; the Discourse I carefully read, but the notes were too learned for me; that however was no fault of yours.—Your poor Aunt Dorothy continues much in her old way—certainly she is no worse. Your Aunt W. is very well, and

[1] *Grace Darling* (*PW* iv. 180), privately printed by Charles Thurnham at Carlisle for circulation among W. W.'s friends (see *Cornell Wordsworth Collection*, nos. 121–4), and published in the *Poems*, 1845. On 7 Sept. 1838, Grace Darling (1815–42), daughter of the Longstone lighthouse keeper on the Farne Islands, had accompanied her father in an open boat to the wreck of the Forfarshire steamboat, and rescued the nine survivors. Her heroism became legendary in her own lifetime. She died on 20 Oct. 1842, and was buried at Bamburgh.

[2] *Communion in Prayer; or, the duty of a Congregation in public worship*, 1843. It consisted of three sermons preached in Winchester College Chapel towards the end of 1842.

[3] *Word dropped out.*

I am recovered, in all but some residue of weakness, from a cold that was injudiciously neglected. Dora is living at Ambleside with her Husband; we see her in fine weather regularly, she has certainly been better in health a good deal than when we were with her in London last Spring—but the other day commenced a severe attack of her old stomach complaint, with pains in the face and head. It is however in some degree abated. We are expecting every hour to hear of poor Mr Southey's release. I shall go over to attend the funeral, and return the same day.—You told me in your letter that you read no Poetry but mine; this disregard of the art does not prevent me send[ing] you the accompanying Verses[1] written within the last two or three weeks. You will undoubtedly remember the event which occurred a few years back. I was impelled to write the Poem, by our late calamitous shipwreck and the cruelty with which the sufferers were treated upon the french Coast. Pray give one of the Copies at your leisure to Mr Keeble.[2]

Best love from all to yourself and dear little Charlotte.

ever your affectionate Uncle
W. Wordsworth

1674. W. W. to C. W.

MS. Mr. Jonathan Wordsworth. Hitherto unpublished.

20th March [1843][3]

My dear Brother,

I ought to have written earlier to express my deep sense of your affectionate kindness to Wm upon the occasion of his intended marriage.[4] He is I know truly grateful for your

[1] For *Grace Darling*, see previous letter.

[2] Keble had been the vicar of Hursley, nr. Winchester, since 1836.

[3] Year added by C. W.

[4] W. W. jnr. had been engaged for rather more than a month to his cousin Mary Monkhouse (see pt. i, L. 50). 'She is a nice girl enough,' E. Q. confided to H. C. R. on 7 Feb., '—just of age, and has a pretty good fortune—I believe not less than £20,000 besides what she will have from her Uncle Monkhouse. In a worldly point of view it is an excellent match for William and in every way we are all inclined to hope and believe not a bad one for either party.' (Morley, i. 476–7). And in welcoming the engagement in her letter to Sir John Taylor

goodness to him, and I doubt not that the object of his choice is the same. An additional proof of your kindness we are delighted to be told of, namely your intention to take so long a journey in order to perform the marriage ceremony. God grant that you may be able to attend, and that Mary and I may not be prevented by ill health or other causes from meeting you at the time, in Herefordshire.

Mary and I were lately at Carlisle with Wm, where we remained ten days, having chiefly gone with a view to his benefitting by his Mother's judgement in looking out for a House, or otherwise establishing themselves, till they could somewhat at leisure procure one to their mind. Our attempt ended as perhaps Wm may have told you, in an arrangement for his taking his Bride to his present Lodgings, and remaining there for some little time that they may look about them jointly.

Mary is very well, so, for her, is our dear Inmate, Miss Fenwick; but Dora has had an attack of her old stomach complaint, and a very severe one. To day she is better, having had a good night, but it is too probable that the complaint may return. It is a species of "Neuralgia" as the Doctors call it, or Tic; do I spell right? About a month or more ago I caught a cold which I neglected at first, and was afterwards obliged, or rather I thought it prudent, to keep House. This, in conjunction with the season, weakened me a good deal; and by medical advice I am now taking bark, with a hope of coming round in due time. Poor dear Sister is no worse, but complaining pretty much in her old way. We rejoice to have heard from Mrs Hoare good accounts of your own much stronger health and better looks. Having been given to understand from Cambridge that the chances were against dear Christopher's success as Candidate for the Professorship,[1] we were of course less disappointed. Of his successful opponent I have no knowledge having never heard his name before. I cannot but much regret Chris. did not succeed,

Coleridge on 22 Mar., Sara Coleridge hinted at a previous attachment: 'Willy deserves to have a nice girl with money, because he was very constant to one who was poor and plain and sickly, till her death released his friends rather than himself, for such freedom was unwelcome to him at the time, from a miserable engagement.' (*Texas University MSS.*). The couple were together at Brinsop in February and returned to Rydal Mount with Mrs. Hutchinson, but the engagement was broken off later this year (see L. 1701 below).

[1] Of Divinity (see L. 1653 above).

and more especially as Dr Mills[1] was not chosen.—

Yesterday we received Charles' three Sermons,[2] by Post. I like them much as far as I have yet had an opportunity of reading them, that is, the 2nd Sermon, half of the third, and half of the 1st. To morrow I shall carefully look over the whole. I trust they will continue to do good.

I send you [a] little Poem[3] written about three weeks ago, and which I got printed when at Carlisle, to send to my Friends. I was impelled to write it chiefly by the disastrous shipwrecks caused by the late storms, and by the Contrast presented on our Coast some few years back to the Cruelty with which the Sufferers were treated lately on the French Coast.

Our Sister would send her love, but She does not know that I am writing, nor does Dora who lives at Ambleside. Mary unites with me in most affectionate remembrances and every kind and good wish. ever my dear Brother, faithfully yours

Wm Wordsworth

We are anxious about Isabella who is looking for her confinement under circumstances that are far from promising. God grant her his gracious protection.

1675. W. W. to THOMAS NOON TALFOURD

MS. Cornell. Hitherto unpublished.

[22 Mar. 1843]

My dear Sergeant Talfourd,

It seems attaching too much importance to the Enclosed copy of Verses,[4] when I send them to you, but as they may give you and Mrs Talfourd some pleasure, I risk that imputation.

I was put upon writing them the other day by the report of the inhumanity with which the Sufferers by Shipwreck had lately been treated upon the French Coast.

[1] The Revd. William Hodge Mill, D.D. (see pt. ii, L. 482), later Regius Professor of Hebrew at Cambridge and Canon of Ely from 1848.

[2] See previous letter.

[3] *Grace Darling.*

[4] *Grace Darling.*

Yesterday about nine in the morning, poor dear Southey breathed his last. Typhus fever gave the finishing blow to his melancholy existence, but he passed away as gently as a child falling into a slumber. His Daughter,[1] who alas has not for some time lived under the same roof, saw him within a few minutes after he ceased to breathe.

I hope Mrs Talfourd and yourself, and your Children, enjoy good health. We are all, except my Daughter, well.

Believe me my dear Sergeant Talfourd

faithfully
[*signature cut away*]

1676. W. W. to C. W. JNR.

MS. British Library.
Mem. (—). *Grosart* (—). *K* (—). *LY iii. 1150* (—).

Rydal
22nd March
1843

My dear Christopher,

The Papers will have informed you, before you receive this, of poor dear Southey's decease. He died yesterday morning about nine o'clock. Some little time since, he was seized with Typhus fever but he passed away without any outward signs of pain, as gently as possible.—We are of course not without sadness, upon the occasion, notwithstanding there has been for years cause why all who knew and loved him should wish for his deliverance.

I enclose for you or rather for Susan a Copy of Verses[2] which I wrote very lately, and of which I had struck off a few impressions when at Carlisle upon a visit along with your Aunt to W^m. I have said I send the Lines to Susan more particularly as they are in honor of her sex.—

I am sorry that you failed to obtain the Professorship, and the more so, because Dr Mills[3] did not succeed. Of the successful Candidate I know nothing. Nor of the secret springs by which the election was swayed. As Mills had no probability of success,

[1] Kate.

[2] *Grace Darling.*

[3] See L. 1674 above.

I think it would have been more becoming, if the Master of Trinity[1] had voted for you. But judging of things at a distance, I am perhaps mistaken.

I do not wish you to take the trouble of acknowledging this Parcel, but at Susan's leisure I shall like to hear how you are in health, that is, whether your health is improved—Give my affectionate love to her, and with a thousand good wishes for yourself and yours, I remain dear Christopher your affectionate

Uncle and faithful friend
Wm Wordsworth

We are all pretty well except Dora who has lately had a severe return of her old stomach complaint with pains in the head and face, a species of Tic or neuralgia.

[*M. W. writes*]

I see your Uncle has omitted to send my dear love to you both which is very remiss in him—or to say that your poor Aunt is in her best way, and always alive to any communication with you and your's—We have good accounts from time to time of your little Darlings[2] thro' Mrs Hoare. We have been reading, with very much pleasure, dear Charles's book[3] which he kindly sent us the other day.

Ever my d^r^ Ch: affly yours
M. Wordsworth

1677. W. W. to MRS. CHARLES JAMES BLOMFIELD[4]

MS. Mr. Robert H. Taylor. Hitherto unpublished.

Rydal Mount
23^d^ March —43.

Dear Mrs Blomfield,

The accompanying Verses[5] I had struck off the other day for circulation among my friends and therefore beg your acceptance of them, particularly as they are an attempt to do honour to one of your sex. It is rather remarkable that since they were

[1] William Whewell.

[2] C. W. jnr.'s two daughters, Elizabeth and Priscilla.

[3] *Communion in Prayer.*

[4] See L. 1523 above.

[5] *Grace Darling.*

composed I have learned that the Queen and Queen Dowager had lately subscribed to a Monument erecting under Archdeacon Thorpe's direction to the memory of the Heroine whose humane Exploit these verses record. Pray present my respects to the Bp, and believe me with the united kind remembrances of Mrs Wordsworth to yourself and yours,

faithfully your obliged
Wm Wordsworth

Dont trouble yourself to acknowledge this note, though I own I should be glad to hear that you were all well. Poor dear Mr Southey has been released after a long and sad illness both of mind and body. He was seized with Typhus very lately, but died without the least apparent suffering, as gently as his dearest Friends could desire—

1678. W. W. to MARY FRANCES HOWLEY

MS. Lambeth Palace Library. Hitherto unpublished.

Rydal Mount
23^d March 43.

Dear Mrs Howley,

The accompanying verses[2] I had struck off lately for circulation among my Friends, and therefore beg your acceptance of them, and particularly as they were written in honour of one of your Sex. It is rather remarkable that I should have written these verses without knowing that at the same time a monument was about to be raised to the memory of the Heroine upon the Spot that witnessed her Exploit, and perhaps you know that the Queen and Queen Dowager have both subscribed to the undertaking. Perhaps dear little Constance may find some pleasure in the lines; I shall be glad not to be mistaken in the supposition.

You did me, dear Madam, a great kindness in writing at such length and so particularly upon the Archbishop's illness; and on the mention you made of your own. I hope that neither of you suffer from the effects of these severe maladies.

[1] See pt. ii, L. 593, and L. 1849 below. The monument was in the new Gothic taste of the Cambridge Camden Society.

[2] *Grace Darling.*

Mrs W unites with me in most respectful remembrances to the Archbishop, and every good and kind wish for him and for yourself and yours and believe [me]

dear Mrs Howley
faithfully your much obliged
Wm Wordsworth

1679. W. W. to GEORGE LEWIS PRENTISS[1]

MS. untraced.
George Lewis Prentiss, A Memoir of S. S. Prentiss, 2 vols., New York, 1879, ii. 265.
LY iii. 1151.

Rydal Mount, near Ambleside, March 23, 1843.

My dear Sir

Your letter, which had for some time been rather anxiously looked for, reached me by yesterday's post. I sincerely thank you for it, and for the pains which you have so kindly taken upon the subject. Nor are we less indebted to your brother[2] for his letter, and for his entering into particulars in the manner he has so considerately and fully done. I feel unwilling to trouble him with a letter, judging that my acknowledgments will be as acceptably conveyed through you. Pray let him know how much we are obliged to him; and say that, for many reasons, we shall be glad to hear from him again, as soon as anything materially affecting the question may occur. The personal

[1] See L. 1637 above.

[2] Seargent Smith Prentiss (1808–50), politician and Congressman, had written to W. W. recently about the prospects for Mississippi bonds. 'There are two classes of Mississippi bonds, issued at different periods, and for different purposes. One class has been repudiated by the legislative body, but the other has not been; nor is the validity of this latter class questioned at all. It is true no provision has been made during several years for the payment of the interest; but the neglect has arisen from other causes than that of repudiation. The bonds in which you are interested, I perceive by a memorandum of my brother's, belong to this class. Their validity is acknowledged on all hands. . . .The doctrine of repudiation has had a momentary and apparent triumph in this State; but its success was accidental. . . .it receives no countenance amongst honest and honourable men.' And he went on to speak of 'my desire to relieve at least a portion of my countrymen from the imputation of intentional dishonesty in the eyes of a poet and philosopher, whose good opinion is capable of adding weight even to the character of a nation.' (*Memoir of S. S. Prentiss*, ii. 261–2).

interest which I attach to it is not [so much] on account of the sum of money that is at stake, as the condition of the proprietors, two of whom, a brother and sister of Mrs Wordsworth, are advanced in life, and one has a large family; and both, owing to various misfortunes, are in very narrow circumstances. The other owner is my only daughter, who is married to a gentleman that has been very unfortunate also. I repeat these particulars, mentioned, I remember, when I had the pleasure of seeing you at Rydal, because I should be very unwilling to give your brother and yourself so much trouble upon a slight occasion. Nothing remains for the suffering parties but patience and hope; for as to the proposal so kindly made of seeking redress through legal process, in which your brother offers his assistance, they have no funds for acting upon that; besides, they could not think of availing themselves of an offer which could not be carried into effect, even were it successful, without occupying your brother's time and thoughts in a way which they would feel unwarrantable. All that you both say respecting the depth and extent of the indignation excited in your country by this shameless dishonesty, we most readily believe; and upon that belief we rest our hopes that justice will be done. But in matters like this, time, as in the case of my relatives, is of infinite importance, and it is to be feared that the two individuals, for whose comfort payment is of the most consequence, may both be in their graves before it comes.[1] Let but taxes, to amount however small, once be imposed exclusively for discharging these obligations, and that measure would be hailed as the dawn of a coming day; but until that is effected, the most sanguine must be subject to fits of despondency.

It gives me much pleasure to learn that you found your mother and sisters in such good health upon your return. What a joyful meeting must it have been after so long a separation. What you say of the nervous fever under which you have been suffering gives me great concern. Had it anything to do with the climate of your country, very different, perhaps, from what you had been accustomed to in Europe?

I cannot but wish that you had seen more of the *mother* country; it is our old English phrase, and I rather grieve to see that many of the present generation, fond of aping German modes of thinking and speech, use father-land instead. England

[1] The policy of repudiation was finally rejected in 1853 and the responsibility of the State for payment upheld.

is certainly the portion of Europe which is the most worthy of American regard, provided it be diligently and carefully noticed and studied.

I send (by way of slight return for your and your brother's kindness) to each of you the last verses from my pen.[1] They were written about three weeks ago, and a few copies struck off for circulation among my friends. I should not like them to be printed, even in America, for they would be sure of finding their way instantly back to England, before, perhaps, I disposed of my own little impression as I could wish. Since the lines were composed, I have heard that our Queen and Queen Dowager have both subscribed pretty largely for the erection of a memorial to the memory of my heroine upon the spot where she lived and was so nobly distinguished. She is since dead. What a contrast, as you will see, does her behavior present to the inhumanity with which lately, upon the French coast, certain ship-wrecked English crews were treated.

Mrs Wordsworth joins me in kind remembrances, and we beg that our respects may be presented to your mother and sisters and believe me to remain,

Sincerely and gratefully, your much obliged,
Wm Wordsworth

1680. W. W. to SIR WILLIAM GOMM

Address: Lieu. Gen. Sir Wm Gomm, Governor of the Mauritius, Mauritius.
MS. Henry E. Huntington Library.
Mem. Grosart. K. LY iii. 1153.

Rydal Mount
March 24th —43.

My dear Sir William,

Nothing should have prevented my answering your kind Letter from the Cape long ago, but the want of matter that seemed worth sending so far, unless I confined myself to what you must be well assured of, my sincere esteem and regard for yourself and Lady Gomm; and the expression of good wishes for your health and happiness. I am still in the same difficulty, but cannot defer writing longer, least I should appear to myself

[1] *Grace Darling.*

unworthy of your Friendship, or respect.—You describe the beauties of Rio Janeiro in glowing colours,[1] and your animated Picture was rendered still more agreeable to me, by the sight which I had enjoyed a little before, of a Panorama of the Scene, executed by a Friend of mine,[2] who in his youth studied at the Academy with a view to practise painting as a Profession. He was a very promising young Artist, but having a Brother a Brazilian Merchant he changed his purpose and went to Rio where he resided many years, and made a little fortune which enabled him to purchase and build in Cumberland, where I saw his splendid Portrait of that magnificent region. What an intricacy of Waters, and what boldness and fantastic variety in the mountains! I suppose taking the Region as a whole it is scarcely any where surpassed. If the different quarters of the globe should ever become subject to one Empire, Rio ought to be the Metropolis, it is so favored in every respect, and so admirably placed for intercourse with all the countries of the Earth. Your approach to the Cape was under awful circumstances, and with those great Wrecks strewn along the Coast of the Bay. Lady Gomm's spirit and fortitude as described by you are worthy of all admiration, and, I am sure she will sympathize with the Verses I send, to commemorate a noble exploit of one of her Sex. The inhumanity with which the shipwrecked were lately treated upon the French Coast impelled me to place in contrast the conduct of an English Woman and her Parents under like circumstances, as it occurred some years ago. Almost immediately after I had composed my tribute to the Memory of *Grace Darling*, I learned that the Queen and Queen Dowager had both just subscribed towards the Erection of a monument to record her Heroism upon the Spot that witnessed it.—

Of public news, I say nothing, as you will have every thing from quarters more worthy of attention. I hope all goes on to your satisfaction, mainly so at least, in your new Government; and that the disposition which you will have taken with you to benefit the people under your rule has not been, nor is likely to be, frustrated in any vexations or painful degree—

[1] In his letter of 23 Oct. 1842 (*WL MSS.*), Gomm had spoken of 'a tumult of wooded mountains, in ranges interminable, seeming on the move to meet our advances, or it might be to dispute our passage, into the finest Haven in the world.'

[2] Richard Carruthers (see *MY* ii. 402; pt. i, L. 45), who painted W. W.'s portrait in 1817.

Yesterday I went over to Keswick to attend the funeral of my excellent Friend Mr Southey.[1] His Genius and abilities are well known to the World, and he was greatly valued for his generous disposition and moral excellence. His illness was long and afflicting—his mind almost extinguished years before the breath departed:—Mr Rogers I have not been in communication with since I saw you in London,[2] but be assured I shall bear in memory your message to him, and deliver [it] if he and I live to meet again. And now my dear Sir Wm, repeating the united best good wishes of Mrs W and myself, for you and Lady Gomm, and for your safe return to your own Country, I remain in the hope of hearing from you again

most faithfully your
much obliged
Wm Wordsworth

My Nephew[3] is still in the Ionian Islands.

1681. W. W. to HENRY REED

Address: Henry Reed Esqre, Philadelphia. [*In M. W.'s hand*]
Postmark: (1) 30 Mar. 1843 (2) 31 Mar. 1843 (3) 2 Apr. 1843 (4) 3 Apr. 1843.
Stamp: (1) Ambleside (2) Boston Ship.
MS. Cornell.
K (—). *Wordsworth and Reed, p. 94.*

Rydal Mount March 27th 43

My dear Mr Reed,

There are many things exclusive of business in your last Letter, dated Novr 15th that required from me much earlier notice, but the farther my Letters have to go, and the greater my obligations to Friends, the more my difficulty in finding matter

[1] W. W. was not invited to the funeral at Crosthwaite Church, but he went all the same with E. Q., who records that as the bearers approached the graveside through the driving rain, two robins suddenly burst into song from a blackthorn hedge nearby (see *Poems, with a Memoir by William Johnston*, 1853, p. 218). Hartley Coleridge, who by mistake arrived too late for the service, implies that the Southey family quarrel was not suspended and that the two factions refused to speak to each other. See *Letters of Hartley Coleridge* (ed. Griggs), p. 264.

[2] The previous May (see *MW*, p. 248).

[3] R. W.'s son, 'Keswick John', now in the army medical service.

worthy of the occasion. Besides, I could not help nourishing the hope that something of public interest might occur which would induce you to write again. But as that has not happened, I now though far too late sit down to thank you for all your kindness and to touch upon the principal parts of your two Letters.[1] I am glad to learn from you that there is no distinction whatever between native and foreign creditors. There is hope in this, because as far as it goes, it proves that an obvious principle of justice is acknowledged. On the other hand Febry has come and you do not write me word, that any vigorous measure of taxation has been resorted to, towards satisfying the Creditors. Till this shall be done, much reliance cannot be placed in common prudence, upon the good intentions of the better, and I trust the larger portion of your community. After all, much as I am interested in this matter on account of my Friends, it is for the reproach which has justly come upon the American name from these proceedings that I am chiefly moved. Even by those States that abhor the infamous doctrine of repudiation no small dishonour has been incurred through their improvidence and unjustifiable eagerness for gain. But let me dismiss the subject with simply observing in reference to myself how strangely things are connected. If the State of Pennsylvania had discharged its obligations, Miss Fenwick would in the ensuing Summer have[2] fulfilled her desire long-cherished of travelling on the Continent, which she has not yet seen. Mrs Wordsworth and I would[3] in all probability have accompanied her and we should have passed, (God willing) the next winter together in Italy. But so considerable a portion of her funds having failed, and the advanced age of us all requiring that we should travel quite at ease as to expense, our joint means are unequal to the undertaking; so that we must remain at home. This, however Mrs W— may regret the cause, is to her no disappointment, for she would rather but for our sakes remain in England, nor do I on my own account much grieve for our inability to carry this scheme into effect, but I should have much liked to have been our dear Friend's cicerone through places and among objects which I have already seen[4], and from which her taste and sensibility would qualify her to draw much enjoyment, and

[1] Reed's letter of 15 Nov. 1842 had a long postscript explaining the latest position on Pennsylvanian bonds. See *Wordsworth and Reed*, pp. 82–8.

[2] *Written* having.

[3] *Written* would have.

[4] *Written* scene.

instruction. In many ways however good comes out of evil, and perhaps by being kept at home we may have the pleasure, as you more than hint,[1] of seeing you and Mrs Reed—Be assured it will give us great delight to welcome you both.

But in writing thus I am checked by the apprehension that the same cause which prevents our rambling may also hinder your visit to England. The account you give of my old Friend, for so, I will presume to call him, Mr Alston was very gratifying to me.[2] As I believe you know, we were made acquainted through Mr Coleridge, who had lived in much intimacy with Mr Alston at Rome. There is a most excellent Portrait of C— by A— about which I am very anxious; not knowing what will become of it; the late owner, Mr Wade for whom it was painted being dead.[3] My wish was, as I expressed to him a year and a half ago, that he should bequeath the Portrait to Mr Coleridges only Daughter for her life, to go after her day to the Fitzwilliam Museum at Cambridge, or the College in that University where he was educated. But I have no knowledge that he acted upon this advice. His own inclination was to send the picture to the Painter. I respected that inclination, and was well aware that Mr Alston would prize it much for his deceased Friend C's sake. I know also that Mr Coleridge had many ardent admirers in America; nevertheless I could not suppress a wish that it should remain in England, it is so admirable a likeness of what that great and good man then was, both as to person, feature, air, and character, and moreover though there are several Pictures of him in existence, and one by an Artist eminent in his day, viz

[1] Reed had explained that the depreciation in investments had affected his own family income. 'After another season I trust I may find a more propitious state of things, when I may revive my hope of visiting England and meeting you—a happiness I ought not to gratify myself in, without Mrs Reed sharing it with me.'

[2] Washington Allston was now living in the suburbs of Boston, where Henry Reed had made his acquaintance the previous summer. 'He goes but little into society but is much cherished by those who know how to appreciate him. He is still engaged in the painting (Belshazzar's Feast) which has been in hand for many years . . . What progress has been made in it is not known, as his intimate friends are not admitted into his painting room. You are probably aware that his habitual difficulty is in satisfying himself with his results on the canvass . . . He talked a great deal about you and his other English friends who seemed to be associated in his memory with you—Lamb and Coleridge and Sir George Beaumont. . .'

[3] See L. 1664 above.

Northcote,[1] there is not one in the least to be compared to that by Mr Alston.

You give me pleasure by the interest you take in the various passages in which I speak of the Poets my contemporaries who are no more. Dear Southey one of the most eminent is just added to the list. A few days ago I went over to Keswick to attend his remains to their last earthly abode. For upwards of three years his mental faculties have been in a state of deplorable deccay, and his powers of recognition except very rarely and but for a moment have been during more than half that period all but extinct. His bodily health also was grievously impaired, and his medical attendant says that he must have died long since but for the very great strength of his natural Constitution. As to his literary Remains, they must be very considerable, but except his Epistolary correspondence none are left unfinished. His Letters cannot but be very numerous, and if carefully collected and judiciously selected, will I doubt not, add greatly to his reputation. He had a fine talent for that species of Compsition and took much delight in throwing off his mind in that way. Mr Taylor, the Dramatic Author, is his literary Executor.

Though I have written at great and I fear tiresome length I will add a few words upon the wish you express that I would pay a tribute to the English Poets of past ages, who never had the praise they are entitled to and have long been almost entirely neglected.[2] Had this been suggested to me earlier in life or had it come into my thoughts the thing in all probability would have been done. At present I can not hope it will—but it may afford you some satisfaction to be told that in the Mss Poem upon my

[1] James Northcote (see *EY*, pp. 593–4).

[2] '. . . what a noble subject it would be for you', Reed had written, '—for you at the present stage of your career—to record in verse your judgment and gratitude to the poets who have enriched our language with their inspirations! Might not a series of sonnets on this subject be to the history of English literature what the ecclesiastical series is to the history of the Church of England? It would serve better than aught else to undo the mischief of Dr. Johnson's 'Lives of the Poets'—for the truth and beauty of poetry would prevail a thousand fold over the fallacy and dogmatism of critical prose. . . . As I have allowed myself to speculate on this subject in your hands, I have thought not only of fit homage to the greatest of the English poets, but of tributes to another class of them which it would be delightful to see rendered by you—I mean such as the world has too much neglected, such as George Wither, Drayton, Daniel, the Beaumonts and others . . .'

own Poetic education there is a whole Book[1] of about 600 lines upon my obligations to writers of imagination, and chiefly the Poets, though I have not expressly named those to whom you allude—and for whom and many others of their age I have a high respect. The character of the School Master[2] about whom you inquire, had like the Wanderer in the Excursion a solid foundation in fact and reality, but like him it was also in some degree a Composition; I will not and need not call it an invention—it was no such thing. But were I to enter into details I fear it would impair the effect of the whole upon your mind, nor could I do it at all to my own satisfaction. I send you, according to your wish the additions to the Ecclesiastical Sonnets[3] and also the last poem from my pen. I threw it off two or three weeks ago, being in a great measure impelled to it by the desire I felt to do justice to the memory of a heroine, whose conduct presented some time ago a striking contrast to the inhumanity with which our Countrymen shipwrecked lately upon the French coast have been mistreated.

Ever most faithfully yours,

Wm Wordsworth

[*In M. W.'s hand*]

I must request that 'Grace Darling' may not be reprinted.

I will be much obliged if you will have the enclosed Sonnets copied and sent to Bp Doane who has not given me his address.

W. W.

[*In John Carter's hand*]

The Sonnet 12 (Sacheverel) is to stand elsewhere and this to be inserted in its place.[4]—

[1] The fifth book of *The Prelude*.

[2] Matthew.

[3] 'What you tell me of additions to the Ecclesiastical Sonnets gives me great gratification,' Reed had written, 'chiefly because I am so deeply assured that that series of poems must exert an important and abiding influence upon the views and feelings of many Churchmen in both our countries—an influence increasing with their completeness. The series has always seemed to me admirably fitted to inspire and guide right feeling in the study of British Church history, and what is remarkable evidence of this, is the fact that it is found adequate to the deeper Church feeling which has been awakened of late years.'

[4] See *PW* iii. 392. This letter establishes the date of the sonnet as late 1842 or early 1843.

Bishops and Priests, how blest are Ye, if deep
(As your's above all offices is high)
Deep in your hearts the sense of duty lie;
Charged as ye are by Christ to feed and keep
From wolves your portion of his chosen sheep;
Laboring as ever in your Master's sight,
Making your hardest task your best delight,
What perfect glory Ye in heaven shall reap!
But in the solemn Office which ye sought
And undertook premonished, if unsound
Your practice prove, faithless though but in thought,
Bishops and Priests, think what a gulf profound
Awaits you then, if they were rightly taught
Who framed the ordinance by your lives disowned!

After the one on the Sacrament comes the following:

[*There follow* The Marriage Ceremony, Thanksgiving after Childbirth, The Commination Service, Forms of Prayer at Sea, Visitation of the Sick, *and* Funeral Service, *as in PW iii. 397–9, with a few minor variations.*]

After this follows the Sonnet on a Rural Ceremony, the first lines altered thus:

Closing the precious Book which long has fed
Our meditations, give we to a day etc

The 15th[1] Sonnet, on the Liturgy, must be altered from the 7th line thus:—

As he approaches them with solemn cheer.
Upon that circle, traced from sacred story,
Here let us cast a more than transient glance;
With harp in hand endeavour to advance,
And mind intent upon the King of Glory—
From his mild advent till his countenance
Shall dissipate the seas and mountains hoary.

[1] Actually the 19th in the final sequence of Part III. (See *PW* iii. 393).

1682. W. W. to EDWARD MOXON

MS. Henry E. Huntington Library.
LY iii. 1155.

[*In M. W.'s hand*]

Wednesday Morn. [29 Mar. 1843][1]

Dear Mr Moxon

We saw Mr Hill[2] on our return from Keswick yesterday, from him we find that Dr Southey[3] had declined to act as his B^r^'s Executor so that his duties are devolved upon Cuth:[4]—and we also understand that Mr Taylor was likely to throw as much of the literary labor upon Cuth: as was consistent with his duty to his departed friend. Mr Hill also said, when the subject of your application was mentioned to him by Mrs W. that he had barely heard the name of Longman mentioned between Dr S. and his nephew. Now I shall to-day write to inform Cuth: of your wish, he goes to London in a few days to meet the Executors, where if you have not left London you may see him—and meanwhile you might if you thought proper see Dr Southey who returned to Town last Monday.

[*W. W. writes*]

Perhaps this intelligence may prevent you coming down into the North; if so I shall be sorry both because if you could spare a few days, you might enjoy yourself, and we should be heartily glad to see you. We might also talk matters over, though I confess I am very indifferent about reprinting in any shape, while there is so little inclination to purchase.

ever faithfully yours
Wm Wordsworth

[1] Date added in another hand.

[2] Southey's son-in-law.

[3] Dr. Henry Southey, the poet's younger brother. He and Cuthbert Southey were on opposing sides in the family quarrel.

[4] Cuthbert Southey had graduated from Queen's College, Oxford, in 1841. He acted as John W.'s curate for a time at Plumbland, and was successively vicar of Ardleigh, Essex (1851–5), Kingsbury Episcopi, Somerset (1855–79), and St. James's, Dudley (1879–85). The point at issue now was whether Moxon was to publish Southey's literary remains. See next letter.

1683. W. W. to HENRY TAYLOR

Endorsed: Letter from Mr Wordsworth and 2 or 3 others respecting Southey's Correspondence.
MS. Bodleian Library.
LY iii. 1155.

Rydal Mount March 31st [1843]

My dear Mr Taylor,

In considering the difficulty of the Editorship of the Papers,[1] you ask what opportunities I have had of judging of Cuthbert's competence to undertake it. *Directly* I have had scarcely more than was afforded while he read to me in MSS his own Portion, which is not little, of the life of Dr Bell.[2] I have no hesitation in saying that I was satisfied with his work, but this gives but slender ground for concluding that he is equal to the arduous office of determining what part of his Father's papers is fit for publication, and what ought to be held back—or destroyed. Mr Hill, who has seen much of C. has a high opinion of his talents, nor independent of that judgement can I doubt that he is a clever young man. But then his education has been altogether irregular, he is unpractised in Literature, and cannot possibly, were it from his youth merely, be competent to decide finally upon the merits of writings so numerous and various in their matter and style, as his Father's must be. He has inherited much of his Father's quickness, and possesses I am told a great deal of information, gathered up, I should think, in a desultory way. But on the whole I cannot entertain the opinion that justice to Southey's memory will be done, if the papers are not for the most part to be looked over by some one of more experience. And to do this, if they be numerous, as there is reason to believe they are, would require more time and labour than any but Cuthbert himself is likely to have to spare. And here, as appears to me, lies the main difficulty of the case; for as to Mrs Warter[3] however painful it may be to the Exrs, she is so much under the influence of her wrong-headed and stupid husband that she must be set aside. The Exrs must take upon themselves this responsi-

[1] Southey's papers. See previous letter.

[2] Cuthbert Southey was responsible for the second and third volumes.

[3] Edith Warter and her husband supported the second Mrs. Southey in the family quarrel, and were therefore on the opposite side to Cuthbert, Kate, and the Hills.

bility, and as to Mr and Mrs Hill and Kate I am sure that they would readily accede to any plan of proceeding that was approved by yourself and Dr Southey.

Mr Hill has *studied* Literature in several of its branches much more carefully I believe than it is possible Cuth: can have done, and could he find time and did opportunity favour, for his uniting his endeavours with Cuthbert's, they might jointly put the papers into such a state that without any unwarrantable demand upon your own time and health you might pass a final judgment upon them with reference to publication. Taking all into consideration this method of managing the important concern seems the most feasible.[1] I have thus without reserve given you my opinion, formed upon careful consideration.

Excuse me if I here add a word upon a matter the decision of which is remote. In a letter I had from Moxon the other day, he begged that if I had any influence in the choice of a Publisher I would say a word on his behalf. The affair being of so delicate a nature, I confine myself to state this wish so communicated to me, for you will know that I have taken an interest in Moxon's welfare, as Mr Southey did, notwithstanding his long connection with Longman and other Publishers.[2]

Ever most faithfully yours
Wm Wordsworth

P.S. I have not said a word about S.'s Letters, being well assured that you will do all in your power to the right management of this piece of the business, which will be of no small difficulty and delicacy.—

[1] After much delay the work was entrusted to Cuthbert Southey, who produced *The Life and Correspondence of the late Robert Southey*, 6 vols., 1849–50. The publisher was Longman not Moxon. Mrs. Southey handed over her collection of Southey letters to John Wood Warter, and these formed the basis of his 4 vol. edition of 1856.

[2] This paragraph and the previous one are in M. W.'s hand.

1684. W. W. to EARL DE LA WARR[1]

Address: The Right Honorable The Earl of De la Warr etc etc etc.
MS. WL.[2]
Mem. Grosart K. LY iii. 1157.

Rydal Mount, Ambleside, April 1st, 1843.

My Lord,

The Recommendation made by your Lordship to the Queen, and graciously approved by Her Majesty, that the vacant Office of Poet Laureat should be offered to me, affords me high gratification. Sincerely am I sensible of this Honor and let me be permitted to add that the being deemed worthy to succeed my lamented and revered friend Mr Southey enhances the pleasure I receive upon this occasion.

The Appointment I feel however imposes Duties which far advanced in life as I am I cannot venture to undertake and I must therefore beg leave to decline the acceptance of an offer that I shall always remember with no unbecoming pride.

Her Majesty will not I trust disapprove of a determination forced upon me by reflections which it is impossible for me to set aside.

Deeply feeling the Distinction conferred upon me and grateful for the terms in which your Lordship has made the communication I have the Honor to be, My Lord

Your Lordship's most obedt Humble Servt,

W. W.

1685. W. W. to LADY FREDERICK BENTINCK

MS. untraced.
Mem. Grosart. K. LY iii. 1158.

[1 Apr. 1843]

. . .The Lord Chamberlain, in terms the most honourable, has, with the Queen's approbation, offered me the vacant laureateship.

[1] Lord Chamberlain, 1841–6 (see also pt. i, L. 203). He had written on 30 Mar. to offer W. W. the Laureateship: 'May I be allowed to add, that it is with feelings of very peculiar gratification, that I find myself in a position to propose this mark of distinction on an Individual whose acceptance of it would shed an additional lustre upon an Office in itself highly honorable.' (*WL MSS.*) See also next letters.

[2] A copy of the letter sent.

Had I been several years younger I should have accepted the office with pride and pleasure; but on Friday I shall enter, God willing, my seventy-fourth year, and on account of so advanced an age I begged permission to decline it, not venturing to undertake its duties. For though, as you are aware, the formal task-work of New Year and Birthday Odes was abolished, when the appointment was given to Mr Southey, he still considered himself obliged in conscience to produce, and did produce, verses—some of very great merit—upon important public occasions. He failed to do so upon the Queen's Coronation, and I know that this omission caused him no little uneasiness. The same might happen to myself upon some important occasion, and I should be uneasy under the possibility; I hope, therefore, that neither you nor Lord Lonsdale, nor any of my friends, will blame me for what I have done.

I was slow to send copies of *Grace Darling* about, except to female friends, lest I should seem to attach too much importance to the production, though it was on a subject which interested the whole nation. But as the verses seem to have given general pleasure, I now venture to send the enclosed copies, one for Mr Colvill,[1] and the other for my old friend Mr O'Callaghan,[2] begging that you would present them at your own convenience. With the best of good wishes, and every kind and respectful remembrance to Lord Lonsdale, who we are happy to learn is doing so well, and also not forgetting Miss Thompson, I remain, dear Lady Frederick,

Most faithfully and affectionately yours,
Wm Wordsworth

[1] Probably Charles Robert Colville (1815–86), of Lullington, Burton-on-Trent, at this time M.P. for South Derbys. In her letter to W. W. from York House, Twickenham, on 27 Mar. (*WL MSS.*), Lady Frederick referred to Mr. Colville's recent visit to her: 'he said he regretted not being *one of your favour'd friends* upon this occasion which I mention in case you might like to include him in that number.'

[2] See pt. i, L. 115.

1686. W. W. to UNKNOWN CORRESPONDENT

MS. untraced.
K (—). *LY iii. 1158.*

Rydal Mount, April 1, 1843.

Dear Sir,

. . . As I advance in life I feel myself more and more incapable of doing justice to the attempts of young authors. The taste and judgment of an old man have too little of aptitude and flexibility for new things; and I am thoroughly convinced that a young writer cannot do worse than lean upon a veteran. It was not my own habit to look out for such guidance. I trusted to myself, and to the principles of criticism which I drew from the practice of the great poets, and not from any observations made upon their works by professed censors. As you are so intimately acquainted with my poems, and as no change has taken place in my manner for the last forty-five years, you will not be at a loss to gather from them upon what principles I write, and what accordingly is likely to be my judgment of your own performances, either as to subject or style.

I remain, my dear sir,
Faithfully, your obliged
Wm Wordsworth

1687. W. W. to EARL DE LA WARR

Address: The Right Honble the Earl of Delawar etc etc etc.
MS. The Royal Library, Windsor.[1]
Mem. Grosart. K. LY iii. 1159.

Rydal Mount
Ambleside
4th April 1843

My Lord,

Being assured by your Lordship's Letter[2] and by one from Sir

[1] A copy of this letter, apparently in John W.'s hand, is among the *WL MSS.*

[2] Lord de la Warr had written on 3 Apr. regretting W. W.'s refusal of the Laureateship and hoping he would change his mind. The duties of the office, he explained, were now merely nominal, 'and could not in any way interfere with your habits of country retirement. I am confident that publick Opinion will bear me out in thus venturing to press the appointment upon you.' (*WL MSS.*)

Robert Peel,[1] both received this day, that the Appointment to the Laureatship is to be considered merely honorary, the apprehensions which at first compelled me to decline accepting the Offer of that Appointment are entirely removed.—

Sir Robert Peel has also done me the Honor of uniting his wish with that which your Lordship has urged in a manner most gratifying to my feelings; so that under these circumstances, and sanctioned as the Recommendation has been by Her Majesty's gracious Approval, it is with unalloyed pleasure that I accept this high Distinction.

I have the Honor to be
my Lord,
most gratefully
your Lordship's obed^{nt} humb^{le} Servt
Wm Wordsworth

1688. W. W. to SIR ROBERT PEEL[2]

Address: The Right Honble Sir Robert Peel Bart, etc etc etc.
Endorsed: 4 Apl/43. Mr Wordsworth accepts the Poet Laureateship.
MS. British Library.
Mem. Grosart. K. LY iii. 1160.

Rydal Mount, Ambleside,
4th April, 1843.

Dear Sir Robert,

Having since my first acquaintance with Horace borne in mind the charge which he tells us frequently thrilled his ear,

[1] See next letter.

[2] Peel had written on 3 Apr. pressing W. W. to reconsider his decision with regard to the Poet Laureateship: 'The offer was made to you by the Lord Chamberlain, with my entire concurrence, not for the purpose of imposing on you any onerous or disagreeable duties, but in order to pay you that tribute of respect which is justly due to the first of living poets. The Queen entirely approved of the nomination, and there is one unanimous feeling on the part of all who have heard of the proposal (and it is pretty generally known) that there could not be a question about the selection. Do not be deterred by the fear of any obligations which the appointment may be supposed to imply. I will undertake that you shall have nothing *required* from you. But the Queen can select no one whose claims for respect and honour, on account of eminence as a poet, can be placed in competition with yours. I trust you will not longer hesitate to accept it.' (*WL MSS.*)

> Solve senescentem maturè sanus equum, ne
> Peccet ad extremum,[1]

I could not but be deterred from incurring responsibilities which I might not prove equal to at so late a period of life; but as my mind has been entirely set at ease by the very kind and most gratifying Letter with which you have honored me, and by a second communication from the Lord Chamberlain[2] to the same effect, and in a like spirit, I have accepted with unqualified pleasure a Distinction sanctioned by her Majesty, and which expresses, upon authority entitled to the highest respect, a sense of the national importance of poetic Literature, and so favorable an opinion of the success with which it has been cultivated by one, who, after this additional mark of your esteem, cannot refrain from again assuring you how deeply sensible he is of the many and great obligations he owes to your goodness, and who has the honor to be, dear Sir Robert,

Most faithfully, your humble Servnt,
William Wordsworth

1689. W. W. to C. W.

MS. WL. Hitherto unpublished.

4th April [1843]

My dear Brother,

After declining the Laureatship, I have accepted the Appointment in a consequence of a renewed offer from the Lord Chamberlain enforced by a Letter from a high Quarter which removed my objection, and left me not at liberty to refuse without the utmost ungratiousness the Appointment.

ever your affectate Br
Wm Wordsworth

[1] *Epistles*, I, i, 8–9.

[2] See previous letter.

1690. W. W. to BENJAMIN ROBERT HAYDON

MS. Georgetown University Library.
Haydon (—). LY iii. 1160.

[6 Apr. 1843][1]

My dear Haydon,

Your Letter and the Print[2] it announced I received on the same day. It is as you say an excellent Impression, and the whole effect a great improvement upon the first sketch, which I owe to your kindness.

With much pleasure I congratulate you upon having finished your Cartoons.[3] Let me thank you also for the sketch on the back of your Letter. My verse days are almost over, as they well may be, for to morrow (God willing) I enter upon my 74th year, so that I can scarcely entertain the least hope of gratifying you by writing a Sonnet on either of the Works which you have just executed.

Lord Lansdown,[4] Sir Robert Peel, and Mr Rogers are, I see by the Papers the Persons who are to decide upon the merits of the several Productions that may be offered. They have all proved how much they are interested in works of Art, and their competence to decide, probably is not inferior to that of any other Gentlemen [on] whom the charge might have devolved. So that I hope and trust, you will have no reason to be dissatisfied with their judgement.[5]—

The Laureatship has just been offered to me. At first I declined it on account of my age, but afterwards it was so urgently pressed upon me, and in so flattering a manner, by the Lord

[1] Dated by the reference to W. W.'s birthday.

[2] Probably the engraving by T. Lupton of W. W.'s head from *Wordsworth on Helvellyn.*

[3] For the proposed frescoes in Westminster Hall (see L. 1604 above). Haydon had written on 30 Mar.: 'I have—God be thanked!—got through my cartoons, one from Milton—the 'Curse'—and one from history—'Edward the Black Prince bringing John (of France) through London after Poitiers.' And he fervently acknowledged the support he had received over the years from his religion. 'Hesitation never enters my mind. If for a moment, I hear "go on" audibly, as if wispered. Your "High is our calling", was from the same awful source.' (Haydon, ii. 55–6). Two pen-and-ink sketches of the cartoons were added to the letter.

[4] See L. 1618 above.

[5] But see L. 1715 below.

Chamberlain, that I could not but alter my determination. I am to hold it as merely honorary.[1]

I send you, or rather I beg Mrs Haydon's acceptance of, a Copy of a Little Poem[2] which I wrote two or three weeks ago, upon a subject which inter[es]ted the whole Nation at the time of the Event.

Admiring your perseverance and firmness, and wishing you all success to which your skill and Genius entitle you

I remain my dear Haydon
ever sincerely yours
Wm Wordsworth

P.S. Since Railways were established advantage is taken to charge most extravagantly. Therefor to save either of us expense, when you favor me again as you have so often done before be so good as send the Parcel or Pacquage to Moxon from whom I am in the habit of receiving things without expense, as I could have done in this last case by a Friend, who is just going to London.

1691. W. W. to M. W.

MS. Dr. Williams's Library.
Morley, i. 485.

[Keswick]
[*c.* 12 Apr. 1843][3]

My dearest Love, As I have no reason to expect you today or tomorrow, I much regret that I ordered the Carriage to come this day, or if the weather were bad tomorrow. The morning is fine; so that undoubtedly it will be here. Your account of dear Isabella is upon the whole as favorable as we could expect if we

[1] Haydon replied on 14 Apr.: 'At first I did not like your soiling your immortal name by any Worldly honor. But your explanation has removed in a great degree the feeling though not altogether. You must know your position. But after having fought and conquered by the main force of Virtue and Genius, I think I would have left the World so.' (*MS. Professor Willard Pope*).

[2] *Grace Darling*.

[3] Dated by reference to L. 1696 below.

encourage hope.[1] When dearest shall I see you again. God bless you and all the family

ever yours W W.

Post Office Keswick

Dearest Mary

In consequence of your Letter just received for which accept my very kindest thanks, I shall wait for you till tomorrow keeping the Carriage if it comes—

1692. W. W. to MRS. RITSON[2]

MS. Henry E. Huntington Library. Hitherto unpublished.

April 13th 1843.

Mr and Mrs Wordsworth of Rydal Mount passed several days in Mrs Ritson's Lodgings as visitors of Miss Fenwick and the whole Party, including Mr Quillinan and Mr Northcott,[3] were much gratified with the attentions paid them, and pleased with the accommodations.

Wm Wordsworth

1693. W. W. to SIR JAMES McGRIGOR[4]

MS. Henry E. Huntington Library.
LY iii. 1162.

Rydal Mount
16th April—1843.

My dear Sir James,

Presuming upon your kindness so often experienced I do not scruple to enclose a part of a Letter just received from my

[1] Isabella W. was threatened with a miscarriage.

[2] Probably the landlady in Bath with whom the Wordsworths stayed just before Dora W.'s marriage to E. Q. in May 1841.

[3] Probably one of I. F.'s Somerset acquaintances, George Barons Northcote (1796–1875), of Somerset Court, Brent Knoll: High Sheriff for Somerset, 1855.

[4] See pt. iii, L. 1336. He replied on 3 May (*WL MSS.*) that he would do anything in his power to help W. W.'s nephew, but feared that he suffered from serious disease.

Nephew, John Wordsworth.[1] Be so good as to cast your eyes over it—It explains itself.

With every good wish and truly sensible of your kind offices

I have the honor to remain
dear Sir James,
faithfully yours
Wm Wordsworth

1694. W. W. to JAMES MONTGOMERY

Address: James Montgomery, The Mount, Sheffield. [*In M. W.'s hand*]
MS. Cornell.
Broughton, p. 82.

Rydal Mount
Ambleside
16th April 1843

My dear Sir,

Allow me to ask if you are acquainted with Mr Ebenezer Elliot the Poet.[2] Mr Southey's Exors, his Brother Dr Southey and Mr Henry Taylor are endeavouring to collect his Letters, and as I have reason to believe, that long ago he wrote several to Mr Elliot, could you ask him in their name and that of the family if he has any objection to their publication, or at least to the publication of extracts or a portion of them. If he is not unwilling that they should be given to the world, can you ask him to be so kind as to send the Pacquet to

Henry Taylor Esq
Blandford Square
London

[1] R. W.'s son had become seriously ill with chronic bronchitis while serving in the Ionian Islands, and was now preparing to return home. The progress of his disease can be traced in several letters he wrote to his mother, Mrs. Lightfoot, 1840–3. (*Mrs. M. J. Roberts MSS.*) He wrote to W. W. again in May from Gibraltar, where he remained for two or three weeks to recruit his strength before completing the voyage home.

[2] See pt. ii, L. 794. His epic *Spirits and Men* was dedicated to James Montgomery. See also Southey, vi. 219–20; Curry, ii. 375, 406.

With many good wishes and the most sincere respect

I remain
my dear Sir
faithfully yours
Wm Wordsworth

1695. W. W. to THOMAS NOON TALFOURD

MS. Carl H. Pforzheimer Library. Hitherto unpublished.

Rydal Mount.
16th April 1843

My dear Sergeant Talfourd,

Thanks for your little Vol:[1] which I have looked over with much pleasure, and also for the elegant and impressive sonnet which accompanies it.

I should have written sooner, but I did not like to trouble you with my Letter, while you were so busy upon the Circuit; but rather than delay my acknowledgment longer I run something of that risk.

It is not likely that I shall be in Town this season unless it be on my way to the Continent, which I regret the more, as I cannot encourage the hope of profiting by your kind invitation. But with respect to London, I will say at once to you as one of its, to me, most interesting Inhabitants, I have too great a weight of years upon my head, to feel equal to the engagements in which I am there entangled; my eyes in particular suffered much last spring from hot rooms, late dinners, and glaring lights.

With a thousand good wishes for yourself and yours, I remain my dear Sergeant

faithfully yours
Wm Wordsworth

[1] *Recollections of a first visit to the Alps, in August and September, 1841*, [privately printed], London, [? 1842]. See *R.M. Cat.*, no. 164 which refers to a MS. sonnet 'on the Reception of the Poet Wordsworth at Oxford', which is presumably the sonnet referred to in this letter.

1696. W. W. to SIR JOHN TAYLOR COLERIDGE

MS. British Library. Hitherto unpublished.

Rydal Mount
17th April 1843

My dear Mr Justice Coleridge,

You have entered completely into my motives upon first declining, and afterwards accepting the Laureateship; and I sincerely thank you for your congratulations—

The dissentions introduced into the family of our lamented Friend[1] by his second marriage have proved most deplorable. But I am happy to report that during a late residence of nearly a week at Keswick I was daily witness of the truly Christian dispositions which prevailed in Miss Southey's[2] heart and mind.

She wrote a most beautiful and touching conciliatory Letter to her sister Edith, which I trust will be met as it ought to be. In respect to Mrs Southey she found a difficulty, not in bringing herself to a proper frame of mind toward Mrs S., but how and through whose mediation she could communicate with Her, so that they might part upon terms of peace and good will mutually declared. This might however be effected through Edith if she receives her Sister's letter in the spirit from which it proceeded.

We are truly sorry that dear Sara has had so much to suffer upon this occasion, and so soon after her sad bereavement.

Mrs Wordsworth, who is in good health as I also am, unites with me in kind remembrances to yourself and Lady Coleridge.

And believe me
My dear Sir
ever faithfully yours
W Wordsworth

[1] Southey.

[2] Kate Southey.

1697. W. W. to GEORGE HUNTLY GORDON[1]

MS. Cornell.
Broughton, p. 48.

Rydal Mount
17th April 1843

My dear Mr Gordon

Absence from home has prevented my replying sooner to your Letter which I was glad to see.

The Report of your decease, that reached me long ago, must no doubt have risen from the frightful accident to which you allude. May you be preserved in future from such mishaps to which you are more exposed by living in that crowded City, than you would be elsewhere.

I am gratified by your liking Grace Darling, so much and send you with pleasure the Enclosed. The only Copy that I have seen in the Newspapers was reprinted from the Sun;[2] and if I may judge from hasty perusal it was correct.—

As no doubt you frequently write to your Father, pray thank him in my name for his kind remembrance in sending me as he did the other day, his Book upon Belgium which I have found very agreeable reading.

Believe me to be
dear Mr Gordon
faithfully yours
Wm Wordsworth

1698. W. W. to DAVID LAING

MS. Edinburgh University Library. Hitherto unpublished.

Rydal Mount
20th April
1843—

Dear Mr Laing,

I was glad to be remembered by you upon the occasion of my being appointed Successor in the Laureateship to my lamented

[1] See pt. i, L. 351.

[2] *Grace Darling* (see L. 1672 above) was reprinted in the *Kentish Observer* on 6 Apr. and thereafter in several London papers. See J. D. Vann, 'The Publication of Wordsworth's *Grace Darling*, *NQ*, ccxxiii (1978), 223–5.

Friend, Southey; and I thank you for your cordial congratulations.

On account of my age I at first declined the honor, but it was so pressed upon me afterwards, and under such circumsances as removed my objection, that I accepted it with pleasure.

I send you a Copy of a little Poem[1] written a few weeks ago upon a subject which interested the Public greatly at the time the event happened. My Verses got surreptitiously into a provincial newspaper, and perhaps you may have met with [them] incorrectly printed, in which case this correct impression may be acceptable.

Believe me my dear Sir
faithfully
your obliged
Wm Wordsworth

1699. W. W. to EDWARD TRAPP PILGRIM[2]

Address: E. T. Pilgrim, Esqre, Mount Radford, Exeter. [*In M. W.'s hand*]
Stamp: Ambleside.
MS. Cornell. Hitherto unpublished.

Rydal Mount
Ambleside
22nd April 1843.

The Poet Laureate, A Septuagenarian, returns thanks to an Octogenarian Pilgrim for the honor of the Verses which he has just received, and for the two little Collections of Poems, which he has not only received but already read, at least much the greater part of them, with much pleasure

Wm Wordsworth

[1] *Grace Darling.*

[2] Author of *Poetical Trifles*, 1785, and *Hymns*, Exeter, 1828 (3rd edn. 1837).

1700. W. W. to GEORGE TICKNOR

MS. Baker Library, Dartmouth College.
Judson Stanley Lyon, 'Wordsworth and Ticknor', PMLA lxvi (1951), 432–40.

Rydal Mount
Ambleside 24th April 43

My dear Mr. Ticknor,

The Exrs of my lamented Friend Southey are engaged in collecting his correspondence, and their views, in performance of this duty, having extended to America, I have undertaken to address you in the hope that you may have some Letters of his writing in your possession; and also that you may happen to know whether he was in correspondence with other gentlemen of your Country. In either of these cases I am pretty sure that the request I have to make viz that you would forward to the Exrs such Letters, as are in your possession or you can procure, will be readily complied with. Of course I mean such as are fit to be published, and likely to prove interesting.

Mr Everett,[1] your Minister thinks that S— had, besides yourself, one or two Correspondents in Boston, and names Mr W. P. Greenwood.[2] He is known to have written to Mrs Brooks,[3] but we are ignorant of her address.—The literary Exr is Henry Taylor Esq Blandford Square London, who will be most happy to receive any communication from you upon this subject.

And now let me express a hope on Mrs Wordsworths part and my own that you and Mrs. Ticknor and your family are in good health, as we ourselves are nowithstanding our advanced age.—Be assured dear Mr Ticknor that we think of you and yours with no little interest and many good wishes—It is

[1] See L. 1613 above.

[2] The Revd. Francis William Pitt Greenwood (1797–1843), author of *The Theology of the Cambridge Divinity School*, Boston, 1830; *A History of King's Chapel, in Boston, the first Episcopal Church in New England*, Boston, 1833; and other religious works.

[3] Mary Gowen Brooks (*c.* 1794–1845) known as 'Maria del Occidente', published *Judith, Esther, and Other Poems, By a Lover of the Fine Arts*, Boston, 1820. She began to correspond with Southey in 1826: in 1831 she came to Europe and stayed at Keswick, and Southey helped with the London publication of her poem *Zophiel*, 1833. (See Warter, iv. 214–5, 361). He called her 'the most expressive and most impassioned of all Poetesses' (see *The Doctor*, Ch. liv). She died in Cuba. See also *R.M.Cat.*, no. 560.

probably not unknown to you that several of my nearest kindred and dearest friends have suffered by their unfortunate confidence in American credit and integrity;[1] you will be pleased to hear that I myself am not one of the sufferers, directly, but that [my] own worldly[2] circumstances are as good as any moderate Man could desire. My younger Son has been appointed my Successor in the office which I held, and a Pension has been granted me. And the other day I had the honor of being appointed Poet Laureat, an office which at first I declined on account of my advanced years, but it was afterwards pressed upon me as *an honor merely*, in such a manner that I should have been ill at ease in my own mind, if I had persisted in my first resolution.

With kindest remembrance to Mrs Ticknor and yourself in which Mrs W. unites I remain

dear Mr Ticknor
faithfully yours
Wm Wordsworth

1701. W. W. to EDWARD MOXON

MS. Henry E. Huntington Library.
LY iii. 1162.

Rydal Mount
27th April.—43

Dear Mr Moxon,

By yesterday's Post I received your Letter containing a Bill for 95–13–8 on account of my Poems lately published, together with my private account—I am glad to hear that we have a prospect of seeing you soon, when we can talk matters over in a much more satisfactory way than we could treat them by Letter. Let us know, as soon as you can, when we may expect you, lest[3] we should be from home.

[1] In his reply of 29 June, Ticknor deplored the continuance of repudiation by the delinquent states: 'I believe it would be necessary for me to travel several hundred miles, in order to discover an individual of any class or condition in society, who would sustain that doctrine in relation to any state in the Union. . . Now throughout the whole country, the condition of the dishonest states is beginning to be felt, as disgrace too severe to be borne.' (*WL MSS.*)

[2] *Written* wordly.

[3] *Written* least.

In regard to Mr Southey's Mss[1] I should be most happy to serve you, were it in my power; but it is not likely that I shall be consulted. Dr Southey and Mr Taylor are the Executors and in all probability the latter will have the management of the literary part. As he is in Town would there be any harm in your calling upon him yourself, and stating your wishes. Mr Rogers is on terms of Friendship with Mr Taylor and might assist in promoting your object, by personal interview, without the formality of express interference which one is naturally delicate about. The well-known friendly disposition of Mr Southey to you as a Publisher, and the kindness which Mr Rogers has ever shewn you, which Mr Taylor must be well aware of, would furnish sufficient grounds for his endeavouring to aid you upon this occasion.—

I enclose for your *own perusal* a little Poem[2] I wrote two or three weeks ago.

You may have heard of your Friend W. W's late proceedings as to matrimony. He will be in Town early next month, solely with reference to this object;[3] so that he will scarcely be able to see so much of his old Friends, at this time, as He and They might wish.

Kindest remembrances to Mrs Moxon and your Sister and Brother, in which Mrs W. unites. How is Miss Lamb?[4]

believe with great regard ever faithfully

yours

Wm Wordsworth

[1] See also L. 1682 above.

[2] *Grace Darling.*

[3] W. W. jnr.'s engagement to Mary Monkhouse (see L. 1674 above) had been broken off. '. . . the obvious fatuity of the poor girl,' E. Q. commented, 'which may still farther degenerate into downright imbecility of mind, if it assume no worse shape, must satisfy him that he has missed a heavy and fearful burthen.' (Morley, i. 493).

[4] '. . . how altered she is!' H. C. R. recorded after visiting Mary Lamb on 19 Mar. 'Deafness has succeeded to her other infirmities. She is a mere wreck of herself.' (*HCR* ii. 630).

1702. W. W. to ALEXANDER DYCE

Address: Rev^{d}. A. Dyce, Grays Inn.
MS. Victoria and Albert Museum. Hitherto unpublished.

Rydal
[? Apr. 1843]

My dear Mr Dyce

Hoping that you may think the verses[1] I send herewith worthy of being inserted in one of the Volumes of your Copy of my poems I beg your acceptance of them. They were composed very lately. Your health I hear is pretty good.

ever faithfully your Servant
Wm Wordsworth

1703. W. W. to SIR WILLIAM ROWAN HAMILTON

MS. Cornell.
Hamilton. Grosart. K (—). LY iii. 1163.

April 1843

My dear Sir W^{m},

The sight of your handwriting was very welcome, and not the less so because your Sister had led me to expect a Letter from you.

The Laureatship was offered to me in the most flattering terms, by the Lord Chamberlain, of course with the approbation of the Queen; but I declined it on account of my advanced age. I then received a 2nd Letter from his Lordship urging my acceptance of it, and assuring me that it was intended merely as an honorary distinction for the past, without the smallest reference to any service to be attached to it. From Sir R. Peel I had also a Letter to the same effect, and the substance and manner of both were such that if I had still rejected the offer, I should have been little at peace with my own mind—

Thank you for your translations. The longer Poem[2] would have given me more pain than pleasure, but for your addition which sets all right.

[1] Probably *Grace Darling*.

[2] A translation of Schiller's *Die Ideale* to which Hamilton added an extra stanza. See *Hamilton*, ii. 252.

The attack upon W. S. L.[1] to which you allude was written by my Son in Law; but without any sanction from me, much less encouragement; in fact I knew nothing about it or the preceding Article of Landor that had called it forth, till after Mr Qu's had appeared. He knew very well that I should have disapproved of his condescending to notice anything that a man so deplorably tormented by ungovernable passion as that unhappy creature might eject. His character may be given in two or three words; a mad-man, a bad-man, yet a man of genius, as many a madman is.—I have not eyesight to spare for Periodical Literature, so with exception of a Newspaper now and then, I never look into anything of the kind, except some particular article may be recommended to me by a Friend upon whose judgement I can rely.

You are quite at liberty to print when and where you like any verses you may do me the honor of writing upon, or addressing to, me—

Your Godson,[2] his Sister, and four Brothers, are all doing well. He is a very clever boy, and more than that, being of an original or rather peculiar structure of intellect, and his heart appears to be not inferior to his head, so that I trust he will as a man do you no discredit.

[*A further sheet missing*]

[1] Landor's second imaginary conversation between Porson and Southey, in which he attacked W. W., appeared in *Blackwood's Magazine*, lii (Dec. 1842), 687–715. See *Works* (ed. Welby and Wheeler), v. 166–213. E. Q.'s reply, which took the form of a dialogue between Landor and 'Christopher North', followed in Apr. 1843 (liii. 518–36). 'As day is partitioned between light and darkness,' North is made to say, 'so has the public taste as to Wordsworth been divided between his reverers and the followers of the Jeffrey heresy. After a lengthened winter, Wordsworth's glory is now in the long summer days: all good judgments that lay torpid have been awakened, and the light prevails against the darkness. But as bats and owls, the haters of light, are ever most restless in the season when nights are shortest, so are purblind egotists most uneasy when their dusky range is contracted by the near approach and sustained ascendency of genius.' The reply was composed in January, but W. W. himself did not see it before publication. See Super, *Walter Savage Landor*, pp. 341–5; Morley, i. 475–6, 478, 480–1; and *HCR* ii. 630. Most of E. Q.'s rejoinder is printed by Morley, ii. 852 ff.

[2] John W.'s son William.

1704. W. W. to EDWARD MOXON

MS. Henry E. Huntington Library.
LY iii. 1164.

[early May 1843]

Dear Mr Moxon,

Excuse my troubling you with the Enclosed. It is, as you will find, from the second Son of Mr Leigh Hunt,[1] and describes the Writer and his family, as in a state of bitter distress. I have known so many instances in which facts have been exaggerated by persons in need, and that from causes for which some allowance may be made, that I apprehend it is possible the like may have occurred here. If you could ascertain whether the Writer is actually in the condition that he describes I should be obliged to you if you would let him have *three Pounds* on my account. More I cannot spare, many of my own near kin being in very narrow circumstances, and demands being made upon me from numerous quarters, with which I have no connection, but as a public Man.—

Be so good as to send directed for me half a dozen Copies of my 7 Volumes, through Whitaker's, to be forwarded in their next Kendal parcel to Hudson and Nicholson Booksellers, Kendal; your Porter having ascertained that Hudson and Nicholson continued to deal with Whitaker.

We are very sorry you did not come down at Easter as you promised, there is no likelihood of my being in London this season—

It was quite out of my power to apply to Lord Lowther[2] as your Brother[3] requested. I did not see him, but he has I know applications a hundred times more numerous than he can listen to, and this from Parties in Cumberland and West^nd^ with whom he is *locally* connected. I am truly sorry that I cannot meet your Brother's wish in this affair for the reason mentioned, and because the Lowther family have conferred so many substantial favors on me and mine.—Besides my Son Wm tells me that the

[1] John Hunt (1812–45). See also Ls. 1708 and 1709 below.

[2] Now Postmaster General, and called to the Upper House (1841) during his father's lifetime.

[3] Moxon had four brothers, two in the law, and two employed by himself. The reference here is to one of the latter, John or Alfred. See Merriam, *Edward Moxon Publisher of Poets*, pp. 189–90.

chances are small for any applicant, unconnected with the Post office Department, yet possibly he might through interest be introduced at the bottom or lowest step of the department. Nothing for its *own sake* worth accepting can be had but by those who have served for many years.

Ever faithfully yours
Wm Wordsworth

1705. W. W. to SARA COLERIDGE

Address: Mrs H. N. Coleridge, Chester Place, Regents Park, London.
Postmark: 2 May 1843.
Stamp: Ambleside.
Endorsed: Mr Wordsworth on Editorship.
MS. Victoria University Library, Toronto. Hitherto unpublished.

Rydal Mount 2nd May 43

My dear Sara,

I feel absolutely certain that your Father never was *Editor* of any periodical Publication whatsoever except The *Watchman*[1] and the *Friend*, neither of which as you know were long continued, and the Friend expressly excluded even allusion to temporary topics; nor, to the best of my remembrance, had the Watchman any thing of the Character of a Newspaper. When he was very young he published several Sonnets in a London Newspaper,[2] I cannot name which, and for these perhaps he might be paid some [? remuneration][3]. Afterwards he was in strict connection with Stuart and Street[4] Editors or at least Proprietors of one or more Newspapers, the Courier and the Morning Post, and in one of these, I think it was the latter, your Father *wrote* a great deal and even for some time he took up his Abode in the House in the Strand where the office of one of these I think the Morning Post was. I am *sure* he lived there for

[1] Published at Bristol at eight-day intervals from 1 Mar. to 13 May, 1796. See *Collected Works of Samuel Taylor Coleridge, The Watchman*, ed. Lewis Patton, 1970.

[2] See 'Sonnets on Eminent Characters', *Morning Chronicle*, Dec. 1794—Jan. 1795; and Griggs, i. 131 ff.

[3] *MS. obscure.*

[4] Daniel Stuart and T. G. Street. See *Collected Works of Samuel Taylor Coleridge, Essays on His Times*, ed. David V. Erdman, 3 vols., 1978.

some time, for I went up to Town on purpose to visit him while there resident. No doubt he would often be seen in that Office, and as he was known to write in the Paper this might have induced the belief to which you allude viz that he was Editor or Proprietor which to my certain knowledge he never was. But if you wish for the *particulars* of his Newspaper connection Mr Daniel Stuart No 9 upper Harley street could furnish you with all that you could possibly require.

As I understand from Miss Fenwick that she is writing to you about dear Kate I need not mention her further than to say that I am entirely satisfied with all that she has done towards her Sister and Mrs S.[1] nay far more than satisfied. I wish that I could think with the least pleasure of the other Parties.

To return a moment to the Newspaper business. So convinced was I of the great Service that your Father rendered Stuarts Paper, far beyond the Payment, which however was liberal, that he received one way or another, that I urged him to put in his claim to be admitted a Proprietor; but this he declined having a great disinclination to any *tie* of that kind. In fact he could not bear being *shackled* in any way. I have heard him say that he should be sorry if any one offered him an Estate, for he should feel the possession would involve cares and duties that would be a clog to him—Mrs Wordsworth left us on Sunday to see her Daughter Isabella, who is in a very precarious state. Dr Ferguson has been written to a 2nd time, and we are looking most anxiously for the Report of his opinion, as to what is to be done. From one circumstance we draw some little Comfort, it is ascertained that there is no *Child* to be looked for, and also what her Complaint is namely an internal inflammation which they must endeavour to subdue.

I am glad to hear so favourable an account of your dear Mother's health: pray remember me most kindly to her, with my best wishes that she may continue to go on well.

My poor Sister is much in the state she has been long in; certainly no worse. Dora is something better, but quite unable to use outdoor exercise except in a Carriage.—

I shall write to the Judge[2] to do all that I can, or assure him of my sympathy with him and the Mother of their Child, upon this afflicting loss.

To comment upon the most important part of your Letter,

[1] Mrs. Southey.

[2] J. T. Coleridge. See next letter.

my dear Sara, that which relates to your Father's religious faith and opinions and your own as governed by them I feel incompetent at present. To do so with any satisfaction to you or myself would require an attentive reperusal of his multifarious theological works, which I could not now undertake. In respect however to the posthumous Work[1] which you specially allude to, I may without scruple repeat what I remember to have written either to yourself or to your departed Husband, that I was greatly pleased with it. Nevertheless there is in it one important point, treated in a manner, which might tend I think to mislead ordinary Readers, or which at any rate is hazardous to half-thinkers—I mean what your Father says upon the inspiration of the Scriptures. When I have the happiness to see you my dear Child for so sanctioned by yourself I will continue to call you we will read that Tract together, and discuss it with a care and frankness of declaration, which I trust may prove profitable to us both. Ever most affectionately and faithfully

yours
Wm Wordsworth

1706. W. W. to SIR JOHN TAYLOR COLERIDGE

MS. Cornell.
K (—). *LY iii. 1165* (—).

Rydal Mount
13th May 43

My dear Mr Justice Coleridge,

Having learned from the newspapers that you have resumed your official duties, I do not scruple to break in upon you for a

[1] *Confessions of an Enquiring Spirit*, published by Henry Nelson Coleridge in 1840. In a letter to W. W. of this year, Sara Coleridge had confessed to a distressing sense of isolation from other believers as a result of adopting her father's views: 'I have often felt it painful to be isolated, as in some measure I am, by the way of looking at certain subjects of universal interest, which a familiarity and sympathy with my Father's mind, so far as I can understand it, has brought me into, and which, I rather think, no one ever unreservedly adopted but *for good*, that is finally. I feel the pain, however, without a wish to have it removed by any means which I can hope to see effectual in my life, even if hereafter general opinion on those subjects should be modified as my Father would have had it.' (*Texas University MSS.*).

moment, though it be only to assure you of what you and Lady Coleridge must be well aware,—my sincere sympathy with you both in your late affliction.[1] In this feeling Mrs W. deeply shares, and unites with me in prayer to the Father of Mercy that you may bear with resignation this, and the other losses of beloved kindred,[2] to which by his will you have so recently in succession been subjected. Our excellent friend Mrs Arnold was so good as to shew me a Letter written to her by yourself immediately after your dear son had been taken from you. A blessed state of mind did these few words indicate; and I trust that, through the Grace of God, you have been able to maintain it. I need say no more. May the rest of your children be preserved to each other and to their parents. I remain,

Yours most faithfully,
Wm Wordsworth

P.S. Pray do not trouble yourself to notice this Letter.—

1707. W. W. to JOHN CRITCHLEY PRINCE[3]

MS. Sir Roger Mynors.
LY iii. 1166.

Rydal Mount Ambleside
May 15th —1843

Mr Wordsworth thanks Mr Prince for his Tribute to the memory of Mr Southey, protesting only however, as he does

[1] The death from typhoid fever on 25 Apr. of their youngest son Frederick.

[2] Sir John Coleridge's only sister Frances, Lady Patterson (see pt. ii, L. 564), had died on 28 Nov. 1842, to be followed on 26 Jan. 1843 by his younger brother Henry Nelson Coleridge (see L. 1668 above). More recently, he had lost his uncle, the Revd. Edward Coleridge (1760–1843), S. T. C.'s elder brother, vicar of Buckerell, nr. Ottery St. Mary. See Ernest Hartley Coleridge, *Life and Correspondence of John Duke Coleridge, Lord Chief Justice of England*, 2 vols., 1904, i. 110–12.

[3] John Critchley Prince (1808–66), born at Wigan, brought out his first volume, *Hours with the Muses*, 1841, while he was still working in a factory. Encouraged by its success (by 1857 it had reached its 6th edn.), he went to Manchester where he kept a small shop, but lived chiefly by his pen. His poem *On the Death of Robert Southey, late Poet Laureate*, as published in his *Poetical Works*, 1880, contains no censure; it was probably cut out as the result of W. W.'s protest. (de Selincourt's note). See R. A. D. Lithgow, *Life of J. C. Prince*, Manchester, 1880.

strongly against the censure passed on his departed Friend towards the conclusion of the Poem, which censure he knows to be utterly undeserved and most unjust. Mr W. will with pleasure subscribe, as also his Friend Miss Fenwick, to Mr Prince's new poem, and thanks him for the offer of the preceding Vol.—

1708. W. W. to EDWARD MOXON

MS. Henry E. Huntington Library.
LY iii. 1166.

[26 May 1843]

Dear Mr Moxon,

I fear you have found it unpleasant and difficult to obtain the information about Leigh Hunt's son,[1] which I hoped you might gain for my guidance.—

I have now [to] request another small favor. Sir William Martins[2] of St James Palace, has written to suggest that some friend of mine should call at his Office there, to receive my appointment as Laureate. Will you be so kind as to render me this service. The Fees upon the occasion, he tells me, may be paid out of the Salary when it becomes due; as it is not likely that I shall be in Town at the time to receive the Salary myself, would you allow me to furnish you with a Power of Att^y^ to receive it when it becomes due. Perhaps by inquiring at Sir Wm's Office you could learn this, when you call for the Appointment.

ever faithfully yours
Wm Wordsworth

[*In M. W.'s hand*]

You need not forward the Appointment—but take care of it till we meet.

[1] See L. 1704 above and next letter.

[2] Sir William Martins had written on 22 Apr., sending the form of oath which W. W. had to take in the presence of a magistrate on his appointment as Poet Laureate. He wrote again on 12 May that the official appointment had now been drawn up, and that the fee of 12 guineas would be deducted from the salary (*WL MSS.*).

1709. W. W. to EDWARD MOXON

MS. Henry E. Huntington Library.
LY iii. 1167.

Rydal Mount
27 May 1843

Dear Mr Moxon,

Before I received yours yesterday, I sent off a Letter in the Post for you, or I need not have troubled you with this—

I am sorry Leigh Hunt has got such a graceless Son—You have done quite well in letting him have no more than a Sovereign. People of this Class cannot be served effectually; assistance is thrown away upon them, and it is rather upon one's own account than theirs, that their requests are at all attended to. There is another sort of request very troublesome, to which I have, I think, become still more liable since I was made Laureate—I mean Solicitations that I would subscribe to Volumes of Poems about to be published. Two of these I have had, within these last few days.

It is well that you only sent 4 sets of the 7 Volumes, they are to supply the Ambleside summer market, and neither of our Booksellers is quite out; what you have sent will prove sufficient.

I dont mean to make any alteration[1] in the Stereotype, so you may go to Press and proceed as rapidly as you like.

Would it not be well to regulate the number you strike off by the Copies of the 7th vol on hand—only not taking off quite so many, so that a few might be spared to be sold separately to those who having the 6 vols, may want the 7th to complete their set.[2]

I am decidedly of Opinion [that the price] should be lowered—at least to 7/- when sold along with the six—perhaps to 5/-.

By the bye the Poem of Grace Darling having been published,[3]

[1] From this point onwards the letter is in M. W.'s hand.

[2] *Poems, Chiefly of Early and Late Years* was issued with an alternative title-page, for the use of those who wished to treat it as the seventh volume of the collected edition, which was now being reprinted. See *Cornell Wordsworth Collection*, nos. 118–9.

[3] See L. 1672 above.

as it were without my knowledge, should be added—to the end of the 7th vol—as it has been much liked.

If you have any Copies of the Excursion send me 4 Copies by any opportunity that may occur. Thanks for your 2d letter and for your readiness of meeting my wish respecting the Laureate's business.

The fees—as Sir Wm Martins mentioned amounting to £12-12 might be paid out of the first payment of the Salary as also the power of Attorney.

With Mrs W's kind regards joined to my own,

believe me ever yours
W Wordsworth

May 28th

We are glad you think still of coming to the North, for my Son John is in great affliction on account of his Wife's illness.

1710. W. W. to JAMES MONTGOMERY

MS. WL.
Life of Montgomery, vi. 160 (—). LY iii. 1168.

Rydal Mount 2nd June 1843.

My dear Sir,

I am very sorry that you have been at all anxious about the result of your application to Mr Elliot.[1] Immediately he wrote to me, and told me that the Letters in his possession should be forwarded, as requested, to Mr Taylor. He was quite earnest in this determination, and strongly expressed his regret that in compliance with the persecuting solicitations of certain American autograph-hunters, he had parted with several letters which he had received from Mr Southey. Mr Taylor, (who you will be sorry to hear is not in good health) has notwithstanding written in many directions to procure as much as could be got together of Mr Southey's correspondence; and to spare him trouble, which he is not equal to, I took upon me to address you upon the subject; otherwise Mr T. would in his character of Exr have himself written to Mr Elliot though not acquainted with that Gentleman.

I have just turned to Mr Elliot's Letter and will transcribe part

[1] Ebenezer Elliott, the Corn Law Rhymer. See L. 1694 above.

of his words—'I have still thirteen Letters of Mr S. which (with others if I can recover them) I will forward as requested in about a week.' So that my dear Sir we may both be easy upon the subject; I must however repeat my regret, that it has occasioned you so much trouble.—

I am truly sensible of the kindness of your expressions upon my appointment of the Laureateship, which I at first refused on account of my advanced age. But it was afterwards pressed upon me so strongly by the Lord Chamberlain, and by Sir Robert Peel himself, that I could not possibly persist in the refusal, and especially as her Majesty's name and approval were again referred to; and I was assured that it was offered me solely in consideration of what I had already done in Literature, and without the least view to future exertion as connected with the honor. It has since gratified me to learn from many quarters, that the Appointment has given universal satisfaction; and I need scarcely add that it has afforded me a *melancholy* pleasure to be thought worthy of succeeding my revered Friend. Believe me faithfully your obliged

Wm Wordsworth

My Letters are all *scrawls*, therefore excuse this.

1711. W. W. to RICHARD PARKINSON

MS. Cornell.
Broughton, p. 83.

Rydal Mount
2nd June 1843

My dear Sir,

It gives me pleasure to send you herewith a Drawing of Seathwaite Chapel copied (and improved) from one done many years ago upon the spot by a deceased Friend of mine. It is a faithful Portrait of the humble Edifice; I cannot, however, but regret that a delineation of the Cottage Parsonage in which *The Wonderful*[1] dwelt so long, and the exterior of which has been little altered, I believe, since his time, is not included in the Sketch; as it stands so very near the Chapel.—I hope you and

[1] The Revd. Robert Walker.

Mrs Parkinson will be able to look in upon us, when you return to Manchester. Believe me my dear Sir,

faithfully yours, Wm Wordsworth

I was very much pleased with your prefatory remarks,[1] and especially by the manner in which you illustrate true Church principles, by the effect of the erroneous proceedings of the good and pious Newton and his Successor, both first rate men in their ways.—

When the Engraver has done with the Drawing, let me have it again, as I should like to preserve it for my Friend's sake who copied it, and also as it is better done than the original sketch, with a view to the probability of its being engraved at some future time for the Duddon Sonnets—Of course any Friend of yours may copy it, if you wish that to be done.

[1] In his introduction to *The Old Church Clock* (see L. 1672 above), Parkinson maintained that the doctrines of the Church could not be preserved by oral teaching alone: they needed to be embodied in external observances, which would commend them to the heart and the imagination of the believer. This was the Prayer Book system, upheld by Robert Walker; and Parkinson contrasted with it the practice of John Newton, the Evangelical curate of Olney (see pt. ii, L. 855), who relied almost entirely on preaching. 'No one can read Cowper's beautiful letters with regard to that place and time, and not be painfully convinced of the evanescent nature of all impressions which are merely made by individual teaching on individual minds, without some external bond of union by which a religious society may be held together when the hand that first combined it has been withdrawn . . . Thus, nearly all the traces of the teaching of that good man disappeared almost as soon as his warning voice had ceased to sound in the ears of his at the time willing hearers.' Newton's successor was another Evangelical, the Biblical commentator Thomas Scott (1747–1821). W. W.'s remarks here are probably influenced by his reading of the second volume of Southey's *Life of Cowper*.

1712. W. W. to ALEXANDER DYCE

Address: The Rev[d] Alex: Dyce, Gray's Inn, London.
Postmark: 8 June 1843.
Stamp: Ambleside.
MS. Victoria and Albert Museum.
LY iii. 1169.

Rydal Mount June 6th '43

Dear Mr Dyce,

A Friend of mine[1] wants to obtain, if possible, *more* copious information about the Institution of the Office of Poet Laureate in this Country, and the earliest Holders of the Office, than is to be got at in Selden,[2] Wood,[3] and those late writers who have echoed T. Warton's Notices from them.[4] He would also be obliged to any one who would would point out to him the sources of any thing *curious* or interesting relative to foreign Laureats; and not to be found in the popular accounts of Petrarch, Tasso, and Metastasio[5] (was Skelton a *Court* Laureate, for Bernard[6] was Laureat to Henry 7 and 8). Knowing that you are not a man of leisure, I would by no means trouble you for more than short hints on the subject of these Queries.

A reply at your early convenience will much oblige dear Sir

faithfully yours
Wm Wordsworth

I am curious about Skelton, and shall be truly glad to receive your Book.[7] Mr Moxon can forward anything to me as arranged

[1] E. Q., who was writing an essay on *The Laureates of England*. See *Mem.* ii. 403.

[2] i.e. in *Titles of Honour* by John Selden (1584–1654), the jurist.

[3] Anthony Wood, *Athenae Oxonienses*.

[4] In his *History of English Poetry*, 3 vols., 1774–81, ii. 130 ff. Thomas Warton the younger was Poet Laureate, 1785–90.

[5] Pietro Metastasio (1698–1782), Italian poet and dramatist: imperial court poet in Vienna from 1730.

[6] Bernard Andreas Tholosatis (*c.* 1456–*c.* 1530), a blind Augustinian friar from Oxford, who joined the courts of Henry VII and Henry VIII and celebrated their achievements in numerous Latin poems. On 21 Nov. 1486 he was granted an annuity of ten marks as Poet Laureate, and this is the first official reference to the office. He was later appointed Historiographer Royal as well. See E. K. Broadus, *The Laureateship*, Oxford, 1921. W. W. probably owed his knowledge of Bernard to Warton's *History* (ii. 132–3).

[7] Dyce's edition of Skelton appeared this year.

between us either in the Kendal Bookseller's weekly parcel, or by a private Friend as may happen. Pray mention how you are in health, and how your worldly affairs are turning out.[1] I heard of those unpleasantnesses with great concern.

1713. W. W. to SIR JOHN TAYLOR COLERIDGE

Endorsed: *1843* June 27th *W. Wordsworth*. Rydal Mount.
MS. British Library.
K (—). *LY iii. 1170* (—).

Rydal Mount
27th June 1843[2]

My dear Mr Justice Coleridge,

Accept my sincere thanks for the moving particulars concerning your departed child,[3] and his sorrowing Mother, which you have so kindly communicated. Truly happy am I to find that after your severe bereavement your own Mind is brought to a state which promises all that could be desired you should aim at, and I hope earnestly that it will not be long before Your Partner in these afflictions is by the grace of God enabled to keep pace with you in submission to his Will and habitual resignation.

It gratifies me to learn that your Uncle's[4] remains are to be removed to Henry's Vault.[5] The change has very much to recommend it, and is liable to no objections.

In respect to Mr Southey's Monument it was not intended that it should interfere in the least with any testimony that might

[1] In an undated letter of early summer 1842, Dyce had acknowledged W. W.'s gift of the *Poems, Chiefly of Early and Late Years*, expressing his 'great delight' with the whole volume, and singling out particularly *The Borderers*, *To the Clouds*, and the *Epistle to Sir G. Beaumont* for praise. He also referred to his own affairs, the quarrel that had broken out in his family, and the suit in chancery he was threatened with. He had lost the greater part of his income as a shareholder in a Scottish bank. (*Dyce MSS., Victoria and Albert Museum*). See also Anthony Burton, 'The Private Life of Alexander Dyce', *Blackwood's Magazine*, cccxxvi (Nov. 1979), 398–409.

[2] *Written* 1834.

[3] Frederick (see L. 1706 above).

[4] i.e. S. T. C.

[5] The vault recently prepared in Highgate churchyard for Henry Nelson Coleridge. Mrs. S. T. C., Sara, and her son Herbert were also eventually interred there. See Griggs, vi. 993–4.

be paid to his Memory at Westminster Abbey. But as he had chosen the Vale of Keswick for his Residence and had lived there for forty years or upwards, some of the neighbouring Gentry (with whom I conversed) were anxious to erect a Tablet in the Church to express their admiration of the life which he had led and their veneration for his Memory. And it was accordingly intended and I believe still is, that the subscription for this purpose should not extend beyond the surrounding district which he had so long benefited and honoured by his presence.

The project which was suspended by the distressed state of the family and the miserable dissentions that prevailed in it will, I have no doubt now that the Sales[1] are over to be resumed forthwith; and for that purpose I shall write to one of the leading Gentlemen of Keswick. Agreeing altogether with you that Monuments to the dead, even in the cases of eminent Men are more touching when connected with local remembrances, I could still wish that Sir R. Inglis and Mr Wynne[2] would persist in the plan of having a memorial placed in Westminster Abbey.[3] In addition to Southey's claim to be so commemorated for his Genius and attainments, his known attachment to the Anglican Church and the Ability with which he supported it by his Writings and his having been educated in the neighbouring School of Westminster give an especial propriety to his being included among the illustrious dead, who are called to remembrance in that beautiful and sacred Edifice, though their Remains have not been deposited there. With regard to the Keswick Monument you shall hear from me again, as soon as any thing is fixed—

Believe me with kind remembrances to Lady Coleridge and to your young family, in which Mrs W. unites,

ever faithfully yours
Wm Wordsworth

[1] See E. Q.'s report to H. C. R., Morley, i. 503. Southey's Portuguese books and manuscripts went to the British Museum.

[2] Charles Watkin Williams Wynn (1775–1850), Southey's friend: M.P. for Old Sarum, 1797–9, and thereafter for Montgomery, President of the Board of Control (1822–8), and Secretary for War under Grey (1830–1). Southey, who received from him an annuity of £160 from the year 1796, dedicated his Welsh poem *Madoc* to him.

[3] A bust of Southey was later placed in Poet's Corner.

[*In M. W.'s hand*]

To the Memory of Robt Southey,[1]

a Man eminent for genius, versatile talents, extensive and accurate knowledge, and habits of the most conscientious industry. Nor was he less distinguished for strict temperance, pure benevolence, and warm affections; but his Mind, such are the awful dispensations of Providence, was prematurely and almost totally obscured by a slowly-working and inscrutable malady, under which he languished till released by death in the 68th year of his age.

Reader! ponder the condition to which this great and good Man, not without merciful alleviations, was doomed; and learn from his example to make timely use of thy endowments and opportunities, and to walk humbly with thy God.

1714. W. W. to UNKNOWN CORRESPONDENT

MS. St. John's College, Cambridge. Hitherto unpublished.

Rydal Mount
Ambleside
June 30
1843

Dear Sir,

Your very obliging Letter, with the accompanying volume, did not reach me till long after its date. You are anxious for my opinion upon your book, much more so than there is any occasion that you should be, both on account of its own great merit, and what I am far more conscious of than you can be, my unfitness to assume the office of a Critic upon the Productions of *young* men of Genius. There is something in *years* that disqualifies a Man, in consequence of long-fixed opinions and familiar habits of feeling, from entering at once into sympathy with Productions, however energetic and powerful, that run at all counter to those opinions and habits. And I must frankly avow that this has been in part the case with me in respect to your work the power of which I feel, but not altogether with the

[1] A suggested wording for the inscription on Southey's monument in Crosthwaite Church. Another copy, in W. W.'s hand, with a few variants, is among the *WL MSS*. The idea of an epitaph of this kind was soon dropped, and W. W. wrote his poetic tribute instead. See Ls. 1753 ff. below.

complacency that I could desire—The momentous and awful event upon which it turns as I have been accustomed to view it, does not admit with me of the interweaving of those fictions which you have ventured upon.—Even in the Paradise Regained of Milton, I have always felt something of the same indispositon to bend to the Poet's *Interpolations* if I may so call them. May I be allowed to particularize a point on which my mind recoiled from sympathy with yours. In the Gospel Story of the sufferings of our Lord Woman is always introduced as sustaining an *amiable* character, so much so, as if the object were to redeem the sex from the stigma of being the Seducer of our first Father previous to the Fall. In the conduct however of your story this delightful impression is done away with, by the Introduction of [Charab ?] as the Tempter to the horrible sin of Judas—I feel the less scruple in being thus open with you, because I greatly admire the poetic ability displayed in your work. Believe me

sincerely yours
Wm Wordsworth

1715. W. W. to BENJAMIN ROBERT HAYDON

MS. Professor Willard Pope.
LY iii. 1171.

Monday Eveng 3d July—1843.

My dear Haydon,

I enclose you a Post Off. order for 5£ as requested, I could not do this sooner having been absent from home 4 days.—I am, believe me, truly sorry for your grievous disappointment,[1] and

[1] Haydon had been unsuccessful in the competition for the Cartoons in Westminster Hall (see L. 1690 above). The successful artists, who won prizes of £300, were Edward Armitage (1817–96), a pupil of Paul Delaroche, for 'Caesar's Invasion of Britain', George Frederick Watts (1817–1904) for 'Caractacus Led in Triumph through the Streets of Rome', and Charles West Cope (1811–90) for 'The First Trial by Jury'. Haydon wrote to W. W. of his disappointment on 5 July: 'I will weather it in the usual way, viz., by another and greater attempt. . . . The decision in favour of a pupil of De La Roche's is most unlucky, and most fortunate: unlucky as giving the French the éclat of beating the English on their own ground, and fortunate as being evidence of such inferior drawing, proportion, character, and taste, as proves in these qualities, of which France boasts, the English are decidedly superior.' (Haydon, ii. 57–8). See also *Diary* (ed. Pope), v. 294–308.

the more so because the numerous claims upon my income deprive me of the power of doing more than offering you and Mrs Haydon my sympathy, and the expression of my deep and sincere regret. Believe me

my dear Haydon
faithfully yours
Wm Wordsworth

1716. W. W. to WILLIAM CRACKANTHORPE[1]

MS. Mr. C. A. Cookson. Hitherto unpublished.

Rydal Mount
7th July 1843.

My dear Cousin,

The account you give of the blessed departure of your beloved Mother[2] from this world is consolatory in the highest degree—

This event carries the thoughts of my Wife and myself much farther back than it can your's; but the sadness which is natural on such an occasion, does in this instance partake largely indeed of feelings of an opposite nature. For what is more enviable in this sphere of our existence than so calm and peaceful a transition after such an active, useful, and so long life? The remembrance of your good Mother, will, my dear Cousin, be a support to you all, till the end of your days; and God grant that the passing away of all of us may resemble hers.

Your Letter will be forwarded by to days Post to Dora, who with her Husband and his Daughters, has through the kindness of Mr and Mrs Curwen been residing at the Island,[3] where they are likely to continue for some weeks. It is a delightful place and they enjoy it much.

We have two of our Grandsons, the 2nd and 3d Wm and John staying with us for a fortnight. They are both fine promising Boys.

[1] Of Newbiggin Hall, W. W.'s cousin.

[2] W. W.'s aunt Charlotte (*EY*, p. 10), widow of Christopher Crackanthorpe Cookson, guardian of the Wordsworth children after their parents' death.

[3] Belle Isle, Windermere. 'We have boats, and are very comfortably independent of neighbours,' E. Q. wrote to H. C. R., 'though by no means without callers.' (Morley, i. 503).

With affectionate remembrances to yourself and your Brother and Sister,[1] in which Mary unites, I remain

My dear Cousin
most faithfully yours
Wm Wordsworth

It would have been gratifying to me to pay my respects by attending the funeral of your Mother, but I was attacked two days ago by an inflammation in my eye; nor have I got rid of a cough which has been troubling me for some weeks,—the remains of a cold caught in the severe weather which we had some time ago—

1717. W. W. and M. W. to ISABELLA FENWICK[2]

MS. Victoria University Library, Toronto. Hitherto unpublished.

Tuesday [11 July 1843]

We are much inconvenienced for want of opportunities for *conveying* our Letters to the Post, unless we send expressly. Yesterday it rained heavily and rains this morning, and as the matter of this letter is not urgent it probably will not go to day. Since the former sheet was written I have had an opportunity of stating to Derwent Coleridge[3] the causes of Mr Lee's[4] apprehensions. To the one about School-Masters he replied that the model School of Stanley Grove,[5] would fit many of the choice

[1] William Crackanthorpe had two sisters, Charlotte and Sarah, but no brother. The reference is probably to his sister and her husband, who had been staying at Newbiggin at the time of his letter to W. W.

[2] A postscript added to M. W.'s letter to I. F. of 10 July (*MW*, p. 267).

[3] Derwent Coleridge was on a visit of two or three weeks to Rydal (*RMVB*), staying with his brother Hartley at the Nab, and preaching in Rydal Chapel. See *Letters of Hartley Coleridge* (ed. Griggs), pp. 266–9.

[4] James Prince Lee (1804–69), Fellow of Trinity College, Cambridge (1829), assistant master at Rugby under Dr. Arnold (1830–8), headmaster of King Edward's School, Birmingham (1838–47), and thereafter first Bishop of Manchester. (See David Newsome, *Godliness and Good Learning, Four Studies on a Victorian Ideal*, 1961, pp. 92–147.) He had called at Rydal Mount the previous December, during a visit to Mrs. Arnold at Fox How, and returned again this July (*RMVB*).

[5] The debate about the role of the Church in national education was continuing. Stanley Grove (see L. 1523 above) had been set up under Derwent Coleridge's direction to train school masters as agents of the church system. But

Pupils for taking Deacons Orders and that he had no doubt they would be ordained, to be maintained by the competent Salaries which such Persons would obtain as Schoolmasters, and that this would furnish a link of connection between the Masters and the Church from which great good might reasonably be expected. He reported many strong facts from his own experience in the neighbourhood of London, tending to prove that the aversion of dissenting Parents to Church-teaching, did not prevail in any thing like the degree which Mr Lee had met with, and above all he dwelt with much feeling upon the danger of giving up a great principle, and the inevitable mischief. He described in a lively manner the bad effects both upon the minds of the teachers and Pupils of the false position in which they would be placed; and added, in conclusion that if Mr Lee's plan were adopted a schism would immediately take place ruinous to the project. I was much gratified with Derwent's observations, and the whole train of his discourse—.

This morning I have again seen Mr Lee and he has promised at his earliest leisure to write to me, and state briefly as he can all that he knows, thinks and feels upon this important subject. Again farewell my beloved Friend, how I long to see you again as does my dear Wife.

ever yours
W. W.

[*M. W. writes*]

I have had a note from Joanna[1] written when prepared to be sent for to Elton—She talks of seeing us, having halted with a friend at Bongate (Appleby) and going forward to the Isle of Man before the Steam Packets [from] Whitehaven cease to ply, viz. 27th of Sep^r^.—How this will *square* with William's plan, could that be adopted I do not see. But as Dora says all will come smooth at last. God bless you—We are going to brave the rain.

M. W.

Dr. Kay's rival institution on non-denominational lines was also prospering. In Nov. 1842 Parliament made it a grant and Prince Albert became its patron, and a year later the management was transferred to the National Society. But many churchmen continued to be apprehensive of its influence. See Sir James Kay-Shuttleworth, *Four Periods of Public Education*, 1862, pp. 294 ff.; Frank Smith, *The Life and Work of Sir James Kay-Shuttleworth*, 1923, pp. 104–27.

[1] Joanna Hutchinson was going to stay with her nephew George Sutton (see *MY* ii. 410) near Stockton-on-Tees.

1718. W. W. to SAMUEL GRINDLEY HOWE[1]

Address: D[r] Howe, Ambleside.
MS. Carl H. Pforzheimer Library. Hitherto unpublished.

Rydal Mount
[mid-July, 1843]

Mr Wordsworth will be at home this Evening, and will be glad to see D[r] and M[rs] Howe[2]—

1719. W. W. TO CHAUNCY HARE TOWNSHEND

Address: Rev[d] C. H. Townsend, Low wood Inn. [*delivered by hand*]
MS. Wisbech Museum. Hitherto unpublished.

Tuesday morn:
half past seven—
[25 July 1843]

My dear Sir,

You were afraid of being thought rude yesterday—I must incur the same risk today, happening to be unfortunately engaged today, in a task which I hoped would have been finished yesterday, and cannot be put off till tomorrow. This is a

[1] Samuel Grindley Howe (1801–76), doctor and philanthropist. As a young man he volunteered in the Greek struggle for independence (see *Letters and Journals of Samuel Grindley Howe during the Greek Revolution*, ed. Laura E. Richards, 2 vols., 1907–9); later he edited *The Commonwealth*, an anti-slavery journal. In 1832 he opened a school for the blind at Boston, which became the foremost institution of its time; and he was associated with Horace Mann, the educationalist, in many other philanthropic projects. Whittier made Howe the subject of his poem *The Hero* (1853). From 1865 to 1874 he was chairman of the Massachussetts Board of State Charities, the first of its kind in the United States. See Julia Ward Howe, *Memoir of Dr. Samuel Grindley Howe*, Boston, 1876. He and his wife were introduced by George Ticknor (*WL MSS.*), and their visit is recorded in *RMVB*.

[2] Julia Ward Howe (1819–1910), poet, abolitionist, and feminist: author of the celebrated *Battle Hymn of the Republic*. She had married Dr. Howe the previous April, and they had travelled to Europe with Horace Mann on an extended tour. According to her *Reminiscences, 1819–1899*, Boston, 1899, p. 116, the visit to W. W. was 'very disappointing'. See also L. 1722 below.

great disappointment to us all—but tomorrow you must come and set all right.

With kindest regards to yourself and circle[1]

I remain faithfully yours
Wm Wordsworth

1720. W. W. to EDWARD MOXON

MS. Henry E. Huntington Library.
LY iii. 1172.

Wednesday morning [? late July 1843][2]

Dear Mr Moxon,

I have been rather puzzled about printing the Female Vagrant;[3] but upon the whole, I think it had better be done. So do Mr Quillinan and Mr Carter. But there is a great awkwardness in encouraging, by any means whatever, the Sale of the six Volumes separate; for if that be done how are we to dispose of the 7th? Now the title page as it stands is

Poems by W. Wordsworth
in *six* Volumes

How can this be got over? Would it not be better to attach a slip of Paper, to the back of the title page announcing the 7th Volume so that the Purchasers of the sixth might be told that there is a seventh. I am quite at a loss as to what is best in this matter. If you were to cancel the present Title page announcing the Poems in six Volumes, that would not allow those 6 to be sold without the 7th. What think you of having a certain number of title pages struck off

Poems by W. Wordsworth
in 7 Volumes

But manage it as you think only having in mind that what I most

[1] According to E. Q.'s letter to H. C. R. of 28 July, Townshend was staying at Ambleside with three ladies, 'two Miss Wigstons (Aunt and Niece) and Miss Townshend, a cousin of Mrs Edward Curwen'. (Morley, i. 508).

[2] The date 22 July 1843 has been added in another hand. But the 22nd was a Saturday.

[3] *The Female Vagrant*, previously published separately, had been included in the 1842 volume as part of *Guilt and Sorrow*.

wish [is] to dispose of the 7th in conjunction with the six, but not to make that rule *absolute*.

Your Brother[1] told Mr Quillinan that the 7th Vol. was now sold separately at 14 shillings—there must be a mistake in charging me 1. 7. 11 per copy for the whole—I have always understood that the six volumes were charged me 1. 1. 6 and at that price I have let Mrs Nicholson have them. And Mr Quillinan told me that he had one of the 7th charged to him wholesale price under 5 shillings—The 7 volumes ought I think to be sold retail, at 36 shillings and wholesale accordingly. I hope you approve of this.

Pray tell me how many of the 7th are still in hand. Excuse this sad scrawl written in extreme haste.

ever dear Mr Moxon faithfully yours
Wm Wordsworth

1721. W. W. to CHRISTOPHER WILSON[2]

MS. Picton Autograph Letters, Synge Collection, Liverpool Public Libraries. Hitherto unpublished.

Rydal Mount
30th July 1843

My dear Sir,

I had the pleasure of meeting your Son,[3] at Mr Branker's Sale; and we talked some time about the School of Ambleside.[4] One of the results of our conversation was, that I venture writing to you to request, that as soon as you conveniently can, you would come over to Lowood Inn, for the purpose of electing a Trustee

[1] See L. 1704 above.

[2] The Kendal banker (see *MY* ii. 417).

[3] Edward Wilson (see *MY* ii. 493; pt. ii, L. 666), of Rigmaden Park.

[4] John Kelsick (1699–1723) of Ambleside, left the bulk of his estate to build a Free Grammar School and provide for a schoolmaster. He set up a board of trustees drawn from the local community, and thereafter the trusteeship descended through a number of prominent local families. Throughout the eighteenth century the offices of curate of Ambleside and schoolmaster were often held by the same person, contrary to Kelsick's original wishes. In the eighteen-forties the curacy was worth £80 a year; the endowment of the school amounted to 32 acres of land and other property, worth altogether about £127 a year. See also L. 1728 below.

for the school, to act in the place of the late Mr Newton.[1] Mr Harrison,[2] of Green Bank, is willing to undertake the office, and I am sure you will be of opinion, that on every account no person more proper could be elected. If you are disposed to come over, it would of course be necessary that you should take the trouble of writing to Mr Jackson,[3] in order that he may meet you at the time which will best suit your convenience.

I am so strongly convinced of the importance of another Trustee being appointed, that I am sure you will not think me an Intruder for having expressed my desire upon the occasion. I have been a Householder for 43 years in the Parish of Grasmere, and since our common School-days, have had an interest in Ambleside and its neighbourhood.

I was much pleased to hear from Mr Edward Wilson that you were in good health, and wishing you the continuance of that and other blessings I remain

faithfully Yours
Wm Wordsworth

1722. W. W. to ISABELLA FENWICK

MS. WL.
LY iii. 1173 (—).

2^d Aug.^t [1843]

My dearest Friend,

I have wished to write you a short Letter for several days, but out of many little matters knew not what to select as most likely to interest you. The Letter I enclose is a copy which Mary was permitted to take from one of Mr Southey in the possession of a young Lady who was here the other day with her Father Dr Jennings[4] of Hampstead. He will endeavour to procure others

[1] Probably William Newton of Waterhead (see *MY* ii. 591; pt. i, L. 20). His place was taken by George Lawton Newton.

[2] Benson Harrison (see *MY* ii. 112; pt. i, L. 313) had lived at Green Bank since 1827, so that he was a comparative newcomer to Ambleside; but he had always taken an energetic part in local affairs, and was later elected a trustee.

[3] Thomas Jackson of Waterhead, representing Lady le Fleming.

[4] Probably a relative of James Jennings, 'the Traumatic Poet' (see Southey, ii. 154; Curry, i. 99).

from the Wade Brown[1] Family, though, as I told him, they have probably been applied to already by the Southeys. I send you also a copy of Verses forwarded to me by their Author, an American, in a very interesting Letter written by him to inform me of the Death of Alstone the Painter,[2] of whom you have often heard me speak. The Letter shall also be sent you, for I think you will deem it well worthy of perusal. Within these two or three last weeks we have had a good number of strangers at the Mount;[3] among others an American Dr Howe,[4] [the same who did such marvels with Laura Bridgeman, born deaf and blind][5] with his Wife and Sister. The Husband is an intelligent Man, and his Wife passes among the Americans as a bright Specimen of the best they produce in female Character. Mary and Dora, however, found her a most disagreeable person. As they were rising to depart I expressed regret to Dr Howe that his visit had been so short, as I should have been glad of his opinion upon Pensylvanian securities, upon which the Wife exclaimed to Mary and Dora; 'wherever we go we are *bored* with repudiation'; and then went on to talk upon the subject in the most offensive way. Her Husband spoke with the utmost consequence of the validity of the Bonds, and said he had not the smallest doubt that the obligations would all be discharged. Curiously enough Chauncey Hare Townsend was present that evening, and one of the Ladies being a Mesmerite, she no doubt thought herself very lucky to fall in with so eminent a Practitioner and so firm a Believer.[6]

[1] Wade Browne (d. 1821), of Ludlow, Southey's friend and correspondent, 'an excellent man, for whom I had a great regard, and in whose house I always found a joyous welcome' (Warter, iii. 287–8). Wade Brown had been a merchant in Leeds, and spent several summers in the Lake District.

[2] See L. 1723 below.

[3] Visitors at this period included Harrison Ainsworth, William Harness, and Dr. John Dalton (1766–1844), the chemist (*RMVB*).

[4] See L. 1718 above.

[5] Words in square brackets added in margin. Laura Dewey Bridgman (1829–89), who from two years of age was blind, deaf, and mute, was received into Dr. Howe's school for the blind at Boston in 1837. He taught her to speak by signs, to write, and to become a skilled needlewoman. She remained in the institution as a teacher, and lived a happy and useful life. Howe's success in treating her, was held at the time to be little short of miraculous, as de Selincourt notes, and his report of it was translated into several languages. Charles Dickens describes a visit to Laura Bridgman in *American Notes*, Ch. iii.

[6] Townshend had become an ardent Mesmerite, and in 1840 had written *Facts in Mesmerism*; in 1854 he wrote *Mesmerism proved True*.

Since Mary wrote to you her Sister[1] has been thrown back by a bilious attack. We saw Mr Bell,[2] Isabella's medical attendant at Mr Branker's sale.[3] He gave a favourable account of her; though I must own, that judging from his Physiognomy we did not think highly of his talents. Dr Davy, I grieve to say, having medically examined my Nephew John W.,[4] gives a less favorable account of the State of his lungs, than John had when examined in London by Dr Ferguson, so that I fear the disease is slowly gaining ground, and he certainly thinks so himself. It is a great pity for he is a very amiable young Man; and his poor Mother will be greatly troubled should she lose him, as indeed he would be much lamented by us all.

Last week I was every day at Mr Branker's Sale, but excepting old wine I bought little. One Print from Leonardo da Vinci, the Virgin and Saint Barbara and Catherine gazing upon the infant Jesus, I purchased, and I hope you will like it. The expression in the face charms me not a little—He is a favorite artist with me.

It is now high time to ask a question or two about yourself. Are you, and have you been pretty well? we half fear not, as we have been expecting a Letter. And how are Mr Taylor, and your other Friends?—My invitation to the Queen's Ball of which perhaps you may have heard did not reach me, when at the Island, till it was too late for me to act upon it;[5] otherwise I probably should have seen you before this time; which would have been sufficient compensation for a journey in itself anything but agreeable. We cannot yet fix when our Journey to Herefordshire is to be made. It will depend upon Isabella and Joanna's state of health. Need I add that I am most lovingly yours and long to see you again. You will find this but a dull Letter though such an one as it seemed fittest to write.

Ever yours
W. W.

Remember me most kindly to Mr and Mrs. Taylor and to other Friends. Wm is here and sends his love. I was delighted with my little nephews, Wm his own dear self again. God bless you.—

[1] Joanna Hutchison.

[2] Of Cockermouth.

[3] James Branker, Hartley Coleridge's friend, was leaving Croft Lodge and returning to Liverpool.

[4] R. W.'s son had now returned from Corfu.

[5] See Morley, i. 507.

1723. W. W. to HENRY REED

Address: Henry Reed Esqre, Philadelphia, U.S. [*In M. W.'s hand*]
Postmark: (1) 4 Aug. 1843 (2) 6 Aug. 1843 (3) 3 Sept.
Stamp: (1) Ambleside (2) Boston Ship.
MS. Cornell.
K (—). *Wordsworth and Reed, p. 108.*

Rydal Mount Aug 2^{d} 1843

My dear Mr Reed

I have been a discreditably long time in your debt, but be assured I was duly sensible of your kindness in giving so long and so often your attention to the disagreeable subject of Pensylvanian Securities, upon my account. I feel much obliged to you for all that you have said upon it for the guidance of my Friends. Nothing has been done by them, and I hope nothing will; though for especial reasons Miss Fenwick has often said she would part with her Bonds, at half the price they cost her. I have striven earnestly to persuade her from doing so; and exhorted her to wait the issue. One question I would wish to put to you. Will they who refuse to accept the offer of the State Property[1] on railways, canals, or other things in part payment, stand, in consequence, upon a less favorable footing than those who do accept? that is, will they forfeit any thing of the strength of their original claim, for such refusal? I hope not, for my own part I would stand upon my Bond; trusting that the State would not evade its obligations under any proposal of that kind. Whatever Natives upon the spot may deem it prudent to do in this case, I should deem it highly imprudent for us on this side of the Atlantic to deal in any such matter; I know not what European Merchants, and Bankers, might do towards turning those Securities to account, but surely for private Individuals such a course is most objectionable; and none of my Friends are likely to enter upon it. And now my dear Sir I have done with the painful subject and beg unless some thing new should occur that you would not trouble yourself more about it on our account.

[1] In his letters of 29 Apr. and 30 May (*Wordsworth and Reed*, pp. 100–108), Reed had explained that the State was proposing to reduce its enormous debt by selling off certain canals and railroads to private companies, to which loanholders could opt to transfer a portion of their claim on the State. The plan was soon dropped, as he disclosed in his letter on 28 Sept.

You have already done so, far too much; only be so kind as reply at your convenience to the question I have asked above—

A few days ago I received a Letter from a Countryman of your's the Rev[d] R. C. Waterston[1] of Boston communicating the intelligence of the death of that admirable artist and amiable Man, my old Friend, Mr Alston.[2] Mr W— and I are not acquainted and therefore I take it very kindly that he should have given me this melancholy information, with most interesting particulars of the last few hours of the life of the Deceased. He also sent me a Copy of verses addressed by himself to me, I presume some little time ago, and printed in the "Christian Souvenir".[3] You have probably seen the Lines, and if so I doubt not you will agree with me that they indicate a true feeling of the leading characteristics of my Poems. At least I am sure that I wished them such as he represents them to be, *too* partially no doubt.

It would give me pleasure could I make this Letter so long due more worthy of perusal by touching upon any topics of a public or private nature that might interest you; but beyond the assurance which I can give you that I and mine are and have been in good health, I know not where to find them. This spring I have not left home for London or any where else and during the progress of it and the Summer I have had much pleasure in noting the flowers and blossoms as they appeared and disappeared successively, an occupation from which, at least with regard to my own grounds, a Residence in Town for the three foregoing spring seasons cut me off. Though my health continues, thank God to be very good, and I am active as most men of my age, my strength for very long walks among the mountains is of course diminishing, but weak or strong in body, I shall ever remain in heart and mind faithfully your much obliged Friend

Wm Wordsworth

P. S. Mr Southeys Literary Ex[rs] are making a collection of his Letters which will prove highly interesting to the Public, they are so gracefully and feelingly written.

[1] The Revd. Robert Cassie Waterston (1812–93), a Boston minister: author of *Thoughts on Moral and Spiritual Culture*, Boston, 1842, and numerous other discourses on social and educational matters.

[2] Washington Allston had died on 9 July. See also L. 1744 below.

[3] W. W. probably means the *Christian Examiner and Theological Review*, published at Boston between 1824 and 1869.

1724. W. W. to [?] ROBERT CHAMBERS[1]

MS. Cornell. Hitherto unpublished.

Rydal Mount
4th Augst
1843

Dear Sir

Absence from home prevented my receiving your Letter as soon as I should otherwise have done. I now write to assure you that you are quite at Liberty to take such Extracts from my Poems as may best suit your purpose; only as Mr Moxon 44 Dover Street my Publisher has a joint pecuniary interest in the Work it will be proper to ask his consent, informing him that I have given mine.

I have the honor to be
dear Sir
sincerely yours
William Wordsworth

1725. W. W. and M. W. to ISABELLA FENWICK

MS. WL.
LY iii. 1176 (—).

Rydal, Wednesday morng [?9] Aug [1843]

Your Letter (received yesterday) announcing that you were about to leave London for Bagborough[2] gave us both very great pleasure, as holding out a pretty confident hope, that if *we* are at liberty to go southward we all may meet at Brinsop and return together to Westmorland, without any sacrifice of feeling on your part, which, as you will learn from my Letter, the fulfillment of my wishes seemed, when it was written, to

[1] Robert Chambers (1802–71), the Edinburgh publisher and author of *Vestiges of the Natural History of Creation* (1844), was preparing his *Cyclopaedia of English Literature*, 2 vols., 1844, and approached W. W. at this time asking for permission to publish extracts from his works (see Merriam, *Edward Moxon Publisher of Poets*, p. 104). His selection (ii. 322–33) was quite extensive, and included *Tintern Abbey*, *Ruth*, *Laodamia*, and passages from *The Excursion*, as well as several sonnets and other short pieces. But see also Ls. 1763 and 1795 below where W. W. implies that he had no direct contact with Chambers.

[2] The residence of I. F.'s sister, nr. Taunton.

require. In fact I apprehended that your stay with your London Friends would be so far prolonged as to render it impossible for us to meet in Herefordshire, without your deferring your visit to Somersetshire for another year;—now all *may* be reconciled, but that will depend still upon circumstances not the least in our power.—

Have you been told that Mr Jackson[1] requires us to pay 60£ per ann: for Rydal Mount, one third more than we have paid hitherto? I said I could not agree without laying the case before Lady Fleming.

The weather clearing up in the afternoon, we went yesterday to the Island[2] and drank tea there. Dora seemed pretty well, as were the rest.—

This is written merely to tell you how happy I was made by the intelligence of your movements.

We hope that it is not bad health, but merely depression of spirits requiring change, that sends Dr Ferguson abroad for so long a period.

We shall not venture to recommend anything in Isabella's case, confining ourselves to the stating of facts. Your kind Letter will be forwarded to her. Mary wrote to her at length last night.

ever most affectionately yours
Wm Wordsworth

[*M. W. writes*]

We think of going to pay our promised visit to Hund[h]ow[3] today—independent of our wished-for two days upon the Island—Dora feeling delicate about prolonging their abode there (the 8 weeks for which they asked for the house being at an end) to admit of our going to them next week.

Tomorrow we dine at Dr Davy's—Friday and Sat. the

[1] Lady le Fleming's agent.

[2] Belle Isle on Windermere. E. Q. and Dora Q. remained there until the end of the month when they moved to Rydal Mount to look after D. W., in the absence of W. W. and M. W. at Elton and Brinsop.

[3] i.e. to Mr. and Mrs. John Harrison, of Hundhow, Burnside, nr. Kendal. They were close friends of the Curwens, and it was probably through them that they came to know the Wordsworths. John Harrison was the son of a former Mayor of Kendal and later a director of the Kendal and Windermere Railway: his wife was apparently author of *Leaves from the Lakeside* (see *R.M.Cat.*, no. 523). See also L. 1748 below.

Whewells[1] are to be here from Keswick, whither they return for Sunday—On Monday we have promised to dine with Lady F.[2] and Mrs Luff—they go in the course of the week to Edinburgh.

You see therefore that we have not much of quiet home-staying. Mesmerising Cha[u]ncey[3] and 3 or 4 Ladies with him (not Mrs T) at Low Wood—Mr and Mrs Milman[4] are at Halsteads, we are to see them in a day or two—and we have had D^{r} and Mrs Lee[5] from Birmingham. If you see Mr Robinson ask him to tell you about that letter which J. Wordsworth sent up to him for Translation.[6]

Poor John![7] we fear is in a most precarious state—indeed neither Dr Davy or Mr Carr entertain much hope of his case. It appears Dr Ferguson, when he was in Town upon examining his lungs told him they were delicate but not diseased—Dr D. has given him a contrary opinion, which I much grieve for—for his spirits have evidently flagged since—and he watches himself in a way that must be injurious. He is still here, God bless you dearest friend.

Affec regards to all around you—M. W.

1726. W. W. to SIR JAMES McGRIGOR[8]

MS. Cornell. Hitherto unpublished.

Rydal Mount
10th August 1843

Dear Sir James,

Remembering with gratitude the ready kindness with which you have always met my wishes, as far as was in your power, in respect to my Nephew, John Wordsworth,[9] I venture to address you once more upon his case, in which I am deeply interested.

1 See *RMVB* and L. 1733 below.

2 Lady Farquhar.

3 Chauncy Hare Townshend (see L. 1722 above).

4 See pt. ii, L. 510.

5 See L. 1717 above.

6 R. W.'s son had asked H. C. R. to obtain a translation of a piece of Russian for him. See *HCR* ii. 633.

7 R. W.'s son.

8 See also L. 1693 above.

9 R. W.'s son.

Since his return to his native Country his health has improved, but is still in a precarious state. He has consulted Dr Davy, who is resident in this neighbourh^d^,[1] several times; and it is Dr Davy's opinion that he should seek the benefit of a milder climate for the ensuing winter; and he proposes Gibraltar or return to the Ionian Islands. The objections to the latter, supposing such return continues open to him, are the length and hazards of the land-journey, liable as he is to taking cold of which he would run great risk in crossing the Alps; and that he would on this account be obliged to begin his journey before he has had an opportunity of fairly profiting by the air of this Country, for as yet we have scarcely had any summer. Should there be a probability of a vacancy on the Gibraltar station in the course of two or three months, his being placed there would combine the advantages of a prolonged stay in this Country, and a comparatively *short* sea-voyage. This is of great importance as he suffered so much from his tedious passage through the Mediterranean.

If you cannot hold out a prospect of his being placed at Gibraltar, we should be glad to learn if his Appointment in the Ionian Islands be still open, so that he may, should his health permit, commence his journey in that direction, in the earlier part of the next Month.[2]

With every good wish I remain, dear Sir James,

With grateful respect your
much obliged
Wm Wordsworth

[1] Dr. and Mrs. Davy had moved from Edinburgh and were building a house just outside Ambleside on the Rydal road.

[2] McGrigor replied on 16 Sept.: 'I regret to read the account which your letter . . . conveys of the health of your nephew, for the restoration of which I will have the greatest pleasure in doing anything in my power, for Mr Wordsworth is a most promising young officer who has gathered golden opinions from all in the Ionian Isles. Unfortunately I have no means of placing him at Gibraltar, the only vacancy which occurred there for the last 15 months was filled . . . but I will keep open his old station for him in the Ionian Isles and do any thing else for him that may tend to the recovery of health of so fine a young man.' (*MS. Mrs. M. J. Roberts*).

1727. W. W. to JOHN WORDSWORTH[1]

MS. WL. Hitherto unpublished.

Monday afternoon
[?14 Aug. 1843]

My dear John,

Your letter of today has caused both your aunt and me great concern, and we should certainly have driven over to see you this afternoon, had it not been for the incessant and heavy rain which we have both reason to fear, on account of rheumatism, to which she is subject, and I being just recovered from a diarrhoea of two days continuance. These repeated inflammations appear to me to render you quite unfit for a long journey, and I am therefore glad that you have given up the thought of crossing the Alps; nor do I at all like considering how much you suffered by your voyage home that you should think of going so far as Corfu by sea.—

As to applying for the situation you name, be assured I would do all in my power to assist you to procure it, were I persuaded that it would be for your benefit; but I cannot help thinking that neither in this situation nor in any other, could you escape exposure to professional duty which might prove very injurious to your health during the approaching winter; I therefore venture to submit to your judgement, whether, giving up the thought of immediate employment, it would not be better to apply for a prolonged leave of absence; and fix yourself in that part of our Island where the climate is least severe and variable, and there to remain till next Spring. I have repeatedly heard from undoubted authority that the South Coast of the Isle of Bute has the most temperate air and the least variable of any part of Great Britain; if you approved of going thither I would with great pleasure visit you on the spot, as I am sure your Cousin W^m would, also to beguile the loneliness of a part of the winter. Should you think this place too remote, I know that Dumfries is very mild and with rather less variation than Falmouth, as was told me the other day by a Person of Cornwall,[2] whose Friend had watched and kept an account of the changes indicated by the Thermometer in Falmouth while the same was doing by a

[1] R. W.'s son, now at Keswick. He had called at Rydal Mount on 28 July.

[2] Probably Mrs. Sarah Fox (see pt. ii, L. 576). See *RMVB*, and *Memories of Old Friends*, ii. 15.

Friend of his in Dumfries, and the account was upon the whole in favor of the latter place.

Do my dear John carefully consider what I have said. I know also that any situation looking Southward from the parish of Millum in Cumberland and the same applies to the coast on Cartmel bay and the other estuaries there about is very mild and temperate. Do let me know by tomorrow's post, what you think of my proposal, if you are against it I will write immediately to Lady Frederic.

If the weather be tolerable tomorrow morning I will ride over and see you for an hours talk

ever your affectionate Uncle
Wm Wordsworth

As an Invalid is seldom the best judge in his own case, suppose you consult Dr Irwin[1] as to my proposal. I should also like to know what Mr Lightfoot and your Mother think of it, unless you be unwilling to agitate your Mother by putting [her][2] upon thinking on a subject in which she must be so deeply interested.

1728. W. W. to EDWARD WILSON[3]

MS. Picton Autograph Letters, Synge Collection, Liverpool Public Libraries. Hitherto unpublished.

Tuesday
15th Augt 1843

My dear Sir,

Owing to absence from home and my usual engagements with Strangers at this season, I have not yet been able to procure the requested information respecting the Feoffes.[4]

Mr Carr, to whom I applied tells me that some time ago he was elected one himself, and perhaps continues to be so; and tells me that Mr Dawes[5] is the most proper person to give the information. I am going this afternoon to the Island, Windermere,

[1] Dr. Ralph Irving of Keswick.

[2] *Word dropped out.*

[3] See also L. 1721 above.

[4] i.e. the Feoffees, the trustees of the endowments of Ambleside School.

[5] The Revd. John Dawes, curate of Ambleside from 1811 until his death in 1845, was also schoolmaster for some years, and had taught John W., W. W. jnr., and Derwent and Hartley Coleridge.

where I shall remain till Friday, but on my way to Bowness this afternoon I will call on M[r] Dawes, and if I see him and procure a list you shall have it enclosed, if not you would do well to write to him in your Father's name, and beg him to send one, which he will, I trust, feel himself obliged to do; though it is too well known what a difficult Person he is to deal with.

M[r] Carr, who as you know, lives close by the School, says that to his belief the Master[1] is regular in attendance, but that there is a universal cry that his Scholars make no progress. M[r] C is confident that nothing can be done against him; so that there is no hope but what you alluded to, and *that* C. fears is but a faint one.

He M[r] C. however suggested a trial.

Pray thank your Father, from me, for his kind letter

I remain
My dear Sir
sincerely Yours
W[m] Wordsworth

P.S. I saw M[r] Dawes, he had not a list of the Trustees, but will procure one, and send it to your Father at Rigmaden as I advised.

Windermere Island
Wednesday Morning.

1729. W. W. to EDWARD MOXON

MS. Henry E. Huntington Library.
LY iii. 1175.

[*In M. W.'s hand*]

17th Aug. [1843]

Dear Mr Moxon,

My nephew D[r] C. Wordsworth will call upon you in a few days, on his way to Rydal Mount—Will you put up 6 more copies of the Excursion, and any other thing that may be lying in Dover St for me, to be ready for him to bring down. I have

[4] The Revd. William Sewell seems to have acted as schoolmaster from 1827, the year he was appointed curate of Troutbeck. In later years he farmed his own land in Troutbeck and hunted. W. W. had already had some reason to doubt his quality as a churchman (see pt. ii, L. 431).

desired him to call upon you with that view before he leaves Town. By the bye I see the 2^{d} Ed: of the 'Yarrow revisited' *neatly got up with gilded leaves* etc, offered in one of our booksellers shops at Ambleside, for 3/6 a vol—How are you able to afford it at so low a price? We find them charged to us 3/7—Mrs Nicholson cannot contend with this.

We like the Sonnets[1] thinking them pleasing compositions—We shall not be offended if you do not adopt any of our alterations.

We see nothing of Hartley—from which we fear you have not heard of him. If you see Mr Rogers tell him how happy we should be, if the North of England had any attractions for him this Autumn.

I have for the last 6 weeks been quite disabled by inflammation in one of my eyes.[2] It is slowly improving.

Very sincerely d^{r} M. Yours

W Wordsworth[3]

How is dear Miss Lamb—Kind remembrances to Mrs M etc.—We hear Troughton[4] gets his *Yarrows* from Longman's.

1730. W. W. to JOHN WORDSWORTH

MS. Mrs. M. J. Roberts. Hitherto unpublished.

Sunday eve [27 Aug. 1843]

My dear John,

We have been much disappointed by your not arriving on this side of the Raise. Your cousin Dora mentioned that it was your intention to be here last Monday—that day being wet we did not expect you but we have had more than one fine day since when you might have ventured, if you had been pretty well. We trust the cause of detaining you has not proceeded from a fresh cold or the continuation of the one you had not quite thrown off when

[1] Moxon's *Sonnets* of 1830 and 1835 had just been reprinted in one volume. This helps to establish the year of this letter.

[2] See also Morley, i. 503, where E. Q.'s letter to H. C. R. on 7 July records the commencement of this inflammation.

[3] Not signed by W. W.

[4] The other Ambleside bookseller.

you left us. The Harrisons[1] who expected you to be their guest have anxiously inquired after you, do dear John write us a line by return of post if we do not see you, for you will be sorry to hear that we have had such a very unfavourable report of my sister Joanna's state as calls for our going to see her immediately. It is therefore the intention of your uncle[2] and myself to set out for Elton on Wednesday and we are hoping to see Dora before we depart. You will therefore see her by watching the Mail pass on Tuesday morning unless she arrives to-morrow which I scarcely expect she can do. You may probably have heard from Dora of the safe arrival of the travellers[3] in London and that Isabella has seen both doctor Ferguson and Dr Locock[4]—they tell her that her disease is over come but have apprehension of something wrong in the lungs.—I have not myself much fear of this, they go to [?][5] on Tuesday for a month during Dr F's absence on the continent. Wm is now at [?Brigham] I believe. God bless you. Love to your mother.

affectionately yours
W. Wordsworth

1731. W. W. to EDWARD MOXON

MS. Henry E. Huntington Library.
LY iii. 1190.

[? Summer 1843]

My dear Mr Moxon,

Thank you for the Laureat remittance, which I shall be obliged to you to send hereafter in the same way, unless you hear to the contrary.

Among the Copies of my Poems sent last year is one that Mrs Nicholson cannot sell on account of the volume, that which contains The White Doe, having leaves answering to the Pages

[1] The Benson Harrisons.

[2] Thomas Hutchinson who had come from Brinsop to accompany M. W. to Elton, nr. Stockon-on-Tees, where Joanna Hutchinson was now seriously ill.

[3] John W. and his wife Isabella. Dora Q. was temporarily looking after their children at Brigham.

[4] See L. 1463 above.

[5] *MS. obscure.* According to E. Q.'s letter to H. C. R. of 25 Aug. (Morley, i. 517), they were going to Tonbridge.

taken from other volumes. This is very faulty negligence in the Person employed, who ought to make up the loss. Unluckily this is not the first time this troublesome inattention has occurred.—I have therefore to beg, that when any Books are sent at my request to Ambleside, that one of your people would carefully examine, to see that they are perfect.

The defective Volume is the 4th, and it has one sheet from the 2nd Vol and one from the 1st—from page 64 to page 97 inclusive—Pray as I shall return the whole set let the Copy be struck out of my account, for it is not worth while to send out another set in its stead

ever faithfully yours
Wm Wordsworth

1732. W. W. to CHARLES THORP[1]

MS. untraced.
Bookseller's Catalogue.

Rydal
near Ambleside.
28 August 1843.

. . . It was probable, that on account of the melancholy illness that has just seized Mrs W's only surviving sister, I should have been in your neighbourhood before this time. Next Wednesday we depart for Mr Sutton's . . . .

[1] The Revd. Charles Thorp, D.D. (1783–1862), Fellow of University College, Oxford (1803), rector of Ryton, Durham (1807), Archdeacon of Durham from 1831, and first Warden of Durham University from 1833. This fragment is part of a letter belatedly thanking Thorp for his 'valuable' Charge, which W. W. had read with pleasure.

1733. W. W. to C. W. JNR.

MS. British Library. Hitherto unpublished.

[*In M. W.'s hand*]

Kirkstall Bridge
Tuesday Morn. [29 Aug. 1843][1]

My dear Christopher,

Here we are on our way from Kendal waiting for the coach.

Your letter was put into my hands as I was getting into Mr Marshall's Carriage which brought us hither. I had a long conversation with Dr Whewell[2] on the subject of yours—I endeavoured alas! in vain—to convince him of the injurious tendency of the proceeding and the discredit which it would throw on the Coll: He said that he had objected to its being placed in the Ante-chapel as first proposed, but he c[d] not admit but that it might stand in the Library as an acknowledgement of the College's Sense of Ld B'[s] great talents.

Any public [comment] from me w[d] be in the highest degree unnecessary—it w[d] be ascribed to personal resentment and probably by many to Envy—in short I have done all I can in the case—

I must conclude for here comes the Coach.

[*unsigned*]

1734. W. W. to UNKNOWN CORRESPONDENT[3]

Endorsed: Wordsworth Sept[r] 9th 1843.
MS. Mr W. Hugh Peal. Hitherto unpublished.

Elton near Stockton
Sept[br] 5th [1843]

My dear Sir,

In fulfilment of my promise I take leave to let you know that I

[1] Dated by reference to E. Q.'s letter to H. C. R. of 1 Sept. (Morley, i. 520), which records the departure of W. W. and M. W. for Elton to visit Joanna Hutchinson.

[2] The Master of Trinity had recently visited Rydal Mount (see L. 1725 above). The rest of this letter concerns the controversy over the placing of Thorwaldsen's statue of Byron, originally intended for Westminster Abbey, in the Library of Trinity College, Cambridge. See pt. iii, L. 1294.

[3] Possibly George Taylor of Witton-le-Wear.

purpose along with my Nephew Mr Sutton of this place to leave Stockton by the first train on next friday morning, and to return by the latest train on the same day. Mr Sutton says we shall be in Durham about ten oclock, at the Waterloo Arms. If Dr Thorp[1] be in College, be so kind as [to] tell him of my intention.

faithfully yours
Wm Wordsworth

1735. W. W. to ISABELLA FENWICK

MS. WL.
LY iii. 1177 (—).

Brinsop Court Sept^br 21st 43

Dr Miss F, Read my letter first

The first word almost Mary said to me upon waking was, You will write to your 'Love' this morning; accordingly I sit down without standing in need of that additional motive, to tell you Beloved Friend, that we reached this place yesterday afternoon, having slept at Birmingham after leaving Stockton early in the morning. Many pages could be filled with an account of but a small part of our discomforts and unhappiness at Elton caused by the excitement and derangement of our Nephew's[2] mind. As arranged between his Stockton medical attendant and myself I called upon Dr Belcomb at York, and he has already sent off a competent Keeper to confine him within his own House, till it shall please God to mitigate the disease of mind under which He is labouring. He was bent upon accompanying us to York, and we had no other resource but to steal away from Elton without his knowledge. What a storm would he be in when he discovered that we were gone; but Wm was there to assist the Family to manage him. Joanna was much shaken by his behaviour latterly but a most desirable lodging has been procured for her and we hope she will remove to it as soon as she has procured a Maid servant to wait upon her. Though very weak she improved decidedly during our Stay.—

We spent six hours at York most agreeably, having had the good fortune to find everyone at home whom we wished to see.

[1] See L. 1732 above.

[2] George Sutton.

Mr Robinson's Brother[1] was our Attendant round the City; Him we found with his Wife at the head of nine interesting Children, descending step by step below each other, and the Mother expecting a tenth in a few days. Upon her and her appearance of character I could dwell at length. She is very handsome with a countenance beautifully intelligent. Never did I see a Woman so near her confinement who gave such dignity to that condition, so lively, so active, so graceful. She is very accomplished, but how she came to take up with Mr H. R. I cannot comprehend. Women do strange things where wedlock is concerned. No doubt her Husband is an active and stirring Member of Society, and may for aught I know be what is called a good Husband, but in appearance certainly no more fit to be mated with her than Vulcan was with Venus.—

We attended service at the Minster, which is still under repair,[2] so that only half of the Building could be seen at once, and the Nave to great disadvantage. Mary and I were placed on opposite sides of the Quire; and about the middle of the service she saw a gentleman leading down from one of the stalls, and down the Aisle, a white-headed Old Man who with a tottering and trailing step accompanied him. She was struck with dismay, for seeing imperfectly she was convinced it was her Husband who was suffering from a sudden seizure. Judge of what she had to endure till that anthem was over and the rest of the service. She was so placed that she could not leave her seat without disturbing the officiating Minister and all those that sat in the same line of seats with herself. What a beautiful Relique is that Ruin at St Mary's Abbey, we were charmed with it, and also with the walk along the Walls.—

We left a quarter past six, had to wait a full hour at Derby, and judge of our vexation, when upon reaching Birmingham at one, we found our large Leather trunk containing almost [all] our wearing apparel was missing. This would not have happened, if I, knowing well Jane's[3] great carefulness had not trusted it and three carpet bags to her vigilance. She however, poor girl, was

[1] Henry Robinson the solicitor (see pt. i, L. 37; pt. ii, L. 434), youngest brother of Capt. Charles Robinson of Ambleside. He married Rosamund, eldest daughter of Dr. Charles Best (1779–1817), physician to the York Asylum, and had thirteen children.

[2] Following the fire in the nave in 1840.

[3] The Rydal Mount housemaid, who died at Brinsop shortly afterwards (see L. 1739 below).

only in fault of her not ascertaining by its direction that the trunk which she saw put in along with the Carpet Bags was ours. It was of the same shape colour and size, and this with the promise of the attendant that he would take care of our luggage and put it all in its proper place deceived her. The trunk she saw put in with the Carpet Bags belonged to another Person. Hereafter I will trust to nobody's eyes but my own. Of course we have taken every possible care; at every place giving directions for the lost Portmanteau's being sent after us. We shall be very uneasy till we receive it; Mrs W. has no clothes to put on; her gowns, her shawls, her linnen, are all left behind, two new Coats of mine, my Waistcoat and all my best wearing apparel, including several things which would have been left at Rydal but on account of our proposed visits with you on our return. This afternoon I shall go to Hereford six miles off to make enquiries. This is a long story—but what has really been of so much concern to us I know cannot be indifferent to you. We found our friends here all well—I mean for them, and Elizabeth[1] wonderfully improved in health.

And now let me say a word upon two points which in none of my letters I have touched upon but which I did not feel the less; I mean your goodness in offering to leave your Friends long before your visits were finished and to come to Rydal in the embarrassment which we were under. Then again we know that but for your love of us you would have gone with Mr Taylor abroad. Both these proofs of your friendship have sunk deep into our hearts. God bless you, best of Friends and most amiable of women. If I could write in seemly penmanship and legibly, I would tell you a hundred little occurrences which it might in some degree please you to hear, but I am really shocked when I look at these misshapen characters and all this blotting, which no care of mine can prevent, for when my pen grows intolerable any attempts to mend it only make it worse.—

The Hotel near the Station at Birmingham where you were so comfortable, had not a bed to spare when we arrived; it was filled with strangers come to the Musical festival. So we were obliged to put up with sorry accommodation in a neighbouring Tavern. From Worcester I was on the outside of the Coach and saw the beautiful country to great advantage, Malvern in particular. We meet with persons who know us or have seen our

[1] Ebba Hutchinson.

place of abode at Rydal everywhere. At Darlington we found in the mailtrain coach where we [were] placed, a lady taking leave of a youth. By his Countenance I was sure he knew who I was. After the train began to move she burst into tears, and sobbed involuntarily. As soon as I could venture to speak to her, I found the youth she had just parted with was her son, and that he was one of ten children. She had lived 20 years in Petersburg where her family had all been born, and she was about to return thither. I led her into this conversation with a hope of beguiling her grief, and I succeeded wonderfully. I learned that she had been at the Lakes some three or four years ago, walked round the grounds of Rydal Mount, and had got a glimpse of me. She proved a very interesting person, intelligent, wellread and informed, with an animated countenance and conversation. She was anything but handsome but expression completely supplied that want, and the tones of her voice from long residence abroad had become more varied and musical than is common with English Ladies. Her sadness would return after we parted, but with much fervour she said, 'this will be a memorable day with me'. Farewell beloved Friend we rely on your joining us here.

W. W.

P.S. It would be *unjust* to our Friends at Leamington[1] to go there without you. I could not get over the disappointment and should be wretched company for them, without you.

1736. W. W. to EDWARD WILSON[2]

MS. Picton Autograph Letters, Synge Collection, Liverpool Public Libraries. Hitherto unpublished.

Brinsop Court
near Hereford
Septer. 21st [18]43

My dear Sir,

I have to thank you for two Letters, which having been moving about were long in reaching me; the latter I found on my arrival at this place yesterday.

I am surprized as you were at Mr Dawes's offer; if he should Keep in the same mind I fear the scheme which you mention will

[1] Particularly Mrs. Hook and Mrs. Ricketts.

[2] See L. 1728 above.

still be found impractible by reason of Mr Sewell's unwillingness to surrender as much of his salary as would be an inducement for a competent person to undertake both offices. The arrangement could only be dependent upon contingencies, and there is this great objection to it, that no single person could adequately perform the duties of Curate and School Master in Ambleside, the population already exceeding 1200. Still it would be an improvement and I heartily wish it may be found practicable.

With you I shall be much pleased if Mr T. Jackson should resign his office of Trustee.[1] But how comes it that you have not named Mr Benson Harrison? Nobody, for many substantial reasons, appears so proper a person to undertake the trust in conjunction With your Father and yourself. Owing to my advanced life, and to my having no property in the Parish I of course feel much disinclined to engage in the Trust, nevertheless were it agreeable to the Electors to appoint me if Mr^r Harrison would accept it I would not refuse, upon the expectation that your Father would not resign unless you were willing to succeed him.

I continue of opinion, in consequence of what Mr Carr said, and what I have heard from others, that it would be difficult if not impossible to make out a case of non-attendance against Mr Sewell.

I shall remain here at least three weeks; if any thing important should occur be so kind as to let me know

I remain, my dear Sir,
faithfully yours
Wm Wordsworth

[1] See L. 1721 above.

1737. W. W. to ANNA RICKETTS

Address: Miss A. Ricketts, Alverston, n^r Stratford upon Avon. [*In M. W.'s hand*]
Postmark: 13 Oct.
Stamp: Hereford.
MS. Berg Collection, New York Public Library. Hitherto unpublished.

[Brinsop]
Friday morn: [13 Oct. 1843]

My dear Anna,

I received your Letter at the Stowe. Mr Monkhouse[1] and I could not reply to it sooner, being dependent on the sad contingency of poor Jane's[2] illness. Mrs W. and I went together to the Stowe with our nephew Geo H.[3] last Monday purposing to stay till to day; but we heard so bad an account of Jane that we returned yesterday, when we found her so much worse that I cannot bring my mind to say positively when I shall be able to leave this place. Except that she suffers from Asthma the medical attendant cannot find out what ails her—her pulse to be sure is *far* from right, but she has no other signs of fever; yet she grows weaker and weaker, though she is able to take food sufficient one would think to restore her strength. I still encourage a hope that before the end of next week I may get to you all at Leamington; though I see not the least prospect of Mary being able to move with the poor Girl. The best we can hope is that she may be in such a state as will allow me to go to Leamington which is only a day's distance from this place and return hither if things grow worse. What poor blind creatures we are—Mary and I thought we had done so cleverly in bringing our faithful Servant along with us to be useful to our departed Sister[4] while at Elton—and see what has come of it.—In this House we have one great consolation that Sarah[5] is now for her very chearful and well, moving about actively.

But our crosses and disasters great and small have been most strange—on Wednesday we went from the Stowe, to see Mr

[1] John Monkhouse, who was now blind.

[2] The maid.

[3] George Hutchinson (see pt. ii, L. 769) had been ordained and was seeking preferment.

[4] Joanna Hutchinson had died towards the end of September.

[5] M. W.'s niece who suffered from a spinal complaint.

George Hutchinson's family, he is Mary's youngest Brother, at his house near Kington. Mary was in one Gig, driven by Mr Monkhouse's Groom, I in another driven by nephew George. When we were about a mile from Kington down came the horse; George leapt out and I was thrown into the road and the ditch. Mary and the Servant who were just before heard the commotion—he leapt out, and gave her the reins, in her consternation she could not manage the Spirited Horse which turned round, backed, and the Carriage went into the ditch, but by God[s] mercy the Horse did not take fright and gallop off so that no mischief ensued and I ran up to hold her Horse. In the meanwhile came by a man with three horses—two led by him, and he in the middle riding the other. The Road was narrow and in passing the Gig the near horse kicked up his heels, and George escaped only by a finger's length—All this happened within 30 yards and three minutes.—Our horses' knees were cut, and one of my fingers hurt but slightly—and that a shake from which I feel no bad effects were all the mischief.—Dearest Anna and you dearest Miss Fenwick and all good Friends about you and elsewhere, avoid single horse chaises on only two wheels. I detest them but we have here no other carriages and are six miles from a Post Town—I can say no more unless I lose the Post. The enclosed from Sir Wm Gomm's Letter[1] just received would give you pleasure.—Love in abundance to each and all. ever faithfully

my dear Anna
your loving Friend
Wm Wordsworth

I had written to Mrs Hook that I hoped to be with her Wednesday next. I must unsay—

1738. W. W. to DORA QUILLINAN

MS. Cornell. Hitherto unpublished.

[Brinsop]
Sat. 14th [Oct. 1843]

Dearest Dora,

Why have I not written? The answer is plain: I had nothing

[1] Gomm had written to W. W. twice—on 8 and 28 June—about his trials as Governor of Mauritius, and praising *Grace Darling* as a work of 'the Laureat of *universal Humanity*' (*WL MSS.*).

scarcely but disappointments and distresses and mishaps to write about, except what you were well aware of—the pleasure we should receive from the kindness of our Friends.

Sarah[1] is quite well, your Uncle suffering a good deal from the cold, your Cousin Thomas[2] has been here, much better than heretofore, though still indisposed, every body else in good health except that poor Jane[3] makes no progress, on the contrary, we found her much worse on our return. Yesterday the Doctor thought so ill of her, that he wished for the advice of a Hereford Physician, *Dr Lye*, [Your Aunt dislikes the *Man*, and had she been within he w^{d} not have been *sent* for, so she has rushed off awkward this m^{g}.][4] who accordingly was written to, to meet him here for a consultation today, but this morning in consequence of Jane seeming a good deal easier, a Messenger was sent off to say the Hereford Doctor need not come. But your Mother thinks that this improvement was only ease and relief from the Weobley Doctor's medicine, probably opiates, and stimulants. He will be here this morning to deliver his opinion; but he has never held out the least hope that she will be able to move for a long time. So you may judge how we are distressed. If she make any step towards recovery by next Wednesday or Thursday, I shall go to Leamington, and there among our friends, as I am of no use here, wait the issue, and after a certain stay there, either return hither or proceed with Miss Fenwick to Rydal, as may be judged best.

On Wednesday we went over to see George[5] and his family. Your mother driven in one Gig by Mr Monkhouse's Groom, and I following in another driven by your Cousin George. When we had got within a mile of Kington down came the Horse which George drove. Off he flew leapt on his feet and I was cast into a ditch, with a good shake, but no apparent harm save a spraining of the little finger of my right hand. The Groom and Mary who were just before saw what was happening—he gave the reins of his Horse to her—the animal was restless and turned round and backed into the ditch, she in her consternation being unable to guide, but God be thanked her horse did not spring forward and run away, else what would have become of her? In the meanwhile passed a Man Leading two horses, he riding upon

[1] M. W.'s niece. [2] M. W.'s nephew (see pt. ii, L. 670).

[3] The maid.

[4] Words in brackets added as a footnote by W. W.

[5] Thomas Hutchinson's younger brother.

a third in the middle; while George was employed in endeavouring to raise our Horse who was lying like a dead thing on his side—the led Horse on George's side gave an ugly kick at him, which he escaped by a finger's length—all this happened within a space of 30 Yards, and within three minutes' time. Was it not a deliverance for which we may all be thankful? I shudder to think of what might have befallen your Mother if her Horse had galloped off in fright. It is a spirited and impatient creature, the same Beast that ran away with its blind Master, owing to the reins having been accidentally dropped by him. I have told you these particulars knowing how every thing that befalls us interests you and yours. I hate Gigs—but here are no other Carriages.—

Here come the *two* Doctors—what can be so unlucky?—but every thing is cross—They are walking about in front of the House, so I shall have to lay down my pen in a minute or two—It is the least cause of regret, though no small one, that this illness of Jane's involves us in great expense—Two sovereigns, by way of an example, for this Man.

The two Doctors are now with Jane—the Hereford has his arm in a sling and has had it paralysed, by a fall from his *Gig*, his horse having come down with him. As I said before I detest these vehicles—

My eyes Thank God continue well—and your Mother is better than she looks. How I long to be fairly at Rydal again. They are waiting to take this Letter to the post. I shall add the Doctors' report when they come from Jane, and then close the Scrawl.

* * *

I am glad that the Hereford Doctor has been here. The result of their joint opinion is unfavorable, though they do not apprehend a fatal termination of *this* attack; but they think that this disease in the liver, and the congestion in the left lung with both of which she is affected, indicate a State of constipation, which will end in water in the [? chest].

There are many strong motives and some urgent reasons of Business, why I should go to London.[1] But my Courage fails

[1] W. W. had probably been discussing his financial affairs with H. C. R. who had spent a few days with the Wordsworths at Brinsop at the end of September, visiting Hereford Cathedral with them on the 28th for 'a lesson in antiquarian architecture' from the Dean, John Merewether. See Morley, i. 528–9; *HCR* ii. 634–5.

in thinking of it, especially as I do not see how your Mother can accompany me; and really I am tired with so little bodily exertion that I am quite afraid of facing the fatigues of London Walking, London Parties and London talking as I used to do. M^r Q's Letter to the Post[1] was quite right, and I hope will be seen by our London Friends, at least by most of them.—

The Miss Pollards[2] have through your Mother [in the most delicate way][3] made to John the munificent offer of 50£ a piece to help him through the expenses inevitable to this long-continued domestic affliction.[4] This is very noble on their part and we are much moved by it, as you will be. Their Letter has been sent to John, and I have begged that after collecting all his Bills, (the Surgeon's will be a very heavy one) and calculating as well as he can all the inevitable emergencies he would decide what portion of the money he can accept

ever
again and again yours
W. W.

Dear Miss Fenwick continues pretty well, Your Mother well too.

1739. W. W. to W. W. JNR.

MS. WL.
LY iii. 1181 (—).

Brinsop Tuesday forenoon [17 Oct. 1843]

My dear William,

I know not whether you have been sufficiently prepared for the event I am to communicate. Dear and good and faithful Jane expired last night at twelve: Her spirit departed so gently that the Housemaid who sate up with her was unconscious of the change. Mr Lomax of Weobley her Doctor saw her at noon, and though he found her a good deal weaker, gave us no reason to think her end was so very near. After the first inflammation was

[1] The *Morning Post*: an untraced item, probably pseudonymous.

[2] Jane Marshall's sisters. Years before, they had made a gift to D. W. (see pt. ii, L. 727).

[3] Words in brackets added by M. W.

[4] John W. was about to take his wife to Madeira in search of health.

subdued by bleeding she suffered no pain at any time, only her breathing was always short and rather difficult.—

I will not dwell on this sad subject, which is through God's mercy attended with much and heartfelt consolations of many kinds.

Your Letter enclosing dear Joanna's[1] will has just arrived, and been read. I grieve to find that all is at George's[2] own disposal; it cannot be helped—I shall speak to him most urgently not to break in upon it by any fond scheme whatever. But perhaps he is already in debt. He will be here on Wednesday, and I will also attempt, but alas it will be in vain—to induce him to fasten the money out of his own power.

Most anxiously do your Mother and I wish that you would call in the assistance of some copying Clerk during Mr Carter's absence, which we regret exceedingly. Also procure a horse, or the immediate use of one till you can procure one to your mind. [Dearest Son I *pray you* do this. M W][3]

—I will write to the Bp of Carlisle[4] as you request. George has been receiving lessons in *chanting* every day—he goes to Hereford on purpose, and in the evening to the Clergyman of Burghill, Mr Hanson,[5] who is skillful in music, as his wife. He has but a poor ear, but he makes encouraging progress.

Do dearest Wm for all our sakes take care of yourself. God bless you. We both have been writing Letters all this morning.

Your affectionate Father
Wm Wordsworth

You cannot say too much in praise of Geo. as a pious minister of the Gospel—and a Man desirous to be all that [he] ought to be as a good Churchman—his heart and soul is in his profession—and I feel confident he will become a *valuable* Member of the Church.

[1] The late Joanna Hutchinson.

[2] M. W.'s nephew (see L. 1737 above) was now seeking a minor canonry at Carlisle. See next letters.

[3] Words in brackets written in by M. W.

[4] Dr. Hugh Percy (see pt. ii, L. 477).

[5] Unidentified, and possibly a temporary curate. Burghill is between Brinsop and Hereford.

1740. W. W. to W. W. JNR.

MS. WL.
LY iii. 1182 (—).

Brinsop Court Wednesday 18th [Oct. 1843]

My dear Wm,

George,[1] who has been in the habit of going every day to Hereford for instruction in chanting, came home yesterday much discouraged. It is certain that he is not gifted with what is called an ear for music, and in consequence has never attended to it. But I have no doubt that He or any one else who earnestly desired to learn and would take pains accordingly would learn in course of time a thing so simple as chanting. Unfortunately in the present case the allowance of time is so very short that G. is almost hopeless; and he is strongly inclined to give up at once.

Now do you know whether it is likely that the Electors would decide altogether by the present competence or rather perfectness of the Candidate in the musical requisite, without suffering the consideration of future improvement to have weight in the matter. If so, I fear your good Cousin would have no chance.

We infer from your Letter that the testimonials include a declaration of *present* fitness; and that there will be no previous trial before the Dean and Chapter—pray is this so? Mr Saul[2] we think will be able to throw light upon the subject of these questions.

George will be at Bishop's Sutton near Pensford, Bristol on Saturday, therefore it will be best to address him there.

Poor dear Jane is to be buried on Friday. George will stay to perform the service. Your uncle George[3] and Mr Monkhouse[4] are both expected here to-day. Love from your dear Mother, and from all

Your affectionate Father
W. Wordsworth

Isabella's letter to be sent to Dora.

[1] George Hutchinson. See previous letter and next letter.

[2] Silas Saul of Castle Street, Carlisle, solicitor to the Dean of Chapter.

[3] M. W.'s younger brother.

[4] *Written* Mrs.

1741. W. W. to WILLIAM HENRY DIXON[1]

MS. untraced.
LY iii. 1182.

Brinsop Court near Hereford 23[d] Oct[br] 43

My dear Sir,

Circumstances of a very distressing kind detained Mrs Wordsworth and myself in the County of Durham so long as to leave us, which we much regretted, no time for our Friends and Relations at York, in which yourself and Mrs Dixon were especially included. I have not taken up the pen to express this regret, for I feel it unnecessary, and I left Mrs Robinson[2] and her Son[3] a message to that effect, but I write upon a matter relating to a Nephew of Mrs Wordsworth in which perhaps your kindness might prompt you to be of some service. A Son of the Archbishop of York,[4] I am told, is a Canon of Carlisle Cathedral, and one of the minor Canonries being vacant it has been suggested by his Cousin my Son William who resides at Carlisle, that he might probably succeed were he to offer himself as a Candidate. The Parents of the Young Man, Mr George Hutchinson, are both natives of Cumberland, (his Mother born at Carlisle) he was educated at Sedbergh School, went to St John's Cambridge, where he took a degree, and afterwards by my advice placed himself under Mr Pinder,[5] principal of the College of Wells. Here he pursued his studies in Divinity with great assiduity and Mr Pinder, I know, thinks very highly of him. I have had the happiness of knowing him from childhood

[1] For W. W.'s cousins Canon and Mrs. Dixon, see pt. ii, L. 37. They were frequent visitors to Rydal Mount in these years (see *RMVB*). He was domestic chaplain to the Archbishop of York, and a wealthy landowner and antiquary. His mother was half-sister to the poet Mason, and he bequeathed important manuscripts of Mason and Gray to the York Minster Library.

[2] Mrs. Dixon's mother, Admiral Robinson's widow.

[3] Henry Robinson the solicitor (see L. 1735 above).

[4] Edward Vernon Harcourt (1757–1847), Bishop of Carlisle, 1791–1807, and thereafter Archbishop of York (see pt. ii, L. 442). His son, the Revd. Charles Vernon Harcourt (d. 1870), formerly Student of Christ Church, Oxford, had been a Canon of Carlisle since 1837.

[5] The Revd. John Hothersall Pinder (1794–1868), educated at Charterhouse and Caius College, Cambridge, was Principal of Codrington College, Barbados, 1829–35, and of Wells Theological College, 1840–65, and a Canon of Wells, 1854–68. He called on W. W. in June 1845 (*RMVB*).

and have been more than satisfied with his conduct through life. Now, what I take the liberty of requesting is that if there be no objection you would express to Mr Harcourt the interest I take in the success of my Nephew's application, and the confidence I feel that were he to be appointed the electors would not be disappointed in their Choice; if you could add that yourself would be gratified if he should be approved of I should be truly thankful. I have taken the liberty of writing to the same effect to the Bishop of Carlisle, though knowing that he is not an elector. Of course testimonials will be prepared and sent in to the Dean and Chapter.

With kindest remembrances to Mrs Dixon and yourself in which Mrs Wordsworth cordially unites,

believe me my dear Sir,
faithfully yours
Wm Wordsworth

We hope to be at home by next Saturday.

1742. W. W. to JAMES PRINCE LEE[1]

Address: The Rev[d] Mr Lee, Master of the Grammar School, Birmingham. [*In M. W.'s hand*]
Postmark: 24 Oct. 1843.
Stamp: (1) Hereford (2) Birmingham.
MS. Lilly Library, Indiana University.
LY iii. 1184.

Brinsop Court near Hereford
Monday 23[d] Oct[r] [1843]

My dear Mr Lee—

Could you contrive to meet me at the Railway Station of the train from Worcester, next Friday, between 12 and 1 at Noon. It would give me great pleasure to see you though only for a few minutes. I will then explain why I did not let you know when I passed through Birmingham to this place. We proceed by the train to Lancaster on the same day.

ever with sincere respect and regard
Yours faithfully
Wm Wordsworth

[1] See L. 1717 above.

1743. W. W. to ANNE HOOK[1]

MS. Mrs. A. Coatalen. Hitherto unpublished.

Tuesday
24th Octbr [1843]

My dear Mrs Hook

Your very kind Letter encreases my regret of the depth of which you may judge by your own disappointment.—I should have been so glad too to see Dr Hook; but every thing since we left home has been either cross or distress, save the proofs which they have given us of the sympathy of our Friends. We are most anxious to be at home as if it would be some Shelter from trouble; but there we should have to meet my Nephew John Wordsworth, the only child of my eldest Brother, long since deceased, in I fear a hopeless state of pulmonary consumption.

About 10 days ago I had the misfortune to be thrown out of a single Horse chaise by the Horse falling. This mishap has left a lameness behind it which requires rest, and in short far more causes than [2] I need enumerate concur to deprive me of the pleasure which I had expected at Leamington.

Another time I may with God's blessing me [be] more favored. Early on Friday Morning we leave this place for Birmingham.

Mrs John Wordsworth and her Husband and two children [?star]t for Madeira on Thursday. Heaven grant her a safe return. What stormy weather for such a voyage, by one so weak.

Believe dear Mrs Hook
faithfully yours
Wm Wordsworth

[1] See pt. ii, Ls. 726–7; pt. iii, L. 970.

[2] *Written* that.

1744. W. W. to RICHARD HENRY DANA[1]

MS. untraced.
Jared B. Flagg, Life and Letters of Washington Allston, New York, 1892. K. LY iii. 1184.

Rydal Mount, Ambleside, [late] October 1843

I had heard much of Mr Allston from Mr Coleridge, and I should have thought it a high privilege to cultivate his friendship had opportunity allowed. Mr Coleridge had lived on terms of intimacy with him at Rome;[2] they returned from Italy about the same time, and it was in London, there only, that I had the pleasure of seeing Mr Allston at his own lodgings.[3] He was well known, both through Coleridge and his own genius, to one of my most intimate friends, Sir George Beaumont, who always passed the spring season in London. Coleridge and he took great delight in referring to Mr Allston's observations upon art and the works of the great masters they had seen together in Rome, and the admiration was no doubt mutual from the commencement of their acquaintance.

By such reports of his conversation and corresponding accounts of his noble qualities of heart and temper, I was led to admire, and with truth I may say to love, Mr Allston, before I had seen him or any of his works. But opportunities did not favor me. His short stay in London occasioned me much regret, less on account of being cut off from his society (though to that I was anything but indifferent) than that I felt strongly that his works would surely be duly appreciated in England.

His own country had a strong claim upon his talents, as it had upon his affections; nevertheless carefully as he had observed the works of the old masters, and deeply as he had studied them, and vivid as were his impressions of their excellence, I could not but entertain some fear, that when by residence in America he was removed from the sight of them, his genius, great as it was, might suffer, and his works fall more or less into mannerism. For my part there was such high promise in the few works of his

[1] Richard Henry Dana (1787–1879), author of *The Buccaneer and Other Poems*, 1827, and *Poems and Prose Writings*, 1833, and brother-in-law of Washington Allston, had written to announce the painter's death on 9 July. Dana was now planning a biography of Allston, but he did not complete it.

[2] In 1805.

[3] Probably both in 1812 and 1815.

pencil which I had the opportunity of seeing, that they stood high in my estimation, much above any artist of his day. They indicated a decided power of higher conceptions, and his skill in dealing with the material of art struck me as far beyond that of any other painter of his time. It was truly as Coleridge used to say, 'coloring, and not color'.

Since Mr Allston went back home[1] I have had short letters from him frequently, introducing his American acquaintances;[2] and friendly messages have often passed between us, which I am certain were mutually acceptable. Your account of his last moments affected me deeply. I thank you sincerely for it. Much do I regret that it is not in my power to dwell more upon particulars, but after such a lapse of time I could not venture to attempt it, and I beg of you to take in good part the scanty tribute to the memory of a great man whom I highly honored.

Sincerely yours,
William Wordsworth

1745. W. W. to UNKNOWN CORRESPONDENT

MS. Yale University Library. Hitherto unpublished.

Rydal Mount
[Nov.][3] 4th 1843

Dear Sir,

An absence from home unexpectedly prolonged, has prevented an earlier acknowledgement of your Letter and its Enclosures; and I must write briefly having found many Letters that demand an answer waiting for me.—

First let me express my sympathy with your sorrows, and a hope that time and reflections acting in concert with God's grace will restore tranquillity to your mind and consolation to your heart. The elegiac poem upon the decease of your Son, you submit to me not merely as a Man who may have suffered as I have in fact done from like bereavements, but also as a Poet and a Critic.—This I somewhat regret for your grief is yet too keen to allow of your treating the Subject in that mitigated tone that

[1] In 1818 (see *MY* ii. 504).

[2] Allston also sent W. W. a copy of his novel *Monaldi*, Boston, 1841 (see *R.M. Cat.*, no. 454).

[3] *Written* Octbr, but Nov. must have been intended.

Poetry requires. And therefore though there are in your verses, many touching passages and profound thoughts, yet as a whole the anguish which is given vent to at such length stands in the way of the general effect. Emotion remembered in a state of mind approaching to tranquillity as I have elsewhere said is more favorable to the production of verses filled to give frequent and general pleasure. Pray do not be hurt at what I have written, which I have had but little scruple in writing as the Lines which you have sent me both upon this sad subject, and upon others afford abundant proof of the poetical mind, while the execution is oftentimes exceedingly happy. I was much pleased with the Stanzas entitled, Poets; with the Sonnet upon Mr Southey, with those upon Guardian Angels; nor must I omit those you have addressed to myself.

I cannot conclude without expressing my satisfaction that my attempts in verse have been productive of so much pleasure and benefit to a mind gifted like yours.

I remain dear Sir
with much respect
faithfully yours
Wm Wordsworth

I concur with all that you say of Mr Southey's character appearance and manner, except as to his voice—in that I differ from you for the tones of it were often to my ear abrupt and unpleasing. On reviewing my Letter I find I have not spoken with sufficient warmth of your Poems, with some of which I was exceedingly delighted. The long ones are certainly however, drawn out to too great length, Grace Darling for instance—you will excuse the Sincerity of this remark.

1746. W. W. to BENJAMIN ROBERT HAYDON

MS. untraced.
LY iii. 1171.

Rydal Mount [? early Nov. 1843]

My dear Haydon,

You have kindly written to me several Letters which have remained unanswered, an omission which I trust you have excused. It gave me very great pleasure to hear that Mrs

Haydon's health was restored, and I am happy to find this favorable account confirmed in your Last.

Your disappointment in the Cartoons[1] vexed me not a little. But the best way of dealing with things of this kind in every concern of life, is, not to be busy in imputing the failures to faults in others, but rigorously to examine one's own doings, so as, if possible, to find out what is amiss there, and amend it for the future; and this is the best mode of avenging one's self upon detractors.

I have had no communication with Mr Rogers[2] upon this matter; and have heard very little about the Cartoons from any one else.—

The state of your affairs as you describe it is very discouraging;[3] and I fear much that the Picture you are doing of me upon Helvellyn,[4] as it is not done by commission, may disappoint you—Had it been summer-time, I think I could have procured a sketch of the view from some part of Helvellyn, but I have no means of doing it at present. Do you know Wm Westall, the Artist? He has made a great number of drawings from this Country some from the mountain tops one of which, viz. from the top of Saddleback I distinctly remember. You might hear of him probably at Murray's,[5] at all events it would not be difficult to find him out; and I am sure he would be gratified by your application and give you all the assistance in his power. I have no other means of assisting you in this difficulty.—

Do you happen to know who engraved the head of Northcote, in Hazlitt's life of that Artist?[6] Alston, the American painter

[1] See L. 1715 above.

[2] Samuel Rogers had been one of the judges, along with Peel, Lord Lansdowne, Sir Richard Westmacott, Richard Cook, R.A., and William Etty, R.A.

[3] By throwing all his energies into the practice of fresco, Haydon had neglected the commissions on which his livelihood depended, and he was now again deeply in debt.

[4] Not *Wordsworth on Helvellyn*, which had been completed the previous year, but almost certainly the unfinished sketch entitled 'Wordsworth on Helvellyn', which is now at Dove Cottage. See Blanshard, *Portraits of Wordsworth*, p. 170. Haydon was at work on this in November (see *Diary*, ed. Pope, v. 326, 328): hence the dating of this letter.

[5] John Murray's, the publisher's.

[6] *Conversations of James Northcote, Esq., R.A.*, 1830. The portrait of Northcote in his eighty-second year was engraved by Thomas Wright (1792–1849), after a drawing by Abraham Wivell (1786–1849). Wright, a pupil of Henry Meyer, was

lately deceased,[1] thought it the best engraved modern head that he had seen.

We are sorry to hear of your Daughter's illness. With best wishes for yourself and Mrs Haydon, in which Mrs W. unites, I remain

dear Haydon
faithfully your's
Wm Wordsworth

1747. W. W. to HENRY REED

MS. untraced.
K (—). Wordsworth and Reed, p. 114.

Rydal Mount
Ambleside
[10 Nov. 1843][2]

My dear Mr Reed,

Your congratulation upon the course which I have all along pursued with my Friends in respect to their Pennsylvanian Bonds gave me much pleasure, and I am glad that you continue to write in so hopeful a strain.[3] You are certainly justified in pointing to the rise in value of the stocks, as a proof of an improved state both of mind and circumstances in the Country; nevertheless I cannot feel confident that justice will be done to the Creditors, till the Government takes some positive step either by imposition of a tax, or sale of some portion of the property it has at command, both for the payment of interest and for reduction of the principal. Of the ability of the State of Pennsylvania to discharge its obligations there can be no doubt;

highly regarded for his engravings of portraits. Much of his time was spent in St. Petersburg, where his brother-in-law George Dawe, R.A., a highly successful portrait-painter, found him ample scope for his talents.

[1] See L. 1744 above. Allston had stated in a letter to Henry Reed, part of which Reed sent on to W. W. (see next letter), that he would have wished his portrait of Coleridge engraved by the same artist.

[2] *Written* Octr 10th 33—but according to Broughton who saw the postmark, the date should be 10 Nov. 1843.

[3] For Reed's letter to W. W. of 28 Sept., see *Wordsworth and Reed*, p. 110. It was largely taken up with a tribute to Washington Allston.

as Mr Webster[1] has told them theirs is one of the richest countries in the world—so that the whole resolves itself into a question of morality. Now I have no doubt that an immense majority of the educated Inhabitants desire nothing more earnestly than that the debt should be provided for; but their opinion is overborne by the sordid mass which will always have a lamentable influence over a community whose institutions are so democratic as yours unfortunately are. Were it not for this evil, I should not have a shadow of doubt as to the Issue; at present, I own, I have. Mr. Webster has spoken manfully, but why does he say so much about the great foreign Capitalists, without giving a word to the very many who in humble life are stripped of their comforts, and even brought to want by these defalcations? It is a sad return for the confidence they placed in the good faith of their transatlantic Brethern. I do not mean to insinuate that the poor creditors should be paid at the expense of the rich; far from it, but it is for that portion of the sufferers that I chiefly grieve; and I mourn even still more for the disgrace brought upon and the discouragement given to, the self-government of nations by the spread of suffrage among the people. For I will not conceal from you that as far as the people are capable of governing themselves I am a Democrat.

I have written to two of Mr. Alston's friends, Mr. Waterston[2] who wrote to me immediately upon his Death and to his Brother in Law[3] also, to whom I should have replied earlier, but that I was discouraged by the expectations which he entertained that I had much to say of his lamented Friend. The fact is, as I have told him, that my direct personal knowledge of Mr. Alston was very slight. I do not think that I ever saw him more than half a dozen times at the utmost, and that was in one place and long ago. But I had heard so much of his character from Mr Coleridge, that I was prepared to set a high value upon his acquaintance, and all that I did see of him personally strengthened my regret that he remained so short a time among us, in England. Your Extracts from his Letter[4] interested me much;

[1] Daniel Webster (see pt. iii, L. 1326), until recently American Secretary of State.

[2] See L. 1723 above. W. W.'s letter to him has not survived.

[3] R. H. Dana. See L. 1744 above.

[4] See *Wordsworth and Reed*, p. 112. Allston had written to Reed shortly before his death expressing agreement with W. W.'s view that his portrait of Coleridge ought to remain in England.

and immediately upon receipt of your's I wrote to a Friend at Bristol,[1] to do what could be done for the fulfilment of Mr Alston's and my own wishes in respect to the Portrait. To that Letter I have not yet received an answer. The Portrait belongs I believe to a nephew or niece of the late Mr Wade, for whom it was painted.

Thanks for your criticism upon the sonnet, let it be altered as you suggest; "*for* rightly were they taught etc."[2] This is a dry Letter but pray do not thence infer that I feel less affectionately towards you, or less sensible of the value of your correspondence, but believe me to remain

ever and truly and faithfully your's

Wm Wordsworth

1748. W. W. to MRS. HARRISON[3]

Address: Mrs Harrison, Hundhow, Kendal.
Postmark: 13 Nov. 1843.
Stamp: (1) Ambleside (2) Kendal.
MS. WL. Hitherto unpublished.

[13 Nov. 1843]

Dear Madam,

Many thanks for your promptness in meeting our invitation; but most unluckily since M[rs] W. wrote our Horse has caught the distemper, so that there is no probability of his being able to take the Journey to Stavely on Tuesday. This Disappointment we are exceedingly sorry for, and I must therefore express a hope that it may suit you to defer your visit for another week, unless some opportunity occurs that You can take advantage of, in which case you can never come wrong.

We received yesterday a Letter from our Son John, dated Funchal Madeira. He speaks in raptures of the climate and their Lodgings, and is in good heart about his dear Wife.

[1] Probably John Peace.

[2] See the sonnet 'Bishops and Priests,' (*PW* iii. 392), l. 13. But this alteration was not finally adopted.

[3] Of Hundhow (see L. 1725 above).

With kin[d] remembrances to Mr Harrison, in which Mrs W. begs to join, and to yourself

I remain, dear Madam
Your much obliged
W[m] Wordsworth

Ambleside

Since the above was written, I have seen Mr Roughsedge who will lend us his Horse for Tuesday. Be so good as to say at what *time* you would wish to be met at Stavely.

1749. W. W. to UNKNOWN CORRESPONDENT

MS. untraced.
Michael Holland, 'A Sussex Library', Book Collectors' Quarterly, iii (1933), no. xii, p. 12.

Rydal Mount
16 Novr., 1843.

Dear Sir,

You ask for more than my *name*, but the choice of words in such a case is not a little perplexing. Pray accept these lines instead.

I remain
truly yours,
Wm Wordsworth

1750. M. W. to JAMES STANGER[1]

Address: James Stanger.
MS. Mr. T. Wilson. Hitherto unpublished.

[mid-Nov. 1843]

My dear Sir,

I have taken the liberty to detain the slip from the Examiner, not wishing Mr Wordsworth to see it until he has expressed

[1] Moves were now under way to set up a permanent memorial to Southey, who had died the previous March. Landor was urging the claims of Bristol, and opened a subscription list in the *Examiner* on 4 Nov., offering at the same time an epitaph of his own composition. (See Super, *Walter Savage Landor*, pp. 346–7.) In

what his own mind suggests for the inscription[1]—but it shall be returned to you when you hear again from Rydal.

Very respectfully, Sir, your's
M. Wordsworth

1751. W. W. to JOSEPH COTTLE

MS. untraced.
Mem. (—). *Grosart* (—). *K* (—). *LY iii. 1186.*

Nov. 24, 1843.

My dear Mr Cottle,

. . . You have treated the momentous subject of socinianism in a masterly manner, which is entirely and absolutely convincing.[2]

Believe me to remain, my good old friend, with great respect,

Faithfully yours,
Wm Wordsworth

1752. W. W. to EDWARD MOXON

MS. Henry E. Huntington Library.
LY iii. 1186.

Rydal 24th Novbr 1843

My dear Mr Moxon,

Pray send by Canal, not by Railroad, (for their charges are most exorbitant) twelve copies of the new edition[3] in 7

the Lake District the appeal was headed by James Stanger, the Keswick churchman and philanthropist, who had now applied to W. W. for an inscription for a monument in Crosthwaite church, where Southey had worshipped for over forty years, and in the churchyard of which he was buried. The appeal provoked some opposition from Dissenters because it also embraced a larger scheme to restore the church fabric.

[1] W. W. first composed a prose epitaph (see L. 1713 above), which was not in the event used, and then his *Inscription for a Monument in Crosthwaite Church, in the Vale of Keswick* (*PW* iv. 278). As succeeding letters show, the poem gave him a good deal of trouble. He submitted successive drafts to Sir John Taylor Coleridge and C. W. jnr. for their comments, and final emendations were still being made as the sculptor set to work incising the marble.

[2] *Essays in reference to Socinianism*, 1842. The first part only was published.

[3] The reissue of the stereotype edition of 1841.

Volumes, of course including the Vol: last published as the 7th, also half a dozen separate Copies of the Excursion in the same Parcel. The Vol: of Sonnets which was printed to gratify my deceased Nephew John Wordsworth[1] has proved a bad concern. What do you do with the Copies—could they be got off at a lower price?—

I see my Poems advertized in the Morning Post 6 volumes; is that politic? how do you propose to get off the 7th. They ought I think to be sold *together* as much as possible; that we may start fairly at the proper time with the double Column Edit.[2]

ever faithfully yours
W. Wordsworth

Turn over.

Eight of the twelve Copies are intended for the Ambleside demand, and are not likely to be disposed of till next summer. The other four I should wish to be at liberty to present among Friends, without their being charged to me.

1753. W. W. to JAMES STANGER

Address: James Stanger. [*delivered by hand*]
MS. Mr. T. Wilson. Hitherto unpublished.

1st Dec. 1843
Rydal

I have no objection whatever to the Epitaph[3] being printed and circulated as you propose. The Copy I now send is slightly altered and has the addition of six lines with a view to characterizing his works which seems adviseable as he was distinguished in so many *different* departments of literature. Upon the marble the lines must be engraved in double column and not large letters, which will admit of the Tablet being better

[1] C. W.'s son.

[2] Publ. 1845.

[3] For Southey's memorial, see L. 1750 above and the next letters. W. W. had now drafted a verse inscription and a simpler biographical statement, which ran as follows: 'Sacred to the memory of Robert Southey whose mortal Remains are interred in the adjoining churchyard. He was born at Bristol October 4th 1774, and died, after a residence of nearly forty years, at Greta Hall in this Parish, March 21st 1843.' Southey's birthday was actually 12 August.

proportioned, and make the Inscription appear not quite so long as it is, which will be an advantage. If it be the opinion of the Committee that 'Poet Laureate, L.L.D.' should be added, it will be necessary that the words "He was" should precede the word "born": For my own part I think the bare name is the best upon a monument to be placed in a Church; besides if these Titles be given why not many others? designating the Academies and Societies of which he was a member. He in the Title-page of the last edition of his Poems calls himself Robert Southey. There is also indeed an Engraved title Page with L.L.D. but that was flourish of the Publisher.

It may be as well to mention that the Sculptor[1] may object to so long an epitaph as being likely to hurt the proportions of his Tablet; but this must not be listened to by the Committee if they approve of the Inscription as it stands.

I remain my dear Sir
faithfully yours
Wm Wordsworth

Pray send a circular to the Rev[d] Dr Wordsworth
Buckstead, Uckfield.
but perhaps I sent this before.
Also send one to

Thomas Hutchinson Esq.
Brinsop Court
Hereford.

Also Wm Crackanthorpe Esq.
Newbiggin Hall
Temple Sowerby

The Marquess of Hastings[2]
Donnington Park Leicestershire

Sir George Beaumont Bart
Coleorton Hall, Ashby de la Zouche.

[1] John Graham Lough (see L. 1622 above). His monument to Southey, a full-length recumbent figure in white marble on a pedestal of Caen stone, was completed in 1846 at a cost of £1,100. A list of subscribers is preserved among the *WL MSS*.

[2] George Augustus Francis Rawdon-Hastings, 2nd Marquess of Hastings and 7th Earl of Loudoun (1808–44), a younger brother of Lady Flora Hastings (see pt. iii, L. 1335).

1754. W. W. to SIR JOHN TAYLOR COLERIDGE

MS. British Library.
K. LY iii. 1187.

2nd Decbr 43.

My dear Mr Justice Coleridge,

Pray accept my thanks for the pains you have taken with the Inscription and excuse the few words I shall have to say upon your remarks.

There are *two* lakes in the vale of Keswick: both which, along with the lateral Vale of Newlands immediately opposite Southey's study window, will be included in the words, 'Ye vales and hills',[1] by every one who is familiar with the neighbourhood.

I quite agree with you that the construction of the lines that particularize his writings is rendered awkward, by so many participles passive, and the more so on account of the transitive verb 'informed'. One of these participles may be got rid of, and I think a better Couplet produced, by this alteration—

> Or judgments sanctioned in the Patriot's mind
> By reverence for the rights of all mankind.

As I have entered into particulars as to the character of S's writings, and they are so various, I thought his Historic works ought by no means to be omitted, and therefore, though unwilling to lengthen the Epitaph, I added the following:

> . . . Labours of his own,
> Whether he traced historic truth with zeal
> For the State's guidance or the Church's weal,
> Or Fancy, disciplined by studious art,
> Informed his pen, or wisdom of the heart,
> Or judgments sanctioned in the Patriot's mind
> By reverence for the rights of all mankind.

I do not feel with you in respect to the word 'so'[2]—it refers of

[1] See *PW* iv. 278, *app. crit.* W. W. had altered the opening of the verse epitaph in response to Sir John Coleridge's comment in his letter of 30 Nov.: 'I desiderate some notice of the Lake—in the third line I could almost venture to turn 'ye loved Books' into 'thou loved Lake'—and end the 4th line with shore.' (*British Library MSS.*)

[2] The original version of ll. 13–14 read:

> Friends, Family—ah wherefore touch that string.
> To them so fondly did the good man cling.

course to the preceding line, and as the reference is to fireside feelings and intimate friends, there appears to me a propriety in an expression inclining to the Colloquial. The Couplet was the dictate of my own feelings, and the construction is accordingly broken and rather dramatic. But too much of this.—If you have any objection to the Couplet as altered be so kind as let me know; if not, on no account trouble yourself to answer this Letter.

'Prematurely'[1] I object to as you do. I used the word with reference to that decay of faculties which is not uncommon in advanced life, and which often leads to Dotage—but the word must not be retained.

We regret much to hear that Lady Coleridge is unwell. Pray present to her our best wishes.—

What could induce the Bp. of London to forbid the choral service at St. Mark's?[2] It was an execution, I understand, above all praise.

ever most faithfully yours,
Wm Wordsworth

[1] This word occurred in the alternative epitaph in prose (see L. 1713 above), which was not used.

[2] Bishop Blomfield's Charge of 1842, in which he recommended strict adherence to the Prayer-Book rubrics, provoked a storm of opposition from both Evangelicals and High-Churchmen. As the Tractarian Movement turned in a Romeward direction, the daily choral service at St. Mark's, with its plainsong chants and intoned prayers, seemed to bear out all his misgivings. See Rainbow, *The Choral Revival in the Anglican Church*, pp. 48 ff. Writing to her cousin Francis on 1 Feb. 1844, Sara Coleridge referred to Derwent Coleridge's difficulties with his bishop: 'Derwent is very much where he was in regard to the affairs of St. Mark's and the choral service. He has to deal with a Bishop who is disinterested, able, and personally well disposed to him,—but whose habit of mind it is to judge of Christian principle by Christian expediency. . . To many it seems, and I own myself to be of their opinion, that the choral service, as conducted at St. Mark's, may be objected to on *principle*: but it is not on such deep ground that the Bishop takes his stand,—so that his arguments appear weak to earnest men, and his authority . . . is becoming more and more reduced to that of his office rather than that of his personal character and his office together.' (*Texas University MSS.*). In his *Second Letter on the National Society's Training College* . . . , 1844, Derwent Coleridge defended the practices at St. Mark's, and denied that they were contrary to the rubrics of the Book of Common Prayer.

1755. W. W. to JAMES STANGER

MS. Mr. Robert H. Taylor. Hitherto unpublished.

[*c.* 3 Dec. 1843]

My dear Sir

Be so good as to alter the 11th and 12th lines thus,

> Or judgements sanctioned in the Patriot's mind
> By reverence for the rights of all mankind.

I should like to have a proof of the circular[1] including of course the Inscription sent me before it is struck off, for correction if there should be any errors. Excuse my troubling you in this way and believe me sincerely yours

Wm Wordsworth

1756. W. W. to EDWARD MOXON

MS. Henry E. Huntington Library.
K (—). LY iii. 1188.

Monday 4th Decbr 43

My dear Mr Moxon,

I answered the American Gentleman's Letter[2] about a month since.

I am as much surprized as you at Mr Gough's Specimens.[3] I expected nothing but a School Book to be sold at a low price. Mr Gough requested of me permission to make a selection mainly of subjects relating to this country, as it was principally intended for circulation among his own Scholars. He was then Master of St. Bees' School, as he is now of the free School of Carlisle. I consented without reluctance, subject to your

[1] A black-bordered quarto sheet containing the first (anon.) printing of W. W.'s *Inscription for a Monument in Crosthwaite Church*. It differs in some detail from the text finally inscribed on the memorial, as is clear from a copy preserved in the British Library.

[2] See L. 1744 above.

[3] *Select Pieces from the Poems of William Wordsworth*, 1843, put out by the London publisher James Burns, with a dedication to Queen Victoria. (See *Cornell Wordsworth Collection*, no. 128). The Revd. Henry Gough (1812–62), Fellow of Queen's College, Oxford, 1846–56, was second master at St. Bees in 1842, and headmaster of Carlisle Grammar School, 1843–9.

permission. I stipulated for no emolument nor even alluded to it, deeming the thing not of sufficient importance. As I have always understood that Mr Gough is a truly respectable man, I am inclined to think that Burns[1] has taken advantage of his inexperience in dealing with Publishers. I shall write to Mr Gough in a Day or two. Burns has sent me by Mail-Train, five Copies and a handsome Quarto Book of common prayer, after the Antique, by way of I suppose of douceur or hush money. But we have both of us had our kindness abused—

ever faithfully
Yours
Wm Wordsworth

PS

As there is not a word from The Excursion nor The White Doe nor Peter Bell etc etc, etc., nor any of the Continental Poems or the Sonnets etc, I hope the Publication will not hurt our Sale, and, if it should not I care nothing about the matter except as far as concerns the behaviour of one or both of these Individuals.—Burns in his Letter alludes to improvements in the Embellishments which he purposes to make if a 2nd Edition be called for; but I shall stop that as soon as I have heard from Mr Gough. I will carefully read the Book you mean to send me. There is a Book or Tract lately published by my Nephew the Master of Harrow entitled Theophilus Anglicanus;[2] I hope he has sent it to you in time to have been forwarded, in your parcel, for I hear it highly spoken of.—

[1] James Burns (1808–71), moved from Forfarshire, where he was intended for the Presbyterian ministry, to London, and set up as publisher and bookseller. He became a keen Tractarian, publishing service books, novels, and tracts for the high-church party. His conversion to Roman Catholicism in 1847 caused him serious hardship, but his business picked up again with Newman's help. The firm later became Burns and Oates.

[2] C. W. jnr.'s exposition of the Anglican *via media* adopted the method of question and answer, followed by supportive quotations from the Fathers and standard Anglican divines. The plan of the work was 'to give the young Churchman a clear and definite conception, first of the Church Catholic, then of the Anglican branch of the Church, and of her true position as regarded Rome on the one side and the various Protestant sects on the other; and finally of her connection, as the National Church of England, with the civil power.' (*Christopher Wordsworth, Bishop of Lincoln*, p. 399.) W. W.'s sonnet addressed to the author was composed on 11 Dec. (see L. 1761 below).

1757. W. W. to SIR JOHN TAYLOR COLERIDGE

MS. British Library.
LY iii. 1189 (—).

Dec[br] 6th [1843]

My dear M[r] Justice Coleridge,

Notwithstanding what I have written before, I could not but wish to meet *your wishes*, upon the points which you mentioned and accordingly have added and altered as on the other side of this paper. If you approve dont trouble yourself to answer

ever faithfully yours
W Wordsworth

Ye torrents foaming down the rocky steeps,
Ye lakes wherein the Spirit of water sleeps,
Ye Vales and hills etc.,
Or judgements sanctioned in the Patriot's mind
By reverence for the rights of all mankind.
Friends, Family—within no human breast
Could private feelings need a holier nest.
His joys, his griefs, have vanished etc.,

These alterations are approved of by friends here, and I hope will please you.

Alteration in the Epitaph[1]

—He to Heaven was vowed

Through a life long and pure; and Christian faith
Calmed in his soul the fear of change and
death

W. W.

[1] The rest of the letter is on a separate slip of paper, and may belong with a later letter to Sir John Coleridge which has not survived.

1758. W. W. to EDWARD MOXON

MS. Henry E. Huntington Library.
LY iii. 1190 (—).

[*c.* 6 Dec. 1843][1]

My dear Mr Moxon,

The Enclosed Paper of directions was left this morning by my Nephew John Wordsworth to go to Burns.[2] He wants to make a present of the Books which have been admired in a Family to which he is greatly obliged. You know that his health is in a precarious state, and as it has obliged him to withdraw from his Profession at present I wish, and therefore I beg, that you would be so kind as to procure for Him the Books at Trade price; for I myself do not wish to have *friendly* communications with Mr Burns. I have written to Mr Gough[3] this morning stating my feelings pretty strongly

ever truly yours
Wm Wordsworth

I have asked Mr Gough to learn for me how many copies have been struck off and told him that I shant give my consent to another edition of the same kind. It is one of *Burns* Selections that my Nephew wishes for, bound as the Paper directs. Pray send the charge along with the Books.

[*John Carter adds*]

Please also to say what would be the *selling* price of the 'Order of Daily Service' same as the one sent to Mr Wordsworth and bound in the same way.

1759. W. W. to C. W.

MS. Mr. Jonathan Wordsworth. Hitherto unpublished.

[? mid-Dec. 1843][4]

. . .John[5] does not get worse, though I am sorry to say we

[1] Dated to the 4th in a later hand, but probably written a day or two later.

[2] James Burns, the publisher (see L. 1756 above).

[3] The Revd. Henry Gough.

[4] Date probably established by E. Q.'s letter to H. C. R. of 9 Dec. (Morley, i. 532), which refers to Dora Q.'s visit to Willy W. at Carlisle.

[5] R. W.'s son.

cannot persuade ourselves that he is much better. He has been and is staying with his kind friends and Relations Mr and Mrs Harrison of Green [Bank], with excellent medical advice [ ][1] of himself [ ][2] Brother with many thanks for your last affectionate letter, and our united love I must bid you farewell.

ever most affectionately yours
Wm Wordsworth

Dora has been on a visit to her Brother and the Crackanthorpes. Her Husband is with her. They return home next Saturday . . .

1760. W. W. to EDWARD MOXON

MS. Henry E. Huntington Library.
LY iii. 1191.

20 Dec^{r} [1843]

My dear Mr Moxon,

I have no objection to the reference you propose; but it cannot be amiss that I should briefly state to *you* some thing of my own feeling on the subject.

I have not yet had either from Mr Gough or Mr Burns the amount of Copies[3] struck off. But I protest entirely whatever that may be against any pecuniary emolument being drawn from the Edition by Mr Burns. Nor do I think that he is entitled to any remuneration of that kind for his personal trouble either in superintending the embellishments or any thing else. In fact he has already renounced every thing of the kind as he well might. For neither you nor I, nor as far as I understand Mr Gough, ever gave his consent to such a publication. We have nothing to do with Mr Burns's motives in this question, we may allow them to be as unselfish as he affirms they were—it is enough that there was to an extraordinary extent, a deviation

[1] *Half a page missing.*

[2] *MS. torn.*

[3] Of Burns's *Select Pieces from the Poems of William Wordsworth* (see L. 1756 above). In 1845 (the date of the new Advertisement) Moxon put out an almost identical volume, with the same selection of poems and embellishments but with different typesetting throughout, presumably by arrangement with James Burns. This volume is incorrectly dated both by the *British Library Catalogue* and the *Cornell Wordsworth Collection* (see no. 127).

from, or opposition to, what you and I had authorized—Next comes the consideration of what Mr Burns is entitled to for actual expenditure, and what is to be done with the embellishments in future. I could wish to leave this matter to your judgement, not doubting that you could state the case on your part and as guardian of our united interests fairly and frankly to the Referee—

I need not repeat that I wish Mr Burns to be dealt with not only without hardness, but as gently as justice and reason will permit.

ever my dear Mr Moxon
faithfully yours
Wm Wordsworth

1761. W. W. to C. W.

MS. WL.
LY iii. 1192.

20 Dec^r [1843][1]

My dear Brother,

Mr Burns has forwarded to me your favorable notice of his Selections from my Poems; your approbation would have been well deserved, if either I or Mr Moxon had given our consent to any such publication. The matter originated thus. The Rev^d Mr Gough, then under master of St. Bees School, and now head master of the Grammar School Carlisle, applied to me for permission to publish Selections from my poems, as an ordinary school-book for his *own* Scholars mainly and for the use of those classes of society which might not have access to so expensive a book as the whole Body of my Poetry. He told me also, that having his own Scholars mainly in view the Selections would principally be of Poems the subjects of which were from the North of England, as being most likely to interest them. Of course I had no difficulty in giving my consent to such a publication under his management, nor to his extending the collection, as far as was consistent with a low price, and reasonable attention to Mr Moxon's interests and my own. In fact I expected that the price of the Book would not exceed half a

[1] Year added by C. W.

crown or three shillings at the utmost, and as neither I nor Mr Moxon nor Mr Gough looked to any pecuniary advantage, or wished for any, the work would have had no expenses to bear of Copyright or Editorship, and might have been sold cheap accordingly. Mr Charles Knight[1] publishes a play of Shakespear (*sometimes* extending to 120 pages) for sixpence—The paper and type are unexceptionable, so that no Copyright profit being in my case looked for, the Selections might have been sold proportionately cheap, care only being taken that they did not go to an extent which would obviously be injurious to the sale of the Works in a Body. Mr Gough was much in fault as he did not let me know what Burns was doing, though he protested against it. Burns was also greatly in fault *whatever might be his motives*, in setting aside Mr Gough's judgement, and disregarding his wishes. In fact he put the work into the hands of another Editor, a Scotch man, who furnished a preface, the first sentence on the 2nd page[2] of which I think very objectionable, as tending to impede the sale of the works in a body, though I trust it was not meant to do so. But too much of this matter. I have read Chris's Work[3] both with profit and pleasure. I have not thanked him for it yet, except through the medium of the Morning Post, in a Sonnet[4] printed in that journal, friday or Saturday last: perhaps you have either seen or heard of it. An Epitaph which I have written for dear Southey, will certainly reach you in a Circular printed Letter.

We look forward with great delight to seeing you here next

[1] Charles Knight (1791–1873), journalist, and publisher of *Knight's Quarterly Magazine* (1823–4), the *Penny Magazine* (1832–45), etc., began issuing his editions of Shakespeare's plays in 1838. His *Pictorial Shakespeare* was completed in 1841. Among his numerous other works were *Half Hours with the Best Authors*, 4 vols., 1847–8, and the autobiographical *Passages of a Working Life*, 3 vols., 1864–5.

[2] The Advertisement recommended W. W.'s poetry as 'one of our direct instruments of education.' 'By no such great poet, besides Shakespeare, has the English tongue been used with equal purity, and yet such flexible command of its resources.' The offending sentence read: 'In the following selection, therefore, the compiler's choice has fallen, as far as possible, on such poems as contain the broader features of Wordsworth's style, as possess a beauty which must reveal itself to all who have the capacity of perceiving beauty, and as have, by this time, taken their place among the classics of the English tongue.'

[3] *Theophilus Anglicanus* (see L. 1756 above).

[4] *To the Rev. Christopher Wordsworth, D.D., Master of Harrow School* (*PW* iii. 59).

Summer. We did not get to Leamington but came strai[gh]t home after leaving Brinsop. Our spirits were too much depressed to allow of our turning out of the way, even to visit friends. I hope Chris's valuable Book will meet with the reception it so amply deserves.

[*unsigned*]

1762. W. W. to SIR JOHN TAYLOR COLERIDGE

MS. British Library.
K. LY iii. 1194.

Rydal Mount
Dec^br^ 23^d^, 43.

My dear Mr Justice Coleridge,

The first line would certainly have more spirit by reading 'your' as you suggest. I had previously considered *that*, but decided in favour of 'the', as 'your', I though, would clog the sentence in sound, there being 'ye' thrice repeated, and followed by 'you' at the close of the 4th line. I also thought that 'your' would interfere with the application of 'you' at the end of the fourth line to the whole of the particular previous images, as I intended it to do. But I don't trouble you with this Letter on that account, but merely to ask you whether the Couplet now standing,

> Large were his aims, yet in no human breast
> Could private feelings find a holier nest,

would not be better thus,

> Could private feelings meet in holier rest.[1]

This alteration does not quite satisfy me, but I can do no better.

[1] W. W. was continuing to alter the text of the *Inscription* as printed in the Circular (see L. 1755 above). Lady Richardson records a discussion of the verses at Mrs. Fletcher's, and her mother's objection to 'holier nest' as not being a correct union of ideas: 'He said there was yet time to change it, and that he should consult Judge Coleridge whether the line as he once had it,

> Did private feeling[s] meet in holier rest

would not be more appropriate to the simplicity of an epitaph where you con every word, and where every word is expected to bear an exact meaning.' (Grosart, iii. 438). But, as de Selincourt notes, the inscription on the monument reverts to 'find a holier nest'.

The word 'nest' both in itself and in conjunction with 'holier' seems to be somewhat bold and rather startling for marble, particularly in a Church. I should not have thought of any alteration in a merely printed poem, but this makes a difference. If you think the proposed alteration better, don't trouble yourself to answer this; if not, pray be so kind as to tell me so by a *single* line. I would not on any account have trespassed on your time but for this public occasion.

We are very sorry to hear of Lady Coleridge's indisposition; pray present to her our kind regards and best wishes for her recovery, united with the greetings of the season both for her and yourself.

And believe me,
faithfully,
your obliged W[m] Wordsworth

1763. W. W. to EDWARD MOXON

MS. Henry E. Huntington Library.
LY iii. 1193.

[23 Dec. 1843]

My dear Mr Moxon

The draft for 75£ has been duly received—also the Books for my Nephew[1] who will pay the amount to me.—

The business is well settled with Mr Burns and I beg that as little may be said about it as possible. The ornaments I have no desire for, and I think that with very few exceptions they will suit any other book as well as ours.[2]

I have written this morning to a Lady[3] through whom Chambers[4] applied to me for permission to make extracts from my poems for his sickly-paddy[5] as Coleridge used to call that class of publication. I gave him leave. But I have desired the Lady to let him know that he must apply to you also, and that he is moderate in the number and length of his Extracts and Selections.

[1] See L. 1758 above.

[2] i.e. Moxon's selection of W. W.'s poems (see L. 1760 above).

[3] Mrs. Fletcher of Lancrigg, according to K.

[4] Robert Chambers (see L. 1724 above).

[5] i.e. his *Cyclopaedia*.

With all the good wishes and greetings of the season to yourself and yours,

I remain
my dear Mr Moxon
Faithfully yours
Wm Wordsworth

We expect Mr Robinson by the Mail to-day.—

1764. W. W. to MRS. HENRY ROBINSON[1]

MS. untraced.
K. LY ii. 1195.

Rydal Mount, 27th Dec., 1843.

Dear Mrs Henry Robinson,

Since I had the pleasure of receiving your kind letter, I have intended every day to thank you for it, but I have been prevented by unlooked-for engagements and occurences, in addition to such as are usual at this season.

It would have been impossible for me to attend in person as sponsor for your little one, and I the less regret it, as I was represented by her father, to whom return my thanks for his service upon this occasion. Advanced in life as I have been for many a long year, it has more than once happened that I have at first refused the office when it was proposed to me by parents; but I have been induced afterwards to accept it by the hope suggested to me that the consciousness of my having stood in that relation to the individual could not but hereafter be salutary, even when I myself was no longer in this world. And it was this feeling, I assure you, which reconciled me to the undertaking the office of sponsor to your child, which I must otherwise have felt bound to decline. May God bless the little infant!—words which I should have written with due solemnity at any season, but the prayer is expressed with a still deeper feeling at this time, between the festival of Christmas Day and the beginning of a New Year. I am happy to share this office with my dear cousin Sarah Crackanthorpe.

[1] Of York, wife of W. W.'s cousin (see L. 1735 above). On 9 Oct. she had given birth to her twelfth child Charlotte Wordsworth Robinson, for whom W. W. stood as godfather.

Mrs Wordsworth unites with me in the kindest greetings of the season to yourself and your husband, and to Mrs Robinson,[1] and also to Mr and Mrs Dixon,[2] and believe me, my dear Mrs H. Robinson, with high respect and sincere regard,

Faithfully yours,
Wm Wordsworth

1765. W. W. to WILLIAM HEATON[3]

MS. untraced.
William Heaton, The Flowers of Calder Dale: Poems, 1847, p. vi.

Rydal Mount, Ambleside,
New Year's Day, 1844.

I cannot suffer this day of the New Year to pass without thanking you, my worthy Friend, for the good wishes you have expressed for me in your Verses of the 23rd of last month. Pray accept mine in return. May it long be permitted you in your humble station, to enjoy opportunities for cultivating that acquaintance with literature, of which the effects are shown, greatly to your credit in the lines you have addressed to me.

I remain, with much respect,
Sincerely yours,
Wm Wordsworth

[1] The Admiral's widow.

[2] See L. 1741 above.

[3] William Heaton (b. 1805), weaver of Luddenden, nr. Halifax, and self-educated poet. He had addressed some congratulatory verses to Wordsworth in 1843 on his appointment to the Laureateship; and these, along with this letter, were later printed in a collection of his poems for which Wordsworth became a subscriber. See also *The Old Soldier; the Wandering Lover; And Other Poems, together with a Sketch of the Author's Life*, 1857, which describes Heaton's early life and humble origins.

1766. W. W. to ALEXANDER DYCE

MS. Victoria and Albert Museum.
LY iii. 1196.

Rydal Mount Jan^{ry} 5th 1844

My dear Mr Dyce,

Your very valuable Present of Skelton's Works[1] edited with your usual industry, judgement and discernment, by yourself reached me a little while ago in a Parcel with other Books, from Mr Moxon. I feel truly obliged by this and the like marks of your attention, and beg you to accept my sincere thanks for the same, which I offer with unavoidable regret that, being so advanced in years, I cannot make that profitable use of your labours, which at an earlier period of life I might have done. I am much in the same situation as Pope[2] when Hall's Satires were first put into his hand. But I will do my best to turn your kindness thus manifested to account.

Believe [me] my dear Sir
Your much obliged
Wm Wordsworth

May the ensuing year be for you a happy one!

1767. W. W. to JAMES STANGER

Address: James Stanger.
MS. Mr. T. Wilson. Hitherto unpublished.

Rydal. Wednesday [early Jan. 1844]

It is thought by some of my friends that the line of Inscription beginning 'Could private feelings' would stand better thus: 'Could private feelings meet in holier rest'.[3] The word 'nest' is deemed too metaphorical, and therefore somewhat startling, for

[1] *The Poetical Works of J. Skelton: with notes and some account of the author and his writings*, 1843.

[2] 'That he gleaned from authors, obscure as well as eminent, what he thought brilliant or useful . . . is not unlikely. When, in his last years, Hall's *Satires* were shewn him, he wished that he had seen them sooner.' (Johnson, *Life of Pope*). Joseph Hall (1574–1656), successively Bishop of Exeter and of Norwich, published satires, meditations and controversial works.

[3] See L. 1762 above.

marble—Probably these critics are right; therefore be so good as to let it stand so in the copy sent to the Sculptor.

1768. W. W. to ROBERT PERCEVAL GRAVES[1]

MS. untraced.
Bookseller's Catalogue.

Rydal Mount
12 January 1844.

. . . From the knowledge which from many years experience I have gained of your Character, your attainments and experience in tuition, I am well assured that you will perform your duty to the great benefit of your pupils . . . nor can I overlook the great advantage which would arise to the Institution from the domestic experience of Mrs Graves, and her excellent judgement.

[*cetera desunt*]

1769. W. W. to UNKNOWN CORRESPONDENT

MS. Lilly Library, Indiana University.
Russell Noyes, 'An Unpublished Letter by Wordsworth on Epitaphs', NQ ccxx (1975), 60–1.

Rydal Mount
Ambleside
13 Jan^{ry} —44

Dear Sir,

I have put off replying to your Letter partly from pressure of engagements; but still more from the embarrassment in which I found myself placed by it. There is no species of composition upon which I should be so unwilling to pass judgement as an Epitaph; for diverse reasons, and chiefly because it is impossible

[1] Part of a letter in which W. W. sent his good wishes to Graves on his application for the Principalship of Elizabeth College, Guernsey, founded 1563 and rebuilt in 1826. He was unsuccessful.

to condemn without wounding personal feelings in the tenderest point. The lamented Individual possessed, I doubt not, the valuable qualities ascribed to her and many more akin to them; but she would not, when alive have been pleased to be told so; and it is reasonable that this truth should be kept constantly in mind, amid the composition of the monumental inscription, regulated and governed by it, more than, as seems to me, has been done upon this occasion. Praise of the departed should be brief; all human beings who deserve it are in exact proportion to their desert, conscious of their own simplicity and frailty, and would shrink accordingly from posthumous encomium, especially when exposed to public view, and in the House of God. Am I then to be understood as forbidding enumeration of the virtues of a beloved Friend or Relative who is no more seen upon earth? I do not go that length—but I deeply feel the exceeding difficulty of publicly recording the truth without some offense to modesty, and I should therefore prefer that instead of a formal proclamation of excellent qualities, the excellence should rather be left to be inferred from the language of gratitude to the Almighty by whom the deceased had been so endowed, or of sorrow for the premature removal of goodness from this world, and from those to whom the person was peculiarly endeared—

I beg pardon for having written so much in which I feel that my notions must have been very imperfectly explained. I have taken the liberty of underlining a few expressions which I think are not suitable in style to an epitaph. I recommend that the whole should be shortened and that one passage should be read thus, "the assurance of a blessed immortality"; an *enduring* immortality is faulty, as endless duration is implied in the word 'immortality'. Here also the epitaph ought to end both for brevity's sake and because the text must be presumed to be known to all readers. In an epitaph I think that the birth-name should be mentioned as well as that of the Husband; which might easily be done without lengthening the Inscription, by leaving the age to be calculated, as the time of birth and death are both recorded.

Excuse this long Letter written without that command of time which a subject so delicate required.

I remain, dear Sir, with much regard
faithfully yours
Wm Wordsworth

1770. W. W. to UNKNOWN CORRESPONDENT

MS. Fitzwilliam Museum, Cambridge.
LY iii. 1196.

Rydal Mount Jan^{ry} 13th—44

Dear Sir

Not long since I received the Vol: of Poems with which you have favoured me. It came along with several other new Publications from Mr Moxon, so that I have not yet read the *whole* of it; but enough to enable me to say with sincerity that there is abundance of interesting and genuine feeling in those performances, and of the elements of Poetry. The only deficiency respects skill in workmanship, of which however there is no want but what more practice would I doubt not supply

I remain
dear Sir truly
Your obliged
Wm Wordsworth

1771. W. W. to C. W. JNR.

MS. British Library.
Christopher Wordsworth, Bishop of Lincoln, p. 66 (—).

[*In M. W.'s hand*]

Tuesday Afternoon
[16 January 1844][1]

My dear Chris:

It is creditable to Mr Southey, and perhaps in some small degree to myself, that the Inscription has given birth to so much minute criticism, and I thank you for taking the pains with it you have done. I question whether there is a couplet in the whole that has not been objected to, by some one or another, and in a way that would surprize you as much, were I to report the instances, as your remarks did me—all but the first, (and a verbal one which I shall notice) viz that referring to the "nest" which for the same reason that induced you to condemn it, I had already altered,[2] tho' not *entirely* to my own satisfaction, thus,

[1] Date added by C. W. jnr.

[2] See Ls. 1762 and 1767 above.

"meet in holier rest". As to the 4 concluding lines, what you dwell upon as a defect I deem exactly the contrary; and it may be as well to say—as you appeal to authorities—that 4 intelligent persons who were present when your remarks were read, were of my opinion.

I have no notion of an "ordinary Christian"; a man is a believer with a life conformable to his belief, and if so, all peculiarities of genius, talent and personal character vanish before the sublime position which he occupies with all Brother-Christians, Children of One Father and saved by the One Redeemer. I had sufficiently raised the Subject of the Inscription above ordinary Men, by the first 16 lines, and this being done, all individual distinctions, are in the conclusion merged, as they ought to be, in a condition compared with which every thing else sinks into insignificance.

[*In Dora Q.'s hand*]

Wednesday Morning. The ambiguity in the word *calmed* has been, and is likely to be felt by others as well as yourself, the word *was* in the previous line inclining, as I was aware, the reader to expect that *calmed* is united with it as a participle; nevertheless for these awkwardnesses, the language is more in fault than any particular author. I have however altered the passage thus:

was vowed,
Through a life long and pure, and Christian faith
Calmed in his Soul the fear of change and death.

This is thought here an improvement and I thank you dear Chris for having expressed your objection. Nothing seems to be lost by the alteration—the ambiguity is avoided and what I as a writer of verse attach more importance to, than the general reader will, the pause in the sense by being transferred from the 4th to the 6th syllable removes a monotony which before I had always felt in the movement of the verse. It gives me much pleasure that you are gratified by my Sonnets and that the circulation of your book[1] is already so considerable. Read the second line "*do* I receive"[2]—two participles passive being too much for one verse. This supposes that I had read the book before I received the copy from you but the literal fact is of no

[1] *Theophilus Anglicanus* (see L. 1756 above).

[2] See *To the Rev. Christopher Wordsworth, D.D.*, l. 2. The final reading was 'Have I received'.

consequence on such an occasion. We are glad to have such good news of the health of you all. We are all well here and expecting William today from Carlisle—Mr Robinson is better[1]—The last reports from Madeira[2] were much more favorable and if our next letters confirm the good news we shall be full of hope. Excuse this letter written not by my own pen (because I am lazy D.Q.). I had just had a long walk and talk when yours was put into my hand, and was so fatigued that I had not spirit to undertake the labour of the penmanship, and this morning I am going off directly on another long walk and talk with your old friend Mr Lee[3] of Birmingham. Love from all to Susan.

faithfully y^r^ affect^e^ Uncle
[*signed*] Wm Wordsworth

1772. W. W. to JAMES STANGER

Address: James Stanger [*delivered by hand*]
MS. Mr. T. Wilson. Hitherto unpublished.

21st Janry 1844

I have to trouble you once more about the inscription which I am very sorry for. The marble I hope has not yet been engraved and I wish that the enclosed should be forwarded to the Sculptor, it contains corrections which are thought improvements and you I have no doubt will be of the same opinion.[4]

[1] H. C. R., who had spent Christmas at Rydal, fell downstairs at his lodgings on Christmas Eve and had to spend several days in bed. See Sadler, iii. 237–9, and Morley, i. 535–6.

[2] i.e. from John and Isabella W.

[3] James Prince Lee (see L. 1717 above). His visit is recorded in *RMVB*.

[4] See de Selincourt's note, *PW* iv. 463. At this late stage, W. W. altered l. 17 to 'Through a life long and pure; and Christian faith', and the earlier reading on the monument had to be erased.

1773. M. W. and W. W. to H. C. R.

Endorsed: 5 Feb: 44. Mrs Wordsworth.
MS. Dr. Williams's Library.
Morley, ii. 540.

5th Febry [1844]

My dear Friend

You have been gone almost a fortnight! and no one, to my knowledge, has written to you—this seems strange and you must have thought us ungrateful; the more so, as you sent us such a nice entertaining letter[1]—but alas! I cannot refer to it, and for why? that involves a long story which I must first explain.

I know not how the remainder of the week after you left us passed, except that with *Willy* or Mr Roughsedge, or Dora, who remained with us till the Friday, we had our evening Rubber.—It was settled as you may not remember that Miss Fenwick was to set off on her expedition into Durham on the Tuesday, and my Husband and myself on that day or the next, to visit our Grandchildren at Brigham—driven by William in our little Carriage—Tuesday arrived, but with stormy, snowy weather—however Miss Fenwick having engaged a proper Carriage, kept to her purpose, and performed her journey safely to Hallsteads—*We* gave up for that day—Dora came to keep house for us, and take care of Aunty[2] in our absence, and to her your letter, received about that time, was given, so that she might beguile her solitude by answering it—'BUT'—(don't be angry if you detect that *that but* is a plagiarism[3] from you) the snow and wind in the night, and a sort of uncertainty about the weather DAUNTED our Gentlemen on Wed: Morng—and neither of them would venture to face the *apprehension* of a storm—therefore—I hope you admire Woman's resolution—When all had been prepared Dora came to me with 'Mother let you and I go'—the bargain was struck—Your friend, James, nothing loth prepared himself to be our Charioteer—and tho' the Lord and Master at first said, '*remember you go against my consent*'—he afterwards gave us in charge to James to return or not, as our way was found to be practicable or otherwise—and we consented to this arrangement—Started and had a journey, pleasant, and without impediment of any sort—Thursday was a glorious day—and we

[1] See Morley, ii. 539.

[2] i.e. D. W.

[3] *Written* plaigarism.

were delighted with the improvement we found in all the dear children, and the joy they had from our visit. More snow fell in the night—yet we were as prompt to return as we had been to go—and had as favourable a drive home—With pleasant incidents at Keswick going and returning. We received a gracious welcoming from the elder and some grumbling from the younger W^m^—who threatened Dora with a storm, worse than she had encountered from her husband—who had been ignorant of her sudden flight—till we were[1] far away. However *his* anger was but a feint—and in our hearts we believe, that he would have been of our Party had he been at Rydal—as would I believe the Poet, but for his faint-hearted Son—who was timid about his Mammy's rashness, and would not be responsible for the consequences—*Hence* your letter remained unanswered, and as it is in Dora's possession so that I cannot refer to it, you must pardon my inability, after such an eventful interval, to recollect what I ought to say in reply, beyond our pleasure at hearing so well of your Brother—but our deep anxiety concerning what you said of your Niece Ere this I trust you have found that what you had heard had been exaggerated—Pray satisfy us on this point as soon as you can—this scrawl will meet you at Bury I expect.

Of dearest Miss Fenwick I can only tell you that she is yet in safe quarters at Hallsteads, our good Friends[2] laid an embargo upon her, and wisely—for no doubt 'Stavemoor's wintry waste' over which she had to cross, is blocked up—This has been a fine day—for exercise, but the snow lies thick upon the ground.

We have had favourable accounts upon the whole from Madeira. John and Isa expressed much concern for your accident Now I must enquire of my husband what he has to say to you—he is left alone after dinner, W being at Green bank chearing his Cousin[3] who I am sorry to hear has not been quite so well—Mr Carr too has had an attack, but is I believe better again.

James is the proudest of the proud in the possession of your gift[4]—which was a consequential companion to him when from time to time we enquired the hour as we travelled to Brigham. He has been somewhat disturbed at the thought 'of his being so

[1] *Written* wear.

[2] The Marshalls.

[3] John, R. W.'s son.

[4] A silver watch, presented to James for looking after H. C. R. during his recent incapacity. See *HCR* ii. 640.

astonished when the Watch was given to him that he believes he did not even thank you for it'—'for he did not know what to think about it'!—

We passed a couple of hours with Mr Stanger on Friday, eat a good dinner and heard much about the Sub: for the Monument—He read us an insolent clever letter (W^m^ bids me tell you this) from Croker in answer to the circular, grounded upon the objection you had heard made[1]—quite in his cutting reviewing style—But Mr S. did not spare him in his reply. M^r^ S told him that the object was not to raise money (for C. even insinuated that they wished to do so under cover of Southey's Monument to spare the Parish of Crosthwaite expence) for he knew one Individual who would rather have done the whole himself—but that it had been considered it would be grateful to others to join in such a mark of respect.—He would much rather that no one Person had sent more than one guinea and he had refused one *large* sum that had been offered. My husband now dictates The Committee had reason to expect there would be some surplus and it was thought it w^d^ be more agreeable to sub^rs^ to be told, if there was any, it should be applied in such a way—rather than return it, in shillings, half-crowns, or larger sums according to the several Subscriptions sent. The vulgar Irishman[2] could neither comprehend this, nor perceive how Crosthwaite Ch: in sight of which Southey lived for nearly 40 years, and where he duly attended public worship etc etc etc could be more to the Sub^rs^ on this occasion than any other Church. Mr Stanger's reply shewed what advantages a good man has over a merely clever one.

I need scarcely add that Dorothy, as she has just told her Brother, sends her love wishing to know how *your* Brother is. She expressed also her concern that your Niece is so unwell. *I* W^m^ have today had a 3rd letter from my Glasgow autograph persecutor—a lyric or a sonnet he again pertinaciously requests. Miss Fletcher called this morn^g^. Our friends are all well of that connection—As are the Arnolds—

[1] H.C. R. had written to his brother on 28 Dec.: 'Kenyon is indignant at the trick of smuggling a subscription for Crossthwaite Church under pretence of doing Southey honour . . . —of whom by the bye it is right to remark that his correspondence with W: Taylor shews that he was very religious from the first and only adopted Jacobinism mistaking it for humanity.' (Morley, i. 536).

[2] J. W. Croker was born in Galway. His father was Surveyor-General of Customs and Excise in Ireland.

It was foolish to print the Epitaph, before it was engraven on the Marble, Lord Ashley,[1] who is not the wisest of men, thinks it not half encomiastic enough—His letter to M[r] Stanger went a *desperate* long way in this strain. How few are there who understand the art of praising either the living or the dead. If you have a copy correct the 2 last lines thus

'Thro a long life and pure and Christian faith
Calmed in his soul the fear of change and death.

With best wishes aff[ly] Your's
W and M. Wordsworth

Excuse all my blunders and awkwardnesses for I cannot have patience to read what I have written

1774. M. W. to H. C. R.

Endorsed: Feb: 6–44. M[rs] Wordsw. The China reced.
MS. Dr. Williams's Library.
Morley, ii. 543.

Feb 6th [1844]

My dear Friend

Since despatching a letter to you at Bury this morn[g] William and I have been engaged in unpacking a box, most dexterously laden with a handsome set of breakfast and tea China—which to my confusion (in having so frequently to refer, to this subject of your generosity) I have to thank *You* for. Indeed my dear friend, tho' I would not receive your gift ungraciously,[2] these annual valuable presents make me feel as[3] if you thought it necessary to

[1] Anthony Ashley Cooper, later 7th Earl of Shaftesbury (1801–85), the social reformer and philanthropist, had been much influenced by Southey's criticisms of the industrial system, and they had corresponded regularly from 1830 until Southey's last illness. On his death Ashley wrote in his Diary: 'I loved and honoured him; that man's noble writings have, more than any man's, advanced God's glory and the inalienable rights of our race. He was essentially the friend of the poor, the young, and the defenceless—no one so true, so eloquent, and so powerful.' See Edwin Hodder, *The Life and Work of the Seventh Earl of Shaftesbury, K.G.*, 3 vols., 1886, i. 113–15, 262. For Southey's opinion of Ashley as 'one of the kindest-warmest-hearted and best of men', see Curry, ii. 385, 394–5.

[2] *Written* uncraciously.

[3] *Written* is.

make some *substantial* addition to the very great pleasure you bestow upon us by affording us your society—In other words to put the matter in a *homely way*—as if you were paying for your board and lodging! and at a high rate.

But truly I must say, that you are a wizard to discover what in the way of household requisites—would not be a superfluous gift to Rydal Mount—I have questioned James whether you had not been sifting him wherein there was a failure—so nicely have you hit upon the right thing to make up a deficiency—for never, since we were housekeepers, did we possess a *Company* Tea Service—and you have before provided spoons suitable to the very elegant and *fashionable*-shaped set—so that our table henceforth will vie with, if not take the lead of those of our neighbours.

We have just returned from taking Dora a drive,[1] and have been charmed by the grandeur of our Mountain scenery—no snow-clad *Alpine* peaks ever appeared more beautiful than our's—and now the beaten snow upon the road allows the wheels to run so glibly, that nothing could be more delightful than our morning drive—Dora and I sate in the Carriage in the Sunshine while the two Williams ran up the hill to see the view from Brathay Chapel, with which they were enchanted.—If ever you go into Redmain's[2] shop in Bond St—to buy yourself a Silk Handkerchief—you might please him by telling him how often the Poet blesses him for that holy deed of his, when he planted the Chapel on that Rock.

We shall long for you after dinner—This M^g my husband was wishing for a *fourth* to make up our evenings Rubber—poor Mr Roughsedge is laid up in the Gout and Quillinan has got a bad Cold.

I hope your good Brother continues in a satisfactory state and that your Niece's health does not cause you encreased anxiety.

With the best wishes of us all for your, and their well doing, and begging you to make our respectful regards acceptable to them believe me ever to be my dear friend affectionately your

much obliged
M. Wordsworth

[1] Dora Q.'s health was giving renewed cause for alarm. 'She is very much of an invalid,' H. C. R. noted on 12 Jan., 'and fills both Mr. and Mrs. Wordsworth with very great anxiety, and not without too much cause, I fear.' (*HCR* ii. 639).

[2] Giles Redmayne (see L. 1669 above).

1775. W. W. to ANNA MARIA HALL[1]

MS. Mr W. Hugh Peal. Hitherto unpublished.

Rydal Mount
8th Febry —44

Dear Madam,

Heartily do I wish you success in your undertaking, but for reasons innumerable, applying personally to myself, I cannot comply with your request. It may be enough to say that I never was connected with, or wrote any thing *for*, a review or magazine, in my life. I am induced, however, to mention that Mr Quillinan my Son in Law, now resident at Ambleside, has had a good deal of practice in writing both in prose and verse and having much leisure, would be happy to employ it in supplying you with articles that would probably suit your purpose. For a specimen of his talent in prose I refer you to his Dialogue between Walter Savage Landor, and the Editor of Blackwood.[2] You will find it in the number for April last. In verse he writes with much spirit, and feeling; and what is rare among modern Poets, with correctness in the workmanship. I should myself be pleased if you come to an arrangement, for he is at present working I think too hard at a translation of Camoens's Lusiad,[3] and it seems to me adviseable that he should vary his literary labours. Of course it will be previously necessary that you should state to him what sort of contributions would suit you best.

Remember me kindly to Mr Hall, and believe me to remain

dear Madam
faithfully yours
Wm Wordsworth

[1] See pt. iii, L. 889 and L. 1481 above. Mrs. Hall was about to take over the editorship of *Sharpe's London Magazine*, which began to appear the following year.

[2] See L. 1703 above. E. Q. had also published a novel *The Conspirators, or the Romance of Military Life* in 1841.

[3] In *ottava rima*. Cantos i–v were published in 1853. E. Q. discussed the project in his letter to H. C. R. on 19 Mar. (Morley, ii. 547–8).

1776. W. W. to UNKNOWN CORRESPONDENT

MS. Cornell.
Broughton, p. 85.

Rydal Mount
Feb^{ry} 8th / 44

Madam,

I have just received through Mr Moxon my Publisher your note of the 4th Decr last, and the accompanying volume, and thank you for your attention.

So *very* numerous are the requests which I receive similar to yours, that I have long been obliged either to return one answer to them all, viz—that I have no time for the purpose of making critical remarks upon productions sent to me, or, as in many instances, have been forced upon the seeming discourtesy of not replying at all. I have the honor to be

truly yours
Wm Wordsworth

1777. W. W. to HENRY ALFORD[1]

MS. untraced.
Mem. Grosart. K. LY iii. 1197.

Rydal Mount, Feb. 28, 1844.

My dear Sir,

I am pleased to hear what you are about, but I am far too advanced in life to venture upon anything so difficult to do as hymns of devotion.

The one of mine which you allude to is quite at your service, only I could wish the first line of the fifth stanza to be altered thus:

Each field is then a hallowed spot.

[1] See also pt. iii, L. 927. This letter, Alford later recalled, 'was written in answer to an inquiry whether Mr Wordsworth had by him any hymns calculated for a collection which I was making, and asking permission to insert his "Noonday Hymn" '. (*Mem.* ii. 406). Alford's collection appeared under the title *Psalms and Hymns adapted to the Sundays and Holydays throughout the year*, 1844, and *The Labourer's Noon-day Hymn* (*PW* iv. 115, 428) was included on p. 139, with the fifth stanza omitted. See *R.M.Cat.*, no. 453.

Or you might omit the stanza altogether, if you thought proper, the piece being long enough without it.

Wishing heartily for your success, and knowing in what able hands the work is,

I remain, my dear sir,
Faithfully yours,
Wm Wordsworth

1778. W. W. to HENRY ALFORD[1]

MS. untraced.
Bookseller's Catalogue.

Rydal Mount
March 6th 1844

. . . Not long since, I made several additions to my Ecclesiastical Sonnets, principally pertaining to the liturgy of the Church Service and among others one upon the 'visitation of the sick'.[2] They are as yet in Mss, and probably may remain so for some time . . . .

I remain dear Sir
faithfully yours
Wm Wordsworth

1779. W. W. to EDWARD MOXON

MS. Cornell. Hitherto unpublished.

[*In the hand of W. W. jnr.*]

Rydal Mount 7th March 1844

My dear Mr Moxon

The enclosed letter will explain itself. Upon the receipt of it a few days ago I wrote to Mr Nicol[3] telling him that as you had been so kind as to receive regularly for me the Laureate's Salary I hoped there would be no objection to your doing the same in respect to the allowance for the butt of sack, and that if I did not

[1] See previous letter. Alford had written again about his proposed collection of hymns.

[2] See L. 1681 above.

[3] Of St. James's Palace.

hear from him to the contrary, I should request you to call upon him for that purpose and as his 2nd letter has come I enclose you his as an introduction to him and I will thank you either to send me the amount by a Bank post Bill, or to pay it over for me in account with Messrs Twining and Co for tea—which ever is most convenient to you—

I hope that Mrs Moxon, your Brothers, Sister and children are all well, as thank God we are here—

The accounts from Madeira received today are more satisfactory than heretofore—John has explored diligently every part of the Island of Madeira and his wife's letter speaks of the more than possibility of his going to Teneriffe. I have urged him to draw up an account of his observations, which might be useful to persons who think of going to Madeira and interesting to their connexions if published either in some periodical or otherwise.

If anything could have made me a Reviewer the indignation I felt from having while looking into the account of W Taylor of Norwich and his correspondence with Mr Southey would have done so.[1] The Quarterly, perhaps as the book is published by Murray, handles him much too softly—[2]he deserves far severer treatment and I hope will get it from some quarter or another.

Farewell
ever faithfully
yours
[*signed*] Wm Wordsworth

Do not fail to mention us to Mr Rogers when you see him

[*W. W. jnr. adds*]

My Kindest regards to all at no. 44 Wm W Jr.
Please return Mr Nicol's letter at yr convenience.

Wm W

[1] have *written twice*. A confused sentence as it stands in the MS. *A memoir of the life and writings of . . . William Taylor of Norwich, containing his correspondence . . . with . . . Robert Southey, and original letters from Sir Walter Scott and other eminent literary men* appeared in 2 vols., 1843. The editor was John Warden Robberds. Southey first met Taylor, the Germanist and free-thinker, at Norwich in 1798, and thereafter they corresponded frequently. For W. W.'s opinion of him, see *MY* i. 469. See also next letter.

[2] In the *Quarterly Review*, lxxiii (1843), 27–68, J. G. Lockhart quoted liberally from the correspondence to demonstate the changes that had taken place in Southey's beliefs between his early years and his maturity.

1780. W. W. to EDWARD MOXON

MS. Henry E. Huntington Library.
K (—). *LY iii. 1197.*

Rydal Mount
11th March 1844

My dear Mr Moxon

Your Check for 68. 15. 8 came safe to hand—

There are several strong reasons why I should go to London this spring, and I hope to do so, yet I become every year less inclined to face the way of life into which I am cast when I am there as a New-comer.—

It appears from the preface to Taylor's correspondence[1] that Mr Southey had (very inconsiderately I think) given consent to the publication; but it also appears that Mr S. must have looked to the Letters being revised by himself before they were given to the world, in which case many passages undoubtedly would have been struck out which the Editor most reprehensibly has not done. There is one passage in particular where S. speaks contemptuously of Mr Cottle's Alfred[2] which will cut the poor old man to the heart. He was so proud of Southey's notice, and when I saw him at Bristol two or three years ago Cottle shewed me several memorials of Southey with the greatest Delight. Besides C. really was, by publishing S's juvenile works,[3] his patron when he stood in need of one. But the licentious opinions in morals which Taylor engrafts upon his unbelief most ostentatiously displayed, are a still greater objection to the

[1] See previous letter. The Preface speaks of the 'ready assent' which Southey had given for the publication of the letters, before his decline in health.

[2] *Alfred; an epic poem, in twenty-four books*, 1800. In a letter from Lisbon on 26 Nov. 1800, Southey wrote: 'I laboured hard and honestly to suppress its birth, and am thrown into a cold sweat by recollecting it.' (*Memoir of . . . William Taylor*, i. 363).

[3] Cottle published *Joan of Arc*, 1796, and in the following year Southey's *Poems* and his *Letters Written during a Short Residence in Spain and Portugal*; he also supported Southey financially until his income from literary work was supplemented by the Wynn annuity. Like others, Southey was annoyed by Cottle's *Early Recollections*. 'Unless you knew him . . . thoroughly,' he wrote to Caroline Bowles in 1837, 'you could not believe that such simple-heartedness and such inordinate vanity were to be found in the same person.' (*Correspondence of Robert Southey with Caroline Bowles*, p. 351).

publication; and these ought to be exposed by some able journalist with the severest condemnation.

It pleases me to learn that my Poems are going off so well. Within the last week I have had three Letters, one from an eminent High-churchman and most popular Poet, the other from a Quaker, and the third from a Scottish Free-Church-man, that prove together how widely the poems interest different classes of men.

What a wonderful Man Mr Rogers is: it would rejoice me to see him again.

ever my dear Mr Moxon
faithfully yours
Wm Wordsworth

1781. W. W. to WILLIAM JACKSON[1]

MS. Berg Collection, New York Public Library. Hitherto unpublished.

Ambleside Wednesday Even.
[20 Mar. 1844]

My dear Dr Jackson,

Pray can you inform me when the funeral of Lord Lonsdale takes place,[2] and whether it is to be private or not.

In great haste to save the Post if possible.

ever yours
Wm Wordsworth

[1] Rector of Lowther.

[2] Lord Lonsdale had died on 19 Mar. Since the previous summer W. W. had been kept informed of his deteriorating health by Lady Frederick Bentinck (*WL MSS.*). He was succeeded as the 2nd Earl by Lord Lowther.

1782. W. W. to JOHN NORTH[1]

MS. WL.
LY iii. 1198.

Rydal Mount 20th March 44

My dear Sir,

In a Letter to his Cousin Mrs Quillinan my Nephew Mr Charles Wordsworth of Winchester College writes thus: 'Tell my Uncle tht I will do my best for young North[2]—who I am glad to find, promises well.' This, I am sure, it will please you to hear—and I know the admirable fitness of the writer for the important office which he fills.

May I, my dear Sir, avail myself of this occasion to venture upon what I feel is a great liberty; viz, to request that along with your Brothers you would take into consideration whether there be any sufficient objection to your having the form of the monument of your lamented Parents now standing in Grasmere Churchyard changed so as to suit better its Situation.[3] The obelisk shape is not only a novelty in the churchyards of this neighbourhood, but in the midst of those lofty mountains its effect is most objectionable. In expressing this opinion I am supported by the judgement of everyone who has spoken of it in my hearing. I must add that I have not for some time closely examined the monument, but it strikes me at this moment, that if the spiral part were removed, it would be less out of harmony with its situation.

Trusting that at all events, you will not take ill what I have written, I remain with kind remembrances to all your family in which Mrs W. unites, faithfully yours

Wm Wordsworth

[1] Solicitor at Liverpool: eldest son of Ford North (1765–1842) and his wife Sarah (1769–1829). The family had occupied Rydal Mount before the Wordsworths and then lived in Ambleside. See also pt. i, L. 23.

[2] John North's eldest son Ford, later Sir Ford, North (b. 1830). Entering Winchester the following year, he went on to University College, Oxford, in 1848, and became a barrister and eventually (1881) a Judge.

[3] John North declined to remove the obelisk, and in a lithograph of the churchyard by J. Brandard (1852), preserved at Dove Cottage, it is depicted *in situ* in a position directly west of the Wordsworth family graves. Some years later it was blown down in a storm and not replaced, and today the base of the monument stands directly behind the graves.

1783. W. W. to WILLIAM EWART GLADSTONE

Endorsed: March 21/44 *Mr Wordsworth*.
MS. British Library.
K. LY iii. 1199.

Rydal Mount, Mar. 21st, 1844.

My dear Mr Gladstone,

Pray accept my thanks for your State and Prospects of the Church,[1] which I have carefully read; I lent it immediately to a neighbouring Clergyman. You have approached the subject in a most becoming spirit, and treated it with admirable ability. From scarcely anything that you have said did I dissent; only felt some little dissatisfaction as to the limits of your Catholicity;[2] for some limits it must have; but probably you acted wisely in not being more precise upon this point. You advert to the formal and open Schism of Methodism, but was not that of Disney,[3] and of others to which Cowper adverts, in some respects of more importance? not as relates to the two or three conspicuous Individuals, who seceded and became preachers in London; but from its leading the way to the transit of so great a number of Presbyterian Clergy, with no small portion of their several congregations, into Unitarianism. This occurred all over

[1] Gladstone, now President of the Board of Trade until his resignation later this year over the Maynooth Grant, had published an article on 'Present Aspects of the Church' in the *Foreign and Colonial Review* for Oct. 1843 (repr. in *Gleanings of Past Years*, 7 vols., 1879, v. 1–80). In the course of a wide-ranging survey of the prospects of the Established Church after *Tract Ninety* and the scheme for the Jerusalem Bishopric, he set out to assess the strength of the Romeward movement which was now giving cause for alarm. C. W. acknowledged the receipt of his copy on 20 Mar.: 'my brother, also, I am persuaded, will set a high value upon his, for he takes a warm interst in questions of this nature.' (*British Library MSS*.)

[2] As a high-churchman, Gladstone had implied that episcopacy was of divine institution, and therefore essential to the organisation and sacramental life of the Church.

[3] John Disney, D.D. (1746–1816), in 1769 given the cures of Swinderby and Panton, Lincs., in 1771 joined a movement to petition Parliament to relieve the clergy from subscription. He dropped from his own services the Athanasian and Nicene creeds and the Litany, and made other changes in Common Prayer. From 1783 he was Secretary of a Unitarian Society for promoting knowledge of the Scriptures and conducted services at Essex Street, London, with a revised prayer book. (de Selincourt's note).

England, and was, I believe, especially remarkable in the city of Norwich, though many there took refuge in the Church of England. Happily there is both in the written Word of God, and in the constitution of his Creature Man, an adequate preservative from that lifeless form of Religion; nevertheless, as it influenced in no small degree what in the Presbyterian and other congregations was called the better educated part of the Community, the result was to be lamented, in some respects more than the Schism of the Wesleyans, which turned mainly, if not exclusively, at first, upon the rejection of episcopal jurisdiction, leaving the great points of Catholic doctrine untouched.

To what you have so justly said upon Tractarianism much in the same spirit might be added. It was a grievous mistake that these Tracts issued from the same place were *numbered*, and at the same time anonymous. Upon the mischief that unavoidably attaches to publications without name, especially, you might have added, corporate publications, you have written with much truth and feeling. But the whole proceeding was wrong, and has led to errors, doubts, and uncertainties, shiftings and ambiguities, not to say absolute double-dealing, injurious to Readers and perilous to those in whom they originated. First, it has caused the great and pernicious error of the Movement being called the *Oxford* Movement, as if it *originated* there, and had sprung up in a moment.[1] But this opinion, which is false in fact, detracts greatly from its dignity, and tends much to narrow and obstruct its range of operation. There is one snare into which it was impossible that Writers so combined should not fall, that of the Individual claiming support for his opinion from the body when it suited him so to do, and rejecting it and resting upon his individuality when that answered his purpose better.

As to Romanism, having lived much in countries where it is dominant, and being not unacquainted with much of its history, my horror of it, I will not use a milder term, notwithstanding all that I love and admire in that Church, is great indeed. I trust with you that there is small reason for believing that it will ever supplant our Church in this Country, but we must never lose sight of its manifold attractions for the two extremes of our artificial society, the opulent and luxurious, never trained to vigorous thinking, and who have outlived the power of

[1] W. W. is thinking here particularly of pre-Tractarian high-churchmen, like Joshua Watson and Bishop Jebb, and those like his brother C. W. and Hugh James Rose, whose affiliations were with Cambridge rather than Oxford.

indulging in their excesses, these on the one hand; and on the other, the extreme poor, who are greatly in danger of falling under the influence of its doctrines, pressed upon them by a priesthood so constituted.

But as my departed Friend Southey said long ago,

Onward in *faith*, and leave the rest to Heaven.[1]

With a thousand thanks for your valuable tract, and the best of good wishes for your health and welfare, I remain, with sincere respect and regard, my dear Mr Gladstone,

Faithfully yours,
Wm Wordsworth

1784. W. W. to THOMAS POWELL

MS. Cornell. Hitherto unpublished.

Rydal Mount
22nd March
[18] 44

My dear Mr Powell,

Some little Time ago we received a Stilton cheese, which we supposed might be a present from you, but as no Letter followed it, we could not undertake to thank you, lest the gift might be from some other person, as we have occasionally been indebted to the kindness of other Friends in a similar way. I was therefore glad to be relieved of this embarrassment by the arrival of your Letter, from which however I learn with much regret that you have been in ill health for some time. Be assured of my sincere and earnest wishes for your entire recovery which you gave us reason to hope will be effected as the Spring advances. We have all been pretty well in this House, free from Influenza colds etc., notwithstanding the severity of the weather during the two last months.[2]

[1] The last line of Southey's *The Retrospect*, dated Oxford, 1794.

[2] 'We have had a roaring storm of wind here,' E. Q. wrote to H. C. R. on 19 Mar., 'which . . . did mischief among trees, but most at Rydal Mount. The two largest of those fine old cherry trees on the terrace nearest the house were uprooted and spread their length over the wall and orchard as far as the kitchen garden; two fir-trees also, both ornamental from their positions, and one especially so from its double stem, have been laid prostrate . . . Such losses will sound trivial at a distance, but they are felt at home. Those cherry trees were old

Mr Quillinan as perhaps he may tell you some time or other, had a striking proof of the truth and nature upon which "We are Seven", which you say has impressed your own boy, is founded. He met in one of his Walks with a little Girl of this neighbourhood, from whom[1] he received a like answer to the common question of how many of you are there? Some it appeared were dead, but she insisted upon the entire number, notwithstanding the bearing of his remarks upon the distinction between the deceased and the living.

I feel not the least curiosity to read a Book so misnamed, as the one you allude to, "The Spirit of *the Age*";[2] "of the *day*," said Mr Quillinan when we were mentioning it. But how absurd to talk of a few Authors or Authorlings, Men, Women, or Children, condensing or exhibiting the Spirit of this or any other age, at any time.

Pray remember Mrs W. and myself kindly to Mrs Powell, and believe us both to be sincerely and faithfully

Yours
Wm Wordsworth

[*M. W. adds*]

By the bye I may mention no tongues arrived with the Cheese—this not mentioned for any reason, but that you may be aware of the fact should you be called upon to pay for them as being sent.[3]

servants and companions—Dora and the birds used (in *her* younger days) to perch together on the boughs, for the fruit.' (Morley, ii. 456–7).

[1] *Written* which.

[2] *A New Spirit of the Age* (1844), by R. H. Horne (see L. 1368 above), written in imitation of Hazlitt's series of studies of leading men of his time. In the new volume W. W. and Leigh Hunt were coupled together as 'highly important connecting links between past and present periods; as the outlivers of many storms; the originators of many opinions and tastes; the sufferers of odium, partly for their virtues, and in some respects for their perversities; and the long wounded but finally victorious experiencers of popular changes of mind during many years.'

[3] This is W. W.'s last known letter to Powell, who subsequently settled in America and repaid the poet's kindness by publishing a highly unflattering account of him in *The Living Authors of England*, New York, 1849, pp. 28–30.

1785. W. W. to UNKNOWN CORRESPONDENT

MS. Princeton University Library. Hitherto unpublished.

Rydal Mount
Ambleside
March 24th —44.

Sir

Mr Wordsworth's Poems are to be had at Mr Moxon's, his Publishers 44 Dover Street Picadilly; they are in seven volumes, Retail Price, thirty nine shillings. It is customary I believe for Book-clubs to procure what they want through their own Booksellers, at a lower rate than the retail price.

I am Sir
yours truly
Wm Wordsworth

1786. W. W. to UNKNOWN CORRESPONDENT

MS. Cornell.
K (—). LY iii. 1201 (—).

Rydal Mount March 26th 1844

Dear Sir,

Two letters from you have at different, and I regret to say, distant times reached me, the letters accompanied by MSS of verses of your own Composition.

You must have thought me ungracious and unkind in not noticing long ago these communications. But you must allow me to state frankly the reasons. So exceedingly numerous are the letters and MSS transmitted to me, that I have sometime since been obliged to leave them unacknowledged, and without any exception, unless they happen to come, which is rare, from persons with whom I am acquainted. You will therefore see that in omitting to notice your's there was no disrespect on my part to yourself. The fact is, my age and domestic position, and an infirmity of eyesight, which disables me from reading at all by candlelight, are insurmountable objections to my meeting the wishes of those who may actually be anxious to have my opinion of their Productions. There is no *young* Person under my roof whom I could employ either as my Reader or

Amanuensis; and my Wife's eyes (she is the same age as myself) are nearly worn out with long and unremitting service in various ways. You will perhaps be surprized when I say that nearly every day, the year through, or rather at the rate of every day in the year, I have either Books sent me, or MSS, or applications for Autographs. I am therefore brought to the necessity above stated, and after what has been said, I cannot doubt from the openness and friendly candour of your last Letter, that you will excuse my Silence hitherto in regard to yourself.

It will be easy for me to send your MSS to any person in London, according to such directions as you might give.

I remain
my dear Sir
with good wishes
respectfully yours
Wm Wordsworth

1787. W. W. to UNKNOWN CORRESPONDENT

MS. Cornell. Hitherto unpublished.

Rydal Mount
March 26th 1844

Sir,

I did receive the Parcel from Mr C. Boner[1] of Ratisbon, after which you enquire. As Mr B. may by this time have changed his Residence, I should be obliged to you to forward to him the Enclosed, if you are acquainted with his private address.

I am Sir
your obed^{nt} Ser^{nt}
Wm Wordsworth

[1] See L. 1882 below.

1788. W. W. to LADY FREDERICK BENTINCK

MS. untraced.
Mem. Grosart. K. LY iii. 1202.

March 31, 1844.

My dear Lady Frederick,

We have known each other too long and too intimately for you not to be well aware of the reasons why I have not earlier condoled with you upon your bereavement.[1] I feel it deeply, and sympathise with you as much and as truly as you possibly could wish. I have also grieved for the rest of your family and household, and not the least for Miss Thompson, whose faithful and strong attachment to your revered father I have, for a long time, witnessed with delight and admiration. Through my kind friend Mr O'Brien[2] I have heard of you both; and in his second letter he informs me, to my great sorrow, that Miss Thompson has been exceedingly ill. God grant that she may soon recover, as you both will stand in need of all your bodily strength to support you under so sad a loss. But, how much is there to be thankful for in every part of Lord Lonsdale's life to its close! How gently was he dealt with in his last moments! and with what fortitude and Christian resignation did he bear such pains as attended his decline, and prepared the way for his quiet dissolution! Of my own feelings upon this loss I shall content myself with saying, that as long as I retain consciousness I shall cherish the memory of your father, for his inestimable worth, as one who honoured me with his friendship, and who was to myself and my children the best benefactor. The sympathy which I now offer, dear Lady Frederick, is shared by my wife, my daughter, and my son William; and will be also participated in by my elder son, when he hears of the sad event.

I wrote to Dr Jackson to inquire whether the funeral was to be strictly private, and learned from him that it is to be so; otherwise I should not have deprived myself of the melancholy satisfaction of attending. Accept, dear Lady Frederick, my best wishes, and be assured of my prayers for your support; and believe me,

Your very affectionate friend,
Wm Wordsworth

[1] The death of Lord Lonsdale. See L. 1781 above.

[2] See *RMVB* for Aug. 1840: probably Augustus Stafford O'Brien (d. 1857), of

1789. W. W. to JOSEPH COTTLE

MS. Cornell. Hitherto unpublished.

Rydal Mount
April 4th 1844

My dear Friend,

Your kind Letter[1] gave me much pleasure, for many reasons, and especially as affording so strong a proof of zeal and activity surviving to so advanced a period of life. Your endeavours to erect in his native City a Monument to the Memory of our excellent Friend cannot but be universally approved; and heartily do I wish a successful conclusion to what has been so well and hopefully begun. You will however not be disappointed when I add, that I cannot promote the object in this neighbourhood. All persons hereabout who were able and willing to commemorate his worth, in that way, have already subscribed to the Monument about to be erected in Crosthwaite Church near Keswick. To this I have myself subscribed five pounds; To The people of Bristol it peculiarly belongs to honour themselves, by paying this token of respect to their distinguished Fellow-Townsman; and I trust that their contributions will not be wanting.

You enquire after the dissentions in Southey's family[2] to which his Brother alludes. You are not ignorant what hazardous things second Marriages are for a Man who has a family by his deceased Wife. Our Lamented Friend built hopes of comfort from taking that step, when his faculties were too much impaired to allow him to judge of the thing wisely, I mean with due discretion. In fact his Mind had become too weak for

Blatherwycke Park, Northants., and Cratloe Woods, Co. Clare: M.P. for the northern vision of Northamptonshire, and Secretary to the Admiralty in 1852.

[1] Cottle had sent a rambling letter the previous month describing his efforts, 'as the oldest of Southey's friends', to promote the Southey memorial appeal in Bristol. The memorial was to take the form of a bust by Edward Hodges Baily R.A. (1788–1867), to be placed in the Cathedral.

[2] Cottle ended his letter by deploring the Southey family quarrel: 'If it were not for my infirmity, I would go up to the North on a mission of peace, to see whether they could not be brought to a right mind. What is it all about? Could you relieve my anxiety? And especially cannot *you*, with your powerful influence, do something to harmonize discordant spirits? (*Bristol University Library MSS.*) See George Lamoine, *Letters from Joseph Cottle to William Wordsworth: 1828–1850*, *Ariel*, iii (Apr. 1972), 84–102.

entering into that state at all. Hence ensued discord between the second M[rs] Southey, and the rest of the family, with the exception of M[rs] Warter, who sided with her Stepmother in a spirit which it would pain me to dwell upon. To enter further into particulars would be unprofitable; and I can assure you that, though I much approve of your Christian and friendly dispositions towards healing this breach, it would be of no avail. The less that is said of the matter and done in it—the better. It must be left to time, and no doubt the painful and unkind feelings are gradually abating through that and other influences. M[rs] W. and My Sister both beg to be kindly remembered to you; Let me add my respects to your Siste[rs]

and believe me my dear old Fri[end]
ever faithfully yours Wm
Wordsworth

I congratulate you on your escape without injury from Your over turn in the carriage.

1790. M. W. to H. C. R.

Endorsed: 7th *April* 1844. M[rs] Wordsworth.
MS. Dr. Williams's Library.
Morley, ii. 550.

Easter Day, April 7th [18]44
The *Laureate's* birth Day

My dear Friend,

In order to do high honor to this great Festival our Breakfast table was this morn[g] graced by the FIRST APPEARANCE of your *latest* contribution to the ornamental and useful arrangements of our household—hitherto reserved for this especial occasion.—And, having this to tell you is a less awkward introduction after my reproachable silence than were I to hunt for excuses to my idleness, tho' perhaps I might not find much difficulty in hitting upon several. It is better however to tell you *why* I write now, than why I have not written sooner—*viz* that my thoughts have thro' the last week been so much drawn towards you as you lay Prisoner at Rydal Mount—and that I have to express my gratitude to your inventive genius,—and for the use of that self-same rope, by which you raised yourself, and which has been *my* help in a state of not less powerlessness than your accident brought upon you. In short, I have been suffering from rather a severe attack of my old Enemy the Lumbago—and tho' I am now well enough to *walk* about something like other folk, I still need the rope—and have not been in plight to go with the rest to Chapel—therefore have thought this a good opportunity to make my peace with you—and learn where you are, and what you are doing; and to enquire after your Brother and your Niece, and to beg you to speak of your own health—as to whether you feel any effect from your Rydal mishap, and of any thing that interests you.

For ourselves, we have been going-on much in our *changeable* fashion—about the middle of last month our dear friend Miss F. returned after a 6 week's absence to Rydal Mount, W^{m} remained with us a few days for the sake of her company, then *he* took his departure—And a week ago we lost our poor Invalid Nephew[1] —who had been our Inmate since the Harrison's left Green bank for Leamington 6 or 7 weeks ago—Poor fellow! his Malady, which had made little or no progress previously, seemed to gain upon him, with the warmer weather, and he is now gone for a little change to Keswick, and to his anxious Mother, and he gives us rather a more favourable report of himself, but we fear his doom is sealed.

From Madeira too we only have very unfavourable reports—In June we expect to see them—Isa: is *ordered* to quit the Island by the end of the present Month—to halt by the way for the sake of change of air—then to pass 4 Months at home, and return to a warmer Climate for the winter—A heartless prospect for us all to look to—but we can only hope and submit.

But let me turn to more cheering matters, and tell you with thankfulness that we are all well at home, were it not for a depressing nervous head-ache of W$^{m's}$ the consequence of too long-continued labour in the attempt to correct what he deems to be faults (*chiefly in the versification*) of the Excursion.[2] I trust however this will soon pass away. Dora has been, and is, our

[1] R. W.'s son.

[2] E. Q. had written to H. C. R. on 19 Mar.: 'Mr Wordsworth has been working very hard lately, to very little purpose, to mend the versification of the Excursion, with some parts of which he is dissatisfied, and no doubt justly: but to mend it without losing more in the freshness and the force of expression than he will gain in variety of cadence is in most cases I believe impracticable: *it will do*, in spite of my Lord Jeffery and its occasional defects in metrical construction etc.' (Morley, ii. 548).

chearful support, since Thursday—and on Tuesday next our good Friend[1] is to make some 3, or 400 School Children happy in giving a fete at Rydal M^{t} to celebrate the Laureate's 74th[2] birth day. How I wish you could be here to see so many proud faces as will present themselves from behind the terrace Wall, which is to be the Tea-table—each with their cup (these they are to bring)—a pretty sight will it be to the Spectators in the Garden below if the weather favors as this bright day promises, and scarcely less interesting will be the glad countenances of the Masters and Mistresses—and here and there a parent—and above all that of the loving, pleasure-giving Donoress of the treat and poor Sister's if able to get out.—But am I not wearying you? Yet you will not think the subject quite unimportant when I tell you that your friends M^{rs} and Miss Fletcher deem it worth while to put off a journey which was fixed for that day, in order to attend this *School fete.—They* are going into Yorkshire, meaning to be absent about 6 weeks.—D^{r} and Mrs Davy I am pleased to tell you, are busy preparing to build upon ground they have lately purchased—where, next to the villagers, they will be our nearest Neighbours on the road to Ambleside—The house will stand in the field on our side of Mr Robinsons,[3] that and the adjoining one, reaching nearly to the Bridge is the Drs Property.

The Arnolds well—Susan gaining ground—Lady Farquhar gone—Mr Carr and his Ladies well, tho' *he* has been a sufferer lately—and at present Mr Q. I am sorry to say has a cold upon him—the Girls are well—and now I must bring this *circumstantial* letter to a close, which I dare say you will think prosy enough—but you know I never expatiate beyond *facts*, and besides they will be coming out of Chapel and we must prepare for roast beef and plumb pudding—birthday fare. So giving vent to the wish that you were here to partake of our festivities believe me to me, with the united best wishes which would be expressed if all were present, ever most affec^{ly}

Yours
M. Wordsworth

Miss F. I believe means to enclose a note in my cover.[4]

[1] I. F. For an account of the festivities, see *Mem*. ii. 446–7.

[2] *Written* 44th.

[3] i.e. Capt. Charles Robinson. The new house was called The Oaks.

[4] See Morley, ii. 549.

Pray tell us about dear Miss Lamb—and your friends the Miss Westons'—[1]

Easter Sunday *Even*[g]. Since writing the above, we have had the pleasure of reading y[r] letter to M[r] Q.—and I may take upon me to say that we hear Thorny-how is engaged.—But if the Serg[t2] really wants to be accommodated, he must state the *time* he means to be here—the number of rooms, and beds they may require—and if they mean to bring their own Servants? They must speak quickly or all the lodgings will be engaged.

1791. W. W. to RICHARD PARKINSON

Address: The Rev[d] R[d] Parkinson, College, Manchester. [*In M. W.'s hand*]
Postmark: (1) 8 Apr. 1844 (2) 9 Apr. 1844.
Stamp: (1) Ambleside (2) Manchester.
MS. Cornell.
LY iii. 1204 (—). *Broughton, p. 86.*

Rydal Mount
8th April [1844]

My dear Sir,

Accept my thanks for the 2nd Edition of your Old Church Clock; and my acknowledgement for the dedication,[3] acceptable on many accounts—

You have fallen into a mistake respecting the Drawing from which the view of Seathwaite Chapel is taken. It was not done by the Barber who married a Grand daughter of Robert Walker, but by a young Friend of mine since dead, the Rev[d] Lionel Frazer.[4] We value the Drawing upon his account. It was given by him to my Daughter; You will know whether it was returned

[1] 'I first saw the Miss Westons in 1839,' H. C. R. later recalled. 'They once lived at Bury, and my name being mentioned, I was introduced by Miss Weston's desire. . . . The Miss Westons went to Rome and I gave them a letter to Miss Mackenzie. On the return our acquaintance became more intimate. Miss Weston was a woman of superior understanding and attainments. She was an admirer of Wordsworth; Kenyon and I brought them together [in May 1842]. Wordsworth professed great respect for her.' (Morley, i. 460).

[2] Probably Talfourd (see Ls. 1812 and 1830 below).

[3] It ran, 'This little book is inscribed to William Wordsworth, as a humble token of admiration and gratitude.'

[4] See pt. ii, L. 784.

to this House, but her Mother and I dont remember that, not having good memories at our time [of][1] life. I beg if it be in your possession or that of the Engraver, you would be so kind as to take care of it with a view to its being returned to the owner at your convenience.

During the very short call you made at Rydal Mount, I showed you an oil Painting of the Vale of Duddon in the neighbourhood of Seathwaite which was given me by the artist, as a token of gratitude for the Memoir I had published of his wife's Grandfather R. Walker; and this has led you into the mistake, which may be corrected in future.

I remain my dear Sir sincerely your much obliged

Wm Wordsworth

1792. W. W. to JOHN PEACE

MS. untraced.
Mem. Grosart. K. LY iii. 1203.

Rydal Mount, April 8, 1844.

My dear Mr Peace,

You have gratified me by what you say of Sir Thomas Browne. I possess his *Religio Medici, Christian Morals, Vulgar Errors*, etc., in separate publications, and value him highly as a most original author. I almost regret that you did not add his treatise upon *Urn Burial* to your publication;[2] it is not long, and very remarkable for the vigour of mind that it displays.

Have you had any communication with Mr Cottle upon the subject of the subscription which he has set on foot for the erection of a *Monument* to Southey in Bristol Cathedral?[3] We are all engaged in a like tribute to be placed in the parish church of Keswick. For my own part, I am not particularly fond of placing monuments in *churches*, at least in modern times. I should prefer their being put in public places in the town with which the party was connected by birth or otherwise; or in the country, if he were a person who lived apart from the bustle of the world. And in Southey's case, I should have liked better a bronze bust, in

[1] *Word dropped out.*

[2] *Religio Medici . . . with resemblant passages from Cowper's Task* [ed. J. Peace], 1844.

[3] See L. 1789 above.

some accessible and not likely to be disturbed part of St. Vincent's Rocks, as a site, than the Cathedral.

Thanks for your congratulations upon my birthday. I have now entered, awful thought! upon my 75th year. God bless you, and believe me, my dear friend,

Ever faithfully yours,
Wm Wordsworth

Mrs Wordsworth begs her kind remembrance, as does Miss Fenwick, who is with us.

1793. W. W. to EDWARD MOXON

MS. Henry E. Huntington Library.
K (—). LY iii. 1205.

15th April 44
Rydal Mount

My dear Mr Moxon,

The enclosed will explain itself. I have referred the Applicant to you, having given my own consent for a small Selection, *provided* you are not disposed to withhold yours.

I could wish you if you consent at all, to define the limits of the selection as to its bulk.

It seems resolved, I am sorry to say, that Mrs John Wordsworth is to remain abroad for another winter. It is a sad thing, but deemed best by her Medical Advisers. Her Husband will be obliged to remain with her.

ever faithfully yours
Wm Wordsworth

I wished you and *yours* could have been with us last Tuesday when upwards of 300 Children and nearly half as many Adults connected with them, or neighbours, were entertained in the grounds and House of Rydal Mount. The treat went off delightfully with music, choral singing, dancing and chasing each other about, in all directions. Young and old, gentle and simple, mingling in every thing.

1794. W. W. to UNKNOWN CORRESPONDENT

Endorsed: Wordsworth. Permission for Selection ap: 44.
MS. Cornell. Hitherto unpublished.

Rydal Mount
15th [Apr.] — 1844

Sir,

I have no objection whatever to you making Selections from my Poems, for the purpose you mention, and upon Scale not exceeding the Specimens you have sent me; but I must add that this permission is not to be acted upon without application being previously made to Mr Moxon for his consent.[1]

The selections published by Mr Burns[2] far exceeded in amount what I was prepared for when I permitted a Clergyman and Schoolmaster with whom I was upon friendly terms, in compliance with his request, to publish a small Vol: to be sold at a low price for the most common use of Schools. This Gentleman turned the matter over to Mr Burns without my having any knowledge that a work so different from what I had consented to was to be produced.

I state this fact not for the purpose of casting blame upon the Parties, but to prevent your supposing I am dealing less liberally with you than I have done with others.

With thanks for the very pretty Books which you have sent me, I remain

Sir
your obliged Ser^{vnt}
Wm Wordsworth

1795. W. W. to EDWARD MOXON

MS. Henry E. Huntington Library.
K (—). LY iii. 1206.

20th Apr [1844]

My dear Mr M

Thanks for your Letter. Every application that shall in future be made to me for leave to print Extracts from my Poems, I shall

[1] Mr Moxon refused it, 19/ Ap: 44 (note by recipient).

[2] See L. 1756 above.

refer at once to you, and inform the Party that such will be my invariable practise. In fact I shall be glad to leave the matter wholly to you as a much better judge than myself. Therefore in the present case make no Scruple to withhold your consent, if you think it expedient so to do, if it is clear that yielding to one application will prepare the way and be an encouragement to others of the same kind.

I am quite shocked to hear that Chambers[1] printed the extracts you have sent me without consulting you. I had no communication *directly* with him; but *through* the Lady, Mrs Fletcher my neighbour, who applied to me at his request. I gave my permission *but* subject entirely to your concurrence. So that he has behaved most unwarrantably and in fact dishonestly; for my permission was null and void without yours. Mrs Fletcher is gone from home; otherwise I should have made a point of seeing her before I wrote; but I am sure she would not neglect the stipulation which I made. You will therefore proceed as you think proper for redress.—As to the length of the Extracts, I merely said, that as the application came to me through such a quarter I could not doubt that they would be kept within reasonable limits, which is indeed far from being the case. As to the Biographical notices, they are grossly erroneous; in particular, it is asserted that I was one of the Pantisocratic Society, though it has been publicly declared by Mr Southey that the project was given up years before I was acquainted either with himself or Mr Coleridge or any one belonging to the Scheme.[2] One-half at least of what is said of Mr Coleridge, as to the facts of his life, is more or less erroneous; and, drolly enough, he marries me to one of my Cousins! He also affirms that my parents were able to send me to college though one died more than ten years before I went thither, and the other four; but these errors are trifles, the other, as to the Pantisocracy, is a piece of reprehensible negligence.

ever faithfully yours,
Wm Wordsworth

[1] See L. 1724 above, and next letter.

[2] W. W.'s memory is at fault here. Southey lost interest in Pantisocracy in the summer of 1795, and announced his withdrawal from the scheme to S. T. C. the following November (see Griggs, i. 163 ff.). But W. W. had already met both of them in the September while staying with the Pinneys at Bristol, on his way to Racedown (see *EY*, p. 153).

1796. W. W. to EDWARD MOXON

MS. Henry E. Huntington Library.
LY iii. 1207.

[29 Apr. 1844][1]

My dear Mr Moxon,

An act of Piracy has no doubt been committed upon me as well as yourself, for, as you know, the consent that I gave was subject to the like consent from you, and without that being given, which was never applied for by Mr Chambers, mine was null and void. Further, my consent was accompanied, (supposing what I have no reason to doubt that Mrs Fletcher faithfully reported my words to Mr C.) with the condition that the Extracts should as to length be *moderate* and a *reasonable* use made of the privilege. That the former condition was utterly disregarded is certain—as to the latter Mr Chambers might be of a different opinion, and others might think with him; all that I need say is, that 1,100 lines and upwards went in the proportion of little less than ten to one beyond which I had presumed, or *thought* I was granting. But as I neglected to make any express stipulation as to the amount, I waive all claim for compensation on the ground of excess, and as to the other ground, I cannot, under all the circumstances (especially with regard to the Lady, through whom Mr C. made the application) accept any pecuniary compensation upon that. It would be inconsistent with my feelings as a Gentleman to do so; though I have, looking at the proceeding in *strictness*, and speaking of it literally an undeniable claim upon Mr Chambers. So as far then as I am directly concerned, let the matter end. I am much pleased however that C. will have to pay you fifty pounds, as smoot money.[2]

I have written without waiting for Mr C.'s Letter to myself, my mind being at once made up upon the subject.

ever faithfully yours
Wm Wordsworth

P.S. Ambleside Monday noon. I have this moment received Mr Chambers's Letter. He says he 'did apply for your permission, but owing to a misdirection of the Letter, it was returned to him through the Post Off: above three weeks after,

[1] Date added in another hand.

[2] Printing slang, as de Selincourt notes, for money paid for casual labour.

when the Sheet had passed through the press, and it was too late to renew the application.'—

He also says 'that he applied through Mrs Fletcher, (which is true) for my permission to make the extracts, *specifying* them almost to the last Piece, and was honoured with my permission in consequence through that Lady'. Mrs Fletcher unfortunately is in Yorkshire, and I cannot refer to her, all I can say is that I have *no remembrance* whatever of any such specification, but a distinct one that I stipulated for a moderate and reasonable use of the permission.[1]

1797. W. W. to T. SHEPHERD[2]

Address: T. Shepherd Esqre, 20 Marlborough St, Chelsea. [*In M. W.'s hand*]
Postmark: (1) 8 May 1844 (2) 9 May 1844.
Stamp: Carlisle.
MS. WL. Hitherto unpublished.

Carlisle
May 9th 44

Sir,

Your obliging Letter has been forwarded to me at this place, and I lose no time in thanking you for it, and the accompanying Volume of Poems which is waiting my return home.

I remain Sir
very truly
your obliged
Wm Wordsworth

[1] Moxon had threatened litigation against Chambers and his associate Robert Carruthers (1799–1878), editor of the *Inverness Courier*, and author of the offending selection of W. W. in Chambers's *Cyclopaedia*. See Morley, ii. 745.

[2] Perhaps Thomas Hosmer Shepherd, the topographical artist.

1798. W. W. to WILLIAM LISLE BOWLES

MS. WL. Hitherto unpublished.

[*In John W.'s hand*]

Rydal Mount
Ambleside
May 17th 1844

My dear Mr Bowles,

The newspapers informed me of your mournful bereavement,[1] and deeply did I sympathize with your sorrows, but I could not bring myself to write to you immediately, being persuaded that my condolence had better be deferred till you had time to feel what through your own heart and mind the goodness of God would effect for your Support and Consolation. It is indeed a sad thing to be left alone, as it were, after having been so long blessed as you have been with a faithful companion; no one can judge of this but they who have been so happily placed, and either have been doomed to a like loss, or, if the tie still be unbroken, are compelled daily to think how soon it certainly must, by one or other being called away. Under this consciousness, I venture to break in upon you, and to offer my heartfelt sympathy. The separation cannot be long between you, nor would I advert to so obvious a reflection were it not that from the advanced age which my wife and I have, through God's blessing, attained together, I feel the power of it to soothe and mitigate and sustain, far beyond what is possible for your young friends to do.—

It is more than half a century since, through your poetry, I became acquainted with your mind and feelings, and felt myself greatly your debtor for the truth and beauty with which you expressed the emotions of a mourner. My Remembrance is thrown back upon those days with a Sadness which is deep, yet far from painful. A beloved Brother with whom I first read your Sonnets[2] (it was in a recess from London Bridge) perished by Shipwreck long ago, and my most valued friends are gone to their graves. 'But not without hope we sorrow and we mourn.' So I wrote when I lost that dear brother. So have I felt ever since,

[1] The death of his wife led to a breakdown in Bowles's health from which he never really recovered. In Jan. 1845 he resigned his living of Bremhill, and retired to Salisbury, where he died five years after, just before W. W. himself.

[2] See *EY*, p. 192.

and so I am sure in my [? heart], you do now. God bless you through time and through eternity. Believe me

faithfully yours
[*signed*] Wm Wordsworth

1799. W. W. to ROBERT SHELTON MACKENZIE[1]

Address: Dr R. Shelton Mackenzie, University Herald Offices, Oxford.
MS. Historical Society of Pennsylvania.
LY iii. 1208.

Rydal Mount 1st June '44

Dear Sir,

I have to acknowledge two Letters from you and an Oxford Newspaper, for which marks of your attention pray accept my thanks.

Your former Letter was the occasion of a good deal of annoyance to me for it was unfortunately mislaid; and I could not find it, and was consequently ignorant of your address, which subjected me to a charge of incivility and seeming neglect—

In your projected Dictionary of living Authors[2] I wish you success. But I apprehend the execution of it will be attended with difficulties, at least if I may judge of others by myself. I much dislike that so insignificant a Biography as mine should have the attention of the Public called to it, and as to the dates of my Publications, I really never thought it worth while to register them. My first Publisher,[3] (in conjunction with Mr Coleridge) was Mr Cottle of Bristol—98—then, I employed Messrs. Longman, and latterly Mr Moxon. And with no others have I been connected.

Your 2nd Letter and the Newspaper would have been noticed earlier; but I was from home at the time of their arrival

I remain
faithfully yours
Wm Wordsworth

[1] See pt. iii, L. 1110.

[2] This project was never completed.

[3] As de Selincourt notes, W. W. seems to have forgotten that in 1793 he published *An Evening Walk* and *Descriptive Sketches* with John Johnson, St. Paul's Churchyard.

I have sent the desired Autograph for your American Friends, as you tell me they are not Collectors of these things; if they had been so, I must have declined complying with a request of a kind which from the great number made to me and from other causes I find rather annoying.

1800. W. W. to the MISSES CONSTABLE[1]

Address: Miss Constable, 16 Cunningham Place, St. John's Wood, London.
MS. Burgess Collection, University of Oregon Library. Hitherto unpublished.

Rydal Mount
June 6th 1844

Mr Wordsworth presents his Compliments to the Misses Constable and thanks them for the acceptable present of the Memoirs of their Father's life[2] which he has just received. He lost no time in perusing the Book with which, on many accounts he has been much interested. Mr Wordsworth had the pleasure of making Mr Constable's acquaintance when he visited this Country long ago; and through their common Friend Sir George Beaumont used often to hear of him, though he had not the good fortune to fall in with him, till the latter part of his life when they met with mutual pleasure. The engravings with which the Memoirs are illustrated, are eminently characteristic of the Painter's mind. Mr W. was not unaquainted with these works, as Mr Constable had gratified him with a Copy of his English Landscape, a work most honorable to his Genius. Pity that he did not prolong his stay in this beautiful country, i.e., that we might have had its features reflected by his pencil.

[1] John Constable left three daughters, Maria (d. 1885), Isabel and Emily.

[2] *Memoirs of the Life of John Constable, R.A., composed chiefly of his letters*, 1843. For W. W.'s contacts with the artist, see pt. iii, L. 1048.

1801. W. W. to JOHN HUDSON

Address: Mr Hudson, Bookseller, Kendal.
MS. untraced.
LY iii. 1209.

Flimby[1]—20th June, 44

Dear Sir

Your letter has followed me to this place.

I have no objection to Mr Dawson[2] making the use he desires of the Extract, provided you approve of the manner in which he acknowledges the Extracts.

I was perfectly aware that Mr Thurnham[3] and Mr Scott[4] were both interested in circulating their own Guides and it was on that very account that I wished you to place yours with some other Bookseller in that city, he giving proper notice at his window or otherwise, so that it might catch the eye of persons coming from Scotland or Newcastle. I think it would be well to do the same at Whitehaven. A large iron steamboat will by next November be launched there that, it is calculated, will perform the voyage between Liverpool and Whitehaven in six hours; at present there are steamboats between those places three times a week that bring many passengers for a Peep at the Lakes. Of course you have an Agent at Ulverstone, it would be well also to have the Book exposed to sale at Penrith; and no doubt you have *that* done at Bowness and at Keswick.—I am persuaded that your Book were it sufficiently put in the way of Tourists would be greatly preferred to any other by most persons.

I remain
dear Sir
truly yours
Wm Wordsworth

[1] A coastal resort south of Maryport, where Dora Q. had gone for her health. R. W.'s son John was also staying there (see *MW*, p. 271).

[2] Joseph Dawson, a Kendal bookseller.

[3] Charles Thurnham, the Carlisle bookseller and publisher of the *Carlisle Patriot*.

[4] Hudson Scott of Messrs. Scott and Benson, Carlisle, who produced the *Monthly Advertiser*: publisher of *A Guide to the Lakes* . . . [1842].

1802. W. W. to ABRAHAM COOPER[1]

MS. British Library.
LY iii. 1210.

Rydal Mount 21st June 1844

Dear Sir,

I cannot help feeling that you treat my remarks upon the Portrait[2] with more deference than they are entitled to. No Man sees his own face when he is absorbed in meditation, with his head downwards, therefore, my opinion of the likeness in such a case can be of little value, and that point must be judged of by others. My Friends object to the eyelid on your right hand as you look at the face and to the projection also beneath the corner of the under lip on the same side of the face. The position of the head in my own opinion merely cannot be favorable to *likeness*, as by shortening the upper lip so much it makes the nose seem much larger than I imagined my own, though undoubtedly large, could in any position appear to be.—I am really sorry you should have so much trouble upon this occasion, and am sensible of your kindness in taking so much pains. I barely *ask* whether the *blackness* under the nose might not be a little softened or mitigated with some advantage. But of this you will be much the best judge, the change might weaken the effect, though to me that point attracts, from being so black, too much attention.

But I cannot endure to puzzle you any longer, and must conclude with a sincere wish that your work may prove satisfactory to the Painter, to yourself, and in general.

Believe me truly yours
Wm Wordsworth

I have been absent from home and to save the Post am obliged to scribble in great haste.

[1] Abraham Cooper, R.A. (1787–1868), painter of animal, battle, and sporting scenes, which were frequently engraved for the Annuals.

[2] Benjamin Robert Haydon's *Wordsworth on Helvellyn*, for which the poet sat during his visit to London in June, 1842.

1803. W. W. to EDWARD MOXON

MS. Henry E. Huntington Libary.
LY iii. 1214.

[*In M. W.'s hand*]

[21 June 1844][1]

My dear Mr Moxon,

Mrs W. holds the pen for me, just come over Kirkstone from Lord Lonsdale's Lowther—I acknowledge with pleasure your Letter, enclosing a cheque for £32. 13. 8, the acc^t of the separate Ed: of the Excursion. I am glad it is disposed of and also that you have another Ed: prepared.

With regard to the Poems, especially the last vol: which encreases the price so much, I fear it will be long before they are off—How can any One when such trashy books as D'Israeli's[2] are run after expect any portion of public attention, unless he confines hims[elf] to personalities or topics of the day.

The Papers had announced that Campbell[3] was dangerously ill at Boulogne, so that I was not unprepared for the account of his decease, which was also announced to me by a Letter from his Physician (I presume) dated Boulogne. Did he seem gratified by your kind visit? or was he too far gone? Poor Fellow one cannot help being sad that he is departed notwithstanding the unhappy habit to which he had given way.

We rejoiced to hear of your intention to visit us, and that Mr Rogers thinks of doing the same. It will be indeed a great treat to see you both, and I hope it may suit you to come together.

To-day, as I rode up Ullswater side, while the vapours were 'curling with unconfirmed intent'[4] on the Mountain sides, and the blue Lake was streaked with silver light, I felt as if no Country could be more beautiful than ours; and certainly there is one point in which our scenery has a striking advantage over that of the greatest part of the Continent. Our forest trees are preserved from that horrible mutilation which prevails almost

[1] Dated to 21 July by another hand, but the contents of the letter indicate June.

[2] Benjamin Disraeli (see also part iii, L. 1335) had just published *Coningsby*, which embodied the political ideals of Young England, and contained thinly-disguised portraits of contemporaries.

[3] Thomas Campbell had died on 15 June.

[4] *To May* (*PW* iv. 118), l. 79.

everywhere in Italy and disfigures the Austrian and Bavarian lakes woefully.

John and his wife are now at Genoa, whence they will proceed to the Baths of Lucca where they mean to pass the Summer. She writes in better spirits than she has ever done, and is stronger, since she left Madeira which was too relaxing for her.

But I must conclude

ever faithfully yours
[*signed*] W. Wordsworth

All the Quillinans are at the Seaside where unfortunately Mrs Q. has taken cold, and with it got a bad cough—The day after tomorrow I go to see her and probably may bring her home, certainly if I do not find her better. Her husband has business in Ireland which calls him away next Tuesday.

1804. W. W. and M. W. to DORA QUILLINAN

Address: Mrs Quillinan, Flimby, Mary-port.
Postmark: 28 June 1844.
Stamp: (1) Ambleside (2) Maryport.
MS. WL. Hitherto unpublished.

[*c.* 28 June 1844]

[*half a sheet missing*]

. . .Joshua and Mary[1] gone to Whitehaven. Called on Mr Dawes who travelled in with me to Mr Lightfoots[2]—eat cold beef and Lamb, at Mrs L's, and left Keswick at three, having called on Mr Myers.[3] Gone to Halsteads: we have had a most pleasant journey, walking up all the Hills. Found Mrs Cookson here and told her about the fish, John[4] here also—looking, I grieve to say very poorly. His Man and Horse both being here, I own I could but be sorry if they were to return tomorrow, but still poor dear Fellow, if he has any comfort here I should wish him to stay. I hope that nothing that passed between us dearest D will at all disturb you or retard your recovery. If I thought so, I should be quite miserable; but I think this will hardly be, as we both spoke

[1] Joshua and Mary Stanger of Field Side, Keswick.
[2] 'Keswick John's' step-father.
[3] The Revd. Frederick Myers.
[4] R. W.'s son.

from our sense of right. Would you like to see your Mother at Brigham. I have just proposed it to her; thinking that James and I could keep House, and she might be spared here for a week. She caught at the Idea at first, but while I am writing she repents and says it cannot be: and full surely it cannot for I forgot and we both forgot that the Boys[1] were here. This will shew at least how strongly we were both [? pushed] with the thought of making you happy. My last word must be, do not on any account let Poor Ebbi's[2] fear of fresh air injure you, but sit in another room where you can have it. In like manner do not let Sara's[3] need of a fire induce you to sit where you are annoyed by one. Sea air must restore you and of that you must have as much as you can get without taking cold or over fatigue. Do not, by any means let your reading together tempt . . . [*half a sheet missing*].

[*M. W. writes*]

Dearest D,

I need not add I suppose to what Daddy may have said—(but I have not read his letter) and you will say you have had *more than enough from me for one day*—I am however overjoyed to hear such a good account of you tonight—and if the cough is really gone, and the perspirations going, I hope you soon may venture into the Sea in fine weather—but *spunge* first with tepid Salt water. John says if it stands all night in a warm room, say the Kitchen, it need not be heated.

I am delighted with the boys—and they are so good and happy!

1805. W. W. to WILLIAM JACKSON

MS. Berg Collection, New York Public Library. Hitherto unpublished.

Rydal
July 4th —44

My dear Dr Jackson,

It is time I should tell you that there is no likelihood of our going from home for some time, except that I shall be two days

[1] Their grandsons, Henry, William, and John.

[2] Ebba Hutchinson from Brinsop (see L. 1809 below).

[3] Sarah Hutchinson.

absent within the course of the next fortnight or so. The Thompsons[1] I met today on the road; they were coming to inquire if they were likely to see you and Mrs Jackson about which they were very anxious as they had already in expectation of your coming refused their Lodgings to more than one Party. Be so good as let them have an answer. I need not say [how][2] pleased Mrs W. and I should be to see you in this neighbourhood.

Believe me
faithfully yours
Wm Wordsworth

No doubt you will have heard from Lady Frederic. They were to quit London today or tomorrow.

1806. W. W. to HENRY REED

Address: Henry Reed Esqre, Philadelphia. [*In M. W.'s hand*]
Postmark: (1) 6 July 1844 (2) 8 July 1844.
Stamp: Ambleside.
MS. Cornell.
Mem. (—). *Grosart* (—). *K* (—). *Wordsworth and Reed*, p. 126.

Rydal Mount 5th July 1844

My dear Mr Reed,

So long have I been in your debt[3] that I am afraid and in some degree ashamed of appearing before you. The only excuse I can offer with the least claim for respect is, that I was loth to write till some thing substantial had been done towards clearing your countrymen from dishonour, and removing the distress which their failure in discharging their pecuniary obligations had caused. Some thing has been done and upon that I sincerely and cordially congratulate you, and every American worthy of the name. We can wait with patience till Feb^ry^ next the period when you expect that payments will be resumed. Let me however ask if what I have heard be correct that there is in your State a large body of land proprietors chiefly Dutch and Germans, men of mean and narrow minds, who care neither for honour nor honesty, and only bent upon escaping taxation at any cost of

[1] Local acquaintances.
[2] *Written* to.
[3] For Reed's recent letters to W. W., see *Wordsworth and Reed*, pp. 116 ff.

both. Supposing this to be true and that such men as I am told have great influence over the Legislature, it is surely very improbable that it will be able to prevent things going on in the right course, now happily begun.

It grieved me much to learn from your last Letter but one that you and Mrs Reed had again suffered a heavy domestic loss,[1] and that Mrs R's health had been impaired in consequence, and by previous anxiety. Be assured of my cordial sympathy and earnest wishes for the reestablishment of your quiet which will bring along with it, I trust restoration of health; so that by next summer you may realize your project of crossing the Atlantic. We shall rejoice to see you and yours under our roof, if our lives and health be prolonged. With the beautiful country around our Residence, I am sure you will be delighted and proud and happy should I be to shew you some of its more retired beauties and interests. I have often mentioned to you my wish to complete my notices of Italy by another tour in that Country; but for many reasons it is not likely to be effected, certainly not this year. And could you come to England next summer you would be almost sure of finding us at home; for should we go on to the Continent it would not be before autumn, and it is very unlikely that we shall move at all.

In your last letter you speak so feelingly of the manner in which my birthday has been noticed, both privately in your country, and somewhat publicly in my own neighbourhood that I cannot forbear saying a word or two upon the subject. It would have delighted you to see the assemblage in front of our House, some dancing upon the gravel platform, old and young, as described in Goldsmiths travels, and others, children I mean, chacing each other upon the little plot of Lawn to which you descend by steps from the platform. We had music of our own preparing, and two sets of casual Itinerants, Italians, and Germans, came in successively, and enlivened the festivity. There were present upward of 300 children, and about 150 adults of both sexes and all ages—the children in their best attire and of that happy and I may say beautiful race which is spread over this highly favoured portion of England. The Tables were tastefully arranged in the open air, oranges and gingerbread in piles decorated with evergreens and spring flowers and all partook of tea, the young in the open air and the old within

[1] Mrs Reed's sister had died shortly after the loss of one of their daughters.

doors. I must own I wish that little commemorations of this kind were more common among us. It is melancholy to think how little that portion of the community which is quite at ease in their circumstances have to do in a *social* way with the humbler classes. They purchase commodities of them, or they employ them as labourers, or they visit them in charity for the sake of supplying the most urgent wants by alms-giving. But this alas is far from enough—One would wish to see the rich mingle with the poor as much as may be upon a footing of fraternal equality. The old feudal dependencies and relations are almost gone from England, and nothing has yet come adequately to supply their place. There are tendencies of the right kind here and there, but they are rather accidental than aught that is established in general manners. Why should not great land-owners look for a substitute for what is lost of feudal Paternity in the higher principles of christianized humanity, and humble-minded Brotherhood. And why should not this extend to those vast communities which crowd so many parts of England, under one head, in the different sorts of manufacture which for the want of it are too often the pests of the social state? We are however improving, and I trust that the example set by some mill owners will not fail to influence others—[1]

It gave me pleasure to be told that Mr Keble's[2] dedication of

[1] W. W. seems to be reflecting here some of the ideals of the Young England Movement, now embodied in Disraeli's *Coningsby* (see L. 1803 above). He had known Lord John Manners (1818–1906) and George Sydney Smythe, later 7th Viscount Strangford (1818–57), since the summer of 1838, while they were both undergraduates at Cambridge. Manners had joined a reading party at Lord Bradford's cottage on Windermere, and he and Smythe had become captivated by Faber's preaching at Ambleside (see pt. iii, L. 1195), and through him they were introduced to W. W. (See *RMVB*; Charles Whibley, *Lord John Manners and His Friends*, 2 vols., 1925, i. 63 ff.; Ronald Chapman, *Father Faber*, 1961, pp. 45 ff.; and *Faber, Poet and Priest, Selected Letters . . .*, ed. Raleigh Addington, 1974, pp. 64 ff.) W. W. received further visits later this summer from Manners and Smythe (*RMVB*) and heard much of Faber (see Ls. 1814 and 1819 below). But any sympathy he may have felt for Young England and its Tractarian allies was dispelled by the Maynooth Grant and the conversions to Rome in 1845. See 'Young England' (*PW* iv. 134).

[2] *Written* Keeble's. His *De Poeticae Vi Medica. Praelectiones Academicae*, was published in 2 vols., Oxford, 1844 (trans. E. K. Francis, 2 vols., 1912). The Dedication, Reed wrote on 29 May, 'does honour to him who gives and to him who is given to. I do not mean because it is so finely worded and so nobly speaks for many of us, but because, coming from one who has deeply studied the best

his Praelectiones had fallen in your way, and that you had been struck by it. It is not for me to say how far I am entitled to the honor which he has done me, but I can sincerely say, that it has been the main scope of my writing to do what he says I have accomplished. And where could I find a more-trustworthy judge? What you advize in respect to a separate Publication of my *Church*-Poetry, I have often turned in my own mind. But I really have done so little in that way compared with the magnitude of the subject, that I have not courage to venture upon such a publication. Besides it would not, I fear pay the expenses. The Sonnets were so published upon the recommendation of a deceased nephew of mine,[1] one of the first Scholars of Europe, and as good as he was learned. The volume did not I believe clear itself, and a great part of the Impression though latterly offered at a reduced price, still remains, I believe, in Mr Moxon's hands. In this country people who do not grudge laying out their money for new publications on personal or fugitive interests, that every one is talking about, are very unwilling to part with it for literature which is unindebted to temporary excitement. If they buy such at all it must be in some form, for the most part that has little to recommend it but low price. One word more upon breach of Faith; have you any means of learning what probability there is of the Missisippi state discharging its obligations. Every one seems to think that honesty is at a lower ebb there than in any other part of the United States. My daughter and others of my kindred has as I have told you, for them, a considerable interest in those funds;

uses of poetry in the service of the Church, and excellently exhibited them, it recognises those higher aims which have long rendered your inspirations auxiliary in the same cause.' (*Wordsworth and Reed*, p. 123). It ran as follows: 'Viro vere philosopho et vati sacro, Gulielmo Wordsworth, cui illud munus tribuit Deus Opt. Max. ut, sive hominum affectus caneret, sive terrarum et coeli pulchritudinem, legentium animos semper ad sanctiora erigeret, semper a pauperum et simpliciorum partibus staret, atque adeo, labente saeculo, existeret non solum dulcissimae poeseos, verum etiam divinae veritatis antistes, unus multorum, qui devinctos se esse sentiunt assiduo nobilium ejus carminum beneficio, hoc qualecunque grati animi testimonium D. D. D. reverentiae, pietatis, amicitiae ergo.' The dedication had been sent in advance to W. W. for his approval. Mrs. Davy recalled that 'he had never seen any estimate of his poetic powers, or more especially of his aims in poetry, that appeared to him so discriminating and so satisfactory.' (Grosart, iii. 441). See also Charles Wordsworth, *Annals of My Early Life*, p. 329.

[1] C. W.'s son, John.

and in a portion of them which has not been repudiated. And I should be glad to learn that there is some chance of getting back what they can so ill spare. But I have a special reason for desiring to have knowledge on this point, as it would in some degree govern my distribution by will of my property among my children.

And now my dear Sir with many thanks for the trouble you have been at, and affectionate wishes for your welfare, believe me faithfully yours

Wm Wordsworth

1807. M. W. to H. C. R.

Endorsed: 1844. *Mrs Wordsworth.*
MS. Dr. Williams's Library.
Morley, ii. 561.

9th July [1844]

My dear Friend

My Husband has written you a very long letter (which is all ready sealed up for the Post) in reply to your's addressed *to me*, but it being upon a subject, quite out of my line he kindly allowed me to prevail upon him to answer it—but, whether from the bad penmanship, or that he feels he has not thoroughly explained himself, I do not exactly know why he will not let me forward it—and he being too tired by hard work in the Hay-field, to turn to the subject at present—*and* as I do not like that you should feel our silence to be unkind, I think it better just to send you this explanation—with a few brief notices concerning ourselves in answer to your enquiries—Know then that we are Darby and Joan-ing it by ourselves, save that 3 of our Grandsons are come to make a sort of holiday—and tho' their company is at times somewhat troublesome, yet we delight in it—for they are 3 fine Lads as one would wish to see in their different ways—none of them much given to learning—but full of activity.

Quillinan is in Ireland gone upon a Mission for his Brother—he left his Wife, and his Daughters by the sea-side on the Cumbd Coast—Poor Dora not having benefitted by this change of air, as we had hoped she might have done had she not had a bad attack of her stomach complaint on their first settling and afterwards brought on a cough by bathing before she was strong enough to do so prudently—She is now thank God better, but very weak.—Her Cousins Eliz and Sarah have been with the *Flimby* Party—and we expect them all at Rydal Mount on Saturday—unless they await M^{r} Q's somewhat uncertain return—for having gone on business, he is now detained visiting old friends.

All our neighbours are well and never forget you—Of Miss F. you know as much, or more than we do—tho' perhaps not, for we heard from her today and she is not at Hampstead—but on a visit to Mrs Ed^{d} Villiers.[1] She will shortly be found at St Ann's Hill, Wandsworth—where Mr Taylor has taken a house for a short time—She tells me that Miss Southey is at Mrs Coleridge's—probably you may see her—and hear something about her Father's Papers, I understand Mr T. is in communication with Mr Wynn[2] upon the subject.

We are indeed deeply interested, (as far as we can speak from the 1st Vol—the only one we have yet read), in D^{r} A's life,[3] and think the Editor has done his work *well*—I wish dear Southey may have as good a one—but alas! there is too much evil astir, to expect any one to have the same advantages that have[4] favoured Mr Stanley.

We are delighted to hear your B^{r} continues so well—and now that your late excitement is at an end I trust you will not continue to live too fast. God bless you I must be done

affec y^{rs}
M Wordsworth

[1] See L. 1379 above.

[2] See L. 1713 above.

[3] A. P. Stanley, *Life and Correspondence of Thomas Arnold, D.D.*, 2 vols., 1844 (5th edn. 1845).

[4] *Written* has.

1808. W. W. to GEORGE WASHINGTON DOANE[1]

Address: The Right Rev[d] G. W. Doane, Riverside, Burlington, New Jersey, favored by the Rev[d] Mr. Dowdney.
MS. Professor Mark Reed. Hitherto unpublished.

Rydal Mount
July 11th 1844

My dear Bishop,

I am most happy in an opportunity just presented[2] of assuring you how sensible I am of the repeated marks of your regard, which in the shape of different writings of yours you have been so kind as to send me from time to time.[3] I have also to request your pardon for not acknowledging earlier these tokens of your respect and esteem, but in Letter writing I have through life been a sad Procrastinator, and this disposition is more difficult to contend with when the Letter has to travel far [and most often seems] accordingly not worth the transport over such extent of Sea as lies between us. But too much of this. You will be glad to hear that my Partner and I through God's blessing both continue to enjoy good health. She is on the point of entering her 75th year and I am several months advanced in mine.

I hear with much pleasure from M[r] Dowdney, that yourself and family are in good health; may that blessing be continued and all good attend you.

Believe me dear Bp to remain faithfully with high respect

your much obliged
W[m] Wordsworth

[1] Bishop of New Jersey. See L. 1536 above.

[2] The visit of the Revd. John Dowdney (*RMVB*), a New York clergyman and friend of the Bishop.

[3] Probably his episcopal Charges, which advocated church revival on Tractarian principles. Doane also wrote hymns, and edited Keble's *Christian Year* for American readers.

1809. W. W. to WILLIAM JACKSON

MS. Berg Collection, New York Public Library. Hitherto unpublished.

Rydal
Thursday Morning [? 11 July 1844]

My dear D[r] Jackson,

I am sorry I did not write to you by return of Post, as I intended, but Mrs Wordsworth said you had better take time to consider about the intended monument[1] and so I put off writing till perhaps my Letter may be too late to be of any service.

I am decidedly still, as I was at the first, in favor of an Obelisk or rather a Column, to be placed on some conspicuous point not far from the line of the Carlisle Railroad, yet so as to be seen if possible, from the roads which lead from North and West to Appleby. Is there not such a place to be found, not far from Emont and Lowther Bridges yet not upon Lord L'[s] own Estate. It would be still better if the funds could afford a Bronze Statue[2] to be placed on the summit; but that I fear would be much too expensive.—

A Statue in the Court House of Carlisle [to] a Lord Lieutenant of that County might have some propriety but it would be seen by few,[3] and for the most part when men's minds were otherwise occupied, or People would have to pay for seeing it, if it should be distinguished as a work of art. Then it is to be remembered that the Lowthers are a Westmorland Family, that he was Lord Lieutenant of Westmorland as well, and there would be some thing invidious in the preference under these circumstances of one County, though so much more important, to the other.

As to the Cathedral, first, I dislike modern monuments in places of worship, for instance in the Choir of Carlisle Cathedral there is one which deporably disfigures the symmetry of that part infinitely the best part, with its fine eastern window, of the Building.[4] Besides neither the late Lord nor any of his Family as

[1] To the late Lord Lonsdale.

[2] Statue *written twice.*

[3] A statue by Musgrave Lewthwaite Watson (1804–47) was erected the following year in Court Square.

[4] The offending monument seems to have been removed since W. W.'s time. It was perhaps identical with the one to Captain John Richard Graham of the Bengal Cavalry who died in the East Indies in 1830, which is now in the north transept. For W. W.'s view on Church monuments, see also Grosart, iii. 450.

far as I know have any especial connection with that Church; it would be altogether I think an intrusion. But I heartily wish our Cathedrals might henceforth be preserved from all such objects, which almost invariably take off from the effect of the architecture, and break in upon that simple solemn devotional feeling which ought to prevail in such places, and with which the Edifices are in themselves so beautifully accordant.

Jane was sent over immediately upon the Receipt of your Letter to The Thompsons. They have let their lodgings etc

ever truly yours
W[m] Wordsworth

[*M. W. writes*]

You enquire d[r] D[r] J. after Dora. Alas she has not hitherto gained much strength—soon after her arrival at Flimby she had a bad attack of her stomach, from over-fatiguing herself. Then she went too soon into the Sea and brought on a bad cough, which tormented her night and day. So that tho' now thank God she is better, she is deplorably weak. She will remain a fortnight longer in the hope of gaining strength—Her Cousins from Herefordsh—[1] who have been with the Party at Flimby come to us on Monday.—Love to Mrs J and the little Girls—

ever y[rs]
M. W.

We have had rather better news of Mrs John[2]—our 3 elder Grandsons are with us—poor lads!

1810. W. W. to RICHARD PARKINSON

Address: The Rev[d]. R. Parkinson, Bolton Sand-side, near Lancaster.
Postmark: 13 July 1844.
Stamp: (1) Ambleside (2) Lancaster.
MS. Cornell.
Broughton, p. 86.

Rydal Mount
July 12th 1844

My dear Sir

I am glad that a 3[d] Edit. of the Old Church Clock is called for, but it is not in my power to send you any contribution towards

[1] Ebba and Sarah Hutchinson. [2] i.e. Isabella W.

it, not having written a word but what is already published upon the subject of your pastoral Hero.[1]

No one would more rejoice than[2] myself that Manchester should become a Bps see,[3] by fair and honorable means, but I should deplore in common with thousands who love the Church to see the Diocese of St Asaph despoiled for that purpose. How is it to be expected that Gods blessing should fall upon a measure arising out of a wrong so grievous! Of the proceedings of the Church Commission in general I have no favorable opinion; mainly they were dictated by timidity and have done mischief which, will, I fear, never be repaired.

I shall be glad to see you as you almost promise and hope that Mrs Parkinson's health will continue to improve by the sea air. Believe [me] to remain my dear Sir

faithfully yours
Wm Wordsworth

1811. W. W. to HENRY INMAN[4]

MS. Cornell. Hitherto unpublished.

Rydal Mount
Near Ambleside
14 July 1844

Sir,

I have just received a Letter from my highly esteemed Friend Mr Reed of Philadelphia, in which he does me the honor of

[1] In the Memoir of the Revd. Robert Walker.

[2] *Written* that.

[3] The Ecclesiastical Commission of 1835 had recommended that the over-large diocese of Chester should be reduced in size, and new provision made for the spiritual needs of the expanding population of Lancashire by the establishment of a bishopric at Manchester. The Established Church Act (1836) empowered the Crown to constitute the see, but it never took effect, and a new Act was required in 1847, when W. W.'s friend James Prince Lee (see L. 1717 above) was nominated to the new bishopric by Lord John Russell. To avoid increasing the number of bishops in the House of Lords the Commission had recommended the fusion of the sees of Bangor and St. Asaph; but this proposal met with so much opposition that it was finally dropped.

[4] Henry Inman (1801–46), American painter of portraits and *genre* scenes, came to Europe with commissions to paint W. W., Macaulay and Dr. Chalmers.

requesting that I should sit for my Portrait by your pencil, and begs that I would lose no time in letting you know, as your stay in England is uncertain, when I shall be at liberty for this purpose. I therefore address this to you, hoping that you will early be able to come thus far, and I shall chearfully meet the wishes of one whom I value so much.

Pray be so kind as let me know when your engagements will permit you to undertake the work; and be assured that I shall be happy to see an Artist of whom Mr Reed thinks so highly.

I am Sir
truly yours
Wm Wordsworth

1812. W. W. to H. C. R.

MS. Dr. Williams's Library.
K (—). *Morley, ii. 563.*

Rydal
14th July
1844

My dear Friend,

I wrote to you at some length immediately on the receipt of your last to M^rs W—but as my Letter turned mainly on the subject of yours, the Dissenters chapel Bill[1] I could not muster

He died soon after his return to America while preparing a series of paintings for the Capitol in Washington. Reed had written on 28 June to commend Inman: '. . . he will, I am confident, produce a likeness that will gratify your family and friends. In the several portraits that have been taken of you, there seems to be some doubt how far this has been accomplished—at least if I may be justified in drawing such an inference from the incidental notices of them I have chanced to meet with. Be this as it may, I hope you will be able to give Mr Inman's talent a chance—especially when it is for the gratification of a distant but affectionate friend of your's.' (*Wordsworth and Reed*, p. 125.) See also L. 1830 below.

[1] This measure, which had engrossed H. C. R.'s attention for several months, legalised the Dissenters' title to hold property. As H. C. R. noted, 'Before this act was passed, the Law Courts had refused to recognise the possibility of men meeting for religious exercises, each unfettered as to his individual ideas of dogmas. They insisted that the mere words, *worship of God*, used by any religionists in their deeds, must essentially mean the annunciation of some peculiar metaphysical views of faith, and that the duty of the Law Courts was to find out and define these views, and to confine such religionists and their

resolution to send it, for I felt it was reviving a matter of which you had had too much.

I was averse to the Bill, and my opinion is not changed. I do not consider the authorities you appeal to as the best judges in a matter of this kind, which it is absurd to treat as mere question of property or any gross material, right or priviledge, say a right of road, or any other thing of the kind for which usage may be pleaded. But the same considerations that prevented my sending the Letter in which the subject was treated at length forbid me to enter again upon it; so let it rest till we have the pleasure of meeting and then, if it be thought worth while we may revert to it.—

Your Correspondent who declined writing to you in answer to a Letter turning upon things which she had not considered, and in which she took no interest begged that I would be her substitute. I have consented though well aware what a dull creature I am at work of this kind. You will be but little concerned to hear that we are now beginning to be overrun with Tourists and summer Visits—a few of whom, I am happy to say will be very welcome. Among others we expect my Brother, and Mr Rogers along with Moxon. I am also looking daily for Mr Salvin[1] the Architect, who is likely to pass through this

successors within them for all futurity. . . . By the effect of the legal decisions in the cases of the Lady Hewley Trust Fund, and of the Wolverhampton Chapel, the Nonconformists of England and Ireland, who held religious opinions at variance with the doctrinal Articles of the Church of England, found that the title to the chapels, burial-grounds, and religious property which had been created by their forefathers, and upheld and added to by themselves, was bad. Though its invalidity had never been previously suspected, these decisions showed that it had been bad for nearly, if not quite, a century.' (Sadler, iii. 249–50). 'I never felt so strong an interest in any measure of legislation,' H. C. R. wrote to W. W. on 7 May, 'Not, if I know my own feelings, from any great interest I take in Unitarians, as such, but because they are standing in the breach in a case of religious liberty,' and he sent W. W. a long answer to this letter on 24 July in which he set out the issues as he understood them (Sadler, iii. 253–7). In retrospect, H. C. R. regarded the part he played in getting the Bill passed as one of the most valuable acts of his life.

[1] Anthony Salvin (1799–1881), specialised in the restoration of castles and country mansions. He was employed on the Tower of London, Windsor Castle, and Alnwick Castle: in the north-west his works included Muncaster Castle (1862–6), and additions to Patterdale Hall for the Marshalls (1845–50) and the rebuilding of the Church (1853). Earlier, he had built St. John's, Keswick, for John Marshall (see pt. iii, L. 933). The cottage for I. F. was never built, owing to Lady le Fleming's opposition.

country on his way to Naworth Castle on the Borders which has been burned down, and which he is employed to rebuild. He is a Relative of Miss Fenwick; and we hope that he will be so kind as to furnish us with a plan for a Cottage which we mean to build for her to occupy, who has been so long looking out in vain for An Abode of her own in this neighbourhood. The Site of the Intended Building will be some part of the field, near our garden, at the top of which runs the green terrace. The views as you remember are very fine; and the approach to the house, as we mean to place it low in the field, will be easy. Among other visitors whom I have reason to expect, is an American Artist, who is just arrived, I believe in London, and purposes at the earnest request of my valued Friend Mr Reed of Philadelphia to take for him my Portrait. Mr Reed speaks highly of this Gentlemans talents, both for portrait and Landscape. His name is Henry Inman Eq which I mention as you may, perhaps fall in with him—his address care of Messrs Wiley and Puttenham No 6 Waterloo place Regent street. To day[1] Mr Julius Hare is expected at Mrs Arnolds, and I am to dine with him there in the course of the week.

Sergeant Talfourd and his family we expect about the middle of August, he has taken Mr Harden's Cottage on the Banks of the Rotha, for ten weeks; I hope they will enjoy themselves. The House is now occupied by Mr Price[2] second Master of Rugby now, as he was in Dr Arnold's time for many years. In the D^r s life by Mr Stanley is inserted a paper of his[3] which no doubt you have read. These pending engagements will prevent my attending the fête about to be given on the Banks of the Dune in honour of the Poet Burns and his Sons. I had an invitation from the Committee seconded by a most urgent one from my old Friend Professor Wilson,[4] who will act as Vicepresident upon the occasion——The Scotch are fond of ceremonials and solemnities and commemorations, partly owing to their nationality, and partly perhaps in opposition to the spirit of the Kirk

[1] *Word deleted.*

[2] Bonamy Price (1807–88), the economist, a former pupil of Dr. Arnold's at Laleham, taught at Rugby 1830–50, and was Professor of Political Economy at Oxford from 1868. He published a Preface to Arnold's *History of the Later Roman Commonwealth*, 1845.

[3] An account of Arnold's Laleham period in Ch. ii.

[4] Wilson had written enthusiastically on 10 July, 'Scotland would exalt—beholding Wordsworth thus honouring Burns.' (*WL MSS.*)

which is austere and forbidding. Then there is to recommend them the intoxication of speechifying: Was it lucky or unlucky for me that I was born and bred before the age of oratory; a qualification which since the reform bill especially no town-council man is without, as the provincial Newspapers give abundant proof.

Dr Arnold's life M^rs W has read diligently, the 1st Vol she read aloud to me, and I have more than skimmed the 2nd. He was a truly good man; of too ardent a mind however to be always judicious on the great points of secular and ecclesiastical politics that occupied his mind and upon which he often wrote and acted under strong prejudices, and with hazardous confidence. But the Book, notwithstanding these objections, must do good, and *great* good.

His benevolence was so earnest, his life so industrious, his affections domestic and social so intense, his faith so warm and firm, and his endeavour to regulate his life by it so constant, that his example cannot but be beneficial even in quarters where his opinions may be most disliked. How he hated sin and loved and thirsted after holiness; O that on this path he were universally followed! Mrs Arnold and all the family are well, Susan[1] recovered from the severe illness which she fell into last winter. The Fletchers and Davies[2] and Harrisons are well. And now let me ask how you have borne with this gossiping Letter. If it has annoyed you, I won't beg pardon, for I cannot write any other kind of Letter to my satisfaction, having scarcely any *thoughts* to which I can do justice either in prose or verse. Pray remember me kindly to all common Friends, especially the Rogers's and Coleridges if you happen to see them, Kenyon also and many more whom I have not space to name; besides my pens are intolerable and I have tried in vain to mend them

[*unsigned*]

[1] Matthew Arnold's younger sister (b. 1830), who married John Wakefield Cropper of Liverpool in 1858. See also L. 1790 above.

[2] i.e. Dr. and Mrs. Davy.

1813. W. W. to C. W.

MS. Mr. Jonathan Wordsworth. Hitherto unpublished.

Rydal
15th July 1844

My dear Brother,

Some time ago you held out a hope that you would come down this summer[1] and see us at Rydal; this intention, I trust has not been abandoned, and I write to remind you of it and to beg earnestly on the part of us all that you would put it into execution, first letting us know when we may expect you.

Our poor Sister continues much in the same state She has been in for several years, yet enfeebled in mind and body as she is, it will delight her to see You. Dora is by the seaside, whither she went in the hope that she might gain strength, and gather flesh; but alas this hope has not been fulfilled, and she will return as lean and as weak as ever, though she writes that she is well, having recovered from a severe cough which she caught in Bathing. We expect her at Rydal next Saturday.

My dear Wife is well, and we have had for nearly 3 weeks three of our Grandchildren with us, the three eldest boys, Henry, Wm and John. They are fine well-looking and promising Boys, of dispositions and powers of mind not a little different from each other, yet each with his respective characteristics that it is pleasing to note.

John and Isabella are at the baths of Lucca where they will remain until the winter sets on. The poor Invalid is upon the whole considerably better, especially as to strength.

Dora has had a Letter giving a favorable account of dear Chris and his Wife from Mrs Hoare. And now my dear Brother farewell. Pray write at your earliest convenience. With kindest love from Mary and our dear Sister,

your affectionate Brother
Wm Wordsworth

[1] C. W. came from Buxted to Rydal Mount in late July, accompanied by his son Charles (*RMVB*).

1814. W. W. to ISABELLA FENWICK

MS. WL.
LY iii. 1211.

Rydal Mount Wednesday morning [17 July 1844]

My beloved Friend,

According to promise I ought to have written to you some time ago, and I have no sufficient excuse for not doing so, nothing indeed but the hope in which I have been disappointed thus far of making my Letter more interesting by the report of Mr Salvin's arrival.[1] We have looked for him day after day in vain and with unreasonable anxiety, we wish so much for his opinion and the guidance of his judgement in respect to the intended Cottage. Mary laughs at my frequent visits to the Site—we have fixed upon and indeed it is a strong object of attraction to me, very sheltered and easy of access, and when part of the rock down which the steps lead shall be quarried out, the House will command a pleasing view towards the Church and the fells, as well as the beautiful one of Rydal lake. We must not however overlook the fact that it is unluckily much too near Mr Ball's Coach House and Stable, not that either need be seen in a short time, but voices will unavoidably be overheard and that is unpleasant. On the whole notwithstanding this objection I am convinced that we cannot do so well in any other part of the field, and I wish earnestly that Mr Salvin may approve, and give us something of a plan, particularly, for internal convenience.—We do not at all relish your making up your mind to pass the winter in the South or West, we are too old and all of us too frail in body to be reconciled to that. Holmes House[2] is too cold and small for you in winter-time, but we are strongly inclined to think that you might be well accommodated in the vale of Grasmere, in that large House lately built by Mr Green, and now occupied in part by three or more Oxonians with their Tutor. The House is a double one and was planned with a view to suit Lodgers; and we do trust that there and under our *own roof*, as this climate seems to agree with you as well or better than any other which you have tried, you may winter as happily and comfortably as you could anywhere far from us. I say this not forgetting what occurred the morning you left us, and without hope that I shall be able to make any material change in

[1] See L. 1812 above. [2] Thorny Howe.

those points of my character, which you felt it your duty to animadvert upon. In the main one I cannot blame myself—therefore I should too probably displease you in that, though I certainly might change my outward manner of shewing it. But my most dear Friend I do feel from the bottom of my heart, that I am unworthy of being constantly in your sight. Your standard is too high for my hourly life;—when I add to what you blame, the knowledge which I bear about all day long of my own internal unworthiness I am oppressed by the consciousness of being an object unfit to be from morning to night in your presence. Among ten thousand causes which I have to thank God for his goodness towards me is that for more than forty years I have had a Companion who can bear with my offences, who forgets them, and enters upon a new course of love with me when I have done wrong, leaving me to the remorse of my own conscience. Of this chastisement I have had my portion and the feeling seems to be gathering strength daily and hourly; only let me believe that I do not love others less, because I seem to hate myself more. But this is being too serious for a letter; a prayer shall conclude what I have to say upon the subject—May God purify and elevate my mind so that I may become more worthy for being in his presence, and of associating with the good and the pure, among the chief of whom that I have had the happiness of knowing through life, forgive me beloved Friend if I say that I reckon yourself—You cannot know how much I think of you.

If I had written sooner I meant to have told you how much I enjoyed my lonely walks on the sea side during the five days I was at Flimby; everything was so different from what we have at home. It is a dead flat coast along which runs a highway between Workington and Maryport bordered by turf dry and smooth as the shaven lawn of any pleasure ground, except that here and there is a thorn bush and a plot of Ayrshire Rose growing wild and cropt almost close to the ground by cattle. It was flowering at the time, and quite deceived me till Dora told me what it was. With these beautiful ground flowers in some places intermingled purple geraniums that crept as close to the ground—and Sea Pinks. Larks were constantly warbling above my head, their song blending with the murmur of the waves, and there there were the high Scotch hills opposite, behind which the sun set three times in the most glorious way possible, sky, mountain, seabeach, cloud and the orb of the sun contending with each other in splendour. These walks and objects, with the knowledge that my presence was useful to Dora, recompensed me in no small degree for unpleasantness of a domestic kind which you are not ignorant of. The worst of it is that Mr Q. seems incapable of regulating his own temper according to the demands which his Wife's indispositions too frequently make upon it. And it is not to be doubted that his way of spending his time is little suited to make the day pass pleasantly for others. He never scarcely *converses* with his wife or children; his papers, his books, or a newspaper engross his whole time. This is surely deplorable, and yet, poor Creature, she is very fond of him; and this I suppose must happen mostly if married pairs do not positively dislike each other—indifference can scarcely exist under that connection except in minds altogether barren or trivial.—

Mr Faber's Brother[1] is dying and his long Poem Sir Lancelot is going through the Press, to be out in September. This we learn from Matthew Harrison[2] just come from him. Mr F. is now, I believe, at Oxford, waiting his Brother's dissolution.

We have reason to expect my Brother. Julius Hare comes either today or tomorrow to Mrs Arnold, Sir Wm Hamilton of Dublin, your co-sponsor,[3] is to be at Mr Graves's, Bowness, in a day or two. We are also to have a visit from an American painter of distinction,[4] who at Mr Reed's request is coming down to paint my Portrait for him. Mr Rogers and Mr Moxon are coming also as you know, besides several others, so that we shall have enough to do. The wet weather or the coach being full has

[1] Francis Faber (see pt. iii, L. 1314) recovered, and left Oxford the following year to become rector of Saunderton, Bucks. Frederick Faber had now been rector of Elton, Hunts. for rather more than a year. He had spent some time the previous summer in Rome, and on his return to his parish his thinking took a more decidedly Catholic direction. But he had written in high spirits to W. W. at 'Halloween, 1843' about the challenge of his new sphere of activity: 'I shall have a difficult game to play, but by God's help I will go through with it: if I cannot save the souls of the Eltonians, the troubles of Elton will probably save my own.' And he went on to deplore the activities of the Methodists: 'I cannot keep the deathbeds of the poor sacred from these fanatics . . .' (*WL MSS.*) He was now about to bring out *Sir Lancelot: a Legend of the Middle Ages*, 1844, which was set in the Lake country.

[2] Benson Harrison's eldest son, and Faber's former pupil, who had accompanied him on his tour to the Continent in 1841.

[3] Of John W.'s son. The words 'your co-sponsor' were added by M. W.

[4] Henry Inman. See L. 1811 above and L. 1816 below.

prevented the arrival of our nieces[1] from Flimby these two days, but not having heard to the contrary we shall look for them today. Dora comes if there is room in the Mail on Saturday. Mr Q. is probably at Liverpool. They will both stay with us till they can procure a servant to be with them during their stay upon the Island at Windermere. All your friends in this neighbourhood are well; we dine with the Fletchers today. I have declined an invitation to the Burns festival[2] of which perhaps you have heard. Professor Wilson was very urgent that I should attend; but it is too far to go upon such a business were I not otherwise engaged and in fact I do not like these displays. I question also whether poor Burns himself would have much enjoyed the thoughts of such a thing—he was too conscious what a failure his life had been notwithstanding his wide-spread popularity. It is high time to release you, a word I ought to say however of our grandchildren. They grow more difficult to manage the longer they stay, but I think you would not have been disappointed with them. Henry has much to recommend him, Wm is an extraordinary Boy. I am sure you would have much delighted in his looks, talk, and ways. He is one of the quickest as his younger brother John is one of the slowest lads I have ever known Farewell and heaven bless you

W. W.

Kind remembrances to Mr Taylor as usual.

1815. W. W. to C. W.

MS. Mr. Jonathan Wordsworth. Hitherto unpublished.

Saturday Evening
20th July [18] 44

My dear Brother,

Any time that may suit you we will contrive shall suit us, only let us know what day we may expect you.

If you leave London by the railway a little before nine in the Morning, it will convey you to Lancaster in less than 12 hours, at least so I suppose, but there has been lately a little change, the Mail arriving an hour sooner than formerly, therefore probably it starts earlier. If you slept at Lancaster you would be at half past

[1] Ebba and Sarah Hutchinson. [2] See L. 1812 above.

eleven next day at Rydal, but probably you would stop at Kendal, and should that be your intention you might probably reach Kendal by Coach that night. It takes the same time if you leave London between eight and nine at night, you reach Lancaster at the same time in the morning, and if you did not stop at Kendal, would reach Rydal by mail at half past eleven.

I dont think it would be judicious in you to go abroad with Charles, your rate of travelling would not suit, and you must either be a clog upon him, or be induced to overexert yourself which in that hot Country would prove very injurious.

Dora arrived to day from the sea-coast apparently stronger than we expected.

We shall all rejoice to see you.

ever your affectionate
Brother
Wm Wordsworth

1816. W. W. to ISABELLA FENWICK

MS. WL.
LY iii. 1216.

[22nd July 1844]

My dear Miss Fenwick,

The summer is passing away and we are most anxious to begin with the Cottage, and Mr Salvin[1] neither makes his appearance nor do we hear any thing about him. I feel it would be such an advantage to have a plan from so distinguished an Architect, after he has seen the ground, that I cannot think[2] of taking a step, even fixing irrevocably the site without the benefit of his advice. If he would be so kind as to furnish us with a plan, including the proportions and size of the rooms, and of the windows and doors, after we had told him what sort of a house we wished for, not a moment should be lost, and we should have hope of getting the House covered in before the severity of the winter commenced. Dr Davy's will be covered in by the end of next month. My present intention is to have the floors, the window frames and doors all executed in Liverpool, and forwarded by sea to Ulverstone; this on account of the certainty

[1] See L. 1812 above.

[2] *Written* thinking.

of not being able to procure in this neighbourhood either seasoned wood or good workmanship. Dora has seen and approves the proposed Site. She is in good health *for her*, but in no strength. She arrived from Brigham by Mail on Saturday. Could you my dearest Friend communicate with Mr Salvin, so as to put us more at ease as to the time when we may hope to see him. I am most anxious about it for the reason mentioned, and in some degree because I would not be absent from home half a day if I could help it, least he should happen to come at the time.

Thanks for your long and affectionate Letter. You scarcely touch upon the point that was nearest to my heart; and I do not see how you well could; so we will let the matter rest till we have the happiness of meeting again and in the meanwhile you must try to think as well of me as you can. To one thing only will I now advert, viz, that I will not bind myself, circumstanced as Dora is, to make her any fixed allowance. I am convinced it would be wrong to do so, as it would only produce in a certain quarter an effect which I should exceedingly deprecate. Be assured I will take care while I live, that she should not *suffer* in mind for scantiness of income. That she may be somewhat straightened, acting as she has chosen to do with my strongest disapprobation I deem fit and right.—But no more of the subject, nor will I return to it again.

Mrs Green has engaged not to let her lodgings, after the university men have vacated them, to the Water Doctor or to any one else without previously letting us know. The only objection I see to that House is that you would be thrown rather too much in the way of Mrs Luff and Mrs Jaffrey;[1] and it might be disagreeable to fight off such very near neighbours. To Thorny Howe you must not go, the house is well enough for a short time during fine weather in Summer, but it would be intolerable through the Winter. It is small, slightly and ill built, and the living Rooms are in the full sweep of the fierce wind that blows down Grasmere vale from Dunmail Raise, and they have no sunshine,—the doors are thin and close to the front door. I am writing in a great hurry to save the Post. My eyes are so much stronger, that I never thought about your kind offer of sending me spectacles. My old ones have not been found. The other pair which want two glasses I will send by Mr Moxon to London to be repaired, and I trust they will suffice for my life—so dearest

[1] Youngest daughter of Thomas Dawson of Allan Bank, who had married the Revd. Edward Jefferes (1815–93), curate and rector of Grasmere for 38 years.

Friend keep your money in your pocket. If I am penurious for myself I am still more so for you; though I trust you are going to be rich; see the enclosed Paper from the *Times*. The American Painter will be here, he thinks, about the 6th of next month,[1] our dear Brother we hope at the same time; and if the Painter succeeds with me we will, if possible, prevail upon my Brother to sit for us. That would be a family treasure. Farewell, beloved Friend! Most tenderly do I embrace you, with a thousand good wishes. Ever yours

Wm Wordsworth

Professors Hamilton[2] and Butler and Mr Graves and Archdeacon Hare[3] dine here to day; and in the evening we have a rout of some thirty or forty; you will think it well you are not here. Mr Hare gave us yesterday what Mrs Wordsworth called a magnificent Sermon. I wish you had heard it. It was one of a series of sermons upon the Prophecies, and he had interwoven with it passages with especial bearing on our neighbourhood as a mountainous Country. The Text was from the Prophet Haggai chapter 1st 7, 8th—and 13th and 14th verses. Love from every Body and pray excuse wretched writing.

[1] Henry Inman actually arrived at Rydal with his daughter Mary on the 20th (*RMVB*), to begin sittings for W. W.'s portrait (see also L. 1849 below). He also made several landscape sketches in the neighbourhood. See Blanshard, *Portraits of Wordsworth*, p. 171.

[2] See *Hamilton*, ii. 459–60 for R. P. Graves's recollections of this visit. Hamilton was his guest at Windermere rectory along with the Revd. William Archer Butler (?1814–48), Professor of Moral Philosophy at Trinity College, Dublin, from 1837, an authority on Plato, who wrote against Newman's Theory of Development, and published poems in *Blackwood's*. See his *Sermons Doctrinal and Practical . . . with a memoir of the author's life*, 1849, pp. 26 ff. Another of W. W.'s visitors at this time was the Revd. Charles Pritchard (1808–93), the astronomer: headmaster of Clapham Grammar School, 1834–62, and Savilian Professor of Astronomy at Oxford, 1870. See *RMVB* for Jan. and Aug. 1844.

[3] See also L. 1824 below.

WORDSWORTH

from the portrait by Henry Inman, 1844

1817. W. W. to UNKNOWN CORRESPONDENT

MS. Henry E. Huntington Library. Hitherto unpublished.

Friday morning — [26 July 1844][1]

My dear Sir,

An application has been made to Mrs Bolton[2] to subscribe towards building a Parsonage House at Langdale. She is ignorant of the Particulars and has requested of me to give her information. I promised to procure it if I could and I dont know any one so likely to enable me to meet her wishes as yourself. Would you then be so kind as to let me know how the project was set on foot; who are the principal Contributors, what is the Sum requisite, and how much is already subscribed; in short any thing needful for her to form a judgement whether there is a call for any assistance from her. The Cure I suppose is in the Patronage of the Rector of Grasmere,[3] and to that Benefice the family of Rydal present, so that it seems that a House for [the] Langdale Curacy ought mainly to be provided by the Patrons assisted by the Township, and perhaps by the Church-building Society. Pray be so kind as to let me know how the matter stands, and I will communicate with Mrs Bolton.

I remain
dear Sir
truly yours
Wm Wordsworth

1818. W. W. to D. S. WILLIAMSON[4]

MS. untraced.
K (—). *LY iii. 1218.*

Rydal Mount, Friday, 27th July, 1844.

. . . It does not surprise me that you feel interested in the Burns festival. So do I, having always thought as highly of him as a poet as any perhaps of his country men may do. But it is quite

[1] Date added in another hand.

[2] Widow of John Bolton of Storrs.

[3] Sir Richard de Fleming (see pt. i, L. 71).

[4] Unidentified.

out of my power to attend as I informed the committee and Professor Wilson[1] in answer to their several invitations. . . .

It gives me pleasure to learn that you approve of the manner in which I have coupled your loftiest and most conspicuous mountain with our own Skiddaw, as forming links of connection between Burns and myself. I have been lately residing on the Cumberland coast at Flimby, from which place I had glorious view of the sun setting upon your line of hills. Nothing can be finer than the effect often was, with the Solway rolling between

Sincerely, your much obliged
Wm Wordsworth

1819. W. W. to FREDERICK WILLIAM FABER[2]

MS. untraced.
The Bookman, 1926. LY iii. 1218.

Rydal Mount August 6th 1844

My dear Mr Faber

You will do me honor by attaching my lines to your life of St Bega.—Be so good as to affix the date of the lines—when the poem was first printed viz. in the Vol. entitled Yarrow Revisited, two of the stanzas exceeded the others in length—a fault which was afterwards corrected in the edition of 1837 as the lines have stood since.—The last stanza I wish you would print thus, that being the only alteration I purpose to make in future

Alas! the genius of our age from Schools
Less humble, draws her lessons, aims, and rules,

[1] See L. 1812 above. In his *Book of Memories*, 1871, pp. 320 ff., S. C. Hall recalls the Burns festival at Ayr on 6 Aug. 1844, at which W. W.'s health was drunk.

[2] Faber had agreed to contribute to the *Lives of the English Saints*, 14 vols., 1844–5, which was being launched under the editorship of John Henry Newman, now living in retirement at Littlemore. Faber wrote nine of the 'Lives', and had approached W. W. for permission to append his *Stanzas Suggested in a Steamboat off Saint Bees' Heads, on the Coast of Cumberland* (*PW* iv. 25) to the *Life of St. Bega* in vol. ii. The lines were duly printed at the end of the volume, with a prefatory note by Faber drawing attention to the date of the poem (1833) as 'a fresh instance of the remarkable way in which his poems did in divers places anticipate the revival of catholic doctrines among us.' (See *PW* iv. 403).

Would merge, Idolatress of formal skill,
In her own systems God's eternal Will.
To her despising faith in things unseen
Matter and spirit are as one machine.
Better, etc.

It will be necessary to notice what is said in the Advertizement to the poem of the new college of St Bee's, otherwise those lines will be unintelligible.

I am concerned about what you say of your eyes. Do remember the old adage of the Goose and golden eggs. You will in the end get far more work out of yourself if you spread it over a larger space of time.

Dear Miss Fenwick is in Somersetshire.

All are pretty well here, and send their best remembrances.

ever my dear Mr Faber
affectionately and faithfully yours
Wm Wordsworth

If you do not object I should like the note upon the Prayers for the dead to be added.[1]

Are not in sooth their requiem's etc.

The note is printed at the end of the Vol:

1820. W. W. to ELIZABETH BARRETT

Address: Miss Barrett, 50 Wimpole St, London. [*In M. W.'s hand*]
MS. Berg Collection, New York Public Library.
K (—). *LY iii. 1219* (—).

Rydal Mount
16th Augst 44

Dear Miss Barrett,

Being exceedingly engaged at this season, as I always am, I think it best to acknowledge immediately my sense of your kindness in sending me the two volumes[2] of your Poems

[1] The note (*PW* iv. 403–4) was omitted.

[2] The first collected edition of her poems, which led to her introduction to Robert Browning the following year. For her view of W. W.'s poetry and its occasional lapses into 'vulgarity' and 'childishness', see *Letters of Elizabeth Barrett Browning*, ed. F. G. Kenyon, 2 vols., 1897, i. 160–1: 'Yes, I *will* be a blind

recently published; from the perusal of which, when I am at leisure, I promise myself great pleasure. It would be a gratification to me if I could learn from any quarter what is the state of your health. I hope it is improved.—

Believe me dear Miss Barrett to remain

with high respect
faithfully yours
Wm Wordsworth

1821. W. W. to LADY LE FLEMING

Address: The Lady le Fleming.
MS. Le Fleming MSS., Record Office, Kendal. Hitherto unpublished.

[*In M. W.'s hand*]

Rydal Mount, Aug. 17th—44.
Saturday.

Dear Madam,

Under the apprehension that having been taken by surprize on the receipt of a letter from Mr. Moser,[1] your Ladyship's Solicitor, I might in the interview with him which immediately followed have failed to express myself with sufficient precision, and, also that he might possibly make some mistake in reporting the conversation that took place between us, I take leave to solicit your Ladyship's attention to the subject, in the hope that when you are accurately informed of all particulars you may be induced to withdraw your opposition to the building of a cottage by me on the site which I fixed upon.

Nearly 20 years go, after a residence of 13 years at Rydal Mount, I had become much attached to the place; and as I had reason to believe it was your Ladyship's wish that Mrs. Huddleston should occupy Rydal Mount, I purchased, at a very high price, of James Backhouse the adjoining Enclosure named The Rash, solely with a view to build upon it.[2] The cottages to which it was attached were no object to me being ignorant that the possession of them would have given me an indisputable right to build otherwise I should have endeavoured to include

admirer of Wordsworth's. I *will* shut my eyes and be blind. Better so, than see too well for the thankfulness which is his due from me.'

[1] Of Messrs. Roger and Robert Moser, Kendal.

[2] See pt. i, L. 206. For James Backhouse, see also pt. ii, L. 747.

them in the purchase; the field was bought without a thought existing in my mind that there was any thing in the Custom of the Manor which could be urged against my acting upon my intention. What strong ground I had for entertaining this notion will sufficiently appear when I recal to your Ladyship's recollection that I then made a request, which you were so kind as immediately to grant, that I might take the stone required for the Building from a Quarry in a field of Rydal Mount Estate which Quarry lay convenient for the purpose. I took other preparatory steps that were known in the neighbourhood without hearing from any quarter a word of opposition.

While this was going on, I was apprized that a change of circumstances had occurred, and that it was not likely I should be called upon to quit Rydal Mount. Accordingly without the least reluctance or rather with pleasure, I gave up all wish to build the House I had intended; and in that state of feeling I have continued ever since till within a few weeks. How I came to be otherwise disposed Mr. Moser must undoubtedly have stated; but it may be as well to repeat that I was led to the undertaking which has been objected to by two motives.

The first and principal one was to accommodate my excellent Friend Miss Fenwick, of whose high character and amiable qualities your Ladyship can scarcely be ignorant. That Lady being strongly attached to myself and family, and finding that this climate agrees with her health, which has long been delicate, better than any other part of England, she has during the last 4 years endeavoured, I regret to say in vain, to hire a suitable house within neighbourly distance of us. Seeing no likelihood of her wishes being gratified I undertook to build a Cottage in which she might have the prospect of living comfortably.

Another motive concurred with this, viz. the hope that my only daughter, to whom the field does in fact belong, might at some future time succeed Miss Fenwick in the occupation of the intended house.

I might earlier have been disposed to build for Miss Fenwick's sake had we not had reason to expect, when the house now occupied by Mr. Burrow was enlarged, that Mr. Carter would have continued to be Tenant, in which case as he must have been absent the greater part of the year, Miss Fenwick would have been satisfied with the use of the house during that absence. Permission was given thro' Mr. Jackson,[1] to Mr. Carter, to

[1] Thomas Jackson, Lady le Fleming's agent.

underlet the Cottage upon which he incurred a heavy expense for furniture, when, to his great disappointment he was told by Mr. Jackson that he would not be allowed to *let* the house for more than *one* year. Under these circumstances for which he was wholly unprepared it became impossible for Mr. Carter to continue the Tenant, and the hope of obtaining a home there for Miss Fenwick vanished with the knowledge of the fact.

I will now ask leave to direct your Ladyship's attention to particulars of less moment but which are however a source of disagreeable feeling to me, in connexion with this little property. Within my recollection the house of which Mr. Ball is owner[1] consisted of a small cottage and Barn, it has since spread, and mainly upon ground before unoccupied to 7 or 8 times the original size, and in a less degree has the house now occupied by Mrs. Ward[2]—and allow me to say that I cannot help thinking it a little hard considering what has been written above, that these Proprietors should have been left at liberty to proceed in that way while I am to be so restricted.

I could add much more tending, I should think, to induce a Lady so distinguished for benevolence as yourself to reconsider your opposition to a plan entered upon with such views. Should I be disappointed in this hope, I cannot omit on the present occasion to thank your Ladyship for the assurance which you once gave me that I should not be disturbed in the occupation of a home, which, thro' the blessing of God, I and mine have so long enjoyed; and let me here repeat what I said to Mr. Moser, that on no account whatever would I litigate the point of your Ladyship's legal right to prevent the Building, were there no other reason than my sense of your kindness.

As the right to build, which I supposed my Daughter possessed as Tenant on the Manor has been disputed it is reasonable that on her part I should request permission to see the Court Rolls in order to ascertain what dues and liabilities the ground is subject to, detached from the Tenements to which it belonged.

In conclusion I would observe that should your Ladyship withdraw your opposition to the Building, that indulgence would not furnish a Precedent, as, with the exception of an acre

[1] Glen Rothay. See pt. iii, L. 1048.

[2] See L. 1625 above.

or two, already built upon, your Ladyship is Owner of the land in the whole Manor in the neighbourhood of Rydal.

I have the honor to be your Ladyship's

Obedient Servt
[*signed*] Wm Wordsworth

1822. W. W. to ROGER MOSER[1]

MS. WL.
LY iii. 1220.

[*In M. W.'s hand*]

Aug: 18th [1844]

Dear Sir,

Your letter rec^{d} yesterday proves to me that the accompanying one was not unnecessary—as it was almost impossible that you should have accurately detailed one hurried conversation, when I had the pleasure of seeing you at Rydal Mount.

With respect to the Cottage occupied by Mr Burrow,[2] it would appear from your last letter that you had understood me as having applied to you for the offer of it—A thing impossible for any Gentleman to do—knowing as I did that Mr B and his family were residing in it. I merely mentioned that had Mr Carter continued to be Tenant in that Cottage, it would have rendered my desire to build unnecessary.

Your memory must also have failed you on another point, of the declaration of her Ladyship as conveyed to me in your letter, that she 'would avail herself of a Court-of-Law to prevent any further building within the Manor of Rydal' was *also* unnecessary, inasmuch as I positively stated that my respect for, and obligation to Lady le Fleming would prevent my having any inclination to litigate the matter as to her Ladyship's legal right, however we might be disposed to consider it doubtful.

Since receiving your yesterday's letter I determined not to send the enclosed prepared for Lady F, but if you will táke the trouble to read it, you will be in full possession of my view of the case before us—and I must beg you to be so kind as to

[1] Lady le Fleming's solicitor. See previous letter.

[2] At Rydal.

correct the two mistakes which I have mentioned, the first opportunity you have to communicate with Lady le Fleming.

In reply to Lady le Fleming's courteous proposal that 'in consideration of my having purchased the Field with a view to build, she would take the purchase off my hands', I have to say that the field belongs to my daughter, who would not bring her mind to part with it for any pecuniary consideration, her attachment to this country is so strong that she lives in the hope at some future day to build a Cottage on some site interesting to her affections.

Permit me then to mention, that at the extremity of the Rydal Property there is a field which Lady le F. might be induced to *exchange* for the one upon which I had proposed to build in the Hamlet of Rydal. This field is adjacent to Dr Pearson's property and is distant about a mile and a half, and terminates not more than a few hundred yards from the Cottage[1] in Grasmere which I inhabited for 8 years, and where my daughter and two of her Brothers were born. If this could be arranged, the whole matter in which our wishes have been so much crossed might terminate satisfactorily to us all, but I may add, that if my daughter could have been induced to *sell* the field it might have been and may be disposed of at a much larger price than the sum which I paid for it.

I may here repeat what I have expressed in the letter addressed to Lady le Fleming, that I think it desirable I should on the part of my daughter see the Court-roll of the Manor, that she, as Tenant, may be aware of the liabilities and restrictions attached to the Land as *de*tached from the Tenements.

Many engagements have prevented my forwarding these letters sooner: which you will be so kind as to excuse.

I am Gen^{t}. yours truly
[*signed*] Wm Wordsworth

[1] Dove Cottage.

1823. W. W. to CHARLES WILLIAM PASLEY

MS. Cornell.
LY iii. 1221.

Rydal Mount
22nd Augst 1844

Dear General Pasley,

My Son, the Revd John Wordsworth, who is abroad with his Wife on account of her state of health, writes that he is very anxious to have the name of his oldest Son,[1] ten years of age, placed upon the list of Candidates to be admitted at a proper age into the Military College of Woolwich.[2] I have therefore presumed upon your kindness, so far as to request the favor of any information which you can give how to set about in the best way for gaining the object.

Believe me,
My dear General
faithfully yours
Wm Wordsworth

1824. W. W. to JULIUS CHARLES HARE[3]

MS. Mr. R. L. Bayne-Powell. Hitherto unpublished.

[late Aug. 1844]

My dear Mr Hare,

A few days after our delightful walk upon Loughrigg Fell[4] I threw off the verses which I enclose, with a view to their being

[1] Henry. See also Ls. 1835 and 1841 below.

[2] Moved from the Arsenal to new buildings on Woolwich Common in 1805–8.

[3] Julius Hare, accompanied by his brother's widow, her son, and Esther, sister of Frederick Denison Maurice (see L. 1503 above), had stayed with Mrs. Arnold at Fox How during July and seen much of the Wordsworths (see L. 1816 above and *RMVB*). In August Hare became engaged to Esther Maurice, and they were married the following November.

[4] R. P. Graves left a long account of this expedition (William Archer Butler, *Sermons Doctrinal and Practical*, pp. 27–8): 'The party consisted of Mr. Wordsworth, Archdeacon Hare, Sir William R. Hamilton, Professor Butler, and two ladies, both by name and mental qualities worthy of the association, besides myself. The day was brilliant, and continued so throughout, as we ascended one

inserted in the Copy of my poems which you presented to Miss Morris.[1] I wrote a short letter to you after these Stanzas were composed, and transcribed them for the purpose I have mentioned, but the letter was not sent off because I seldom have the resolution to part with verses immediately, as I always apprehend that there may be some thing wrong in them which would shew itself in a little time.—I am truly glad of the delay, for Mrs Arnold was so kind yesterday to read to us the most interesting Letter in which you communicate your engagement with Miss Morris. We rejoice to hear of it and you both have *our* fervent wishes and earnest prayers for God's blessing upon a course so well begun. Be assured that the nearest approach that can be made to happiness upon earth is by a union such as you have in prospect. You both have had an opportunity of being long and intimately acquainted with each other, so that you can judge of and feel your natural suitableness, the want of which previous knowledge is the most common cause of the unhappiness that wedlock often produces. Will you be so kind as to present to the object of your affections the united remembrances

of the ravines of Loughrigg Fell, opposite to Rydal . . . I remember that not only poetry and philosophy, with other lighter matters, formed topics of conversation, but that religious subjects also, and especially the doctrine of the Resurrection, were spoken of with a reverent and cordial interest. Our eminent countrymen excited admiration from all, by the ample share they contributed, in the way both of original remark and brilliantly apposite quotation, to the fund of intellectual treasure then poured forth. . . . When we reached the side of Loughrigg Tarn . . . the loveliness of the scene arrested our steps and fixed our gaze . . . and when the poet's eyes were satisfied with their feast on the beauty familiar to them, they sought relief in the search, for them a happy vital habit, for new beauty in the flower-enamelled turf at his feet. There his attention was attracted by a fair, smooth stone, of the size of an ostrich's egg, seeming to embed at its centre, and, at the same time, to display a dark star-shaped fossil of most distinct outline. Upon closer inspection this proved to be the shadow of a daisy projected upon it with extraordinary precision by the intense light of an almost vertical sun. The poet drew the attention of the rest of the party to the minute, but beautiful phenomenon, and gave expression at the time to thoughts suggested by it . . . The little poem, in which some of those thoughts were afterwards crystallized, commences with the stanza,

So fair, so sweet, withal so sensitive,
Would that the little flowers were born to live,
Conscious of half the pleasure that they give.'

(*PW* iv. 125)

[1] i.e. Esther Maurice.

of this Family, not omitting that we should be most happy to see you both again in our beautiful Country, which your Letter to Mrs Arnold makes us think still better of, if possible.

Believe me to be
my dear, Mr Hare
very faithfully yours
Wm Wordsworth

1825. W. W. to FREDERICK WILLIAM FABER

MS. Dr. E. L. McAdam, jnr. Hitherto unpublished.

Rydal Mount —
10th Sep^br [18]44

My dear Mr Faber,

You will think me a strange Creature for not having yet read your Poem.[1] In fact I have for some weeks been almost hurried out of my life by company and moving about; and also greatly untuned by disappointment respecting the House which I intended to build for Miss Fenwick; and till that business is settled one way or the other it would be quite unfair to your Poetry or any one's else to meddle with it. I have to thank you also for Your little book of the lives of English Saints. I have read enough of this to be assured that the whole will interest me though I cannot go to your lenghts.[2] You shall hear from me as soon as I can write with some satisfaction. Ever faithfully

Yours Wm Wordsworth

(turn over)

Mrs W. begs her love; Your Letter to Miss Fenwick will be forward[ed] to her at Mr Popham's where she will remain a week or ten days, after which for a short time her address will be Kelston Knoll near Bath.—On Thursday we go to Mr Marshall's for a few days, then to Levens and afterward to Underleigh, M^r

[1] *Sir Lancelot* (see L. 1814 above).

[2] W. W. is probably referring to Faber's *Life of St. Wilfrid*, which took up vol. v. of *The Lives of the English Saints*. It provoked much hostility on account of its openly-expressed sympathy for the Roman Catholic system and uncritical acceptance of legendary material.

Alderman Thompson's,[1] after which unsettling, I hope we shall be quiet for the winter.—Today we dine with the Harrisons to meet Mathew's Intended and her Father and Mother.[2] I ought not to omit that last Friday and Saturday I was on the banks of the Duddon, with Miss Fletcher—an engagement of two years standing. What a bewitching Vale it is!—

1826. W. W. to EDWARD MOXON

MS. Henry E. Huntington Library.
LY iii. 1204 (—).

Rydal Mount
Sept[br] 12th 1844

My dear Mr Moxon,

I understand that the last Vol: of Thirlwall's[3] History of Greece is just published. The whole work consists, I am told, of eight Vols. of which I possess the first four; would you be so kind as to procure for me the remaining four, and forward them with the Excursions you mean to send. I suppose of course you can procure the 4 vols of the History separate and at trade price. The parcel will reach me free of expense if directed and forwarded to Mrs Harrison of Hundow 65 Old Broad Street, at your early leisure.

We have had swarms of Company since you left us, a great part of whom we would willingly have exchanged for a few days more of your society—Yesterday we had two Sons of the

[1] William Thompson (d. 1854), a wealthy iron-master who made money from railways, became M.P. for the City of London in 1826, Lord Mayor in 1829, and eventually senior Alderman. He subsequently represented Sunderland as a liberal (1837–41), but stood as a conservative for Westmorland when Lord Lowther moved to the House of Lords in 1841, and sat for that constituency till 1854. His mansion, Underley Hall, nr. Kirkby Lonsdale, was built by George Webster, the Kendal architect, in 1825, for Alexander Nowell (see pt. ii, L. 610), who had died in 1842. Thompson's only daughter Amelia (d. 1864) married in 1842 Thomas Taylor, Earl of Bective, later 3rd Marquess of Headfort (1822–94), who succeeded him as M.P. for Westmorland. Lord and Lady Bective had visited W. W. in August (*RMVB*).

[2] Matthew Benson Harrison was married to Catherine (d. 1862), daughter of the Revd. George Day, rector of Earsham, Norfolk, on 11 Dec. 1845.

[3] Connop Thirlwall (see also pt. ii, L. 827) published his *History of Greece*, 8 vols., 1835–44, in Lardner's *Cabinet Encyclopaedia*.

Poet Burns, and Lord and Lady Monteagle, to-day Professor Sedgewick, these all are good exceptions to the above remark.[1] Kindest remembrances to you and yours, in which all unite. In half an hour we set off for Halsteads, Mr Marshall's, on the Banks of Ulleswater. We spent two delightful days upon the Duddon since you left us. You would have liked to have been of the party.

ever faithfully yours
Wm Wordsworth

1827. W. W. to C. W.

Address: The Revd Dr Wordsworth, Buxtead, near Uckfield.
Postmark: (1) 19 Sept. 1844 (2) 20 Sept. 1844 (3) 21 Sept. 1844.
Stamp: (1) Ambleside (2) Uckfield.
MS. Mr. Jonathan Wordsworth. Hitherto unpublished.

Rydal
18th Sept^{r} [18] 44

My dear Brother,

I have been some time in your debt for a kind Letter giving an account of your proceedings till—(here I was interrupted, as usual, by visitors; three ladies of the name of Marriat, distant relations of ours through our Grandmother Robinson)[2] they are gone but I fear I shall not be long at liberty to proceed, but I will finish my Sentence—till you reached your quiet and lonely home. I have been moving about a good deal since you left us—two days in the neighbourhood of Kendal, two on the banks of the Duddon, and five at Hallsteads, including the going and coming. Mary was with me at the latter place, where we found the old people in dejected Spirits; Mr Marshall being threatened with incurable blindness, and Mrs M. not well. The

[1] Other visitors (see *RMVB*) included Aubrey de Vere from Ireland, Edward Bulwer (see also pt. iii, L. 1197), Whewell, W. W.'s Quaker connections Mrs. Crewdson and J. Bevan Braithwaite, and William Winstanley Hull (1794–1873) the Evangelical, who was staying at Fox How. In October, Bunsen (see pt. iii, L. 1063) and W. C. Lake (see L. 2124 below) called, and Caroline Fox and her sister, who found the poet 'in great force.' For their conversations, see *Memoirs of Old Friends*, ii. 37–44, and L. 1839 below.

[2] Mary Robinson (1700–73), who married W. W.'s grandfather Richard Wordsworth of Sockbridge.

Whewells were there, enjoying themselves as much as their sad circumstances could permit. Loss of sight will cut off Mr Marshall from the two chief sources of his minor enjoyments, reading, and the beauty of the Country, to which he has always been peculiarly sensible; and his poor Wife seems less able than himself to bear the thought of such privation. He has a hired Reader who attends him three hours in the day—but for the other loss there can be found no substitute. On our return home on Monday we found Dora had been suffering, and was still suffering greatly, under severe cold, no voice left, and she had neither eaten nor slept for three days and nights. A sad welcome for us; she had caught the cold upon Windermere in going down to keep an appointment unfortunately made, and the malady was no doubt aggravated by her coming back to Rydal, to take care of our Sister during our absence. Dr Davy has been so kind as to visit her regularly; once he came twice in the same day. She is thank God! something better. If she improves we shall leave home again on Saturday for a week, and then commences, we hope, an undisturbed Season, undisturbed I mean as far as company-engagements are concerned. You have heard, I believe, of the obstacle to the Exchange,[1] supposed to exist in the unfortunate marriage settlement. Sergeant Talfourd, and an Eminent Solicitor[2] of Huddersfield who happened to be here are both of the opinion, that the settlement need not prevent a satisfactory arrangement, should Lady Fleming continue in the same mind. I forwarded both the Settlement and the opinions to her Solicitor at Kendal, but have not yet heard from him in reply. These repeated delays and disappointments have worried me more than they ought to have done; but we cannot meet with a suitable House for Miss Fenwick, and the motive of supplying her with one would determine one to build; as the *situation* is one of the most eligible in the whole of this beautiful region.

We are truly glad that you had such good health and enjoyed yourself so much while among us; and the more so because we trust you will be tempted to come again, and not infrequently, should our lives and health be prolonged.

Mr Branker[3] has made another proposal to Charles, which I

[1] The possibility of an exchange of land with Lady le Fleming (see L. 1822 above). The marriage settlement W. W. goes on to refer to is Dora Q.'s.

[2] Mr. Laycock, a friend of Mrs. Fletcher.

[3] Formerly of Croft Lodge.

begged him not to think a moment about, the place being quite unsuitable to his purpose. He must come down at Christmas and look about him at leisure.

Chris: returned, I hope, in somewhat improved health. His Residence in Paris must have added greatly to his knowledge of important matters.—*19th*—I was again interrupted yesterday when I was on the point of concluding in time for the Post. Dora was something better last night, but she coughs upon the slightest excitement. Wm is with us and is to accompany us on our visit to Underley.[1] I have heard from Lady F's Solicitor and he seems to think that the difficulty arising out of the Settlement may be overcome. If so I shall be pleased, as I should like our family to have a *lien* upon the beautiful and much-loved vale of Grasmere. I have nothing more to add than the best love of us all, not enumerating the family individually. Sister is much as usual, and has a ride in her chair almost every day, though the weather has a sharp autumnal feel.

ever your affectionate Brother
Wm Wordsworth

1828. W. W. and M. W. to ISABELLA FENWICK

Address: Miss Fenwick, Kelston Knoll, Nr Bath. [*In M. W.'s hand*]
Postmark: (1) [19] Sept. 1844 (2) 22 Sept. 1844.
Stamp: (1) Ambleside (2) Bath.
MS. WL.
LY iii. 1222 (—).

Rydal—Thursday [19 Sept. 1844]

I have been prevented, my beloved Friend, from writing to you for some time, by a succession of vexations and disappointments, which I have met with in my anxious wish and endeavour to build a House for you, where if so disposed you might have a home for the Remainder of your life. The possession of the Wishing-gate Field seems now attainable provided we can agree as to the price. Observe Mr Jackson cannot molest us in the least; if the field be sold it becomes at once freehold, and he has no power either over, or in connection with it all—he can only do us harm by putting the Solr on making a harder bargain than

[1] Residence of Alderman Thompson (see L. 1825 above).

otherwise he would be inclined to. But such obstacles as exist in the marriage Settlement of Dora, may be got over; in this opinion Lady F's Sol[r] coincides with Sergeant Talfourd and Mr Laycock, Mrs Fletcher's legal Friend. If the purchase be effected, I should propose, with your approbation, to build for you, my dear Friend, a Cottage residence upon this plot of ground, endeared to me by so many touching remembrances. But if you neither think that the situation would suit you, nor can get over the objections you once expressed in strong terms, to having a house built for you, while Dora was without one, then I shall abandon all thoughts of building, and must be contented with the thought of the field being Dora's after my day and her Mothers with the power to leave it in the end after her husband's life to one of her Brothers which would I doubt not be Wm. It would gratify me [to] think that some one of my family had that substantial connection with a place where we first took root in this beautiful Country. Now I must here repeat what I have said to you before, that building for Dora, situated as she is, I cannot think of, and if you would not be comfortable in occupation of the House, then there is an end of the matter; how much to my sorrow and regret I shall not say. So my dear Miss Fenwick think the matter over dispassionately, and let me know the result. The field and House if built will be left to Dora after her Mother's and my time subject to no condition but that you are to be Tenant as long as you live and that after her Husband's decease if he survive her it is to go to whomsoever she shall name.—Grasmere is a little too far from us at our time of life, but I think we could manage to see much of each other, though far from as much as I could wish, did I not feel myself in so many respects unworthy of your love and too likely to become more so. Worldly-minded I am not, nor indifferent to the welfare of my fellow creatures; on the contrary, my wish to benefit them within my humble sphere strengthens, seemingly, in exact proportion to my inability to realise those wishes, in any project which I may engage in. What I lament most is that the spirituality of my Nature does not expand and rise the nearer I approach the grave, as yours does, and as it fares with my beloved Partner. The pleasure which I derive from God's works in his visible creation is not with me I think impaired, but no kind of reading interests me as it used to do, and I feel that I am becoming daily a much less instructive Companion to others.— Excuse this Egotism, I feel it necessary to your understanding what I am, and how little you would gain by habitual intercourse with me, however greatly *I* might benefit from intercourse with you. I know not whether you have been told how much Miss Fletcher enjoyed her Tour to, and upon the banks of the Duddon.[1] Mr Quillinan was charioteer, and nobody could be kinder or more ready to serve, or more generally amiable than he was. Neither this nor anything else however reconciles me to his course of life. You say he could not procure employment—I say, that he does not *try*. He has now taken again to hard labour on his translation of Camoens,[2] a work which can not possibly turn to profit of any kind either pecuniary or intellectual. All that ought to be looked to from it is his own amusement at *leisure* hours. The fact is he cannot bring himself to stoop in the direction he ought to stoop in. His pride looks and works the wrong way; and I am hopeless of a cure—but I am resolved not to minister to it, because it ought not to exist, circumstanced as he is. His inaction mortifies me the more because his talents are greatly superior to those of most men who earn a handsome livelihood by Literature.—Dora has been and is, I am sorry to say, very unwell. She caught a severe cold in passing to and fro upon Windermere, and [on] our return from Hallsteads we found her suffering greatly—Three days and nights she has been without sleep, and without food unless tea may be called so—for the state of her stomach wont allow [her] to take solids of any kind. This is very grievous, and she looks of course deplorably thin and ill. Her voice however is returning, and we hope the fever is a good deal abated. Friday Morning. We think Dora rather better, though she had an uneasy night. Tomorrow I start with Wm for Alderman Thompson's near Kirkby Lonsdale. These visits are most irksome unless Mary can go along with me which she cannot now do. If the Howards of Levens can receive me I go from Underley to them on Wednesday with some faint hope that Mary may be able to join me there.—We are at our wits' end to find a House for you. Yesterday Miss Fletcher called and talked about a House at Grasmere lately rebuilt and decorated by Captn Philips in the water-doctor connection. She says it is an excellent House and she thought you might have [it] in [the] spring. We have since

[1] For Lady Richardson's recollections of the tour, see Grosart, iii. 445–8. They were accompanied by Thomas Hutchinson, jnr. and his sister who were staying at Rydal Mount.

[2] See L. 1775 above.

learned that this is quite a mistake. Philips means it for some[one] himself and should be change his mind it is previously engaged to the Cooksons, in conjunction with their Brother. As to Thorny How it is I am sure the coldest situation in the whole Country, and you would be sadly cut off from us. If you could get a House at or near Ambleside so constant is the communication between the Fletchers and Davies[1] that you could not fail seeing much of them; and would be within our easy reach. As to Bowness you might almost as well be in Somersetshire as far as concerns us, and better for yourself. Bowness is upwards of nine miles from Rydal, quite out of neighbourly winter distance. As love's almost last shift Mary and I are going to look at Mr North's large House,[2] known by the forbidding and odious name of Mr North's new Poor House. But Mrs Nicholson[3] tells me, that but for the entrance front to and so near the road, it would be no objectionable residence. The view from it across the Vale would be excellent she says by converting one of the bed rooms into a drawing room. But we will make our report before this Letter is closed. Mr Quillinan is here and would have written to you a long and no doubt an entertaining Letter, but he deferred a few days [? knowing] I am before hand with him. You dont say much about Kate's[4] health, we are anxious to know whether her weakness is at all got the better of. Hartley is just come in, and says that his Mother is anxious to know whether she means to remain at Warwick,[5] or what she intends. Perhaps she will write herself to Mrs Coleridge, who appears to be in a state of much suffering. Sarah is returned Home. We should have had more pleasure in hearing of your [? kind] intention to visit Brinsop but for the steep stairs. Poor Jane[6] [said] not long before she died, 'O poor Miss Fenwick could never get up these stairs!' It is nevertheless possible or you might take the way back. They would, I am sure rejoice to see you.—

[*M. W. writes*]

Well, dearest friend, we have seen all in the way of lodgings that is to be seen in Ambleside. Mrs. Landsborough's which is

[1] i.e. Dr. and Mrs. Davy. [2] In Ambleside.

[3] The Ambleside bookseller.

[4] Probably Kate Southey

[5] i.e. with Bertha and Herbert Hill.

[6] Their old servant, who had died at Brinsop.

one of those 2 pleasant looking dwellings (from their facing the Valley towards Loughrigg) you pass, going to Miss Thompson's, may be had at the same rate the Qs[1] pay, viz £5 a month—attendance and Kitchen four pound—the rooms, tho' not so high quite, are somewhat larger than Miss T's 4 bed rooms but furniture not so nice and Mrs Nicholson says Mrs L's temper is so bad no one can be in comfort with her. Fisher beck (bearing the opprobrious title [of] the new Poor house) is a roomy house, 2 shabby little Parlours looking to the road from which you know it is entered. 4 stairs carry you from the door to these—then 2 good sized rooms—the drawing and dining room are behind, and have a pleasing view, only you have to pass your eye over a vulgar sort of yard walled in by a high wall, but which does not impede the view, the house being raised.—There are then 5 sufficiently sized bed-rooms—4 with beds, on the first floor—and 4 bed rooms above—the staircase not tempting me to mount! It is furnished with Mr North's furniture—not handsome but I suppose sufficient for use. Add to these there was what might be a room for housekeeper, Butler's Pantry etc, and they said good cellars—but not a convenience conveniently situated. This Mrs N, who is inclined to think you might be comfortable here, thinks, as there is so much *room* in the house, that you need not be annoyed by *this want*! You might, if you could make up your mind to bear the vulgar entrance etc, have this house for the winter for £5 a month. We are inclined to think it preferable to Thorney how, but tell us your '*sentiments*'. They say Lady F has purchased Mrs Ward's house etc, so all Rydal except neighbour Bales will be hers. Every dearest wish

Yrs M W

P.S. Willy's dear love.

1829. W. W. to ROGER MOSER[2]

MS. WL.
LY iii. 1225.

19th Sept. 1844

My dear Sir

I have delayed sending you the marriage settlement[3] for the

[1] The Quillinans. [2] Lady le Fleming's solicitor.

[3] Dora Q.'s. See L. 1827 above.

purpose of submitting it to Sergeant Talfourd and to an eminent solicitor and conveyancer etc. of Huddersfield, Mr Laycock, who both happen to be in this neighbourhood and I enclose you their several opinions. The former will remain here for several weeks and I am sure it would give him pleasure to meet you if you should wish it. The settlement does not contain as I expected any express allusion to a power of selling the field to my son Wm; but both Mr Quillinan and I distinctly recollect that in the draft for the settlement that condition was inserted. What induced Mr Cookson[1] to omit it, I cannot recollect, but no doubt we must have understood each other at the time and I must have been satisfied with his reasons which were probably of a technical trend. I hope that you will find no obstacle to a satisfactory settlement of the business as soon as may be. I leave home today to be absent till Monday. In the course of next week I shall have to pass through Kendal, and will do myself the pleasure of calling upon you; but perhaps you may be at Rydal before that time.

I remain dear Sir sincerely yours,
Wm Wordsworth

1830. M. W. to H. C. R.

Endorsed: 23 Sept. 44 *Mrs Wordsworth.*
MS. Dr. Williams's Library.
Morley, ii. 569.

23rd Sepr [1844]

My dear Friend

I deputed Mr Q—, whose home is now upon the Island, but who was here when your very interesting letter arrived,—to answer it for me—feeling my incapacity to do so adequately myself—However he has left your letter behind so that I must just thank you for it, and gossip a little in my own way—and the first thing I shall say is, that we are beginning to reckon the weeks that must intervene before we see you at Rydal Mount—and tell you that your favourite bed has advanced from one side of the room to the other to meet you—but it shall march back to its old station if you like it better

Such a summer we have had for visitors tires me to look back

[1] Strickland Cookson, W. W.'s London solicitor.

upon—the tide is in a measure stemmed—and I am quietly interrupted from proceeding on a course of visits with my husband by Dora having unluckily caught a bad influenza—She came to be housekeeper and her Aunt's Companion in our absence—and on our return from Hallsteads last Monday we found her so ill that I could not leave her again.—So that the two Williams were obliged to go to Underley to visit Alderman and Mrs Thompson without me, where they now are, Willy on his road to Carlisle—and I am happy to say that Dora, tho' very weak and languid, is so much better, that if my husband insists on my meeting him at Levens on Wednesday next I am bound, tho' loth to do so—for I must confess paying these kind of visits is become as distasteful to me as letter-writing. This coming visit over, and a few weeks more (in the course of which I hope to take Dora to the sea side for us both to have a ½ a doz or so, warm sea baths to stave off the Rheumatism in the winter)—then we shall be well prepared for our campaign at the whist table with you dear friend—Mr Roughsedge is panting for the season already. We do not reckon poor Mr R. to be in a good state—he has alarming attacks in the head, which increase upon him and keep his wife very anxious. Your accounts of your good Brother delight[1] us much, but you say nothing of yourself. I hope you have forgotten all about your accident? and to finish the subject of health I may just tell you at once that we ourselves, including old Aunty, are well—and that poor John Wordsworth seems to be no worse—in many points better, but this he does not himself allow—and none of his Medical Advisers give him any encouragement to take upon himself any professional duty—he is just now at Keswick.

From our Wanderers we have better acc^ts^ of M^rs^ J Ws health, they are now about leaving the baths of Lucca, where they have been for about the last 3 months—intending to spend a Month between Florence and Sienna and then on to Rome along with and by the advice of a favourite Doctor, who Isabella thinks has been of more use to her than *all* her previous ones. It is a pity that she had not met with him sooner.

Notwithstanding we have been often tired out (for we are not so young as we once were) by our numerous visitors we have seen many interesting People—and interesting occurences have taken place—for instance a marriage which promises much

[1] *Written* delights.

happiness has been settled among our Mountains—Our Friend Julius Hare and a fair Companion of his travels and visit along with his Sister-in-law, to Mrs Arnold—have here made up their minds to become one[1]—She is sister to Mr Maurice of Guys Hospital—the pious Divine. Then we still have the Serg^t[2] and his family—all of whom seem to be very much enjoying themselves—and we have had great pleasure and no little profit from his residence—as you will hear hereafter—And Mrs T. has afforded, by her appearance and bearing, no little amusement to the Natives.

Have you been told by any one of the New Portrait? the last and best that has been taken of the Poet—The Painter is an American—deputed to carry the Laureate's Head to our unseen friend Mr Reed of Philadelphia. And thither ere this the picture is on its way, but Mr Inman has promised us a Copy[3]—of what appeared to us to be a marvel inasmuch as it only occupied the Artist and Sitter scarcely 4½ hours to produce it. All agreed that no Englishman could do the like.

We *did* see the B^p of Norwich[4] and his family with whom we were well pleased—but W^m never entered upon the subject of your Grand Bill[5]—The Hares gave way to the Bp etc at Fox-how and went into the Cottage which Mr Price[6] (the 2nd Master of Rugby and his family had left) and in which the Talfourds now are—Rothay bridge—Dear old Mr Harden with his eldest daughter Jane—you know he has lost Jessy[7] also—are now at Miller Bridge—he as gay as ever—and I believe his son John is likewise with him at present. We have had Baron and Lady Park[8] also—who told W^m that he had by recommending to them

[1] See L. 1824 above.

[2] Sergeant Talfourd.

[3] Henry Reed's copy of the portrait now belongs to the University of Pennsylvania. The copy commissioned by the Wordsworths (see also L. 1849 below) has descended through the family and now hangs again at Rydal Mount.

[4] Edward Stanley (see pt. iii, L. 983), consecrated 1837. He supported the Dissenters' Chapels Bill, and other Whig measures. The visit of his family is recorded in *RMVB* in August.

[5] The Dissenters' Chapels Bill.

[6] Bonamy Price (see L. 1812 above).

[7] John Harden's sixth child Jessie (1814–1908) had married in 1843 the Revd. John Clay (d. 1877), Fellow of St. John's College, Cambridge (1836), and vicar of Stapenhill, Derbys. (1837–75). Jane had married in 1840 (see pt. i, L. 50).

[8] See pt. iii, L. 1275. Lady Parke was Cecilia, youngest daughter of Samuel Barlow of Middlethorpe, Yorks.

to take the tour of the Langdales afforded him 'One of the pleasantest excursions he had ever made'—and I mention this to shew you[1] we are not insensible to the gratification we ourselves have derived in return for the interruptions which I have in some sort complained of—the pleasure remains while the annoyance passes away. An advantage which also abides with us after the *pains* of travelling.

We saw all about the Canterbury meeting[2] but it was not till after your own report reached us, that we looked more minutely into the matter. When I saw your name as being the proposer of a vote of thanks—

We have not heard a word of M[r] Moxon since he was here—his was a hurried visit—and he was at home sooner than he intended to be when we parted from him at the Lake side, after crossing together from the Island to Bowness—for in a day or two M[r] Q. rec[d] *from London* a pair of Gloves which he had run away with. He had talked of a visit by the way.

Our dear Miss F. is now on her duties to her Somersetshire friends—and whether she will come northward in Nov[r] or not, depends upon our being able to find a habitation for her near us, where she can give accommodation to visitors—and this is doubtful—You perhaps know not of W[ms] intention of building for her—and of our being hitherto deterred by threatenings of Manorial impediments and—but this is a long subject that you must hear of viva voce—As also all about the Railway[3] that is to our annoyance—unless M[r] Q. enters upon these subjects. But if not it will be all in good time when we meet. Thanks for your news from Playford[4]—pray forget not when you write to communicate our love to, and interest in them and their

[1] M. W. first wrote 'So you see we', and left the first three words undeleted.

[2] The British Archaeological Association met on 9 Aug. See Sadler, iii. 244–6.

[3] The proposed Kendal and Windermere Railway. See L. 1839 below.

[4] 'Old Clarkson is really a wonderful creature.' H. C. R. had written on 18 Sept., 'were he only contemplated as an animal. There he is in his 85th year as laborious and calmly strenuous in his pursuits as he was fifty and sixty years ago, . . .writing letters assiduously both to private friends and for the press And all for his Africans.—He is happy in this that he really cannot see difficulties or dangers or doubts in any interest he has embraced or in any act he has to do—No one ever more faithfully discharged the duty of *hoping*, which the poet has laid down.' (Morley, ii. 568.)

concerns. And poor dear Mary Lamb[1]—What of her?—And now I think I have tired you by all this gossip—*Mind* you ask for it. One question I have not answered I find—and truly I cannot be sure but I think it was *this* spring that the Archbp of Dublin and his family were at Fox how. Best love from old Aunty and Dora with that of y^r affec

M. Wordsworth

You will observe that among our visitors I have not enumerated the family ones—our dear B^r and his son Ch Wordsworth and my nephew T. H.[2] and his Sister. The d^r Doctor was with us 3 happy weeks before the *height* of the season.

1831. W. W. to M. W.

MS. Fitzpark Museum, Keswick.
LY iii. 1381.

Underley Park
12 o'clock noon Tuesday
[24 Sept. 1844]

My dearest Mary,

Your letter most anxiously expected did not reach me till this moment. I rejoice that Dora appears to be recovering—I did not write earlier because not hearing either from yourself or Mrs Howard I was at a loss what to say or do. The way is now plain before me. I shall take Wm to Kendal tomorrow and wait for you, to convey you to Levens where we can arrive in time for dinner. I should recommend that you go to Ambleside before the arrival of the mail tomorrow, and bespeak a car to take you to Kendal, should there not be a place in the Mail, I mean to bespeak the car on that condition, and should there be no room in the mail must then come on in your Car.

We have passed our time very agreeably here except that on Sunday soon after coming out of Church I was seized with a violent attack in my bowels which were greatly disturbed all that day and part of yesterday; as you may recollect they were

[1] H. C. R. had not apparently seen Mary Lamb lately. He called on her on 21 Dec. with a Christmas present of a handsome shawl and had 'a nice chat'. (*HCR* ii. 647).

[2] Thomas Hutchinson, jnr.

attacked at Whitehaven a few years ago. I had a quiet night last night, but I fear the thing is not quite gone off. I long to see you again and also to be at home. Yesterday we went to the M[r] G[reene][1] two miles below Kirby L. and today we shall drive further, to Hornby Castle.[2] W[m] is out shooting, as he was all yesterday. He seems very well. Since my attack I live as plain as possible—meat and rice and no drink but two glasses of sherry and two small cups of tea. God bless you and Sister and Dora, and dearest love to all. Ever your affectionate Husband Wm Wordsworth.

Bad news from America. M[r] Thompson[3] is a Creditor upon a large scale. His Agent in America tells him that the taxes imposed for paying the interest, which payment was expected to be resumed next February are mere moonshine; for the act of congress did not authorize enforcing payment of the Taxes in case the persons liable refused; so that it is in vain to look for their voluntary payment, and if an act has not passed next session empowering the tax-gatherer to enforce payment things will be as bad as ever. In fact there is no honesty in the [? matter].

1832. W. W. to H. C. R.

Endorsed: 29th Septr 1844. Wordsworth.
MS. Dr. Williams's Library.
Morley, ii. 573.

Rydal Mount
29th Sept. 1844

My dear friend,

On returning home after an absence of a week I find your note of the 23rd I have tried in vain to find a substitute for tenacious; but see no objection to change the passage thus.

[1] Thomas Greene (1794–1872), of Slyne, and Whittington Hall, Lancs., M.P. for Lancaster, 1824–57, had rebuilt the Hall in an ambitious Tudor style, *c.* 1831.

[2] Hornby Castle, originally a pele tower of the 13th century, had passed through many hands before it became a focus of attention in the celebrated case of Wright v. Tatham (see pt. iii, L. 1066). In the 1840s the estate was acquired by Pudsey Dawson, a financier, who rebuilt the Castle to spectacular effect (1849–52).

[3] Alderman Thompson (see L. 1825 above) had numerous banking interests.

Our fond regrets, all that our hopes would grasp?
The sage's theory etc—[1]

M[rs] Quillinan was ill in a severe cold when I went away, it turned to an influenza and she still continues very poorly. I left home without M[rs] W— who remained to nurse her Daughter, but she joined me at Levens on Wednesday, and we returned together yesterday. viz, Saturday. My sister is as well as usual. My first visit was to M[r] Alderman Thompson's, a pretty place near Kirkby Lonsdale. During my stay (W[m] was with me) I saw a good deal of the rich and beautiful Vale of the Lune; among other places Hornby Castle, once the property and residence of the infamous Chartres.[2] They show a small turret room upon the top of the old Tower to be entered only by a trap door, in the floor; where some of his enormities were committed or attempted. The situation of the Castle is grand, commanding a noble view of Ingleborough 14 miles distant at the termination of a rich and spatious Vale.—

We have just heard from Miss Fenwick; her Letters have distressed us much, as she seems conscious of a change in the state of her health that is somewhat alarming, not, I mean, as to immediate effects, but causing apprehension. God grant that she may be mistaken. We are not likely to see her in West[nd] this Winter, which we exceedingly regret.

I find an accumulation of Letters requiring answers, so you must be content with this scrawl, sent because yours required as speedy an answer as I could give.

ever faithfully and affectionately yours
W. Wordsworth

[1] See *Roman Antiquities* (*PW* iii. 278) in the *Yarrow Revisited* volume of 1835. 'Tenacious' in l. 10 was an emendation of 1837 which W. W. in the end retained.

[2] Col. Francis Charteris (1675–1732), notorious swindler, satirised by Pope and Hogarth. His daughter Janet married James, 5th Earl of Wemyss (1699–1756), whose family possessed the Hornby Castle estates for a time.

1833. W. W. to EDWARD MOXON

MS. Henry E. Huntington Library.
LY iii. 1226.

Rydal
30th $Sept^{r}$ —44

My dear Mr Moxon,

Is there in existence a Rail-way Guide, to answer the purpose of Paterson's Book of Roads,[1] if not, I think it might answer for you to publish one. I have long wished that you had some book or Books like Murray's hand-books, for regular and constant Sale. I send you a sort of Specimen drawn by Mrs Howard of Levens, who has often wished for some thing of the kind. It ought to express by small drawings the object signified, a Church, a Castle, a Gentleman's Seat, a conspicuous hill, brook or river, or any other prominent object, marking its distance from the line. Verbum sat. Mrs Quillinan thanks you very much for executing so speedily and well her Miltonian Commission. She has had a shocking Influenza but is we hope getting better. We were glad of so good an account of Miss Lamb.

ever faithfully yours
Wm Wordsworth

I have been absent 10 days lately.—

We were all very sorry to hear that Mrs Moxon was poorly. The Morning Herald has been behaving ill to Mr C. Southey, and your neighbour Murray has been obliged to cry out 'peccavi' upon this same occasion.[2]

1834. W. W. to ISABELLA FENWICK

MS. WL.
LY iii. 1227.

[late Sept. *or* early Oct. 1844]

Your Letter, my beloved Friend, was but a sad greeting when Mary and I returned home, yesterday. It troubled us much;

[1] *A New and Accurate Description of all the Direct and Principal Cross Roads in Great Britain*, 1771 (18th enlarged edn., *c.* 1832). Daniel Paterson (1739–1825) was for many years assistant to the Quartermaster-General at the Horse Guards, and from 1812 Lieutenant-Governor of Quebec.

[2] See L. 1779 above.

Dora also we found but little improved. She has a better appetite, but coughs upon any exertion of talking or otherwise, and is also very weak. She says nevertheless, that she is going on favorably upon the whole. My poor Sister is as usual, better I think in point of health than any of the family.

We dread the notion of your wintering in London. The place never agreed with you, and Mr Taylor's House,[1] and its staircase particularly you always described as being most unfavourable to your health and comfort. On the other hand—but Mary has come in and I find has expressed what I was going to say about your health in connection with the place. She has also anticipated me in other matters, better expressed than I could have done. So I will confine myself to the main point; and I will come to it at once. Only assure me that you will not judge of my faults and infirmities so severely, perhaps I ought to say so *strictly* as you have done, and allow me to declare that I will *endeavour to mend*, and then, pressing you to my heart of hearts, I would exclaim, come once more and live under our roof till we can find or make a house for you to your mind. I am too conscious my dear Friend that I am unworthy of being always in your sight—but feelings of this kind in respect to some or other object must in every reflecting man's mind be incident to his humanity. It is all a question of degrees; be you tolerant, nay *indulgent*, and we shall do well together, if but I endeavour to improve as I promise you I will. Take these words as more than a promise—as a vow, and let me give you a Brother's kiss upon it.

I am aware of another obstacle to your becoming again our Inmate, Hannah being obliged to do work for which she is unfit, and which it is painful to you, and indeed to us all that she should have to do. Were she younger and freer from infirmity the objection would not exist; a fact too obvious to call for the remark from me. Dora has just come in and I have read her this last sentence. She suggests that Jane should take the waiting, and for the winter, at least, become a *parlour servant*—in which case our Housemaid could do *all* the Housemaid's work in *your room*. I am most thankful for this suggestion, for it seems entirely to remove an objection which I could not get over to my satisfaction—So once again let me entreat you to come to us. We will join you at Leamington and may return together.—I have said nothing about the house in the Wishing-gate Field.[2] Lady

[1] In Blandford Square, Regent's Park.

[2] See L. 1828 above, and *DWJ* i. 184.

F's Solicitor is in Ireland and nothing can be done about the exchange or purchase till his return; besides, all this may be settled when we meet. I am told also that I must conclude as this letter is to go to the Post immediately. Dora seems to have got a little more cold caused by the change of weather yesterday, when it rained a good deal. To day is very bright.—And now farewell, ever most affectionately and faithfully yours

Wm Wordsworth

1835. W. W. to CHARLES WILLIAM PASLEY[1]

Address: Major Gen: Pasley. [*To be delivered by hand?*]
MS. Mr. E. L. McAdam jnr. Hitherto unpublished.

[?Oct. 1844]

My dear General Pasley,

May I take the liberty to introduce my Son the Rev[d] John Wordsworth to You. He is about to prepare his eldest Son for Woolwich, and it has struck me that your friendly advice on the subject would be of very great use to him; and I am well assured that you would give it with pleasure.

Believe me
dear General
to be
faithfully yours
W[m] Wordsworth

[1] A letter of introduction provided for John W., but not necessarily used by him. It was probably written soon after L. 1823 above, and clearly before Pasley was made a K.C.B. in 1846. See also L. 1841 below.

1836. W. W. to BASIL MONTAGU

Endorsed: Wordsworth's letter sending me a lock of his Hair B. M. The last I ever received.

MS. Cambridge University Library.

Mem. (—). *Grosart* (—). *K* (—). *LY iii. 1228* (—).

Rydal Mount
Oct^br 1st 1844

My dear Montagu,

Absence from home has prevented my replying earlier to your Letter, which gave me much pleasure on many accounts, and particularly as I learned from it that you are so industrious and to such good effect. You have done well in complying with my request, and I rejoice that you burned my Letters and papers. Southey and Lamb both took pleasure in throwing off their thoughts and feelings with a pen in their hands. Southey used to say that his pen was his magic wand—with me it was and is quite otherwise—the touch of it half benumbs me. But see how they are treating my dear Friend—a Volume has been published already stuffed with S's Letters,[1] many of them containing opinions and expressions which ought never to have been given to the world; and every body else is served much in the same way. I dont wonder at your mention of the Friends whom we have lost by death. Bowles the poet still lives, and Rogers, all that survive of the poetical fraternity with whom I have had any intimacy. Southey Campbell and Cary[2] are no more. Of my class-fellow and school-fellows very few remain; my *intimate* associates of my own College are all gone long since. Myers[3] my cousin, Terrot,[4] Jones my Fellow-traveller,[5] Fleming[6] and his brother Raincock[7] of Pembroke, Bp Middleton[8] of the same

[1] For the *Memoir of William Taylor of Norwich*, see L. 1779 above.

[2] Henry Francis Cary had died at Willesden on 14 Aug. He was buried in Westminster Abbey, not far from the spot where Campbell had been laid to rest a few weeks before.

[3] John Myers (see pt. i, L. 2 and *EY*, p. 112).

[4] William Terrot (see *EY*, p. 49).

[5] Robert Jones, W. W.'s companion on the 'pedestrian tour' of 1790, and a life-long friend (see pt. iii, L. 920).

[6] The Revd. John Fleming of Rayrigg (see pt. iii, L. 861).

[7] Fletcher Raincock (see pt. i, L. 26, and *EY*, p. 70).

[8] Thomas Fanshaw Middleton (1769–1822), Bishop of Calcutta from 1814. He had been at Christ's Hospital with S. T. C. and Lamb, who described him in

College—it has pleased God that I should survive them all. Then there are none left but Joseph Cottle of the many Friends I made at Bristol, and in Somersetshire—yet we are only in our 75th year. But enough of this sad subject: let us be resigned under all dispensations and thankful for that is our duty however difficult it may be to perform it. I send you the lock of hair which you desired, white as snow, and taken from a residue which is thinning rapidly.

You neither mention your own health nor Mrs Montagu's, I conclude therefore that both of you are doing well. Pray remember me kindly to her and believe me my dear Montagu

your faithful and affectionate Friend,
Wm Wordsworth

In speaking of our Bristol Friends I forgot to mention John Pinney,[1] but him I have neither seen nor heard of for many years.

1837. W. W. to SARA COLERIDGE

MS. Victoria University Library, Toronto. Hitherto unpublished.

2nd Oct. 1844
R.M.

My dear Sarah,

Yesterday Dora showed me a Letter which she had just received from you; and I cannot forbear writing a line or two in consequence.

Pray do not be troubled because you cannot in justice to others supply your Brother Hartley with money.[2] He has quite enough for his reasonable wants, and any addition would only put it in his power to do himself more harm. Be assured I would not make this assertion without due knowledge and consideration. We were all sorry that you had harrassed yourself about the

Christ's Hospital Five and Thirty Years Ago as 'a scholar and a gentleman in his teens.' See also Griggs, i. 15, 18, 21, 26, 112.

[1] John Frederick Pinney (see *EY*, p. 148), who had inherited Racedown on his father's death in 1818. He died in 1845.

[2] Hartley's finances were a constant source of irritation to the Wordsworths, as M. W.'s MS. letters to Mrs. S. T. C. in the Victoria University Library, Toronto, show. 'I feel *at our age*', she wrote on 27 Aug. 1845, 'we should not defer to correct mistakes which might cause trouble to others.'

matter. Should Mr and Mrs Richardson resolve to give him up as a Lodger, which is not, we think, likely, it will then be time to think where he had best be placed. To one thing all his friends must make up their minds—that he would not stay in any house where he was to be watched and controuled as much as his infirmity would dispose his friends to do. As far as one can judge his health has suffered little, if at all, from his sad propensity—which is mainly owing to a cause that the command of more money would not do away with. M^r or Mrs Quillinan would give answers to the questions you put concerning your Father's Residence with us, which was only during our abode at Allan Bank, whither we went in the summer of [180]8. The whole of the Friend was written in that place by Sarah Hutchinson from your Father's dictation; it went from her pen to the Printer no transcript being taken.

I should have been a considerable Contributor to the Work, but your Father always beg[ged] me to wait till he had laid down his principles, which was never done. You are of course aware that it was much enlarged in the after Edition[1]—Ever my dear Sarah your most affectionate Friend and Father in heart-feeling

Wm Wordsworth

1838. W. W. to ISABELLA FENWICK

MS. WL.
LY iii. 1229.

5th Oct. [1844]

Your last Letter, my dear Friend, gave us upon the whole much comfort. The apprehensions which we had felt for the state of your health had been more painful than we would have ventured to express. Though not removed they are certainly mitigated by the contents of your last; and we were greatly relieved by being told that it was not to Mr Taylor's House in *London* that you were going, but to another, which he had taken in the Country. We readily acknowledge his strong claims upon your society and we are reconciled to the plan you have fixed upon for the winter, and look forward with pleasure to spending a fortnight

[1] The 3 vol. edition, published in Nov. 1818. For the textual history, see *The Collected Works of Samuel Taylor Coleridge, The Friend*, ed. Barbara E. Rooke, 2 vols., 1969, i. xxxv–xcvii.

ISABELLA FENWICK

from the miniature by Margaret Gillies, 1839

with you and our other dear Friends at Leamington. Our plan is to arrive there as near as may be at your time. The family of Ricketts, to whom we owe a visit, will not think it indicates less regard for them if we pay that visit at a time when we all may meet under their roof. They must feel that our age, and your infirmities beloved Friend considered, we cannot but be anxious to see as much of you as your engagements and duties will permit. Therefore pray let us know when you have fixed the time for your visit to Leamington. If it be not convenient for Mrs R— to welcome us under her own roof we hope there will be no difficulty in finding a lodging near. And all this must be settled before we start.—

Dora's illness continues to abate; but as she is so susceptible of taking cold, Dr Davy does not think it advisable that she should venture on a journey and residence at the sea-side so late in the year. That plan is therefore given up, which leaves us at liberty to move from home, at the time which may suit you and our other Friends.—

Mr Faber is at Green bank, and his health seems already much improved. He is inclined to prolong his stay though it was limited by his medical adviser to three or four days, the sea air being strongly recommended in preference to any other—He gives a very interesting account of the improvement he has wrought in his parish,[1] in every respect. It is, however too obvious that he is in the habit of using strong expressions, so that what he says must be taken with some qualification. This practise in so very pious, good and able a man is deeply to be regretted. Mary says to me, tell him of it; but if it be a specific fact, say of numbers or quantity in respect to which his accounts at different times have varied, it is surely an awkward thing to mention that to a gentleman. And if the diversity of statements concerns vague and indefinite matters, one does not see how one could fasten the charge upon the Speaker so as to produce any effect.

I have told him what I thought of his Poem[2] as far as I have read it. It is a mine of description, and valuable thought and feeling; but too minute and diffusive, and disproportioned; and in the workmanship very defective. The Poem was begun too

[1] For a full account of Faber's work at Elton, Hunts., see Chapman, *Father Faber*, pp. 93 ff. But he had already put himself under the direction of Newman, and felt drawn towards Rome.

[2] *Sir Lancelot.*

soon and carried on too rapidly before he had attained sufficient experience in the art of writing, and this he candidly and readily admits. Some of his Friends wish and urge him to continue writing verse. I had a long conversation with him upon the subject yesterday, in which he gave me such an account of himself that I could not concur with those advisers in their opinion. A man like him cannot serve two Masters. He has vowed himself as a Minister of the Gospel to the service of God. He is of that temperament that if he writes verse the Spirit must *possess* him, and the practise master him, to the great injury of his work as a Priest. Look at the case of Milton, he thought it his duty to take an active part in the troubles of his country, and consequently from his early manhood to the decline of his life he abandoned Poetry. Dante wrote his Poem in a great measure, perhaps entirely, when exile had separated him from the passions and what he thought the social duties, of his native City.[1] Cervantes, Camoens[2] and other illustrious foreigners wrote in prison and in exile, when they were cut off from all other employments. So will it be found with most others, they composed either under similar circumstances, or like Virgil and Horace, at entire leisure, in which they were placed by Patronage, and charged themselves with no other leading duty than fulfilling their mission in their several ways as Poets. Now I do believe as I told Mr Faber, that no man can write verses that will live in the hearts of his Fellow creatures but through an over powering impulse in his own mind, involving him often times in labour that he cannot dismiss or escape from, though his duty to himself and others may require it. Observe the difference of execution in the Poems of Coleridge and Southey, how masterly is the workmanship of the former, compared with the latter; the one persevered in labour unremittingly, the other could lay down his work at pleasure and turn to any thing else. But what was the result? Southey's Poems, notwithstanding the care and forethought with which most of them were planned after the material had been diligently collected, are read once but how

[1] Dante completed his *Divine Comedy* at Ravenna, in exile from his native Florence.

[2] Cervantes was imprisoned in Algiers (1575–80), and later Valladolid (1603–4), and some of his early poems and plays reflect his experiences. Camoens spent much of his adult life in exile in Portuguese India and Mozambique, only returning to Lisbon (1570) for the last decade of his life, during which his *Lusiads* appeared (1572).

rarely are they recurred to! how seldom quoted, and how few passages, notwithstanding the great merit of the works in many respects, are gotten by heart. You may think that I took a great deal of fruitless pains in stating all this and much more to my Friend, which he readily acknowledged—I think so too, being convinced that if he gives himself up exclusively to his sacred calling, it must be done through the firm conviction drawn from high and holier sources than external observations of his own or others however just.—

Yesterday I had a Letter from my Brother in which he tells me that his Son Chris. has been presented to a Stall at Westminster.[1] We are all truly glad of this, for Harrow was breaking up his health; and he was obviously from some cause or other unsuited to the situation. I have now scrawled you, my beloved Friend, a long and I fear unreadable Letter; but I am sure you will do your best to decypher it for my sake. God bless you now and for ever—Most affectionately and faithfully yours

Wm Wordsworth

1839. W. W. to WILLIAM EWART GLADSTONE[2]

MS. British Library.
LY iii. 1232.

Rydal Mount Oct. 15th—44.

My dear Mr Gladstone

We are in this neighbourhood all in consternation, that is, every man of taste and feeling, at the stir which is made for carrying a branch Railway from Kendal to the head of

[1] Peel had previously offered the canonry to C. W., but at his request it was transferred to his son. See *Christopher Wordsworth, Bishop of Lincoln*, pp. 110–11.

[2] *Endorsed: Mr Wordsworth*. Pleading the Cause of the Lake Scenery against the proposed Kendal and Windermere Railway, and sending a sonnet on the subject. The parties have been at this office on the subject, and W. Laing does not see much probability of the line being thrown overboard here on the grounds put forward by Mr W. who has written also to Genl Pasley.

Windermere.[1] When the subject comes before you officially,[2] as I suppose it will, pray give it more attention than its apparent importance may call for. In fact, the project if carried into effect will destroy the *staple* of the Country which is its beauty, and, on the Lord's day particularly, will prove subversive of its quiet, and be highly injurious to its morals. At present I shall say no more, only let me beg of you to cast your eye over a Letter which I propose shortly to address thro' the public Press to our two county Members upon the occasion.[3]

Believe me my dear Mr Gladstone
faithfully your much obliged
Wm Wordsworth

[1] The Lancaster and Carlisle Railway had been completed the previous summer, and it was now proposed to connect Kendal with it by means of a junction at Oxenholme, and to carry the branch line as far as Windermere. In his sonnet (1833) on *Steamboats, Viaducts and Railways* (*PW* iv. 47), and in conversation with Caroline Fox on 6 Oct., W. W. had expressed guarded approval of railways: 'He grieves that the ravens and eagles should be disturbed in their meditations, and fears that their endeavours after lyric poetry will be checked. However, he admits that railroads and all the mechanical achievements of this day are doing wonders for the next generation; indeed, it is the appropriate work of this age and this country, and it is doing it gloriously.' (*Memories of Old Friends*, ii. 37). But as subsequent letters show, he now set himself to oppose a development that would encroach on the beauty and retirement of his native region. For a full survey of the controversy that ensued, see *Prose Works*, iii. 331 ff. In the end, the poet's opposition was of no avail, and the branch line to Bowness was completed in 1846–7.

[2] As President of the Board of Trade, Gladstone had to present the Board's reports on all railway bills to Parliament.

[3] W. W. enclosed a copy in M. W.'s hand of his sonnet *On the Projected Kendal and Windermere Railway* (*PW* iii. 61), dated 12 Oct., which was to be published in the *Morning Post* on the 16th and thereafter in other local and national papers. The 'letter' to the county members which he also sent was not apparently published, but it probably rehearsed the arguments he was to use later in his two letters to the *Morning Post* in December (see L. 1855 below). Gladstone replied to W. W. on the 19th: 'It had been my hope that Orrest Head, and other like projections on the earth's surface, would have pleaded for themselves in terms intelligible to engineers and speculators—in other words that the expected traffic between Kendal and Winandermere, when compared with the natural obstacles to be overcome, would not have sustained the project of a Railway. You will observe that I do not refer to this as a reason preferable to yours, but as one which would more readily have brought about that practical solution of the question which you desire.' (*WL MSS.*)

1840. W. W. to CHARLES WILLIAM PASLEY

Endorsed: Mr Wordsworth the 15th Novr 1844.
MS. British Library. Hitherto unpublished.

Rydal Mount 15th Octr [1844]

My dear General Pasley,

All the old resident Gentlemen and Proprietors of this neighbourhood are greatly annoyed, with scarcely an exception, by the project of a Railway from Kendal to the head of Windermere.[1] The shares are already subscribed for and at a premium, which will not surprize you who are better, probably, than any one else, acquainted with the excesses to which the Railway Mania drives people on the present superabundances of Capital. Excuse my writing to you upon this occasion which I do to beg that when it comes before you, as probably it will, you would give it more attention than its apparent importance may call for. The traffic will be found quite contemptible, the *staple* of this country is its beauty and that will be destroyed by such a nuisance being carried through these narrow vales. At present nothing is publicly said of its being carried farther than within a mile of Ambleside,[2] but that is all nonsense. Attempts will assuredly be made and at no distant Period, to carry it on to Keswick, to Maryport, notwithstanding the high ground that parts Westmorland from Cumberland.

I purpose to address through the public Press, a Letter to our two County members, in opposition to the Scheme, and beg that you would condescend to give it a Perusal.

Yesterday I had the pleasure of a call from Captain Smyth[3] of the Royal Navy, and he has the same opinion of the affair as myself. He promised me that he would talk to you about it.

Mrs Wordsworth unites with me in kind remembrances to

[1] See previous letter. General Pasley was now Inspector General of Railways, having retired from the Chatham Arsenal in 1841.

[2] The original plan was that the line should terminate at Low Wood, but Bowness was substituted when it was proposed to supplement the railway with a Lake steamer. A cutting in the woods on St. Catherine's Walk is now all that remains of the original intention to carry the railway through Ambleside, Rydal, and Grasmere, to link up with another line being constructed between Keswick and Cockermouth. It may be that W. W.'s opposition was provoked in the first instance by the very real threat to his own property.

[3] See pt. iii, L. 1329.

yourself and Mrs Pasley, and believe me faithfully

yours
Wm Wordsworth

Could you aid me in having my Grandson's name, Henry Curwen Wordsworth, entered upon the list at Woolwich with a view to his being admitted at a proper age, as a Student. He is the eldest of five Sons, a promising lad ten years old, and his Father and Mother design him for your Profession—

1841. W. W. to CHARLES WILLIAM PASLEY

MS. Dr. E. L. McAdam, jnr. Hitherto unpublished.

Leamington 28th October
[1844]

My dear General Pasley,

Your very friendly Letter has followed me to this place[1] and I now write to thank you for the consideration you have given to both points upon which my Letter to you turned.

I have written as you suggest by this Post to Sir George Murray,[2] and will inform you of the result, as soon as I receive his answer.

I have had a very kind Letter from Mr Gladstone,[3] whom I have the honor of reckoning among my Friends, upon the subject of the Railway, and another from your Friend Captn Smyth. Both these Gentlemen lament a project which if carried into effect would so disturb and disfigure our beautiful Country. I would fain hope that if it should come before Paliament, we may with due exertion muster strong against it.

Believe me
faithfully your
much obliged
Wm Wordsworth

[1] Where the Wordsworths had arranged to meet I. F. and other friends.

[2] About his grandson Henry. General Sir George Murray, Bart. (1772–1846) performed distinguished service throughout the Napoleonic Wars, and became Governor of Sandhurst (1819–24), Commander-in-Chief, Ireland (1825–8), M.P. for Perth (1823–32, and 1834), Colonial Secretary under Wellington (1828–30), and finally Master-General of the Ordnance, a post he held until 1846. He edited *The Letters and Dispatches of John Churchill, first Duke of Marlborough, from 1702 to 1712*, 5 vols., 1845.

[3] See L. 1839 above.

1842. W. W. to C. W. JNR.

MS. untraced.
Christopher Wordsworth. Bishop of Lincoln, p. 66.

November, 1844

My dear Nephew,

Heartily do we all rejoice in the event[1] of which we had before heard from your father. We are glad especially on account of your health, that you are leaving Harrow; and this new situation seems exactly fitted for you, provided you can unite with it some parochial work which may not be too much for your strength. A residence in London will enable you to serve the Church in many ways through her various societies, and bring you near to her several heads, for her benefit; as I cannot but confidently hope.

[*cetera desunt*]

1843. M. W. to H. C. R.

Endorsed: 1844. Mrs Wordsworth.
MS. Dr. Williams's Library.
Morley, ii. 575.

Rydal Mount Nov 4th [1844]

My dear Friend

Your interesting *double* letter bearing date the 1st and 6th inst was fowarded to us by Dora to Cambridge and, as she told us at the same time that, as a reward for the privilege of reading it, her husband had answered it for me, knowing we were *upon the move*—and as he would naturally give you some account of our proceedings—I have nothing to say in *reply* to your communication which I have re-read this morng—than, to express my deep sympathy in your family perplexities and the cause thereof—the necessity of an uprooting for your dear Brother is truly a sad grievance—and yet the reason for contemplating such a wrench justifies it. Not for a moment dear friend must (if *necessity* requires the sacrifice) you think of us and our severe disappointment—but we do hope arrangements may be decided upon that may not deprive us of what we now deem our rightful

[1] His preferment to a Canonry of Westminster. See L. 1838 above.

gratification and claim upon you—I know you will do your best to come to us—*but* if duty and affection says nay—why, we must submit with the best grace we can.

My husband and I passed a most pleasant Month in Company with our beloved Friend,[1] paying our several visits—particulars of which, I must still venture to reserve for our after-dinner chat—before we draw round the Whist table—by the bye we *now* pass *one* hour each evening, thus profitably employed—which amuses poor Dora (Mr Carter is our 4th) whom you will be sorry to hear we found very unwell on our arrival at home—and that she continues exceedingly weak, and unable to join her family upon the Island. In the course of next week Mr Q. and his daughters return to winter quarters in Ambleside when I trust poor Dora may be strong enough to go to them—altho' at present she is obliged to keep to the Sofa most part of the day.

Our dear friend Miss Fenwick is with the Taylors—you will probably find a note upon your Table from her, as I told her you were to be in Town on the 26th, if not I may as well tell you that her address is 'Ladon House Mortlake Surry'. There she remains till Feb^{ry} when, with God's blessing, she will return to Mrs Peddar's house in Ambleside which she has taken for the following 3 or 4 Months—afterwards we trust she will be again our Inmate. What do you think of dear Mrs Arnold having volunteered to come and play Whist with us tomorrow Even^{g}!!—We have never seen or even heard of The Fragments,[2] except from your letter. 'The Life etc'[3] sells swim[m]ingly and is universally read with delight—but—(tho' perhaps I ought not to speak of it—and Mr S. does not wish that the profits should be his)—but they are and the family has *hitherto* (by their own decision) no benefit from the work. Is this right circumstances considered?—

Our Neighbours are all in their usual way—Mr Carr been a sufferer of late—it will be a disappointment—a great one to him if you do not come—and as for y^{r} Friend James, I know not how he will be pacified—by the by I must tell you what he said to me upon my asking him for a certain newspaper the other day—He observed he had not read one for a very long time, indeed he seldom did, '*natural* books were more to his fancy'.

[1] I. F. From Leamington they also visited Herbert and Bertha Hill at Warwick School.

[2] Arnold's *Fragments on Church and State*, publ. 1844.

[3] A. P. Stanley's biography.

I hope you will be able to send us good tidings not only of yourself, but of your brother and Niece, and believe me with the united love of the household affec my dear Friend

Your's
M Wordsworth.

P.S. I was glad to hear so favorable an acct of dear Mary Lamb, and of Miss Rogers. The Coleridges too—to all of whom kindest remembrances.

1844. W. W. to SAMUEL CROMPTON[1]

MS. untraced.
K (—). *LY iii. 1232* (—).

Rydal Mount, Nov. 14, 1844.

Dear Sir,

On returning home yesterday, I found your letter. The facts are most important, and ought to be circulated all the world over, and highly satisfactory would it be to me to assist in making them known. . . . An edition of my poems in double columns or some other cheap form is indeed likely to be published at no distant period, and I might attach to the description of the blind man in *The Excursion* a note such as you desire. Your conjecture concerning that passage is remarkable; Mr Gough[2] of Kendal, whom I had the pleasure of knowing, was the person from whom I drew the picture, which is in no respect exaggerated. He was an extraordinary person, highly gifted; and how painful is it to think that in all probability his sight was lost to him by want of the knowledge which you are anxious to circulate. The sadness which the contemplation of blindness always produces was in Mr Gough's case tempered by admiration and wonder in the most affecting manner. During my late absence I stayed some time at Leamington, and there became acquainted with two blind ladies, the one named Buchanan, the other Williams; both of them interested me greatly. Mrs B.'s case was, I apprehend, inflammation of the optic nerve; she suffered from violent pains in the head. Her

[1] A Manchester surgeon 'who thinks that a great proportion of the blindness in this country might be prevented by attention to the diseases of the eye in the young'. (Lady Richardson, quoted by K.)

[2] See *MY* ii. 115.

husband took [her] the round of the German baths, and placed her under the most eminent physicians of the country, but without any benefit. The particulars of Miss W.'s case I could learn, and would transmit them to you if you desire it. She became blind young, as appears from the verses written by her father, which I send you, and is now past middle age—a most intelligent woman—

. . . You could have scarcely mentioned the influence of my Poems over your mind in any way so likely to gratify me, as by coupling them with that delightful and precious book, Walton's Lives. It is singular that this individual Book is the only one which tempted me to any thing like reading during the last month while I have been moving from place to place. . . .[1]

I remain, dear Sir, with great respect sincerely yours,

Wm Wordsworth

1845. W. W. to [?] HORATIO SMITH[2]

MS. Cornell.
LY iii. 1232.

Rydal Mount
Nov. 14th 1844

Sir,

Having been a Wanderer for the last month I could not thank you earlier for your threnody on your departed Friend, the Poet Campbell. You have done justice to his memory in a manner which does equal credit to the Mourned and to the Mourner.

Believe me sincerely
Your much obliged
Wm Wordsworth

[1] This paragraph supplied from a bookseller's catalogue.

[2] Horatio Smith (1779–1849), poet, historical novelist, and co-author with his brother James of *Rejected Addresses*, 1812. The poem referred to here is probably *Campbell's Funeral* (*Poetical Works*, 2 vols., 1846, i. 121). Like other close friends of Campbell, Horace Smith deplored the decision to inter his remains in Westminster Abbey rather than beside his beloved Clyde.

1846. W. W. to BERNARD BARTON

MS. Swarthmore College Library.
J. E. Wells, 'Wordsworth and Railways in 1844–1845', Modern Language Quarterly, vi (1945), 35–50.

15 Nov^er [44]

Dear Friend,

You pay my Effusion[1] too great a Compliment in desiring a Copy of it. I send it however as a tribute to the sympathy with my views of the subject which you feelingly express.

This Railway is a mere gambling speculation, and not only uncalled for, but the Country through which it is to pass when it comes in view of Windermere is almost to a Man against it.

Believe me with much respect very faithfully yours

Wm Wordsworth

I have been a month from home or your's would have been earlier acknowledged

1847. W. W. to CHARLES WILLIAM PASLEY

Endorsed: W. Wordsworth.
MS. Cornell.
Broughton, p. 87.

Rydal Mount
Nov. 16th — 1844.

My dear General Paisley,

I am just returned home after a long ramble, and can sit down with more satisfaction to thank you for the trouble you kindly

[1] W. W. and Bernard Barton corresponded occasionally about business matters and poetry. 'Moxon's edition is quite a treasure to me,' Barton had written on 3 Feb. 1840, 'but I still wish to see more from the same source.' And he wrote again on 21 Nov. 1844 to thank W. W. for his sonnet on the Kendal and Windermere Railway: 'My own dislike to the uncalled for and absurd multiplication of rail-roads would have induced me to read with interest and sympathy any tolerable protest against a growing nuisance, which I could believe to be genuine and heart-felt. I must needs admire, and cordially love thine—and earnestly wish it could arrest the progress of so barbarous an intrusion on the beautiful romance of thy fairy region . . .' (*WL MSS.*) Not all of W. W.'s friends viewed his intervention so favourably, however. See, for example, Barron Field's letters to H. C. R. of 21 Oct. 1844 and 16 Feb. 1845 (Morley, ii. 575, 591).

took in my little Grandsons behalf.[1] Sir George Murray in the kindest terms wrote telling me that he had put the Boy in nomination upon the List. If he succeeds in being elected I hope he will prove worthy of his noble profession.

The managers of the obnoxious Kendal and Windermere Railway have determined to change the terminus, which is now designed to come no further than within a mile of Bowness.[2] It is an absurd Project and cannot but be attended with great loss to those who remain shareholders after the persons who have set it on foot have sold out. It is to be hoped that the Board of Trade will look sharply to these Schemes of which no few originate in mere gambling speculation, taking advantage of those who have money they don't know what to do with, and little wit.

I remain my dear General faithfully your

much obliged
Wm Wordsworth

1848. W. W. to MRS. HARRISON[3]

MS. WL.
LY iii. 1233.

Rydal Mount Novr 17th 1844

Dear Mrs Harrison,

Both parcels, the small and the large One, which you kindly forwarded, arrived safe without any injury from damp as you feared. Mrs Quillinan for whom I hold the pen would have written to you with thanks for your kind note had she not thought it better to wait till she could announce our arrival, but unfortunately she has had a severe attack of her old complaint, and is still unable to do anything.

Like yourself Mrs Wordsworth and I have had a sight of the Queen.[4] We met her Majesty and her retinue in the Town of

[1] See L. 1840 above.

[2] The line terminated at the hamlet of Birthwaite, then separated by open country from Bowness.

[3] Of Hundhow.

[4] Queen Victoria and Prince Albert had travelled by the Birmingham railway on their way to Burghley House, Stamford, for the christening of Victoria, later Lady Carbery, younger daughter of Brownlow Cecil, 2nd Marquess of Exeter (1795–1867). Lord Exeter was Steward of the Royal Household, 1858–9.

Northampton, were we [were] stopped two hours by the arrangements and the crowd. The most interesting sight of the day for us was the decoration of the villages and small towns before we reached Northampton. We passed under many triumphal Arches ornamented with laurel boughs and flowers, and every little cottage had its sprig or branch either at the threshold or over one or more of the Windows. How the Queen looked I could not say, or more than that I saw a woman's face under a black bonnet, from the top of the Coach which I had mounted for the sake of the view.

We were absent a month all but one day, a fortnight at Leamington, and the remainder of the time at Cambridge, and Elton, Mr Faber's parish where we found him doing a great deal of good, among a flock which had been long neglected.

It is about three weeks since we heard of Isabella and her Husband. Her health appeared to be improving. The Letter was dated *Sienna* and they were on their way to Rome.

Mr and Mrs Quillinan will take up their abode in Ambleside at their old Lodgings on the third of next Month. Mrs Q. will remain with us till that time; her Husband and his Daughters are at the Island, which he enjoys mightily. It is indeed an enchanting place.

With kind remembrances from all to yourself and Mr Harrison, I remain, dear Mrs H. faithfully yours

Wm Wordsworth

1849. W. W. to HENRY REED

Address: Henry Reed Esqre, Philadelphia. U.S. *paid.*
Postmark: (1) 19 Nov. 1844 (2) 20 Nov. 1844.
Stamp: Ambleside.
MS. Pennsylvania University Library.
Mem. (—). *Grosart* (—). *K* (—). *Wordsworth and Reed, p. 135.*

Novr 18th 1844

My dear Mr Reed

Mrs Wordsworth and I have been absent from home for a month past, and we deferred acknowledging your acceptable Letter[1] till our return. Among the places to which we went on

[1] Henry Reed had written on 14 Oct. about W. W.'s birthday celebrations (see L. 1790 above): 'I could not help thinking how much more truth—living, active

visits to our Friends was Cambridge, where I was happy to learn that great improvement was going on among the young Men. They were become much more regular in their conduct and attentive to their duties. Our Host was the Master of Trinity College, Dr Whewell, Successor to my Brother Dr Wordsworth, who filled the office for more than 20 years highly to his honor, and resigned before he was disqualified by age lest[1] as his years advanced his judgment might be impaired and his powers become unfit for the responsibility without his being aware of it. This, you will agree with me was a noble example; may it be followed by others. In matter of religion to which the thoughts of the Youth in general are much more turned than heretofore, I was pleased to learn that what is commonly called low church, is quite in disrepute, without any tendency to Popery as far as appears.[2] On our return home we were detained two hours at Northampton by the vast crowd assembled to greet the Queen on her way to Burleigh House. Shouts and ringing of bells there were in abundance; but these are things of course—it did please us however greatly to see every village we passed through for the space of 22 miles decorated with triumphal arches, and every cottage however humble with its little display of laurel boughs and flowers, hung from the windows and the doors. The people young and old were all making a holy day, and the Queen if she had the least of a human heart in her could not but be affected with these universal manifestations of affectionate loyalty. As I

truth there was in such a festivity than in the cold subtleties of speculative Science, and is it not becoming plainer every year that the Political Economy, which has heretofore for the most part assumed to be sole arbiter, will only make the Poor-Law perplexities a thousand-fold more perplexed,—especially where there is a fearful disparity between the rich and poor, unless the Church and her members restore some of her neglected Catholic attributes in order somewhat to realize socially that brotherhood of man and man that exists in the Church, but can be found in no political system that ever was devised by *human* skill.' (*Wordsworth and Reed*, pp. 130–1).

[1] *Written* least.

[2] On 7 Nov. W. W. had attended a meeting of the Cambridge Camden Society, the high-church group devoted to the revival of true ecclesiological principles in the Church of England. Its President, Thomas Thorp (see pt. ii, L. 593) stated that W. W. 'might be considered one of the founders of the Society. He had sown the seed which was breaking out now among them, as in other directions, to the recall of whatever was pure and imaginative, whatever was not merely utilitarian, to the service of both Church and State.' See James F. White, *The Cambridge Movement, The Ecclesiologists and the Gothic Revival*, 1962, p. 28.

have said we were detained two hours and I much regret that it did not strike me at the moment to throw off my feelings in verse, for I had ample time to have done so, and might perhaps have contrived to present through some of the authorities the tribute to my royal Mistress. How must these words shock your republican ears! But you are too well acquainted with mankind and their history not to be aware that love of country can clothe itself in many shapes!

From a private quarter I heard lately an unpromising account respecting the resumption of payment by your State. The public papers however speak more hopefully. It was told me that as there was no clause *compelling* the payment of the taxes to be raised—the act would be of no effect. I trust that the people will be honest enough to do their duty without such compulsion, or if it should not prove so, that the Legislature will supply what is necessary.

I need not say what pleasure it would give us to see you and Mrs Reed in our beautiful place of abode.

I have no wish to see the Review of my Poems to which you allude,[1] nor should I heed it if it fell in my way. It is too late in life for me to profit by censure, and I am indifferent to praise merely as such.

Mrs Wordsworth will be happy to write her opinion of the Portrait[2] as you request. Believe me my dear Mr Reed faithfully yours Wm Wordsworth—Excuse haste—have an accumulation of Letters to answer—

[1] 'Wordsworth's Poetical Works', *North American Review*, lix (1844) 352–84, a discussion of Henry Reed's Philadelphia edition of 1837, which examined W. W. as 'the pioneer of the new school' of poetry, 'for many years its martyr, and now its patriarch.' The article claimed to detect ambiguities in W. W.'s political views: 'In truth, when Wordsworth deals with virtue, freedom, justice, and truth in the abstract, or blends them with majestic images drawn from the sublimest aspects of the universe, no poet can be more grand and impressive; but when he connects these with the acts and policies of English Tory politicians, or with the state and church of England, we are conscious that the analogy is false, if not ludicrous.' In his letter, Reed had deplored the lack of 'any adequate disquisition on the political character of your poetry'.

[2] Inman's. Reed had written that: 'It will be more valued by me and mine that I can venture to express to you—and will, I trust, be prized by my children after me, as the likeness of one whom (besides his literary fame) it was their father's privilege to call his friend—on many accounts his friend and benefactor.'

[*M. W. adds*]

My dear Sir

It is gratifying to me to be able to answer the questions you have done me the honor to ask with perfect sincerity, in a way that must be satisfactory to you; for I can have no hesitation in saying that in my opinion, and what is of more value to *my feelings* Mr Inman's Portrait of my Husband is the best likeness that has been taken of him. And I am happy on this occasion to congratulate you and Mrs Reed upon the possession of so valuable a treasure: at the same time I must express the obligations I feel to the Painter for having produced so faithfully a Record. To this testimony I may add that my daughter and her younger Brother—(her Elder is abroad and has not seen it) are as much satisfied with the Portrait of their Father as I am.

Believe me dear Sir with respectful regards to Mrs Reed very sincerely your obliged

M. Wordsworth

1850. W. W. to PATRICK ROBERTSON, LORD ROBERTSON[1]

MS. Hornby Library MSS., Liverpool Public Libraries. Hitherto unpublished.

Rydal Mount
24th Novr 1844

My Lord,

I have seldom written an Autograph with more pleasure than I am doing now as a return for the gratification which your "Leaves from a Journal" have afforded me, scarcely less by your Pictures of the Scenes which I have beheld, than of others which untoward circumstances of the time did not permit me to see.

You have carried with You to Italy much Learning, and a poetic sensibility dictating lively expression; and, that being every where obvious, imperfections of mere Workmanship, for

[1] Patrick Robertson, Lord Robertson (1794–1855), wit and *bon viveur*, was called to the Scottish bar along with his lifelong friend John Wilson in 1815, became a judge in 1843, and Rector of Aberdeen University in 1848. He published *Leaves from a Journal*, Edinburgh [privately printed], 1844, and several other indifferent volumes of verse. In *Peter's Letters to his Kinsfolk*, Lockhart gives a vivid picture of Robertson's prowess as a dinner-table raconteur and master of ceremonies.

these you are aware your Verses are not without, will, by such persons as you desire to please, be little regarded.

I have the honor to be
My Lord
Your obliged
Wm Wordsworth

1851. W. W. to EDWARD MOXON

MS. Henry E. Huntington Library.
LY iii. 1234.

Rydal Mount
29th Novr 1844

My dear Mr Moxon,

We are all most concerned at the account in the Papers of the Robbery at Mr Rogers's Bank. Pray tell us about it; and how it is likely to affect our excellent Friend and his Sister if the stolen property should not be recovered.[1] But we trust this cannot happen. Give our affectionate condolences upon this distressing occasion; and mention anything that may have come to your knowledge about it which, you think, would interest us.

We were sorry to be so near London lately without seeing you and other Friends. But it would have kept us longer from home than we could be spared; besides the season for persons of our age was unsuitable to moving about. We are all pretty well though Mrs Quillinan has lately been much the contrary. Mr Q. is still at the Island, his wife with us: In a few days they go to Ambleside for the winter.

We hope you are all well, pray remember us kindly to your family; and believe [me] my dear Mr Moxon

faithfully yours
Wm Wordsworth

[1] On the previous Sunday the Bank of which Rogers was Chairman was robbed of over £46,000, mostly in notes. In the race which ensued between the Bank and the robbers, as to who could first get into touch with the foreign banks, the Bank won, and did not in the end lose very heavily. Rogers met the affair with cheerful fortitude. 'I should be ashamed of myself,' he said, 'if I were unable to bear a shock like this at my age.' See *Rogers*, ii. 253–5; Morley, ii. 578.

1852. W. W. to SARA COLERIDGE

MS. Victoria University Library, Toronto. Hitherto unpublished.

Rydal Mount Novr last day 1844

My very dear Sara,

I have written to Lord Lonsdale[1] and unless I lose this day's Post, I have only time to tell you so, as I must myself be the Bearer to Ambleside of both letters.

I trust this beautiful weather is doing you good. Dora is wonderfully improved within these two days.

Love to your Mother—and ever most affectionately yours

Wm Wordsworth

[*M. W. adds*]

Dr S.[2] Pray give the enclosed bill to y^r Mother. God bless you and yrs.

1853. W. W. to SARA COLERIDGE

MS. Victoria University Library, Toronto. Hitherto unpublished.

Rydal Mount
1st Dec 1844

My dear Sara,

Lord Lonsdale writes me that he has no influence over the Proctorship,[3] that is wholly at the disposal of Sir R. Peel. He adds, that if he had any power it would be exerted in favour of a gentleman whom he names, Mr Mandell.[4] Mr Townsend therefore as perhaps he has already learned, has nothing to expect from that quarter. I shall be sorry if he is disappointed.

I hope that your health continues to mend. Our weather here has been most beautiful—today a brilliant sunshine after a calm

[1] See next letter.

[2] i.e. Dear Sara.

[3] W. W. had agreed to approach the new Lord Lonsdale on behalf of Chauncy Hare Townshend who was seeking ecclesiastical preferment.

[4] Probably the Revd. John Mandell, of Bolton, Cumb. He graduated from St. Catherine's College, Cambridge, in 1826, and served as curate of Colne, Hunts., *c.* 1841–3, but his name disappears from the *Clergy Lists* in 1844. His brother William Mandell (1781–1843), Fellow of Queens' from 1803, was a notable Cambridge Evangelical.

night of hoar frost for the first time. Dora is going on well. She leaves us tomorrow for her winter Quarters at her old Residence in Ambleside. Mrs W. has been in general [in] very good health, but she over-exerts herself in walking to Ambleside and in other quarters. My dear Sister goes on much as usual. Hartley is quite well. He has been defending me in a Kendal Newspaper against a clamor raised by my opposition to the railway between Kendal and Windermere.[1] My friendship for Dr Arnold has induced me to look into certain Reviews of his life; Aversion to his opinions theological and ecclesiastical especially the latter coloured the several writers' views of his character as a man.[2]

ever faithfully my dear Sara
your affectionate Friend
W W.

1854. W. W. and M. W. to EDWARD MOXON

MS. Henry E. Huntington Library.
LY iii. 1235 (—).

Rydal Mount
4 Dec^br^ 1844

My dear Mr Moxon,

Many thanks for your Note.—I have written to Mr [? Haslan][3] Secretary to the Sanatorium[4] to request he would apply to you for the payment of my Subscription to that Institution—one guinea. Be so kind as to let him have the money.

ever faithfully
your much obliged
Wm Wordsworth

Say all that is affectionate and kind to Mr Rogers. He bears this cross[5] as I had no doubt he would, and I sincerely wish that in the end the loss may prove inconsiderable. It is a shocking affair.

[1] Hartley Coleridge's letter in the *Kendal Mercury* on 23 Nov. (repr. by Wells, op. cit.), protested against any wish on W. W.'s part to 'keep the Lakes to himself and his wealthier friends'.

[2] See also L. 1812 above.

[3] *MS. obscure.*

[4] Dr. Southwood Smith's sanatorium. See L. 1382 above.

[5] See L. 1851 above.

[*M. W. writes*]

My dear Mr Moxon

In addition to my Husband's request for the payment of a Guinea on his acc^t—I must beg you at some *convenient* opportunity to pay for me £1—in the name of Mrs Lockwood London. The Some[1] was given to Mr W. by one of our Tourists last Summer, to whom he shewed the accompanying Prospectus—He feeling an interest in the Project.

Your much obliged
M. Wordsworth

P.S.

I *think* I have not sent to you before on this acc^t—if so you will just take no notice of it. My memory fails me sadly.

1855. W. W. to H. C. R.

Endorsed: 8th Decr 1844. Wordsworth.
MS. Dr. Williams's Library.
Morley, ii. 579.

Rydal. 8th Dec^br 1844

My dear Friend

Miss Martineau[2] is coming to Mr Gregg,[3] at the head of Windermere, and we shall have you and the Mesmerism Convert in all your glory! and for us all yourself included there is a still better thing in prospect, Miss Fenwick in the 2nd week of next month and probably, along with her, our dear little Friend, Anna Rickettes. We rejoice that the state of your Brother's health is not so threatening as to require your being in attendance, and pray assure him of our best wishes.[4]

[1] i.e. Sum.

[2] Harriet Martineau was about to move from Tynemouth to Ambleside. After a prolonged period of ill-health she had, on Basil Montagu's advice, turned to mesmerism.

[3] William Rathbone Greg (1809–81), mill-owner, essayist and political commentator, settled in Ambleside in 1842 for the sake of his wife's health. His best-known work was *The Creed of Christendom*, 1851. He became a Commissioner at the Board of Customs (1856) and Comptroller of the Stationery Office (1864–77), and published several volumes of essays which Lord Morley discussed in his *Miscellanies*. He was, according to H. C. R., 'a whig radical and a man of some literature.' (Morley ii. 584).

[4] Thomas Robinson (d. 1860) suffered from epileptic fits.

8 December 1844

We have had very fine bright weather since our return, though the frost has been for some days most severe. The Thermometer, Dr Briggs[1] says, never so low since—96. I know not what you may think of public affairs, but we are all much concerned for the distracted state of the Church,[2] and for the privations of so many among the labouring poor. As to the former, it may in time work to some good, for the latter I cannot foresee any material benefit. They multiply in all directions the standard of civilization being so low among them, and evil proceeding from ignorance for which the upper classes have not virtue enough to prepare a remedy or material palliation. Then there is America growing worse and worse; and state murders committed in Spain[3] without remorse.

You will have an opportunity of reading here, a Book which though somewhat over minute and consequently in parts tedious has interested us much. It is written by the Librarian at Lambeth,[4] and entitled, the dark ages. It confirms, without alluding to any thing of mine all that I had previously thrown out upon the benefits conferred by monastic institutions, and exposing the ignorance of Robertson[5] Milner[6] Mosheim[7] and others upon this subject—repels most successfully their calumnies.

[1] Hartley Coleridge's 'excellent, aged friend Dr. Briggs' of Ambleside. For the family, see *Letters of Hartley Coleridge* (ed. Griggs), p. 280.

[2] The Romeward movement at Oxford was now gathering momentum, under the influence of W. G. Ward's *Ideal of a Christian Church* (1844), which pushed Tractarian principles to extremes.

[3] After the close of the Carlist wars in 1839, rival generals became the arbiters of Spanish political life: first Espartero, and then (1844–54) Ramón Maria Narvaez, who introduced a new constitution. The country was split into rival factions and was constantly disturbed by plots and counter-plots.

[4] Samuel Roffey Maitland (1792–1866), Librarian at Lambeth Palace from 1838. His contributions to the *British Magazine* were republished in *The Dark Ages*, 1844, and *Essays on subjects connected with the Reformation in England*, 1849.

[5] Dr. William Robertson (1721–93), historian and Principal of Edinburgh University, 1762–92: author of *The History of the Reign of the Emperor Charles V, with a view of the progress of Society in Europe, from the subversion of the Roman Empire to the beginning of the sixteenth century*, 3 vols., 1769.

[6] Joseph Milner (1744–97), Evangelical churchman: author of *History of the Church of Christ*, 1794–7, edited and continued by his brother Isaac, Wilberforce's friend.

[7] Johann Lorenz von Mosheim (1694–1755), Lutheran historian and Professor at Göttingen from 1747. His *Institutiones Historiae Ecclesiasticae* went through numerous editions and translations in W. W.'s lifetime.

I have just sent a long letter, probably much too long for insertion in their Paper, to the Editor of the Morning Post,[1] upon the Railway with which we are threatened by some gambling Speculators.[2] I am not so simple as to think that my paper if published would stop the nuisance, but collaterally it might set opinion right in some quarters. Many thanks for your notice of Rogers's misfortune. It is well borne by the parties— We have heard twice from Moxon on the subject

Ever faithfully yours
Wm Wordsworth

1856. W. W. to WILLIAM JACKSON

MS. Cornell. Hitherto unpublished.

Rydal Mount Decr 12th
[1844]

My dear Friend,

(I M. W. am holding the pen for my husband)

As you conjecture I received a letter from John,[3] written the day after he had attended the Funeral and by yesterday's Post I despatched a letter of condolence to Lady Frederic. We were grievously shocked by the sad news. Miss Thompson[4] was a most excellent Person and beloved by every one, who had opportunities of knowing her intimately, and her loss coming so soon after that of her dear Friend,[5] is doubly affecting. We are comforted by hearing from you that Lady F., tho' writing from her bed describes herself as not ill—but how sad must be her

[1] W. W.'s first letter on the Kendal and Windermere railway, dated 9 Dec. and published in the *Morning Post* on the 11th (repr. in the *Westmorland Gazette* on the 21st). By this time W. W. was convinced that the grounds of his opposition to the scheme had been misunderstood and widely misrepresented, as he complained to Lady Richardson on 21 Nov. (see Grosart, iii. 448), and in this letter, and a second on 20 Dec. (see L. 1858 below), he sought to explain his objections more fully than had been possible in his sonnet, and mobilise public opinion against the proposal. For the revised texts of the two letters, see Ls. 1867 and 1875 below.

[2] *Written* Specutors.

[3] John W., now in Rome.

[4] Miss Thompson, close friend of the Lowther Castle circle, had just died in Italy.

[5] The late Lord Lonsdale.

thoughts in finding her intentions towards her Friend thus suddenly frustrated.

From John's letter we gather no particulars beyond what you mention, relating to the sad events, except his fear that vigorous measures had not been resorted to in time. Of course *he* could know nothing of the matter, except what he might hear from others—perhaps from the Physician who attended his Wife for some time at the Baths of Lucca, and under whose care she now is at Rome. I trust however there is no foundation for such a report—and it is better not to mention it. Only I know that good medical advice is not procurable at Rome or in any part of Italy. We are most anxious to hear what step Lady F. will take, and will be greatly obliged by any tidings you may be able to send us. I hope however she will write to me herself.

John writes in bad spirits, shocked by this event, and suffering much anxiety from the state of his Wife's health; the long journey over bad roads was too much for her, and brought back painful symptoms of her original complaint, and probably from a sudden change of weather to severe frost, she has had a return of inflammatory action in her chest—So that poor fellow! he is greatly to be pitied—such renewal of anxiety on his Wife's account returning after so long an absence from his home, and his Parish—and bearing in mind how advanced in Life his Parents are—and the weak state of his Sister's health—his expences also are unavoidably great for his means—and then he is sadly annoyed by what he hears of the Workington and Cockermouth Railway[1] being to pass within 10 yards of his dining-room Window—cutting between him and the River, thro his Garden and little pleasure-ground—in a great measure the work of his own hands. Do you not think that Ld. Lonsdale, being the Patron of the Living, might interfere, so far at least as to have the Line diverted—to a reasonable distance on the other side of the House i.e., between the entrance to the Parsonage and the high road—this would still be bad, but the other must make the House uninhabitable. John thinks that the *damage money* saved by such alteration would pay the expence of it.

On the subject of the Kendal and Windermere Railway see, if you have opportunity, a long letter of mine in the Morning Post of yesterday.[2]

We are much concerned to hear no better account of M^rs^ J's

[1] Opened Apr. 1847. See also Ls. 1859 and 1860 below.

[2] See previous letter.

health—which seems to be much in the same state as that of poor Dora. She was not able, from weakness, after her severe attack in our absence, to return to the Island—and did not leave Rydal till last Thursday, when her Husband and she took possession of their Winter Quarters in Ambleside. Pray give our joint love and best wishes for Mrs Jackson's recovery—and that you may all escape colds during this very severe season believe me ever to be your

affectionate friend
[*signed*] Wm Wordsworth

1857. W. W. to THOMAS BOYLES MURRAY[1]

Address: To The Rev. T. B. Murray.
MS. WL transcript. Hitherto unpublished.

Rydal Mount
12 Decr 1844.

My dear Sir,

Notwithstanding the privilege you have allowed me of not replying to your Letter, I cannot refrain from thanking you, and for the little Book[2] which you have kindly sent me. I have looked it over and am so much pleased with its contents, that I shall make a point of putting it into the hands of my Grandchildren, who, I have no doubt, will con it with pleasure and profit.

Thanks for your obliging offer to send me intelligence respecting the proceedings of the ecclesiastical commission. At present I have no enquiries to make, but am not less interested in that important subject than heretofore.

Believe me my dear Sir
faithfully your much obliged
Wm Wordsworth

[1] See L. 1448 above.
[2] *An Alphabet of Emblems*, 1844.

1858. M. W. and W. W. to ISABELLA FENWICK

MS. WL.
LY iii. 1236 (—).

14 Dec^r [1844]

My dear Friend,

Your letter with its charitable enclosure (£20) has just reached us, and W^m and Mr Carter have taken the ½ thereof to *Ambleside*, to leave with Dora—the other shall be desposed of as you desire.

For some days d^r Friend we have only resisted writing to you in the hope that next Post would bring us news of you—and *now* we find that our fears your prolonged silence cause us, are justified. Truly do we grieve that you have been suffering—The season indeed, even here, has been, and still is, very severe. W^m feels it very, *very* much—the keen frost, and hot rooms (tho' he does not expose his legs to the fire) cannot but aggravate the irritation in his legs and this seems to create a general chilliness beyond what he used to be subject to, tho' in all other respects he is quite well. So that we cannot wonder you, beloved friend! have been suffering—in a situation so near the river[1] and where probably the Soil is of a damp character.

It is a great disappointment to us to gather from your letter of today that we are not to have you among our sheltering hills so soon as your previous one gave us reason to hope might be the case. Mrs Pedder's House will not be ready for you till the 2^d week in Feb^ry but we had calculated upon having you and dear Anna[2] at least a month under our own roof—and I do plead that you will hasten to us as soon as you can, being assured that no other good can make us so happy as your presence at Rydal Mount.

We grieve for the report of y^r Brother's health, and your consequent anxiety. Sincerely do we hope to hear of his recovery—What tidings have you from France? Our's from Rome are discouraging—but I will not give you details from poor John's letter, but in a few days [will] send it to you to speak for itself. The account of Miss Thompson's death has afflicted us much, especially for the bereavement dear Lady Frederic must feel. Miss T. was an excellent Person, and all who knew her, as

[1] I. F. was staying with Henry Taylor at Mortlake.

[2] Anna Ricketts.

my husband did, will sincerely mourn her loss. John attended her funeral on the 24th.

Dora, I am thankful to say, is better, but she does not gather strength. We have taken her out most days since she left us (last Thursday week) but today, tho' they tell me the frost is less intense, I was myself too starved to venture, having been writing for Wm at a cold window, the day being too dark to see elsewhere, all the morning. You must look to the Morng Post for his labours. If you have not seen it, refer to last Wednesday's number—for the long-promised letter on the Rail-way, and in a few days you may see its sequel,[1] with another Sonnet thrown off yesterday morning. We have seen many reports of Miss Martineau's strange letters taken from the Atheneum.[2] I will leave Wm to answer your question as to 'what we shall do with her when she comes to Windermere'. Our mutual friend[3] being here at the same time will perhaps bring us more together than we otherwise should be, and *perhaps* more often than we should like. But he shall *pay* his visits alone, for we have made up our minds to avail ourselves of our advanced years etc, to excuse our not being out, beyond Rydal, in the evenings during the winter—*You* will not quarrel with this arrangement dr friend when you are one of us.

Mrs Fletcher has had a bad attack from Cold—and Mary from her usual head-ache but they are both afloat again.—

Now comes in Wm. Beloved friend, I won't repeat anything that Mary has said, being assured you will take it all as coming from me also—except the words '*hot rooms*'; the rooms measured by the Thermometer have never been hot, but her pulse goes one third quicker than mine, and thence I suppose it is that she is often heated when I am starved.

As to Miss M. I feel no little resentment against her, for the sake of her sex, far more, than on acct of herself, at having been the cause of her infirmities and *internal* complaints being discussed as I have seen them in the newspapers. Mesmerism is

1 W. W.'s second letter on the Kendal and Windermere Railway, dated 17 Dec., was published in the *Morning Post* on the 20th. It closed with the sonnet 'Proud were ye, Mountains' (*PW* iii. 62), the precise date of which is established by this letter. See also L. 1861 below.

2 A series of papers on mesmerism, contributed to the *Athenaeum* between 23 Nov. and 21 Dec. 1844. See R. K. Webb, *Harriet Martineau, A Radical Victorian*, 1960, pp. 230–53.

3 H. C. R.

no doubt a Power, a very noticeable power, but I have no faith in its having effected her cure, more than any application or occurrence would have done, which in the then state of her body had suddenly put her upon exerting herself. Time, rest, and nature were bringing about her cure and Mesmerism came luckily in for the honor of the achievement. Miss Fleming of Rayrigg[1] lay in bed for 5 successive years—Her Father came suddenly into the house after an absence—she arose from her bed and ran to the stairs to meet him and thenceforward went about like any body else. Had she been mesmerised the change would have been ascribed to that agent. Thank you for thinking of my poor dear sister—Time hangs heavy upon her in the Evenings—she was grievously disappointed when I told her just now it was only 7 oC—her hour for going to bed is 8. If I had far more confidence in Miss M's remedy than I can muster, I durst not trust her to its influence—being quite unable to conjecture what, in her case, might come of it. The responsibility would alarm me. As to the Maid's clairvoyance and the Brandy, of that we have only vaguely heard, and of course I can give no opinion of it except that it seemed monstrous and absurd.

Pray do come to us as soon as you can, surely by this time we understand each other, do come, pray come, ever most tenderly and faithfully yours

[*signed*] Wm Wordsworth

1859. W. W. to WILLIAM JACKSON

MS. Berg Collection, New York Public Library. Hitherto unpublished.

[*In M. W.'s hand*]

Rydal M^t^ 15th Dec^r^ [1844]

My dear Friend,

I am going to trouble you about the Cockermouth and Workington Railway—a business which under any circumstances would have given the family much concern, but, in the unavoidably protracted absence of John perplexes us very much. I learn by a letter from his Brigham Curate today that the Railway *is* to pass between his house and the River—in short his letter confirms the report we had had before, and which if [I]

[1] Youngest daughter of the late John Fleming of Rayrigg. His first two girls had died in infancy.

recollect right I mentioned to you in my last—The space between the house and the edge of the River bank is scarcely more than the rail road must of necessity occupy, so that the premises will become uninhabitable by him or any future Vicar who may have a family. Now I want to know what way to proceed, if I can act at all, in the matter, for procuring sufficient damages—To whom shall I apply in the first instance—Would you recommend my writing to Ld Lonsdale not only as *Patron* of the Living; but having probably great sway in the management of the business, might be able to turn the course—The damage will not be confined to the house, garden, and bit of Pleasure ground, the latter of which it must entirely destroy—but it will extend thro a great part of his glebe. All his friends and the friends of the Church, must be anxious to have the damage fairly assessed. Have the Church Commissioners any thing to do with such matters, and if so how is one to apply?

I need not say more at present

believe me faithfully y^rs^
[*signed*] Wm Wordsworth

We have heard nothing further from Rome.

1860. W. W. to UNKNOWN CORRESPONDENT[1]

MS. Harvard University Library.
LY iii. 1237.

Rydal Mount 18th Dec^br^ —44

Dear Sir

A notice and Schedule headed Cockermouth and Workington Railway, has been forwarded this day to me from Brigham. It is dated Cockermouth 11th Nov^r^, but was not delivered at the Vicar's House at Brigham untill the 17th In^st^, leaving only four days to give an assent or Dissent. You are aware that the melancholy state of my Son's wife's health compels him to remain at Rome, therefore it is out of his power to have a choice either of assent or dissent. His absence is most unfortunate, for I see by the Schedule that the proposed line will pass within a few yards of his House, will cut up and destroy his bit of pleasure

[1] Perhaps the Revd. Henry Curwen, John W.'s brother-in-law (see pt. ii, L. 482; pt. iii, Ls. 957 and 1103). See also L. 1863 below.

ground and pass through a great part of his Glebe. The Damages therefore must be great; the old Vicarage House as you know was uninhabitable, and quite unfit for a Clergyman to dwell in; that house repaired,[1] for the Residence of a Farmer, receiving nothing for dilapidations, and built a suitable one for the Vicar of the Parish.[2] This was done at the expense of at least £800 of his own and his Friends' money, in addition to £200 from the Patron, the late Earl of Lonsdale, and a like sum from Church-building Bounty, (I do not recollect from what fund).—It seems to me that this undertaking will make the House uninhabitable by a Gentleman with young Children, and whose Wife is in such delicate health as Mrs John Wordsworth, and it appears that any *allowed* deviation would be of no advantage, but the contrary. Having had no communication with my Son upon the subject, I have merely stated my own conjectures, and would thank you to tell me how his interests, *as Vicar*, are to be represented? Have the Church Commissioners or the Patron anything to do in the case, or what course in his unavoidably protracted absence is to be pursued?

I remain dear Sir
Yours truly
Wm Wordsworth

1861. W. W. to ROBERT PERCEVAL GRAVES

Endorsed: Dec^br^ 19/184[4].
MS. Harvard University Library.
LY iii. 1238.

Rydal 19th Dec^br^ [1844]

My dear Mr Graves,

You will be surprized when you see the accompanying Paper, it contains a list of all the Proprietors along the line of the proposed Railway from Kendal to your neighbourhood.

Look it over and if you have any influence either directly or through the medium of friends or acquaintances over any of the Persons named, or even an acquaintance with them, pray endeavour to induce them to sign Dissent to a Paper which they will receive; if they sign neuter, in parliamentary construction it

[1] So MS.

[2] See pt. ii, Ls. 753 and 778.

will mean favorable. The signature will involved them in no expense. It is of prime importance for the defeating of this object, that as many signatures as possible should be procured against—I write in great Haste this being the 4th Letter I have written this morning upon this annoying subject.

ever most faithfully yours
Wm Wordsworth

Do call upon Mrs Bolton and beg she would desire her Steward to speak to Mr Braithwaite[1] of Orrest Head—he is one of the chief proprietors. I know he dislikes the project; but he declared I believe some time since that he would be neuter, but this change which brings the terminus so near him, would complete[ly] release him from any tie which he might think attached to such declaration—and this might be explained to him. A second Letter of mine on the subject will appear in the Morning Post of Saturday next,[2] pray read it.

1862. W. W. to UNKNOWN CORRESPONDENT

MS. Bryn Mawr College Library.
Frederika Beatty, William Wordsworth of Rydal Mount, New York, 1939, p. 180.

Rydal Mount
Decr 21st 1844.

Dear Sir,

Absence from home and much occupation partly consequent upon it, have prevented the expression of sympathy with you upon the occasion of the brutal assault to which you have been subjected; I say the *expression* to you of sympathy, for I assure you I resented it most deeply when I first heard of it. I presume it is yourself whom I have to thank for two Copies of your Journal giving an account of the case.

I hope you were not much injured, and that the effects of the ferocious violence are entirely gone off. Pray let me know if this be so—

This detestable action will at all events have called out the

[1] William, son of John Braithwaite of Orrest Head (1749–1818), a pupil at Hawkshead School in the early 1790s.

[2] It actually appeared the next day, Friday the 20th.

sound feelings of your friends and supporters towards you in a way which must have been highly gratifying.

Believe me with every good wish

Sincerely dear Sir your obliged
Wm Wordsworth

1863. W. W. to UNKNOWN CORRESPONDENT[1]

Endorsed: Dec 1844, Letter from W. Wordsworth.
MS. Harvard University Library.
LY iii. 1238.

Rydal Mount [late] Dec^br 44

Dear Sir

Accept my thanks for your Letter. To-day I shall write to my Son[2] and inform him of its Contents. The Railway must undoubtedly under any circumstances form a great annoyance to the Parsonage House, so great a one that if it could have been foreseen that such a thing would be, another Site for the House would have been chosen. As to any *Dissent* on the part of my Son, it is quite out of the Question. He will never think of it. But I do earnestly entreat on his behalf and for those who will succeed him that every possible attention may be paid to render the Railway as little hurtful to the House and its Inhabitants, and the glebe in general as the case will admit. Your expression, that 'a River-wall will be created for the Railway to *pass over*' I am sorry to say I do not understand. Is it intended that the Line is to be entirely scooped out of the Bank, or is a portion of the space it will require to be taken from the bed of the River by the creation of a Wall? If the whole passage is to be scooped out of the Bank the Railway will of course come so much nearer the House, to the greater annoyance of the Inhabitants, and possibly to shaking its foundations, as the House is at so small a distance from the Bank. In addition to the Wall which you say will be created to *support the Bank* an iron railing will be required along its top, to protect the ground between it and the House, and for the safety of the children and other inhabitants. A wall would not answer, as it would entirely shut out the prospect.

I am encouraged to hope from what you write that ample compensation will be made for damage of every kind.

[1] See L. 1860 above.

[2] John W.

After Mrs Curwen has seen the plan could a Section of it be forwarded to me? with any observations explanatory of it, or in answer to what I have written.

I remain
dear Sir
Truly yours
Wm Wordsworth

1864. W. W. to JOHN MOULTRIE[1]

MS. Cornell.
K (—). *LY iii. 1271* (—).

Rydal Mount
Monday
[early 1845]

My dear Sir,

My copy of the Ode,[2] in Gray's own hand-writing has

Ah, happy Hills, ah, pleasant Shade.

I wonder how Bentley could ever have substituted 'Rills,' a reading which has no support in the context. The common copies read, a few lines below—

Full many a sprightly race.

Gray's own copy

Full many a smil*e*ing (for so he spells the word).

Throughout the whole poem the substantives are written in Capital Letters. He writes 'Fury-Passions', and not, as commonly printed, the 'fury-passions'. What is the reason that our modern Compositors are so unwilling to employ Capital Letters? believe me

my dear sir

faithfully yours
Wm Wordsworth

[1] See pt. i, L. 24. Moultrie's edition of Gray's *Poetical Works* appeared in 1845. Hence the dating of this letter.

[2] *Ode on a Distant Prospect of Eton College* (see ll. 11, 22, 61): the edition of 1768 reads 'hills', 'sprightly', 'fury Passions'.

1865. W. W. to SAMUEL CROMPTON[1]

MS. untraced.
K (—). LY iii. 1239.

Rydal Mount, Jan. 3[d], 1845.

My dear Sir,

. . . You mention an American review of my poems.[2] There is nothing I am less disposed to read than things of that kind—in fact I never look at them, for if fault be found justly, I am too old to mend, and praise I care nothing about.

I remain, my dear Sir, your much obliged,
Wm Wordsworth

1866. W. W. to [?] JOHN HOLLAND[3]

MS. Cornell. Hitherto unpublished.

[early Jan. 1845]

Sir,

I have strong reasons for not wishing my name to appear as a Subscriber to Works about to be published, and therefore beg it may be suppressed on this occasion. But if 4 Copies of your Book are sent addressed to

Henry Crabbe Robinson Esq
No. 30 Russell Square
London

they will be paid for. He is at present a guest in my House and does not object to his name being inserted in your list for two Copies, the other two, my self being one, I wish to be anonymous.

Wishing you success
I remain yours sincerely
W[m] Wordsworth

I have not had for more than a Century any family connection with Yorkshire.[4] My Grandfather settled in West[nd] early in the

[1] The Manchester surgeon. See L. 1844 above.

[2] Probably the review mentioned in L. 1849 above.

[3] See L. 1881 below.

[4] See pt. ii, Ls. 648 and 672.

last Century. The Extract you give is correct,—except that my Brother's name, is Christopher, and not W^{m} which is mine.

1867. W. W. to ISABELLA FENWICK

MS. WL.
LY iii. 1240.

[early Jan. 1845]

My most dear Friend,

We are delighted to think that we have good reason for expecting you so soon; only bear this in mind that much as we wish to see dear Anna[1] as your Companion, we cannot reconcile ourselves, at least I cannot, to the thought of your remaining at Leamington until a Letter may arrive from some distant part of the world, or of *deferring* your journey upon account of a thing so uncertain.—It is unfortunate for *you* that Mr Taylor's residence should have stood in so cold a situation, but every where the Winter has been unusually cold, and I have myself, while in the House but only then, been annoyed by it along the surface of my skin to an extreme which I never knew before. On the other hand the *beauty* of the season with us has exceeded anything—such glorious effects of sunshine and shadow, and skies that are quite heavenly in the evenings especially; with moon and mountain-clouds setting each other off in a way that really has transported us to look upon.

My legs you will be glad to hear are going on as well as could be desired, scarcely any trace being left of the late discomfort.—Dora who is on the Sofa exclaims, what a lovely day—pray tell Miss Fenwick what enchanting weather we have had—not a flake of snow, nor a hailstone has fallen in the valley, no wind, clear frost, charming ice on which poor John Wordsworth[2] has skaited several times. He told us yesterday that he had not felt so well for weeks past. James is quite a model for the Learners of that art, in fact he is the good-natured *Skaiting-Master* of young Dr Davy,[3] Master Maude, and half a dozen more of like age. What a kind-hearted Creature he is. He was set up not long ago

[1] Anna Ricketts.

[2] R. W.'s son.

[3] His son Archibald, who entered the Navy. 'Master Maude' is perhaps a grandson of T. H. Maude (see *MY* ii. 417).

as a pattern by good Mrs Fletcher to her tall red-faced Coachman (your Jackson's twin) in little handy-jobs about the House. 'To be sure' was the reply 'I am not so clever in such matters, but then James, Ma'am, does just as he pleases'—

Mrs Carrick, Wm's second Mother[1] for the last 12 years, is no more. She is just dead of apoplexy—a sad desolation for them all—Her poor Daughters had been out, Christmasing with their Mother's Brother and his Bride, and Wm had to fetch, first, the Doctor, and then the poor Girls, and to announce that their mother was in a state of insensibility.—We are anxious to learn what arrangements Wm can make for the future.—Our reports from Rome are far from good. Were you told (Dora says you were) that a Railway is to drive within a few yards of John's House[2]—I am glad you approve my Railway Letter, but it has drawn upon me as I knew it would, from the low-minded and ill-bred a torrent of abuse through the Press—both in London Glasgow and elsewhere, but as it has afforded me an opportunity of directing attention to some important truths I care little for such rancorous scurrility, the natural outbreak of self conceit and stupid ignorance. The two Letters, with some additional matter interwoven, would have been reprinted by this time at Kendal[3] but for the interruption of the Christmas Holiday.

Mr Robinson arrived on Christmas day, when the family were at church, he is in his usually good spirits and health; deep in divinity,[4] but he seems never to get any deeper, his mind every now and then coming up to the surface of what I cannot give a name to, for the state seems quite anomalous. He has however publicly professed himself a Unitarian, having been made to perceive that the wide embrace of that belief does not exclude Arianism.—But all his aberrations of faith we can bear with for a hundred reasons and not the least his love and admiration of you. Mary is pretty well, Dora only so so—

[1] His Carlisle landlady. [2] Brigham vicarage.

[3] W. W. had extensively revised his two letters during the first week of January (see *HCR* ii. 648), and they were now being republished in pamphlet form at Kendal for private circulation. See L. 1875 below. 'In their new form they will have gained a permanent value', H. C. R. wrote to his brother on 8 Jan. (Morley, ii. 583).

[4] See Morley, ii. 580–2 for H. C. R.'s comments to his brother about W. W.'s 'unreasonable dislike' of Unitarians, and the fears about Puseyite excesses which he shared with the poet. A few days later he described W. W. as 'shrinking' from Tractarianism.

You wont be surprized to hear that Miss Monkhouse[1] has cast off the Queen's Messenger, having found out on his return from Spain that his affections were fixed upon her purse and not her person and that he owned to a debt of a thousand pounds, upon which she took her Aunt Sinclair's[2] advice and turned him adrift; and we do not hear that his heart is broken in consequence. Here is a man this moment come in for your address, to present you a plan of a Railway intended to pass through your fields. I gave him a bit of my mind upon the many rotten branches of Railway that the Country is about to be pestered with.—But I must bid you good bye, with a thousand kind wishes. How I long to see you!

ever most tenderly yours
Wm Wordsworth

1868. W. W. to ROBERT PERCEVAL GRAVES

Address: The Rev^{d}. R. P. Graves Esqr, Bowness. [*In M. W.'s hand*]
Endorsed: Jan 17th / 42.
MS. Harvard University Library.
LY iii. 1109.

Sat: Morning 17th Jan^{ry} [1845][3]

My dear Mr Graves,

Your Letter was indeed most acceptable; and we all sincerely and cordially congratulate you and your Relatives upon your convalescence.

Understanding as we do that your illness was ag[g]ravated by undertaking more duty in the earlier stages of it than you were equal to, we earnestly entreat that you would be more cautious hereafter, as a Relapse might otherwise come on, and that might prove serious indeed and not improbably dangerous.

[1] Mary Monkhouse (see also L. 1674 above). Her new suitor is unidentified.

[2] See pt. i, L. 199.

[3] The endorsement must be incorrect, for in 1842 the 17th was a Monday. 1845 is almost certainly the year, though in that year Saturday was the 18th January. But this is the kind of slip that W. W. often makes in dating. The sonnet referred to in the letter is undoubtedly the one which Graves addressed *To Mrs. Fletcher, On the Seventy-Fifth Anniversary of Her Birthday*, dated 15 Jan. 1845. See *Autobiography of Mrs. Fletcher*, pp. 255–6.

Many thanks for your Sonnet both on account of the affectionate sentiments it so well expresses, as for the proof it gave that you were going on well.

Pray do not on any account be hasty to visit us. It is our duty as it is our inclination to look after you, which in the earlier part of next week we intend to do, if our Horse be sufficiently recovered from the cold and cough which he at present has.

I was sorry to learn that your Brother[1] had suffered in health from his journey. I thought him looking but thin and poorly, when he was so kind as to come and see us. We should be glad to hear that your Sisters[2] continue to go on well, and that your Mother keeps in good health.

Ever with best wishes in which Mrs W. and my Daughter unite

affectionately and faithfully yours
Wm Wordsworth

1869. W. W. to RICHARD CHARLES COXE[3]

MS. untraced.
Bookseller's Catalogue.

Rydal Mount,
Ambleside.
23 January —45.

. . . There are many tender touches in the longer Poem particularly which might recommend it to general Perusal in spite of the local dialect, but with that view, I think the Narrative ought to be somewhat compressed, and perhaps it would be as well that the catastrophe should not be anticipated in the Title, and so early in the Poem . . . mine was suggested by the footprints of a child being found in a snow-storm *half way* across the Lock of a Canal in Yorkshire. It is entitled Lucy Gray.[4]

[1] J. T. Graves (see pt. iii, L. 1221). [2] See pt. iii, L. 1048.

[3] The Revd. Richard Charles Coxe (1800–65), vicar of Newcastle from 1841, Archdeacon of Lindisfarne and vicar of Eglingham from 1853, and Canon of Durham from 1857. He published two ballads, which are the subject of this letter: *The Mercy at Marsden Rocks*, 1844, and *The Snow Shroud; or, The Lost Bairn o' Biddleston Edge*, 1845.

[4] See *PW* i. 234 and the I. F. note, p. 360.

1870. W. W. to EDWARD MOXON

MS. Henry E. Huntington Library.
K (—). LY iii. 1242.

Rydal—
Thursday 23[d] Jan[ry] 1845

My dear Mr Moxon,

Mr Robinson, who leaves us today, will report to you all I think about your proposal of printing my prose-writings in a separate Volume.[1]

He will also I hope in passing through Kendal today receive from the Printer a few Copies of my two Letters to the Morning Post upon the Railway,[2] they are revised, one paragraph omitted as leading the Reader from the main point, and another towards the conclusion of the 2nd Letter added. You observe that the Morning Post nobody reads—this is not correct. Its circulation, among the Aristocracy, is very considerable; all the Ladies look at it and that puts it in the way of the Gentlemen. Besides, the pains which it takes to support the Landed interest against 'free trade' and the league is the cause of its being a favorite with a great number of the landed Gentry. Furthermore, Mr Johnstone,[3] who writes the leading Articles, has long been an intimate acquaintance of mine. It is a pity that Quillinan has not access to Books, or he might have been of great use to your Dictionary of dates, for he is wonderfully industrious, a most pains-taking Man. I wish you could put into his hands some literary labour by which he could add to his very scanty Income. Do think about it. As to any light work of his own choice, I am sure it would never sell unless he would condescend, which he never will do, to traffic in the trade of praise with London Authorlings, who write in newspapers, Magazines and Reviews. You Publishers are quite at the mercy of these Knots and Cabals of Scribblers whose publications are of the day, the week, the month, or the Quarter. I do not mean their writing merely in Periodicals, but also what they give to the world individually,

[1] Nothing came of this, and other proposals, to publish W. W.'s prose writings. It was left to his early editors—Alexander Grosart in 1876, and William Knight in 1896—to draw up the canon and decide in doubtful cases what should be included. See also L. 2019 below.

[2] See L. 1875 below.

[3] For William Johnston see pt. iii, L. 1234.

whatever shape it may assume, or through whatever vehicle it may be offered to the Public. It is a sad condition of things, but I see no remedy—

Mr Robinson has enjoyed himself much, and seen a great deal of Miss Martineau, who is staying within three miles of us.[1] Mrs Wordsworth with her kind regards thanks you for Miss Martineau's Letters.[2]

ever faithfully yours
Wm Wordsworth

1871. W. W. to C. W.

MS. Mr. Jonathan Wordsworth.
Charles Wordsworth, Annals of my Early Life (—).

Rydal Mount
24 Jany 1845

My dear Brother,

Mr Reed's Letter[3] was sent to Miss Fenwick and by her to you, from London. I have more than once thanked Mr R. in your name and shall do so again.—Allow me to say that notwithstanding the very probable resumption of Payments of interest in Feb^{ry}, there is nothing like certainty that the same will be continued in August; and were it to be so, I certainly would not leave my Money if I had any in America, after the Stock had reached or even approached Par.—For my part I have no confidence in the American character, nor should I have in any absolute Democracy, in any part of the World, or in any Government where Democracy was the commanding Element.[4]

[1] With W. R. Greg (see L. 1855 above).

[2] *Letters on Mesmerism.*

[3] Reed had written on 13 Dec. 1844, counselling patience over the State Loans of Pennsylvania: 'I pray you therefore help me in keeping your friends in good heart—in good temper with us, and I trust we shall prove not unworthy of the magnanimous forbearance which you have manifested.' (*Wordsworth and Reed*, pp. 134–5). W. W.'s sonnet *To the Pennsylvanians* (*PW* iv. 132) probably belongs to this time. See Grosart, iii. 450.

[4] The United States, under its new President James Knox Polk (1795–1849), was about to enter on a rapid period of further expansion, which would include the settlement of the Oregon boundary question with Great Britain in the north, and the acquisition of California from Mexico in the west.

There are crisises in which it has had far too much to do in our own, and such will occur again. I hope you will sell out after a while if the Pensylvania Stock should continue to rise in value as I hope it will.—I wish I could send you better news from Rome. I think Isabella is in a very precarious state—and poor John's heart must be full of anxiety. Lady F. Bentinck who is in Rome, gives an unfavorable account of Isabella, whom she has seen, and has also seen her Physician. John's two children who are with them at Rome; the eldest Jane, and the youngest but one Charles, Lady F. says are delightful children, and good Italians.—You will be sorry to learn that the Railway from Workington to Cockermouth, will pass so close to John's Vicarage, as to destroy the only bit of pleasure ground he has, and will make the House, I fear, uninhabitable for his Family, and undo all he has done there.—

Miss Fenwick has seen Charles at Leamington, he has been introduced to all our Friends there. Miss F. was exceedingly struck with Charles's likeness to his relations at Rydal, especially to Dora and our Sister: Dr Jephson[1] appears to be doing him good; but he must take care not to overwork himself or all will be in vain. I have just received a Vol. of Sermons from Chris:[2] but as I cannot read by Candlelight and have been very much occupied during the daylight in various ways I have not yet been able to gratify my wish by perusing it. I am afraid he too will suffer from too much work. I am however truly glad that he has left Harrow. Of Dora's health I cannot give a favorable account; she suffers continually almost from a pain in her stomach but especially after eating. John[3] is with us and I regret to say also, that his stomach is much out of order; and he suffers also after his meals—Our Sister, Mary and I are all as well as usual.

In a day or two I hope to be able to send you my Railway Letters Revised, with omissions and additions.[4] If you could interest any member of Parliament in this matter so far as to induce him to vote against the Bill being sent to a Committee, it would be doing good service. It is like most of the Projects at present a vile Gambling Speculation.

Wm is waiting to take this to the Post office, and I have to

[1] See pt. iii, L. 1277.

[2] C. W. jnr.'s *Discourses on Public Education*, 1844.

[3] R. W.'s son.

[4] See L. 1875 below.

attend a meeting of Railway Opposition, so I must bid you farewell, ever my dear Brother, with love from us all,

faithfully yours
Wm Wordsworth

1872. W. W. to ISABELLA FENWICK

MS. WL.
LY iii. 1243.

Rydal Mount, Sat. 25th Janry —45

Your Letter, my beloved Friend, was most welcome. We could not help being anxious about your having so much travelling at this cold season, with so many and such sudden changes in the temperature of the air. Pray take care of yourself, and if you return in good health that will be the best compensation we can have for our disappointment in not seeing you under our own roof as we had reason to expect.—We shall be truly glad if you find your Brother better than you expect after his distressing accident; it is a melancholy thing for so active a Person as he is—You will not fail to let us know as soon as you can when we may expect you. Mr Robinson went on Thursday; what with talking, I can scarcely say conversing, sleeping, reading, playing at Whist all the evening when at home, dining out, now and then, and making friendly calls on all his acquaintance during the day, especially on his *intended* as we call her, the dear Martineau, he passed his time most agreeably. *You* are strongly infected with the mesmeric mania, I am therefore pleased to tell you that the Herald and Proclaimer of the Virtues of the process is desirous of obtaining a Lodging in these parts so that you have good prospect of a favorable opportunity for cultivating her acquaintance. She has dined with the Fletchers, with Dr Davy,[1] and drank tea with Mrs Arnold—and they are all charmed with her. Mr Robinson has taken great pains to make arrangements for your meeting, as he intends you to be great Friends—I have only seen her twice, once at Dr Davy's where I sat by her at

[1] On 16 Jan., according to H. C. R., 'Wordsworth sat next Miss M: And they chatted very freely on indifferent subjects—but Mesmerism was not once alluded to. This was judicious— . . . Anything like a dispassionate discussion was out of the question.' (Morley, ii. 584). Soon after, Harriet Martineau called at Rydal Mount (*RMVB*). See also *HCR* ii. 650.

Dinner, and about ten minutes in our own House. I have not the least doubt of her proving a highly interesting neighbour, and a good deal more, but to me her manner of uttering her opinions, not on mesmerism for that subject was not touched, but on any miscellaneous matter was a little abrupt and peremptory—But it might be that I was mistaken, I mean in not making sufficient allowance first for her being a Dissenter, and next for being what is somewhat vulgarly called a 'BLUE', and this class of *Women* (I dare not say *Females*) I have never lived with, and therefore it is probable that as far as I was not pleased I ought rather to have imputed it to her sect and class than to herself individually; for everybody else seems to like her without the least draw-back. Did we tell you that Mr Robinson and some of the Arnolds were present when Mrs Winyard[1] performed upon Jane.[2] Mary Arnold[3] has taken most accurate memorandums of all that occurred, and you may see them yourself, but it should seem that nothing at all decisive happened, except that when the organ of veneration was touched the sleeper assumed an attitude and expression of devotion more beautiful than anything he, Mr R, ever beheld. When Miss M. drank tea at Mrs Arnold's on *Thursday*, Mrs Wynyard could not be of the Party, because Jane was by all means to be mesmerised on *that* day, it being *Thursday*, and on Thursdays the effects are always the *most striking*. What say you my dear one, to this? Mr Gregg[4] who is a Mesmeriser has undertaken Miss Martineau with a view to relieve or cure her deafness.—Enough of this.

Wm is here, looking very ill, and being very far from well. I must consult Dr Davy about him. He sends his love, and adds, that he would be happy to go to Leamington and escort you home. But *that* I am sure you would not wish him to do, unless he were disposed to take Jephson's advice which he stands much in need of; his stomach being greatly out of order. As to diet nobody has been less self indulgent than he is—he scarcely eats anything, and the little he takes seems invariably to disagree with him. He must return to Carlisle on the 13th of Feb^ry^, within a day or two of the time when your House will be ready to receive you. He is hurried home five weeks earlier than he

[1] Miss Martineau's friend.

[2] Jane Arnold (see L. 1540 above).

[3] b. 1825, she married (1) Aldred Twining (d. 1848), and (2) The Revd. J. S. Hiley (in 1858).

[4] See L. 1855 above.

thought of, in consequence of his being called upon to learn the mode of collecting new Duties which are about to be imposed upon him. This addition we should some years back have been glad of, when he was my Sub^r and had more leisure and Government work was better paid. Now the Rule is to get as much work out of a man as possible, without incurring the charge of murder, man-slaughter not being a Capital offence. But seriously this is very wrong. Were the allowance tolerably liberal, he might keep an additional clerk without inconvenience, and moving about to collect the Revenue, through the two Counties, might possibly be favourable to his Health. Dora has been something better during the last few days.

Now for your Pensylvanians;[1] do not rely too confidently upon your Riches. You will be paid, I doubt not, this quarter, but I am far from certain that they will not tire of their honesty; and that when August comes the half year's payment that will then be due, will not be paid, and you and the other creditors will be no better off than before. This apprehension may prove erroneous, but pray do not let your generosity and benevolence build upon it at present.—

If in the course of your wanderings you meet with any Member of Parliament or other influential Person who takes an interest in our Lake-district pray request him to vote against the Railway Bill being sent to a Committee of the House. It is a vile job contrived by juggling speculators.

Mr Liddell,[2] Mrs Villiers' Brother, will in all probability have the same additional Collection of Duties imposed upon him as Wm has had.—It has taken a month to reprint my two Railway Letters,[3] such is the expedition of Kendal workmen. I hope that a Parcel of them may reach me to day, and then I shall enclose one which I should be glad to think you and Mrs Villiers may read with interest. Pray remember us affectionately to her with our good wishes. Love of the tenderest kind to yourself. My legs are quite well. Nevertheless we are both growing old, though Mary is a wonder and so am I thought to be by many. Old Aunty[4] seems set in earthly immortality.

W. W.

[1] Pennsylvanian stock. See previous letter.

[2] One of the younger brothers of H. T. Liddell (see pt. iii, L. 875), either Thomas (1800–56) or John (1803–65).

[3] See L. 1867 above and L. 1875 below.

[4] i.e. D. W.

1873. W. W. to THOMAS HUTCHINSON JNR.

Address: Rev[d] T. Hutchinson, Grantsfield, Leominster.
Postmark: 29 Jan. 1845.
Stamp: (1) Ambleside (2) Leominster.
MS. Mr. Jonathan Wordsworth.
LY iii. 1246.

Rydal
28th Jan[ry] 45

Dear Thomas,

Perhaps it may amuse you to cast your eyes over the Enclosed,[1]—but as a Copy has been sent to Brinsop which you may see at your leisure, I should not have troubled you with this but to request you would be so kind as to forward it with my Compts to your Friend the Clergyman[2] and Esquire whom along with his Brother I had the pleasure of seeing at your House. For the life of me I cannot recall at present the name of these three Brothers, and therefore cannot enclose a note of thanks to the one, the eldest I think, who was so obliging as to write to me a few weeks ago, in consequence of having seen one or both of these Letters when they first appeared in the Morning Post. Pray represent me on this occasion and thank him in my name for his obliging Letter.

Your Aunt is quite well except that she is annoyed from time to time with a giddiness or swimming in her head. Dora is but so so. Nor is W[m] well who has been here some little time. My poor Sister is much as usual—I hope that you suffer less than when you were with us; all send their love and believe me my dear Thomas

your affectionate Uncle

W[m] Wordsworth

P.S. The accounts of Isabella are far from good.

[1] W. W.'s pamphlet, *Kendal and Windermere Railway. Two Letters Re-Printed from the Morning Post.* See L. 1875 below.

[2] According to a note on the MS., this was the Revd. Joseph Kirkham Miller (see pt. ii, L. 658), vicar of Walkeringham, Notts., who was also perpetual curate of Brockleton, Herefordshire, 1830–50. His brother was Thomas Elton Miller (1783–1857), of Brockleton.

1874. W. W. to LORD LONSDALE[1]

Endorsed: W. Wordsworth Jany 1845 answ[d].
MS. Berg Collection, New York Public Library. Hitherto unpublished.

Rydal Mount
28th Jan[ry] —45

Dear Lord Lonsdale,

Pray excuse my sending you the Enclosed.[2] I can scarcely expect that you will be able to find time for looking into, much less for reading, the whole of so long an affair, nevertheless I could not be satisfied without putting into your way the reasons that have induced me and others to oppose the Kendal and Windermere Railway—

The more I think about the Brigham Vicarage as it will be affected by the Railway, the more am I convinced, that justice to the Church and the present Incumbent, requires the Insertion in the Act of a clause enjoining the Erection of a new Parsonage.—[3]

I had the pleasure of receiving [? some days] ago a Letter from Lady Frederic. She speaks of her health being good except for a cold.

Many thanks for your last Letter in reply to mine respecting that unaccountable Report.

Believe me ever
dear Lord Lonsdale
faithfully
your much obliged
W[m] Wordsworth

[1] The 2nd Earl.

[2] *Kendal and Windermere Railway. Two Letters* . . . See next letter.

[3] The Railway Company finally agreed to this, and a new vicarage was built two years later, before the new line was opened.

1875. W. W. to H. C. R.

Endorsed: *5th Apl*: 1845. Wordsworth.
MS. Dr. Williams's Library.
Morley, ii. 589.

Rydal
2nd Feb [18]45

My dear Friend,

Thanks for your Letter—I write in great haste having several Copies of the two Letters[1] to send off, and my purpose is to mention that having forgotten that I had allowed you to publish the 'Young England'[2] when and where you liked; I now beg that if it is still in MS. you keep it so. Mr Johnston of the Post to whom Mr Quillinan sent the Sonnet showed it to Lockhart who relished it much; and most likely would be able to find a place for it in the Quarterly which would introduce it to notice better than as a flying Squib in a daily or weekly Journal.

We called on Miss Martineau yesterday. We found her alone, the Greggs being from home—She relates strong things of cures by Mesmerism, which would be entitled as far as they depend upon her own testimony to more respect, if she were not really of *unsound mind* upon the subject of claire-voyance. Besides, I hardly think it safe for any one's Wits to be possessed on the manner this extraordinary person is by one subject be it what it may.—

Your suggestion of *is* for *was*[3] etc will be attended to. I have given permission to the Kendal Publisher to strike off as many Copies as he thinks proper for sale.—I have not the least hope of preventing the Bill being sent to a Committee, but my Letters may prepare an efficient Opposition to another which will

[1] W. W.'s pamphlet *Kendal and Windermere Railway. Two Letters Re-Printed from the Morning Post*, which opened and closed with W. W.'s two sonnets on the subject, was jointly published by Whittaker and Co. and Edward Moxon in London and R. Branthwaite and Son, Kendal. It sold for fourpence. See *Cornell Wordsworth Collection*, nos. 133 and 134, and *Prose Works*, iii. 337 ff. H. C. R. had written to M. W. on 27 Jan.: 'I have read over the letters again with very great pleasure And am satisfied his [W. W.'s] argument is essentially and incontrovertibly true—It will convince every body, except I fear all those by whom the ultimate decision will be given decisive of the fate of the lakes.' (Morley, ii. 586).

[2] 'Young England—what is then become of Old' (*PW* iv. 134), publ. 1845. According to *HCR* ii. 649, it was composed on 14 Jan.

[3] In l. 1 of the sonnet *On the Projected Kendal and Windermere Railway*.

surely follow this; namely a Bill to carry the railway through the Country to join the one that will soon be brought from Cockermouth to Keswick.—

ever my dear Friend
faithfully your's
Wm Wordsworth

1876. W. W. to CHARLES WORDSWORTH

MS. Swarthmore College Library. Hitherto unpublished.

Rydal
2nd Febry [18]45

My dear Charles,

This Letter speaks for itself, I have only to add, that the Writer[1] is a most worthy man, born and bred in Ambleside where his Father and Mother lived and died. The whole Family were most excellent people, and I have no Doubt that this Boy will prove worthy of any attention which consistent with the rules of the School and your personal convenience you can pay to him.

We were very sorry to hear of your Indisposition. Do write a line and tell me how you are. We have heard of you through our Friends Miss Fenwick and the family of Ricketts, they thought you had benefitted under Jephson.[2] Dora, I grieve to say, continues to suffer, and Does not gather strength. Wm is here, and is also far from well—the rest of us as usual. best love from all—I write in great haste, having several Copies [of the] [? little] Pamphlet[3] to send off.

your affectionate Uncle
W. W.

[1] John North (see L. 1782 above).

[2] The Leamington doctor.

[3] *MS. torn.* The reference is to *Kendal and Windermere Railway.*

1877. W. W. to EDWARD MOXON

MS. Henry E. Huntington Library.
LY iii. 1246.

17th Feb^{ry} [1845]

My dear Mr Moxon,

I have no recollection of the matter to which the enclosed Letters refer. My consent must have been given before you told me how much such liberty had been abused, or I must have referred the Applicant to you.

You may send the two Copies he speaks of at any time when there shall be an opportunity, but first look over the Contents and if you object to the length or number, tell the person so. I have apprized her[1] that I have referred the matter to you. I am sadly plagued by these things, and the number of tracts, Poems, etc etc that are sent to me. You know how much I dislike writing Letters of acknowledgement

ever faithfully yours
W Wordsworth

If you have got my two Railway Letters read the two last pages of the 2nd; the blank verses[2] are not inferior to any I have written.

1878. W. W. to UNKNOWN CORRESPONDENT[3]

MS. Cornell. Hitherto unpublished.

Rydal Mount 20 Feb^{ry} — 45

Dear Sir

Your Plants were received with much pleasure, and you will be glad to learn that they, are not injured. My garden lies in

[1] An unidentified anthologist, who had applied for permission to use some of W. W.'s poems.

[2] *The Simplon Pass* (*PW* ii. 212), the lines from *The Prelude* recording W. W.'s crossing of the Alps in 1790 during his 'pedestrian tour' with Robert Jones. See *Prel.*, pp. 210–11. On 9 Feb. Lady Richardson recalled that W. W. spoke 'with pleasure of having heard that Mr. Lockhart had been struck by his lines from a MSS. poem, printed in his Railway-Sonnet pamphlet.' (Grosart, iii. 450).

[3] Perhaps William Pearson.

something of a hollow and is yet covered with snow, but they are placed in sheltered plots in front of the House, and will be transferred to the Garden as soon as the season will permit.

You were right in inferring that the Fir was a favourite tree with me, indeed, as perhaps I have told you before, I prefer it to all others, except the Oak, taking into consideration its beauty in winter, and by moonlight and in the evening.

Accept my sincere thanks for this mark of your attention and even still more for your good wishes so feelingly expressed.

I remain
dear Sir
faithfully your obliged
Wm Wordsworth

There seems to be no reason for fearing that the plants will not do well, but perhaps it would be prudent to wait a little before you carry your kindness into effect by sending more. If these should fail you will certainly hear from me.

1879. W. W. to EDWARD MOXON

MS. Henry E. Huntington Library.
LY iii. 1247.

[March 5th 1845][1]

My dear Mr Moxon,

You have so frequently and so kindly exerted yourself at my request, that I hope you will be able to take some trouble upon the present occasion. The Paper which I enclose will explain itself—I have only to add, that the Applicant is the Mother of an excellent young woman, a Servant in my house. Her Father's case was a peculiarly hard one; he had invested the whole of his property in building a little vessel of which he was master, and was wrecked in the Solway, the ship lost and the lives of the crew and his own also. A Lighthouse has since been erected on the Spot where the Vessel perished.—

If you can, be so good as to have the thing done according to the poor Widow's request.

A request petition stating particulars has been presented to the Trinity house—at the proper time I suppose.

[1] Date added in another hand.

I have looked over your Statement of Sale. The Early and Late[1] are doing full as well as I expected, so few persons seem to know of the existence of that Vol: as a separate publication.

I do not find how many of the six Vol:[2] are still on hand, nor do you give an opinion as to when it is likely that we should be justified in preparing a cheaper Edition; nor am I at all anxious about it, being confident that unpuffed publications have a poor chance of competing with puffed ones. The other day I was told of a Lady of some Note in Literature, who previous to one of her late Publications, thought it expedient to beat about for means of getting at more than 20 periodicals, in which she succeeded to admiration.

You know, I think, the beautiful situation of John's Parsonage.[3] A railway is to be drawn within 18 yards of his drawing room window, cutting him off from the River, and running through both ends of his little garden. So much for an Englishman's home being his Castle. I have petitioned Parliament for compensation

ever faithfully yours
Wm Wordsworth

1880. W. W. to JAMES DAVID FORBES[4]

MS. St. Andrews University Library. Hitherto unpublished.

Rydal Mount
March [1845]

Sir,

Accept my thanks for your Letter announcing that at a general Meeting of the Royal Society of Edinburgh I had been elected an Honorary Fellow of that Body; and let me beg the Society may

[1] *Poems, Chiefly of Early and Late Years*, 1842.

[2] The 6 vol. *Poetical Works* of 1843.

[3] At Brigham.

[4] James David Forbes, F.R.S. (1809–68), Professor of Natural Philosophy at Edinburgh University from 1833, Secretary of the Royal Society of Edinburgh, 1840–51, and Principal of St. Andrews University from 1859: an authority on glaciers. See also *RMVB* for May, 1846.

be assured that I am duly sensible of the distinction thus conferred upon me.

I have the honor
to be, Sir,
Your most obedient
humble Servant
Wm Wordsworth

1881. W. W. to [?] JOHN HOLLAND[1]

MS. Cornell. Hitherto unpublished.

Rydal Mount
April 4. 1845

Mr Wordsworth having just heard from his Friend Mr C. Robinson that a parcel has reached him containing two Volumes

"The Poets of Yorkshire"[2]

Mr Wordsworth not having remembered the directions which he must have given to Mr Holland on this subject, begs to know if any mention was made in his Letter of the Person's name for whom the 2nd Copy was intended. This request Mr W. makes because he has forgotten the particulars, yet is assured that one of the Copies must have been ordered for him for some one of his Friends or acquaintance, but for whom he does not know.

[1] John Holland (1794–1872), friend and biographer of James Montgomery, succeeded him as editor of the *Sheffield Iris*, edited the *Sheffield Mercury*, 1835–48, and published poetry and historical works.

[2] William Cartwright Newsam, *The Poets of Yorkshire*, completed and published by J. Holland, 1845.

1882. W. W. to CHARLES BONER[1]

MS. Harvard University Library.
LY iii. 1249.

Rydal Mount April 10th—1845

My dear Sir

I regret that it is not in my power to speak *positively* in answer to your inquiry. All I can say is, that I have no intention of being absent during the spring or any great part of the summer; but I do mean to go down to the seaside in the course of it, but during what particular time I am unable to say—and of course I cannot bind myself—only let me add that it would give me much pleasure if our times should suit—

With many and sincere good wishes
believe me my dear Sir
faithfully yours
Wm Wordsworth

1883. W. W. to MESSRS. COLNAGHI AND CO.[2]

Endorsed: 1845 April 10 W. Wordsworth Ansd Apl 25.
MS. Henry E. Huntington Library.
LY iii. 1250.

Rydal Mount
April 10th—1845

Mr Wordsworth presents his Compts to Messrs Colnaghi and Co and returns his thanks for a Print of the Virgin and Child which appears to have reached him through their hands.

This beautiful Work, he sees, is from a picture of Lady M. Alford,[3] and if it be a Prese[n]t from her Ladyship Mr W would

[1] Charles Boner (1815–70) lived twenty years with the family of Prince Thurn and Taxis at Ratisbon, and achieved some reputation as a translator of Hans Andersen, and for his articles on German poets. He was a friend of Mary Russell Mitford, and for a time acted as Constable's secretary. He saw a good deal of W. W. this summer during a visit to Rydal, 31 Aug.—6 Sept. (*RMVB*). For their conversations on poetry, see *Memoir and Letters of Charles Boner*, ed. R. M. Kettle, 1871, i. 59–62. See also L. 1915 below.

[2] See pt. iii, L. 1018.

[3] Lady Marian Alford (1817–88), elder daughter of W. W.'s friend Lord Northampton, married (1841) John Hume Cust, Viscount Alford (1812–51),

wish his thanks to be conveyed to her, and his acknowledgement for the pleasure this proof of feeling and skill has given him—

1884. W. W. to EDWARD MOXON

MS. Henry E. Huntington Library.
K (—). LY iii. 1248.

10th April 1845
Now I am in my 76th year alas alas!

My dear Mr Moxon,

My nephew, Dr C Wordsworth, writes me that he has forwarded a Pamphlet to you for me, also Mr Robinson has a couple of books which he says he will send to you for the same purpose. Will you be so kind as to forward these or any others which you may have, with following address

Miss Dowling[1]
4 Norfolk Street
Strand
for Mr Wordsworth of Rydal Mount

If Mr R's Books have not reached you be so kind as to send your Messenger for them. As I don't exactly know how long Miss Dowling means to stay in London, the sooner you could do me this little service the better.—

Having long wished that an Edition of my Poems should be published without the Prefaces and Supplement, I submit to your consideration whether that would not be well, (printing, however, the prose now attached to the Volumes as a portion of the Prose Volume which you meditate).[2] The Prefaces etc contain many important observations upon Poetry—but they were written solely to gratify Coleridge; and, for my own part, being quite against any thing of the kind, and having always been of opinion that Poetry should stand upon its own merits, I would not even attach to the Poems any explanation of the grounds of their arrangement. I should however by [all] means wish that the Vol: of prose should be printed uniform with the Poems, whether they be printed in double column which most

M.P. for Bedfordshire, eldest son of the 1st Earl Brownlow. She was a painter and patron of the arts.

[1] Jane Dowling (see pt. i, L. 121).

[2] See L. 1870 above.

of my Friends, especially the Ladies, dislike, or in a type somewhat larger than Mr Taylor's.—

Thanks for your detailed account of the volumes on hand.

I cannot muster courage to face the fatigues and late dinners of London, and therefore do not think it likely I shall leave home for the purpose.

We are expecting my Son John from Italy to look after his parish and affairs. The account of his Wife's health is not cheering. My son Wm is also far from well. My Nephew John Wordsworth suffering under a slow but incurable disease of the lungs, caught among the Ionian Islands, and lastly poor Mrs Quillinan is very weak. So that you see we are not in a state for moving from home. Mrs Q. has given up the thought of going to Portugal. Mr Q. however *is* going shortly

ever faithfully yours
Wm Wordsworth

Kindest remembrances to Mr Rogers and his Sister, and other enquiring Friends.

1885. W. W. to C. W. JNR.

MS. Cornell.
Broughton, p. 88.

Rydal Mount
10th April—45
I am in my 76th year—eheu fugaces!

My dear Nephew

We are truly glad of the good [news][1] you give of your new-born, and hope that she will continue to go on as well—

It gave me also much pleasure to learn that you have been so much better employed than in writing to me; and I shall look with impatience for your Pamphlet.[2] I have written to Mr

[1] *Word dropped out.* The reference is to his third daughter Mary, born at Leamington.

[2] *Maynooth, the Crown and the Country*, 1845 (3rd enlarged edn., 1845), the first of C. W. jnr.'s three anonymous pamphlets on the Maynooth Endowment Grant. In his attempts to conciliate O'Connell and the Repeal Association, Peel had the previous year proposed a new method for financing the Maynooth Seminary, founded in 1795 during the French Revolution. The original grant had

Moxon about it, and directed him to send it to a Lady of Ambleside now in London but expected home shortly. No subject is more difficult to handle than the course of treatment towards Ireland. For my own part in the present state of things I can not see that any good can be done by what Sir R. Peel and others call conciliation.[1] Every step in that direction will only serve to promote more injurious and insolent demands. The only *positive* good that can be done would be the establishment, at any cost of a strong government in Ireland for the protection of person and property. Capital would then, but cannot otherwise flow into the Country and Absentees would have less cause and less pretext for abandoning their Country. Were this effected the standard of civilization in spite of the Priests might be gradually raised, the people's ignorance giving way at the same time, and their violent passions being brought under some subjection.—If a strong government is not established we must prepare ourself for a civil war, or give up the Country at once.—

I am glad also to hear that Theophilus[2] is going on so well.—It seems however right I should mention to you that its circulation has been obstructed in some quarters, perhaps many, by the political doctrines advanced towards the close of the Book.[3] Mr

been made by the Irish Parliament, and accepted as part of the Union settlement. Peel's new plan, by making the annual grant permanent, tripling the amount, incorporating the trustees, and providing for the maintenance of the fabric, seemed to establish a new and closer link between the State and the College, and aroused considerable apprehension among churchmen. The Maynooth Bill, which received its Second Reading on 11 Apr., led to the resignation of Gladstone from the Board of Trade, and the break-up of the Young England party.

[1] In addition to the Maynooth proposals, Peel passed a Charitable Bequests Act to facilitate the endowment of the Irish Catholic Church, and put forward a controversial scheme for setting up colleges in Cork, Galway and Belfast, to raise the general level of education in the country. Earlier, in summer 1843, he had appointed a commission under the chairmanship of Lord Devon to look into the question of Irish land reform, but the potato famine occurred in autumn 1845, before any of its contentious proposals could be implemented.

[2] C. W. jnr.'s *Theophilus Anglicanus*. See L. 1756 above.

[3] W. W. is probably referring to Part III, 'The Church of England in its Civil Relations,' especially Ch. iii, 'On the Church of England as the Spiritual Mother of Christians in this Country', where C. W. jnr. writes: 'As *Christians* . . . Schismatics are Members, though *unsound* members, of the Church, and must be objects of her regard, as she *ought* to be an object of reverence to them; they are *children* of the Church, though *not obedient* ones; and as long as she is a Church,

Crabb Robinson told me that a Friend of his purposed to send his Sons to Harrow school, but was so *shocked* at what he called the 'slavish' doctrine there inculcated as to be prevented from doing so—he added that not less than Seven of his friends had acted upon the same principle.—My House is at present in entire disorder under an Easter cleaning, so that I cannot refer to your Book; but I remember when I read that passage feeling regret at the mode in which you had expressed yourself upon those points.—

Dora has given up the thought of going to Portugal, in consequence of her Mother (who knows her constitution perfectly,) being averse to her doing so when the summer heats are so near.—We rejoice that your Father is well—I wish I could send you better accounts of our Invalids—Mrs Q. is no stronger and John[1] very poorly. You seem pleased at the thought of your new Dean—[2] I cannot be so, notwithstanding his great talents; I fear he is an *insincere* man—however he may not prove so. He has great influence over the Queen and Prince Albert.—

With best love to Susan and yourself from all hereabouts—I remain My dear Chris. your

affectionate Uncle
Wm Wordsworth

We are looking for John who was to quit Rome about this time.

1886. W. W. to EDWARD MOXON

MS. Henry E. Huntington Library.
K (—). LY iii. 1250.

Friday 18th April—[1845]

My dear Moxon,

An invitation from the Lord Chamberlain to attend the

and as long as they are Christians, neither can she forget her maternal love to them, nor can they cast off their filial duty to her.' He supported his arguments with quotations from Hooker, Cyprian and Augustine.

[1] R. W.'s son.

[2] Samuel Wilberforce (see L. 1633 above) was Dean of Westminster for a few months in 1845 before he became Bishop of Oxford. A favourite at court, he was talked of as a possible tutor for the infant Prince of Wales; but on his installation in May, he came under some criticism in the press for retaining his benefice of Alverstoke.

Queen's Ball on Friday the 25th left me without a choice as to visiting London,[1] and in consequence I purpose to start on Wednesday next with Mr and Mrs Quillinan who are going to Oporto,[2] he to attend his Brother's marriage, and she accompanying him in the hope of benefiting her health which as you know has been declining for several years. I should prefer arriving at your house rather than Mr Robinson's if I could be received there early on Thursday Morning, your maid-servant having provided me a bed to lie down upon for two or three hours, as I am but a poor Traveller in the night Season. If it be in your power to accomodate me pray let me know by return of Post. I have another favor to ask, which is that you would mention my errand to Mr Rogers, and perhaps he could put me in the way of being properly introduced, and instructed how to behave in a situation, I am not sorry to say, altogether new to me.[3] My stay in London for several cogent reasons will be very short. Hoping that my proposal of coming first to you may not prove inconvenient to Mrs Moxon, and your Household,

I remain my dear Mr Moxon
faithfully yours
Wm Wordsworth

[1] W. W. spent just over two weeks in London, dividing his time between Moxon's and Mrs. Hoare's at Hampstead. Shortly after his presentation at court by Lord Northampton, he told Dyce that 'the Queen talked to him very kindly and at considerable length both about his own poetry and on other subjects.' (*Reminiscences of Alexander Dyce*, ed. R. J. Schrader, Ohio, 1972, p. 182). Aubrey de Vere brought Tennyson (see pt. ii, L. 582, and L. 1903 below) to Hampstead on 4 May. On 6 May W. W. dined at Moxon's with Tennyson, Henry Lushington, later Chief Secretary at Malta (see L. 1449 above), Harness, Dyce and William Henry Brookfield. (See Ward, *Aubrey de Vere*, pp. 70–4; Charles and Frances Brookfield, *Mrs. Brookfield and Her Circle*, 2 vols., 1905, i. 150–1).

[2] 'My Brother has a pretty marine villa at the mouth of the Douro, 3 miles from Oporto,' E. Q. explained to H. C. R. on 4 Apr. '—he has offered it to us with all sorts of accommodation for as many months as we choose . . .' (Morley, ii. 594). E. Q., Dora Q., and Rotha Q. left Southampton for Portugal on 7 May.

[3] In a letter to I. F., Aubrey de Vere described meeting W. W. soon after his arrival in London. 'I never saw him in greater force or energy, either of body or mind. He gave us a lively account of his visit to Mr. Rogers, and his trying on Mr. Rogers's court dress which fortunately fits him so well that, with the help of Sir Humphry Davy's sword "science and art being thus fraternally united" he will have no trouble about his apparel.' (Una Taylor, *Guests and Memories*, 1924, p. 164.) See also *Rogers*, ii. 232.

1887. W. W. to GEORGE WILLIAMS FULCHER[1]

MS. untraced.
G. W. Fulcher, Spencer Farm, With Some Account of Its Owners, 1845, pp. vi–viii.
K (—). LY iii. 1251 (—).

22nd April, 1845, Rydal Mount

My dear Friend,

The little book you have sent to me consisting of the Memoirs of Mr. G. L. Way[2] and his Son the Rev. Lewis Way,[3] I have read with great interest. Their lives harmonize beautifully as both being strictly governed by principles of duty, while they contrast more strikingly as to the manner in which those principles put themselves into action.

Mr. Ellis[4] fell into a mistake, when speaking of Mr. G. L. Way, he says, that "happiness is the only rational object of pursuit"; but he is right, when in the same sentence he affirms that the means of happiness (he ought to have said the *only* means) are to be found in the practice of religion. Mr. Way's own words are, "I endeavour upon principle to have no business but my duty," and he adds, my amusements are excited by duty, and the rule of duty he gathers from his Bible, with the assistance of wise and good men.

The whole of the little Volume, (with the exception that for ordinary perusal too much space is given to Mr. G. L. Way's literary pursuits,) I found so interesting as earnestly to desire to see it printed in some shape that would give it a wide circulation; and this would perhaps be most effectually done, if it could be included in some collection of brief biographies confined exclusively to the lives of men of remarkable virtues and talents, though not universally or generally known. The number of these, if sought for, would be found considerable, and I cannot but think they would tend more to excite imitation than accounts of men so pre-eminent in genius and so favoured by opportunity, as rather to discourage than inspire emulation.

[1] See pt. ii, L. 756.

[2] Gregory Lewis Way (1757–99) Merewether's father-in-law (see L. 1404 above), of Spencer Farm, Essex: naturalist and translator of Le Grand's Fabliaux (1796, 1800).

[3] The Revd. Lewis Way, educated at Eton and Trinity College, Cambridge, held various curacies in Essex while residing at Spencer Farm.

[4] George Ellis (1753–1815), Scott's friend: author of *Specimens of the Early English Poets*, 1790, and *Specimens of the Early English Romances in Metre*, 1805.

One word more:—every intelligent Reader must be struck by the sound judgment with which Mr. Way manages his nervous depressions and apprehensions, and how he makes them subservient to the improvement of his own character. Would that others, who have like infirmities to contend with, might be induced to follow his example, and prove equally successful!

Pray do not impute it to any want of desire to meet your wishes, if I feel myself obliged to declare that I cannot presume to write anything that would deserve the name of a preface upon this occasion. If I were to put down in writing but a small portion of the thoughts raised in my mind by the perusal of these well-paired memoirs, you would have to read a volume larger than that which you sent, and which I now return to you with sincere thanks. My mind has been lately, and continues to be so much disturbed by sickness among near kindred, and other causes, that I am quite unable to give my thoughts upon this or any other subject a definite shape; and more by way of excuse for not complying with your request need not be said.

Wm Wordsworth

1888. W. W. to EDWARD MOXON

MS. Henry E. Huntington Library.
K (—). LY iii. 1252.

[*In I. F.'s hand*]

Rydal Mount
12th May—[1845]

My dear Mr Moxon,

I slept—my journey in the Coupée[1] with Genl Pasley proved very pleasant. I saw the country with great convenience and his conversation was interesting and most agreeable to me because there was no occasion I should talk much myself. The next day was also bright and fine and I was enchanted when I came into the Lake District a little above Bowness ('that beautiful romance of nature'). Every object—fields, woods, Lake, and Mountains, Sun-shine and shade were seen all the way in the utmost perfection of Spring beauty—reached home a little after 11 all well—my eyes better for the journey though I am still glad to employ an amanuensis, who on this occasion is Miss F, M^rs

[1] The end compartment in a railway carriage, with seating on one side only.

Wordsworth not being in the house. I was miserably mistaken about the plaid shawl and beg your and Miss Moxon's pardon for the trouble I gave you and your household to search for it. I found I had not taken it with me—has not this confusion of impressions something to do with age?—I must endeavour to draw a lesson from it for the future; others of my friends younger than myself I find have come to the same point. I forgot to remind you of the books you might possibly have spared for the Ambleside Library, but there is no hurry about this—

Having other letters to write I can only add I shall never forget your and Mrs Moxon's kindness to me during my late residence with you, nor Miss Moxon's never ceasing attentions—remember me affectionately to all and pray mention the substance of this letter to Mr Rogers and to any other friends who may enquire after me. Mr Rogers's care and concern for me were you know unbounded and I shall ever remain duly sensible of it—Mrs Wordsworth, were she in the house, would unite with me in the best of good wishes for you all not forgetting the New-born.

I remain
faithfully yours
[*signed*] Wm Wordsworth

1889. W. W. to WILLIAM WHEWELL

MS. Trinity College, Cambridge.
I. Todhunter, William Whewell . . . An Account of his Writings, with Selections from his Letters and Scientific Correspondence, 2 vols., 1876, i. 250 (—).

[*In I. F.'s hand*]

Rydal Mount
12 May 1845.

My dear Mr Whewell,

Your very kind letter and the vols that it accompanyed were put into my hands a couple of days before I left London where and at Hampstead I suffered so much from an attack in my Eyes which seized me almost upon my arrival that I was disabled both as to reading and writing as I continue to be tho' decidedly better for my journey and the quiet twenty four hours I have had since reaching home. I regretted very much missing you when you were so good as to call on me in Dover Street also that I could not thank you immediately for your two Vols on the Elements of Morality[1] and express my sense of the honor I have received by your dedicating them to me and *that* in terms which all my friends have read with the greatest pleasure and indeed you must allow me to say that both for delicacy, warmth of feeling and importance of the points touched upon I have scarcely seen the dedication of a Work which was more honorable to both parties. As soon as I am able I shall not fail to peruse the Vols with the utmost care. I have however no doubt that the subject will be so treated as not to stand in need of any comments from me, tho' should any thing occur to my mind worthy of your notice I will not fail to communicate it.

Pray remember us affectionately to Cordelia whose anxiety for her father[2] we think much of, and with every good wish for yourself and her—Believe me my dear Mr Whewell

Yours most faithfully
[*signed*] Wm Wordsworth

1890. W. W. to WILLIAM EDWARDS[3]

MS. Mr. R. E. Whitaker. Hitherto unpublished.

Rydal Mount
24th May 1845.

Dear Sir,

I take it very kindly that you did not leave to accident my being informed of the decease of your excellent Father, for whose virtues and talents I entertained a high respect; and

[1] *The Elements of Morality*, 2 vols., 1845. The dedicatory epistle ran as follows: My dear Mr. Wordsworth, I am desirous that, if the present book finds its way to the next generation, it should make known to them that I had the great privilege of your friendship. And there is no one to whom I could with more propriety dedicate such a work: since in your Poems, at the season of life when the mind and the heart are most wrought on by poetry, I, along with many others, found a spirit of pure and comprehensive morality, operating to raise your readers above the moral temper of those times. I shall rejoice if it appear from the following pages, that such influences have not been wasted upon me. That you may long enjoy the reverence and affection with which England, on such grounds, regards you, is the wish and prayer of . . . Your cordial friend and admirer, W. Whewell.

[2] John Marshall had gone blind. He died later this year.

[3] The Revd. William Edwards, son of John Edwards of Derby (see *MY* i. 470, ii. 562; and pt. iii, L. 1054). He apparently edited the *Moravian Magazine* in 1853.

sincerely can I say that I am sad at the thought of our never meeting again in this world. The way in which he managed to unite the cultivation of literature with activity in business was highly to his honor; nor can I think with you that his intellectual powers are overrated in the brief account which the *Derby Mercury* has given of him. The writer I am inclined to think is mistaken in his opinion that the Poem upon All Saints Church was the means of making us acquainted. Mr. Coleridge was at one time intimate with the Messrs. Streete of Derby, and I believe that it was through him that I was first introduced to your Father. But this is a matter of no consequence. I always deemed myself fortunate when circumstances brought your lamented Father and myself together.

It will give me much pleasure to renew my acquaintance with you should you again visit this country. Believe [me] with many good wishes

Faithfully your
much obliged
Wm Wordsworth

As to the time when I am likely to be at home I am quite unable to fix it, it depends upon circumstances which I cannot exactly foresee so that, with the rest of my friends, you must take your chance.

1891. W. W. to EDWARD MOXON

MS. Henry E. Huntington Library.
LY iii. 1253.

Rydal Mount
2nd June—1845

Dear Mr Moxon,

Since we first heard of this frightful fire so near your Premises, we have been very anxious about yourself and your family, particularly about Mrs Moxon. Pray write a line to tell us how you got through this awful trial—One Paper says your House was slightly damaged, but do let us know some thing, as our apprehensions as far as you are concerned may be worse than the reality proved—

I have just begun with the assistance of Mr Carter to prepare for the new Edition.[1] You will remember that I am quite set upon having fewer lines in a page than Murray and Longman have in their double-column Editions—and I am sorry to say that I am cried out against from many quarters for consenting to this shape of publication at all. But I have an answer to this, that it will put my Poems within the reach of so many persons of too small means to purchase them when confined to their present comparatively expensive shape.

Pray send me a specimen of what you propose at leisure—

My eye is much better though still weak.

Kind remembrances to all friends—especially of your own household and to Mr and Miss Rogers.

ever most faithfully yours
Wm Wordsworth

1892. W. W. to EDWARD MOXON

MS. Henry E. Huntington Library.
LY iii. 1254.

[June 1845]

My dear Mr Moxon,

My Friend Miss Fletcher has been twice at Rydal Mount taking a drawing of the House[2] from the best point of view—and I expect to be able to send it you very soon; I hope that the Printing will now go on with speed, and regularly. Great confusion and delay as I said before was caused by one proof being sent to me and another to Mr Carter.

ever faithfully yours
Wm Wordsworth

Pray send the other page to the Printer—it would be well that I should be favoured with his name, so that I might write to him directly.

[1] *The Poems of William Wordsworth*, 1845, the one-volume edition in double column which sold at one guinea.

[2] A vignette of Rydal Mount was to be engraved by W. Finden for the title-page of the new edition of W. W.'s poems. As subsequent letters show, W. W. was not satisfied with Miss Fletcher's efforts, and a drawing by G. Howse (d. 1860), a professional water-colour artist, was substituted.

1893. W. W. to EDWARD MOXON

MS. Henry E. Huntington Library.
K (—). LY iii. 1254.

[June 1845]

My dear Mr Moxon,

Herewith you have my Friend Miss Fletcher's Drawing of the House. It is very faithful, only the Engraver will of course have to reduce it.[1] Keep the drawing for a gift [when] the engraver has done with it.

I think I mentioned to you that I had an utter dislike of the Print from Pickersgill prefixed to the Poems. It does me and him also great injustice. Pray what would be the lowest expense of a respectable engraving from Chantrey's Bust?[2] That I should like infinitely better.

You have never told me how many copies of this Edition you mean to strike off, and whether it would answer to stereotype it; probably not.—

I have an impression of your having mentioned to me when I was with you in London, that in the course of the summer you would have a remittance to make to me. Was this so?—I know that since that time you advanced 20 pounds to Mr Quillinan on my account. I have not mentioned the matter as being in want of the money, but only to ask whether I am right in the impression, that I may regulate my summer expenses accordingly.

I enclose you a note from Mr Carter to me, showing how much importance he as well as I attach to the Stanzas not being broken. Do prevail upon the Printer to meet our wishes in this particular. They seem to have no notions on this subject. Sometimes you will have a line of a couplet, and a page must be turned over before one can get at the other.

Our Son William is just arrived, looking, for him, very well.—He begs to be kindly remembered to you.

Ever my dear Mr Moxon
faithfully yours
Wm Wordsworth

I am suffering a good deal from a violent fall, owing to my own carelessness.

[1] See previous letter.

[2] The Frontispiece of the new volume was an engraving by W. Finden of the Chantrey bust (see pt. ii, L. 500).

1894. W. W. to EDWARD MOXON

MS. Henry E. Huntington Library.
LY iii. 1255.

June 16th—45

My dear Mr Moxon,

The little Box contains my artificial teeth which want repairs. Be so good as to take them if you can find time, or let them be sent, if you cannot, to the Dentist. He did live a few years ago and I hope does still in Bedford Row, on the west side, and about half way down the street. I am sorry I have forgotten his name, but I think it was either Heath or Barclay—his predecessor I am persuaded bore one of these names, and he the other, but which of the two I do not know. When you have ascertained this will you be so kind as to direct the accompanying note which is for him, and may be taken along with the Box.—

We have been wishing for the Specimen Sheet as Mr Carter quits us tomorrow. Pray let the paper be stouter than is used in these editions and send the specimen upon it.

ever faithfully yours
Wm Wordsworth

1895. W. W. to JOHN PEACE

MS. WL transcript. Hitherto unpublished.

Rydal Mount
19th June, 1845.

My dear Mr Peace,

. . .I should like to think that your Descants[1] may be collected into a little volume. As you wrote so admirably upon the official maltreatment of cathedrals,[2] could not you be tempted to give a touch on Maynooth and its still more serious misdemeanours, the Establishment of colleges where Religion is to be thrown

[1] Peace published anonymously *A Descant on the Penny Postage*, 1841, *A Descant upon Railways*, 1842, and *A Descant upon Weather-wisdom*, 1845.

[2] In his *Apology for Cathedral Service*, 1839.

overboard.[1] This is surely one of the worse signs of the times that we have had. . .

ever faithfully yours,
Wm Wordsworth

1896. M. W. and W. W. to H. C. R.

Endorsed: Wordsw: Mrs Wordsw.
MS. Dr. Williams's Library.
Morley, ii. 600.

[*M. W. writes*]

21 June [1845] Rydal Mt.

My dear Friend

We want to know something of your whereabouts, and how your B^{r} is, and all about you—that we are so ignorant on these points, wch are always interesting to us, is no fault of yours, but of my own, who have been so long disinclined to write to any one unless from[2] dire necessity—which I am sorry to say has of late been but too frequent. We have had from various causes an anxious and I may say saddening Season—Dora's departure, her subsequent illness which is still hanging about us—Father returning from town with disordered eyes—which tho thank God are better, yet still require attention—And John's arrival from Italy, and hasty return with his 4 boys, who are now poor things travelling onward thro' France to the Baths of Lucca, the youngest 4 years old! to join their sick Mother—They left us at 5 oC. on Tuesday morning and got thro' London as fast as the business John had to do, about the rail-road which is to destroy his house—and getting Passports etc would allow—Hence probably neither you nor any of his friends save Moxon saw aught of him. His Boys were under the care of a connection of their Mother while he was making these preparations. You will guess our thoughts are travelling with them.

Mrs Fletcher mentioned to me one day, that you had given her reason to understand you intended giving us a *Summers Call*

[1] The Maynooth Bill (see L. 1885 above) received its Third Reading in the Lords on 16 June. The Bill for setting up the Queen's Colleges, where it was proposed that no provision should be made for religious instruction, went into Committee on the 13th.

[2] *Written* form.

some of these days. Is this true? I hope it may be, for be it but an hour's chat, it is worth a doz letters—if one had time to write them.

Miss Fenwick with Kate Southey returned last night to R. M. from a 2 days Excursion to Newby Bridge and Furness Abbey with the Miss Arnolds—they had the pain (tho it was a picturesque appearance) of seeing the Old Abbey occupied by the 'Navys'[1] at their meal, who are carrying a rail-way, so near to the East window that from it Persons might shake hands with the Passengers!!

The weather is beautiful for Tourists, and the Country is going to swarm—but some of our Neighbours mean to fly—for instance Mrs A. and her brood mean to go about the 14th to the Isle of Man for a few weeks. *We* shall be stationary, till about Sepr when *I* at least hope to go for a farewell visit to Brinsop—which the family leave in the Spring—Willy—if his health which is far from what it ought to be poor fellow, does not require to seek advice elsewhere will go with me

Our dear Sister keeps in her usual way—her B^r^ is at this moment drawing his Sister's Carriage in *the front*, they together with our dear friend beg their affec. remembrances along with me, hoping that you will excuse this scrubby letter and believe me ever affly

Yours
M. Wordsworth

My dear Friend,

I congratulate you upon the Premier doing so stoutly the devil's work in fellowship with your Friends the Whigs and the Radicals. The ignorance of fact, Law, and human nature shown in Parliament upon this occasion[2] is truly deplorable. Let Sir Robert look to the state of France to learn whither leads the course he is taking—ever faithfully yours

W W.

I hope your dear Brother is doing well.—

[1] i.e. the navvies of the Furness Railway Company. See W. W.'s sonnet *At Furness Abbey* (*PW* iii. 63), dated 21 June 1845.

[2] See previous letter.

1897. W. W. to GEORGE HUNTLY GORDON

Address: Geo. Huntley Gordon Esq., Stationery Office, London.
MS. Cornell. Hitherto unpublished.

Rydal Mount
June 24th— [18]45

My dear Sir

When I had but a glimpse of you at Mr Moxon's I was troubled with an inflammation in one of my eyes from which I am only just recovered and you must kindly accept this as excuse for not replying sooner to your friendly Letter. The Extract which [you] have sent me is very pleasing, but I do not feel I could make any thing of it in a poem, as you recommend. Besides, there is some thing wayward in matters of this kind. When a subject was proposed to Gainsborough[1] for a picture, if he liked it he used to say, "What a pity I did not think of it myself".

My own practise is odd even in respect to subjects of my own chusing. It was only a few days ago that I was able to put into Verse the Matter of a short Poem which had been in my mind with a determination and a strong desire to write upon it for more than thirty years;[2] nor is this the first time when the like has occurred.

I had a short Letter from your Father[3] some little time ago to introduce one of his Friends; pray tell him that I am pleased to hear of him upon any occasion and believe me with great sincerity your much obliged

Wm Wordsworth

[1] Thomas Gainsborough, R.A. (1727–88).

[2] 'Forth from a jutting ridge' (*PW* ii. 123), recalling the two rocks in Bainriggs from which M. W. and S. H. had been wont to admire the prospect of Rydal and Grasmere. Aubrey de Vere wrote to Henry Taylor from Ambleside on 9 Mar.: 'It is one of the wonders of the world to hear him [W. W.] talk over his own poetry and give you its secret history. I verily believe that not an object he ever saw or sound he ever heard has been lost upon him.' (*Correspondence of Henry Taylor*, p. 156).

[3] For Major Pryse Gordon, see pt. i, L. 351.

1898. W. W. to ANNA BROWNELL JAMESON[1]

MS. Cornell. Hitherto unpublished.

Sunday Evening
[June 1845]

Dear Mrs Jameson

I am truly sorry that you did not think of drawing our Gate towards you in which case you would have found no difficulty in approaching this House. We shall be very glad to see you to morrow at any time which may suit you. We drink tea at 6 oclock and at any time in the course of the afternoon you would be welcome; or if it should suit your arrangements better to call in the morning you will be sure to find us at home. I trust you will excuse my calling upon you, as I shall have my Haymakers to look after in the field in front of my House.

Believe me sincerely yours

W Wordsworth

1899. W. W. to MARY JANE RUDD

Address: Miss Rudd, Cockermouth.
MS. Cornell. Hitherto unpublished.

Rydal Mount
26 June — 1845

Dear Miss Rudd,

I take the liberty of thus addressing you in the belief that you are a Daughter of a much valued School fellow and University

[1] Mrs. Jameson (see *MY* i. 331; pt. i, L. 246) authoress of *Characteristics of Women*, 2 vols., 1832, had lived in Germany, 1834–6, and then in North America, where her husband was Attorney General of Toronto; but she had now returned alone to England. According to H. C. R., 'She has lately risen much in the estimation of society, and is now received in the highest literary circles, and this has not made her offensively confident' (*HCR* ii. 651). She had expressed her admiration of W. W. in a letter to Mrs. Austin of 9 Jan. 1832: 'Shelley's address to the skylark is like its own warble—it is a gush of joyous music, Wordsworth's is a strain of contemplative harmony—they are so unlike, that one may *like* both equally, but were I to make a choice I prefer Wordsworth's—' (*Pierpont Morgan Library MSS.*). The date of this letter is established by *RMVB*.

Friend of mine;[1] and can with truth assure you that I have much pleasure in subscribing myself

Sincerely yours
Wm Wordsworth

1900. W. W. to ANNA BROWNELL JAMESON

MS. Harvard University Library. Hitherto unpublished.

past 2 oclock. [June 1845]

Dear Mrs Jameson,

We have just heard that owing to Mrs Davy's illness the Party at Mrs Fletcher's does not hold. If you have an hour or two to spare we should [be] very glad to see you here as soon as convenient. We drink tea at six but pray come as much earlier as you like.

faithfully yours,
Wm Wordsworth

1901. W. W. to C. W. JNR.

Address: The Rev. Chris Wordsworth DD, Leamington, Warwickshire. [*In M. W.'s hand*]
Postmark: (1) 30 June 1845 (2) 1 July 1845.
Stamp: (1) Ambleside (2) Leamington.
MS. British Library.
Grosart (—). *K* (—). *LY iii. 1256* (—).

Monday noon [30 June 1845]

My dear Christopher,

I ought to have acknowledged my debt to you long ago, but the inflammation in one of my eyes which seized me on my first arrival in London kept its ground for a long time. I had your two first Pamphlets[2] read to me, and immediately put them into

[1] For John Rudd, see pt. iii, L. 865.

[2] On the Maynooth Question (see also L. 1885 above). The second, entitled *Church Principles and Church Measures: a Letter to Lord John Manners*, 1845, was an answer to Manners's *Past and Present Policy of England towards Ireland*, 1845 (see also L. 1806 above), which had supported the Maynooth grant and Peel's conciliatory policy (see *Lord John Manners and his Friends*, i. 181–4). C. W. jnr.'s third pamphlet was *A Review of the Maynooth Endowment Bill . . . and of the debates*

circulation among my Friends in this neighbourhood; but wishing to read them myself, I did not like to write to you till I had done so, as there were one or two passages on which I wished to make a remark. I have however not yet had an opportunity of doing so, and therefore must at present content myself with saying that the passages referred to some expressions upon Romanism which I thought too harsh and severe. My abhorrence of the system is as great as yours can probably be, but still in controversial writing one's language ought to be more guarded than I thought yours in the words to which I refer, though I cannot now turn to them having only just got back the Pamphlets. As to your arguments, they are unanswerable, and the three tracts do you the greatest possible credit; but the torrent cannot be stemmed, unless we can construct a body—I will not call it a party—upon a new and true principle of action, as you have set forth. Certain questions are forced by the present conduct of Government upon the mind of every observing and thinking person. First and foremost: are we to have a *national* English Church, or is the Church of England to be regarded merely as a sect, and is the right to the throne to be put upon a new foundation. Is the present ministry prepared for this and all that must proceed and follow it? Is Ireland an integral and inseparable portion of the empire or not; if it be, I cannot listen to the argument in favour of enduring Romanism upon the ground of superiority of numbers. The Romanists are not a majority in England and Ireland, taken, as they ought to be, together. As to Scotland, it has its separate Kirk by especial covenant. Are the ministers prepared to alter fundamentally the basis of the Union between England and Ireland, and to construct a new one. If they be, let them tell us so at once. In short, they are involving themselves and the Nation in difficulties from which there is no escape: for them, at least, none. What I have seen of your letter to Lord John Manners I like as well as your two former tracts, and I shall read it carefully at my first leisure moment.—

Pray thank dear Susan for her Letter which Mrs W. would have answered had I not been writing; but she is really overwhelmed with correspondence. We thank you sincerely in our name and W$^{m's}$ for your kind invitation to Leamington but alas we cannot profit by it, being overwhelmed with business

in the Commons . . . with a proposal for the conciliation of the contending parties in Ireland, 1845.

from morning to night. In fact since the most injudicious union upon principles of false economy of the two offices of Stamps and Taxes the Commissioners have not time to consider what is either expedient or right with respect to the administration of the several Distributorships of Stamps, which in their circumstances differ so widely from each other. The consequence is that W^{m} has work heaped upon him which no man even twice as strong would be equal to. And therefore I do exceedingly regret that he cannot find or make leisure for an excursion from home at present nor is it clear when he will be able to do so.—If he has not written to yourself or Susan the reason must be that at this time he is employed from 7 in the morning till nine or ten at night often, with the exception of a couple of hours or so for meals and a short ride.—He has some hope however (but that is dependent upon the arrangements of the board) of his being able to give a week to his Cousins at Newbiggin.[1]

The *Present and past Policy*[2] is your own; Mr Moxon meant it as a present to yourself, he gave me one at the same time. You have handled the shallow Author as he deserves.

Dora is convalescent, but still weak. We had a Letter yesterday, written in *good* and *chearful spirits*. Of Isabella the accounts are not very satisfactory. We think that the disease is telling much upon her mind—her Letters are so contradictory of each other. Her Physicians write to Mrs Curwen that the main bodily ailment is [? haemarroidial]. John writes that he had a most prosperous journey with his 4 sons to Paris where he meant to halt for two days, then would proceed to Chalons sur Soane by Diligence—the rest of the journey would be by water first to Marseilles, and then to Leghorn, by railway to Pisa, and then, no great distance, by carriage to the Baths of Lucca—

You see by this long scrawl that my eyes are better—pray excuse the wretched penmanship.—Your Cousin John Wordsworth is languishing under a malady which he is convinced is making progress, but surely it is very slow, and he may live for many years poor Fellow! Susan does not mention your Father or Charles. We hope both are well. Kindest Love to you both, in which dear old Auntie joins

your affectionate Uncle,

W. W.

[1] The Crackanthorpes.

[2] i.e. Lord John Manners's pamphlet.

Herbert[1] and Emmie Fisher are just arrived. He is gone to Grasmere where he will spend the next two months with a Tutor Mr Clough,[2] and she will remain with us the greatest part of the time.—Miss Southey is also with us so that Emmie and she will be companions. Miss Fenwick will remain with us for three weeks yet.

1902. W. W. to CHARLES SCARLE and CHARLES BAKER[3]

MS. Mr. Leopold Hughman. Hitherto unpublished.

[late June, 1845]

My Dear Young Friends,

Innumerable engagements, absence from home and other reasons must be accepted as an excuse for not replying sooner to your communications. I have read, which I rarely do in respect to Mss. *both* your poems, as you requested, and will frankly tell you that neither of them is of first-rate merit; but perhaps the one with the motto from Thomson is the better, at least my grandsons, school-boys like yourselves, think so. Don't be discouraged by my not extolling your productions, for I am very difficult to please, my own being included, and I remember that when at School I first began to write, my attempts were much below what you have sent me.

[1] Herbert William Fisher (see *RMVB*), eldest son of W. W.'s cousin, Mrs. Fisher of Salisbury, now a barrister and Student of Christ Church, Oxford: later private secretary to the Prince of Wales (1861–70), and vice-warden of the Stannaries. He was the father of H. A. L. Fisher, the historian.

[2] Arthur Hugh Clough (1819–61), the poet and friend of Matthew Arnold: Fellow of Oriel College, Oxford, 1842–8. Educated at Rugby under Dr. Arnold, he subsequently fell under the influence of Newman and W. G. Ward, and eventually resigned his Fellowship. Clough had toured the Lakes this month with his sister Anne Jemima Clough (1820–92), first Principal of Newnham College, Cambridge, and they had met W. W. See Blanche Athena Clough, *A Memoir of Anne Jemima Clough*, 1897, pp. 54–6.

[3] Pupils at Mill Hill School, Yoxford, nr. Ipswich. Their master, Robert Hughman (b. 1813), author of *The Foil: an historical poem*, 1843, had sent on 3 June his 'Lines addressed to Wm Wordsworth Esq., Poet Laureate, . . . requesting him to award the mimic wreath to the most deserving candidate for the Poet-Laureateship of my school—Chas. Scarle and Chas. Baker competitors, subject Alfred . . .' Hughman's verses, with W. W.'s reply, were copied into his notebook: the original MS. has not survived.

With best wishes for your future welfare, believe me, my young friends,

Sincerely Yours,
Wm Wordsworth

Excuse great haste.

I like your Hero mightily, indeed above every other that I ever heard of.

1903. W. W. to HENRY REED

Address: Henry Reed Esqre, Philadelphia, U.S. P^{r} packet from Liverpool.
Postmark: (1) 1 July 1845 (2) 2 July.
Stamp: Ambleside.
MS. Cornell.
Mem. Grosart. Wordsworth and Reed, p. 142.

Rydal Mount Ambleside
July 1st—45

My dear Mr Reed

I have as usual been long in your debt, which I am pretty sure you will excuse as heretofore. It gave me much pleasure to have a glimpse of your Brother,[1] under circumstances which no doubt he will have described to you. He spoke of his health as improved, and I hope it will continue to do so. I understood from him that it was probable he should call at Rydal before his return to his own Country. I need not say to you I shall be glad, truly glad to see him both for his own sake and as so nearly connected with you. My absence from home lately was of more than three weeks. I took the journey to London solely to pay my respects to the Queen upon my appointment to the Laureatship upon the decease of my Friend Mr Southey. The weather was very cold, and I caught an inflammation in one of my eyes which rendered my stay in the South very uncomfortable. I nevertheless did in respect to the object of my journey all that was required. The reception given me by the young Queen at her Ball was most gracious. Mrs Everett[2] the wife of your minister

[1] William B. Reed, formerly Attorney General for Pennsylvania. (*RMVB*). See also L. 1908 below.

[2] Wife of the American Minister Edward Everett (see L. 1613 above). She was Charlotte, daughter of Peter Chardon Brooks (1767–1849), Boston merchant, reputedly one of the wealthiest men in New England.

among many others was a witness to it; without knowing who I was. It moved her to the shedding of tears. This effect was in part produced, I suppose by American habits of feeling, as pertaining to a republican government like yours.[1] To see a grey haired Man 75 years of age kneeling down in a large assembly, to kiss the hand of a young Woman is a sight for which institutions essentially democratic do not prepare a spectator of either sex, and must naturally place the opinions upon which a Republic is founded, and the sentiments which support it, in strong contrast with a government based and upheld as our's is. I am not therefore surprized that Mrs Everett was moved as she herself described to persons of my acquaintance, among others to Mr Rogers the Poet. By the bye this Gentleman, now I believe in his 83[d] year I saw more of than of any other Person except my Host Mr Moxon, while I was in London. He is singularly fresh and strong for his years, and his mental faculties (with the exception of his memory a little) not at all impaired. It is remarkable that he and the Rev[d] W. Bowles were both distinguished as Poets when I was a school-boy, and they have survived almost all their eminent contemporaries, several of whom came into notice long after them. Since they became known Burns, Cowper, Mason[2] the author of Caractacus and friend of Gray have died. Thomas Warton Laureate, then Byron, Shelley, Keats, and a good deal latter Scott, Coleridge, Crabbe, Southey, Lamb, the Ettrick Shepherd, Cary the Translator of Dante, Crowe[3] the author of Lewesdon Hill, and others of more or less distinction have disappeared. And now of English Poets advanced in life, I cannot recall any but James Montgomery, Thomas Moore, and myself who are living, except the Octogenarian with whom I began. I saw Tennyson[4]

[1] In his letter of 29 Mar., Reed professed himself 'much interested' in W. W.'s account (see L. 1849 above) of the demonstrations of enthusiasm for the Queen: 'Pray do not suppose that our republicanism is so democratic and Jacobinical, as, by narrowing and perverting our thoughts and feelings, to unfit us for understanding and sympathising with such expressions of patriotism and affectionate loyalty.' (*Wordsworth and Reed*, p. 140).

[2] William Mason (1724–97), friend and biographer of Gray, author of *Caractacus*, 1759.

[3] William Crowe (1745–1829), rector of Alton Barnes, Wilts. from 1787. See also *EY*, p. 166.

[4] See L. 1886 above. Tennyson's reputation was consolidated by his 1842 volume. He was now at work on *The Princess* (1847), and the elegies which were later combined in *In Memoriam* (1850).

when I was in London, several times. He is decidedly the first of our living Poets, and I hope will live to give the world still better things. You will be pleased to hear that he expressed in the strongest terms his gratitude to my writings. To this I was far from indifferent though persuaded that he is not much in sympathy with what I should myself most value in my attempts, viz the spirituality with which I have endeavored to invest the material Universe, and the moral relation under which I have wished to exhibit its most ordinary appearances. I ought not to conclude this first portion of my letter without telling you that I have now under my Roof, a Cousin, who some time ago was introduced, improperly I think, she being then a child, to the notice of the public, as one of the English Poetesses, in an article of the Quarterly so Entitled.[1] Her name is Emmeline Fisher and her mother is my first cousin. What advances she may have made in latter years I do not know, but her productions from the age of eight to twelve, were not less than astonishing. She only arrived yesterday, and we promise ourselves much pleasure in seeing more of her. Our dear Friend Miss Fenwick is also under our Roof, so is Katharine Southey, her late Fathers youngest daughter, so that we reckon our Household rich; though our only daughter is far from us, being gone to Oporto with her Husband on account of her enfeebled frame, and most unfortunately soon after her arrival she was seized with a violent attack of Rheumatic fever caused by exposure to the evening air. We have also been obliged lately to part with four grandsons, very fine boys, who are gone with their Father to Italy to visit their mother, kept there by severe illness which sent her abroad two years ago. Under these circumstances we old people keep our spirits as well as we can, trusting the end to God's goodness.

Now for the enclosed Poem[2] which I wrote the other day, which I send to you, hoping it may give you some pleasure as a scanty repayment for all that we owe you. Our dear Friend Miss Fenwick, is especially desirous that her warm thanks shall be returned to you for all the trouble you have taken about her

[1] 'Modern English Poetesses', *Quarterly Review*, lxvi (1840), 374–418, a discussion of works by (among others) Mrs. Caroline Norton, Elizabeth Barrett, Caroline Southey, and Sara Coleridge, in which Emmie Fisher was presented as 'a bud among the flowers', with a specimen of her poetry. The author of the article was Henry Nelson Coleridge.

[2] The earlier version of *The Westmoreland Girl, To My Grandchildren* (*PW* i. 255), dated Rydal Mount, 6 June 1845. See also L. 1908 below.

Bonds. But to return to the verses, if you approve, pray forward them with my compts and thanks for his letter to Wm P. Atkinson,[1] West Roxbury St. Boston, Massachusetts.

In his Letter he states that with others he is strenuously exerting himself in endeavours to abolish slavery, and as one of the means of disposing the public mind to that measure, he is about to publish selections from various authors in behalf of *humanity*. He begs an original composition from me. I have nothing bearing directly upon slavery, but if you think this little piece would serve his cause indirectly pray be so kind as to forward it to him. He speaks of himself as deeply indebted to my writings.

I have not left room to subscribe myself more than affectionately yours

W Wordsworth

1904. W. W. to EDWARD MOXON

MS. Henry E. Huntington Library.
LY iii. 1257.

[*In M. W.'s hand*]

Rydal Mount
July 14th —45

Dear Mr Moxon,

Mr Carter writes to me for direction as to the *Heading* of the Pages—I think it best not to attend to this till we see the Proof sheets, when we can determine according to the matter contained thereon.[2]

Would it not be desireable that the Work should be out against the time that Christmas presents are called for? But this must depend upon what number of the present Ed: remains on hand.

My Nephew Mr Charles W. will call upon you in a day or two, previous to his coming down here. Will you please send by him, together with any parcel you may have for us, a few quires

[1] William P. Atkinson (1820–90), Boston abolitionist, who wrote on 25 May asking for a contribution to a volume of poetry in support of the cause and acknowledging his obligations to W. W.: 'In times of peculiar spiritual loneliness, when my mind was but half developed, my principles half formed, your words were more to me than anything save the Gospels.' (*WL MSS.*)

[2] W. W. was now revising his poems for the 1845 edition.

of the thinnest paper, for foreign postage, that is to be had. The Quillinans complain of the heavy rate of Postage they are charged in Oporto—Mrs Q has had a severe illness, but I am thankful to say she is now convalescent. We have not heard of John's arrival with *his* charge at Lucca,—but his last letter announced their safety as far as Avignon. Send me by Mr C. W. three copies of the Excursion.

If you do not go on to the Continent we should be glad if you could run down here in the course of the present, or next Month. In Septr we mean to go into Herefordshire.

ever faithfully yours
[*signed*] Wm Wordsworth

We have had Mr Bryant[1] the American Poet and his friend here, they seemed to enjoy the day much.

1905. M. W. and W. W. to CHARLES WORDSWORTH

MS. Mr. Jonathan Wordsworth. Hitherto unpublished.

[*c.* 14 July 1845]

My dear Charles,

We are truly glad to find you are turning your thoughts hitherwards, and I need not say how happy your Uncle, Aunt and myself shall be to see you and your's.[2] We have no intention of leaving home before September, at that time it is our wish to pay a short visit to my Brother and his family in Herefordshire —but that will not interfere with your holiday.

[1] William Cullen Bryant (see pt. iii, L. 1184), came to Rydal Mount on 10 July with an introduction from H. C. R. (see *HCR* ii. 654 and *RMVB*): 'Mr. Wordsworth was in the garden, in a white broad-brimmed, low-crowned hat; he received me very kindly; showed me over his grounds, his study etc.' (Park Godwin, *A Biography of William Cullen Bryant*, ii. 8). His companion was Charles Leupp (see L. 1984 below).

[2] i.e. his daughter with her governess, Miss Searle, and his sister-in-law and her aunt. Miss Searle's *Diary* (*MS. Miss Bell*) records visits to Rydal Mount on 23 and 30 July, 2, 7, and 21 Aug. ('. . . the poet said the first voluntary verses he ever wrote were written after walking 6 miles to attend a dance at Egremont. . .'), and a farewell visit on the 23rd: 'Poor Miss Wordsworth was in the garden so I talked to her, it is quite wonderful that she should talk so sensibly at times.'

I lost no time in applying for the lodgings which I think would best suit you—those which the Quillinans occupied, near Ambleside Chapel, kept by two Sisters, for whom Dora feels almost the respect of a Sister—but I am not quite sure that this House may be at liberty for you—You must however write me a line by return of Post, and mention the day you are likely to be here, and for how *long a time you* may require the lodgings. If I am disappointed here, I will use my best endeavours to have you comfortably accommodated elswhere—but the Country is likely to be very full of Strangers—and lodgings scarce.

[*W. W. writes*]

My dear Charles,

I am very glad that we are likely to see you and yours so soon, and should be still more so were I sure that you can procure the Lodgings your aunt inquired after yesterday, as I think they would exactly suit you. Chris: has done himself great credit by his late publications,[1] and I see with pleasure that his French Diary[2] is advertized. The Publication is well-timed. Pray bring it down with you, and should it be convenient, but not otherwise, call at Moxon's to inquire if he has any small parcel for me.

You do not mention your health. I hope therefore it is improved. Dora has been very ill since she went to Oporto—an attack of Rheumatic fever. By the last account she is convalescent, but still very weak. John has been here and is gone back to Italy with his 4 Sons. We have heard of them from Avignon, where they had arrived without mishap of any kind, and all in good health. He travels with a Servant Male or Female, and the Boys behaved wonderfully well. We think your Cousin John[3] a good deal better.

Your affectionate Uncle, W Wordsworth

The accounts of John's Wife Isabella are rather more favorable—

[1] His three pamphlets on the Maynooth Question. See Ls. 1885 and 1901 above.

[2] *Diary in France, Mainly on Topics concerning Education and the Church*, 1845. It was dedicated to Joshua Watson, and described C. W. jnr.'s visit to France the previous summer.

[3] R. W.'s son.

1906. W. W. to UNKNOWN CORRESPONDENT

Endorsed: W Wordsworth July 15 1845.
MS. WL.
LY iii. 1258.

Rydal Mount July 15th—1845

Dear Sir,

Accept my thanks for your obliging Invitation to attend the opening of the Windermere Steam Yacht[1] but my engagements are no[t] likely to allow me that pleasure.

I remain
truly
your obliged
Wm Wordsworth

1907. W. W. to EDWARD MOXON

Address: Mr Moxon —
MS. Henry E. Huntington Library.
LY iii. 1258.

[July 1845]

Dear Mr Moxon,

I shall speak to Miss Fletcher about the want of character in the trees of the drawing,[2] and I hope she will be able to correct it.

[1] *Written* yatch. A steamer had now been provided to carry passengers from the railway terminus at Bowness to Low Wood. See W. Rollinson, *Life and Tradition in the Lake District*, 1974, p. 175. W. W.'s opposition seems to have led to a temporary misunderstanding with Lord Lonsdale, who had written on 8 Jan.: 'I have now been long enough acquainted with the world to be well aware that from equally good motives men may take very different views of what is generally useful, or, for any other reason, proper to be done. I never supposed that any other than good motives actuated you in what you may have said or done about this Steamer. I consented to it, because it never occurred to me that it would be looked upon as any thing else than a general advantage. I am well aware that from our long friendship, you would yourself have communicated directly with me if you saw good reason why a consent should not have been given by me. And on the same ground if I had any thing to say against the part which you have taken, I should at once have said it to yourself.' (*WL MSS.*)

[2] See L. 1892 above.

I am well aware of the difficulty of avoiding breaks in the Stanzas, but with due care a good deal may be done to prevent the disadvantage, though certainly not in all cases.—I hope we shall get on speedily.

ever faithfully yours
W Wordsworth

Sunday morning. I am glad you mean to stereotype, as I shall make no more alterations.

1908. W. W. to HENRY REED

Address: Henry Reed Esqre, Philadelphia. [*In M. W.'s hand*]
MS. Cornell.
Wordsworth and Reed, p. 146.

Rydal Mount
31st July—45

My dear Mr Reed

Your Brother[1] who is kindly coming from Liverpool to bid me good bye will be the Bearer of this, the principal object of which is, to mention the two volumes entitled Glossary of Architecture[2] with which I hope he will be able to charge himself, are from Miss Fenwick, who begs your acceptance of them as an acknowledgement of the unwearied attention you have paid to her interests in the matter of the Pennsylvania Bonds. She regrets much that she has not an opportunity here of getting the work bound, but not knowing when so favorable an opportunity may again occur for sending it she hopes it may be acceptable to you though only in its present state.

I know not what we are to expect as to the future; but I would fain hope that a regard for their own honor, if no superior motive, will constrain the State to continue to discharge its

[1] See L. 1903 above. Another visitor from America in August was Dr. Charles Meigs (1792–1869) the Philadelphia obstetrician, also introduced by Henry Reed.

[2] Probably *A Glossary of Terms used in Grecian, Roman, Italian, and Gothic Architecture, Exemplified by one hundred and fifty wood-cuts*, 1836 (4th edn. enlarged, 1845). The author was John Henry Parker (1806–84), an Oxford bookseller who published for the high-church party, and became first Keeper of the Ashmolean Museum, 1870–84.

obligations. At all events whatever may occur or is likely to happen in this matter, I am pretty sure you will let me know.

I am at present carrying through the Press an Edition in double column of my Poems including the last. The contents of which will be interspersed in their several places. In the Heading of the Pages I have followed the example of your Edition[1] by extending the classification of imagination far beyond what it has hitherto been except in your Edition. The Book will be by no means so well-looking as your's; as the Contents will be more crowded. The new matter is not of much consequence but will amount to about 300 lines. The little Poem[2] which I ventured to send you lately I thought might interest you on account of the fact as exhibiting what sort of characters our mountains breed. It is truth to the Letter. If you have a copy pray insert after the words sharp tooth'd Pike" this stanza

Merciful Protectress, kindling
Into anger or disdain,
Many a Captive hath she rescued,
Others saved from lingering pain.

and after "Maid of Arc" at the conclusion, stanza,

Leave that word—and here be offer[ed]
Prayer that Grace divine would raise
This humane courageous Spirit
Up to heaven, through peaceful ways.

It was thought by some of my Friends that the other conclusion took the mind too much away from the subject

ever most faithfully W W.

[1] The Philadelphia edition of 1837.

[2] *The Westmoreland Girl* (see L. 1903 above).

1909. W. W. to GEORGE WASHINGTON DOANE

Address: Bishop Doane, Rounde, Burlington, N.J. [*In M. W.'s hand*]
Postmark: 22 Aug. [ ].
Stamp: Philadelphia, Pa.
MS. Columbia University Library. Hitherto unpublished.

[early Aug. 1845][1]

My dear Bishop,

I had scarcely subscribed my name to the foregoing, when I was more agreeably surprized by receiving a note from you, presented by your Friend and Fellow Country man Mr Williamson.[2] From him I learned that you were neighbours, and that your children were under the same Schoolmaster. By him also I was told that your purposed voyage to Europe had been prevented, but I hope we may see you at some future time. I did not see quite as much as I wished of Mr Williamson, for it happened that I was engaged through the whole of the day with a succession of Visitors, two of whom however he seemed pleased to meet—one Mr La Trobe[3] the Moravian Missionary and the other Mr Wm Howit[4] the Author of Rural life in England and other known works.

[1] This letter was apparently taken away by an American visitor, probably Henry Reed's brother, and posted in the U.S. Hence the dating.

[2] General Williamson of Pennsylvania called at Rydal Mount on 30 July (*RMVB*).

[3] James Montgomery had written on 25 July to introduce the Revd. Peter Latrobe and his brother (*WL MSS.*), and their visit is recorded in *RMVB* under 30 July. Peter Latrobe (1795–1863), son of Christian Ignatius Latrobe (1758–1836), the Moravian missionary and composer, succeeded his father as secretary of the Moravian missions. He was an organist and wrote an *Introduction on the Progress of the Church Psalmody* for an edition of 'Moravian Hymn Tunes.' His brother John (1799–1878), took orders in the Church of England, and after several curacies became incumbent of St. Thomas's, Kendal, 1840–65. He was author of *The Music of the Church considered in its various branches, Congregational and Choral*, 1831, and *The Chant: its character explained, and its use recommended*, 1838, and compiled his own church hymnary which included some of his own compositions.

[4] William Howitt (see pt. i, L. 293; pt. ii, Ls. 608 and 785) had published *The Rural Life of England*, 2 vols., 1838, and was now planning *Homes and Haunts of the Most Eminent British Poets*. In her *Autobiography*, ii. 32, Mary Howitt recalls their visit to Rydal Mount: '. . . dear Mrs. Wordsworth sat mending her shoe, while the room was full of strangers, who had called to honour the poet. There

I hope that your Episcopal church continues to make progress, and that you are upon the whole well pleased with its condition and prospects. When I was in London in the Spring, I saw more than once our common Friend Sir R. H. Inglis as well as active and as profitably employed as ever. Believe me my dear Bishop as before said faithfully your much obliged

Wm Wordsworth

1910. W. W. to H. C. R.

MS. Dr. Williams's Library.
Morley, ii. 605.

Rydal Mount 7th Aug^t [18]45

My dear Friend,

I must begin with a little matter of business—A few months ago you kindly presented me with two Vols, entitled a Glossary of Architecture.[1] They were very acceptable as a memorial of yourself, and for their contents; but I have felt obliged to part with the Book; and I will tell you—How. Miss Fenwick was very desirous of making an acknowledgement to Mr Reed of Philadelphia for the trouble he had taken mainly on her account about the Pennsylvanian bonds. Mr Reed's Brother came hither from Liverpool to bid me good bye, just before his departure for America. I showed him this Book and asked if he thought it was in his Brother's library. He said he was sure it was not; I then proposed to Miss Fenwick that as there was no time to procure any other, She should avail herself of the opportunity to send the Volumes in her own name. This accordingly was done, and they are now better half of the way to Pensylvania.—Now what I have to beg is that you would procure another Copy of this work write your name in it as a present from you to me, have it sent to Moxon to be forwarded by the first convenient opportunity, and request him to put the cost of the Volumes

was, among others, an American general there, an advocate of slavery, with whom William and Mr. Wordsworth had a great argument. All the day afterwards Wordsworth kept rejoicing that they had defeated the general. "To think of the man" said he, "coming, of all things, to this house with a defence of slavery! But he got nothing by it. Mr. Howitt and I gave it to him pretty well." ' See also L. 2032 below.

[1] See L. 1908 above.

down to me. In this way Miss F. will have attained her wish, and things will stand on the same footing as before.

You ask how we get on with Miss Martineau. She has had with her 4 Aunts and 9 Cousins, and innumerable acquaintances occasionally, so that it has been utterly impossible for us to have more than two or three interviews with her, one of which was at our own house, where she was kind enough to drink tea with us. I have however heard from others that she is as entêtée as ever upon the ground of mesmerism, and will only see and hear as suits her passionate credulity. A striking instance of this in connection with her prime agent, Jane,[1] shall be told you with all particulars when we meet. At present I will confine myself to observing that in this and all matters, her quickness of mind, in leaping to conclusions, in conjunction with her imperfect hearing, has much to do in misleading her, and makes her in many respects ever a dangerous companion. Of this also You shall have an instance, in which the Fletchers were concerned and with which they were a good deal hurt.—I have not been well lately from two causes; I overlaboured and overheated myself with my axe and saw, and caught cold in the evening. And when I was recovering from this I had [a] very ugly fall from the top of the Mount, which shook me sadly, and of which I shall feel the effects for some time. M[rs] W and Miss Fenwick are both pretty well—You do not mention your Brother. The reprinting of my Poems is going on regularly, the Book will be stereotyped and from what I hear through the Bookseller, there will be no small demand for it; partly for its own sake, and partly to class with Byron and Southey etc who are already in the same forms. The alterations of which you heard, are almost exclusively confined to a few of the Juvenile Poems—I am at the end of my paper and my time and so my dear Friend farewell, with a thousand good wishes—ever

most faithfully yours
W. Wordsworth

[1] Jane Arnold.

1911. M. W. to H. C. R.

MS. Dr. Williams's Library.
Morley, ii. 606.

[7 Aug. 1845]

My dear Friend

I have forwarded your note to good Mrs Hoare and unless she be gone to Cromer as is her usual custom about this season I have no doubt Miss Weston[1] will soon have a visit from her and Miss Hoare.

I have indeed been very remiss in leaving you so long in the dark about us—but truly my thoughts have been so much disturbed of late in connection with our Absentees, and our time has been so taken up by daily visitors[2] which under existing circumstances (My husband's derangement from his fall etc) have been rather oppressive than otherwise, so that I have shrunk from the pen, as much as I possibly could,—and hence I have presumed upon your forbearance.

I am now thankful to tell you that we have delightful reports of Dora's improvement since the illness which interupted the flattering account she gave of herself after her first arrival in Portugal—She now rides a beautiful Andalusian poney and is in the 7th Heaven.

From Lucca our letters give, I grieve to say, a very different report, Mrs J. W. not seeming to make any progress—and the heat of the present season oppressive to them all—tho' the Father and the little fellows all performed their journey admirably. Notwithstanding what I have said about our being overrun by visitors We sh^d be delighted were your Lady friend to succeed in her desire to elope hitherward with you. Miss F. is now in residence, and entertaining the H. Taylors and other inmates, at Fox how.—Our nephew Charles W. and his daughter, with three other Lady friends are occupying the Quillinan's lodgings at Ambleside.—Mr Monkhouse[3] after a visit of a fortnight's stay

[1] See L. 1790 above.

[2] Recent visitors (*RMVB*), not mentioned elsewhere, included H. S. Tremenheere (see L. 1942 below), Edward Denison (see pt. iii, L. 983), J. W. Blakesley (see pt. ii, L. 706), and J. J. Gurney, the Quaker, Elizabeth Fry's brother (see J. B. Braithwaite, *Memoirs of Joseph John Gurney*, 2 vols., 1854, ii. 467–8).

[3] John Monkhouse of The Stow.

left us yesterday—The youthful Poetess Emmie Fisher is our guest—as also Kate Southey has been, and will be again we expect tomorrow—She went to Keswick for a few days to be present at the re-opening of Crosthwaite Church,[1] which Mr Stanger, that munificent Man, has been beautifying preparatory to M^r^ S's Monument being received therein.

Ever my dear friend
affly yours
M. Wordsworth

By the date of *Fathers* letter you will discover that William is now with us and I am thankful to say in better health than during his last visit.

1912. W. W. to C. W. JNR.

MS. Cornell. Hitherto unpublished.

[*In the hand of W. W. Jnr.*]

Rydal Mount
7th Augt 1845

. . . Pray give my blessing with a kiss to my little Maria Wordsworth.[2] We like the name much—This is penned by W^m^ who desires his kindest regards.—

[*signed*] Wm Wordsworth

1913. W. W. to C. W. JNR.

MS. British Library. Hitherto unpublished.

[*c.* 8 Aug. 1845]

My dear Christopher,

I have not yet heard of your Books[3] sent to Ambleside but I shall inquire after them immediately.

One Copy I have myself, and have read with very great interest and much instruction, so that I wish it were read by every person of station or consideration in the Country. I hope it

[1] James Stanger of Lairthwaite had donated £4,000 for the restoration of the roof and interior.

[2] C. W. jnr.'s third daughter Mary.

[3] Probably copies of his third Maynooth pamphlet (see L. 1901 above).

has been noticed in periodical Publications, though I myself have seen no *other* notice of it than in two numbers of the *Morning Post*. Mr Johnston, an Irishman who writes the Leading Articles in that Journal is an old and intimate Acquaintance of mine and spent last Sunday with us. Your Book has greatly interested him; and the more so because he knows his native Country so well.

Charles and W^{m} went yesterday by Coniston and down the Vale of Duddon, and by Broughton to Dalton where they would sleep. It was a beautiful grey day, and this is a splendid sunshining one, most favorable to the continuance of their Tour. Their first object this morning would be Furness Abbey. They return this Evening. What do you think of a Railway being driven as it now is, close to the magnificent memorial of the piety of our ancestors?[1] Many of the trees which embowered the ruin have been felled to make way for this pestilential nuisance. We have also surveyors at work with our beautiful Valley the line meditated to pass through Rydal Park and immediately behind Rydal Mount.

We are sorry that we are not likely to see our dear Brother. At our age one cannot but be strongly desirous of making the most of opportunities of intercourse whenever they present themselves. Emmie Fisher is still with us and will remain another week or so, when she will go to Keswick with Miss Fenwick; and her brother[2] who has been residing at Grasmere, will come here for a few days, and follow her to Keswick; whence they both will proceed to Newbiggin on their way homeward—we like them both very much.

You say nothing about your health, I hope it has been benefited by your Residence at Leamington; pray mention it, when you write again.

Your Aunt Dorothy often complains but on the whole I am persuaded she is no worse than she has been for many years. Pray when do you think of going into Italy, and how, and by what route do you mean to travel? You cannot be an acceptable visitor to the authorities of Rome; you may be pretty sure that they are not ignorant of the character and tendency of your writings, and I should not at all wonder if you were to receive a hint that you would do well to quit the Country. But I may be in error on this point; and you are likely to know much better than

[1] See also L. 1896 above.

[2] Herbert (see L. 1901 above).

I how things would stand with you. If we do not hear more satisfactory accounts than we have done lately—old as we are, it is not improbable that Mary and I may go to Pisa to visit Isabella. I earnestly hope however that such a long journey may not be necessary for us. An Edition of my Poems in double column is passing through the Press, the Book will not I hope extend beyond 400 pages.[1] Southey's I see contains 1000.

Best love to Susan in which Mary and Aunt unite with me ever Your affectionate Uncle

W Wordsworth—

1914. W. W. to UNKNOWN CORRESPONDENT[2]

MS. Mr. W. Hugh Peal. Hitherto unpublished.

Rydal Mount
29th Augst 45

Dear Sir,

You were not mistaken in supposing that I should be pleased with the sight of a Book which does so much credit to the Press of Newcastle as the One which you were so kind as to send me. My thanks ought to have been returned much earlier and would have been so, but I wished to make myself acquainted with the Poems, which I had not leisure to do, or to write, my time at this season of the year being so taken up with Visitors, and Strangers crowding in from morning to night. I can now assure you that I have looked over your Volume with much pleasure.

Let me particularly thank you for the Poem upon the Legend with which your Volume closes. It is written with much Spirit and the subject is really important. No man can travel through Ireland, as it has been my lot to do, without indignation and sorrow, at the Proofs he will meet with of the disgrace incurred by the Roman Catholic Church in not pulling down the Superstitions that prevail in that country, to an extent which would be utterly impossible, if they were not connived at by the Priests, not to say encouraged and participated by some of the most ignorant among them.

[1] It actually extended to over 600 pages.

[2] Possibly John Adamson (see L. 2107 below).

Repeating my thanks for so agreeable a mark of your attention, I remain my dear Sir

Sincerely your
much obliged
Wm Wordsworth

1915. W. W. to JOHN GIBSON LOCKHART

MS. Hunter Baillie Collection, Royal College of Surgeons. Hitherto unpublished.

Rydal Mount
Septr 6th—1845

My dear Mr Lockhart

Pray excuse the liberty I take by introducing to you the Bearer which I should not have done but from some hope that you might serve him in some degree without inconvenience to yourself. The Gentleman's name is Boner,[1] an Englishman by birth and Education, but who has been for the last six years as he continues to be Tutor to the sons of a German Prince whose principal Residence is at Ratisbon. Tour and Taxis I think is his name. This young man has a good deal of leisure, is thoroughly acquainted with Germany and German literature and versed in other Departments of knowledge, and in consequence is desirous of an opening for literary Employment, but owing to his absence from his native Country, he has no personal knowledge either of Publishers or Editors. Allow me then to ask if you would look over some one of his productions, especially an Article which he tells me he has written upon Germany, and which might prove not unsuitable to the *Quarterly Review*, especially if upon looking into it you should approve of it so far as to suggest any additions or omissions by which it might be better adapted to such a purpose. As I hope Mr Boner may be so fortunate as to have an interview I need not say any more upon the subject, and must conclude by again entreating you to excuse the liberty I have taken.

Believe me faithfully
Wm Wordsworth

You will be pleased to hear that my Daughter's health has been greatly benefited by a Residence at the mouth of the

[1] See L. 1882 above.

Douro, whither she went with her Husband Mr Quillinan a few months back. He is labouring hard at a Translation of the *Lusiad* into English verse; which he has been induced to undertake from his love of Portugal (his native Country) and with the view of doing something like justice to a Poet who has been so miserably *mis*translated in our language. I am sorry he has undertaken this work, and should have much rather that *you* could have given him an opening in your Journal, his talents for periodical writing being in my judgement great and it would be convenient that they should be turned to account.

W. W.

1916. M. W. to H. C. R.

Endorsed: *16 Septr 1845. M^{rs}* Wordsworth.
MS. Dr. Williams's Library.
Morley, ii. 608.

16 Sept. [1845]

My dear Friend

I am going to give you as briefly as I can an account of what we have been doing, and what we are going to do—for I have not time to write a regular letter but first I must thank you for y^{r} comfortable report of y^{r} B^{r} and answer your main question as to Dora's health—and to this I am most thankful to tell you that we have, since the severe illness, which attacked her soon after her arrival in Portugal, and which lasted about a month, had nothing but flourishing accounts of her improvement; and among a host of letters, which we found upon the table on our return after a week's absence yesterday, was one from her from which I will extract a passage just to shew you how her ambitious spirit is mounting

'Shall I tell you why we are so very careful of our pence. We have a grand project in view (*if*—*if*—*if*—you may fill up my *ifs*)—when we leave Oporto for England to turn South instead of North, and [instead of] giving our £40 to a Steamer just to be made miserable for 5 days and see nothing—we wish to add enough to this £40 to enable us to see Lisbon, Cintra, Cadiz, Seville, Gibraltar, Grenada, the Alhambra!! and so coach it on to Marseilles and home up the Rhone. This is all very easy but *I* am so ambitious as to ask, Cannot we go from Grenada to Madrid and thence home by the Pyrenees? Old Daddy, Mammy and dearest Miss F. you must give us the meeting among those mountains'—

What do you think of this flight? It will serve to answer your questions after her health in the happiest words I could make use of. But for ourselves, and your dear friend first of all I must tell you that yesterday week my husband and I as we passed the 'Descenting Shop' saw your friend,[1] as we thought behind that building staking out the foundation for her house, on our return yesterday to our surprize the walls had risen half-roof high—Surely she must have mesmerized her workmen for our builders are never so alert as her's must have been. We have seen little of her for She has been so much engaged with her relations and friends—Poor Law Commissioners—Educationalists etc etc to whom she has been the Shew Woman—ranging over the mountains, the Leader, and *Tirer*-out of all the said Commissioners etc She is truly the marvel of the Country by her exertions—but she is now about to exclude herself from all society for several hours a day being to be engaged in some most important work that is to enlighten the world and which is much needed—I will speak to her of you as you wish when I see her.

We have, THRO THE SEASON been beset by strangers—among those we liked best was the Poet Bryant[2] he was an agreeable modest person—and my husband enjoyed his society—and he my husband is much pleased that you approve of the disposal of the book being sent by Miss F. to Mr Reed—by the bye W^m had a letter from that Gen^t yesterday giving *almost* an assurance that Miss F's interest will in future be paid—Miss F. is not further from us, than the house at the end of Ambleside *as yet*, and I trust some abode may be found for her near[er] to us than Rayrigg which is the house you must have heard of.

Mrs Arnold and her daughter and eldest son[3] are returned from the Isle of Man and Ireland in good health to Fox-how, and enjoying the place if possible more than ever.—Tom[4] and

[1] Miss Martineau.

[2] See L. 1904 above.

[3] Matthew Arnold (1822–88) had won the Newdigate in 1843 and was now a Fellow of Oriel. His first volume, *The Strayed Reveller, and other Poems*, appeared in 1849, and *Empedocles on Etna, and other Poems* in 1852. He was Professor of Poetry at Oxford, 1857–67.

[4] Tom (1823–1900) had recently graduated from University College, Oxford. After some years in New Zealand and Tasmania, he became a Roman Catholic

Edward[1] are in Scotland—the 2 youngest boys[2] gone back to School. We had but just seen them before our departure—Good Mrs Davy bears her widowhood with chearfulness in her comfortable new house—and is now and then cheered by good tidings from her husband at Barbadoes—the Fletchers are well—I do not imagine the *Miff* to which you allude between them and H. M. has caused very great difference in their several feelings toward each other. I do not enter into particulars not having any distinct notion of the cause of the misunderstanding further than we all think your friend has been the dupe and continues to be duped.

My Husband and Son W^m^ go to Brigham next Thursday to fix upon a site to which the Parsonage house is to be removed *out of the way* of the horrid Railroad which is to be carried upon the very ground on which that building a doz years ago was fixed by the choice of the Father and Son—Alas we have no good news from Lucca save that the Children are all well, I fear they are to be left by their Father who is coming to take the duty not at Brigham, but at his other Incumbency Plumbland. This latter arrangement is very satisfactory to us, as he can be of no use to his Wife—that he should be where his Professional duty requires his presence. Isabella hopes to be able in the spring to leave her D^r^ under whose care she means to return to Rome for the winter, with her younger children—the Elder boys being left with a clergyman who takes Pupils now in Lucca, and at Pisa in the winter. To such matter of fact people as myself these seem strange proceedings, but we are old-fashioned people and can only submit—I will not say without disturbance of mind.

Next week my husband and I hope to set out for Brinsop to pay a farewell visit to that place—You know perhaps that they[3] have given up their Farm, and are going to live with their eldest son Thos near Presteyn.

(1856), and Professor of English Literature at Newman's Catholic University in Dublin. His *Passages in a Wandering Life*, 1900, contains reminiscences of W. W. during the Kendal and Windermere Railway controversy.

[1] Edward (1826–78) now an undergraduate at Balliol: later a Schools Inspector in Cornwall.

[2] William (1828–59), later an Anglo-Indian official, and author of *Oakfield* (1853); and Walter (b. 1835), who entered the Navy.

[3] The Hutchinsons.

But W. waits for my letter and I must be done—with all affec remembrances from all ever y^r much obliged friend

M Wordsworth

Go and see Miss Rogers with my Love—Christmas is coming fast upon us.

1917. W. W. to MRS. HARRISON

Address: Mrs Harrison, Hundhow. [*In M. W.'s hand*]
MS. WL. Hitherto unpublished.

Rydal Mount
Tuesday Morn:
[Sepr 17th 1845][1]

Dear Mrs Harrison,

The Shades which you have been so kind as to make for me suit exactly both as to Shape and Material and I am much gratified by your thinking of me in this way. Pray accept my sincere thanks and believe me dear Mrs H. faithfully your

Much obliged
Wm Wordsworth

1918. W. W. to EDWARD MOXON

MS. Henry E. Huntington Library.
LY iii. 1258.

Rydal Mount
20th Septr 45

My dear Mr Moxon,

A Gentleman, by name Boner,[2] whom I should be glad to serve, is anxious for an introduction to you. He has been employed six years as Tutor to the Sons of a German prince, and during that time has resided at Ratisbon, whither he purposes shortly to return and resume his office. I had never seen him before he took the trouble of coming down some weeks since to Rydal, in order to make my acquaintance, we having had

[1] Date added in another hand.
[2] See L. 1882 above.

previously some correspondence by Letter. Mr B. has a good deal of leisure time, which he gives to various departments of literature, and wishes to find out some channel for the publication of such productions of his pen as he has finished or may be induced by that hope to bring to a conclusion. Will you allow him some conversation with you to specify what his objects are, and if you shall see an opening for rendering him a service, as I have before said, I should be grateful. I have already given him a Letter to Mr Lockhart[1] who is well disposed to meet his wishes if an Article which he has written upon Germany should suit the Quarterly Review.

I had no wish whatever that my Volume should be sold under twenty shillings. I noticed the subject merely to express my wonder how Longman could possibly afford to sell 800 pages for a guinea, and that is still to me a mystery. Our printers do their work with great accuracy, but they might frequently, by more attention, make the columns of each page more uniform. They seem desirous of having the bottom uniform at any cost to the appearance of the top. This I think an error, but in neither case is it necessary there should be so great a difference as often occurs in the top.—

This is Saturday, and next Tuesday Mrs W. and I set off to visit her Brother in Herefordshire. We shall be absent, I calculate, about six weeks as we mean to stop at York and at Leeds on our return; and our stay in Herefordshire will be little less than [a] month. My address

Thomas Hutchinson's Esq.
Brinsop Court
near Hereford.

ever faithfully yours
Wm Wordsworth

[1] See L. 1915 above.

1919. W. W. to HENRY REED

Address: Henry Reed Esqre, Philadelphia. [*In M. W.'s hand*]
Postmark: (1) 27 Sept. 1845 (2) 29 Sept.
Stamp: Hereford.
MS. Cornell.
Mem. (—). *Grosart* (—). *Wordsworth and Reed, p. 152.*

Brinsop Court Sep^{br} 27th [1845]

My dear Mr Reed,

The sight of your Letter was very welcome, and its contents proved most agreeable. It was well that you did not forward my little Poem to the Party, he entertaining the opinions he holds and being of the character you describe.[1] I shall therefore be gratified if you, as you propose, write him a note expressing that I have nothing among my Mss that would suit his purpose. The verses are already printed in the new Edition of my Poems (double Column) which is going through the Press. It will contain about 300 verses not found in the previous Edition. I do not remember whether I have mentioned to you that following your example I have greatly extended the class entitled Poems of the Imagination, thinking as you must have done that if Imagination were predominant in the class, it was not indispensable that it should[2] pervade every poem which it contained. Limiting the class as I had done before seemed to imply, and to the uncandid or observing did so, that the faculty which[3] is the primum mobile in Poetry had little to do, in the estimation of the author, with Pieces not arranged under that head. I therefore feel much obliged to you for suggesting by your practice the plan which I have adopted. In respect to the prefaces my own wish would be that now the Poems should be left to speak for themselves without them, but I know that this would not

[1] See L. 1903 above. In his letter of 28 Aug. Reed had expressed misgivings about sending *The Westmoreland Girl* for inclusion in Atkinson's publication. '. . . I beg you especially to be assured that my objection is not suggested by the smallest sympathy with Slavery, which . . . is truly odious alike to my feelings and my judgment, and the removal of which from our soil I should hail as a most precious social reform. . . . But indulge me in saying that I should regret seeing your name brought into a connection, where it might be perverted as sanctioning (if only by the connection) a spirit and modes of "Reform" which I am satisfied you have no sympathy with.' (*Wordsworth and Reed*, pp. 149–50).

[2] it *written again*.

[3] *Written* what.

answer for the purposes of sale. They will therefore be printed at the end of the Volume, and to this I am in some degree reconciled by the matter they contain relating to Poetry in general, and the principles they inculcate.

I hope that upon the whole the Edition will please you. In a very few instances I have altered the expression for the worse, on account of the same feeling and word occuring rather too near the passage. For example the Sonnet on Baptism[1] begins

Blest be the church—

But unfortunately the word occurs some three or [four][2] places just before or after,—I have therefore though reluctantly substituted the less impressive word

Dear be the church.

I mention this solely to prevent blame on your part in this and a few similar cases where an injurious change has been made. The Book will be off my hands I hope in about two months.

The prospect of a continued payment on the Pensylvanian debt which you hold out is very gratifying. Let us trust that nothing will tempt the State again to forfeit its character. It is melancholy to observe how widely and deeply has been and are felt through England the ill consequences of this breach of faith in the different states. In the House from which I now write, my Brother in Law's, are two young Ladies,[3] who are robbed of 40 pounds a piece of annual income by the dishonesty of the State of Missisippi. My own daughter as I have told you before is precisely in the same situation, the money having been left to all the parties by a beloved Sister of Mrs Wordsworth, who being unwisely advised entrusted the whole of her little Fortune to that Communialty.[4] Ofen and often have I felt a sort of melancholy satisfaction that this dear Person died soon after that investment was made. She was a noble-minded Person, of a most generous spirit, and I fear to think how painful it would have been to her to be thrown, in destitution, upon her Friends for a maintenance. But too much of this.

Mrs W— and I left home four days ago and, do not intend to return, if all goes well in less than 5 or six weeks from this time. We purpose on our way home to visit York, the Cathedral of which city has been restored; and thence we shall go to Leeds on a visit to our Friend Mr James Marshall, in full expectation that

[1] *PW* iii. 394.

[2] *Word dropped out.*

[3] Elizabeth and Sarah Hutchinson.

[4] *Word indistinct.*

we shall be highly delighted by the humane and judicious manner in which his Manufactor[y] is managed, and by inspecting the schools which he and his Brothers have established and superintend. We also promise our selves much pleasure from the sight of the magnificent Church[1] which upon the foundation of the old Parish Church of that Town has been built through the exertion and by the munificence of the present Incumbent, that excellent and able man Dr Hook, whom I have the honor of reckoning among my Friends. This letter is written by the side of my Brother in Law who eight years ago became a cripple confined to his Chair by the accident of his Horse falling with him in the high road, where he lay without power to move either hand or leg, but left in perfect possession of his faculties.

His bodily sufferings are by this time *somewhat* abated, but they still continue severe. His patience and chearfulness are so admirable, that I could not forbear mentioning him to you. He is an example to us all, and most undeserving should we be if we did not profit by it. His family have lately succeeded in persuading [him][2] to have his Portrait taken as he sits in his arm chair.[3] It is an excellent likeness, one of the best I ever saw, and will be invaluable to his family. This reminds me of Mr Inman and a promise which he made us that he would send us a copy of your Portrait of myself—I say a promise, though it scarcely amounted to that absolutely, but it was little short of it. Do you think he could find time to act upon his own wish in this matter, in which I feel interested on Mrs Wordsworth['s] account, who reckons that Portrait much the best both as to likeness and execution of all that have been made of me, and she is an excellent Judge. In advertin[g] to this subject I of course presume that you would have no objection to the Picture being copied if the artist were inclined to do it. My paper admonishes me that I must conclude. Pray let me know in your next how Mrs Reed and your family are in health and present my good wishes to her.

Ever your faithful and much obliged Friend

Wm Wordsworth

[1] St. Saviour's.

[2] *Word dropped out.*

[3] This letter establishes the date of the portrait of Thomas Hutchinson reproduced in pt. ii, facing p. 571.

1920. W. W. to DERWENT COLERIDGE

MS. Pierpont Morgan Library transcript.[1]
K. LY iii. 1259.

Brinsop Court Hereford 29th Sep 45.

My dear Derwent,

Your Letter announcing the decease of our long-tried Friend, your excellent Mother,[2] followed Mrs Wordsworth and me to this place. It was a great shock to us, being so sudden, and the recent correspondence between your good Mother and Mrs W, not having made mention of her health being in a *worse* state, and shewing that her faculties were unimpaired. It was very kind in you to enter into particulars as you did, and also to let us know how dear Sara bore her afflicting loss: pray give our kindest love and most earnest and affectionate wishes to her. The privation must be deeply felt by her. It is a rare thing to see a Mother and Daughter so long and so closely and tenderly united as they have been since Sara was an infant. More than 50 years have elapsed since I first became acquainted with your mother, and her departure naturally sends back my mind into long past events and circumstances, which cause in me feelings, with which it is impossible you can adequately sympathise. Her memory will for the short remainder of my days continue in a high degree interesting to me. Link after link is broken, and yet for the most part we do not bear those severings in mind as we ought to do.

The good family under whose roof we are, thank God, are all well and healthy. Mr Hutchinson gaining power though very slowly and though suffering much yet less and less in some degree every year. He is an example of patience and chearful resignation beyond almost what one could have conceived possible.

God bless you my dear Derwent
Your affectionate and faithful Friend
Wm Wordsworth

[1] By Ernest Hartley Coleridge.

[2] Mrs. S. T. C. had died at Chester Place on 24 Sept., while Sara Coleridge was away at Eton.

1921. W. W. to C. W. JNR.

MS. Cornell.
Broughton, p. 84.

Brinsop Court
Oct 13th [1845]

My dear Nephew,

I enclose a Letter from G. H.[1] from which you will learn that his acceptance of Mathon depends upon the wishes and determination of his Father's family—We have been giving the subject every consideration; and there appears to us no difficulty in the way which they are not prepared to meet, except the requisite expenditure of between two and three hundred pounds, as mentioned in my last, to furnish stabling, fences for the garden, gates, shaping the ground about the House etc etc. Now it does seem quite unreasonable that upon the first Incumbent should fall, (out of a Stipend 100 per Ann) this heavey expense. If you have not written touching upon this point, pray let us know immediately (for there is no time to lose) if there be any means that you are aware of for raising the requisite Sum. If this cannot be done, I *fear* George will be compelled to decline this in many respects advantageous offer, but of course you will hear again on or before the 18th.

Ever your affectionate Uncle
Wm Wordsworth

I enclose also a Letter to me from the Bp of Hereford,[2] from which you will see that he concurs with me, as [to] the errors of the Ecclesiastical[3] Commissioners in respect to [the][4] new Parsonage House. Of course the contents of the Bps Letter are confided to you only.

[1] M. W.'s nephew George Hutchinson, who was seeking the living of Mathon, nr. Malvern, which was in the gift of the Dean and Chapter of Westminster. See next letter and Ls. 1924, 1927 and 1937 below.

[2] Thomas Musgrave (1788–1860), Bishop of Hereford from 1837, translated to York in 1847: a Whig and an Evangelical.

[3] *Written* Eclesastical.

[4] *Word dropped out.*

1922. W. W. to C. W. JNR.

MS. WL. Hitherto unpublished.

Friday 24 Oct —45
Handley[1] near Upton upon Severn.

My dear Nephew,

We are thus far on our way homewards, meaning to go by York and Leeds, at each of which places we shall stay a few days and then strait for Rydal.—Yesterday we visited Mathon St James's, along with Mrs Hutchinson and her Son Thomas. The House as you are probably aware stands high upon the edge of the common, not a tree upon the slip of Common Ground attached to it, but the situation as to prospect and scenery beyond measure beautiful, the ground for several miles below, broken on either hand, into little vallies with hills wooded or bare, of various elevations and shapes, and beyond these, a vast extent of prospects stretching over Herefordshire and terminated by the Welsh hills.—It is really magnificent.

But now to business. We saw the Incumbent Mr Shelgard[2] and had a long conversation with him about the place. He is anxious to leave when his Successor will receive his Nomination,[3] and therefore I beg that you would be so kind as to write to Mr George Hutchinson, informing him, as well as you can when he may expect it; I need not add that the sooner it is made out the better for both parties. In your last Letter to me you recommended that the matter should still be considered in abeyance; on this I suppose you merely alluded to objections on George's part, but he had made up his mind at all events to accept the Benefices; therefore do not deem that any obstacle exists on his part which he is not willing to meet.—It happened that Mr McCann the Worcester Builder was also present. He speaks confidently of the House being ready by Feb^ry^, should the weather continue favorable. From all that I could learn, I am of opinion, that not less than 300£ will be necessary for offices, including stable, small yd and provision for Garden wall, draining the Garden, making walks, shaping the grounds, which will require a great cost of Labour to fill up, furnishing the premises with gates, etc

[1] i.e. Hanley, the seat of the Lechmere family, to members of which W. W. had presumably been introduced.

[2] Unidentified.

[3] See previous letter.

etc. Indeed nothing can be in a worse state than the place will be left by the Builder, he confining himself merely to the Dwelling House. Now it appears that the net Income will not exceed ninety-one Pounds some odd shillings; so that three years stipend at least will be required to make the Premises comfortable or respectable. Now to supply this money would bear hard on any Incumbent; very few persons unless of handsome fortune, and the House would be too small for such Persons, would I think undertake it.—George is so moderate in his desires and so anxious to find a . . .

[*cetera desunt*]

1923. W. W. to CHARLES HENRY PARRY[1]

MS. WL.
LY iii. 1260.

York, 28th Oct. '45.

My dear Sir,

The accompanying Letter is from my late Clerk, Mr Carter; I regret that his inquiries have not proved more decisive. The reason is, that Dale-head Hall the residence of Mr Russel Scot[2] is not less than 9 miles from Ambleside, on the road to Keswick. Mr R. S. has no doubt his Letter-bag made up at Ambleside, to be dropped as the Post goes northward.

Dale-head is six miles from Keswick; and Keswick is no doubt the market town of the place, so that probably better information might be gained by applying to some one resident in Keswick. It would give me pleasure to assist you in this endeavour if you approve of it. A Letter addressed by you to John Lightfoot Esq,[3] Keswick I think would be of use; and I beg that you would use my name as your Introduction if you think proper to write to him. For my own part I should be loth to let a Residence like yours, and to incur expense also, without satisfactory knowledge of the Party, and this I think particularly desirable in cases of Strangers applying from our neighbourhood, where so many fanciful and irregular people are apt to take up their abode for a short time.

[1] Of Bath. See L. 1408 above.

[2] Apparently a tenant. Dale Head Hall, Wythburn, belonged to Thomas Leathes.

[3] The Keswick attorney, who had married R. W.'s widow.

On Thursday I go to Mr Marshall's, Headingley, Leeds, to remain till Tuesday following, and then home.

I cannot conclude without renewing the expression of my deep sympathy with your domestic distresses, and my most earnest wish and prayer that the lives of your other Daughters may be spared.

Believe me, my dear Dr Parry, very faithfully yours
Wm Wordsworth

1924. W. W. to C. W. JNR.

MS. British Library. Hitherto unpublished.

Friday 31st Octr 45.
Headingley
near Leeds

My dear Nephew,

I am very sorry that I did not request your Letter to be directed to York as we could not leave that place till yesterday (Thursday) afternoon—

I feel much obliged by the kind and careful consideration which you gave to the nomination to Mathon;[1] but I cannot but regret that in my Letter, I dwelt so much upon the weight of debt which must be incurred by George H. to make the Environs comfortable and respectable. I regret that I did so, because G. H. so deeply feels the desirableness of having a House to receive his Parents and Sisters in; and above all his Father who cannot move from place to place without great pain; and probability of serious injury. I *do hope* therefore that still he may have the option of *Mathon*, on the supposition of its being declined by others.

Your Letter will be forwarded to him by this day's post, but it will have to go round by Brinsop as we have not his address correctly.

I have just mentioned the particulars of the case to Mr James Marshall, having told him that I should have given £16 towards diminishing George's debt, and he kindly and generously said that he would add £30 towards the same purpose. This encourages me to hope that with due exertion among personal Friends, and friends of the Church, George might have been so

[1] See L. 1921 above.

far assisted as greatly to diminish this *only* objection of importance, every thing else being so much in its favor.

A Letter addressed here could not reach me in time, but on Tuesday we hope to be at Rydal—and I should be very glad to hear from you again if you have any thing to communicate.

I am delighted to hear that your Father's health is improved.

Your
affectionate Uncle
Wm Wordsworth

1925. W. W. to EDWARD MOXON

MS. Henry E. Huntington Library.
LY iii. 1261.

[Rydal Mount]
[4 Nov. 1845]

My dear Mr Moxon,

My late wanderings have unavoidably caused some delay, but the next sheet will conclude the Poetry and bring us to the Notes, which will be followed by the Prefaces and then we shall be done with this tedious work. Looking over the Proofs has been trying to my eyes, but I feel much indebted to Mr Carter, as I am sure you will also, for the care which he has taken in correcting the proofs; I feel obliged to you also for your own attentions to this important part of the concern. I have not yet seen (Mr Carter being now at Carlisle) a specimen of the Sheet as struck off; my only fear is that the margin will not be broad enough for binding as one could wish—will it not be cramped? We are about to publish this expensive Vol. at a most unfavorable time. Nothing is now thought of but railway shares. The Savings-banks are almost emptied of their old deposits, and scarcely any thing has come into them—all gone to Railway Speculation—a deplorable state of things.

Are the engraving of the Bust and the view of the House finished?

Mr Carter is making an Index of first lines which I hope will be of some use, for it is impossible to give titles to a third part of this multifarious collection of Poems.—

ever my dear Mr Moxon
faithfully yours
W. W.

What say you to the Title standing merely thus

THE POEMS
OF
WILLIAM WORDSWORTH D.C.L.
POET LAUREAT ETC—

I would have added Honorary Member of the Royal Society of Edinborough, if I could have joined with it and of the Royal *Irish Academy*, (that I think is the title) but they will not [? elect][1] till after Christmas.

I was offered that distinction some years ago, but thought it best to decline it then.

1926. W. W. to EDWARD MOXON

MS. Henry E. Huntington Library.
K (—). LY iii. 1262.

Nov^r [5th 1845][2]

My dear Mr Moxon,

I reply to yours of yesterday's post received after mine was sent off; I have to say 1st—that the House I live in has no name but Rydal Mount. I have considered and reconsidered the title, and I cannot make up my mind to adhere to any but simply

THE POEMS
OF
WILLIAM WORDSWORTH.

I hope that you wont object to this, bald as it is.

There is a small poem, beginning

If thou indeed derive thy light from Heaven[3]

which the Printer has been directed to place before the Poems. I mean it to serve as a sort of preface. All the prose prefaces, and in fact all the prose, except a few brief Notes printed at the bottom of the page of the verse, will be printed at the end of the Volume, it being now my wish that the poems should be left to speak for themselves though I did not think it prudent to

[1] *Paper torn away.*

[2] Day of month and year added in another hand.

[3] See *PW* i. 317. First published in 1827, among *Poems of Sentiment and Reflection*, and now moved to the head of the volume.

suppress any considerable portion of the Prose, thinking this would hurt the sale of the work.

What must we do with the Stereotype of the 6 Volumes; I ask because I know that many persons would prefer that shape to the double column and not a few would have the[m] both—the 7 vol: for ordinary reading, and the double column for travelling.

ever faithfully yours

W. W.

1927. W. W. to C. W. JNR.

MS. British Library. Hitherto unpublished.

[Nov. 1845]

My dear Chris

Mr Thomas Hutchinson[1] went over to make inquiries upon the spot—the result will best appear by a Copy of his Letter to Mr [? Chalk]; which I enclose.

There can be no doubt that there has been much unnecessary delay in building the House—Before you proceed with this Note read the Copy of the Letter—

It would surely be much better that in the plans of the London Builder submitted to the Ecclesiastical Commissioners, or in their selection from the places submitted, more consideration should be paid to what is most needful in Benefices so small as this of Mathon. You mentioned that those in the gift of the Dean and Chapter are for the most part small; and surely it would be worth while for the members of that Body to take care that there are no such unnecessary expenses as have been incurred in this instance.

If the inside of the house is to be finished like the outside, with cornice centre-pieces on the ceilings etc., the sum required for Both would probably have met all the Outlay needful for the *indispensible* conveniences as mentioned in Mr H's Letter and for which there will not be a farthing of surplus—

There are 20 acres of Land belonging to the Dean and Chapter of Westminster, which lie close to the House. They are let out upon a Lease to a Mr Featherstone-Haugh[2] and underlet by him.

[1] i.e. Thomas Hutchinson, jnr.

[2] Alexander Stephenson Fetherstonehaugh (1798–1875), of Hopton Court, Worcs.

It would be a very great advantage to Mathon, if these Lands could be placed at the option of the Incumbents. But I find that Mr Hutchinson wrote a sketch of a Note upon this subject, which he wished to be written over and more neatly expressed, as he was in a great hurry. But I do not scruple to enclose it to you, as it states the case quite intelligibly.

I hope some means may be contrived for meeting the large deficit, and that in that expectation, George will accept the Benefice. I need not ask you to use your endeavour to have the work forwarded, and the whole concern made as eligible as possible.

Your affectionate Uncle
W. W.

1928. M. W. and W. W. to SARA COLERIDGE[1]

Address: Mrs H. N. Coleridge, 10 Chester Place, Regents Park, London.
Postmark: (1) 7 Nov. 1845 (2) 8 Nov. 1845.
Stamp: Ambleside.
MS. Victoria University Library, Toronto.
K (—). *LY iii. 1263* (—).

[7 Nov. 1845]

. . . With my husband's tender love to you, he bids me say in reply to a question you have put to him thro' Miss Fenwick, that he has not as distinct a remembrance as he could wish, of the time when he first saw your Father and your Uncle Southey but the impression upon his mind is, that he first saw them both, and your Mother and Aunt Edith[2] at the same time in a lodging in Bristol, this must have been about the year 1795.[3] Your father he says, 'came afterwards to see us at Racedown, where I was then living with my Sister. We have both a distinct remembrance of his arrival—he did not keep to the high road, but leapt over a gate and bounded down the pathless field, by which he cut off an angle. We both retain the liveliest possible image of his appearance at that moment. My poor Sister has just been

[1] The conclusion of a long letter about Hartley's affairs and her mother's character.

[2] i.e. Mrs. Southey.

[3] *Written* 1895. It was in fact in Sept. 1795 (see *EY*, p. 153). S. T. C. visited W. W. and D. W. at Racedown on 5 June 1797 (*EY*, pp. 187–8; Griggs, i. 326).

speaking of it to me with much feeling and tenderness.' Ever, dear Sara,

Most affectionately yours,
M. Wordsworth.

1929. M. W. to H. C. R.

Endorsed: M[rs] Wordsworth. *Nov*. 1845.
MS. Dr. Williams's Library.
Morley, ii. 610.

Rydal M[t] Nov[r] 7th [1845]

My dear Friend

My husband and I reached home after an absence of six weeks last Tuesday night—and I have so many things that I *could* say to you, and so many things that I *must* say to numerous others—that I merely take this sheet to remind you that Christmas is fast approaching when we can each relate our adventures viva voce—

Meanwhile, I must express our regret that you did not favor us with at least one of your pleasant letters while we were at Brinsop—were it not that good M[rs] Hoare has spoken of you to us, we should not have known if you were in the land of the living—Do let us hear of your Brother, of yourself and your doings—We have had a pleasant bustling time while absent—and find plenty of occupation awaiting our return. From Oporto we have delightful tidings of Dora's improved health—and rather more favorable of M[rs] I. Wordsworth's.

Your friend Miss Martineau, whose house, as W[m] told her yesterday, he expected was to be like the Lark's, nestling in the earth—is soaring to the skies—as, truly are her spirits—she is the gayest of the gay, and perfectly well—indeed we have found all our friends flourishing and all enquired after you, and when we are to see you—You must enable me to answer this question—and I hope satisfactorily.

Yesterday evening we had M[rs] Arnold with us at our Tea-table and this even[g] M[rs] and Miss Fletcher—with whom we have also had pleasant chat, in which you were not forgotten

W[m] bids me say that he paid 9 visits, i.e. passed one or more nights in different houses during our absence—we were 4 or 5 days at York and the like in the neighbourhood and Leeds, and took great pains to see the leading Lions of these places.[1] York is in fact in[ex]haustible.

We found our Sister had been well and comfortable during our absence—and think her much improved in many points.—The 2 books to replace those that went from Miss F. to America have found their way to Rydal—and your name must be written therein when you arrive.

With our joint affec regards believe me to be very sincerely your's

M. Wordsworth.

Moxon tells us that the Trade have taken off the last copies of the 6 vols—the new Ed: is nearly ready

1930. W. W. to FREDERICK WESTLEY[2]

Address: Fred Westley Esq, Rockfort Villa, Lower Tulse Hill, London.
MS. WL.
LY iii. 1264.

Rydal Mount, Novr. 13th '45

My dear Sir,

The one Vol: Edit: of my Poems will soon be out; and I have directed Mr Moxon, before it is published to send three Copies to you, one for yourself, one which you will be so kind as to bind for me, and one which I intend as a bridal Present for my Friend Lady Rolfe.[3]—The mode of binding this last I refer especially to your own taste, I have no wish that it should be superb; that would be ostentatious—perhaps white vellum with some gilding would suit the occasion, but I leave this wholly to your better judgement. Your 'Holy Living'[4] is much admired by every one who has seen it, as also is the good taste of the Commines[5]—I remain my dear Sir

faithfully your much obliged
Wm Wordsworth

I could conveniently pay you through Mr Moxon for the

[1] Including the Archbishop of York, Edward Harcourt, and Daniel Wilson, Bishop of Calcutta. See pt. ii, L. 442.

[2] The bookbinder.

[3] See L. 1381 above.

[4] Jeremy Taylor's treatise. See pt. i, L. 296.

[5] The *Memoirs* of Philip de Commines (*c.* 1446–*c.* 1511).

Binding of the two Copies—It would, I believe, enhance the Value of the Volume in your eyes if it had my Autograph and I have accordingly sent it as you will see.

W. W.

Be so good as to return the book for me when bound, to Mr Moxon, directed for me—and the other for Lady Rolfe, to 8 New St Spring Gardens.

1931. W. W. to ELIZABETH FRANCES OGLE[1]

MS. Yale University Library. Hitherto unpublished.

Rydal Mount
Nov^{br} 15th [1845]

Dear Madam,

According to the rule of manners in the old school which my years at least give me some title to belong to, a Letter from a Lady ought never to remain [un]acknowledged. I therefore take leave to return my thanks for the favor of your Last, slow though I am in general to employ the pen, and inexpert as you have proof before you in the use of it.—

To obviate in part an objection to the sequel of the Norman Boy which you have been so well [? natured] as to be pleased with, I have added a Stanza near the Conclusion as follows.—

But oh! that Countryman of thine dear Boy, whose eye can see
A pledge of endless bliss, in acts of early piety,
In verse which to thy ear might come, would treat this simple theme
Nor leave unsung our happy flight dear Boy in that adventurous dream.
Alas the dream to thee poor Boy! to thee from whom it flowed
Was nothing, scarcely can be aught, yet 'twas bounteously bestowed

This addition connects however faintly the Boy at least, with a knowledge etc of the dream in which he has a leading part.—

And now dear Madam with many good wishes and with

[1] See L. 1407 above. This letter refers to ll. 73–6 added in 1845 to *The Poet's Dream* (*PW* i. 253), the sequel to *The Norman Boy*.

thanks, I must bid you goodbye, and believe me to be sincerely your obliged

Wm Wordsworth—

1932. W. W. to EDWARD MOXON

MS. Henry E. Huntington Library.
K (—). *LY iii. 1264* (—).

Monday Morning
17th Nov. 45

My dear Mr Moxon,

We have carefully compared the Engraving of the Bust with the Plaster Cast given by Sir F. Chantrey to Mrs Wordsworth. Upon the whole we prefer it much to the print from Mr Pickersgill's Picture,[1] but we think it may be a good deal improved both as to likeness and general effect. If the Engraving be taken from your *Bronze* Bust, which must have been done from a Plaster Cast, the Marble not being accessible, I should by all means recommend to Mr Finden[2] to take the trouble of comparing his work with a plaster cast (Mr Crabb Robinson possesses one, and so does Mr Henry Taylor) he would then perceive that the Line of the Nose in his Engraving is not sufficient[ly] curved. A still greater defect we think is in the eyes which are somewhat too small or rather they have a peering look as eyes have when they shun a strong light and strive to see a distant object. In my own opinion also they more resemble the eyes of a Picture than of a Bust; I feel assured that Mr Finden will be able to remove both these objections.

The Print of the House is faulty as to the Porch, and this was probably the consequence of a defect in the Drawing, which was not by a professional Artist.[3] The Porch looks more like a substantial adjunct to the House than a trellis-work, as it is, and open in Front. Could this effect be given by the Engraver—it would be a great improvement, only a few flowers and plants hanging against and upon the trellis-work. The drawing was taken from a distance, by which all the lower windows were hidden. I would like one to be seen by taking away a few of the boughs which hide it, but perhaps this is impracticable.

[1] See pt. ii, L. 717.
[2] See pt. ii, L. 500.
[3] See L. 1892 above.

I omitted to mention as a strong additional inducement for your coming down to Rydal that Miss Martineau would I am sure be much pleased to see you. She speaks to her friends with much delight of your generous behaviour as her Publisher.

Care shall be taken to forward to you, by some opportunity, the Copy from which the One Vol: Edit. was made. I fear the expense of accomodating the changes to the 6 Volumes of stereotype would be found scarcely prudent to enter upon; but this may be considered.

I should have been sorely disappointed if the double column had not been stereotyped.

ever my dear Mr Moxon
faithfully yours
Wm Wordsworth

[*In M. W.'s hand*]

Mrs W. wishes to know the price of the book you sent to Dora—it was ordered at the request of a friend who wished to make her a present.

1933. W. W. to FREDERICK WESTLEY

MS. Carl H. Pforzheimer Library. Hitherto unpublished.

Rydal Mount
Sat.—Nov. 18th —45

My dear Sir,

I enclose a paper which I will thank you to have bound up with the Vol: to be presented to Lady Rolfe. As to the binding I have nothing to add, but that the leaves must be *gilt*, and if you approve of my suggestion of white vellum, that as much gilding should be used as to your taste may seem becoming, where there is a wish to avoid any thing like ostentation.—

I remain my dear Sir
truly your obliged
Wm Wordsworth

1934. W. W. to EDWARD MOXON

MS. Cornell. Hitherto unpublished.

19th Novbr [1845]
Rydal

Pray take care of the Drawing after the Engraver has done with [it].

My dear Mr Moxon

What I now send will be[1] I fear too late for the Engraver to profit by it. The former drawing was taken in summer, when the trees hid the House,[2] in a great measure. Besides, the point was not well chosen—The present gives the form of the House, and its structure, much better—without much expense or loss of time. If it could be adopted in preference, I should like that to be done—

The Bust ought also to be altered as decided before both on the eyes and the nose, neither is the upper lip what it ought to be.—There is both in my face and in the bust a swelling or projection rather, above the upper lip where as in the bust it sinks. The Engraver if he works carefully must at once recognise that—

I am sorry to give so much work, but really my Friends here are so dissatisfied that I could not but dwell on these particulars.

ever faithfully yours
Wm Wordsworth

Mr Edward Coleridge[3] of Eton has applied to me for a subscription to St Augustines College, Canterbury[4]—be so good as to let him have 5 pounds, if he calls for it or any body authorized by him.—

Faber (Frederic) has gone over to what he calls the Church, [? I mean] what others call the Church of Rome.[5]

[1] arrive *written above the line.*

[2] Rydal Mount. See L. 1932 above.

[3] See pt. i, L. 126.

[4] Founded 1848 for the training of missionaries, and built in the ruins of St. Augustine's Abbey.

[5] Faber was received into the Roman Catholic Church at Northampton on 17 November. W. W. had received a laconic note of one sentence announcing the news (*WL MSS.*).

1935. W. W. to FREDERICK WESTLEY

MS. untraced.
Bookseller's Catalogue.

[19 Nov. 1845]

All I have written about the Binding of Lady Rolfes Copy was but suggestion subject to your superior taste—Let it be by all means exclusively what you yourself approve of . . . I hope the leaf I sent yesterday to indicate the Presentation may be bound up without disfiguring the Vol. . . .

[*cetera desunt*]

1936. W. W. to EDWARD MOXON

MS. Henry E. Huntington Libray.
K (—). LY iii. 1266.

[*In John Carter's hand*]

Rydal Mount
25 Novr 1845.

My dear Mr Moxon,

I think both the Engraving of the Bust and of the House considerably improved, and hope they will do credit to the Publication.[1] The Title page also is much approved in appearance.

Let a dozen Copies be sent down to me for sale—that is for the use of Mrs Nicholson and Mr Troughton, and as many as you think reasonable to myself to distribute among my friends. You will please to remember what I said some little time ago about the three Copies to be sent to Mr Westley. I suppose the Book will be out in a few days, the sooner the better for the sake of Christmas presents. Send the Package by Canal. Mrs Wordsworth begs to say that a pair of Hares was sent off the other day by this conveyance, and she hopes they will arrive in good condition.

Miss Martineau called here to-day. She is in excellent health

[1] There follows some eleven lines, apparently erased by W. W.: 'and I have nothing further to observe but that I can see no reason why there should be a Table of Contents in the beginning and another at the end, the only difference being that the latter is called an Index. There cannot be any need of both. Let one of them be suppressed. I leave it to you to determine which. Let the one which is paged in be retained.'

and spirits, very busy with house-building and book-writing, by which latter operation I hope you will profit.[1] Pray remember me most kindly to Mr Rogers and his Sister if ever you see her, and to dear old Miss Lamb, in which wishes Mrs W. joins. My Son John is still here, in very good health, and taking very long walks every day. Give our very kind regards to Mrs Moxon and your Sister, not forgetting your Brothers, and believe me

V^y faithfully Y^rs
[*signed*] Wm Wordsworth

1937. W. W. to C. W. JNR.

MS. Cornell. Hitherto unpublished.

[Dec. 1845]

My dear Nephew

We are exceedingly pleased to hear that G. H. has been nominated to Mathon.[2] The whole family had their hearts set upon it, as a harbour to retire into, and I cannot help repeating that the benefit to the District I am sure, will be such as you and the Dean and Chapter will be thankful for.—Had the result been different I should not have been free from self-reproach, as having caused it by dwelling in my Letter to you upon the unfavorable circumstance of so large an Outlay being necessary which I did solely from the hope that by making you fully acquainted with the state of the case, it might be in your power to assist among the friends of the Church, in lessening the objection. Your good and generous Father without any communication between him and me upon the subject, and solely in consequence of the Letter you sent him, has offered 20 pounds in case nothing considerable can be procured from a public Body—I think I told you that Mr James Marshall had offered thirty, so that we have a very good beginning—Accept the repetition of your Aunt's warm thanks and mine for this good

[1] After his success with her *Letters on Mesmerism*, Moxon went on to publish her *Forest and Game Law Tales*, 3 vols., 1845–6.

[2] See L. 1921 above.

service done to those whom we esteem so highly. With love to Susan and yourself in which your Aunt unites, I remain

my dear Christopher—
your affectionate Uncle
Wm Wordsworth

PS Your welcome Letter would have been answered immediately but for incessant engagements consequent upon our absence—and my inability to write by candlelight. Your Aunt Dorothy goes on as usual, she is still wheel[ed] about in her Carriage twice a day—but this will soon be stopped by the Cold, which seems to do her some harm already.

1938. W. W. to JOSEPH COTTLE

MS. untraced.
Joseph Cottle, Alfred; an epic poem, 4th edn. 1850, p. cxx (—).
Grosart. K. LY iii. 1266.

Rydal Mount, Dec. 6, 1845.

My dear old Friend,

Now for your little tract, *Heresiarch Church of Rome.*[1] I have perused it carefully, and go the whole length with you in condemnation of Romanism, and probably much further, by reason of my having passed at least three years of life in countries where Romanism was the prevailing or exclusive religion; and if we are to trust the declaration, 'By their fruits ye shall know them', I have stronger reasons, in the privilege I have named, for passing a severe condemnation upon leading parts of their faith and courses of their practice than others who have never been eye-witnesses of the evils to which I allude. Your little publication is well-timed, and will, I trust, have such an effect as you aimed at upon the minds of its readers.

And now let me bid you affectionately good-bye, with assurance that I do and shall retain to the last a remembrance of your kindness and of the many pleasant and happy hours which,

[1] An earlier, separate printing of Cottle's strictures on the Church of Rome and its superstitious and persecuting spirit. The version appended to the 4th edition of *Alfred* extended the condemnation to the Puseyites, and listed recent converts to Rome, including Newman, Faber, Coffin, and Burder.

at one of the most interesting periods of my life, I passed in your neighbourhood and in your company.[1]

Ever most faithfully yours
William Wordsworth

1939. M. W. to H. C. R.

Endorsed: *9 Decr 45* [shd be *8th*] Mrs Wordsw.
MS. Dr. Williams's Library.
Morley, ii. 613.

9th [8th] Decr [1845]
Rydal Mt

My dear Friend

James tells me that you 'took a fancy' to the Candles that were in use at Rydal Mount and that he gave you the address whence they were to be procured in London—This said address *we* cannot find, so will you excuse my making you useful before you leave Town (which I hope and expect you mean soon to do on your Northward course) by requesting that you will order to be sent immediately to Rydal Mount *per Canal a doz: Packets* of 'Price's Composite Candles *short fours* in the pound' also, if to[2] be had at the same place, *2 doz lbs* of Moulds (shorts 8ths in the lb)—And, I must further request that you will desire the Vendor to take the bill to Mr Moxon (*before he sends off the Candles*) whom I will request to discharge it—and who will be prepared to give a parcel to be forwarded in the Box. I am afraid you will think me very troublesome, and, but for my husbands encouragement I scarcely should have ventured upon what I have done.

We are all looking forward with much pleasure to your visit; and we trust nothing may occur to cause disappointment to so many of your friends. At present the weather is deplorable—and we are as stupid as needs be, but you will chear us up spite of the *Potatoe disease*[3] etc etc

[1] W. W. possibly saw Cottle once more, during his visit to Bath in Mar. 1847. On 5 July 1850, after W. W.'s death, Cottle sent D. W. his condolences through M. W. '. . . say that I not infrequently revolve on past scenes, when Dorothy Wordsworth was the life of every company, by her discriminating remarks, her vivacity, and warm-heartedness.' (*WL MSS.*)

[2] *First written* which no doubt may: 'which' *undeleted*.

[3] The Irish potato famine.

I forget if I have before thanked you for your last kind letter which brought so good an account of[1] y^{r} dear Brother—of course you will bring the latest news of Miss Rogers and dear Miss Lamb—to whom when you make your farewell call[2] give our best remembrances—and wishing you a good journey and our happy meeting believe me very aff^{ly}

Yours M. W.

1940. W. W. to EDWARD MOXON

MS. Henry E. Huntington Library.
LY iii. 1267.

Rydal M^{t} 9th Dec^{r} [1845]

My dear Mr Moxon,

I have this moment received the intelligence, that I have just been elected an honorary Member of the Royal Irish Academy[3] as I was not long ago of the Royal Society of Edinburgh. Perhaps it would be as well to add these distinctions to the Title page of the next Edition of the Poems. I did not think it worth while to notice the one till the other had been conferred—

ever faithfully yours
Wm Wordsworth

1941. M. W. to H. C. R.

Endorsed: 9th Decr 45. Mrs Wordsworth.
MS. Dr. Williams's Library.
Morley, ii. 614.

Decr 9th [1845]

My dear Friend

I forwarded you a troublesome note yesterday—and our plaguy Post Mistress has detained our letter today too late for

[1] *Written* for.

[2] See Morley, ii. 615: '. . . in addition to her other infirmities, her articulation is become so indistinct that I do not understand her, and that displeases her—What a relief is death from such infirmities!'

[3] W. W. was elected a member of the Royal Irish Academy on 29 Nov. 1845. See also L. 1976 below.

me to reply to yours by return of Post I can only say that come when you will we shall rejoice to see you—and *why* you mean to antedate our pleasure I have no business to enquire—and as we do not see the Times[1] cannot guess—but I must premise that we are not to have your visit curtailed. So let us know *how soon* we are to expect you. I am only sorry that William will miss much of your company—for his holidays do not commence till towards the middle of January I fear. We have M[r] Carter till about the 20th of the present Month—when their tug of business begins at the Stamp Office.

I shall be very much obliged by your bringing us a supply of stationary. You selected so well before that I can only request to have, if you cannot *conveniently* bring more, at least, a duplicate of that same parcel—for which by the bye we are still indebted to you.

The parcel I yesterday begged the *Candleman* to call for at Moxon's (via my note to[2] you) is to contain a copy of Southey's P.W.[3] double column and 4 copies of Oliver Newman,[4] and is for Miss Fenwick—I suppose it would be too large a one for you to be troubled with—so I will not ask you to bring it. I suppose the Box by Canal may arrive in time for the books being disposed of as Xtmas presents, for such is, I believe their destination.

Faithfully dear friend
Yours
M Wordsworth

Along with the Candles, if not too late might I ask you to order ½ doz lbs of *Windsor* (or other) soap—I think you were curious in this article—I mean it for bed-rooms. *Scold* me if I am taking a liberty, but dont think me presuming and be silent.

[1] See H. C. R.'s cryptic explanation in his letter of 8 Dec. (Morley, ii. 613).

[2] to *written twice*.

[3] *Poetical Works*.

[4] See L. 1960 below.

1942. W. W. to HUGH SEYMOUR TREMENHEERE[1]

MS. WL transcript.
LY iii. 1267.

16th Decr 1845.

My dear Sir,

I have been long in your debt; but, as I believe you are aware, I was from home during six weeks of autumn, and on my return I found numerous engagements pressing upon me in consequence. Besides as I scarcely am able to read or write by candlelight my allowance of time for the pen is but scanty during these short days. The acknowledgment of yr Kindness was not among the least important of those engagements, but I felt that I could not make it with much satisfaction till I had read yr second Report and the Volumes which thro' yr suggestion were transmitted to me from the Committee of the Council on Education. These I shall have an opporty of returning in the course of a fortnight. Yr own Report and every one in the two Vols. which you pointed out to me, I have carefully perused; and had I an opporty of conversing with you upon the subject I might perhaps be able to make upon the details, some remarks not wholly unworthy of attention, but I could say little by Letter which could be satisfactory either to you or myself. I must therefore be confined to a general observation or two. First however let me express

[1] Hugh Seymour Tremenheere (1804–93), Fellow of New College, Oxford, 1824–56, and an Inspector of Schools from 1840, made his name on numerous royal commissions which produced reforming legislation on education, child labour, and working practices. While staying on Windermere the previous July, he had called at Rydal Mount with his colleague Henry Tufnell (1805–54), M.P. for Devonport and Secretary to the Treasury under Lord John Russell (see *RMVB*, L. 1911 above, and Harriet Martineau's *Autobiography*, Period vi, section ii), and he had written at length on 19 Sept., enclosing the Minutes of the Committee of the Privy Council on Education and his Report on the Mining Population, and urging W. W. to write on these urgent problems. An essay, he maintained, 'embodying your present impression on the subject of elementary education for the lower classes, would be of much value, and would greatly help to increase that growing sense of responsibility, which has been so long in abeyance among those whose positions, whether as Landlords or Manufacturers, make them answerable to a great extent for the condition of the lower classes on their estates or in their neighbourhoods. Happily, your voice is now more and more listened to; and (permit me to add) you may feel conscious that it will be more so yet. A word or two from you, in the present stage of public opinion on this subject, would not, I am sure, be in vain.' (*WL MSS.*)

my gratitude to all the Reporters, yourself especially, for the information and instruction I have gained from their labours, and also my admiration of the perseverance and judgment with which their important work has been carried on. The prospect surely is upon the whole full as promising as could have been expected. Generation after Generation will I trust start from a higher point than the preceding one, and the improvement be progressive accordingly. Encouraged by this belief the Inspectors, to whom we already owe so much, will not relax their efforts, in which all good and wise men will concur.—Having given vent to these feelings, let me ask you, dear Sir, whether throughout the Minutes too little value is not set upon the occupations of Children out of doors, under the direction, or by permission, of their Parents, comparatively with what they do or acquire in school? Is not the Knowledge inculcated by the Teacher, or derived under his managem^t^, from books, too exclusively dwelt upon, so as almost to put out of sight that which comes, without being sought for, from intercourse with nature and from experience in the actual employments and duties which a child's situation in the Country, however unfavorable, will lead him to or impose upon him? How much of what is precious comes into our minds, in all ranks of society, not as Knowledge entering formally in the shape of Knowledge, but as infused thro' the constitution of things and by the grace of God.[1] There is no condition of life, however unpromising, that does not daily exhibit something of this truth. I do not relish the words of one of the Reporters (Mr Allen[2] I believe whose notices are generally very valuable) in which he would reconcile the Parents to the expence of having their Children educated in school by remarking that the wear and tear of clothes will be less; and an equivalent thus saved in shoe-leather.—Excuse this disagreement in opinion, as coming from one who spent half of his boyhood in running wild among the Mountains.

It struck me also that, from the same cause, too little attention is paid to books of imagination which are eminently useful in calling forth intellectual power. We must not only have Knowledge but the means of wielding it, and that is done infinitely more thro' the imaginative faculty assisting both in the

[1] See also pt. ii, L. 408.
[2] A Schools Inspector.

collection and application of facts than is generally believed. But I must conclude.

Believe me, My dear Sir,
with many thanks,
Sincerely y[r] much obliged
W[m] Wordsworth

1943. W. W. to MARY HOWITT

MS. Harvard University Library.
LY iii. 1269.

Dec[br] 17th 1845
Rydal Mount

Dear Mrs Howitt,

The resolution which the numerous applications for Autographs have compelled me to make is pretty much what you conjecture. I take no notice of the requests of strangers but never fail to comply with those of my Friends, either made for themselves or for those in whom they are interested, though persons unknown to myself. But even here I do not often write more than my name; penmanship, which was never attractive to me, having long been disagreeable.

You will excuse me therefore for having confined myself to four lines even upon your application.

I remain, dear Mrs Howitt, with kind regards to yourself and Mr Howitt in which Mrs W. unites,

faithfully yours
Wm Wordsworth

We continue to receive most favourable accounts of Mrs Quillinan's health and strength.

[*There follows* Written in the Album of a Child *as in PW iv. 178, followed by W. W.'s signature.*]

1944. W. W. to EDWARD MOXON

MS. Henry E. Huntington Library.
K (—). LY iii. 1270.

Rydal Mount
Decr 20th 1845

My dear Mr Moxon,

We have received the Books, and they are all distributed—I have thought it proper to give a Copy to each of the Ladies who furnished the Drawings of the House, and the remainder of my Copies are also distributed chiefly among my female Friends in this neighbourhood; and pleased and proud they are on having been, as they express it, so honored.—Yesterday I had a Letter from a Gentleman of St Andrews, unknown to me, who says that he has already given 8 Copies among his Relations and Friends, and means to make presents of more in the same way; so that it seems probable that the Edition will not remain long on hand; at all events it is clear that we have done well by printing the Book in this Shape.—

Mr Robinson arrived yesterday; and does not take from us the hope of seeing you. Nevertheless as according to him your Stay will be only two or three days, I can scarcely wish that at this unfavorable season you should take so much trouble and put yourself to the expense. Should you come however I need not say that you will be most welcome.

Did you observe or hear of the favorable Report of the Poems which Mr Johnstone gave the other day in the Morning Post.[1] He has always been very friendly to any publications of mine; and should he fall in your way pray be more than civil to him; with the best good wishes of the season for you and yours I remain my dear Mr Moxon

faithfully yours
W. Wordsworth

[1] A brief notice of the one-volume edition on 16 Dec., which argued W. W.'s superiority to every poet since Milton. '. . . Wordsworth offers great variety, and any one may find entertainment in his works who has a natural relish for the truth and simplicity of nature.'

1945. W. W. to EDWARD MOXON

MS. Henry E. Huntington Library.
LY iii. 1271.

Rydal Mount
22nd Decr 45

My dear Mr Moxon,

It has been strongly recommended to me to send a Copy of our Volume to the Queen; and for the purpose of having it bound I beg you would send one in Sheets to Mr Westley, with the best impression of the Print and Title-page you can select.

Every one as I mentioned before admires the getting up of the Book, but several, (Ladies especially) complain that the weight prevents their keeping the Book as long as they would like in hand.

What do you say to have a second Title page for a 2nd vol. to be inserted by those that chuse to divide the 600 and odd pages into two parts. This might easily be done by placing the 2nd Title page immediately before the 280th page:—The Egyptian Maiden. Of course every thing, pages etc, remaining in other respects just as it is—

faithfully yours
W. Wordsworth

[*In M. W.'s hand*]

After all you may think it better to defer this till another Ed. is to be struck off—

Pray do not mention the Presentation Copy to *any one*.

1946. W. W. to FREDERICK WESTLEY

MS. Cornell. Hitherto unpublished.

Rydal Mount
Decr 22nd 1845

My dear Sir

Mrs W. kindly allows me her hand to spare you the trouble of decyphering my impatient penmanship.

It has been strongly recommended to me to present a Copy of my New Edition to her Majesty, and I believe your beautiful binding had not a little to do in putting the proposal into my

Friends' thoughts, as I am sure it did much to reconcile me to an act that might be thought presumptuous. It is probable you must have bound Volumes for a like purpose, and therefore know in what style my Offering ought to be executed. I therefore leave it to your taste, with only submitting what is most likely needless, whether the Royal Arms ought not to be introduced. I must beg you to insert a leaf of superior Paper to receive a *written* address of presentation from my own hand.

I will desire Mr Moxon to send you a Copy of the Volume immediately and as I have reason to expect a visit from him shortly, it would be well if you could learn from himself whether you could have the book ready for him to bring down, should he come. This would be very desirable as he could take it back with him and have it conveyed to the hands of the Ld Chamberlain[1] by whom I wish to have it presented to the Queen, as I have the honour of his Acquaintance.

It gives me pleasure to add that the Binding of my Volume is universally admired.

With the best of good wishes of the Season to you and Yours, I remain dear Mr Westley

Your much obliged
Wm Wordsworth

Pray do not mention this my present intention to any one

1947. M. W. and W. W. to EDWARD MOXON

MS. Henry E. Huntington Library. Hitherto unpublished.

Sat: night [22 Dec. 1845][2]

Dear Mr Moxon

Your Cheque for £100 has arrived safely.

The enclosed reached us after a letter was posted for you from my husband today, acknowledging the arrival of the Box—Mr Robinson reached Rydal, and in excellent Spirits yesterday. I trust we shall see you soon, and pray when you come bring me a Copy of Dr Arnold's Life.[3] You have forgotten my desire to

[1] Earl de la Warr (see L. 1684 above).

[2] Date added in another hand.

[3] A. P. Stanley's biography (see L. 1807 above).

possess this book—You put me off till a second Ed: which was *expected* soon after you were last in West[d].

Sincerely d[r] Mr M
yours
M Wordsworth

[*W. W. adds*]

I was much pleased with your liberal present of Books to Mr Carter—he well deserved such notice.

1948. W. W. to UNKNOWN CORRESPONDENT

MS. Liverpool Public Libraries. Hitherto unpublished.

[?late Dec. 1845]

My dear Sir,

Accept my thanks for your obliging Letter and the accompanying sketch of your Work, now forth coming. Had you called at M[r] Moxon's only two or three days before I should have received it through the Hands of a Friend, who is now upon a visit to us, and I have had within these few Weeks two other opportunities of receiving Books from the same quarter in the same way. Others are likely to occur, so that if you send your Volume thither, I shall be sure to get it, though not perhaps quite so soon as either of us might wish. This is however of less consequence at this season when the days are so short as to allow me little time for reading; my eyes not permitting me to use them for that purpose by candle light; and I have no young Persons about me to supply the want, which I have long felt.

Believe me with
The best wishes of the season
faithfully
Your much obliged
W[m] Wordsworth

1949. W. W. to FREDERICK WESTLEY

MS. Cornell. Hitherto unpublished.

Rydal Mount
[26][1] Dec[br] —45

My dear Sir,

As far as concerns the presentation of the Vol:[2] there need not be at this anxious time any hurry about it. I wish however, that you could finish it without inconvenience, so as to be returned to London by the hands of Mr Robinson a Friend who is now with us, and will remain I believe a fortnight longer. Mr Moxon also comes to morrow,[3] but he can only spare a few days.—With you, I prefer green for the binding and am glad to leave the whole to your taste, in which I can entirely confide.

The Books for the college of Columba[4] will be sent by Mr Moxon—they are now at Rydal. In the binding of these nothing but plain and respectable durability will I think be required. But this also I readily submit to your taste. The one Volume which Miss Fenwick presents, she wishes, to be substantially, and *handsomely* bound.

Pray excuse the blundering manner in which I have begun this Letter on the wrong page and believe me

dear Mr Westley
faithfully yours
W[m] Wordsworth

[*M. W. adds*]

My husband has forgotten to mention an important point, viz, that the page or pages he wished to be of a good paper to

[1] Day of month added by M. W.

[2] The copy of W. W.'s poems intended for the Queen (see L. 1945 above).

[3] See *HCR* ii. 656. 'His arrival very much improved our conversations in vivacity, as he brought with him a good deal of book gossip.' Aubrey de Vere also joined the Wordsworth circle for a few days this Christmas, staying with I. F. at Ambleside. See Ward, *Aubrey de Vere*, p. 99.

[4] The Irish public school founded in 1840 by William Sewell (see L. 1458 above) to forward the revival of the Church of Ireland. The project grew out of a tour of Ireland, when he made the acquaintance of Sir William Hamilton, Lord Adare, and Aubrey de Vere. See *Hamilton*, ii. 323, 325–6. W. W.'s earlier letter to Westley, of 18 Dec. (*Bookseller's Catalogue*), which has not come to light, had referred to his intention of presenting 'my Poems in the Edition of Seven Volumes, now out of print' to St. Columba's.

receive writing, will be required for 6 Stanzas[1] of 10 Syllables like Gray's Elegy.

1950. W. W. to UNKNOWN CORRESPONDENT

MS. Yale University Library. Hitherto unpublished.

[1845]

[*In M. W.'s hand*]

Dear Sir,

I have looked the enclosed over and having made one slight correction think it quite correct. I understand Mr Coleridge[2] has not been at his lodgings since your papers were put into his hands.

Y^rs etc
[*signed*] W. Wordsworth

1951. W. W. to ELIZABETH FISHER

MS. untraced.
LY iii. 1272.

2 Jan^ry 1846

My dear Cousin

The testimony of love and affection to Mrs Quillinan given under the circumstances which you mention, will I know move her deeply; and Mrs Wordsworth, my poor Sister and myself, have all been touched by it. My Son Wm being a Trustee for managing her little money affairs, you had best send him a draught in payment of this gift.

We were very thankful to hear that your dear Sister is in the way of recovery from her severe illness. Pray present to her our very kind love, and best good wishes.

On Christmas Eve we received a Letter from Mrs John Wordsworth then and still at Rome communicating the death of her youngest Son,[3] nearly five years old, and also reported that two other of her Children she had been obliged to send, under

[1] The dedicatory verses to the Queen ran to seven stanzas. See L. 1957 below.

[2] Hartley Coleridge.

[3] Edward (b. 1841). See also L. 1957 below.

the care of an English Nurse, for change of air to Albano, a third being kept with her at Rome by an attack of fever, the same we apprehend which brought on the convulsions of which his Brother died. This lamentable news, in conju[n]ction with his Wife's weakness of body and distressed state of mind, has driven him to Rome, with a view to have his family removed, and brought to England as soon as the Season will allow. He passed this house in the Mail on New year's day without calling, so dislocated was he in mind, as appears from a Letter which he left as he went by. His only Daughter was one of the indisposed who was sent to Albano, and the child he has lost was one of the noblest Creatures both in mind and body I ever saw. With this loss we couple that of our dear Cousin Sarah,[1] happening so nearly at the same time, and I am sure you will sympathize with our sorrow and trouble.

I must not dwell longer on these sad topics but beg you to accept, my kindest remembrances joined with those of Mrs W— and my Sister, and believe me with many thanks your

affectionate Cousin
Wm Wordsworth

1952. W. W. to WILLIAM JACKSON

MS. Berg Collection, New York Public Library. Hitherto unpublished.

Rydal Mount
Jan^{ry} 2nd —46.

My dear Friend,

Our poor John has been driven to Rome by the distressing intelligence that he has received of the death of his youngest Son[2] (one of the noblest Boys both in mind and body I ever saw) and the sickness of two other of his children, and the consequent exhaustion of his afflicted wife. He passed through Rydal on New Year's day in so distracted a State of mind, as appears from a Letter which he left, rather than have to contend with any objections which he feared we might urge to detain him. In his Letter are these words, 'I leave you dear Father, to make my peace with the B^{p} of Carlisle through Dr Jackson's kind consideration of my Sufferings. I believe my original Licence of

[1] Sarah Crackanthorpe.

[2] See previous letter.

non-residence does not expire till the end of Jan^{ry}. The B^{p}, I fear, is not in a state of health to attend to such matters for I hear he has had a Relapse—I have engaged the Revd J. Gilbanks,[1] who his Father tells me came with a high character from his last Curacy, and is a Favorite with the B^{p} of Carlisle, a break certainly will not be later than the first Sunday in Jan^{ry}.' Thus far John, I hope they will all come earlier if the season should allow his wife to be removed, at all events he is determined to bring the children home. Mrs Jackson, who I hope continues to gain ground, will sympathize with our distress. Excuse my saying more at this time, and believe me

very faithfully yours
Wm Wordsworth

1953. W. W. to GEORGE JOHN STEVENSON[2]

Address: Geo. John Stevenson Esq. St John's College, Battersea.
Postmark: (1) 3 Jan. 1846 (2) 5 Jan. 1846.
Stamp: Ambleside.
MS. Harvard University Library.
LY iii. 1273.

[*In M. W.'s hand*]

Rydal Mount
3^{d} Jan.^{ry} 1846.

Mr Wordsworth presents his Comp^{ts} to Mr Stevenson and begs to say that he thinks Mr S. scarcely authorized to entertain the expectation that, during his Mr W's life-time, there should have been a biographical Memoir prefixed to the Vol: referred to. As Mr W. has long ago made a point of not reading any Reviews of his own Works and indeed scarcely ever looks at a Review or

[1] The Revd. Jackson Gilbanks (b. 1819), educated at Sedbergh and St. John's College, Cambridge: sometime curate of Gilsland, Cumb., but later resided at Whitefield House, nr. Bassenthwaite.

[2] George John Stevenson (1818–88) Methodist hymnologist, entered St. John's College, Battersea in 1844 for teacher training under the National Society, and became headmaster first of a remedial centre for criminals in Southwark (1846), and then of a parish school at Lambeth Green (1848). From 1855 he set up as a publisher, and edited the *Wesleyan Times*, 1861–7. He published *The Methodist Hymn Book*, 1869 (enlarged 1883), and studies of Spurgeon and other Methodist figures.

Magazine he is totally unable to give Mr Stevenson the information he requests.

There have been Prints from three different Paintings made of Mr W.—one a large size by Mr Wilkin,[1] another by Mr Boxall[2] and a third from Miss Marg^t Gillies[3]—any of which may probably be heard of at the Print Shops or at the Residence of the Painters which Mr [W] does not at present know. As to which is the best opinions vary.

In 1831 Mr Wilkin's Print might have been had at No 144 New Bond S^t.

[*unsigned*]

1954. W. W. to WILLIAM JACKSON

MS. Berg Collection, New York Public Library. Hitherto unpublished.

Rydal
8th Jan^ry —46

My dear Friend,

Mrs Wordsworth and I are truly thankful for your kindness in respect to the Bp,[4] and equally so for the sympathy you and Mrs Jackson express with our trouble and anxiety.

We thank you also for offering to write yourself to John, but it would be so melancholy an office that we wish to spare you undertaking it. I will add that so desirable, so necessary, is it that the Children should be brought away as soon as possible from Italy, the Father returning with them, that we think it much better that his term of absence should not be lengthened beyond the end of May. We will communicate to John the substance of your Letter, only omitting the mention of your friendly desire to procure him the liberty of absence for a longer term—By the end of the month we hope for a Letter from John, and if it contains any important particulars we will not fail to inform you of them. My poor wife has been much shattered by these events, but she is easier in mind since John's departure. May God support us all

[1] See pt. ii, L. 639.

[2] See pt. ii, Ls. 603 and 750.

[3] See pt. iii, Ls. 1345 and 1350, and L. 1541 above.

[4] The Bishop of Carlisle, Dr. Hugh Percy.

my dear Friend under such afflictions. With Mrs W's affectionate remembrances to your self and Mrs Jackson, I remain

ever faithfully your much obliged
Wm Wordsworth

We understand Mr Fell[1] has accepted the Ambleside Curacy.—

1955. W. W. to JOSEPH SNOW[2]

MS. Carl H. Pforzheimer Library. Hitherto unpublished.

Rydal Mount
8th Janry 1846.

Sir,

You are quite at Liberty to make such use of my Essay upon Epitaphs as you may think suitable to your intended Publication—

I am Sir, with thanks for your specimens,

Yours truly
Wm Wordsworth

1956. W. W. to FREDERICK WESTLEY

MS. Cornell. Hitherto unpublished.

[*c.* 9 Jan. 1846]

My dear Sir,

Thank you for the Book intended for the Queen. The Binding is just what I wished; nevertheless comparing it with the One which you so kindly sent before, I cannot but say that I prefer the effect of the former, principally because I like white better than green. But they are both excellent. The Book will be taken to London, by Mr Robinson, and I have written to the Lord Chamberlain to beg that he would present it so that I hope it will be in the Queen's hands before the end of next week.

Miss Fenwick's Vol: to be collected will be sent from Mr Moxon.

[1] Samuel Irton Fell (b. 1801), of Queen's College, Oxford, perpetual curate of Ambleside, 1846–60, in succession to Mr. Dawes, who had died in 1845.

[2] Author of *Lyra Memorialis. Original Epitaphs and Churchyard Thoughts in Verse*, 1847, which reprinted W. W.'s essay from *The Friend*.

Pray insert in the 6th Vol: either by Pasting it or otherwise the Accompanying Paper

ever faithfully
My dear Sir
Your much obliged
Wm Wordsworth

Miss Fenwick will write to you what she wishes to have inserted in the Copy presented by her.

1957. W. W. to C. W. JNR.

MS. British Library. Hitherto unpublished.

[*c.* 10 Jan. 1846]

My dear Christopher,

Three of Isabella's children have had the fever at Rome, of which the youngest has died. What our loss is you will find imperfectly expressed in the Lines upon the other leaf. The Departed was the youngest, Edward, your Godson, and his Father entreats that we would inform you of the sad event, which he himself could not find heart to do, when he passed through London last week on his way to Rome, his object being to support his afflicted Wife and bring them all to England as soon as the season will allow. He also felt that the Mother being disabled his presence was necessary to protect them from further mischief, to be apprehended from the dangerous climate or any other cause. The beloved Boy would have been five years old if he had lived till April. What effect these anxieties, and this distress may have had on the poor Mother's health she can scarcely know, but John will be able to tell us soon after his arrival at Rome—Pray forward this Letter to your Father, who I know will sympathize with us all in our sorrow.

I ought to have acknowledged the receipt of your last kind Letter earlier, but under such circumstances I need not plead for your excuse. You are aware of the value I set upon your Theophilus, and I need scarcely say that I was glad to hear of the intended Translation.[1]

George Hutchinson will write to your Father; perhaps he has

[1] A Greek version of *Theophilus Anglicanus* was published by Rivington in 1847. The work was translated into French by Dr. Frédéric Godfray in 1861.

already written to thank him for his generous offer, and let him know when and how to pay the money.

Pray forward this Letter to him and believe me Your affectionate

Uncle
Wm Wordsworth

Love as usual to Susan—

I have sent my last Edition to the Queen with a copy of Verses prefixed—7 Quatrains.[1] The book sells very well especially considering how the Public mind has been occupied for some time.

[*In M. W.'s hand*[

Why should we weep or mourn! Angelic Boy,
For such thou wert ere from our sight removed;
Holy and ever dutiful—beloved
From day to day with never-ceasing joy,
And hopes as dear as could the heart employ
In aught to Earth pertaining. Death hath proved
His might, nor less his mercy—as behoved,
Death, conscious that he only could destroy
The bodily frame. That beauty is laid low
To moulder in a far-off field of Rome;
But Heaven is now blest Child! thy Spirit's home;
When that divine communion, which we know,
Is felt,—thy Roman burial-place will be
Surely a sweet remembrancer of thee.[2]

W. W.

1958. W. W. to EDWARD MOXON

Address: Edward Moxon Esqre, 44 Dover St, London. [*In M. W.'s hand*]
Postmark: (1) 15 Jan. 1846 (2) 16 Jan. 1846.
MS. Henry E. Huntington Library.
LY iii. 1273.

15 Jan^ry—1846

My dear Mr Moxon,

Of the half a dozen Copies of the new Edition we have only

[1] See *PW* iv. 391. Dated 9 Jan. 1846: first printed 1876.
[2] See *PW* iv. 266.

one left; and Mrs Nicholson is desirous of more. I think at least a dozen ought to be sent here, and if the demand is not likely to be greater as the spring advances, in London, you might send us 20, which I think would certainly go off in the course of the summer. If I am not mistaken you took with you the direction for the cheaper conveyance. But dont send the Books till you have procured the bottle of lustre varnish which Mr Cottle of Bristol gave orders should wait for my call at Mr D. Green's 36 King Wm Street, London Bridge.

Pray be so good as to procure this immediately and send it in the same package with the Books—or rather dont send the Books without it. I have in my house three large Pictures which my Son John sent from Italy; though much damaged by Time and neglect they are worth repairing and luckily a respectable Painter is now for a short time at Ambleside and he would do the needful as to cleaning etc under my own eye. Of this lustre varnish my Friend Cottle gave so flattering an account that I am anxious to have it tried—the Varnish is of C's own invention, and by a series of experiments carried on at different periods through his long life he thinks he has brought it to perfection.

I hope my Vol: will be in the Queen's hands before the end of the week. We have heard nothing more from Italy, that is from our Friends there, but from another quarter that the sickness is very formidable, which makes us most anxious. We however have heard of John's safe arrival at Paris on the Saturday night—to go forward on Monday morning

ever faithfully yours
Wm Wordsworth

1959. W. W. to MARY ANN DIXON[1]

MS. Cornell. Hitherto unpublished.

Rydal Mount
22nd Jan^{ry} —46

My dear Cousin,

I cannot content myself, with sending my thanks through your Brother, or one of your nieces, for the little presents that I have just received. Be assured that I shall value both for the

[1] W. W.'s cousin (see pt. i, L. 37 and L. 1741 above). W. W. had stayed with the Dixons during his recent visit to York.

Donors sake and its own, and it will take its place among several memorials, some [from] Greece, some from Italy which I possess through the kindness of Friends.—

I was glad to hear from your Brother a favorable account of your good Mother and my other valued Relatives in your neighbourhood. Pray remember me Kindly to Mr Dixon and believe me sincerely and affectionately

your much obliged
Wm Wordsworth

1960. W. W. to HERBERT HILL[1]

Address: Revd H. Hill, College, Warwick.
Postmark: (1) 22 Jan. 1846 (2) 24 Jan. 1846.
Stamp: (1) Ambleside (2) Warwick.
MS. Harvard University Library.
LY iii. 1274.

Rydal
Jan. 22nd—1846

My dear Mr Hill

Some time ago I received from Cockermouth 'Oliver Newman',[2] and read in print your touching dedication of the little Vol: to my Wife and me. I felt strongly that my acknowledgements for such a mark of your affections in thus uniting us all, ought to have been made at once, but being sure that you would give me credit for feeling upon this occasion as became me I was induced to defer writing till I could read the Vol: in a state of mind sufficiently at liberty to do it justice. But in fact for many weeks troubles have multiplied for us in a degree that has been very distressing; first the sudden decease of our dear Cousin Sarah Crackenthorp, who on her return from Edinburgh where she died was to come to visit us, next a Letter from Rome, announcing the dangerous illness of our dear Grandchild, John's

[1] Bertha Southey's husband.

[2] *Oliver Newman: A New-England Tale (Unfinished); With Other Poetical Remains*, 1845. The dedication ran: 'To William and Mary Wordsworth, the old and dear friends of Robert Southey, these last productions, the imperfect "Autumn Leaves" of his poetical genius, are inscribed, with filial reverence and affection by the Editor.' The poem was first conceived as early as 1809 (see Curry, ii. 5, and Southey, iii. 293–4).

youngest Son, as fine a Boy as could be seen, and soon after came the tidings of his decease. Poor John was distracted, for the same Letters announced that his Daughter and another Son were ill of the same fever. Notwithstanding all his cares and duties at home, he could not help setting off immediately for Rome and passed our door without calling in the fear that we might endeavor to stop him. He would reach Rome last Saturday if no mishap delayed him. Lastly came the news that my last-surviving Brother the late Master of Trinity was alarmingly ill, and he still continues in a very feeble state, so that my dear Mr Hill, you will not wonder that I did not feel my mind sufficiently open to be interested as I wished and ought to be in any poetical production of my departed Friend. I have however read the Volume and most of it more than once. The beautiful parts of Oliver are I think fully equal to any preceding work of their Author, and the whole of it with some correction and softening from his pen, which he undoubtedly would have given, would have met the desires of his most judicious Friends. The speech of the Governor is too long and somewhat dry and prosaic, and a few expressions in Randolph's mouth partake in my opinion of vulgarity; with these exceptions, I like the fragment exceedingly and several parts of it cannot be over-estimated.

You will be sure that we are most anxious for tidings from Rome, which we cannot have till the middle of next week; and the more so because we learn through Mr Price[1] that Dr Babbington's[2] whole time has been engrossed by Patients suffering from this sickness, which is of such a character that he has been obliged to visit several Patients three times a day, and the others at least once every day. On the other side we hear from Isabella that all the children were well, except Jane who is suffering from a nervous complaint, aggravated by her late attack of fever, on account of which with her Brother John, who had the same illness, she had been sent to Albano, but both have returned to Rome. Whatever becomes of the poor Mother the children must be brought to England, their lives must not be sacrificed, and it is for this purpose that their Father is gone again to Italy.

Pray give our very kind love to Bertha, accept the same

[3] Bonamy Price (see L. 1812 above).

[4] Dr. Benjamin Guy Babington, F.R.S. (1794–1866), physician at Guy's Hospital, 1840–55.

yourself, and believe me with a thousand good wishes for you and yours

your sincere Friend
Wm Wordsworth

1961. W. W. to HENRY REED

Address: Henry Reed, Philadelphia, U.S. Via L-pool packet.
Postmark: (1) 23 Jan. 1846 (2) 26 Jan.
Stamp: Ambleside.
MS. Cornell.
Mem. (—). *Grosart* (—). *Wordsworth and Reed, p. 160.*

Rydal Mt Jan^{ry} 23^{d}—46

My dear Mr Reed

After a delay at Liverpool under which we were not a little impatient, the Portrait has reached us, and Mrs W— returns her grateful thanks to you and Mrs Reed for a Present on which she sets so high a value, both for its own sake, and as coming from Friends for whom she entertains a high respect.[1] In these thanks we beg Mr Inman may be included; but regretting the expense to which you have been put, I cannot forbear to observe that the subject was mentioned to your Brother solely because Mr Inman had said that "if it pleased Mrs W— she should have a copy though He was afraid that he could not find time to do it during his stay in England." This hope was of course held out upon the supposition, that it would be rather pleasing to you than otherwise, that it should be fulfilled. As to the copy now happily in Mrs W's possession she begs me to say that it quite answers her expectation, so indeed it does mine, as far as the likeness of feature is concerned; but the expression which one would have wished for, was not aimed at, and probably the artist did well in not attempting more than what he has performed a striking

[1] See L. 1830 above. Reed had written on 27 Nov. 1845: 'The original picture is so highly prized by Mrs. Reed and myself and we derive so constant an enjoyment from the possession of it, that I can well conceive the gratification such a likeness will afford to Mrs. Wordsworth and the rest of your family. . . . The wonderfully life-like face in the picture has become such a familiar presence to us, that when it was sent to New York for Mr. Inman to make the copy, we felt the blank as if one of our household were away.' (*Wordsworth and Reed*, p. 158). The portrait now hangs at Rydal Mount.

resemblance in this respect to his subject; and therefore as Mrs W— values the work so highly, you may be sure that in the main points it is all that one would desire. I hope to be able to send you an impression of an Engraving from a Picture of Mr Haydon representing me in the act of climbing Helvellyn.[1] There is great merit in this work and the sight of it will shew my meaning on the subject of *expression*. This I think is attained, but then, I am stooping and the inclination of the head necessarily causes a foreshortening of the features below the nose which takes from the likeness accordingly; so that upon the whole your's has the advantage, especially under the circumstances of your having never seen the original. Mrs W— has been looking over your Letters in vain to find the address of the Person in London through whose hands any parcels for you might be sent—pray take the trouble of repeating the address in your next Letter—and your request shall be attended to of sending you my two Letters upon the offensive subject of a Railway to, and through our beautiful neighbourhood. A Copy of my Poems in one Vol. double column I hope you will accept at the same time.

Now let me ask you whether there is sufficient cause for apprehending a war between your country and ours[2]—Heaven forbid it should be so, but ignorant multitudes have so much to do in governing your affairs and such is the language held among you in some quarters by men high at least from their unmerited position that one cannot help being under some alarm for the consequences. Do tell me what you think.

You will be sorry to hear that Mrs W and I have been, and still are under great trouble and anxiety. Our Daughter in Law fell into bad health between three and four [years][3] ago. She went with her Husband to Madeira, where they remained nearly a year; she was then advised to go to Italy—after a prolonged Residence there her 6 Children whom her Husband returned to England for, went at her earnest request to that Country, under their Father's guidance—there he was obliged on account of his duty as a Clergyman to leave them. Four of the number resided

[1] See next letter.

[2] The American title to the Oregon territory remained in dispute until the treaty with Britain in June 1846 settled the northern boundary of the United States and Canada along the 49th Parallel. In his reply of 26 Feb. Reed deplored 'the wanton wickedness of war between two such nations' on such a question. (*Wordsworth and Reed*, p. 164).

[3] *Word dropped out.*

with their mother at Rome, three of whom took a fever there of which the youngest, as noble a boy of nearly five years as ever was seen died, being seized with convulsions when the fever was somewhat subdued. The Father in a distracted state of mind is just gone back to Italy, and we are most anxious to hear the result. My only surviving Brother also the late Master of Trin. Coll. Cambridge and an inestimable person is also in an alarming state of health, and the only child of my eldest Brother long since deceased, is now languishing under mortal illness at Ambleside. He was educated to the medical Profession, and caught his illness while on duty in the Mediterranean. He is a truly amiable and excellent young man and will be universally regretted. These sad occurrences with others of like kind have thrown my mind into a state of feeling which the other day vented itself in the two Sonnets which Mrs W. will transcribe as the best acknowledgement she can make for Mrs Reed's and your kindness.—

[*unsigned*]

[*There follows in M. W.'s hand* Why should we weep or mourn Angelic Boy, *as in L. 1957 above, except that in l. 12 read* this *for* that; *and* Where lies the truth? *as in PW iv. 19, except that in l. 6 read* Who that lies down, and may not wake to sorrow, *and in l. 9* this *for* as.]

1962. W. W. to BENJAMIN ROBERT HAYDON

MS. untraced.
LY iii. 1276.

Rydal Mount, Jan. 24th, 1846.

My dear Haydon,

I was sorry that I could not give a more satisfactory answer to your request for a Motto to the Engraving[1] from your admirable Portrait of my ascent towards the top of Helvellyn. My Son Wm who is here has just been with me to look at the impression of the Print in the unfinished state, as we have it. But from the first he has been exceedingly pleased with it, so much so that he would be truly happy to be put into possession of it as it then was, if an impression could be procured for him, and would

[1] The engraving of the head by T. Lupton.

readily pay for it if purchaseable. Pray let me have a few impressions, when it is finished, sent to Moxon, as I myself think that it is the best likeness, that is the most characteristic, which has been done of me. I wish to send one also to America according to directions which will be hereafter given.

I hope you get on with your labours to your satisfaction.

Believe me dear Haydon

faithfully your obliged Friend
Wm Wordsworth

1963. W. W. to EDWARD MOXON

MS. Henry E. Huntington Library.
LY iii. 1322 (—).

[1 Feb. 1846][1]

My dear Mr Moxon,

Your Communication came at a bad time, one of my eyes being inflamed; besides, I really am tired with getting up these Poems, as you witnessed when you were here. When we were together at Rydal we agreed upon what was to be done, and I have no fear of entrusting the work to your superintendence. Should you think it would be better to refer the Sheets to Mr Carter you can do so directing to him, Stamp off. Carlisle—

I approve of your arrangement, the Excursion to stand last. As a new Title page will be necessary the volumes being 7, it would be well to add—with such abreviations as are usual on like occasions—

Honorary Member of the Royal Society
of Edinburgh and of the Royal Irish
Academy etc etc.

You do not mention whether the last Edition continues to go off, I am aware that its time of publication is as unfavorable as possible—

ever faithfully yours
Wm Wordsworth

My Son Wm sets off to morrow as Miss Fenwick's Escort to

[1] Dated to 1847 in another hand,—but the letter is clearly about the preparation of the edn. of 1846 in 7 vols.

London,[1] where he hopes to arrive on Friday; He means to take his bed according to promise at Mr Robinsons, and will take with him the Vol. you sent; He will remain in Town a fortnight or so, and can bring any thing you may have to send to me—

In the Volume sent to me the Text to be printed from, you will bear in mind, is that of the last Edition in one Vol: because there are some corrections and some errata of the printer, also, corrected.—

1964. W. W. to H. C. R.

Address: H. C. Robinson Esqre, 30 Russel Sq^re^, London. [*In M. W.'s hand*]
Postmark: (1) 2 Feb. 1846 (2) 3 Feb. 1846
Stamp: Ambleside.
Endorsed: 2^d^ Feb: 46. Wordsworth. Autograph.
MS. Dr. Williams's Library.
Morley, ii. 619.

Rydal Feb^ry^ 2nd [18]46

My dear Friend

You kindly desired me to tell you of our news from Rome—John arrived safely and found his Children well—tho' as he says looking miserably, his wife greatly shattered, but, in some respects better than when he left her. We have been and are in sad distress. My Brother D^r^ W— is dying—The last letter said that it was not thought he could survive another 24 hours, our Nephew John Mr Fell thinks, may be taken off at any moment, he is sinking so rapidly, We have other causes of great distress with which you need not be trouble[d][2] So that my poor Wife's frame is sadly shaken. My dear Sister continues much the same.—

[1] His visit was postponed owing to I. F.'s illness (see *HCR* ii. 657).

[2] W. W. may be referring here to his anxiety about John W.'s deteriorating relationship with his wife, which Sara Coleridge described in an undated letter to I. F. of this period: '. . .The circumstances of his eldest son are enough to depress him. Even if his wife recovers her health, nothing can heal the worse and sorer sicknesses which through her illness have grown up and been fully revealed—nothing, I fear, can turn *her* into a wise woman or *him* into an energetic high-minded man. . . . A wearisome wasting thing it will be, from year to year, to see that couple wronging each other and mismanaging their children—one pulling this way and the other that.' (*Texas University MSS.*).

I have heard nothing from the Queen, which I only care about for her own sake, concluding that she must have been anxious about and occupied by the state of public affairs,[1] or that She cares little about Literature—

Dear Miss Fenwick was the other night along with Jemima Quillinan overturned in one of Donaldsons carriages, they were dragged about 2 yards and then lifted out of the Window—Miss F a good deal shaken throughout the frame, the effects of which she feels more now than she did at first. But we all hope that no permanent mischief has ensued. The accident took place a few yards from Mrs Arnolds door. In a few days I hope we shall be able to write again—but at present we are in a sad state of anxiety,

ever your affectionate Friend
Wm Wordsworth

[*M. W. adds*]

D^r^ friend do not let Miss F. accident get abroad—else she will be inundated by letters of enquiry—

1965. W. W. to HENRY REED

Address: Henry Reed Esqre, Philadelphia. [*In M. W.'s hand*]
Postmark: (1) 3 Feb. 1846 (2) 4 Feb. 1846.
Stamp: Ambleside.
MS. Cornell.
Mem. (—). *Grosart* (—). *Wordsworth and Reed, p. 165.*

3^d^ Feb^ry^ [1846]

My dear Mr Reed,

I was much shocked to find that my last had been despatched without acknowledgement for your kindness in sending me the admirable engraving of Bp White which I was delighted, on many accounts to receive. This omission was owing to the distressed state of mind in which I wrote, and which I throw myself on your goodness to excuse. I ought to have written again by next Post but we really have been, and still are, in such trouble from various causes that I could not take up the pen and now must beg you to accept this statement as the only excuse

[1] The Corn Law crisis. See L. 1974 below.

which I can offer. We have had such accounts from my Daughter in Law at Rome, that her Mother and Brother are just gone thither to support her, her mother being 70 years of age.

Do you know any thing of a wretched set of Religionists in your Country, *Superstitionists* I ought to say, called Mormonites or Latter-day-saints.[1] Would you believe it, a niece of Mrs W's has just embarked, *we believe* at Liverpool, with a set of the deluded Followers of that wretch, in an atempt to join their society. her name is Margaret Hutchinson,[2] a young woman of good abilities and well educated, but early in life she took from her Mother and *her* connections, a Methodistical turn and has gone on in a course of what she supposes to be piety till she has come to this miserable close. If you should by chance hear any thing about her pray let us know.[3]

The Report of my Brother's decease we look for every day has not yet reached us, and my Nephew is still languishing on, from day to day.

ever faithfully and affectionately yours
Wm Wordsworth

The Print of Bp White is noble, every thing indeed that could be wished—[4]

[1] The Church of Jesus Christ of Latter-Day Saints was founded at Manchester, New York, in 1830 by Joseph Smith (1805–44), to whom the 'Book of Mormon', the Bible of the sect, was revealed. In 1843 he received another revelation sanctioning polygamy. His successor Brigham Young (1801–77) moved the headquarters of the sect to Salt Lake City, Utah.

[2] See also L. 1523 above. Her mother, *née* Margaret Roberts, was M. W.'s sister in law, and had married George Hutchinson in 1812.

[3] 'I know nothing of those wretched and wicked fanatics,' Reed replied on 30 Mar., 'except the accounts, which from time to time have reached us, of the scenes of tumult in the region occupied by them. They are at a great distance in the West and since the death of their chief leader—the Prime Impostor—they have moved off in mass to a more remote West. It would be only by some lucky chance that I should be likely to hear anything of a person who had joined them. . . . If correspondence is continued with her, it might be desirable to put her in possession of my address—as one she might apply to as a friend of yours: experience may dispel her unhappy delusion, and she may unexpectedly find herself . . . in great want of friendly counsel and assistance.' (*Wordsworth and Reed*, pp. 166–7).

[4] This is W. W.'s last letter to Reed, who, however, continued to write to the poet intermittently until Dec. 1849 (see *Wordsworth and Reed*, pp. 168 ff.). After W. W.'s death, he supervised the publication of *Mem.* in America, and continued to correspond with M. W., particularly about American participation in the

1966. W. W. to THOMAS BOYLES MURRAY[1]

Address: Rev[d] T. B. Murray.
MS. WL transcript. Hitherto unpublished.

Rydal Mount
Feb[ry] 4th — 46

Dear Sir,

Your obliging note of Jan[ry] 17, and the little Volume which it accompanied, I have not been able to acknowledge earlier for several reasons, with which I forbear to trouble you, as they were of a distressing kind.

Your little Book,[2] as far as I can judge, is well suited for its purpose, and I trust will be read with advantage by young persons; and the more, if it prove the cause of the passages in Scripture on which the Verses are founded, being more frequently read.

With many thanks and good wishes,

I remain dear Sir
faithfully your much obliged
W[m] Wordsworth

1967. W. W. to ELIZABETH FISHER

MS. Mr. P. G. Gates. Hitherto unpublished.

Rydal
Feby 5th 1846

My dear Cousin,

It was kind in you to write, and I thank you sincerely for your sympathizing letter. My beloved Brother's sufferings which were severe closed between three and four on *Monday* morning.[3] The information you must have had from Carlisle was premature. *We* only received the intelligence of his decease by the same Post which brought your Letter of condolence, but a Letter from

Wordsworth memorial in Ambleside Church (*WL MSS.*). In 1854 he finally came to Europe and visited Rydal Mount.

[1] See L. 1448 above.

[2] Perhaps *Lays of Christmas*, 1847 (*R.M.Cat.* no. 523): in which case W. W. inadvertently misdated the letter to the previous year.

[3] C. W. had died at Buxted on 2 Feb. See C. W. jnr.'s tribute to him in *Mem.* ii. 426 ff.

Buxted, written a few days before, had informed us that it was not likely that he could survive more than 24 hours. In the opinion of his Uckfield medical attendant his death was mainly caused by an injury done to the spine many years ago at Cambridge when he had the misfortune to be thrown from his Horse, which was run against by a reckless Coach-driver. His Son Charles was with him to the last, so was Christopher at the *close* and for some days previous. He is expecting his Wife's confinement every day. Charles' letter received yesterday has been forwarded to W^{m}, and it shall be sent to you, if it has not been done by him already.

I say nothing of our sorrow upon this bereavement; you know too well how good a Man he was, for that to be necessary.

We regret much that you cannot give us a more favorable account of your dear Sister's state; pray present to her our kind love and best wishes, accept the same yourself, and believe me my dear Cousin,

affectionately and faithfully yours
Wm Wordsworth

1968. W. W. to CHARLES WORDSWORTH

MS. Mr. Jonathan Wordsworth. Hitherto unpublished.[1]

5th Feb^{ry} [1846]

My dear Charles,

We had as you were aware been sufficiently prepared for the sad intelligence contained in your last Letter, and that being so, the announcement of our dear Brother's departure from this life,[2] brought with it its due share of consolation. As your Father's trial of suffering was borne with the patience and resignation of a Christian, even thus when the suffering has ceased They who loved him find pure sources of comfort and support after so heavy a loss. To you or your Brother I need not say how dear he was to me and how I reverenced his virtues. Your Aunt Dorothy notwithstanding her enfeebled state of mind has been much troubled by the tidings, and your Aunt Wordsworth sympathizes with us all very deeply. So does William, and so will his poor Sister, when She shall receive the

[1] A single sentence appears in *Annals of My Early Life.*

[2] See previous letter.

tidings following so closely upon the loss of her Cousin Sarah Crackanthorp, and her dear Nephew little Edward, as promising a child as could be seen. Then will come to her the tidings of John's decease. In your view of the loss which the Church and the Country will have in the removal of such a Friend as your beloved Father I entirely concur. His activity, his zeal and his judgement were in no quarter surpassed.

Your Cousin John[1] continues to sink hourly, we go every day to him. He is quite prepared for dissolution—Farewell my dear Charles, may God support you and your Brother. Your most affectionate Uncle

W W.

We are anxious to hear of Susan's safe confinement.

1969. W. W. to ROBERT SHELTON MACKENZIE[2]

Address: R. Shelton Mackenzie Esq, 73 Albert Street, Mornington Road, London.
MS. Cornell.
Broughton, p. 89.

Rydal Mount
17th Febry 1846.

Dear Sir,

I wish you success in your projected Magazine,[3] but it is quite out of my power to serve you by contributing to it. In the whole course of my life I have never written a word for a Magazine or Review, and must not surely think of such a thing now—

Thanks for your enquiries after my health. It is in a good state, and I hope your's is the same.

Believe me, dear Sir,
faithfully yours
Wm Wordsworth

[1] R. W.'s son.
[2] See pt. iii, L. 1110.
[3] Perhaps the railway journal which he is recorded as editing at this time,—or some other unrealised project.

1970. W. W. to EDWARD MOXON

MS. Henry E. Huntington Library.
LY iii. 1277.

23^{d} Feb^{ry} [1846]

Dear Mr Moxon,

The entanglement of public Affairs seems to have prevented my receiving an earlier acknowledgement from the Queen of the offering of our Volume—Yesterday however a Letter arrived from the Ld Chamberlain conveying her M—y's thanks and the expression of her admiration of the verses in the fly leaf.[1] The Queen has also sent me 4 lithographic Copies of the Portraits of [her] several children.[2] The Ld Chamberlain's words are 'I have placed your beautiful Volume before Her Majesty'.

I will thank you to pay my debt to Mr Westley when his bill is presented.

Dont forget to [? rub] up Burns[3] for any thing that may be due to us. I am sorry to be forced to allude to this Subject, but I have been hardly drawn upon lately by various causes—

I was much grieved to be obliged to return the volume as I did—as to carry it thro' the press correctly will I fear impose much trouble upon you. Do not however fail to transmit the Sheets as they are struck off to Mr Carter if you think it will be of use—only avoiding to break in upon him between the 20th of March and the middle of Ap. a time when he is busy in the Off.—after that time he will be at Rydal—Only the proofs need be sent—but pray procure the old Copy of the Excursion *especially*

Aff^{dy} yours
Wm Wordsworth

I will send you soon as they can be transcribed 6 Sonnets and 2 other small Poems to be inserted in the last Vol.[4]

[1] See L. 1957 above.

[2] Victoria (see L. 1463), later Crown Princess of Prussia; Albert Edward (1841–1910), Prince of Wales; Alice (1843–78), later Grand Duchess of Hesse-Darmstadt; and Alfred (1844–1900), Duke of Edinburgh. A fifth child Helena (1846–1923), later Princess Christian of Schleswig-Holstein, was born on 25 May.

[3] The publisher (see L. 1756 above).

[4] i.e. vol. vi of the new 7 vol. edition which was now in preparation.

1971. W. W. to FREDERICK WESTLEY

MS. Cornell. Hitherto unpublished.

[*In M. W.'s hand*]

Rydal Mt Feb^{ry} 23^{d}. [1846]

Dear Sir

The entanglement of public Affairs seems to have prevented my receiving an earlier acknowledgment from the Queen of the Offering of my Volume. Yesterday however a letter arrived from the Ld Chamberlain conveying her Majesty's thanks, and the expression of her admiration of the Verses on the fly leaf. The Queen also sent me Copies from the Portraits of her 4 Children. The Ld Chamberlain's words are "I have placed your beautiful Volume before her Majesty."

I must request you to present the account of whatever may be due from me to you for the books you have bound for Miss Fenwick and myself to Mr Moxon, whom I have deputed to discharge my debt.

I so very much admire your taste and execution in binding, that were I a rich Man I should often have recourse to you.

Believe me to remain with much regard

faithfully your greatly obliged

[*signed*] Wm Wordsworth

An inflammation in one of my eyes has compelled me to employ an Amanuensis

1972. W. W. to EDWARD MOXON

MS. Henry E. Huntington Library.
LY iii. 1277.

[*In unidentified hand*]

[late Feb. 1846]

My dear Mr Moxon,

I send you the little Poems as promised.[1] Insert them in succession—after the Sonnets I should suppose, but wherever you think best. I should like the proofs of the sheet that contains them to be sent down to me. Mr Westley as I mentioned before will have to call for a copy of the last edition which you will set

[1] See L. 1970 above.

down to my account, it being intended as a present from Miss Fenwick to the Boys School in the new Protestant College of St Columba, Ireland.[1] Do you happen to know what bookseller in London that College communicates with? Miss Fenwick had the address but having packed up her things she could not find it again without trouble. The Copy both of my 7 volumes (and Miss Fenwick's) which Mr Westley has bound for me were both to be sent through that Publisher.—Don't trouble yourself to answer the above question unless you can tell us who the Bookseller is.

Ever faithfully yours
[*signed*] Wm Wordsworth

My eye is better but not well enough to allow me to write.

1973. W. W. to ROBERT PERCEVAL GRAVES

MS. Lilly Library, Indiana University. Hitherto unpublished.

Rydal Mount
Saturday Evening. [early 1846]

My dear Mr Graves,

I am sorry that I cannot be of use to your Brother[2] upon this occasion. Mr Blamire[3] is a cousin of my Daughter in law, but I never saw him, nor have any means of communication with Him. Had Isabella been in England I should without scruple have forwarded through her to Mr Blamire your letter. With the other two persons I have no connection.

Your Brother will have an advantage in his application, being so distinguished as he is for legal knowledge, and I heartily wish him success.

Believe me ever faithfully yours
Wm Wordsworth

[1] See L. 1949 above.

[2] John Thomas Graves (see pt. iii, L. 1221). This letter almost certainly refers to his application for appointment as an assistant poor-law commissioner. Hence the dating.

[3] William Blamire (see pt. ii, L. 610).

1974. W. W. to WILLIAM JACKSON

MS. Berg Collection, New York Public Library.
LY iii. 1278 (—).

[Mar. 1846]

My dear Friend,

My first words must be to beg pardon for not having written to you, both to inform you of what had been done, and to acknowledge your great kindness. But the fact is we have been subject for some time to anxieties and sorrows in no common degree; and we wanted courage to communicate with our friends, in consequence; and in addition to this I have for more than a month been obliged to abstain both from writing and reading and what is still worse almost from thinking by my old complaint—inflammation in one of my eyes. Sincerely do I thank you for your condolence upon the death of my excellent and beloved Brother; it is gratifying to me to be told that you saw so much of him lately. The Church has lost in him one of her most zealous and judicious defenders, and this at a time when such men can be ill-spared. Our dear and amiable Nephew, John Wordsworth of Sockbridge is also soon to be taken from us. He has a House at Ambleside, and some one of our family visits him daily. Poor Fellow, he is growing weaker and weaker every day, and is quite aware that his dissolution is approaching.—Now to come to business. John requested me to thank you for your kind exertions, and for your Letter, which he thought to spare you expense of postage, and other reasons, he thought might be better done through me. This I regret to say, from causes above stated was omitted by his Mother and me; and I again ask your pardon for the fault. We bear in mind the debt for postage which we owe you for the Papers you sent to Rome to be signed, which he duly returned to the Bishop, stating to his Lordship at the time that he was afraid he should not be able to return to England before June. *But* since that time Mrs Curwen having gone to Rome to her Daughter, whom she hopes to bring home when the season will permit, we have reason to believe that John will be here by the end of the month; with his two elder Boys. But there is great embarrassment connected with the residence of these Children abroad. Upon hearing the death of his darling Son, and at the same time a

Letter having been seen by me from a Sister of Dr Babbington[1] at home, giving an account of the dangerous character of the fever then prevailing, John determined to remove the children out of the City, a resolution which I entirely approved. My wish was that they should have gone to Pisa, but he took them to Florence which I regret, as it is not a healthy place.—

We are sorry to hear so poor an account of Mrs Jackson's health, pray present to her our united good wishes and accept the same yourself. I remain my dear Friend very faithfully

your much obliged
Wm Wordsworth

W^m is gone to London chiefly to escort Miss Fenwick, who has lately suffered from severe colds. He will see Lady Frederic,[2] who must be much grieved by the death of Colonel Howard,[3] a loss of which I am truly sensible—

As to public affairs I cannot bear to think of them. Sir R. Peel is infatuated;[4] he is playing the part of that weak man, Necker,[5] in the beginning of the French Revolution. The Queen sent me the other day 4 portraits of her several children as a return for the One Volume Edition of my Poems which I sent to her with a copy of Mss Verses on the fly Leaf.

[1] See L. 1960 above.

[2] Lady Frederick Bentinck.

[3] Of Levens. See L. 1648 above.

[4] The potato disease of 1845 had led to widespread famine in Ireland, which could only be alleviated by repeal of the Corn Law of 1842, and the importation of foreign corn. Peel had resigned on the issue of repeal on 5 Dec. 1845, but Lord John Russell failed to form an alternative government, and Peel was back in office on the 20th. In the early months of 1846 he committed himself to repeal, and on 25 June, after five months of debate, his Corn Bill finally passed the Lords and all duties on imported grain were drastically reduced.

[5] Jacques Necker (1732–1804), French minister and financier under Louis XVI, whose vacillation and weakness in the early years of the Revolution were widely criticised.

1975. W. W. to CHARLES WORDSWORTH

MS. WL.
Annals of my Early Life, p. 305. LY iii. 1279.

Rydal—12th March 1846

My dear Charles,

Many thanks for your Farewell Sermon[1] which your Aunt has read to me. It is well suited to the occasion and very touching, and cannot but be remembered by your Pupils who heard it, to their future benefit. In every part I went along with it, except when you speak in praise of emulation;[2] on that subject I was not entirely in accord with you. I know well that you have St Paul in your favour in one or two passages. Homer also, and other wise and good men among the heathen: I am aware too that you have had greater experience among Boys, and the way of usefully influencing their minds, than has been my lot, yet still I cannot help being afraid of encouraging emulation—it proves too often closely akin to envy, in spite of the christian spirit you recommend. My own case is, I am aware, a peculiar one in many respects, but I can sincerely affirm, that I am not indebted to emulation for my attainments whatever they be. I have from my Youth down to this late day cultivated the habit of valuing knowledge for its own sake and for the good that may and ought to come out of it, the unmixed pure good. I used often to press this view of the subject upon the late Dr Bell, in whose system of Tuition this was a master-spring.[3]—Pray my dear Charles let us hear of you from time to time—above all don't omit telling us immediately, when any plan of life, or course of employment, may open upon you.[4] We hear of Chris: and his Family from Wm who is now for a few days in London.

I am truly glad to see your Winchester Discourses[5] advertised.

[1] *The better gifts and the more excellent way, A Farewell Sermon, preached in Winchester College Chapel on Quinquagesima Sunday*, 1846: on 1 Corinthians xii. 31.

[2] 'Zeal, emulation, rivalry are among the great and happy advantages which a public system of education, such as is pursued in this place, enjoys over systems which are more private. And be assured from this language of the Apostle these things are not unlawful: only let them be exerted in a Christian temper, and applied to their proper objects.' (p. 7).

[3] See pt. i, L. 384 and *Mem.* ii. 463–4.

[4] See L. 2009 below.

[5] *Christian Boyhood at a Public School*, 1846.

Notwithstanding our anxieties and distresses, we are pretty well, though your Aunt has been a good deal shattered lately.

ever my dear Charles your affectionate Uncle
W. Wordsworth

1976. W. W. to SIR WILLIAM ROWAN HAMILTON

MS. untraced.
Hamilton. K. LY iii. 1280.

Rydal Mount, March 14, 1846.

My dear Sir William,

Having just received from you a notification that the Royal Irish Academy has conferred upon me the distinction of electing me an honorary member of their body, I beg you will express to the council and to the academy my deep sense of the honour of being admitted into a society so eminent for Science and Literature; let me add that the interest I have always taken in the sister country, and in everything calculated to promote its welfare, greatly enhances the gratification afforded me by this act of the academy.

The diploma to which you refer has not yet reached me, or I should, of course, have acknowledged it. As the matter stands, this answer to your notification will, I hope, arrive in time to be read by you to the academy before you resign the chair, and be accepted by their courtesy in place of a more formal acknowledgment. I cannot conclude without expressing my sincere regret that the society is about to lose the benefit of your services as president, and the honour of having your name at its head. It is impossible that any personal consideration could have made the honour which I now acknowledge more acceptable than its having been proposed by one holding so high a position as you do in the scientific and literary world, and filling an equally high place in the private regards of your friends, among whom I have long thought it a great happiness to be numbered.

Believe me, my dear Sir William,
Ever most faithfully, your much obliged
William Wordsworth

1977. W. W. to JACKSON GILBANKS[1]

MS. Keswick Museum.
LY ii. 1280.

[*In M. W.'s hand*]

Rydal Mount March 21st—46.

Revd Sir,

My Son, the Revd John Wordsworth, who is now on his route from Italy, has desired me to inform you that he hopes to be at home to resume his duty early next month

I am Sir, Yrs etc.
[*signed*] W. Wordsworth

1978. W. W. to UNKNOWN CORRESPONDENT

MS. Amherst College Library.
LY iii. 1281.

23 March—46

Dear Sir,

Having carefully read your Passages from the life of George Herbert,[2] I have no hesitation in saying that I greatly approve of what you have done, circumstances being as they are, and your purpose so commendable.

It is not fair to call your abridgement a mutilation, you have kept closely to the two main points, setting in view the peculiar temptation, which the subject of your work was under to continue a man of the world and a scholar ambitious of secular distinction, and how he overcame all these and devoted himself entirely to the service of his Lord and Saviour. This transition is brought before the Reader with little or no intervening matter, and becomes in consequence especially fitted to strike the mind and affect the heart of the young Reader.

Surely there is no sufficient ground for a feeling that Walton's beautiful performance has not its share of due respect by being treated in this way for such an object as yours. His Book of Lives is matchless and no abridgement of any part of it can make the

[1] John W.'s temporary curate at Brigham (see L. 1952 above).

[2] One of several abridgments of Isaac Walton's *Life* (1670) in the 1840s. For W. W.'s admiration of Walton's *Lives*, see *PW* iii. 387.

volume less sought after by those who have the means of procuring it.

I remain dear Sir with thanks for the sight of this precious penny-worth in my own name, and that of your pupils.

Your much obliged
Wm Wordsworth

1979. W. W. to EDWARD MOXON

MS. Henry E. Huntington Library.
LY iii. 1281.

Rydal
April 2nd—46

My dear Mr Moxon,

Thank you for Burns' Check: 65–5–[1] My expenses in connection with my Son John's journies to and fro to Italy, and heavy outlays there, have made this sum very acceptable and I am duly sensible of your liberality in regard to it.

The new title Page will do quite well; a few days ago I received my Diploma from the Royal Irish Academy, and they have caused to be printed in a Dublin Newspaper my Letter to Sir Wm Hamilton, upon this honor being conferred upon me.—I am truly sorry that you have been so unwell. Pray take care of yourself. Your life and health are highly important not only to your Wife and Family and personal Friends; but also in no small degree to the community; your conduct as a Publisher being eminently liberal, and serviceable in proportion.

I am not at all surprized at the unfavorable report you give of the Book trade—public affairs are so unhinged, that it could not be otherwise.

My own health is daily improving—though I am still inconvenienced by a shortness of breathing, and now and then I feel the pain in the parts lately affected, when I take a deep respiration—In a few days I expect to be quite well.

You will be sure to see John with his Children in a day or two, if none of them have been ill on the road. Did I tell you that they were at Lausanne on the 23d [of] last month, and hoped to be in London in eight days.

[1] See L. 1970 above.

Mr and Mrs Quillinan were to leave Oporto for Lisbon on the first of this month. If her strength should be equal to the exertion, they will visit Seville, Granada etc and go by the coast of Spain visiting all the coast Towns, and so on to Marseilles, meaning to return by Paris, but perhaps I told you this before.

ever my dear Mr Moxon faithfully yours

W W

1980. W. W. to EDWARD GIRDLESTONE[1]

Address: Rev. E. Girdlestone.
MS. Cornell. Hitherto unpublished.

Rydal 6th April
—46

My dear Sir

My Son arrived here yesterday with his Sons[2] whom we propose to send tomorrow week to the Rossall Hill School. The Papers and Queries have been filled up and signed as you directed, and sent to the Revd St Vincent Beechey.[3] In short every direction given in your Letter of the 26 March has been strictly followed.

The Quarter till Midsummer will be paid, at the rate of 40£ per ann: Any nomination by which this sum may for the future be reduced will be gratefully acknowledged.

The Boys are in perfect health. As they have never been at any *School* some allowance will I hope, be kindly made for them at first, on that account. The Younger Boy as I said before is as quick as need be desired, and I believe well and steadily disposed to learn. The elder is by no means wanting in talents, but it is rather difficult to keep his attention up to his studies. His future Profession is not determined, but it is his Father's wish and mine, and that if he should prove equal to the Employment he

[1] The Revd. Edward Girdlestone (1804–84), Canon of Bristol (1852), and vicar of Deane, Lancs., 1830–55. See also *RMVB* for Jan. 1846 and L. 1985 below.

[2] Henry and William, John W.'s eldest sons.

[3] The Revd. St. Vincent Beechey (1806–99), son of Sir William Beechey, R.A., and founder of Rossall School (1844): perpetual curate of Fleetwood, Lancs., from 1842, vicar of Worsley from 1850, and Canon of Manchester, 1868–90. See *RMVB* for June 1846.

should be a Civil Engineer. His Brother is destined for College, either at Oxford or Cambridge as may be thought best.

Allow me to repeat once more my sincere thanks, and to add those of his Father, for your continued good offices upon this important occasion. And believe me my dear Sir faithfully your much obliged

Wm Wordsworth

Tomorrow, God willing, I enter my 77th year,—an awful consideration!

1981. W. W. to ISABELLA FENWICK

MS. WL. Hitherto unpublished.

Rydal
7th April—1846

My beloved Friend, this morning must not pass without sending you a greeting. I have now entered, as you are no doubt aware, my 77th year; can I be other than seriously stricken by the thought? Your good wishes and prayers attend me I know at all times and I feel especial confidence that they attend me now.

At eight o'clock Sunday morning John arrived with his four Sons, having slept at Kendal. The Boys are all well, so was Jane whom at our earnest request, and his Wife's desire John left at Hendon with Mrs Gee. She requires the discipline of a School, which she has never had. By her Father's account her abilities are very remarkable. I hope she may do well notwithstanding all her Grandfather Curwen did to spoil her. Henry is a fine stout Boy, quick enough in learning, but inattentive, Wm both quick and attentive when required to be so; his physical frame is not in strength or growth equal to his Brothers. John is very nearly as tall as Wm, and a fine boy, but slow in book-learning, nevertheless on examining him as to what he had seen in the course of their long journey, he proved himself an attentive observer, full as much as any of his Brothers. Poor Fellow, he is very humble-minded and modest. Charles the youngest has greatly improved in health since his Father took him from Rome, and especially during his journey. He seems an amiable and tractable Boy, which latter quality I cannot [think] the two eldest are remarkable for. They are a little too fond of their own ways and pursuits; obedient however when necessary, but it requires some urgency and trouble to make them so. I look for good results from the school education upon which they will enter Wednesday week, at the seminary near Fleetwood. John will go to live with his Father at Plumbland, and Charles will remain here, till his Mothers return which we still hope may be towards the end of Spring. Pray excuse the above minute particulars; we dwell in our Letters to you upon what most interests us. Mary sends her kindest love but every moment of her time is taken up in preparing for the departure of her Grandsons and in writing letters to those correspondents in respect to whom I cannot represent her, as I to you dearest Miss Fenwick. It is now time to thank you for Dear Dora's letter which was most acceptable. Heaven grant that she may preserve her health till her return; but all cannot be well as she makes no mention of increased powers of walking, or that she has gained what the Scotch Ladies elegantly call "Beef"!—For yourself, we are pleased to hear, very much pleased, that you are recovering regularly though slowly. The attack on your digestion while it grieves surprizes me much. It seems quite a new thing with you. Could the brown bread at all differ in quality or in the making from what you were accustomed to, have? Dora inquires after your accident at Foxhow; pray tell us if you feel any ill effect from it.—Dora's Letter to you is gone to Wm and he will return it. Sockbridge John languishes on as usual. I have not seen him since my attack; the weather the last three days has been so stormy as to prevent my attempting it. Jemima is gone with the Harrisons to Bardsey near Ulverstone, for a fortnight. And now my beloved Friend, I must bid you goodbye, hoping you will excuse this dull Letter—Mary is quite well, and seems getting the better of her depression, which hurt her health and impaired her strength much. I am quite well, except that my eyes are still somewhat weak; and my skin suffers from the severe cold, as it has done in some degree for many years. God bless you—ever most affectionately yours

Wm Wordsworth

Kindest remembrances to your Niece and to Mrs Tudor.

1982. W. W. to WILLIAM JACKSON

MS. Amherst College Library.
LY iii. 1282.

Apr. 28th [1846]

My dear Friend,

I am much pleased to hear of your appointment to the Chancellorship of Carlisle, both as a personal distinction to which you are so well entitled, and from a conviction that the duties of the office will be faithfully and zealously discharged by you. The Bishop, as perhaps you are aware, has more than once invited me to Rose Castle, and in the course of the summer I hope to be able to visit Wm at Carlisle, in which case I shall profit by his Lordship's invitation, and will not fail to express the satisfaction with which your appointment was learned by me, and by your Friends in this neighbourhood. To write expressly to the Bp upon the subject, would[1] . . .

. . . not like to leave my Sister for any length of time, I should be strongly inclined to pass the next winter in the South of France, about Nice, if I could tempt Mrs W. to accompany me. So little is passing in England to my mind, that it would be a relief to me to get out of the way of daily hearing of it. With best wishes for yourself and Mrs Jackson in which Mrs W. cordially unites, I remain my dear Dr Jackson your sincere friend

W. W.

P.S. Mr and Mrs Quillinan are we hope in France on their way to Paris. If you or Mrs Jackson should be inclined once more to see our excellent Friend Mrs Gee, at Hendon, who is in a declining state, you will find our Granddaughter Jane under her care, where she was left by her Father on his return with all his children from Italy. The two eldest Boys are placed at the Establishment near Fleetwood. Isabella with her Mother will we hope be in England by the end of next month at the latest. As you do not mention your Daughters we hope they are both well.

Once more farewell

W W

[1] The two parts, indicated by dots, may be portions of separate letters, as de Selincourt notes, or there may be an intermediate sheet missing.

1983. W. W. to EDWARD MOXON

MS. Mr. W. Hugh Peal. Hitherto unpublished.

[early May 1846]

My dear Mr Moxon,

I am truly glad that your health is improved; so is my own though I have not yet quite recovered my usual strength.

Be so good as to give to the accompanying Letter, such answer as you think proper. Whatever you determine upon, will I am sure be approved by me—I have referred the writer to you, you will therefore probably hear from her.

My Son John has been with us since Monday, he is gone to his Living of Plumbland this morning. He is in good health—His wife is expected about the end of this month.

Believe me dear Mr Moxon most faithfully yours

Wm Wordsworth

We are a Letter in debt to good Mr Robinson, and mean to write to him shortly. Thanks for your news of Mr and Mrs Quillinan—

1984. W. W. to CHARLES M. LEUPP[1]

MS. Mrs. Alvin Lewis. Hitherto unpublished.

Rydal Mount
9th May 1846

My dear Sir,

I have received through the hands of Mr Christie[2] of Manchester a Walking-stick of Hickory from Goat's Island Niagera falls, for which I cordially thank you, and also for the accompanying Letter. Both are valued as marks of your kind regard.—I live in a quiet country and have no need of a Stick for defense, and though advanced in life I may thank heaven still say, with Dr Johnson in his imitation of Juvenal 'as yet no steady staff my step sustains'; nevertheless your Present will be taken good care of, and shewn to my Friends among other Memorials of like kind—

[1] An American merchant and patron of the arts, who had visited W. W. with his friend William Cullen Bryant the previous July (see L. 1904 above).

[2] Probably a business contact of Leupp's.

Mr Inman[1] was obviously in ill health when he was in this Country, and I was truly sorry to hear of his decease some time ago from our common Friend Mr Reid of Philadelphia.[2] He appeared to be an amiable man and was assuredly an excellent artist. He is a loss to his Country, and will be greatly regretted by his Friends and Family.

Thank you for communicating to him my sentiments in regard to his Portrait of myself—it is thought to be an excellent likeness, and certainly is so as to Features and general effect, and what is wanting in expression is not to be attributed to inability in the artist but to want of familiar opportunity for witnessing the varying expressions of countenance.

May I beg you to present my kind remembrances to Mr Bryant, with those of Mrs Wordsworth. We both regret that we saw so little of him, as of yourself. I must now bid you good bye, with every kind wish for your health and happiness.

Believe me dear Sir
faithfully
your much obliged
Wm Wordsworth

1985. W. W. to ISABELLA FENWICK

Address: Miss Fenwick, Bagboro' House, n^r Taunton, Somerset. [*In M. W.'s hand*]
Postmark: (1) 13 May 1846 (2) 14 May 1846.
Stamp: (1) Ambleside (2) Taunton.
MS. WL.
LY iii. 1283.

[13 May 1846]

My dearest Friend,

I put off writing in the hope that we might have heard from Dora, by the last South of Europe Mail; but we have been disappointed, and cannot hear from her till the beginning of next week, I believe. We have no news for you respecting ourselves. Two of the Children are still with us, as is their father for two or three days. Things look no brighter in that quarter—Isabella and her Mother are on their way homeward, under the guidance and

[1] See L. 1811 above.
[2] See *Wordsworth and Reed*, p. 163.

protection of the indispensable Doctor. Mrs Arnold has the Archbishop of Dublin with her, and the Fletchers are enjoying their pretty place much. Miss Martineau seems happy as the day is long in her new House—a well managed abode, which with shaping the ground which was rather expensive has cost her under £600—The Cooksons are about going in their new abode[1]—I should be sorry to leave the old one.—Mrs Davy's House[2] and Garden cost two thousand but that is a large affair. Mr Mathew Harrison[3] is filling up his Father's House, which the Combs occupied. He and his poor Wife, who is in a family way, were over turned by the breaking of the axle of the Mail-coach in Kendal street,—neither received any injury—He was on the roof, and she of course inside. We find Jemima a very good natured and obliging Inmate, but the most observant unreflecting Creature that ever professed any talent. Company and amusement are all she seems to live for. To day she is in her glory, gone with the Gerdlestones[4] to Easedale Tarn, an object well worth visiting by any one capable of receiving what it can give.—Mrs Arnold has told me from a Letter of yours what your plan is till next year or after this time. It does not hold out any hope of our meeting, which I need not say I was sorry for, as there is no likelihood of our remaining at Mathon till you leave Mr Taylor's—Mr Angus Fletcher[5] who is here was assured lately in France, that the hatred the French bear the English is quite monstrous. He was told by a French Gentleman that were a war to break out between the two nations, a massacre of all the English residents in France would be not unlikely to take place. This is not to be believed; nevertheless that any Frenchman of birth and education could have reason so to speak is frightful. I understand that Mrs Fletcher considers herself as having taken leave of Edinburgh for life—Miss F continues subject to her old Headaches, and the Physicians tell her that her complaint is Gout in the head.—My dear Wife keeps herself quite well by marvellous activity of mind and body. I wish I could do the same—but many things do not touch her which depress me, public affairs in particular—my contempt for the management

[1] Howe Foot.

[2] Lesketh How.

[3] Benson Harrison's son (see Ls. 1814 and 1825 above). For Mr.Combe see L. 1379 above.

[4] See L. 1980 above.

[5] Mrs. Fletcher's son, the sculptor. See L. 2025 below.

of these both in England and Ireland is quite painful. I have almost confined myself in this sheet to personal news, and I must beg you my dear Friend excuse the dullness of what I write. My pleasures are among Birds and Flowers, and of these enjoyments, thank God, I retain enough; but my interests in Literature and books in general seem to be dying away unreasonably fast—nor do I look or much care for a revival in them. This I do not suppose to be a universal attendant upon the age which I have reached, but I fear it is very common. Mason the Poet[1] used to say latterly that he read no poetry but his own. I could not speak in this strain, for I read my own less than any other—and often think that my life has been in a great measure wasted. I will now lay down my pen as we are going to see my poor nephew, who continues to languish and waste as he may for months to come.—As Mary purposes to write as soon as we hear from Dora which we confidently expect to do by the Pacquet due on the 16th I do not scruple to conclude this with blank paper before me. Ever most affectionately and faithfully yours

Wm Wordsworth

13th May—the 11th was the 5th anniversary of Dora's wedding day which you will remember, not forgetting Alfoxden and Nether-Stowey where we were all together the next day. Yesterday Wm completed his 34th year, pray look out for a wife for him, he has no time to lose.

[*M. W. adds*]

Wm sometimes talks of our going to London for a fortnight—I wish to defer this if we move at all till there is a chance of our meeting the Qs—but do not like to discourage it altogether—for *he does* seem to require some change—a *change* in spirits and habits I am sorry to say has taken place since the time I mentioned to you before—he sits more over the fire in silence etc etc and is sooner tired on his walks—which he is ever unwilling to commence unaccompanied by me—but dearest friend I must be done.

[1] See L. 1903 above.

1986. W. W. to H. C. R.

MS. Dr. Williams's Library.
Morley, ii. 623.

Rydal Mount
Wednesday
[20] May 46

My dear Friend,

Our debt to you would have been discharged much earlier, if we had been able to tell you anything that would have been likely to interest you; but in our course of life one day is just a repetition of its predecessor. Persons we see few except our old Neighbours, and new books none. Yesterday indeed furnished an exception. We had an influx of two parties; one a clergyman by name Stewart and his wife, Friends of Mrs Harrison of Hundhow,[1] who accompanied them; and the other Professor Forbes,[2] and three Ladies one his Wife. The Professor is a very active Man, known for his diligent researches in Geology especially among the Alps; he has been much delighted with his residence in this Country, especially at Conistone where the Copper mines interested him much. He is a modest man of what I reckon sound opinions, but he seems to be taking too much out of himself by habits of over exertion, in mind and body. We talked a good deal about David Hume, and a recent Publication referring to him a sort of addition to his life, with some Letters;[3] but by the Professor's account there is not much in the Book—Mr Stewart is on his way to Paisley there to settle as a minister of the Episcopal Church, a church which has at least one apostolic characteristic, namely, that it is very poor—

We have Archbishop Whateley staying with Mrs Arnold; they called on us yesterday. His Grace is rather too fond of talking; but is nevertheless not a little entertaining by means of his various information, and his habits of minute observation. He amuses himself also and his hearer, with theories as fanciful as

[1] See L. 1725 above. The visit of her friend Mr. Stewart is recorded in *RMVB*, but nothing else is known about him beyond what W. W. adds below.

[2] The glaciologist (see L. 1880 above), friend of Whewell, Airy, etc. He had married (1843) Alicia, eldest daughter of George Wauchope. See *RMVB*.

[3] John Hill Burton, *Life and Correspondence of David Hume from the papers bequeathed by his nephew to the Royal Society of Edinburgh*, 1846, a landmark in Hume studies and a notable portrait of the man.

Swift's in his Gullivers travels. He scarcely touched upon the state of Ireland, except with reference to O'connel,[1] whom he branded as a hypocritical Patriot, and a selfish Agitator—Good Miss Martineau is as busy and active and healthy as ever—Her mesmeric and magnetic speculations engage her I believe as much as, or more than ever;[2] the fever seems to have had an access from the presence of Dr Gregory[3] of Edinburgh, who was lately a visitor of her's, and who, I understand, is in Edinburgh thought to be travelling and not slowly towards a state of mind not well adapted for filling a professorial chair with credit to himself, or benefit to his audience—But to matters of more importance: I am indignant with our Ministers especially Sir James Graham[4] who told us the other day in his place in parliament, that we are, and of course ought to be, more and more a manufacturing people—in other words the white negroes of all the world—If those opinions mean anything it is this, that with the British Agriculture should henceforth be considered as holding a subordinate place to manufacture and commerce, and the one be encouraged by government at the expense of the other if necessary. My own opinions on this matter were given to the world more than thirty years ago,[5] and I have since found no reason for changing them, and therefore I cannot but hold in detestation this doctrine of our present Governors—Southey and I were of one mind on this subject and in his writings he has frequently expresst himself with genuine feelings upon it.

[1] O'Connell was calling in Parliament for measures to relieve the potato famine in Ireland, but the Government, while promising relief, responded with coercion.

[2] 'His mind is always completely full of the thing that is in it', Miss Martineau had written about W. W. to H. C. R. on 8 Feb., 'And there he was on Wednesday his face all gloom and tears at two O'Clock from the tidings of his brother's death . . . And lo! at three he was all animation discussing the rationale of my extraordinary discourses (in the Mesmeric state)—his mind so wholly occupied that he was quite happy for the time. . . . His mind must always have been essentially liberal, but now it is more obviously and charmingly so than I understand it used to appear—The mildness of age has succeeded to what used to be thought a rather harsh peculiarity of opinion and manners'. (Morley, ii. 620–1).

[3] William Gregory (1803–58), Professor of Medicine in the University of Edinburgh from 1844: author of *Outlines of Chemistry*, 1845.

[4] Home Secretary (see *MY* ii. 536), and Peel's closest ally in the battle for repeal of the Corn Laws.

[5] In *The Convention of Cintra* (1809).

The Carrs as you know are in London, your other Friends are all well, and enjoying this most beautiful season. The other day James drove M[rs] W— Miss Quillinan and myself down Windermere side, and home by Hawkshead, and the beautiful Vale, my old School-day haunts which I make a point of seeing every year—but how changed! In my time we had more than a 100 Boys playing and roaming about the Vale; now not one was to be seen, the School being utterly deserted.—

Miss Fenwick is still near Taunton—Bagboro', which she means to leave at the beginning of next month for Havre, where she is to meet her Brother and his Family who reside at Rennes as I believe you know. She will return from Havre (but this perhaps I have told you before) to the Taylors on the bank of the Thames,[1] winter at Bath and not visit Westmorland till next summer. The last letter we had from the Quillinans, was dated Cadiz; they had been at Seville with which they were much pleased. There they fell in with the reigning Duke of Saxe Cobourg[2] and his Duchess—He had heard of Drawings which Dora was making of the objects she met with in that neighbourhood, and though somewhat to her discomfort got a sight of them, and appears to have been gratified by her performance. Our Friends will make a point of seeing Granada, and thence will coast it to Marseilles. God grant that our dear Daughters health may not suffer from that excitement to which she will be subject, and the fatigue which she will put herself upon encountering. We long for their safe return. M[rs] John Wordsworth was to leave Rome at beginning of this month. Her Mother is with her and they purpose returning by land, though, she writes, she stands in awe of the journey.—When you see Sergeant Talfourd pray remember me to him; and the like to M[r] Rogers and other Friends—particularly M[r] Kenyon. And let us hear from you as often as you feel inclined to write.

With good wishes for yourself and your Brother, in which my Wife unites, believe me, my dear Friend, ever faithfully yours

W. Wordsworth

I send no message to Moxon as I hear from him every now and then.—

[1] Henry Taylor and his wife had left Blandford Square in 1844 and taken a house at Mortlake.

[2] Ernest II, Duke of Saxe-Coburg-Gotha (1818–93), elder brother of Prince Albert.

[*M. W. adds*]

As soon as I can tell you any good news of our Travellers I will write to you, if you will receive a letter from me after my long delinquency. M. W.

1987. W. W. to WILLIAM BOXALL

MS. Mr. M. J. Liversidge.
M. J. Liversidge, John Ruskin and William Boxall, Unpublished Correspondence, Apollo, lxxxv (1967), 39–44.

[21 May 1846]

My dear Mr. Boxall,

I shall be well pleased to receive Mr Ruskin's 2nd volume[1] both for its own sake and as a token of your kind remembrance. In your letter, for which accept my sincere thanks, I wish you had been able to mention that you found for your Pencil more interesting employment than mere Portraits,—but I am afraid that little else is suitable to English demand.

Turner[2] is undoubtedly a man of extraordinary genius, but

[1] The second volume of *Modern Painters: Their Superiority in the Art of Landscape Painting to all the Ancient Masters, proved by examples of the True, the Beautiful and the Intellectual from the works of Modern Artists, especially from those of J. M. W. Turner Esq. R.A. By a Graduate of Oxford.* John Ruskin (1819–1900) visited the Lakes as a child in 1824, 1826 and 1830, embodying his experiences in youthful verse (*Works*, ed. E. T. Cook and A. D. O. Wedderburn, 39 vols., 1903–12, ii. 265 ff.), and catching sight of W. W. in Rydal Chapel. His first meeting with the poet was probably during the Oxford Commemoration in 1839 (see pt. iii, L. 1328), and his admiration for W. W. is writ large over *Modern Painters*, the first volume of which appeared in 1843 with a motto from *Exc.* iv. 978 ff. (*PW* v. 140). For his comparative estimate of W. W. and S. T. C. in 1843, see *Works*, iv. 390 ff. Ruskin had written to Boxall on 19 Apr. 1846 with an order for the second volume of *Modern Painters*, 'in case you might think that Wordsworth would have any pleasure in seeing the frequent use made of him. Don't bother him with it—only send it in case the old man might be pleased.' A year later, in Mar. 1847, he called at Rydal Mount (*RMVB*), apparently for the first time.

[2] Joseph Mallord William Turner, R.A. (1775–1851), whose genius was celebrated in *Modern Painters*. W. W. would also be familiar with his illustrations in Rogers's *Italy* and his *Poems* (see pt. ii, L. 773; pt. iii, L. 1131; and Rogers, ii. 3–6). W. W. had met the artist at one of Rogers's breakfast parties in May 1815. Both appear in a painting of the gathering by Charles Mottram in the Victoria and Albert Museum. See also *HCR* ii. 459.

like many others he has not foreborne abusing his gift. It pleases me to learn that Mr Ruskin has modified some of his extreme opinions concerning this artist, because, as I believe you know, I think very highly of Mr R's talents and that he has given abundant proof how closely he has observed and how deeply he has reflected. I shall have the pleasure of receiving your Present of his volume in ten days or a fortnight at the latest through the hands of some Ambleside Friends now in London.

I don't know whether you are acquainted with the works of Lucca Giordano[1]—he is a clever painter. My son picked up at Lucca three large Pictures of his which now hang in my staircase, which they exactly fill. One is Vulcan presenting to Venus the armour he has forged for Aneas, the other Diana hanging over Endymion on Mount Latmos, and the third, a Scene from Ariosto or Tasso, of a Lady bending over her dead lover, who has been slain. These Pictures cost John but little on the spot and I shall take care that he does not lose by the Purchase. They have cost me a good deal putting into order etc.

Mrs W is glad to be remembered by you and joins me in kind regards.

Believe me, dear Mr. Boxall, faithfully your much obliged

Wm Wordsworth

Rydal Mount—1846
21st May—a glorious day for beauty, I wish you could see how lovely our Country is at this fine season.

1988. W. W. to GEORGE LEWIS PRENTISS[2]

MS. Mr. W. Hugh Peal.
LY iii. 1286.

Rydal Mount
Ambleside
May 21st 1846

My dear Sir,

Accept my sincere thanks for your bearing in mind my Daughter's property in Missisippi Bonds, and your kind services in the matter. I have written to Governor Brown[3] authorizing

[1] Lucca Giordano (1632–1705), Neapolitan Painter. See also W. W.'s sonnet to this artist, *PW* iv. 18.

[2] See L. 1637 above.

[3] Of the Mississippi State Bank.

him to sell the Bonds if it can be done at the rate he mentions 75 cents—it is a sad loss to my Daughter's small means and still more to others of her Relatives. I feel much obliged to Governor Brown upon this occasion, and also to your Friend Mr Casson,[1] to whom I beg you would present my thanks.

You have gratified me not a little by entering into particulars respecting your situation in life;[2] and pray accept my sincere congratulations upon your marriage, with every good wish to yourself and the Partner of your life, and especially for the recovery of your own health.—

I wish you could see the beauty of our situation from the green Terrace at the end of which you and I sat together. More than once every day I visit the Spot, when the weather is tolerable. I am glad you are pleasantly located, and that your Congregation is one in which you find satisfaction. With many good wishes and sincere thanks, I remain

dear Sir
Your much obliged Friend
Wm Wordsworth

1989. W. W. to UNKNOWN CORRESPONDENT

MS. Lancashire Record Office. Hitherto unpublished.

Rydal Mount
25 May—1846

Dear Sir,

In reply to your enquiry respecting Mr Troughton[3] it gives me pleasure to say that though my own personal intercourse with him was but slight, I believe him to be an excellent person, both from general report and upon the authority of others whose judgement I respect! In his attention to the poor and to the discharge of his pastoral office among all ranks, he was

[1] Unidentified.

[2] Prentiss had been appointed Pastor of the South Trinitarian Church, New Bedford, Mass., the previous year, and had married Elizabeth Payson (1818–78), author of *Stepping Heavenward*, 1869, and numerous other religious and children's books.

[3] The Revd. Thomas Troughton, of Trinity College, Cambridge, formerly a temporary curate at Ambleside: perpetual curate of Haverthwaite, Lancs., 1846–51, and of Clandown, Somerset, 1852–8.

exemplary, and his discourses from the pulpit were entirely satisfactory to judicious friends of mine resident in Ambleside who were his constant hearer[s] during the two years he resided there.—I may add that he was disinterested [ly] charitable which his means enabled him to be, for I understand that his private fortune is good, and likely to be very considerable. His wife also was his zealous coadjutor, to the great benefit of the poor and suffering in the Chapelry.

I am happy to bear this testimony in favor of so good a man as I believe him to be and remain dear Sir

sincerely yours
Wm Wordsworth

1990. W. W. to ADAM WHITE[1]

MS. British Library. Hitherto unpublished.

Rydal Mount,
29th May 46

Dear Sir,

I return your paper upon the Museum with thanks, and beg you to accept the same for your accompanying Letter. Upon the Museum, as you will find, I had no remarks to make, but having spoken of Gray the Poet in connection with the place,[2] I think you ought to have mentioned the late Cary,[3] the Translator of Dante, who had an office there and lived many years within its walls. I was not *intimate* with Flaxman, but I have seen him several times both at his Studio and in company.[4] He was a Man as he has proved to the understanding part of the world of fine Genius but somewhat limited in its exercise by want of bodily strength. The people of England during his life time were little

[1] The Scottish naturalist (see L. 1529 above).

[2] Thomas Gray became a regular reader in the British Museum soon after its opening in 1759, while he was resident in Southampton Row.

[3] See pt. iii, L. 1031.

[4] See pt. i, Ls. 97, 168, and 274. From 1795 Flaxman lived off Fitzroy Square, and became a regular student of the Classical antiquities in the British Museum, actively supporting the acquisition of the Elgin Marbles in 1816. W. W. had met him in May 1815 at Samuel Rogers's breakfast party, recorded by Charles Mottram (see L. 1987 above).

capable of estimating his[1] works nor are they likely to become so perhaps for some generations. In his manner of talking there was some thing which I took at first for affectation; but if it had ever been any thing of the kind it had ceased to be so, and had become natural.

—The notices of natural History which you think of publishing[2] cannot but interest that portion of the public whom you would most wish to please. The British Museum is rather a trite subject.

I remain dear Sir
sincerely your obliged
Wm Wordsworth

I cannot assist you to any handwriting of Mr Coleridge or Southey, having long since given away all that I could part with. If any should come into my hands I will remember your request.—

1991. W. W. to C. W. JNR.

MS. British Library. Hitherto unpublished.

Sunday Morning
8 o'clock
[late May 1846]

My dear Christopher,

I was obliged to write you the other day a painful letter respecting George Hutchinson.[3] We have since heard twice from

[1] his *written twice.*

[2] His contributions to *List of the Specimens of British Animals* . . . , 1848, etc., published by the British Museum.

[3] M. W.'s nephew (see pt. ii, L. 769; pt. iii, L. 977; and Ls. 1921 ff. above) had withdrawn from his parish of Mathon in an overwrought state of mind, in circumstances recalled by M. W. in her letter to Derwent Coleridge of 16 Jan. 1847 (*Texas University MSS.*): 'From a child, G. H. has been naturally a pious character, and as there is, as far as we can tell, no family tendency to insanity, we can only attribute this aberration of mind on this one point to an overwrought brain. . . . At present I need mention only its first public outbreak which shewed itself to the whole Congregation, it was upon the Ascension day, his Father and Uncle Monkhouse being present, and to their consternation he delivered extempore a long Calvinistic Discourse, with so much heat and eloquence as astounded them . . . , his poor infirm Father specially, whose dismay drew from

his Mother, and learn that what we apprehended has actually taken place, and the conflict of opinion and feeling has produced unquestionable derangement of mind, which shows itself in several ways, and among others in paroxysms of anger against the Woman who has been at the bottom of all the mischief. We may look for one good result from this access of malady namely, the probability of its inducing Miss R. to give up all thoughts of connecting herself with poor George in marriage,[1] and then, (for we cannot but hope that the malady will pass away), all may go on as happily as before. You shall hear from me again upon the subject as soon as I have any thing of moment to communicate.

Your affectionate Uncle
Wm Wordsworth

We had a Letter from Mrs Hutchinson yesterday. George had written to his Father from Newport Magna[2] whither he had gone having run from the Lady at Wolverlow, who, he says had bewitched him, not this to his Father but to his Friend, Mr Garbol. He is aware of his state, and has put himself under guardianship; and tells his Father that he will soon be home. It is a singular case; but I am very hopeful that the cloud will pass away, and that he will soon be himself again. The derangement has obviously risen from a conflict of new religious opinions instilled by this Woman, and old affections. Pray excuse this bad writing—I have had a very troublesome cough hanging upon me for some time, it seems going off this morning.

1992. W. W. to C. W. JNR.

MS. WL. Hitherto unpublished.

[early June 1846]

My dear Chris,

As you kindly wished to know how poor George[3] was going on, you will not think it a trouble to read this copy of a note

him reproof so strong that his Son left the House—and what followed I will not enter upon—but he was for some time certainly in a state of *derangement* . . .'

[1] Miss R. is unidentified: some years later George Hutchinson married Selina Valince.

[2] A village on the other side of Herefordshire. Wolverlow is about 20 miles north of Mathon.

[3] George Hutchinson.

from Mr Resser under whose care he now is, and also one from himself to his mother.

W. W.

1993. W. W. to HENRY CROFTS[1]

Endorsed: addressed to the Rev[d] Henry Crofts, Linton, Yorkshire—
MS. Mr. W. Hugh Peal. Hitherto unpublished.

Rydal Mount
11th June 1846

Dear Sir,

Absence from home and Indisposition have prevented my giving an earlier reply to your Letter.

I do not think it at all likely that such an Audience could be procured for D[r] Wolff[2] as would make it worth his while to come to Ambleside; at all events owing to the cause above mentioned and other reasons, I could not assist in promoting the object.

I remain
dear Sir
Sincerely yours
W[m] Wordsworth

1994. W. W. to C. W. JNR.

MS. British Library. Hitherto unpublished.

11th June —46

My dear Christopher,

I have at last the comfort of telling you that poor George Hutchinson is apparently quite recovered from his late lamentable

[1] The Revd. Henry Crofts (b. 1809), of University College, Oxford: rector of Linton, Yorks.

[2] The Revd. Joseph Wolff (1795–1862), 'the Protestant Xavier'. A Jew by birth, he was baptised in youth, and made numerous missionary journeys in the near east. Later, he was ordained by the Bishop of Dromore and became rector of Linthwaite, Yorks., and Ile Brewers, Somerset (1845), publishing many journals and accounts of his travels.

delusions.[1] The Reports from his Friends at Birmingham, and the Surgeon with whom he has been are as favorable as could be desired; and the evidence from his own Letters to his parents is of like favorable character.

He is now, we believe, at Mathon, previously to his going to the sea-side as recommended by his Medical Friend. Meanwhile it is a happy circumstance that a Gentleman, a sound Churchman, and a Man of excellent character, who being engaged in a school is at liberty during the Summer Vacation, will take up his Abode with the family in the Parsonage, which is a great relief to his poor Mother who has been a great sufferer to the no small injury of her Health. His Father can only be moved about in his chair. The last account we had speaks of him as being seated in the churchyard superintending the Levellin[g] of the ground above the Parsonage, which will become very pretty under their Management, if as I trust all may go on well with their Son; but *that* I think will depend entirely upon all connection being for ever broken off with the Person who has been the principal cause of his errors, *and* we have the strongest reason to hope that this will be so. Every thing in his power has already been *done* by him to prove to her that he has recovered from his misjudgements, and that all intercourse between them must cease. We hope that Susan and her Babe continue well. Best love to her. You will hear of Dora through Mrs Hoare—Poor John is still alive.

Your affectionate Uncle
Wm Wordsworth

1995. W. W. to H. C. R.

Endorsed: 22^d^ *June* 1846. *Wordsworth*. Autograph.
MS. Dr. Williams's Library.
Morley, ii. 630.

Rydal 22nd June 1846

My dear Friend

M^rs^ W— and I were absent three days during last week and since our return all our time has been occupied by our Son John his Wife, their four Boys, and by Strangers; a more than

[1] See L. 1991 above.

sufficient excuse for your last letter not having received an earlier answer. I regret also to say that in this confusion it has been mislaid, and we have diligently sought for it in vain, this morning.

Yesterday we called upon Mr Carr and received from Miss Eliza Dowling[1] your little pacquet—They were all well, and grateful for your attentions to them. M^rs^ W— says you shall her from her as soon [as] your Commission is concluded, at present she is over head and ears in business of all kinds—

The Queries of M^rs^ N— Coleridge[2] I could but answer very imperfectly even if I had your letter before me. If M^rs^ C— had been a reader of Milton she would have known that 'harsh and of dissonant mood from his Complaint is from a chorus—in the Samson Agonistes—beginning 'Many are the sayings of the Wise',[3] and if of Akenside, she would not have been ignorant, that 'The gayest happiest attitude of things' is the concluding line of the first Paragraph of the Pleasures of Imagination.[4]

There are two Poems, perhaps more, in the English Language bearing the Title of the 'Excursion', one by David Mallet,[5] and another by William Wordsworth; in the latter, is to be found within 60 lines or so of the beginning the line and wou[l]d

rejoice
In the plain presence of his dignity'.—[6]

The Quillinans are now with Miss Fenwick at Ride, Isle of Wight; and expect to be with Mrs Hoare Hampstead Heath to morrow or next day, and we hope they will be at Rydal at the end of this Week or the beginning of next: Miss Fenwick was much shocked with the first appearance of poor Q— but he is mending every day.—Dora is well and strong for her,[7] but not stouter in appearance—

[1] Mr. Carr's sister in law. See also Morley ii. 628.

[2] Sara Coleridge had sought help in identifying quotations for her edition of S. T. C.'s *Biographia Literaria* (see L. 2020 below).

[3] l. 652.

[4] l. 30, The gayest happiest attitudes of things.

[5] David Mallet (?1705–65), minor poet, dramatist, and friend of Thomson, published *The Excursion* in two books in 1728, 'a desultory and capricious view of such scenes of nature as his fancy led him, or his knowledge enabled him, to describe.' (Johnson)

[6] *Exc.* i. 76 (*PW* v. 10).

[7] 'Dora looks like a rose', Sara Coleridge wrote to H. C. R. on the 27th, 'The improvement in her is marvellous.' (Morley, ii. 631).

We hope it will be in your power to go and see them,[1] but they are of course very anxious to be at home, as soon as possible.

I need not tell you that this hot weather puts us all in to Falstaffs state; but it will pass away in due time

We are glad to hear so favorable an account of your Brother.

faithfully and
affectionately yours
Wm Wordsworth

1996. W. W. to ORLANDO HYMAN[2]

MS. untraced.
LY iii. 1286.

Rydal Mount July 1st [1846]

Sir,

I should be happy to promote the interests of my lamented Friend's family[3] as far as lies in my power; but I cannot hope to do much, because almost all of those Persons to whom I could apply are themselves disposed, I have no doubt, to come forward, having seen more of Mr Haydon than my own opportunities, for some years past, have allowed me to do. I will not however omit my best endeavours to promote the subscription as soon as it is set on foot. Had I been in London I could have been of some considerable use in quickening the good intentions of others—as it is, I will do my best.—Every one must acknowledge that Mr Haydon had no common claim as an Artist upon the gratitude of the Country, both for what he executed himself, and for the zealous pains which he took to teach and incite others to aim at a style of art, both in its subjects and execution, of much higher character than was the general practise.

[1] H. C. R. saw them on the 29th (*HCR* ii. 659).

[2] Orlando Bridgeman Hyman (1814–78), Benjamin Robert Haydon's elder stepson: Fellow of Wadham College, Oxford, from 1835.

[3] Haydon's gruesome suicide on 22 June (see *Diary*, ed. Pope, v. 555 ff.) had shocked his friends, and at a meeting on 30 June in Talfourd's chambers, Lord Morpeth had launched a Subscription for the widow and daughter. Mrs. Haydon was also granted a Civil List pension of £50 a year. See Eric George, *The Life and Death of Benjamin Robert Haydon*, 2nd edn., 1967, pp. 297–8.

Pray present my most sincere condolence to the afflicted Widow, and best wishes for her future comfort and peace.

I remain
faithfully yours
Wm Wordsworth

Your Letter was not received till some time after its date, having been misdirected to Keswick. My address is, simply

Rydal Mount
Ambleside

which is a post Town, perfectly well known at the Head office.

1997. W. W. to EDWARD MOXON

MS. Henry E. Huntington Library.
LY iii. 1287.

Rydal Mount
18th July—1846.

My dear Mr Moxon,

Yours enclosing the Laureate's salary was duly received.

Be so good as to send me when an opportunity occurs four Copies of the 7 Volumes as I have occasionally a demand for one of them—

Would you be so kind as to pay for me five Pounds to the Haydon Subscription. Poor Fellow! what a shocking end to come to—[1]

I understand you are going on a summer excursion with Alfred Tennyson.[2] I hope all will go on well with you and that you may enjoy yourselves. If the alps be your object, you will of course include the Italian Lakes—

I wish much for an Excursion myself along with my good wife, but we are detained here by our poor Nephew John Wordsworth who grows feebler every day.—Were we at liberty my object would be the Pyrenees.

Mrs Quillinan is gradually strengthening.[3] She has been sadly

[1] See previous letter.

[2] See *Alfred Lord Tennyson, A Memoir, By his Son*, 2 vols., 1897, i. 230 ff; Merriam, *Edward Moxon, Publisher of Poets*, p. 175; and R. B. Martin, *Tennyson, The Unquiet Heart*, 1980, pp. 306 ff.

[3] The Quillinans had now taken up residence at Loughrigg Holme.

pulled down. Mrs W. is wonderfully well; I am quite well also.

With every good wish for you and yours I remain my dear Mr Moxon

faithfully your much obliged
Wm Wordsworth

1998. W. W. to MARTIN FARQUHAR TUPPER[1]

MS. Cornell. Hitherto unpublished.

Rydal Mount
21st July 1846

Dear Sir,

Let me thank you for Your Thousand Lines,[2] and the accompanying Letter. Of the Poems I have received two Copies, one of which I shall take the liberty of presenting to the Mechanics' Book-Society of Ambleside, being well assured that Verses like yours cannot be read by the intelligent in such a Society without profit. I have only to add along with my thanks, that as far as this busy season would allow me time, I have read your poems and with much pleasure; and if I am not yet acquainted with the whole it is because you write with thought and reflection which preclude the possibility of going over the ground at a hasty pace.

Believe me to be with sincere thanks

your much obliged
Wm Wordsworth

1999. W. W. to C. W. JNR.

MS. British Library. Hitherto unpublished.

[late July 1846]

My dear Chris,

We sate up last night till twelve an hour later than usual—Your dear Aunt reading aloud to me your Article on Dr Hook.[3]

[1] See L. 1663 above.

[2] *A Thousand Lines: now first offered to the World we live in*, [anon.], 1845.

[3] W. F. Hook (see pt. ii, L. 726) had just published a letter to Connop Thirlwall, Bishop of St. David's (see pt. ii, L. 827), entitled *How to Render more*

You have treated his shallowness as it deserves—These mock High Churchmen ought to be pulled down from their Stools as you have pulled him—He is a much more shallow man than I thought, till I had read his Letter—

His position as Vicar of Leeds is an influential one, and that makes his doings and sayings of more consequence than they could otherwise pretend to.

George Hutchinson appears to be still somewhat unsettled — He has however resumed his duties at Mathon. How it will end seems to be yet uncertain; but he is so conscientious a Man, that I do not apprehend any mischief to the Parish, from any doubts or misgivings that he may fall into—We feel very much for his family, especially for his Parents—

With kindest love in which your aunts unite,

I remain my dear Chris:
Your affectionate Uncle
Wm Wordsworth

Your Aunt Dorothy continues much the same. Mrs Quillinan is quite well.

2000. W. W. to LADY FREDERICK BENTINCK

MS. Mr W. Hugh Peal.
LY iii. 1288.

Rydal Mount
Friday Morning [Aug. 1846]

Dear Lady Frederic

With much regret I feel that I must now give up the hope of seeing you and Lord Lonsdale at this season. I have tried the motion of a carriage and I find it so injurious, where the road is

Efficient the Education of the People, in which he argued that it was now beyond the power of the voluntary agencies to provide a national system of education. State action was necessary; but the state could not educate the people upon a religious basis that was not common to the whole. He therefore advocated state schools in which secular instruction would be regularly supplemented by religious teaching from the parish clergy or Dissenting ministers. His scheme stirred up a storm of controversy, and though favoured by liberals, it was strongly condemned by churchmen and Dissenters. According to E. Q.'s letter to Sara Coleridge of 15 Aug. 1846 (*WL MSS.*), C. W. jnr.'s answer to Hook appeared anonymously in *The English Review*.

at all rough that I dare not venture. The best thing I could do would I think be to get down to the sea-side, but I would much rather for many reasons go southward.

Do you know Mr Milman?[1] He and Mrs Milman spent the evening with us yesterday; and such is the variety of his information, that we found his conversation both entertaining and instructive, though his manner is much against him. We have had visits from several Americans; one a literary Lady[2] of some note in her own Country; her look and manner any thing but pleasing. Our greatest enjoyment is, that every day we see our Daughter Mrs Quillinan, whose accounts of what she saw in Spain and Portugal are very interesting.—

How dear Lady Frederic do you bear this hot weather?—it is now only a little past nine—I invited Mrs W to take a walk in the garden, but the heat overpowered her; and she is now, though in very good health and strength, lying on the sofa as if quite exhausted—I hope you have better accounts of Lady Elizabeth.[3]

Mrs W. unites with me in affectionate remembrances—ever dear Lady Frederic—faithfully yours

W Wordsworth

I am sorry to hear from Dr Jackson that Mrs Jackson is so poorly—Lord Lonsdale's appointment of Dr Parkinson[4] to the Headship of St Bees, will give great satisfaction to every judicious person.—

[1] H. H. Milman (see pt. ii, L. 510), who had first met W. W. *c.* 1812 (see Arthur Milman, *Henry Hart Milman, . . . A Biographical Sketch*, 1900, p. 25).

[2] Margaret Fuller (1810–50) of Boston (*RMVB*), author and feminist, co-editor of *The Dial* with Emerson and George Ripley. For her visit see *Memoirs of Margaret Fuller Ossoli*, 3 vols., 1852, ii. 80 ff.: 'Mr. Wordsworth spoke with more liberality than we expected of the recent measures about the Corn-Laws, saying that "the principle was certainly right, though whether existing interests had been as carefully attended to as was right, he was not prepared to say", etc.' See also her *Papers on Literature and Art*, 2 vols., New York, 1846, (*R.M.Cat.*, no. 551). Other American visitors this summer included Professor Bela Bates Edwards of Andover College, the Biblical scholar and Classicist (*RMVB*).

[3] Lady Frederick's sister.

[4] Richard Parkinson.

2001. W. W. to [?] JOHN MOXON

Address:—Moxon Esqre, 44 Dover Street, London. [*In M. W.'s hand*]
Postmark: 6 Aug. 1846.
Stamp: Ambleside.
MS. Berg Collection, New York Public Library.
LY iii. 1289.

Rydal Mount
6th August—1846

Dear Sir,

In the absence of your Brother I write to request that you would procure a Copy of Mr Southey's Poems in one Vol:[1] at trade price for me and have it bound well and neatly but in no costly manner, and uniform with a Copy of my own Poems to be bound also and both to be charged to me, and kept till you receive directions (which you shall do in a few days) whither they are to be sent. Let me know the price of the 2 Vols, *when bound*.

I should like also that 6 new Copies of the 7 Volumes and as many of the one Volume should be sent to me at Rydal by the usual conveyance i.e. the luggage Train. They are not wanted immediately.—

We duly received the Check your Brother sent (on the eve of his departure), for one hundred and twelve pound, four and ten pence—

With our kind regards to Mrs Moxon and your Sister, who we hope are well I remain

My dear Sir
faithfully yours
Wm Wordsworth

[1] Publ. 1845.

2002. W. W. to [?] JOHN MOXON[1]

Address: Ed: Moxon Esq, 44 Dover Street, London. [*In M. W.'s hand*]
Postmark: 14 Aug. 1846.
Stamp: Ambleside.
MS. Berg Collection, New York Public Library.
LY iii. 1290.

Rydal Mount
14th Augst 1846

Dear Sir,

Mr Reed, Professor of English Literature in the university of Philadelphia writes to me thus.

'I think the new Edition of your Poems will have to some extent an American Circulation. I have already met with several Copies of it in private hands; and the Copies which I noticed in some of the importing Houses appear to have been soon disposed of. I should rejoice if part of the Edition found a Sale in this Country. I mention the subject as one which may deserve Mr Moxon's consideration especially as there is at present no complete American Edition.'[2]

To the above I have only to add my own opinion that it would be well to keep the American market supplied—W. W.

I hope you have good accounts of your Brother, and that he and his Companion enjoy themselves upon their Tour.

Believe me dear
Sir faithfully yours
Wm Wordsworth

2003. W. W. to HENRY TAYLOR

MS. Bodleian Library.
LY iii. 1291.

Tuesday Morning Rydal Mount
[Aug. 1846]

Dear Mr Taylor,

My Letter to Miss Fenwick anticipated a reply to the one you were so kind as to write to me.

[1] Addressed to Edward Moxon, but clearly intended for his brother.
[2] See *Wordsworth and Reed*, p. 170.

Many thanks for your invitation to Mortlake, but I can scarcely hope to profit by it. I feel indeed that it is expedient that I should move from home, yet I seem fastened to this Spot—everything about us is so soothing and beautiful. Before I had this little attack of some thing like rheumatism I talked big about going as far as the Pyrenees, and now I am afraid of the rough road of Kirkstone and Patterdale; I mean in a carriage, for I could walk on foot from morning to night without injury or fatigue.

Your account of dear Miss Fenwick gave us much concern. She writes with pleasure of the beauty of your situation. But I am sorry to see in the Newspapers that you are not without annoyances. Tell Miss Fenwick that Mr Quillinan, who by the bye is everlastingly industrious, employs himself from morning to night with Portuguese Literature, especially the works of their earliest Dramatist 'Gilvincente',[1] a name I imagine scarcely ever heard of in England.—

Kate Southey is still with us; we talk much about her Father's letters; and I, who cannot be long in this world, am much grieved that there is no prospect of their being collected and a selection of them published, a duty which would naturally devolve upon his Son, and which I cannot but think he is quite equal to.[2] How untoward has been our dear Friend's fate in these later years.

Mr and Mrs Milman[3] passed the evening with us yesterday—they have taken for several weeks a house in this neighbourhood. His manner is very much against him, but to me who have read little his conversation is both instructive and entertaining.

ever faithfully yours
Wm Wordsworth

[1] Gil Vicente (?1465–?1536), dramatist in Portuguese and Spanish. See E. Q.'s 'Ancient Portuguese drama; *Works of Gil Vicente*', *Quarterly Review*, lxxix (Dec. 1846), 168–202, and Ls. 2010 and 2024 below.

[2] See L. 1683 above and Morley, ii. 666.

[3] See L. 2000 above.

2004. W. W. to MRS. HARRISON[1]

MS. WL. Hitherto unpublished.

Rydal Mount
Wednesday Morning—
[19 Aug. 1846]

Dear Mrs Harrison,

I meant to have written to you yesterday but was interrupted by a succession of Visitors—

My dear Nephew's[2] long illness terminated yesterday morning at 7 o'clock. His Mother was with him, and so was his Cousin W^m^. He expired without any suffering, Nature being quite worn out. He will be interred on Saturday in the Churchyard of Grasmere—

We are sorry that circumstances allowed us to see so little of Louisa[3] when she was at Ambleside, but that loss will I trust be supplied at no very distant period.

The week after next Mrs W. and I will probably move southward, though I still have an attack of the rheumatic kind to get rid of, before I can venture from home. It is far from severe; and I would fain believe will not last long.

I have to thank you for a Ham which was dressed yesterday, and proved excellent—

We heard from Isabella eight or ten days ago—She had Clara[4] with her—She complains as usual.

We expect John before the end of the week to attend the funeral of his Cousin—

We have Miss Southey staying with us, and W^m^ will not depart immediately after the funeral—He is his Cousin's Executor.

I have nothing more to add but our affectionate remembrances —Believe me dear Mrs Harrison

faithfully yours
Wm Wordsworth

[1] Of Hundhow.

[2] R. W.'s son, 'Keswick John'.

[3] Apparently Mrs. Harrison's daughter (or niece).

[4] Unidentified.

2005. W. W. to [?] JAMES DAWSON[1]

Address: —Dawson, Esq. [*delivered by hand*]
MS. Picton Autograph Collection, Liverpool Public Libraries. Hitherto unpublished.

Rydal Mount
20th August, 1846

Dear Sir,

My poor nephew John Wordsworth, as probably you will have heard is no more. He died on Tuesday Morning; it will give you pleasure to learn that the Water-bed, which is now returned with thanks was a great relief to him; and he often expressed regret that it had not been earlier procured for him.

Pray present my kind regards to Mrs Dawson; and believe me faithfully

Your much obliged
Wm Wordsworth

2006. W. W. to JOHN GARDNER[2]

Address: Jno. Gardner Esqre.
MS. Miriam Lutcher Stark Library, University of Texas.
LY iii. 1290.

Rydal Mount Ambleside
Augst 20—1846

My dear Sir

The illness under which your Pupil and Friend John Wordsworth has been declining so long, terminated on Tuesday last. He died at his Residence in Ambleside being gradually worn out. His Mother was with him, and also his Cousin William, my Son. On Saturday he will be laid in Grasmere Churchyard. I ought to mention that his mind was clear and bright to the very last; I need not add that he will long be greatly lamented by all who enjoyed an intimacy with him.

Believe me
my dear Sir
sincerely and faithfully yours
Wm Wordsworth

[1] Probably Dr. James Dawson (1779–1875), the retired Liverpool surgeon, who built Wray Castle (1840–7) on the west bank of Windermere and the church of St. Margaret nearby (1845). See also *Westmorland Gazette*, 24 Apr. 1847.

[2] See pt. ii, L. 515.

2007. W. W. to REGINALD GRAHAM[1]

MS. WL. Hitherto unpublished.

Rydal Mount
14th Septr 1846

My dear Sir,

My Son W^m has intimated to me that he thinks it would be agreeable to you to hear from myself that the communication he has made to his mother and me of his engagement with your Daughter has given us both much pleasure. My wife, I understand, has already expressed her satisfaction to her intended Daughter-in-Law; and I must request you to accept my congratulations upon the prospect of an event which, from what I have heard, I trust will confer happiness upon our children, and prove a comfort to their Parents. Your Daughter will, I hope, accept through you, my blessing.—We shall be glad to welcome her as a Guest under our roof whenever it shall be mutually convenient, which will not be on our part for some time as we propose going from home in a few days. I need not add that we shall be glad to see Fanny's Escort whether it may be yourself or her Brother.

Believe me to remain, dear Sir, with much respect

faithfully yours
Wm Wordsworth

[*M. W. adds*]

To Miss Graham, the Sister of our intended Daughter, we should wish to be aff^ly remembered; and trust that it will not be long before we have the pleasure of seeing her at Rydal Mt.

M. W.

[1] Reginald Graham, a retired stockbroker, originally of Kirklinton, Cumb., now living at Brighton, whose younger daughter Fanny Elizabeth (b. 1820) was engaged to W. W. jnr. They were married at Brighton on 20 Jan. 1847. 'W. W.'s Intended,' E. Q. wrote to Sara Coleridge on 15 Aug., 'is, I am told, a pretty and very pleasing person. She is no heiress nor anything of the sort: her family are I believe in very moderate circumstances but Mr. and Mrs. W. and Dora are all well satisfied with the match.' (*WL MSS.*). According to Dora Q.'s letter to Mrs. Lightfoot of 23 Sept. (*MS. Mrs. M. J. Roberts*), Willy had known his fiancée for fourteen years. 'Dora Harrison knows her well and likes her much. She jumped off her chair and clapped her hands when we told her of William's engagement.' See also *MW*, pp. 276–7.

2008. W. W. and M. W. to THOMAS HUTCHINSON JNR. and MRS. HUTCHINSON

MS. Mr. Jonathan Wordsworth. Hitherto unpublished.

Rydal Mount Sept^{r} [24th] 46

My dear Thomas,

The unsettled state of your Brother's mind continues to give his Aunt and me much uneasiness;[1] and I write to you upon it rather than directly to his dear Mother, because I think it probable from the habit of the House, a Letter from Rydal would be read as common property by all. My purpose is to recommend that poor George may be prevented from taking steps towards vacating his Incumbency in the hope and trust that the scruples which still seem to disturb him may erelong give way to sounder views, and that he may perform his offices of a Clergyman of the Church of England, not only with a [?] ease, but with earnest care and sincere contentment and pleasure. Should it prove otherwise (which God forbid) he himself will have the assurance that he has not come to the determination of vacating his benefice hastily, and all his family will find less difficulty in bearing with an act so much to be lamented as that would be. When one recalls to mind under what circumstances his doubts originated, and by what influences they were sustained and cherished, that connection being now broken, it is surely not unreasonable to expect that erelong all may be set right again.—

Your Aunt is at present suffering from an attack of Rheumatism in one of her shoulders, owing I imagine to the season. Mrs. Quillinan is quite well, poor Miss Wordsworth much in her old way. Pray remember me most kindly to the Brothers Miller[2] when you see them, and believe me my dear Thomas, with your Aunt's kindest remembrances,

Your affectionate Uncle,
Wm Wordsworth

P.S. It would surely be much better for George to procure a Curate if necessary. This of course could not be done without considerable expense, perhaps equal to the income of the Living—but then the expense of removal would be spared, and there is house, already furnished, provided for the family—

[1] See L. 1994 above. [2] See L. 1873 above.

24 September 1846

[*M. W. writes*]

My dearest Sister,

Our family habit of correspondence being in common, is not always convenient as we must have felt all of us lately. I have been fearful of saying aught that might not be good for dear George to see—as for instance, in the case of our coming to Mathon. No doubt much comfort might attend our being together at this time of y^r perplexity, and in your last letter you say such intercourse might be serviceable to poor George—but dear Mary might it not be the *reverse*—would it not be running a great risk?—Bearing in mind the effect excitement of any kind, especially our being with you, when dearest Sarah[1] was in her nervous way, I confess I should be fearful of the result. Therefore, tho' I have the strongest desire to see you all, and you my dear Sister and B^r especially in this time of doubt and sorrow, it is the safest to suspend our determination as to visiting you for a few weeks at any rate. I quite agree with what my husband has said ab^t giving up the incumbency till Geo: is in a more decisively sound state of mind. Higher considerations out of the question, *your* convenience ought to be considered, to give you time of fixing a new residence if necessary—especially as dearest Thos'^s Parsonage[2] is in the course of being built, where it would best please you to settle, unless indeed he chuses to follow his Cousin Willy's example and take unto himself a Wife[3]—in that case I should like you to draw towards your ain Countree.—Marriage seems to be the order of the day—At the end of next Month Charles Wordsworth is to be married[4] to a young Lady scarcely ½ his age—no wise thing *we* think,—but he says this does not go by years but character, and her's is fitted to be a companion and help-mate to himself as a Teacher, yet not too old to be fitted to be a Play-fellow to his daughter! A happy combination, which I trust may be realized for he is abundantly fitted to be a happy husband, as indeed he proved himself to be. Willy's chosen one is I guess full young for him but nothing like Charles's. God bless you all dearest friends.

M. W.

[1] Sarah Hutchinson jnr., M. W.'s niece.

[2] At Kimbolton (see pt. ii, L. 670).

[3] See previous letter.

[4] See next letter.

2009. W. W. to CHARLES WORDSWORTH

MS. Mr. Jonathan Wordsworth. Hitherto unpublished.

Rydal Mount
Sept[r] 25—1846

My dear Charles,

It gave your Aunt and myself much pleasure to have confirmed by your own pen the intelligence of your engagement[1] which we had previously heard through Mrs Hoare. Be assured you have our sincere and earnest wishes for your happiness, which may be reasonably expected through the blessing of God, as you must have been favored with excellent opportunities for being *intimately* acquainted with the character of the young Lady who is the object of your choice.—

Your Aunt and I had intended to go abroad for a month or so—but that is now out of the question; the season is too far advanced and she, I am sorry to say is suffering from an attack of rheumatism. Your Cousin Wm's marriage,[2] I believe is not likely to take place till the early Spring; otherwise he might have been so fortunate as to fall in with you and Chris: at Rome or elsewhere on the Continent; as after his marriage, he proposes to apply to his Superiors, for leave of six months absence; which if granted will allow him to go as far as Sicily, with his Bride, who has near Relatives residing at Messina.

I am glad to learn that Chris: has taken D[r] Hook in hand.[3] The spirit of his Letter to the Bishop of St Davids, is not good, and one or two sentences are particularly obnoxious. Indeed why should such a man have addressed a Letter to that quarter at all. I cannot impute to Dr H. in a matter of such moment any selfish motives; but surely it is unlucky that this liberalism should have come out immediately before the Whigs and Radicals, etc., came in.[4]

We had hoped to see you on our return from Scotland.[5]

[1] To Katharine, eldest daughter of the Revd. William Brudenell Barter (1788–1858), formerly Fellow of Oriel College, Oxford, and rector of Burghclere, Hants., from 1836. She was a niece of the Warden of Winchester College. Charles Wordsworth had visited Rydal Mount in July (*RMVB*).

[2] See L. 2007 above.

[3] See L. 1999 above.

[4] Peel had resigned on 29 June, following the defeat of his coercion bill for Ireland, and Lord John Russell succeeded him as Prime Minister.

[5] Charles Wordsworth had been appointed Warden of the new Episcopal

Accept our thanks for the Perth Newspaper, and by all means let us have your address when it shall be printed. We are obliged to Chris: for the Guardian Newspaper which he sends us weekly, and which we forward to John. There is little chance of our being gratified by being present at your marriage, which we much regret. Where do you mean to leave Charlotte[1] when you go abroad?

[*cetera desunt*]

2010. W. W. to EDWARD MOXON

MS. Henry E. Huntington Library.
LY iii. 1292.

Rydal Mount
Oct[br] 1st 1846

Dear Mr Moxon,

If a Mr Freeman (He is a near connection of Mrs Nicholson of Ambleside) should call,[2] let him have half a dozen Copies of my one Volume, and place them to my account. More Copies are likely to be wanted and may be sent by any future opportunity.

I hope you and Mr Tennyson had a pleasant ramble on the Continent.[3] Mrs W. and I were prepared for a journey to our Friends in Herefordshire, but it is prevented by the Illness of one of the Family; so that we shall not leave home in all probability till next Spring.

Mr Quillinan has been very busy with Portuguese Literature, and an Article from his pen will appear on that subject in the next Quarterly.[4] Mrs Q. is about finishing the copying of her journal.[5] Had she seen more of Portugal and Spain, it would have been well worth sending to the Press; but in regard to the former she was prevented by bad weather. Women observe

College at Glenalmond, largely at the instigation of Gladstone. He attended the laying of the foundation stone on 8 Sept. and delivered an Address. See *Annals of My Early Life*, pp. 317–8, and L. 2056 below.

[1] His daughter.

[2] should call *written twice*.

[3] See L. 1997 above.

[4] See L. 2003 above.

[5] See L. 2031 below.

many particulars of manners and opinions which are apt to escape the notice of the Lords of the Creation.

We hope that you and yours are all well—

Believe me dear Mr Moxon
faithfully yours
Wm Wordsworth

How are Mr and Miss Rogers?

Dont mention what I have said about Mr Q. and the Quarterly as I am not aware that he wishes it to be known. I rather think not.—

2011. W. W. to CATHERINE CLARKSON

MS. untraced.
K (—). *LY iii. 1293* (—).

Rydal Mount, 2^{d} Oct^{br}, 1846

My dear Mrs Clarkson,

We condole with you most sincerely on the separation[1] which you have just had to suffer, and pray that the Almighty will comfort and support you in your distress. You will find abundant consolation in looking back upon your Husband's services in the cause of humanity, commenced in his youth and continued for such a length of time with unremitting zeal. We are very sorry that Mr C. Robinson happens to be abroad at this time, as probably he might have been of no small service to you; and we feel persuaded that he will hasten his return home as soon as he hears of the event, which might well be called a sad one, were it not that your husband died so full of years. . . . We are both well and write in affectionate love to our old Friend.[2] I remain

Faithfully and affectionately yours,
Wm Wordsworth

[1] Thomas Clarkson had died on 26 Sept. See also L. 2025 below.

[2] This last sentence added from bookseller's catalogue.

2012. W. W. to UNKNOWN CORRESPONDENT

MS. Cornell. Hitherto unpublished.

Rydal Mount
Ambleside
[?4th][1] Oct. 1846

Dear Sir

You must not take it ill if I cannot answer your Letter as you would wish. In fact I receive so many poetical Publications or Mss that it is quite out of my power, advanced in life as I am, and obliged to spare my eyes, to give them the attention which I have no doubt many of them deserve. This has been the case with your own, and pray do not consider it as a slight; for it is no such thing; I am sensible of your kind consideration and doubt not but for the reasons mentioned I should have been much pleased with your Production.

Believe me dear Sir
sincerely your obliged
Wm Wordsworth

2013. W. W. to EDWARD MOXON

MS. Henry E. Huntington Library.
K (—). LY iii. 1293.

Rydal Mount
12 Octr—1846

My dear Mr Moxon,

Thanks for your Letter. We were not aware that Mrs Q. had actually made up her mind to publish her journal.[2] This she never could have done or could have thought of but for the hope of raising a little money.—Please do not speak of this publication (whatever shape it may take) in connection with her. Her mother and I don't like it, and *she* would shrink from notoriety.

I am pleased that you saw those parts of Switzerland which you mention. They are all well known to me; but the Alpine Passes have lost much of their effect by the good roads that have been made through so many of them.—

[1] *Blot on MS.*

[2] Of her residence in Portugal. See L. 2031 below.

No doubt you will have Copies of my Poems bound ready for Christmas Presents. I know they are in request as prizes at Schools, in particular—I certainly did not expect as good a Sale of the 7 Vols as you report.—

I am truly glad to hear so good a report of Messrs Rogers and Maltby[1] as you give. If it had not been so far off, I should have much liked to have seen them and you at Broadstairs. In spring if all goes well with myself and Family, I *do* mean to go to Paris along with Mrs W. and should be glad to think we might have your company during some part of our visit there.—

Miss Barrett, I am pleased to learn, is so much recovered as to have taken to herself a Husband.[2] Her choice is a very able man, and I trust that it will be a happy union, not doubting that they will speak more intelligibly to each other than, notwithstanding their abilities, they have yet done to the Public.

Pray where is Mr Robinson? The news of good Mr Clarkson's decease[3] will probably hasten his return home?—We expect him here as usual at Christmas, and if you could accompany him or join him, so much the better. You know that Wm is about to marry;[4] we expect a visit from the young lady next month. We are not yet personally acquainted with her.

And now good bye.

ever faithfully yours—
Wm Wordsworth

[1] Samuel Rogers's friend William Maltby, whom he had known since his schooldays in Hackney. A Dissenter, Maltby did not take his degree at Cambridge but practised as a solicitor, and was Librarian of the London Institution (1809–34) in succession to Porson. He was related to Edward Maltby, Bishop of Durham from 1836.

[2] Elizabeth Barrett had secretly married Robert Browning at St. Pancras Church on 12 Sept.

[3] See L. 2011 above.

[4] See L. 2007 above.

2014. W. W. to EDWARD MOXON

MS. Henry E. Huntington Library.
LY iii. 1294.

Rydal Mount
16 Oct^{br} 1846

My dear Mr Moxon,

Pray cast your eye over this Letter just received. It seems to me a bold proceeding on the part of the writer who describes herself as patronized by Mr Rogers. If she really has been much noticed by him and is not in very easy circumstances, you may send her the one vol. Edition of my Poems if you think proper.

Some time ago you kindly gave us a useful Pocket map of England; it has disappeared, some person having taken a fancy to it. Would you supply us with another, of clear easy print and reference, and put down to my account.—

ever faithfully yours
Wm Wordsworth

Of course you need not send the map till an opportunity occurs of its reaching us without expence to either yourself or to me.—

2015. W. W. to JAMES HUTCHESON[1]

MS. WL.[2]
LY iii. 1296.

[Oct. 1846]

Unavoidable engagements have prevented my replying to y^{r} letter by return of Post. Whether I consider the distinguished place which the University of Glasgow has always held in general estimation, or recal to mind the number of eminent Persons who have filled the Office of Lord Rector, I must needs regard the proposal made to me of allowing myself to be named as a Candidate for it at the forthcoming Election as a high Honor; and one which would have been received with unmingled

[1] Secretary of the Wordsworth Committee for the Rectorial Election. W. W. had declined to stand once before, in 1838 (see pt. iii, L. 1278). See also Ls. 2020 and 2026 below.

[2] M. W.'s copy of W. W.'s answer, made for W. W. jnr. and sent on to him.

pleasure had circumstances permitted me to meet the wishes of the Committee, on the part of whom you write.

As I cannot doubt that they will give me credit for having carefully weighed the reasons which have led me to decline the honor, I feel myself at liberty to declare at once the satisfaction which I have derived from this occurrence as an evidence of the sense entertained among the Students in your University of the importance of imaginative Literature. A right understanding upon the subject, and a just feeling is at all times momentous, but especially so in the present state of society, and the opinions now so prevalent respecting the relative value of intellectual pursuits.

Allow me to conclude with the expression of a hope, that my inability to comply with the request of your Committee will in no way obstruct or interfere with the salutary or benign influence my humble endeavours in literature may have upon the understandings and affections of the Students who have thought of me at this time as worthy to be placed in so conspicuous a Station.

2016. W. W. to ISABELLA FENWICK

MS. WL.
LY iii. 1295.

Rydal, Monday morn. 19th Octr. 1846

My very very dear Friend

Your generosity to Wm and the *manner* in which it has showed itself have quite overpowered me even to the shedding of tears. I can only say in return God bless you for ever and ever, adding an earnest entreaty that you would be with us as much as you possibly can consistent with the claims of other Friends upon your time and your affections.—You say nothing of your health, we therefore hope that it is at least as good as usual. Of ourselves or our common Friends in the neighbourhood I am glad to have nothing much amiss to report. Mary Wordsworth's rheumatism is much better—I have been troubled with a cold for about a week and the rainy weather is unfavorable to getting rid of it; but be assured I have committed none of those indiscretions against which you so kindly guarded me. The cold was caught at church and it has been prolonged as I have said—Dora is wonderfully strong and well, and Mr Q— appears to be hardening against the Winter.—

Mary seems anxious that we should visit you this winter at Bath; I own I should much prefer going abroad with you in Spring, and showing you as much of the Continent as your strength would allow, taking the railway to Cologne and the steam boat up the Rhine—all to be done with the least possible fatigue. But all this is looking forward more than perhaps is becoming.—

We had yesterday a Letter from Wm in which with a full heart he spoke of your intended gifts to him in four gilded Frames, beside the Queen, brightening the dark corner of their room, and Lord Bacon, though with much regret on our part, has given place to Ben Jonson, which we thought a more suitable companion to the other Poets. These Worthies remind me of dear Anna Ricketts whom I have not had courage to write to since she changed her name.[1]—It is awkward to write to a wife whose Husband one does not know; and the Pamphlet[2] which dear Miss Taylor, in her pride, sent me, though cleverly written upon the whole, impressed me unfavorably in spite of the soundness of its opinions. There was in style an air of conceit and a flippancy which I could not but dislike.—

And now dearest Friend with a thousand good wishes I must bid you farewell.

Most affectionately and faithfully yours
Wm Wordsworth

2017. W. W. to UNKNOWN CORRESPONDENT

MS. Cornell. Hitherto unpublished.

Rydal Mount Ambleside
24 Octr 1846

Dear Sir

Allow me to thank you for your spirited verses and the Compliment they convey—

[1] Anna Ricketts (see pt. iii, Ls. 1276 and 1317) had married, as his second wife, Chandos Wren-Hoskyns (see L. 2047 below) on 9 July.

[2] Probably by Chandos Wren-Hoskyns. It is not clear which Miss Taylor W. W. is referring to here: possibly Mrs. Lutwidge's niece (see L. 1369 above).

It was expedient as a set off to the rest[1] that some melancholy objects should be encountered on my voyage, and therefore Saturn was naturally enough selected, though perhaps with some injustice.

Hoping that my Poetry may continue to interest you as you in so lively a manner describe,

I remain dear Sir
your obliged
Wm Wordsworth

2018. W. W. to CAROLINE HAVILAND[2]

MS. Cornell. Hitherto unpublished.

Rydal Mount
Tuesday — 28th October, I believe [1846]

My dear Cousin,

Accept my warm thanks for the Memorial you have sent me of the unfortunate Abergavenny; for the Print of the pretty churchyard[3] in which were deposited the Remains of my lamented Brother, and for the care with which you point out the place of his interment. That the Stone which marked it out has been removed, is little to the credit of those who had had the superintendence of the Churchyard, and I do not see what could be done in the case; for if another Stone were put up what assurance could be had that it would not shortly meet with the same fate? A brass plate might possibly be placed in some not obscure part of the Church briefly relating the calamitous shipwreck and pointing out the place where the Commander of the Vessel was interred. Ask your Father what he thinks of that; I should be somewhat more desirous of this being done if my own Poems had not widely spread the knowledge of my poor Brother's fate.

Pray tell your Sister Elizabeth that I have unhappily mislaid her Letter, and do not remember what office it was which her Husband thought he might be assisted in attaining by means of

[1] as a set off to the rest *written twice*. See *Peter Bell*, l. 41.

[2] Eldest daughter of W. W.'s cousin Robinson Wordsworth. See L. 1477 above.

[3] At Wyke Regis, nr. Weymouth (see *EY*, p. 574).

Sergeant Talfourd. Pray let me know; and I will address a letter to him at his own House, but I am not aware that he is returned.

We shall be truly glad to see you again at Green Bank.[1]

Remember me kindly to your Father, and my other Relations, and believe me my dear Cousin

faithfully yours
Wm Wordsworth

[*M. W. writes*]

Thanks dear Caroline for your letter. We are delighted to hear that your Mother's health is so much improved—our best wishes for its continuance.

The name of W$^{m's}$ betrothed is Fanny Graham—H. Cookson or Dora Harrison[2] can tell you more about her than I am able to do: but I shall know her shortly, as she means to pay us a visit about the 10th of next month. With affec love to y^{r} Sister Eliz, and to your own household believe me ever y^{rs}

M. W.

We shall be most glad to see you again in West^{d}.

2019. W. W. to UNKNOWN CORRESPONDENT[3]

MS. University of Iowa Library. Hitherto unpublished.

Rydal Mount
30th Octr 1846.

My dear Sir,

Thank you for your notice of the Convention of Cintra. The price is quite unreasonable; but in fact I do not want it, as Mr Moxon intends to publish soon all my prose-writings (which are but inconsiderable) in a separate Volume.[4]

The Edition of my Poems in one Vol: double column published last year, is nearly out of print; and Mr Moxon is going to press with another—the last was two thousand copies.—The annual sale[5] for the last nine years annually has

[1] The Ambleside home of the Benson Harrisons.

[2] i.e. Mrs. Benson Harrison.

[3] Presumably a publisher who was proposing to reprint W. W.'s pamphlet *The Convention of Cintra*.

[4] This plan was never carried out.

[5] *Written* sold.

been about a thousand, which is remarkable as it is upwards of half a century since I began to publish.

Mrs Wordsworth begs me to present her kind regards.

Believe me very faithfully
your obliged
Wm Wordsworth

2020. W. W. to ISABELLA FENWICK

MS. WL.
LY iii. 1297 (—).

Rydal Mount [early Nov. 1846]

My beloved Friend

We have been delighted to hear from Mr Robinson that he never saw you looking better; God grant that you may continue as well through the winter. Of ourselves I may say with gratitude that we have little [to] complain of, only it is true that Mary has been overexerted in going up and down stairs (you know her pace) in attendance upon poor Elizabeth, who is recovering but very slowly—She is, however, able to come down stairs, which would be very well if she could bring herself to sit quietly and abstain from work. Having begun I will go on with my bulletin—The Arnolds appear to be quite well. Mr Roughsedge is suffering under the gout, nevertheless he and Mrs R are going this day to Beetham.[1] He drank tea with us yesterday and appeared to enjoy himself. The Quillinans are quite well, except that Jemima has not yet cast off a cold and Dora was somewhat overdone by a fortnight's anxiety while Elizabeth was so ill—reminding her of her old Enemy. Quiet has set her right I hope. We dined with them yesterday,[2] and see some of them daily notwithstanding the unsettled weather. The season has not been a healthy one in this neighbourhood, but I hope the worst is over. Mrs Davy has been unwell, not so her Mother and Sister. I will conclude this rather tedious account with telling you that the troublesome sensation in my throat and the cough are much abated, and I hope will soon be entirely gone—

The papers will have told you that I was proposed as a

[1] Nr. Milnthorpe.
[2] At Loughrigg Holme.

candidate for the Lord Rectorship University of Glasgow,[1] and had a majority of votes, 21 I believe out of 200; but owing to the *form* of Election the decision fell to the Lord Rector, whose deputy voted for the opposing Candidate Lord John Russell. Be assured I am truly glad of this, as if Lord J. accepts the Office, I shall be spared the disagreeableness of a refusal, or what would be still worse at this season a journey to Glasgow, and a public exhibition there to which I should be exceedingly averse.—

Dora with the assistance of her Husband has just concluded the Revision of her Journal.[2] I am anxious to read it, or rather that Mary should read it aloud to me during our lonely Evenings. It never before happened to us to pass so much time together without other companionship; and what cause have we to be thankful that neither by bodily infirmity, or any other evil we are prevented from mutual enjoyment, though we cannot help earnestly wishing that you, our beloved Friend, were with us to make a Third in our society.—We are reading the Life of that true Philanthropist Wm Allen,[3] the Quaker. His knowledge of mankind was not equal to his earnest wish and unabating endeavour to serve them—And we were told yesterday by two Quakers who knew him intimately, that his disappointment in many of his benevolent schemes, did in the latter part of his life ruffle his temper to a degree which gave his Friends a good deal of concern. He lived in much intimacy with Sir Humphrey Davy, and often supplied his place as a Lecturer in Physics at the royal Institution. But what a contrast in their characters. With all his intellectual power and extensive knowledge Davy was a sensualist, and a slave of rank and worldly station—I knew him well, and it grieved me much to see that a Man so endowed could not pass his daily life in a higher moral sphere.—You have seen, I understand, not a little of Sara Coleridge. I rather tremble for the Notice she is engaged in giving of her Father's life.[4] Her opportunities of knowing any thing about him were too small for such an Employment, which would be very difficult to manage for any one, nor could her judgement be free from bias unfavorable to truth. Pray remember me very kindly to Lady Rolfe, and also to Mr and Mrs Taylor. The account which Lady Monteagle gives of Mrs Marshall is discouraging, she will

[1] See L. 2015 above and L. 2027 below.

[2] Of her residence in Portugal. See L. 2031 below.

[3] See *MY* ii. 230, 589. His *Life* was published in 3 vols., 1846.

[4] See L. 1995 above and L. 2037 below.

remain at Halsteads through the winter. And now dearest Friend farewell. God's blessing be with you. Ever most affectionately yours

Wm Wordsworth

[*M. W. writes*]

Tell us dearest friend if you hear aught of poor Faber.[1] Some time ago we saw a Paragraph stating he had a dangerous Stroke of Paralysis, and had rec^{d} the last Sacrament of the Romish Ch: no contradiction—or further notice—makes us fear he is lingering in a hopeless state. God bless you! The enclosed letter from the Bp of Oxford to Mrs C.[2] is creditable to himself and may be interesting to you. It was in reply to one she wrote which I also enclose—and you will return them when you write. Dear love to Lady R. You will see Willie in a few days—God bless you dearest Friend. M. W.

Our poor Sister is going on as usual.

2021. W. W. and M. W. to FANNY ELIZA GRAHAM

MS. WL. Hitherto unpublished.

Rydal Mount
11th Nov^{r} — 1846

My dear Fanny,

I cannot let Wm depart for Brighton without a word from my pen expressive of the great pleasure which his Mother and I feel in the expectation of [? his] being soon united to One whom he loves so sincerely, and whose love we are confident he will deserve by his own amiable qualities of which an affectionate heart has ever been the foremost.

[1] Earlier this autumn, W. W. had met John Bill (d. 1853), of Farley Hall, Cheadle, Staffs., who reported that Frederick Faber was now settled with his Wilfridian brethren at Cotton Hall, with the help of Lord Shrewsbury, and running a Catholic mission there. (*WL MSS.*). In Oct., at the end of a retreat in preparation for his ordination as a Roman Catholic priest, Faber collapsed and was given the last sacraments; but he recovered soon afterwards.

[2] i.e. from Samuel Wilberforce to Mrs. Clarkson, presumably about Thomas Clarkson's 'last thoughts on slavery' (see L. 2025 below).

We deeply regret the cause which has prevented us seeing you under our roof at this Season as we expected; and earnestly wish that all anxiety upon your dear Sister's account may speedily be removed.—Wm is charged with the expression of our most friendly regards to your Father and Brother; and with every kind and loving wish and sincere prayers we remain dear Fanny

faithfully yours
William, and allow me to add, Mary,
Wordsworth.

2022. W. W. to FRED WESTLEY

MS. Cornell. Hitherto unpublished.

Rydal Mount
Novr 11th 1846

Dear Mr Westley,

I thought that I had written to you some time ago, but to my great regret I find an empty cover addressed to you which must have been lying over looked in my Portfolio—

The purport of the letter I supposed to have been written was to express that the Engraver was at Liberty to dispose of the Plate from Haydon's Portrait of me as might be convenient to himself or he might think proper. My second Son would have been glad to purchase it but he is in the point of taking to himself a wife, which step with the furnishing of his House will take all the money that he can command—

Mrs W. and I have great pride in shewing the Copy of my Poems so beautifully bound which you presented to me; it is unusually admired. 2,000 Copies were struck off in —45 and Mr Moxon is going to strike off another Edition, which you will be pleased to hear—

I need scarcely add that we shall always be glad to see you at Rydal Mount, or that I remain with sincere regard and esteem

faithfully yours
Wm Wordsworth

2023. W. W. to C. W. JNR.

MS. British Library.
Mem. (—). *LY iii. 1299* (—).

12th Nov — 1846

Thank you my dear Chris: for the trouble you have taken about the "Guardian", which lately has come quite regularly. Mr Quillinan does not know from whom he receives his Copy.

The Passage which you have been so kind as to comment upon in one of the Ecclesiastical Sonnets, was altered several years ago by my pen in a Copy of my Poems which I possess, but the correction was not printed till a place was given it in the last Edition, printed last year, in one Vol—It there stands, "Their Church reformed!"[1] Though for my own part, as I mentioned some time since in a Letter I had occasion to write to the Bp of London,[2] I do not like the term, "*reformed*"; if taken in its literal sense as a *transformation*, it is very objectionable.

Your account of the state of things as to opinion etc., in the University of Cambridge gives me much pleasure.[3] Though the Voice of the *Body* as such may not have much weight, it is of infinite importance what notions civil or ecclesiastical the persons educated there take with them into respective positions in society.

Pray my dear Chris, take care not to overwork yourself; every body says you look very thin.

Charles has done well to go abroad. We are glad to have so favorable an account of his Bride[4]—I cannot however help wishing that the disparity in their years had not been so great. Best love to Susan from your Aunts, Mrs Q., and myself, and pray accept the same yourself.

Your affectionate Uncle
W. Wordsworth

[1] See *Ecclesiastical Sonnets* II, xl. 4 (*PW* iii. 381). The original reading was 'their new-born Church!'

[2] C. J. Blomfield.

[3] See also *Christopher Wordsworth, Bishop of Lincoln*, p. 127.

[4] See L. 2009 above.

2024. W. W. to JOHN GIBSON LOCKHART

MS. National Library of Scotland.
LY iii. 1300.

14th Novr 1846

My dear Mr Lockhart,

The intelligence conveyed to Mrs W. and myself, through Mr Quillinan, at your kind request, gave us much pleasure. Pray present our congratulations to your Daughter,[1] and our best wishes for her health and happiness through a long life. The connection, as you represent it to be, is one which I feel assured would have been highly gratifying to her Grandfather, Sir Walter, had he survived to see her settled so favorably in his own Country and yours.—Mrs W. to whom as well as to myself it would give great pleasure to see your Daughter here, tells me that she once had a half promise from your daughter to visit Rydal Mount. Could you not manage to take us in your way southward for a day or two, and longer if in your power. Mr Quillinan lives only half a mile from us, and he and his Wife would be much gratified by meeting you here.—

I hope you have good news of your Son,[2] and that India agrees with his health. I remain faithfully yours Wm Wordsworth.

(Turn over)

Be so good as to present my kind regards to your Brother who I hope is well. I have read in the proof the Article upon Gil Vincente:[3] it is well done and I think it will be a pleasing variety in the Quarterly.—

[1] Charlotte Lockhart (1828–58) was engaged to James Robert Hope (1812–73), barrister, Tractarian, and friend of Gladstone, who became a Roman Catholic after the Gorham Judgment (1851). They were married in Aug. 1847 and moved to Abbotsford the following year. In 1853, at the death of her brother, he inherited the estate and changed his name to Hope-Scott.

[2] Lockhart's younger son Walter Lockhart Scott (1826–53), an army officer, who died young at Versailles after an undistinguished career.

[3] See L. 2003 above.

2025. W. W. to H. C. R.

Endorsed: 16 Nov: 1846. Wordsworth.
MS. Dr. Williams's Library.
Morley, ii. 637.

Rydal Mount
16 Nov[r]—1846

My dear Friend

M[rs] Wordsworth being much engaged in attendance upon one of our Servants who is unwell, and otherwise occupied, I sit down to thank you in her name and my own for your Letter, which we much wished for.—Great part of the ground which you have been over is known to her, and all of it except the passage from Spluge to Chiavenna is known to me. In my twentieth year I went from Spluge with my Friend Jones down that branch of the Rhine and turned up the other to Dissentis and so over to Urseven.[1]

We are glad to hear so good an account of your Brothers health and sincerely wish that it may continue. M[r] Clarkson died[2] full of years and rich in good works. We have read with interest the unfinished Paper (so discreditably published) which he was writing upon Slavery in America. The truths it contains cannot but prove galling to Numbers in America.—We rely confidently upon your usual Christmas Visit.[3] Perhaps you may have learned from Miss Fenwick that we think of going to see her in Bath, during the month of Feb[ry]—Your account of her looks rejoiced us much.—Except M[r] Roughsedge now recovering from Gout, your Friends here are all well. M[r4] and Miss Fletcher

[1] See *EY*, pp. 34, 40.

[2] On 26 Sept. (see L. 2011 above). Subsequently, on 2 Nov., C. C. wrote to W. W. about the efforts of American emancipationists to enlist Thomas Clarkson in their cause, and of the 'perfidy' of William Lloyd Garrison in publishing Clarkson's 'last thoughts on slavery' in the Press and involving him in their feuds over the place of women in the Anti-Slavery Society. Garrison was unquestionably 'a fine noble fellow', she wrote on 28 Dec., 'But he seems to have adopted all sorts of wild notions and to imagine that if all the Governments upon earth could be up rooted—all forms of religion (not religion itself) could be destroyed, the earth would be restored to a paradisical state. This I call fanaticism . . .' (*WL MSS.*)

[3] Curtailed, this year, to a fortnight. See *HCR* ii. 660–1.

[4] Angus Fletcher (1799–1862), Mrs. Fletcher's son, sculptor and pupil of Chantrey. His works included a medallion of his mother in Grasmere Church,

are staying with M[rs] Davy. We intend to call upon them this morning. M[rs] Arnold is and looks very well,—M[r] Carr as usual, so is my poor Sister—I say nothing about public affairs, which appear to be as mute and quiet as any sincere Quaker-politician could wish.

The Quillinans are well—M[r] Q. busy in drawing up an account of a Portuguese poet, by name Gil Vicente[1] who flourished about 100 years before our Milton. I should not have ventured upon so dull a Letter as this were it not for a trust that any thing will be acceptable from this House, ever faithfully yours

W. W.

2026. W. W. to SIR WILLIAM GOMM

Address: To Sir W[m] Gomm Bart etc etc etc Port Louis, Mauritius. *Paid*. [*In M. W.'s hand*]
Postmark: (1) 23 Nov. 1846 (2) 24 Nov. 1846.
Stamp: (1) Ambleside (2) Fetter [Lane] London (3) Mauritius.
MS. Henry E. Huntington Library.
Mem. (—). *Grosart* (—). *K* (—). *LY iii. 1301*.

Nov[r] 23—1846
Rydal Mount
Ambleside

Dear Sir William

Your kind Letter of the 4th of August I have just received, and I thank you sincerely for this mark of your attention, and for the gratification it afforded me. It is pleasing to see fancy amusements giving Birth to works of solid profit, as under the auspices of Lady Gomm they are doing in your Island.

Your Sonnet addressed to the unfinished monument of Governor Malartic[2] is conceived with appropriate feeling, and

Dora Q.'s headstone in the churchyard, and a posthumous (1852) bust of W. W. (see *HCR* ii. 715 and Blanshard, *Portraits of Wordsworth*, pp. 179–80).

[1] See L. 2003 above.

[2] Anne Joseph Hippolyte de Maurès de Malartic (1730–1800) served in Canada under Montcalm, and was Governor of Ile de France, later Mauritius, 1792–1800. Refusing to enforce the French revolutionary edicts (including the abolition of slavery), he ruled through the local assembly of planters, and led the colony to virtual independence from Paris, thereby preparing the way for the

just discrimination. Long may the finished Monument last as a tribute to departed worth, and as a check and restraint upon intemperate desires for change, to which the Inhabitants of the Island may hereafter be liable.

Before this Letter reaches you, the Newspapers will probably have told you that I have been recently put in nomination unknown to myself for the high office of Lord Rector of the University of Glasgow;[1] and that there was a majority of 21 votes in my favor, in opposition to the Premier, Lord John Russell. The forms of the election, however, allowed Lord John to be returned; through the single vote of the sub-rector voting for his Superior, who, if I am not mistaken, was Mr Macaulay. To say the truth I am glad of this result, being too advanced in life to undertake with comfort any considerable public duty, and it might have seemed ungracious to decline the office.

Men of rank, or of high station, with the exception of the Poet Campbell who was, I believe educated at this University, have almost invariably been chosen Lord Rectors of this antient University, and that another exception was made in my favor by a considerable majority affords a proof that Literature independent of Office does not want due estimation. I should not have dwelt so long upon this subject, had any thing personal to myself occurred in which you could have taken interest.

As you do not mention your own health or that of Lady Gomm, I infer with pleasure that the climate agrees with you both. That this may continue to be so is my earnest and sincere wish, in which Mrs Wordsworth cordially unites. Believe me dear Sir William

faithfully yours
William Wordsworth

My dear Nephew[2] about whom you so kindly enquire, I grieve to say returned to England in bad health and after languishing more than two years died at Ambleside three

British occupation from 1810. His tomb by the architect Gastambide in the Champ de Mars, Port Louis, remained unfinished until the late 1840s, when it was completed through the efforts of Gomm. In his letter to W. W. deploring the racial dissensions in the island, Gomm described the project as 'the only cause in which the *french* party, the *brown* party, the English party, and *all others*, would be found heartily to draw together. . .', and he paid tribute to the Comte de Malartic, 'who stemmed the Revolutionary fury at its wildest, and saved the Colony from the horrors of the Guillotine'. (*WL MSS.*)

[1] See Ls. 2015 and 2020 above.

[2] R. W.'s son.

months ago leaving his afflicted Mother and all who knew him intimately, to lament his loss. He was the only child of my eldest Brother long since deceased. He was thought highly of by Sir James Macgregor[1] as a most promising Officer, and much beloved by us all—

2027. W. W. to EDWARD MOXON

MS. Henry E. Huntington Library.
K (—). *LY iii. 1299.*

Nov. 23rd 1846[2]

My dear Mr Moxon,

Your check for £61. 4. 1 has been duly received; I hope you will be able to dispose of the remaining Copies of the 'Early and Late'[3] in a satisfactory way.—

The death of Mr Alsager[4] following upon that of poor Haydon has shocked me much; I became acquainted with him through Charles Lamb, in whose chambers I have not infrequently seen him, as well as in the City. I always looked upon him as a man of sober mind and sound judgement, and that he was so in other respects makes this Catastrophe the more deplorable.

ever faithfully yours
Wm Wordsworth

P.S.

We had a letter from Mr Robinson the other day; and as he says nothing to the contrary we hope to see him at Rydal before Christmas. I much regret you cannot join him. My going to Paris in the Spring is uncertain.

I find I have not alluded to the Lord Rectorship of Glasgow University. I am glad I was not elected (I knew nothing of

[1] See pt. iii, L. 1336 and L. 1693 above.

[2] So dated in another hand.

[3] i.e. *Poems, Chiefly of Early and Late Years* (1842).

[4] Thomas Massa Alsager (1779–1846), writer of City articles and musical criticism for *The Times*, and a close friend of H. C. R. and Charles Lamb (see *HCR* ii. 616 and Sadler, i. 483), had died on 15 Nov. after cutting his throat a week earlier. He had recently been dismissed from *The Times*, and it had apparently preyed on his mind. See D. E. Wickham, 'Thomas Massa Alsager: An Elian Shade Illuminated', *The Charles Lamb Bulletin*, no. 35 (July 1981), pp. 45–62.

having been nominated) as I should have much disliked being compelled to go to Glasgow, and above all being obliged to make a public exhibition of myself, and to stumble through a speech, a work in which I have had no experience whatever.

2028. W. W. to MR. and MRS. WILLIAM BENNETT[1]

Address: M[rs] Bennett.
MS. WL. Hitherto unpublished.

[*In Dora Q.'s hand*]

Rydal Mount
Tuesday M[ng]—[late Nov. 1846]

Mr Wordsworth will have much pleasure in taking tea tomorrow E[ng] with Mr and Mrs Bennett: he will be with them at 5 o'clock. Mrs Wordsworth much regrets that the serious indisposition of one of her servants must keep her at home. Mr William Wordsworth leaves the Mount by Mail for the south otherwise it would have given him much pleasure to have accompanied his Father.

[1] A Quaker couple, who had called on W. W. on 24 Nov. (*RMVB*). William Bennett left a detailed account of his conversation about the art of poetry, contemporary poets, and Quakerism past and present (*WL MSS.*). 'Goethe and Byron are deficient in the true elements of life and immortality, both having written when and how they pleased from mere impulse, without steady culture or special aim, and the latter wholly without a conception of the moral and religious end of our being, and perfectly careless of fact or falsehood, to produce an effect . . . Shelley was gifted with a far higher talent, and more artistic power than Lord Byron.' W. W. had argued for Shelley's superiority to Byron as early as 1826. See *Letters of John James Tayler*, ed. John Hamilton Thom, 2 vols., 1872, i. 74.

2029. W. W. to C. MARKS[1]

Address: To C. Marks, 59 Princess St., Leicester Square, London. [*In unidentified hand*]
MS. Mr. Basil Cottle.
Basil Cottle, 'Wordsworth and His Portraits', NQ ccxviii (Aug. 1973), 285–6.

Rydal Mount
29th Novr 1846

Sir

Accept my thanks for your obliging offer of the Portrait of myself painted by my much lamented Friend B. R. Haydon.[2] Being in possession of an excellent likeness by the same hand,[3] and really having in my small House no place proper to hang it up in, I must decli[ne] the offer, with the hope that you will be able to dispose of the work to some one else at a higher price than that which you have kindly put upon it for me.

I am Sir
yours truly
Wm Wordsworth

2030. W. W. to WILLIAM ELLIS[4]

MS. untraced.
LY iii. 1302.

Rydal Mount Decr. 3d [1846, ?1837]

Dear Sir

Accept my thanks for your valuable and elegant present, the Christian Keepsake; the purpose of the Work is excellent; and

[1] Unidentified. Apparently a connection of Theodore and Simon Marks, paper stainers, of this address.

[2] Of the four portraits by Haydon which might be referred to here, the most likely one is the best known, *Wordsworth on Helvellyn*. At the time of Haydon's suicide (see L. 1996 above) this picture had been lodged with Elizabeth Barrett and then with Lupton the engraver (*Diary*, ed. Pope, v. 552, 556); but it was subsequently sent to Kendal, where it remained for some time on sale before it was bought by Cornelius Nicholson (see pt. iii, L. 935). How it came to pass through Mr. Marks's hands is not clear, but it seems likely he was acting for the vendor, who would naturally offer it to W. W. first.

[3] The chalk drawing of 1818 (see *MY* ii. 577; pt. ii, L. 619).

[4] William Ellis (1794–1872), secretary of the London Missionary Society,

the execution, as far as I have seen, highly creditable to those concerned in it. I must confine my notice however, to the Memoir of that great and good Man, Thomas Clarkson:[1] it is carefully compiled, and the matter, as a piece of Biography, judiciously proportioned; if your limits would have allowed, the narrative might have been profitably extended, but my long and intimate acquaintance with Mr Clarkson enables me to say, that *any* report of his labours and perils in accomplishing his part of that great Work, the Abolition of the Slave Trade, must on account of his modesty and humility of mind fall very far short of the truth.

It would have given me pleasure to comply with your request, by sending something to a Work that promises to be so interesting and beneficial, but I cannot do so, having found it expedient to decline being a Contributor to any periodical publication whatsoever.

With best wishes for the success of your Undertaking, I remain Sir, Your obliged

Wm Wordsworth

2031. W. W. to ISABELLA FENWICK

MS. WL.
LY iii. 1303.

Monday Morning [Dec. 14th 1846]

My beloved Friend

While Mary and Dora are engaged in the melancholy office, for such I feel it to be, of opening out your Plate, I sit down to write to you a few lines. Notwithstanding the disposal you are

1830–41, and editor of the *Christian Keepsake and Missionary Annual* from 1835: author of *A History of Madagascar*, 2 vols., 1838, and *A History of the London Missionary Society*, 1844. He married (1837) Sarah Stickney (d. 1872), author of *The Women of England* and other popular works. According to his biographer (J. E. Ellis, *Life of William Ellis*, 1873), he submitted an epic poem on the overthrow of idolatry in the South Seas to W. W., Montgomery, and Southey, *c.* 1830; but in spite of their commendations, it was not apparently published.

[1] This letter was dated by de Selincourt to 1846, presumably on the strength of the reference to Clarkson. But W. W.'s remarks do not necessarily imply a posthumous memoir, and the letter may possibly have been written up to a decade earlier. A biographical notice of Thomas Clarkson appeared in the *Annual* for 1837 (pp. 42–61), and that is probably the year of this letter.

making of these things, I cannot but feel sad upon the occasion. The reasons must suggest themselves to your own heart and mind, which spares me the pain of dwelling upon them, and I will turn to other subjects. First let me tell you that your Friends here the Fletchers, Mrs Davy and her family, and the Arnolds, with the exception of Edward who is suffering from a disease in his skin, are all well. Of the Roughsedges I am sorry to say so much cannot be said. Mr Roughsedge's carriage was overturned on driving towards Lancaster from Beetham and she was injured in the spine and had two ribs broken, and he himself did not escape without injury. Perhaps I told you this before.—Mrs Wordsworth is quite well, so is Dora, and I have nothing to complain of except that my skin continues to plague me more than little, though not, thank God, beyond my patience. The severe frost which we have had for some days, has carried away the low fever by which many people were suffering, especially in Grasmere. The weather is beautiful of its kind. The sun has taken away the sprinkling of snow; only the mountain tops are still white.

I have nothing to say of our doings beyond the simple fact that we are reading Agnes Strickland's[1] Memoir of Queen Elizabeth, who sinks more and more in one's esteem the more one knows of her private life, and the character of the Woman. A pretty Gloriana she was for the Poet Spenser, and 'Virgin of the West', for his greater Contemporary.—

John is coming to day by the Coach and on Wednesday the three Boys for one day. I shall make time to ascertain their progress in their Books. If it is only poor I shall not be disappointed. They will do better I hope in future; they had lost so much time. Mr Faber[2] we hear is quite well though he had a frightful accident, having fallen down the mouth of a Coal pit.—Mr Moxon has behaved very liberally towards Dora; offering her two thirds of the profits of her Notices of Portugal and Spain,[3] if any, and taking all the risk upon himself. I have

[1] Agnes Strickland (1796–1874), author, with her sister Elizabeth, of the popular *Lives of the Queens of England*, 1840–8.

[2] See L. 2020 above.

[3] Dora Q.'s *Journal of a Few Months' Residence in Portugal and Glimpses of the South of Spain*, was published (anon.) in 2 vols., 1847. E. Q. was somewhat sceptical about its success, writing to I. F. on 21 Apr. 1847, 'Portugal is so little known, and so slightly interesting to English Readers, that I am afraid a mere clever Journal like D.'s will hardly go of itself without a go-cart such as a leading Review might furnish.' (*WL MSS.*)

written my dearest Friend with a discouraging feeling that everything contained in this sheet has been told to you before, if so pray excuse it, also this ugly blot which stared me in the face when I turned over the sheet; pray excuse also this bad penmanship—I have nothing but a metallic pen and can scarcely get it to mark the paper. I will conclude with heartfelt thanks for your last Letter, which was most welcome, we were so anxious to hear of your safe arrival. My dear Wife is a wonderful woman; she is so active, and never complains, God bless her, and you also my very very dear Friend—

Most affectionately
yours
Wm Wordsworth

2032. W. W. to WILLIAM HOWITT

Address: W. Howitt, Esq.
MS. Lilly Library, Indiana University. Hitherto unpublished.

[*In John Carter's hand*]

[late 1846]

Hoc op' fiebat A° D'ni M CCCCC XXV ex sūptu Will'mi Wordesworth, filii W. fil. Joh. fil. W. fil. Nich. viri Elizabeth filiae et hered. W. P'ctor de Penysto qorū anēabus p'picietur De'.[1]

[*W. W. writes*]

Dear Mr Howitt,

If you should print the above, pray let it not be understood that I have any thing to do with giving publicity to this memorial of one of my Ancestors. I consider it to be an unpleasant characteristic of these times that there is so little delicacy observed in respect to the domestic life and concerns of

[1] The inscription on the Wordsworth family aumbry (see pt. ii, L. 648). William Howitt was now writing his *Homes and Haunts of the Most Eminent British Poets*, 2 vols., 1847, in which he describes the aumbry and quotes the inscription (ii. 288). Earlier this year, in *The People's Journal*, i (Feb. 1846), 43–5, he had written of W. W.'s contribution to the cause of the people: 'This grand old conservative is at the same time, unknown to himself, the grandest of levellers.'

Individuals who happen to have attracted public attention in any way.

Believe me dear Sir
faithfully yours
Wm Wordsworth

2033. W. W. to UNKNOWN CORRESPONDENT

MS. National Library of Scotland.
LY iii. 1304 (—).

Jan^ry^ 2nd 1847

My dear Sir,

The Print of the Head of Burns[1] which I owe to your kindness is hung up in the room where I am now writing.

I like it much—better upon the whole than either of the two others in my possession; one of which was given me by his Sons.[2] He is in good company, for in the same apartment hang Shakespear, Chaucer, Spenser, Milton, Ben Jonson, Cowper, and Southey, and others; but I regret to say not my Friend Coleridge of whom I fear no Print exists, except a poor Performance of Northcote[3] done long ago.—

Let me beg your acceptance of two Prints of myself—the one from a miniature by Miss Gillies,[4] and the other from an oil painting by Boxall.[5] That by Miss Gillies is more like as far as features go, but the other which was done many years before, has the advantage, at least in the outline.

Believe me to remain my dear Sir

faithfully yours
Wm Wordsworth

Let me offer you the good wishes of the season. W. W.

[1] At least seven portraits of Burns are recorded, and six of them were engraved. The most authentic (and the one probably referred to here) is that by Alexander Nasmyth (1758–1840) of 1787, now in the National Gallery of Scotland. It was first engraved by John Beugo for the Edinburgh edition, and subsequently (1830) by Samuel Cousins.

[2] Major James Glencairn Burns sent this engraving on 14 Oct. 1844, as a gift from himself and his brother, Col. W. N. Burns (*WL MSS.*).

[3] See L. 1681 above.

[4] See L. 1541 above.

[5] See pt. ii, Ls. 603 and 750.

[*In Dora W.'s hand*]

The prints shall be forwarded to the care of my Son at Carlisle the first opportunity and he will forward them thence to Glasgow.

2034. W. W. to UNKNOWN CORRESPONDENT

MS. McGill University Library. Hitherto unpublished.

Rydal Mount
Jan^ry^ 2nd 1847

Sir,

I regret to say that you have been led into mistake, in supposing that documents concerning Lord Byron, are in my possession. Nothing of the kind is now or ever was: my acquaintance with Lord B. was very slight. I never saw him but twice, both times in the house of Mr Rogers, and in one instance only for a few minutes.[1]—

Not doubting that your Memoir[2] will prove highly interesting and wishing that it may answer every purpose you have in view

I remain Sir
truly yours
Wm Wordsworth

2035. M. W. and W. W. to ISABELLA FENWICK

MS. WL. Hitherto unpublished.

[5 Jan. 1847]

The hope my beloved friend that, with God's blessing, we shall meet so soon—and that we shall be the day thro' together, is so ever-present in my thoughts, that my writing, *to myself*, appears useless, especially as dear Dora (who has not the like happy

[1] W. W. first met Byron in May 1812: 'a Man who is now the rage in London, in consequence of his Late Poem Childe Haroldes pilgrimage. He wrote a satire some time since in which Coleridge and I were abused, but these are little thought of . . .' (W. W. to M. W., 9–13 May 1812, to be included in the forthcoming *Middle Years: A Supplement*). The second occasion was at Rogers's breakfast party in May 1815 (see Ls. 1987 and 1990 above).

[2] Untraced: apparently unpublished.

prospect before her) generally lets you hear how all is going on among us, when she is staying for a few days at Rydal Mt. as was the case last week. But as my husband is continually saying 'we ought to write to dear Miss Fenwick'—and you know he is slow to begin I will do that for him, being left alone while he M. Hutchinson and Mr Q.[1] walk thro a drizzly gloomy day to enquire after poor Mr Carr who is so very unwell that the day before yesterday he thought himself dying. I trust however they may bring a favorable report, as he was easier yesterday.

Your New-year's greeting dear friend, was like all that comes from you, gratifying to us all—but tho' you did not tell us your health continued to improve, we are unwilling to conclude from the omission that any interruption has taken place—but we shall be thankful to be told that you have not suffered from going about in this very cold weather—for tho' the frost is gone, warmth has not succeeded—

[*W. W. writes*]

Dearest Mary was interrupted at this place yesterday and this morning being Ascension day[2] and she having a good deal upon her hands before she goes to Church, I take up the pen to add a few words on both our parts. It cannot be said that your wishes have been fulf[ill]ed in our having even a chearful Christmas owing to dear Mrs Hutchinson having such a weight upon her mind. It is obvious that her Son George is never absent from her thoughts, and one does not see how to comfort her. For my own part I cannot but think it almost a hopeless case;[3] but I remember what I have said elsewhere 'In all men it is sinful to be slow to hope'—to which is added, 'in parents sinful above all'.[4]—His case seems to bear a strong resemblance to that of Cowper the Poet, in the time of his dejection.—

Your Friends in this neighbourhood are all well; (we see them frequently;) for outselves we are the same, except that I feel myself not able to take as long walks as usual, on account of something of irritation or anger in the great Toe of my right

[1] Mary Hutchinson, who was on a visit to Rydal Mount, and E. Q.

[2] W. W. means Epiphany.

[3] See L. 2008 above. Writing to Derwent Coleridge on 16 Jan. (*Texas University MSS.*), M. W. described George Hutchinson as 'sunk into utter hopelessness and despondency regarding himself', having left his parish of Mathon and put in a curate. See L. 2040 below.

[4] W. W.'s sonnet 'Desponding Father!' (*PW* iii. 33) ll. 13–14, publ. 1835.

foot—in all other respects, the irritation of my skin being gone, I am thank God, quite as well as usual—and as to dear Mary she is an absolute wonder, for health strength and spirits.

By and bye, you must let us know how we can most conveniently pursue our journey from Birmingham to Bath.[1] I suppose we shall have to go round by Bristol. I am always sad when I think of leaving my poor Sister alone with Servants; and I could not bring myself to do so, were it not that Dora, by aid of her Donkey will be able to see her I trust almost every day, and the Servants vie with each other in kind attentions to her. At this moment she happens to be alone and I hear her striking the floor to signify her wish for a Companion.

Mary has just come in to the room, and tells me that I have done wrong in mentioning her health at all—and in fact that my statement is erroneous—for that she is much annoyed by giddiness specially when she rises from her chair. All things of this kind she keeps to herself so that in future I shall not presume to say any thing about them—

Wm's marriage as probably you know is to take place this day week.[2] He goes to London on Saturday night. I am sorry to say that he has been overworked and has suffered in health in consequence. We expect Mr Robinson tomorrow—[3]

Mr Roughsedge is here for a few days and gave a good account of Mrs R. who however does not seem to return to Foxghyll till she can bear the journey without risk.

And now I have told you every thing, and said all I have to say, except on the inexhaustible subject of our love of you, and our wish to embrace you once more. God almighty bless you—your most affectionate and faithful Friend

Wm Wordsworth

We shall have to sleep, I presume, at Birmingham—

[1] Their proposed visit to Bath the following month (see L. 2041 below).

[2] It was delayed until the 20th.

[3] H. C. R. arrived on the 13th.

2036. W. W. to WILLIAM BELL[1]

Address: Wm Bell Esqr, 3 Coleman St Buildings, Moorgate, London.
MS. Cornell. Hitherto unpublished.

Rydal Mount
Jan^ry^ 7th 1847

Dear Sir,

Your Draft for 32. .2. .10 has been duly received, and I thank you sincerely for all the trouble you take on my account. Notwithstanding this trouble, I shall be sorry if I live till this connection between us ceases, for on more accounts than one it has always been a pleasure to hear from You. I hope your Nephews and Niece Courtenay are well. I should like to be remembered by them.

Returning your good wishes for the season I remain, dear Sir

faithfully
Your much obliged
Wm Wordsworth

2037. W. W. to SARA COLERIDGE

Postmark: 5 Feb. 1847.
Stamp: Ambleside.
Endorsed: Mr Wordsworth on Dedication of *B.L.* received Feby 5.
MS. Victoria University Library, Toronto. Hitherto unpublished.

[*c.*4 Feb. 1847]

My dear Sara,

Mr R.[2] sent me the substance of your Letter from Kendal; and I should have replied to your request immediately, had I not been prevented by an influx of Callers who came to pay their respects to the Bride.[3] I shall be pleased to have my name united with your dear Father's in the way you propose, particularly as no one else seems to have so good a claim, though after he left Cumberland and West^nd^ I saw little of him compared with what I wished. Some regret I feel that I have not seen you previous to

[1] W. W.'s stockbroker (see pt. i, L. 157), apparently connected with the late Philip Courtenay (see L. 1569 above).

[2] H. C. R.

[3] W. W. jnr.'s wife Fanny (see L. 2021 above).

preparing the Edit. of the B.L.[1]—as I might probably have mentioned a few particulars which you might have deemed worthy of being recorded, and corrected others in which you may have been innocently misled.

Allow me to ask whether you know what Mrs Green[2] is doing with your Father's MSS. I hope they will be more fortunate than your Uncle Southey's have hitherto been. We like our new Daughter very much, and I think W^m^ has been greatly favoured in his choice. She is in person tall and well-looking, and her face anything but commonplace—her manners are quiet gentle and mild, her voice sweet, which as we have upon high authority is "an excellent thing in Woman."—[3]

We have our Sister "in law" (I dislike the last two words) Mrs Hutchinson, now of Mathon near Malvern, staying with us—I wish you had an opportunity of knowing her, for she is among the best of Women, both in heart and judgment. My poor sister is much in her old way.—Dora is suffering from a cold, other wise she is well—so is M^r^ Q.

Mrs W. and I mean to go to Bath about the end of this month,[4] and probably shall take a peep at London before we return in which case we shall have much pleasure in seeing you and yours—As one grows old the interest attached to *things* decays; but by no means in like degree to *persons*, but rather the contrary—as I strongly feel at this moment. Farewell my dear Sara—your affectionate Father in spirit.

Wm Wordsworth

[1] Sara Coleridge had asked that she might dedicate to W. W. her edition of *Biographia Literaria* completed after her husband's death. This second edition of the work, by H. N. Coleridge and Sara Coleridge, was published in 1847 with a dedicatory Letter to W. W. which ended thus: 'I remain, dear Mr Wordsworth, with deep affection, admiration, and respect, Your Child in heart and faithful Friend, Sara Coleridge'. See also next letter.

[2] Wife of S. T. C.'s literary executor (see pt. ii, Ls. 653, 844).

[3] See *Lear*, v, iii. 274.

[4] They arrived to stay with I. F. in Bath *c.* 2 Mar., after a visit to Mathon. See L. 2041 below.

2038. W. W. to ISABELLA FENWICK

MS. WL. Hitherto unpublished.

Rydal Mount
5th Febry —47

This House, my beloved Friend has been owing you a Letter for some time; and I ought to have written having so much leisure; but to say the truth I have been a good deal annoyed by a cold in my head and eyes, which is going away but not gone. It was a good deal encreased by attending our neighbour Irving's[1] funeral. He died suddenly, no doubt the consequence of his propensity to excess in drinking.—We hope that you support pretty well this rather severe season. All our neighbours as far as I know are in a good way; except that Dora has her usual winter cold. Mr Q. seems quite well—and is very busy with antient Portugese literature.—

But it is time to say a few words of our new Daughter. Wm is gone to Carlisle for a week, but she is with us. We like her very much; and it is fortunate that her Aunt Hutchinson is with us. They walk together and with mutual pleasure see much of each other. Wm we think has been very judicious in his choice. She is likely to make him an excellent wife, and there is every probability of their being more than usually happy together provided she keeps her Health. She is quite well and strong now, but one cannot forget that there has been much mortality in her family. I don't suppose that she is of bookish habits: which upon the whole I am not sorry for, as she might have been too much so; as our Grand daughter Jane is, caring for little else than Books, and whether by the seaside or among the mountains, always reading. Her mother is at Hastings with her youngest Son, so that the Husband[2] is left quite alone—How I wish you were here, instead of our being obliged to go to you. As to bathing I dont now require it at all, and Mary is as well as Woman can be. [*M. W. adds*: but longing to be with you M. W.]

Sara Coleridge is about to publish a new Edition of her Father's Literary Biography,[3] which she has asked permission to dedicate to me; which I could not refuse, though [the] Book contains many things not at all to my taste as far as I am

[1] Probably Thomas Irving, who lived at Fox How some time before the Arnolds.

[2] i.e. John W.

[3] i.e. *Biographia Literaria*.

individually concerned. It appears by the newspaper, that Mrs Southey the widow has got into a Squabble with that literary Marauder Howitt the ex-quaker.[1] I am sorry for it.

Mary sends her dear love, adding that she thinks a deal about the pleasure of seeing you[2]—as I do.

Your most affectionate Friend
Wm Wordsworth

2039. W. W. to SARA COLERIDGE

Postmark: 10 Feb. 1847.
Stamp: Ambleside.
Endorsed: Mr. Wordsworth's remarks on the Dedication.
MS. Victoria University Library, Toronto. Hitherto unpublished.

[*c.* 9 Feb. 1847]

Two or three [times] my dear Sara, have I sate down to answer your last Letter, and been interrupted by persons calling, chiefly on the Bride's account.

Upon your dedication,[3] for which accept my cordial thanks, I have little to suggest. "The latest writings of my dear Henry" is quite natural for you to write, and in a *private* letter it would have no objectionable [?] but as the dedication is to be published would it not be better to say something like my dear deceased Husband or my "deeply lamented husband" or "ever to be lamented Husband". There is no need of "plea" or any word of like meaning—enough to say, but my chief motive (or reason) for dedicating the Book to you is that etc.[4]

"More and more inwardly" would to most readers be obscure, and in truth, one is "thought of" rather than spoken of *inwardly*.

[1] Caroline Southey had publicly taken exception to some remarks in *The Athenaeum*, 30 Jan. 1847, about Howitt's *Homes and Haunts of the Most Eminent British Poets* (see also L. 2032 above), and his treatment of Southey (ii. 246 ff.). Mrs. Southey had returned to Lymington after her husband's death, and was eventually (1852) granted a Civil List pension, as Howitt had advocated.

[2] At Bath.

[3] See previous letters.

[4] Sara Coleridge acted on all three of these suggestions: for 'my dear Henry' the printed text of 1847 reads 'my dear departed Husband'; for the sentence in which 'plea' was introduced,—'my chief reason for dedicating it to you is that . . .'; and for 'more and more inwardly',—'more and more fully and widely'.

Did I ever tell you of the origin of the Antient Mariner, or rather how it came to be written. If not you shall know when we meet at Bath, which I look forward to with great pleasure.

We are all well under this roof; if my poor Sister may be said to be so, who is however just as usual. My son John is here for a few days, a happy contented Creature though with much in his situation which would make others discontented.

Hill and valley are around us covered with snow lying rather deep; and the sharpness of the weather, prevents us seeing as much of Dora as we wish—whose cough keeps her at home.

There is a notice in the Newspaper of Warter[1] having refused, on account of the *delicate* health of his family, a valuable Living offered him by the Arch Bp of C.[2] We wish his Grace would transfer the offer to Cuthbert, but I believe he is in the habit of confining himself in a great measure to the Clergy of his diocese. Can you tell us anything about the health of the family, especially Edith's?

Yours most affectionately
W. W.

2040. M. W. and W. W. to C. W. JNR.

MS. WL. Hitherto unpublished.

St. James' Mathon
Sat: Feb. 27th [1847]

My dear Christopher,

I hold the pen for your Uncle, to save his eyes, he having caught a cold upon this exposed hillside when we arrived on Wed:—and in remembrances of the correspondence which has passed between you about our poor Nephew[3] and the family settling here, he thinks you will like to hear from him, how we find the Parish attended to under the peculiarly painful circumstances which have since occurred.

M. W.

[*In M. W.'s hand*]

My dr nephew, Mrs Hutchinson was our fellow Traveller,

[1] Edith Southey's husband.

[2] Dr. Howley, Archbishop of Canterbury.

[3] George Hutchinson. See Ls. 2008 and 2035 above.

having been so kind as to pay us a visit of 7 weeks at Rydal; we remain here till Tuesday next when if weather permit, we shall depart for Bath, to join our friend Miss Fenwick, and after a stay there of not less than 5 weeks we think of returning home by London. The engagement of going to Bath was made some time ago, when I was suffering from an irritation in my skin, and thought that the Baths might do me good, and tho' that reason for leaving home has ceased I keep to my promise on Miss Fenwick's account. We left your Aunt and Dora as usual, save that Dora has had her accustomed cough and winter cold, which happily does not prevent her enjoying herself. I may mention to you that for the sake of repaying herself some of the expences of the journey, she has been induced at Moxon's request to prepare some account of what she saw in Portugal and the South of Spain on their way home by Marsailles. In what concerns the north of Portugal a considerable part will be supplied by M^r^ Q, who was born at Oporto, and had visited parts of the Country Dora had not seen. The book (2 vols) will enter into the Subject of the early literature of Portugal, of which the Portugese themselves know very little. Of course D will not give her name, therefore it would be well not to speak of this, even among our common acquaintance. Your Cousin W^m^ and his wife (whom we like very much) have been with us at Rydal, since about a week after their marriage, and we left them there on Tuesday. They are now returned to Brighton upon a most sad occasion, to visit Fanny's dying Sister, as they supposed, but she was no more, having died the very day they set out from Rydal. This is a great trouble; tho' not an unexpected one, at the outset of married life.

We had the pleasure of hearing of Charles from Miss Hoare, who we suppose may be looked for soon. I had a rather narrow escape from being connected with Scotland, a *2^d^ time*,[1] by an application of

[*cetera desunt*]

[1] See L. 2015 above.

2041. W. W. to EMMELINE FISHER[1]

MS. Cornell. Hitherto unpublished.

Bath[2] 4th March
1847.—

Dearest Emmie

A single word from me I hope will not be unacceptable. Ten days ago we left Rydal Mount, my Sister and Dora quite well except the latter as too often happens at this season with her was annoyed by a cough and irritation in the throat.

Our dear Friend Miss Fenwick you will grieve to hear is not looking any thing like so well as she used to do in Westmorland, but we hope the warm weather when it comes will benefit her.

It gave us much concern to hear that Your dear Mother's health had suffered. May we trust that it is improving—Pray remember us affectionately to her and to your Aunt[3] when you write. If all goes well we shall scarcely return home before two months are over, as we think of taking a look at our Friends in London. And now my dear Emmie with a thousand good wishes for You and Yours,[4] I must bid you good bye. Mrs W. sends her kind Love; ever affectionately and faithfully your Friend and Cousin

Wm Wordsworth

Pray remember us also to your Father.

[1] Se Ls. 1515, 1547 and 1570 above.

[2] I. F. had taken a house near Bath for some weeks in order to be near her relatives at Kelston Knoll, and had invited W. W. and M. W. to stay with her. Sara Coleridge and her daughter joined them on the 18th and her letters (*Texas University MSS.*) give a full account of their activities together and the aged poet's appearance. 'He can walk seven or eight miles very well,' she wrote to Sir John Taylor Coleridge on 29 Mar., 'but is always losing his way, and making out *he* is obliged to look sharp after his wife, whose eyesight is grown so bad that she is not to be trusted.' See also *Memoir and Letters of Sara Coleridge*, ii. 41 ff.

[3] See pt. iii, L. 1323.

[4] Emmie, now engaged to her future husband, visited the Wordsworths at Bath later this month. 'This young lady has a capacious brow and very fine eyes, but her attractiveness is sadly spoilt by a whining drawl in speaking,' Sara Coleridge commented in her letter.

2042. W. W. and M. W. to EDWARD MOXON

MS. Henry E. Huntington Library.
LY iii. 1305 (—).

8 Queen Square
Bath
[12 Mar. 1847][1]

My dear Mr Moxon,

I have to thank you for a Letter and the two Volumes of Mr Cary's Life.[2] The Publication I fear will scarcely repay you as the Incidents of a Scholar's Life can scarcely be of interest to the Public at large.

Mr C. Robinson is here moving about in his usual excellent health and spirits.[3] I cannot say exactly the same of myself as I caught a cold upon my first coming here which is not inclined to leave me.

I hope you will not lose any thing by my Daughter's notices of Portugal etc, which you have kindly undertaken to publish—

We still think of taking London on our way homeward.

With very kind regards in which Mrs W. unites I remain my dear Mr Moxon

faithfully yours
Wm Wordsworth

[*M. W. writes*]

Dr Mr M,

I venture (observe without my husband's authority, so keep the secret) to suggest that if you intend to reprint Burns' Ed,[4] that it ought to be in the very cheapest form, to be for the benefit of *School* boys of all classes. The price you mention is far out of the reach, or ought to be, of all such.

affly yrs M W.

[1] Date added in another hand.

[2] Henry Cary, *Memoir of the Revd. Henry Francis Cary . . . with his Literary Journal and Letters*, 2 vols., 1847. See pt. iii, L. 1031.

[3] See *HCR* ii. 662–3.

[4] See Ls. 1756 and 1760 above.

2043. W. W. to the HON. CHARLES BEAUMONT PHIPPS[1]

Address: The Honble C. B. Phipps etc etc etc.
MS. The Royal Library, Windsor Castle.
Sir Theodore Martin, Life of His Royal Highness the Prince Consort, 1875–80, i. 392.
K. LY iii. 1305.

Bath
15th March 1847

Sir,

The request with which through your hands his Royal Highness the Prince Albert has honored me, could not but be highly gratifying; and I hope that I may be able upon this interesting occasion to retouch a harp which, I will not say with Tasso, oppressed by misfortunes and years, has been hung up upon a cypress, but which has however for some time been laid aside.

I have the honor to be
with sincere respect,
faithfully your
most obedient Serv^nt
William Wordsworth

[1] Charles Beaumont Phipps (1801–66), second son of Henry, 1st Earl of Mulgrave (see *MY* ii. 663): equerry to the Queen from 1846, and private secretary to the Prince Consort from 1847. He had written from Buckingham Palace on 12 Mar. to convey Prince Albert's wish that W. W. would write an Ode to celebrate his installation as Chancellor of Cambridge University, which was to take place the following July: 'His Royal Highness would have felt considerable hesitation in thus breaking in upon your retirement were it not that His Royal Highness felt that he thus might bear testimony to His admiration of your Genius, and might be the means of procuring for the University of Cambridge another valuable work of one of her most distinguished Sons.' (*WL MSS.*). See next letter and L. 2057 below.

2044. W. W. to THOMAS ATTWOOD WALMISLEY[1]

MS. WL. Hitherto unpublished.

Bath March 26
1847

Dear Sir,

Your obliging Letter has been forwarded from Rydal to this place; and I lose no time in thanking you for it.

I cannot but wish you had a Fellow-labourer more worthy of his office than myself—for it is some time since I ceased to write verse, and gave up the intention of ever resuming the employment—All I can say at present is, that though I have not yet composed a Line, I will endeavour to meet your wish speedily; only be so kind as to let me know, whether you would prefer an irregular style of versification Like Gray's Ode on the Installation of the Duke of Grafton,[2] or a regular form of stanza to be repeated to the conclusion—As soon as I am apprized of this, I shall set about to work in order to comply with your request without delay.[3]

I have the honor to be
dear Sir
Sincerely yours
Wm Wordsworth

[1] See pt. ii, L. 732. Walmisley had been appointed Professor of Music at Cambridge in 1836.

[2] *Ode performed in the Senate House at Cambridge, July 1, 1769, At the Installation of his Grace Augustus-Henry Fitzroy, Duke of Grafton, Chancellor of the University. Set to music by Dr. Randal, Professor of Music.* Gray had obtained the Regius Professorship of Modern History the previous year, through the Duke's influence.

[3] See *PW* iv. 392. According to a note by M. W. in a copy of the Installation Ode at the *WL*, 'The plan and composition of this Ode was chiefly prepared by Mr. Quillinan, but carefully revised in MS. by Mr. Wordsworth, who, being in a state of deep domestic affliction, could not otherwise have been able to fulfil the engagement with Prince Albert, previously made, in time for the installation.' The 'domestic affliction' referred to was Dora Q.'s last illness. See also Ls. 2046, 2050 and 2051 below.

2045. W. W. to UNKNOWN CORRESPONDENT

MS. Cornell.
LY iii. 1306.

Rydal Mount
March 27, 1847[1]

Sir,

You do me justice; I never spoke with acrimony of Lord Byron, notwithstanding the noble poet's public poetical attacks —perhaps the worst, because the most enduring of all. His review of my poems was a very serious one, but Lord B. laughed at it, and thus disarmed me if I had been inclined to be angry—You say that Prof. Wilson declared 'that it was Wordsworth who first taught Byron to look at a mountain'—but I must disclaim the honour of being his lordship's poetical guide—notwithstanding the dictum of Christopher North.

I remain
Sir
truly yours
Wm Wordsworth

2046. W. W. and M. W. to D. W.

MS. Keswick Museum.
LY iii. 1306 (—).

Hampstead Heath 9th April 47

My very very dear Sister,

Your few lines were most welcome; and I thank you most cordially for them.

We left Miss Fenwick yesterday and reached this place in little more than three hours. Mrs and Miss Hoare are both well—we found your Nephew Charles and his young wife. You are aware that they are just returned from Rome. We expect to see Chris: and his wife, Susan, about one o'clock. Mr Moxon kindly met us at the Railway Station, yesterday, and will call here today.

We are most anxious to hear that Dora is better. I need not say how glad I am to hear that you have a ride every day in your chair, as often as the weather permits.—

[1] Either misdated, or, more likely, dated from Rydal Mount by mistake.

And now my dear Sister farewell—I know you don't like long Letters and in fact I have nothing to say but that I shall be most glad to see you all again.

[*unsigned*]

[*M. W. writes*]

[ ][1] and poor Mrs [ ] has been here just now—looking very ill and almost voiceless, but she says she is *much better*—her visit prevented me writing more than this hurried scrall. She prolonged her stay in hope of hearing about you by post—She is very anxious about [you]. God grant we may have good news tomorrow—Aff^{dy} and lovingly your M. W.

[ ] send yours by John who I hope we shall see on his return—Miss C.[2] speaks well of Jane—The Ode[3] unbegun yet!

2047. W. W. to CHANDOS WREN-HOSKINS[4]

Address: Chandos Wren-Hoskins Esqr.
MS. WL. Hitherto unpublished.

Hampstead Heath
April 19th 1847

My dear Sir

It gives me great pleasure to learn from your obliging Note of yesterday that the Gentlemen of the Town and neighbourhood of Stratford-upon-Avon purpose to institute a Shakespear Anniversary, to be celebrated in that Town: nor can I be other than gratified by the expression of their wish that I should be present at the approaching meeting.

Much do I regret that circumstances will not allow me to avail myself of the Committee's invitation, but, as my earnest good wishes will attend the occasion, may I venture to say that in my

[1] MS. damaged, but apparently part of a second sheet.

[2] Unidentified.

[3] The Installation Ode. 'I am sorry he has this *incubus* of an Installation Ode lying upon him,' Sara Coleridge had written in her letter of 29 Mar. to Sir John Coleridge. 'He says that Gray has exhausted the subject.' (*Texas University MSS.*).

[4] Chandos Wren-Hoskyns (1812–76) of Wroxhall Abbey, Warwickshire, 2nd son of Sir Hungerford Hoskyns, 7th Bart., of Harewood, Herefordshire: agriculturalist, land reformer, and M.P. for Hereford, 1869–74. He married Anna Ricketts in 1846 (see L. 2016 above).

judgement a *triennial* meeting would be preferable to an annual one; as it is to be apprehended that so frequent a recurrence of the Celebration though for the first few years it might be met with pride and pleasure, would in no long course of time lose its spirit. The expression of this opinion will, I trust, be taken in good part by the Gentlemen of the Committee; who will accept my cordial thanks for the honor they have done me by their invitation.—Let me also thank you my dear Sir for the trouble you have taken.

Believe me to remain faithfully your much obliged

Wm Wordsworth

2048. W. W. to FANNY ELIZA WORDSWORTH

MS. WL. Hitherto unpublished.

Hampstead Heath
20th April [1847]

I cannot allow this Letter from Hannah Cookson[1] to be forwarded to you without a word or two from my pen. And first let me congratulate you, particularly for dear Dora's sake, upon the improved state of the weather, which has been very sharp and trying to Invalids, but today the temperature of the air is *much* improved.

Our present intentions are to leave our kind Friends here on Saturday for the Cloisters Westminster,[2] and remain there till the morning of the Saturday after when we propose to start for home. But of course this depends upon the tidings which we receive from Rydal, if they prove at all unfavorable we shall set off for Home instantly.—[3]

Since we came to London and to this place, nothing has occurred, and we have seen nothing, that requires particular notice—My principal enjoyment has been under this roof, and on the beautiful lawn, in front of the room where I am now

[1] Daughter of Mrs. Cookson, now of Howe Foot, Grasmere.

[2] Residence of C. W. jnr.

[3] Dora Q.'s worsening condition was giving increased cause for concern. She had not recovered from a chill she had caught at Carlisle the previous December while preparing W. W. jnr.'s house for his return with his bride.

writing.[1] Mary and I when I lay down the pen mean to set off for High-gate to visit the spot where Coleridge is interred[2]—We have seen Anna Ricketts[3] that was and her Husband also; she is and looks quite well and happy. She brought hither her Step-daughter, a very engaging Child. Mrs Wordsworth is just come in to the Room, prepared to start. She unites with me in affectionate remembrances.

faithfully yours
W Wordsworth

I ordered Dora's Book[4] to be sent you, I have only had time to look into it, but like what I have seen. O that we were less anxious about her—We remain here and in London solely because we think she will do better without than with us. Again most affectionately farewell.

2049. W. W. to H. C. R.

Address: H. C. Robinson Esq, 30 Russel Sq.
Postmark: 24 Apr. 1947.
Stamp: Hampstead Heath.
Endorsed: *1847. Wordsworth. Autograph.*
MS. Dr. Williams's Library.
Morley, ii. 645.

Hampstead
Ap 24/47 Saturday forenoon

My dear Friend—

I am very sorry we have seen so little of you—This afternoon we go to the Cloisters Westminster—At 10 on Monday morning

[1] 'He has looked remarkably well since he came to town,' Sara Coleridge wrote of W. W. to I. F. on the 26th. 'Mr. Henry Taylor too was struck with his vigour in conversation, and thought him in as much force as he had known him for years. Some others who met him at Mrs. Hoare's thought him drowsy and feeble.' (*Texas University MSS.*).

[2] S. T. C. had been buried in Highgate Churchyard, but in 1843 his remains were transferred to a new family vault where Henry Nelson Coleridge and Mrs. S. T. C. were interred. In 1961 the remains of S. T. C. and the other members of the family were transferred to St. Michael's Church. See Griggs, vi. 993–7.

[3] See previous letter.

[4] Her *Journal of a Few Months' Residence in Portugal*.

your Medalist Friend[1] comes again to me, so that, if it should suit to call at that time, you would be sure to find me at home— and M[rs] W— also.

Ever faithfully yours
W[m] Wordsworth

2050. W. W. to THOMAS ATTWOOD WALMISLEY

MS. Amherst College Library.
Amherst Wordsworth Collection, p. 66. LY iii. 1307.

Rydal Mount 29[2] April 1847

My dear Sir

Here is the promised Ode[3] corrected as well as under distressing domestic circumstances I was able to do it—

My Nephew Dr Wordsworth gave me hope that it would answer our mutual purpose, that is, that the words would suit your music.

Believe me
with much respect
faithfully yours
W[m] Wordsworth

I was glad to have been assured by you that you would not shew the Ode to any one till it shall be called into use.

[1] Leonard Charles Wyon (1826–91), cousin of E. W. Wyon (see pt. iii, L. 930), and chief engraver at the Mint from 1851. At H. C. R.'s request, he had done a chalk drawing of W. W. on 21 Apr., and he returned on the 26th (see *HCR* ii. 665) to model the poet's head for a silver medallion which was issued in 1848. See Blanshard, *Portraits of Wordsworth*, pp. 173–4.

[2] Or 27th?

[3] The Installation Ode. See L. 2044 above.

2051. W. W. to THOMAS ATTWOOD WALMISLEY

MS. untraced.
K. LY iii. 1307.

Rydal Mount, May 5, 1847.

My dear Sir,

I quite agree in most of your remarks.[1] The alterations were made in the notion, mistaken as it seems, that they might better suit your music. Be pleased to understand that you may adopt or reject any alterations as they suit you or not, and whether the note you suggest for the printed Ode may be requisite we will leave to after-consideration. The only alteration that I wish to stand is *lore* instead of *path*,[2] because it is intended to mark her *education* as a girl, the means by which she acquired a fitting knowledge of the manner in which she was to tread the path of peculiar duty when grown up. The alteration 'past' and 'clarion's blast' was to get rid of the word *trumpet*, which is required near the end of the Ode, but it may be repeated if you like. I will try to supply you with the sort of chorus you wish to conclude with.[3] I felt the need of it, but I was willing to leave the matter where it was, till I was sure that you were desirous of an addition.

The heavy domestic affliction that presses on me, the very dangerous illness of my only daughter, makes it impossible for me to exert myself satisfactorily in this task. I am, dear sir,

Yours truly,
Wm Wordsworth

P.S.—Do not misunderstand the word *task*. I only feel it one in reference to the great anxiety that I have alluded to, for I was not called on to furnish the *Installation Ode* in my capacity of Laureate, but simply as a poet to whom His Royal Highness was pleased to apply on the occasion.

W. W.

[1] Walmisley had written several times, suggesting modifications in W. W.'s text of the Installation Ode (*WL MSS.*).

[2] In the 4th Stanza, describing the Queen's upbringing.

[3] Writing on 3 May, Walmisley had complained about the proposed ending of the Ode: 'Could you add another Stanza which would cause the Ode to end more joyously than the present termination, which seems rather sombre. This I submit to your judgment; for my own part, I should like a few words added, to which I might write a spirit-stirring Chorus.'

2052. M. W. to LADY MONTEAGLE[1]

MS. WL.
LY iii. 1308.

Sat. May 7th [1847]

My dear Mary Anne,

This sad week must not close without my telling you that your loving friend recd your note with tender gratitude—she gave it to me saying put it into my dressing case, for I would not lose it for a great deal'. She was then in as hopeless a state, tho stronger far than she is at present. Since that time her lower limbs have lost their power,—the voice is gone—the cough and perspirations encreased—but happily her *suffering* from the cough is not so tearing as it had been. Her mind is clear—and her heavenward aspirations are, I doubt not, *tho' in silence*, her support. Excitement of any kind she strives to avoid—and hence we are all upon our guard—but our task is a hard one. Her dear tender-hearted and much oppressed Brother has paid a comforting visit to us of 3 days and left his only beloved Sister and early companion, apparently *for ever*, this morng for his solitary home and his Parish duty.

You may believe we have had a trying season, and I know my dear friend we have had your sympathy and prayers—and we are rich in kind friends.

I have scarcely had heart to write to any one. Mr Q. spares me the overpowering excitement of communicating with our saintly friend at Kelston[2] and Jemima sends a daily bulletin to good Mrs. Hoare from whom, dear Mary-Anne, you may be able to hear about us—should you become anxious. To all of your own belongings you will kindly give our affectionate remembrances—especially to those dear ones at Bath.

Ever my dear friend shall I look to you in times of trial as I shd have done to your now blessed Mother[3]—do not feel that this, or any of these out-pourings of mine need a reply—to *feel* that you know how we are going on is my only motive for now writing—to *feel* we are in communion, as I shall do, is more congenial to me just now than to receive letters. You will understand this, and God bless you.

M. Wordsworth.

[1] Formerly Mary Anne Marshall. [2] I. F.
[3] Jane Marshall, who had died on 25 Jan. 1847.

To those kind friends who enquire to you about us pray say all that is affectionate.

2053. M. W. to SARA COLERIDGE

Address: Mrs H. N. Coleridge, Post Office, Hearne Bay, Kent.
MS. untraced.
LY iii. 1309.

25th May 1847.

My dear Sara,

From your note to Jemima recd to-day I find the vague reports she gives, or indeed *can* give, little convey to you (from your expression 'if' it is proper to tell her so) that state of heavenly composure and preparation in which your early friend remains awaiting her dismissal—but at the same time with an increased love of, and drawing towards all that she has taken an interest in on earth. So that she has not only been told but has read to her, all the letters we receive, and her overflowing heart is in full sympathy with all the expressions of love and consolation which her many friends [?] to her, and yet more *towards* us all. But she was afraid to trust herself to the excitement of seeing dear Mary Stanger[1] the other day—for both their sakes; for her own, she dreads being drawn from that tranquillity which she has endeavoured to preserve ever since she was aware of her real state.—She has not even seen Coz. Dorothy Harrison—none but her Brothers. Her sisterly love of you, Kate,[2] and Mary Stanger is very near her heart, and I am sure she rests in humblest hope that the broken tie will be, thro' our blessed Saviour, reunited in the kingdom of our heavenly Father.

Such, dear Sara, being her present blessed state, what may we not trust will it be after her removal—and selfish mortals should we be were we not to *try* to be resigned to the short separation. Yet alas human nature is hard to overcome, but we do our best, and I have cause for peculiar thankfulness that my strength allows me to participate in her present holy occupations, and attend to her—when we think it improper for dearest H. Cookson[3] to be in her room, after it is closed for the night. H. C. is a treasure to us—being an incomparable nurse—so thoughtful—

[1] Formerly Mary Calvert, Dora Q.'s schoolfriend.
[2] Southey. [3] Hannah Cookson.

tender and such presence of mind! as under such circumstances is scarcely to be looked for in one whose heart and affections are so deeply interested. I remain with her till towards two o'cl.—then one of our own attached servants, who has had rest till that time, takes my place and remains with her till she has her windows opened abt 5 or 6 as it may happen. She can then occupy herself with reading, which is a blessing she was unable to enjoy at the commencement of her illness—her eyes not then being equal i.e. everything danced before them. Of late when I returned to her room between 7 and 8 ocl. I have found her busy with her pen,—the same indefatigable mind will live to the last! She is now, thank God asleep (10 o'cl—May 26th) having had little or none the 2 last nights, the cough being so troublesome—but as she says does not hurt her. Her patience does not allow that she suffers any pain. Her frequent expression is 'How mercifully I am dealt with'.

Dearest S. I have felt this detail due to you as one if not her first companion-friend—you a babe were in the house when she was born.[1] God bless you prays your old friend M. W.

2054. M. W. to LADY MONTEAGLE

MS. WL.
LY iii. 1310.

June 1st [1847]

My dear, very dear friend,

It does seem unnatural that I should have restrained the expression of your sympathy which is such a comfort to me—but when I did so, I did not think it possible our Treasure should have remained with us many hours. Weaker much she is now than she was then, still the experience we have gained tells us her end is not *so near*.[2] Yet none of the wasting power is

[1] See *EY*, p. 496.

[2] For the progress of Dora Q.'s decline, see Morley, ii. 647 ff.; *MW*, pp. 278 ff., and *Letters of Hartley Coleridge* (ed. Griggs), p. 294. 'She asked me several particulars,' E. Q. wrote, 'to every one of which I answered faithfully; so she was put in full possession of the truth. The spirit with which she received the awful intimation, and with which she continues to bear to look it in the face, is in every respect admirable; so humble, so self-censuring for faults of temper which the delicacy of her conscience magnifies, yet so cheerful, so hopeful of the mercy

relaxed—but the spirit remains, and life is tenacious. The prayers of so many good friends *must* be availing and with all her humility, her repentance, resignation, faith, and hope which is unbounded there are times—(and one has occurred this morn[g] after an unusually comfortable night, I mean of natural sleep,) when the mind is overshadowed by some awful thought. These moments are bitter ones, which she calls the *pangs of death*, and on these occasions (two only have occurred) she requires the fervent prayers of her friends. Thank God these trials are followed by that joy and peace which passeth understanding.

We are thank God wonderfully supported. The afflicted Father, not having the consolatory *duty* of nursing to turn his thoughts from our deep sorrow—in this season of suspense, suffers most. But I trust he, as well as the rest of us, will be upheld to the close, by the sustaining will of our blessed Redeemer.

Thanks a thousand times for sparing our communicating with so many whose sympathy is so grateful to our feelings. Y[r] dear aunt and sisters especially—to all of whom give our united tenderest love, including our Darling who did she know I was writing would be able to send her thanks and blessings. You will hear from herself another time.

Ever dear M. A.,[1] your old and sorrowing, but I trust resigned, friend

M. Wordsworth

2055. W. W. to [?] JAMES DAWSON[2]

MS. Swarthmore College Library.
LY iii. 1311.

Rydal Mount
Tuesday afternoon [8 June 1847][3]

My dear Sir,

I grieve deeply to have to say that my only Daughter M[rs] Quillinan has been for some time wasting away in a pulmonary

of God, so willing to live yet so resigned to die, and so loving withal, and so considerate.' (*Poems*, p. xxxviii).

[1] Mary Anne.

[2] See L. 2005 above.

[3] This letter is endorsed: 'Mr Dawson when he gave me this Letter of Mr. Wordsworth told me it was written June 8th 1847.'

consumption. Her mother and I think that the Water-bed which about this time last year, you kindly lent to her poor Cousin when suffering in the same way would afford our beloved Child some relief. In the hope that the Bed may be at liberty and that you will most readily meet our wishes in this matter, I have sent a Man with a Horse and Cart to bring what we so much desire, to Rydal Mount.

Begging to be kindly remembered to Mrs Dawson in which wish Mrs W— sincerely unites as well as in good wishes to yourself, I remain my dear Sir

Your much obliged
Wm Wordsworth

2056. W. W. to CHARLES WORDSWORTH

MS. WL.
Annals of My Life, 1847–1856, p. 19. LY iii. 1312.

Rydal Mount 9th July 1847

My dear Charles,

It is my mournful duty to announce to you that it has pleased God to remove from this world the Spirit of your dear Cousin Dora. She expired a quarter before one this morning. Her bodily suffering for some time past had been great; but were borne with true christian resignation—and she retained the possession of her faculties until the last moment. Of her Husband and your dear Aunt I need not speak; they know and feel what they have to bear, and God will I trust support them.

With kind love to Catharine[1] I remain my dear Charles

your affectionate Uncle
Wm Wordsworth

You will not fail to give us the benefit of your prayers. Sincere thanks for your interesting Letter,[2] which would have been at once acknowledged but for our affliction.

[1] His second wife.

[2] On 8 June Charles Wordsworth had sent W. W. a long account of his busy new life at Trinity College, Glenalmond—'. . .provided I have strength to go through with it, there is no situation in which I could be happier'—and sought his advice on the laying out of the grounds of the new College. (*WL MSS.*). He remained there until shortly after his election to the Bishopric of St. Andrews in 1853.

2057. W. W. to C. W. JNR. and SUSAN W.[1]

Endorsed: Received 10 July 1847.
MS. Yale University Library.
Mem. (—). *Grosart* (—). *K* (—). *LY iii. 1312* (—).

[9 July 1847]

My dear Christopher and Susan,

Last night, I ought to have [said][2] a quarter before One this morning it pleased God to take to himself the Spirit of our beloved Daughter and your truly affectionate Cousin. She had latterly much bodily suffering under which she supported herself by prayer and gratitude to her heavenly Father for granting her to the End so many of his blessings.

I need not write more. Your Aunt bears up under the affliction as becomes a Christian.

Kindest love to Susan of whose sympathey we are fully assured.—

Your affectionate Uncle, and the more so for
this affliction
Wm Wordsworth

Pray for us!

[1] C. W. jnr. had written on 8 July about the Installation ceremony at Cambridge (see L. 2043 above): 'I was in the Senate House on Tuesday during the performance of the Installation Ode, and being on the platform very near Her Majesty and the Chancellor, and among all the grandees I had the best opportunity of hearing and seeing the effect it produced, and I assure you that no thing could be more gratifying than the manner in which it was received. All seemed to admire the patriotic and moral spirit of the Ode, and I think it did good to many hearts, as well as gave pleasure to many ears. . . . It is I hope some comfort to you my dear Uncle in your own private sorrow that you have been affording pleasure to others, and have dignified and sanctified the joy of a great Academic festival.' The next day C. B. Phipps wrote to convey the Queen's and Prince's gratification: 'The force and beauty of the ideas, and the elegance of the Versification fully proved to Her Majesty and the Prince that Time had been powerless over the Mind or Skill of the Poet.' (*WL MSS.*)

[2] *Word dropped out.*

2058. W. W. and M. W. to ISABELLA FENWICK

MS. WL.
LY iii. 1313.

Rydal Mount Monday Morning [July 1847]

We are much comforted beloved Friend by learning from your letter to Mr Quillinan that you are able to come to us. To no other quarter could we look for support so precious as we shall have in and from you.—Wm is here and will be able to stay till the end of the week—I enter into no particulars as you will soon hear every thing from our own mouths. Pray make all the arrangements you can to facilitate your remaining with us as long as possible—

God almighty bless you!—ever your most affectionate Friends

William and Mary Wordsworth

You say nothing about your Brother—does he still think of coming to England? or rather is he able to encounter the journey?—

2059. W. W. to EDWARD MOXON

MS. Henry E. Huntington Library.
LY iii. 1313 (—).

Rydal Mount
9th Augst 1847.

My dear Mr Moxon,

The Parcel has been received, containing the draft for 40£ 19. 3 on account of the Excursion.

I enclose a Page to be inserted in a Copy of my Poems in one Vol: to be strongly and handsomely bound for the use of a School (a large one)—and pray forward it as soon as is convenient in your Bookseller's Parcel, Fleetwood, if such there be, if not to Preston, Lancashire—directed to the Revd Dr Woolley[1] Rossall Hall near Fleetwood, Lancashire.

[1] The Revd. John Woolley (1816–66), Fellow of Exeter College, Oxford (1841), headmaster of Rossall (1844) and of King Edward's School, Norwich (1849), and first Principal of the University of Sydney, Australia, from 1852.

We bear up under our affliction as well as God enables us to do, but O my dear Friend our loss is immeasurable—

God bless you and yours—
ever faithfully your obliged
Wm Wordsworth

2060. W. W. to C. W. JNR.

MS. British Library. Hitherto unpublished.

Rydal Mount
August 9th 1847.

My dear Christopher,

Our Friend Miss Fenwick (who, you will remember, made you a Co-Trustee together with your dear Cousin Dora and Mr Strickland Cookson, when, for the education of her Godson my Grandson Wm, she invested 500£ in the Stocks) is anxious to make thro' you some inquiries as to the expence and otherwise about the Westminster School, where she expresses a wish to have him sent bye and bye if you approve of the School, and if so would there be any likelihood through your interest or otherwise, to have him placed upon the Foundation—Rossall School where he now is, we are not quite satisfied with, thinking the Under-Masters not being equal to their work: the cheapness of the terms not affording[1] a sufficient renumeration for men of experience and ability.—

We bear up under our affliction through God's Grace but the Sense of it will never be out of our hearts.—

I was forgetting to mention that my Grandson Henry is desirous of spending his Pocket money on some good monthly Publication suitable to his years. He named Sharp's Magazine,[2] but on learning from him that he had opportunity of seeing this at home, I recommended to him to have a different one. Do you know of any that would be proper to put into his hands? I have an impression that Murray publishes something that might do.[3] I am very sorry, knowing how constantly you are engaged, to

[1] *Written* afforded.

[2] See L. 1775 above.

[3] John Murray (see pt. i, L. 164) had projected *Murray's Magazine* as early as 1816, but it was not started until many years later by his son John Murray II (1808–92), in 1887.

trouble you; but the little Fellow is impatient and I do not like that a wrong choice should be made.

Kindest love to Susan and yourself, in which your Aunt cordially joins. Love to the children.

Your affectionate Uncle
W. Wordsworth

2061. W. W. to MRS. JOHN BOLTON[1]

MS. Harvard University Library.
LY iii. 1314.

[*In M. W.'s hand*]

Rydal Mount Augt. 18th [? 1847][2]

Be assured dear Mrs Bolton that it is with great reluctance I make this representation, knowing what demands must be made upon you, as upon all Persons, who like yourself, are distinguished for humanity and benevolence.

This morning Mrs W. and I enquired of Mrs Robinson of York, who is upon a visit to her Son,[3] about Mrs Hale—our questions were put with the requisite delicacy, and Mrs R. said she was never heard to make any complaint—that she always appeared at Church dressed as a Gentlewoman, and that she had lately been ill—but Mrs R. was aware of her *poverty*—for so I must call it upon the statement of our Sister—tho as I have said her exact income I forget. You are probably aware that Mrs Hale is above fourscore years of age. It is fit I should state from Mrs Robinson that she does not know whether her sister Douglas be alive, she having had no communication with her for some years—this is strange—and who is in fault I do not know, but I should think *not* Mrs Hale.

I have now dear Madam discharged a painful duty, which nothing but a knowledge of your goodness would have induced me to do; and in whatever light the matter strikes you, I trust I shall not appear guilty of an unwarrantable liberty in presenting this poor Old Lady to your remembrance.

I remain dear Madam, in kindest regards and best wishes in

[1] Of Storrs.

[2] The year is purely conjectural.

[3] Capt. Charles Robinson of Ambleside.

which Mrs W. unites; and with Comp^{ts} to Mrs Sutherland[1] and the Young Ladies, Yours very faithfully

[*signed*] Wm Wordsworth

2062. W. W. to UNKNOWN CORRESPONDENT

MS. Lilly Library, Indiana University. Hitherto unpublished.

Rydal Mount
Ambleside
Augst 30th 1847

Dear Sir,

I have been anxiously expecting and enquiring after the Package containing the Cast of the Boy with the Shell[2] which Mr Kirk has done me the honor of presenting to me, and which as your Letter announced has been forwarded; but it has not arrived. I think it therefore necessary to request that enquiries should be made at the place from which you despatched it, as my present ignorance does not allow me to do more than I have already done.

Believe me dear Sir
faithfully your obliged
Wm Wordsworth

PS

My little Shell-boy is just arrived and I am greatly pleased with it.

[1] A connection of Mrs. Bolton's.

[2] Probably the statue of 'The Curious Child', based on *Exc.* iv. 1132 ff., and now at Rydal Mount. The artist's name is unclear in the MS., but the reference is possibly to Thomas Kirk (1784–1845), the Dublin sculptor, or his son.

2063. W. W. to JOHN THORNTON[1]

MS. Lady Thornton. Hitherto unpublished.

Brigham
near Cockermouth
21st September 1847.

My dear Sir,

I take the liberty of writing to you in consequence of having heard from my Son that the Collection of the Coach and Railway duties is to be transferred from his Office to that of the Excise, by which arrangement his Income from the Stamp Office will be reduced to the amount of between £100 and £120 per annum.

Bearing in mind the expenses incident to the performance of his duty, viz Office-rent, Clerk's salary (which is considerable) Stationery[2] etc etc, taken from a moderate Income I cannot but feel a strong wish to know that some compensation is intended; or if not, allow me to ask your friendly advice as to what steps he might take without impropriety to represent his case to the Board, or to the Government, with a view to some remuneration.

I cannot forbear mentioning to you and Mrs Thornton, who have had like trials to undergo, that I and my wife are under much affliction from the recent decease of our only Daughter, who was to us everything that a Parent could wish—

Mrs Wordsworth unites with me in kind remembrances to yourself and Mrs Thornton. Believe me to remain, my dear Sir, faithfully

your much obliged
Wm Wordsworth

[1] The Commissioner of Stamps (see pt. ii, L. 780).

[2] *Written* Stationary.

2064. W. W. to [?] JOHN THORNTON[1]

MS. Cornell. Hitherto unpublished.

Septr 25th 1847
Vicarage Brigham
near Cockermouth

My dear Sir,

Many thanks for your prompt reply to my enquiries, unfavorable as it is.

I have forwarded your Letter to my Son, though I do not think that he will act upon the suggestion of reducing his Clerk's Salary who after 33 or 34 years' faithful service in the Stamp Office under me and himself might rather look for an augmentation than a reduction of his income. W^{m} must himself reduce his expenditure, moderate as it is, which, if he had known of the change a year ago (before his Marriage) might have been more easily effected. I think He will be able to explain that he has not misled me by stating the supposed reduction about to take place in his poundage to fall heavier upon him than it will prove. I wish he *may* be under a mistake.

Allow me to repeat my thanks, and believe me my dear Sir

faithfully your
much obliged
Wm Wordsworth

On Monday next I go to Carlisle for a few days.

2065. W. W. to UNKNOWN CORRESPONDENT

MS. Princeton University Library. Hitherto unpublished.

Novr 21st [1847][2]

Sir,

Had I offered myself as a Candidate for the office of Lord Rector of the antient University of Glasgow, it might have been

[1] See previous letter.

[2] Year added in another hand. For the Rectorial Election at Glasgow, see L. 2015 above. W. W.'s correspondent here seems to have sought out his views on Church and State, particularly perhaps in relation to the patronage question which had agitated the Established Church of Scotland and led to the Disruption four years previously.

incumbent upon me to give a direct answer to the Queries put in your Letter received yesterday; but not wishing, on account of my advanced age for such high honor that would impose duties upon me which it might be inconvenient to fulfil I need only refer you for a knowledge of my opinions and principles to writings which have long been before the Public, specially to the Series of Ecclesiastical Sonnets—

I have the honor to be sincerely yours

William Wordsworth

2066. W. W. to ISABELLA FENWICK

MS. WL.
LY iii. 1314 (—).

6th Decbr [1847]

I ought to have written to you my very very dear Friend upon our return hither, and *perhaps* I *did*, for I really have no distinct remembrance of anything that passes.—The thing I have to say is that the Mother of our departed Child preserves her health and stirs about the House upon every occasion as heretofore. You kindly express a hope that Mr Quillinan and I walk together—this has not been so, I cannot bear to cross the Bridge and Field that leads to his Abode; and he does not come hither,[1] so that except once on the highway, and once or twice at Church, and one evening when he dined here with Mr Scott,[2] his Friend, I have not seen him at all.

It pleases me to hear that Mr H. Taylor is so actively employed. His health and strength not being better he has surely done right in declining Mr Steeven's office.[3]

[1] 'It is a *horrible desolation*, and I cannot yet call it anything else,' E. Q. had written to I. F. on 13 Oct. about his wife's death. '—All my usual occupations were so blended with her presence and encouragement, that I *cannot* yet fix myself to any of them.' But he was returning to his translation of Camoens. 'I hate the drudgery of translation . . . but so much nonsense has been written *for* and *of* Camoens that I would fain make an effort to do him some little justice . . .' (*WL MSS.*). See also L. 1775 above.

[2] Unidentified.

[3] Sir James Stephen (see pt. ii, L. 607) had just resigned as Under Secretary of State for the Colonies, and the post had been offered to Taylor. See *Autobiography of Henry Taylor*, ii. 25 ff.

We expect Henry and Wm from School on Thursday—I shall carefully examine them. Henry, we are told, has more application than Wm; but I will do my utmost to impress Wm with the duty of being diligent.—

The weather here as is usual at this season is much broken, and as I have had a troublesome cold I have seldom ventured lately further than the walks of the Terrace and the Garden. Hannah Cookson[1] has been staying with us a few days. No one can be kinder and she is very useful to me in many ways. I suffer most in head and mind before I leave my bed in a morning—Daily used She to come to my bedside and greet me and her Mother and *now* the blank is terrible. But I must stop. She is ever with me and will be so to the last moment of my life.—

We don't hear from Mr Robinson, but I suppose he intends to come here before Christmas.

Mrs Arnold is so kind as to call from time to time; she seems very well. Mrs Hornsby's[2] eldest child has been poorly, but is recovering as I hear—The Mother endeared herself to me by the tears she shed, in her first interview with me after our loss.

And now my beloved Friend, I must bid you farewell with a prayer that our sorrows may, through God's mercy, prove a help to us, an unfailing help on our way to Heaven.

Again farewell, most faithfully and affectionately yours

Wm Wordsworth

[*M.W. writes*]

Beloved friend I am thankful that this one solitary effort has been made—tho' it too painfully speaks of my poor Husband's state, and this will be a pain to you—

With a chance that it will find you at Mortlake I will direct to that place, where I trust you are and in tolerable plight. We shall be most thankful to hear that you perform your journey to Kelston and find your B^r^ and his belongings comfortable. Is Mrs Fenwick[3] with him? My love to dear Louisa[4] when you see her, and meanwhile to all our Kind and dear friends where you are. God bless you my beloved Miss Fenwick.

M.W.

[1] See L. 2048 above.

[2] Unidentified. Does W. W. mean Mrs. Hornby?

[3] I. F.'s sister in law.

[4] One of her nieces.

2067. W. W. to EDWARD MOXON

MS. Henry E. Huntington Library.
LY iii. 1316.

Rydal Mount 29 Dec[r] 1847

Dear Mr Moxon

Your draft for £109 11*s*, 7*d*. was duly received yesterday.

It seems from your Letter the Book trade is not flourishing, nor can one be surprized at that, the state of the times considered.

Mr Robinson is here still,[1] he will leave us at the end of next week. He is in his usual good health and spirits. Yesterday he drank tea at Mrs Davy's, where he met Miss Martineau. She is busy in writing an account of her travels[2]—She rises every morning at six—takes a long walk before breakfast—and after breakfast works until two o'clock. You and your family have, we hope, escaped the influenza, of which one heard so much.

We bear up as well as we are able under our sorrowful bereavement. We see little of poor Mr Quillinan, Mrs W. seldom goes down to the hill, and I have not courage to go to his House.[3] Our sorrow, I feel, is for life—but God's will be done.—

Pray give our kind remembrances to Mrs Moxon, and to your Sister, and accept the same yourself.

ever faithfully yours
Wm Wordsworth

[1] H. C. R. found the Wordsworths sunk in grief and averse to society (see *HCR* ii. 670–3).

[2] See L. 2078 below.

[3] H. C. R. feared the possibility of 'a lasting estrangement' between W. W. and E. Q. (see Morley, ii. 655–6). In the event, their relationship gradually improved, but meanwhile W. W. had accepted C. W. jnr.'s offer (made during his visit in November) to prepare the posthumous *Memoirs* and act as his uncle's literary executor. See Morley, ii. 660, 728, and *MW*, p. 291.

2068. W. W. to W. W. JNR.

MS. WL. Hitherto unpublished.

Mond: morn. (late 1847]

Dearest William,

Circumstances are much changed since I thought the House you speak of might be a desirable purchase from your benefit. At present it might prove an inadvisable Entanglement. A Residence a little way out of the Town, the place for instance where Mr Graham formerly lived[1] might suit both Fanny and you much better. It would be airy and pleasant. Therefore think this over, very carefully.

Your dear Mother continues well, though sadly dejected—as I am; Time doing nothing for one—

We are anxious to hear from Fanny. Miss Hannah Cookson kindly continues with us—

your affectionate Father

W W

[*M. W. adds*]

Just read y^{rs}—we would much rather you *rented* than bought a house—prove whether the *Town* suits dear Fanny before you buy. Mr C. says the situation that suited her was *out* of Town—But you must not think of remaining at Briscoe[2] under present impressions M. W.

2069. W. W. to MAURICE MORGAN JAMESON[3]

MS. Harvard University Library. Hitherto unpublished.

Rydal Mount
5th Jan^{ry} 1848

Sir,

It is with pleasure that I accept the honor of being elected by

[1] Kirklinton.

[2] A suburb on the south side of Carlisle.

[3] Foreign Corresponding Secretary of the American Union of Literature and Art, founded by Benjamin Franklin in 1748 'for the encouragement of learning in the American Colonies.' He had written from Utica, New York, on 4 Dec. 1847 to announce that W. W. had been elected an honorary member in succession to Southey. (*Cornell MSS.*)

"The American Union of Literature and Art", a member of their antient and distinguished Society.

Thanking you for the Communication of this intelligence

I remain, Sir,
your obliged
Wm Wordsworth

2070. W. W. to GEORGE JABET[1]

MS. untraced.
Bookseller's Catalogue.

Rydal Mount
2 February 1848

. . .I did not mean to imply that the Lily of the Vale was without scent, but that it was only found thriving in shady and sunless places. This is particularly the case in those Islands of Windermere, which bear the name of the Lily of the Valley Islands. . . .

[*cetera desunt*]

2071. W. W. to SIR JOHN FREDERICK WILLIAM HERSCHEL[2]

MS. Lilly Library, Indiana University. Hitherto unpublished.

Rydal Mount
near Ambleside
Feb^ry 3^d—1848

Dear Sir John,

The Bearer of this note is Mr Carrick[3] a distinguished Miniature Painter upon a large scale. He is a native of Carlisle at

[1] Author of *Nasology: or Hints towards a classification of Noses*, 1848, and (under the pseudonym of Eden Warwick) *The Poet's Pleasaunce; or Garden of all sorts of Pleasant Flowers, which our pleasant poets have in past time, for pastime, planted*, 1847. In this letter W. W. is acknowledging 'the innocent and profitable enjoyment' this work afforded, and referring to *An Evening Walk*, ll. 233–4 (*PW* i. 24).

[2] Sir John Frederick William Herschel, 1st Bart., F.R.S. (1792–1871), astronomer. See also pt. iii, L. 1328.

[3] Thomas Heathfield Carrick (1802–75), miniaturist, had taken W. W.'s portrait in Oct. 1847 (see *MW*, pp. 288–9): 'the most striking likeness I have yet

which place he drew a Portrait of me last summer, and he is desirous of being permitted to take your Likeness. His Practice, I understand, is to have his Portraits engraved and published in pairs; and he would be happy to unite mine with yours which I should consider as no small honor; particularly when I bear in mind that both our Portraits are at present in our College of St John's Cambridge.

Not doubting that you will excuse my troubling you upon this occasion I have the honor to remain dear Sir John

faithfully yours
Wm Wordsworth

2072. W. W. to UNKNOWN CORRESPONDENT[1]

MS. Historical Society of Pennsylvania.
James A. Butler, 'Two New Wordsworth Letters', NQ ccxx (1975), 61–3.

Rydal Mount
21st Feb^ry 1848.

Sir,

The Book of Mr Bryant's Poems[2] did not reach me 'till three days ago, I beg you would accept my thanks for this acceptable mark of your attention.

Believe me to be
sincerely your
obliged
Wm Wordsworth

seen of Wordsworth,' H. C. R. noted, 'But it is too sad a likeness, it has an expression of fixed and irremovable grief.' (*HCR* ii. 674). The original is now at Dove Cottage. See Blanshard, *Portraits of Wordsworth*, pp. 174–5, and L. 2074 below.

[1] Perhaps R. W. Emerson (see L. 1537 above), who was now in England and paid his second visit to W. W. on 28 Feb. See *English Traits*, Ch. xvii. 'I heard that he talked for an hour with Emerson, an American writer of some reputation,' Sara Coleridge wrote to I. F. on 3 Apr., 'and afterwards expressed regret that he had not known at the time with whom he was conversing.' (*Texas University MSS.*).

[2] See L. 1904 above.

2073. M. W. to KATE SOUTHEY

MS. untraced.
K (—).

Feb 23d [? 1848]

This is a gloomy season with me—but what season *now* is not gloomy with us? . . . Mr. Wordsworth's spirits are so overwhelmed that I can fix upon nothing . . . Never a day passes that my husband does not mourn over the injustice that has been done to your father's memory by the suppression of his invaluable works, not to speak of the injury that bad passions have caused to the fortunes of you all; but this is even a trifle when we think how your hearts have been riven and your spirits wounded . . . I will only add that I am ever your tender friend, and that *we* consider you as our own.

M. Wordsworth

2074. W. W. to SAMUEL ROGERS

MS. Sharpe Collection, University College, London.
Rogers. LY iii. 1316.

Rydal Mount
16th March 1848

My dear Friend,

I have just received the enclosed, which I hope you will be so kind as to peruse. It is from Mr Carrick[1] a miniature painter, who took my Portrait when I met him not long ago at his native place, Carlisle. If you could comply with his wish I should be gratified, and should deem it an honour to be associated with you in this way. You preserve your health, I hope, in this severe March weather. You and your dear Sister[2] have both the good wishes of those that remain of this afflicted family.

Believe me, my Friend of nearly half a Century

very affectionately and faithfully yours
W Wordsworth

[1] See L. 2071 above. W. W. was successful in this application to Rogers, and the pair of miniatures were exhibited at the Royal Academy later this year (see Blanshard, *Portraits of Wordsworth*, pp. 100–1).

[2] Sarah Rogers had had an attack of paralysis.

P.S. On second thoughts it is not worth while troubling you to read Mr Carrick's letter, which was simply that I might strengthen his application that you would be so kind as to give him a little of your time.[1]

2075. W. W. to WILLIAM WALKER[2]

MS. Cornell. Hitherto unpublished.

[*In M. W.'s hand*]

Carlisle April 11th —48

Mr Wordsworth being from home did not hear until last evening of the arrival of the Engraving[3] at Rydal Mount.

As requested by Mr Walker, Mr W. now encloses a Post Off. order for £1–13.

2076. W. W. to CHARLES KNIGHT[4]

MS. Henry E. Huntington Library.
LY iii. 1317.

Rydal Mount
near Ambleside
May 20th 1848

Dear Sir,

On returning home after an absence of six weeks, I have had the pleasure of receiving the third Volume of your Half-hours[5]

[1] Rogers replied: 'You must be sure that I could not hesitate for a moment to consent to such a fellowship as you propose, or to any testimonial of a friendship so long and so uninterrupted as ours. What delightful days we have passed together, walking and sitting wherever we were, and more especially among the rocks and waters of your enchanting country. On that they were to come over again! You may well conceive how much you were in my mind during your long, long trial. Pray remember me to those who remain with you . . .' (Rogers, ii. 324).

[2] William Walker (1793–1867), Scottish engraver, who settled in London in 1832. He specialised in portraits and historical works, publishing them himself from his studio in Margaret Street.

[3] Almost certainly his engraving of George Richmond's drawing of Charles Wordsworth, publ. 1 Mar. 1848.

[4] See L. 1761 above.

[5] *Half Hours with the Best Authors*, which includes a tribute to W. W. as 'the

etc, and thank you cordially for it and the preceding Volumes. The Selections appear to be judiciously made; though I regret to find that there are no extracts from the Works of Lord Bacon, one of the greatest Writers that our Country has produced.

Thanking you for these valuable marks of your regard, I rema[in]

dear Sir
faithfully
your much obliged
Wm Wordsworth

2077. W. W. to JAMES BUSH[1]

Address: Rev^d. James Bush, Dale Head, Keswick.
Postmark: July 1848.
MS. University Library, Davis, California. Hitherto unpublished.

Rydal Mount
4th June 1848

My dear Sir

Accept my thanks for your obliging communication from Archdeacon Bailey.[2] It is gratifying to be thought of in this manner by an amiable and pious man living so long at such a distance. This is the second proof of his regard and esteem which I have received from your hands. Pray when you write to Mr Bailey present him my thanks for these repeated favors.

I cannot omit this opportunity to offer You and Mrs Bush the congratulations of Mrs Wordsworth and myself upon your

greatest name in the literature of our age' (i. 144). Charles Knight met W. W. the following year at Harriet Martineau's, and visited Rydal Mount: 'I was surprised at the very slight acquaintance with the more eminent writers of the previous ten or twenty years which he manifested. . . . He has been reproached with wilfully ignoring the merits of his contemporaries. I doubt whether it might with justice be attributed either to envy or to affectation when he told me that he felt no interest in any modern book except in Layard's Nineveh, which had then been recently published.' (*Passages of a Working Life*, iii. 28–9).

[1] See L. 1564 above.

[2] Of Colombo (see pt. ii, L. 638). Twice recently, Bush had forwarded sonnets from Bailey, 'in the land of his exile . . . For an exile it is, though a useful and an honourable one.' (*WL MSS.*)

Daughter Charlotte's marriage and our sincere wishes for her happiness.

I remain my dear Sir
very respectfully
your much obliged
Wm Wordsworth

2078. M. W. to H. C. R.

Endorsed: June 7th Mrs Wordsworth.
MS. Dr. Williams's Library.
Morley, ii. 667.

7th June 1848

My dear Friend

I should be very unworthy of your persevering kindness in writing to me, were I not roused to thank you *myself* for the comforting news I received from you yesterday of our dear friend's[1] good looks and cheerfulness—Sara Coleridge had given but an unsatisfactory report of her, in a letter which Kate Southey (who is now with us) had from her cousin the other day—so that your's was most welcome—more especially as we are always in fear while Miss F. is in, or near, London where she is doing and seeing *too much*—and excitement always tells upon her bodily health. I hope, as she is to visit Lady Rolfe that you will have a quiet chat with her having been disappointed by such an influx of visitors at Mortlake.

Poor dear Mrs Davys sojourn in London has robbed her of her previous good looks and store of health, tho' I am very thankful to say that she feels herself gaining strength in her quiet home—altho' the unlooked-for prolongation of her Husband's absence makes her anxious—She had expected his return about this time, but he, from some cause, delays the quitting his Post[2] till Sepr and she cannot but dread his remaining the 2 next months in that climate from which he suffered last year. I have just *seen* Mrs Fletcher and Lady Richardson[3] *once*—not *the family* at all—but I hear that the Old Lady much enjoys having the young ones about her, when it pleases her to *call for them*—Lady R made a judicious arrangement, so that they might not be an *annoyance*

[1] I. F.'s. H. C. R. had seen her on 3 June at Henry Taylor's. See *HCR* ii. 677.

[2] In Barbados.

[3] Formerly Mary Fletcher (see pt. iii, L. 1157).

to her Mother, by placing the Children,[1] with their Governess in the next cottage to Lancrigg: and the alternate visits between Mother and Daughter go on as heretofore.

Dear Mrs Arnold has been enjoying the presence of her little Sailor Boy[2] for the last 10 days—but a sad separation I fear will take place today—the little *important* fellow is expecting to be recalled to join his Ship at Sheerness,—and the rest are arranging matters to pass a couple of months at the sea-side—where I believe they expect poor M^rs^ A Twining[3] to join them. The Quillinans are at home, and well—The Roughsedges absent with their daughter at Ormskirk. The Cooksons as usual, except that Mary after a very long absence, has returned home much changed in appearance—having lost her beauty—first I suppose from too much racketting and latterly from anxious attendance upon her friend with whom, in the neighbourhood of Manchester she was staying, and whose health is now in a very dangerous state—and poor Mary's looks are just now anything but hopeful.

This is all I can tell you of our neighbour-friends.

For ourselves, were you here I think you would be comforted; tho' my husband still shrinks from turning his steps towards Loughrigg which *was* such a happy walk to us all—or to go beyond the Cookson's house[4] in our *own* Vale of Grasmere. Yet you would be pleased to find us *at home* more as we used to be—but this is a trying time to us—and I must not dwell upon it. However do give a favorable report of us to dear Mrs Clarkson. How well I should like once more to see her. Thank you for the mention of other friends—but you do not speak of the Miss Westons,[5] of whom I always like to hear. What a *prodigy* Mr Rogers is! I do not see why he should not once more visit the Lakes, I can scarcely say how much good his presence might not do to his old friend, tell him this with my love. Moxon is under an engagement to come down, at least he spoke of this some time ago—but it is long since we have heard from him.

You will grieve to hear, tho' it will not surprize you, that our dear-daughter-in Law, Fanny is in a very weak state, and

[1] Sir John Richardson's four sons and two daughters by his second marriage to a niece of Sir John Franklin.

[2] Her son Walter.

[3] Formerly Mary Arnold (see L. 1872 above).

[4] Howe Foot, south of Dove Cottage.

[5] See L. 1790 above.

without any apparent cause—change of air, which was recommended to her, has failed and she is now, accompanied by her Father, gone for medical advice to Edinborough—and probably she may, when her husband is at liberty to go with her, be inclined to consult her former Dr Sir James Clerk,[1] we cannot but feel sad at the prospect of our Son—whose peculiar sensitive mind has been so often tried—and now, save on the score of health, seemed to be blessed by a wife suited in all respects to him so admirably.

This, dear friend, is a less chearing detail than I should have wished to send you—but such as it is you will take in good part—of our family at Brigham all is going on as well as can be looked for,[2] where the Wife and Mother is so far away in search of health. The trial of another winter is to be made. From Pisa Isabella and her Brother have removed for the summer to Lucca. The report of her health is somewhat better, but that her return to England, as we had expected this season, would impede her recovery they say.

I have not seen M^r Q since I rec^d your letter, but as you suggest, he shall reply to the *political* portion of it.[3] From me you must be content with *Personalities*—and I fear I have tired you—What are your plans of travel this season? Shall we get a glimpse of you?—But I must not leave Miss H. M. unmentioned. She is the briskest and most active Person in the vale—has had

[1] Sir James Clark, 1st Bart., F. R. S. (1788–1870), physician to Queen Victoria since her accession: an unpopular figure owing to his misdiagnosis in the case of Lady Flora Hastings (1839), which encouraged the scandalous allegations against her (see pt. iii, L. 1335).

[2] W. W. and M. W. had spent a fortnight at Brigham in May.

[3] H. C. R. had written to M. W. on 7 Mar. about W. W.'s politics: 'I recollect once hearing Mr W. say, half in joke, half in earnest—"I have no respect whatever for Whigs, but I have a great deal of the Chartist in me". To be sure he has. His earlier poems are full of that intense love of the people, as such, which becomes Chartism when the attempt is formally made to make their interests the especial object of legislation as of deeper importance than the positive rights hitherto accorded to the privileged orders.' (Morley, ii. 665). Cf. W. W.'s conversation (1846), recorded by Thomas Cooper the Chartist: 'You were right . . . I have always said the people were right in what they asked; but you went the wrong way about it. . . .There is nothing unreasonable in your Charter: it is the foolish attempt at physical force, for which many of you have been blameable. . . .The people are sure to have the franchise . . . as knowledge increases; but you will not get all you seek at once—and you must never seek it again by physical force . . . (*Life, written by himself*, 1872, pp. 290–4).

her fellow-traveller Mr Ewart[1] with her, a fine looking interesting man—who called with her here on Sunday, walked in the Garden—and after our return from Chapel, sate with us a ¼ of an hour.—She going about the hills and vales to prepare some acc^t^ of the Country for Mr Knight—a *Martineau* guide[2] in addition to so many upon Mrs Nicholsons[3] Counter. She describes admirably. I have read, and *skipped* nearly thro' her three volumes, with much pleasure, but more dis[satis]faction I grieve to say—but *this between* ourselves. God bless you dear f^d^. ever aff^ly^ yours

M. Wordsworth

2079. W. W. to C. W. JNR.

Endorsed: First week in July—1848.
MS. Mr. W. A. Strutz. Hitherto unpublished.

Rydal Mount
[early July 1848]

My dear Christopher,

The Bearer is the Revd E. Hornby[4] whose Letter I forwarded to you lately.

Your affectionate Uncle, W. Wordsworth

[1] Harriet Martineau's companion on her visit to Egypt and the Holy Land, which formed the subject of *Eastern Life, Past and Present*, 3 vols., 1848. See also her letter to H. C. R. of 8 June (Morley, ii. 671–2).

[2] Charles Knight (see L. 2076 above) had commissioned her to write an account of the Lake District for a volume called 'The Land we Live in'. Her *Complete Guide to the English Lakes* appeared in 1855.

[3] The Ambleside bookseller.

[4] The Revd. Edward Hornby (b. 1817), of Merton College, Oxford, rector of Winnithrop, Lancs.: rector of Bury, Lancs., from 1850, and Canon of Manchester from 1855. A pupil of Faber's, he had married Miss Roughsedge of Fox Ghyll (see *MW*, p. 189), and was now seeking preferment. W. W. also knew his father, the Revd. James Hornby (1777–1855), rector of Winwick, Lancs. from 1813, and editor of the *Remains* of Alexander Knox (see pt. ii, L. 740).

2080. M. W. to H. C. R.

MS. Dr. Williams's Library.
Morley, ii. 700.

July 22nd [1848] Rydal Mt

My dear friend

Strong expressions are apt to alarm, or I should say that the report of your accident[1] SHOCKED *us all* very much, especially as you say your plan of life must be changed, 'You will not be able to continue your habit of taking long walks'—we fear, tho' this *does* not yet tell upon your general health—its effect will in time do so—and this does not make us exult with you in what you call 'The best part of the story' the getting forward with your reminiscences[2]—these I well know will be not only very entertaining and valuable—but I would rather that the work were left to other hands, than done at the expense of your being cut off from your pleasant ramblings, which have been such a gratification to yourself—and the source whence you have drawn such a pleasant portion of the mass from which the selections are to be made.

Your mention of this, your occupation, suggests to me that your letters in our possession might be of use, in which case, if you will say so, they shall be sent to you by any safe conveyance that may present itself—or, as you say, your plans for the summer are 'open to any rational proposal' why not come and fetch them, or select such as you thought proper during a friendly visit to us. I do not mean to interfere with the annual one which is our due.

Poor dear Mrs C.[3] What a change from her steady hand—I return you the document that shows her heart and her interests are as lively and faithful as heretofore.

We have good chearful Mr Monkhouse[4] with us, John left us this morning after a Clergyman's week's visit—his two younger sons have had a long holiday with us, and are still here and Mr Hill and one of his youngsters came to us this morng on their way to Warwick from Keswick—they will depart on Monday. Mr H. brings a good report of Cuth's[5] progress with his Father's

[1] H. C. R. had slipped and strained his leg.

[2] Begun about three years earlier, and eventually carried to the close of 1843.

[3] Clarkson.

[4] John Monkhouse of the Stow.

[5] Cuthbert Southey. See also L. 1683 above.

Biography (Letters) a volume of which he expects to send to Press almost immediately.

I am sorry for your acc[t] of poor Miss Weston['s] inability, from lameness, to profit by the improvement of her health. I hope I may say that the health of William's precious wife is, for the present at least, more hopeful—They are now paying visits to friends of her's in Cheshire—and we hope to see them in the course of a fortnight. M[rs] Davy thinks herself better—as for M[rs] Fletcher she is off, unattended but by her two Grandaughters (Davys) gadding about in Yorkshire—Lady Richardson occupied at Lancrigg with her Family of Children—suffering from a Gum boil just at this time but happy in her Charge. The Cooksons all well. The Arnolds at Redcar a bathing place on the Yorkshire Coast, n[r] Gisbro where M[rs] A. Twining had already joined her, when you wrote to me the message I was to deliver to her Mother—'that you had seen her daughter' who begins to smile again. This we were all glad to hear.

M[r] Q. I am happy to tell you is better—and that my dear Husband, our Sister and myself are all perfectly well *in health*, and join most cordially in the hope that you may be out in your prophesy when you say you must no more indulge in long walks.

God bless you
aff[ly] yours
M. Wordsworth

2081. W. W. to JOHN PRINGLE NICHOL[1]

MS. Cornell.
K (—). LY iii. 1317 (—). Broughton, p. 90.

Rydal Mount
near Ambleside
Aug[st] 1848.

Mr Wordsworth is much obliged by Professor Nichol's kindness in transmitting to him Mr Longfellow's Poem, Evangeline.[2]

[1] John Pringle Nichol (1804–59), Scottish schoolmaster and friend of John Stuart Mill: from 1836 Professor of Astronomy at the University of Glasgow, where De Quincey was his guest in 1841.

[2] Longfellow's narrative poem on the Acadians of Canada, publ. 1847. Henry Wadsworth Longfellow (1807–82), author of *Voices of the Night*, 1839, *Ballads*

Mr W— is sorry for the mistake which occasioned Mr Nichol some additional trouble—

Mr Longfellow's Poem is obviously in metre and in manner and matter, after the model of Voss' Louisie[1] a Poem which used to be as popular in Germany as the *Metre* would allow, which does not suit modern Languages. In our own we have no spondees, and are therefor obliged to substitute trochaics, or to make spondees out of the end of one word and the beginning of the next.

What M[r] Nichol says of the attention paid to Mr W's Poems in America accords with what Mr W has had the pleasure of hearing from several other quarters. What a momentous obligation does the spread of the English Language impose upon the Persons who write in it. It has already taken the lead of the French, and will I must hope keep the precedence

2082. W. W. to DAVID LEITCH[2]

MS. Cornell.
K (—). *LY iii. 1318* (—).

[*In M. W.'s hand*]

Rydal Mount
Sep[r] 18th —48

Dear Sir

I am sorry that I cannot meet your wishes in respect to parting with any portion of my little Property at Applethwaite;[3] it is endeared to me by so many sacred and personal recollections,

and Other Poems, 1842, *The Song of Hiawatha*, 1855, *Tales of a Wayside Inn*, 1863, etc., succeeded Ticknor as Professor of French and Spanish at Harvard in 1836. In a letter to Henry Reed in 1852 about the proposed Wordsworth Memorial in Ambleside Church (*WL MSS.*), Longfellow paid a notable tribute to W. W.'s influence. See also *R.M.Cat.*, nos. 553, 588.

[1] *Luise*, by Johann Heinrich Voss (1751–1826), which S. T. C. had planned to translate into English hexameters. See Griggs, ii. 856.

[2] David Ross Leitch (1809–81), physician, of Derwent Bank, nr. Keswick: author of *A Memoir of Jonathan Otley*, [1857], prefixed to Otley's *Guide*.

[3] The farmstead presented to W. W. by Sir George Beaumont in 1803 (see *EY*, p. 406; *MY* i. 76). It is now clear from documents in the Record Office, Carlisle, that W. W. had enlarged his holding in 1814 by purchase (see *MY* ii. 97), and also by taking advantage of an allotment of enclosed common land in 1815. See also next letter and L. 2089 below.

some of very long standing, that I much regretted the erection of that small Mill when it took place, and had I known of the intention, the fulfilment of which so much impaired the privacy of the Place, I should have done my utmost by purchase, or otherwise, to have prevented such an intrusion.

Circumstances frustrated my original intention of building at Applethwaite, and at my advanced Age I am not likely [to] do so, but that may not be the case with some of my family.[1]

If your intention was to fix the Site of your Cottage upon the ground bounded on both sides by my property, I certainly should feel much obliged by your selecting some other Spot, and one which might interfere as little as possible with the prospect and character of the Dell.

Believe me dear Sir, to be sensible of the kind expressions you use towards me, and sincerely yours

[*signed*] William Wordsworth

2083. W. W. to DAVID LEITCH[2]

MS. Mrs. Spence Clepham. Hitherto unpublished.

Rydal Mount, 10th Octr 1848

My dear Sir,

I trust you have attributed my tardiness in replying to your very obliging and gratifying Letter received, I am sorry to say, a fortnight ago, in some measure to its right cause, *viz*: its reaching me at a time when the distressing circumstance of my Daughter-in-law's somewhat sudden death in a foreign Country[3] gave a great shock to the Family. Moreover I thought an opportunity was at hand for me to have a personal interview with You.

It would be less difficult and painful to my feelings to express by *words* than by writing the reasons for my non-compliance with your wishes. At present I need only say, that my original acquisition of, subsequent appropriation, and long-continued possession of that little Property are accompanied with a *sacred* feeling which puts it out of my power to make any change

[1] W. W. never lived at Applethwaite himself, but his son Willy did, at a later date.

[2] See previous letter.

[3] Isabella W. had died at Pisa the previous month.

which I can avoid; and I can only say, that I exceedingly regret standing in the way of wishes with which I sincerely sympathize.

I am much obliged by your offer to transfer your purchase, and shall readily accept it if it meets with the approbation of my younger Son, and my Son-in-law who has, during his life, an interest in the Property.

Let me add, that I have some hope of being able ere long to go over to Keswick myself, in which case I hope to have an interview with you. Believe me my dear Sir to remain with great respect

sincerely Yours
Wm Wordsworth

2084. M. W. to [?] JAMES GREGOR GRANT[1]

MS. Yale University Library. Hitherto unpublished.

Rydal M[t]
Nov[r] 6th [1848]

My dear Sir

I am very sorry that I did not in my husband's name acknowledge your very gratifying letter accompanying 2 Copies of your Poems at the time of their being delivered by your Friend at Rydal Mount—for it is with pain I am compelled to state to you, that anxious as he is to express his thanks to you *himself*, he is, even now, as unable to bring his mind to write upon aught that *interests him* as at the time when our deep sorrow was recent, and when the letter to which you so delicately allude was written.

You will therefore thro' me accept the assurance that Mr Wordsworth has been much interested by several of your Poems that have been read to him, and that he feels gratified by your having connected his name with a Publication which promises to be useful, and to be an honour to yourself.

I remain dear Sir, begging to express the pleasure I myself have derived from your Volumes, very sincerely

Yours
M Wordsworth

[1] Author of *Madonna Pia, and Other Poems*, 2 vols., 1848, dedicated to W. W. The presentation copy is at the *WL*. Grant had visited W. W. in 1836.

2085. W. W. to [?] JAMES GREGOR GRANT

MS. Yale University Library. Hitherto unpublished.

Rydal Mount
7th Novr 1848.

My dear Sir,

Mrs Wordsworth kindly undertook yesterday to acknowledge my obligations to you; nevertheless I do not feel satisfied without thanking you by my own pen for the two Volumes of Poems which you have done me the honour of dedicating to me; and also for your two Letters in which you feelingly express your sympathy with my severe affliction.

Believe me
my dear Sir
to be faithfully
your much obliged
Wm Wordsworth

2086. W. W. to ISABELLA FENWICK

MS. WL. Hitherto unpublished.

[mid-November 1848]

. . . We have excellent accounts from good authority of the two Boys at Sedbergh. They appear to be doing very well at school; and Mrs Green the Matron with whom they lodge said to us that they were very good Boys. One thing is however rather against their being together that William is taking the lead of Henry in his class. He writes Verses that surprize his Schoolfellows; and Hartley Coleridge spoke to us in praise of some that He had seen—Wms School fellows for this, and perhaps other reasons, call him "Grandfather". But I must have tried you my dear Friend, with these minute accounts.

We have had Cuthbert Southey with us on Saturday Afternoon, and Sunday till noon. [*M. W. adds*: John and he exchanged their several duties to give us this opportunity of seeing him: We were much interested in him.] He is very much improved in his style of reading; and gave us such an excellent discourse upon the text "Take no thought for the Morrow" which was feelingly treated by Him and from no one with a better grace for he acts up to it.

His wife is in a dreadfully nervous state. She cannot bear the sound of voices in the room below Her. Mrs Lovell lives with them—We shall see Cuthbert again in the course of the week, and he will bring with him a specimen of the volumes which he is preparing—of his Father's Letters. He is a most deserving young Man, and were there in the country a proper feeling of his Father's merits and his own He would not be long without some preferment [*M. W. adds*: but he is at present perfectly contented and the situation suits his work.]

Now let me inquire how you are in health and how your brother and the rest of your kindred are, at home and abroad. I had a letter the other day from Mr Peace. He reminds me of a Verse in the Epistle to the Ephesians, which I quoted the first time I saw him, 5th Chapter 20th verse—giving thanks etc., etc., Such consolation I do need, and shall need as long as I remain in this sorrowful world. But I must stop with my love and blessing. God grant that we may meet again. Ever most tenderly—and faithfully yours

Wm Wordsworth

My dear Sister continues quite well—

2087. W. W. to JOHN PEACE

Postmark: 18 Nov. 1848.
MS. untraced.
Mem. Grosart. K. LY iii. 1318.

Brigham [*c.* 17 Nov. 1848]

My dear Friend,

Mrs Wordsworth has deputed to me the acceptable office of answering your friendly letter, which has followed us to Brigham, upon the banks of the river Derwent, near Cockermouth, the birthplace of four brothers and their sister. Of these four I, the second, am now the only one left. Am I wrong in supposing that you have been here? The house was driven out of its place by a railway, and stands now not nearly so advantageously for a prospect of this beautiful country, though at only a small distance from its former situation.

We are expecting Cuthbert Southey to-day from his curacy[1]

[1] Plumbland.

seven or eight miles distant. He is busy in carrying through the press the first volume of his father's letters, or rather collecting and preparing them for it. Do you happen to have any in your possession? If so, be so kind as to let me or his son know what they are, if you think they contain anything which would interest the public. . . .

Mrs W. and I are, thank God, both in good health, and possessing a degree of strength beyond what is usual at our age, being both in our seventy-ninth year. The beloved daughter whom it has pleased God to remove from this anxious and sorrowful world I have not mentioned; but I can judge of the depth of your fellow-feeling for us. Many thanks to you for referring to the text in Scripture which I quoted to you so long ago. 'Thy kingdom come. Thy will be done.' He who does not find support and consolation there will find it nowhere. God grant that it may be continued to me and mine, and to all sufferers! Believe me, with Mrs W.'s very kind remembrance,

Faithfully yours,
Wm Wordsworth

2088. W. W. and M. W. to ISABELLA FENWICK

MS. WL.
LY iii. 1319 (—).

Rydal 7th Decr. [1848]

Your affectionate Letter, beloved Friend, just received was most welcome to us both, notwithstanding its contents in what regards your health are far from what we wish—

It is a week to day since we reached home, having stayed one day with Mr and Mrs Joshua Stanger[1] at their house near Keswick. We have now little to say about our Household but that our dear Sister is well, though she complains a little in her own way. Jemima and Rotha have been residing with us. They are gone home this morning in the expectation of their Father's arrival. He has been suffering from cold in his face, and also from having hit his foot against a trunk in his bed-room while he was walking quickly to and fro to get rid in part of his pain.—

Mrs Lightfoot[2] is here for a couple of days, I see her just

[1] See pt. i, L. 166.

[2] R. W.'s widow, married to the Keswick attorney.

returned from Ambleside where she has been to visit those Friends who were most kind to her Son, on whose memory she seems to dwell with unabated love and sorrow.

Our return home was most mournful, but Mary bears up with a religious resignation, which is in the true spirit of the Gospel of Christ. I wish I could come nearer her excellence in this and every respect—

All that you wish Mrs Cookson and the rest to do will be carefully told her. I saw her and her family yesterday all well.[1] They give a somewhat better account of George Hutchinson though far from what is to be wished. He is duly attentive to the duties of his sacred Calling, but moody often towards his own family. Mr Hutchinson continues wonderfully patient and even chearful.—Fanny W. thinks the air of Rydal does not agree with her health, so we must reconcile ourselves to seeing little of her.—

Carlisle is to me a painful place, from a conviction in my mind that our Child hastened her dissolution by over-exertion there, in furnishing Wm's House. But alas! wherever she was, she sacrificed Herself to others, and the consequence is a deep sorrow to the remainder of our days. But God's Will be done!

Be assured that we sympathise with all you have to suffer in body and in mind. I will now with earnest blessings give up the pen to Mary—ever your devoted Friend

Wm Wordsworth

We see Mrs Arnold from time to time. She has been unwell but is recovered—Mrs Davy expects her Husband to day or to morrow. W. W.

[*M. W. writes*]

Beloved friend, I am so thankful when I am able to rouse my poor dear Husband to take the pen for your sake, and his own for he will pass a happier day, after having been in communion with you—You would be thankful to see how well he works, and to hear how every one expresses the impression that his looks bespeak which convinces me *I* do not deceive myself—and indeed he never makes one *bodily* complaint.

We are thankful too for the release of your suffering from Miss Trevelyon.[2] She was a good woman and is gone to her reward.

[1] Mrs. Cookson had been staying at Mathon.

[2] Unidentified.

When dear Louisa[1] returns will you tell her with my love that I will thank her to call upon Mrs Pollard[2] now and then at her convenience to say how you are. That good Lady has an affec[te] regard for you and always anxious[ly] enquires after your health. The weather was so unfavourable while we were at Keswick that we could not get to see Mrs Myers[3] or Mrs Lightfoot—we called by the way upon Kate[4] and She remained at the Stangers till we left them. She looks and is I think quite well. Cuth's[5] Children have left her for the present—how soon to return I fear to say—their poor weak mother is I believe nearly confined to bed so nervous as not to look at her Children, and Mrs L. has but seen her once since her return several months ago. She has borne another *fine* Child—who is to be *Robert.*

But I shall miss the Post. Dear love to all

ever lovingly y[r]
M Wordsworth

2089. W. W. to DAVID LEITCH[6]

MS. Cornell. Hitherto unpublished.

Friday—8 Dec[br] 1848—

My dear Sir,

You have obliged me much by the attention which you have so readily paid to the little Property at Applethwaite, which as you know is interesting to me far beyond its pecuniary value.

My wishes are that encroachments should be prevented upon what is now Common, and that the Larches in the Plantation should give way to the Oaks wherever the latter are likely to thrive;—and that reasonable repairs when wanted should be made in the Dwelling House or Houses. This, with the repetition of my sincere thanks, is all that I have to say at present.

[1] I. F.'s niece.

[2] Of Bath (see pt. iii, L. 1301).

[3] Wife of the Revd. Frederick Myers (see L. 1487 above).

[4] Kate Southey.

[5] Cuthbert Southey's.

[6] See Ls. 2082 and 2083 above.

Early in spring if our lives are spared and our health continues Mary and I will profit by your hospitality again.

We have no news from this neighbourhood.

Kind love to Mary[1] and yourself in which my Wife joins—

ever faithfully
your *much* obliged
Wm Wordsworth

2090. W. W. to WILLIAM WILKIE COLLINS[2]

MS. Pierpont Morgan Library.
LY iii. 1320.

Rydal Mount, 10th Decr 1848

Dear Sir,

I hope to receive in a few days the Memoir of your Father which you announce as having been left for me at Mr Moxon's—My Son is at present in the south and will bring [it][3] down to me.—It will I am sure interest me in no small degree. The last time I saw your Father was at Rome, the evening before he set out from that place for Naples[4]—

With kind wishes
I remain
My dear Sir
sincerely your's
Wm Wordsworth

[1] Leitch's daughter.

[2] William Wilkie Collins (1824–89), eldest son of the painter who had died in London on 17 Feb. 1847, published *Memoirs of the Life of William Collins, R.A.*, 2 vols., 1848, and wrote for *Household Words* and *All the Year Round* under Dickens's editorship: author of *The Woman in White*, 1860, *The Moonstone*, 1868, etc.

[3] *Word dropped out.*

[4] In 1837. See pt. iii, L. 1137.

2091. W. W. to JOHN GIBSON[1]

Address: John Gibson Esq. Post Office, Whitehaven.
MS. untraced.
LY iii. 1321.

Rydal Mount Dec. 1848.

My dear Sir,

Accept my cordial thanks for the beautiful apples which were received yesterday.

There is a French Poet now living by name Beranger[2] who would do justice to the Poems of Burns as far as that is possible. He is a man of extraordinary genius, and the french language under his management seems equal to any thing which Lyrical Poetry requires.

I remain
my dear Sir
faithfully
your much obliged
Wm. Wordsworth

2092. W. W. to W. W. JNR.

Address: Wm Wordsworth Esq., 25 Norfolk Square, Brighton.
Postmark: (1) 13 Dec. 1848 (2) 14 Dec. 1848.
Stamp: (1) Ambleside (2) Brighton.
MS. WL. Hitherto unpublished.

Rydal
13th Dec^{br} 48—

My dear W^{m},

I see no objection to Mr Ellwood's[3] proposal; presuming that he will put me to no further expense than is absolutely

[1] Postmaster at Whitehaven. De Selincourt notes that Gibson had in his possession a French version of *Burns* by Léon de Wailly (Paris, 1843); W. W.'s letter may refer to some query about the value of this version.

[2] Pierre-Jean de Béranger (1780–1857), author of the immensely popular *Chansons* and satires on Restoration society, who glorified the Napoleonic era and became a Bonapartist deputy in 1848. See also *HCR* ii. 517.

[3] Probably Thomas Ellwood, farmer, of Sockbridge. W. W. continued to oversee the estate after the death of R. W.'s son.

necessary, especially as he must know that I derive no profit whatever from the Sockbridge Estate.

The [? Tracks][1] I have no objection to pay for; and as to the draining I am desirous it should be done *at proper seasons*, whenever it is adviseable.—Dr Davy has just returned, in good health, he wears one of those new fashioned *paletot* overcoats,[2] very light and apparently waterproof—I think it would answer for me to have one if you could bring it. But observe that among the numerous advertisements some are[3] priced *three* guineas, whereas the Doctors only cost one or a pound.

Best love to yourself and Fanny—Pray call at Moxon's he has one book at least for me

Your affectionate Father W W

2093. W. W. to JOHN GIBSON

Address: John Gibson Esqre Post Office, Whitehaven.
MS. untraced.
LY iii. 1321.

Rydal Mount 14th Dec. 1848

My dear Sir,

You have gratified me much by your kind remembrance of me; and I shall be happy to receive whatever you have to send me from your American parcel. Believe me to be my dear Sir

sincerely yours
Wm Wordsworth

2094. W. W. to UNKNOWN CORRESPONDENT

MS. Mrs. Mary Hyde. Hitherto unpublished.

29th Jan^ry^ 1849

Dear Sir,

Be assured I regret much my not being able to comply with your request that I would furnish you with a Libretto for your Oratorio. If I live untill the 7th of next April I shall then enter my

[1] *MS. obscure.*
[2] A loose coat or cloak which became popular in the 1840s.
[3] *Written* a.

80th year, a greater age than any English poet of eminence, with the exception of the Author of the Night Thoughts Dr Young, has attained.

This fact you will not be unwilling to admit is a sufficient excuse for my not venturing on the work which your partial opinion of my fitness for it, induces you to propose to me. Wishing that it may be executed to your liking by some one else, I remain

dear Sir
sincerely yours
Wm Wordsworth

Pray keep clear of Lord Byron.—

2095. W. W. to SIR JOHN TAYLOR COLERIDGE

MS. British Library.
K (—). *LY iii. 1322* (—).

Rydal Mount
19th Febry 1849

Dear Mr Justice Coleridge,

In common with Mrs Arnold and her family, Mrs Wordsworth and I are very sorry that we shall not see you among us:—What a pity that there is not some Power to gag prating and prolix Advocates. I have been led to believe that the more a Council[lor] talks the higher do the common People rate him, whether what he says be good or bad.

It must be gratifying to dear Hartley's[1] Friends, that from the

[1] Hartley Coleridge's health had broken down the previous autumn. 'No doubt the origin of this was owing to his own sad habits which occasioned his being exposed on stormy nights,' M. W. confided to I. F. on 28 Dec. (*Victoria University Library MSS., Toronto*). By Christmas his condition had worsened and on 4 Jan. he seemed to be 'hanging between life and death.' He died on 6 Jan. 1849, and was buried in Grasmere churchyard. 'It soothes me to think,' Sara Coleridge wrote to Edward Coleridge on the 15th, 'that my dear brother the greater part of whose life has been spent in our dear old friends' daily sight, should in death not be parted from them . . . that his remains should rest beside those of dear bright-minded kind-hearted Dora who never mentioned his name but to say something of praise or affection.' And she recalled W. W.'s praise of Hartley during their conversations at Bath in 1847. 'It showed me that he was esteemed in heart by one who knew him well . . . one not too lenient in his moral

beginning of his illness until his decease, every possible care was taken of him. The affectionate kindness of his Hostess and Host[1] was admirable; and for medical advice He had all that could be wished, in frequent, I might say constant attention [from] Mr Fell his old Friend, Dr Green[2] recently from Dublin, Dr Davy and Dr Stolterforth who was 20 years in full practice at Dover. Derwent took away all his Books and papers, and will probably write a Memoir of Him.[3] Before he publishes it, I could wish you to see it that the work might profit by your observations. Hartley used to write a great deal, but rarely, I suppose, finished any thing.[4]

I dare not speak of my departed child further than to thank you in my own name and that of her Mother for the affectionate expression of your sympathy. "Thy Will be done" is perpetually in my thoughts. Upon that rock our consolation is built. May You my dear Friend be supported under all trials, with the blessing of God upon You and Yours—

Believe me

affectionately and faithfully

Your Friend

Wm Wordsworth

P.S. Pray excuse my recurring to what I have said upon Derwent's probable notice of Hartley. His fraternal partiality might, I fear lead him to speak in a tone of unqualified eulogy, which while poor Hartley's irregularities are so fresh in memory had much better be avoided.

judgments.' (*Memoir and Letters of Sara Coleridge*, ii. 154). But see *HCR* ii. 685 and Morley, ii. 680–1, 684, for H. C. R.'s harsher verdict on Hartley's 'worthless life' and 'intense sottishness'.

[1] The Richardsons of the Nab, with whom M. W. had many dealings over the years in trying to sort out Hartley's finances.

[2] Dr. Thomas Green, Hartley's former pupil.

[3] Derwent's memoir, prefixed to his *Poems of Hartley Coleridge*, 2 vols., 1851, contains a detailed account of his last hours and funeral.

[4] Derwent brought out Hartley Coleridge's *Essays and Marginalia* in 1851. Poetry apart, Hartley wrote little in his last years, but he made money from lectures and poetry readings for the Kendal Natural History and Scientific Society. (*Minute Books, Kendal Public Library*).

2096. M. W. to H. C. R.

Endorsed: 24th Feb. 49. Mrs Wordsworth.
MS. Dr. Williams's Library.
Morley, ii. 687.

Rydal Mt
Feb 24th [1849]

My dear Friend

What you speak of in your very interesting letter, as being the '*lowest object*' upon which you treat, i.e. *yourself*, is the one which impels me to take up my lazy pen at once. But before I tell you *Why* I must state that, you prefaced the subject in a way (referring to *Willy* as being best able to appreciate the *importance* of a change in your domicile etc) that made me *at first* ask myself Is he going to commit Matrimony?!! On 2nd thoughts however I remembered the opportunity Wm had of seeing and *feeling* how comfortably you were established with your present Attendants.

But waiving badinage. We enter so anxiously into the matter of your unsettling that Dr and Mrs Davy (who have just been with us) coming in while we were considering the subject, we could not forbear *speaking* of it—At once the Dr suggested, which his wife heartily responded to,—a Person who would be the very man for you—(a 2d James I should say tho' I hope with a better memory) if he should be at liberty—which is doubtful—but the Dr thinks, as you might make the enquiry without much trouble, it would be worth while. The Person in question, and whom he can thoroughly recommend for his faithfulness and trust-worthiness, from a Years experience, when they were together in Constantinople—where he found him competent *he thinks* to be your Attendant in health or in *sickness* should you require such an one. *Mrs* Davy says, when she parted with her Husband on that occasion, she committed him to the care of this Attendant with perfect confidence.—He had been a sergeant in the Army, and left on acct of a hurt in his hand—He is married to a nice sort of person who had lived in a Gentleman's family. Now, the question comes, is this Man at liberty? which is doubtful—but as the Dr says it is worth your while to enquire. He was about to take a house in the precincts of the London University, with an intention to accommodate Students—but if, as is possible, this scheme was not accomplished, the Dr thinks still, he might there be heard of. It would be a mutual accommodation if M[r] *John Bowen* and his wife were to become your Servants—I neglected to enquire if it was when D[r] D was *last in* Town that this arrangement was pending, otherwise I think he scarcely would have mentioned the matter. It will, believe me be a real comfort to us when you are suited with a personal Servant, upon whom you and your friends can depend.

Now dear friend to the other interesting points in your letter—and first I must thank you for your acc[t] of Layard[1]—It is a subject in which we have been deeply interested since M[rs] Austin introduced us to the knowledge of her Nephew; and my Husband has talked and thought more about him than I can well make you understand, since he has been brought before the public—Often and of[t] has he exclaimed 'that fine fellow should have some public honor conferred upon him'—we read the review of his book with avidity, and longed to see his book—and are not without hope, that *in time* we may be able to borrow it, as D[r] Davy tells us that it has been ordered by the *Baroness.*[2]—I do not know if you have heard of such a Person—or seen her Italian Villa at Bowness. So I may tell you that she is one of our Cumberland ladies of fortune who chose, for a title I suppose to bestow herself (I hope not her money) for they are parted upon a German.—Observe this is not the *Polish* Count of Keswick notoriety—The publication I understand is a ten guinea concern—so that this is our only chance of getting a peep at it—at least in this neighbourhood.

'A prating Barrister' as Judge Coleridge expressed himself in a letter to my husband, disappointed us of the pleasure of seeing him at Rydal—which we much regretted on many accounts, especially as a personal interview would have afforded a better opportunity for my husband to impress upon him the desirableness that he, the Judge, should if he had the power to check any rodomontade which may be prepared for publication upon the subject of poor frail Hartley.[3] By note M[r] W. said what Delicacy would allow him to do writing to one of *the Name. I* say, 'the least said is soonest mended'—and I do wish poor dear

[1] The explorer and diplomat (see pt. iii, L. 1331), who published the results of his excavations in *Nineveh and its Remains*, 2 vols., 1849. His uncle, Henry Austen, a solicitor, had called at Rydal Mount with Mrs. Austen in Aug. 1846 (see Morley, ii. 635). See L. 2076 above and L. 2100 below.

[2] Possibly Baroness Bysham, whose husband called at Rydal Mount in summer 1846 (*RMVB*).

[3] See previous letter.

indefatigable Sara would let her Father's character rest.[1] Surely that great spirit has left sufficient to gratify the craving for literary fame in any one, without that dear Creature worrying her brain in her endeavours to increase, or justify it—which with all her pains she will never accomplish. I cannot imagine any one to have sent the paragraph you allude to to the Atheneem.—except D.[2] himself—and he did speak to me of his impressions on the day of the funeral in a strain that might have produced this folly—Quillinan at once fixed it upon D.

A report of dear Mrs Clarkson is always what I look for in your letters, and I rejoice to find that dear friend still retains her animated powers to converse upon the treasured subject. But we cannot but grieve to see her former steady hand so much shaken. Our tenderest love to her when you write or see her.

And now to speak of ourselves, and the 'goings-on in the Valley'. Of our *personal selves* I may reply to your question in the words of an old Dalesman 'We're varra well o' ourselves, but its no' but' rhewmatis'—The fact is, it will be a fortnight tomorrow since, after attending our Chapel twice—the rainy weather having caused it to be unusually damp—my husband was suddenly seized by lumbago—not of the worst kind, but sufficient to have deprived him, (without *much pain*) of being able to move, hence he has been almost confined to the house—and I am only thankful that this has not been attended with worse consequences—I hope it is now going off, and, if we could have a little more warm sunshine, in a few days the inconvenience will pass away. He is now walking upon the Terrace with my Sister Hutchinson who is with us from Mathon—I too have been a little plagued with the rheumatism—but this is no novelty—and of little consequence. Our dear Sister is in her usual way, no change of weather makes any change in her.[3]

Of your friends in the *Valley*—to remember them all I must

[1] Sara Coleridge published S. T. C.'s *Notes and Lectures on Shakespeare* this year.

[2] Derwent Coleridge. 'Derwent apparently fosters a diseased impression of the extent of Hartley's poetical and philosophising powers', H. C. R. wrote to I. F. on 15 Jan. 'But this, I am told, is a family weakness'. (Morley, ii. 686).

[3] 'Dear Mrs Wordsworth is what she always was', H. C. R. wrote after his Christmas visit to Rydal Mount. '—I see no change in her, but that the wrinkles of her careworn countenance are somewhat deeper. Poor Miss W: I thought sunk still deeper in insensibility . . .' (Morley, ii.685).

begin to speak of good Mrs Fletcher—who is left at one extreme point—to the care of her Son Angus,[1] and a Miss Crake (I know not if she was here before you left us) a *Border* friend I believe. Lady Richardson, with her Children who were at Lancrigg, and expecting to winter with her Mother, having found it necessary to join her Husband's eldest daughter at Haslem,[2] whither *she* had been previously sent to be under medical and surgical skill. The dear old Lady is well and visiting her friends and dispensing hospitality as usual. Mrs H.[3] and I dined at Lancrygg one day—where by accident we found Miss M.[4] to whom it was a treat to my sister to have seen.—She was in her unfailing good spirits, talking of her Farm her building schemes etc etc—

Lady F. and Mrs L.[5] we have scarcely seen or heard of since you saw them—but I believe they are well as Mrs L. always is when stone and mortar occupy her thoughts—her Companion is ever happy.

The Cooksons,—some of whom we see almost daily—dear Hannah is now with her B^r^ on Highbury Terrace, and Mary returned home—The only change in that establish^t^—The Flemings[6] are at Bath—Mrs Arnold and her daughters all well, cheared occasionally—frequently I may say, by interesting details from her absent Sons. And your report of her daughter, the widowed Mary[7] agrees with her own. D^r^ and Mrs Davy being restored to each other, seem as happy as a new married Pair and *her* health is perfectly reestablished—Poor Mrs Roughsedge does not look so well as we should like to see her—and her weakness confines her to her *solitary* home, for her husband, when his Gout permits him to move, see-saws to and fro like a weaver's shuttle, between Beetham and Fox Ghyll—Mr Carr and his Ladies are in statu quo—the Lutwidges[8] are in Bath—and now I think I have traversed the Valley and mentioned all I can tell you of your old friends Q. you hear from himself, And the thought of Bath reminds me that you will be glad to hear that our Beloved Miss F. is much better than she herself ever expected to be after the severe attacks of cold which

[1] See L. 2025 above.

[2] The Royal Naval Hospital, Haslar, Gosport (founded 1746), where Sir John Richardson had been physician since 1838.

[3] Mary Hutchinson.

[4] Martineau.

[5] Lady Farquhar and Mrs. Luff.

[6] Fletcher Fleming, curate of Rydal, and his wife.

[7] Mrs. Aldred Twining.

[8] See L. 1369 above.

followed so quickly upon each other in the Autumn. She is now alone at Kelston Knoll. Her brother, and niece (who is a comfort to her) being in Bath but often with her during the absence of M^rs^ and Miss Tudor.

You do not speak of your own health—nor particularly of that of your *Brother's* so that I trust all is well with you. And that you may both continue to be so, and that you may not be annoyed with this, I fear wearisome, letter, is my sincere wish—with our united affectionate remembrances to all friends who enquire for us—retaining a double portion to yourself, ever believe me to be your sincere and obliged friend

M. Wordsworth

Excuse all blots and blunders for I am become an awkard blind body—Even as you can say a careless one

P.S Mrs Arnold says that H.M.[1] had made some speech or observations *on the funeral* which tho' not from Miss M. herself had appeared in print—so they may be what you mention from the Athenæum

2097. W. W. to DAVID LEITCH

MS. WL. (Moorsom Papers).

Rydal Mount
28th Feb^ry^ 1849

My dear Sir,

I feel much obliged by your taking the trouble to cast a look upon my little Plantation.[2] It is a place in which I am interested far beyond its pecuniary value; and I should like to have it possessed by some one or other of my family for generations to come.

Mrs Wordsworth and I and our Sister Mrs Hutchinson are going to Carlisle by way of Brigham; but we shall not have time to see you and Mary, as we *must* see Miss Southey; we shall visit you later in the Spring; as that may be somewhat too late for cutting the oaks, I should be glad to refer the matter entirely to your judgement, and would thank you to give such directions as you may think proper.—

[1] Harriet Martineau.

[2] At Applethwaite. See L. 2082 above.

My Sister continues as well as usual, and we all join in love to you and Mary.

Believe me my dear Sir faithfully your much obliged

William Wordsworth

2098. W. W. to ROBERT PERCEVAL GRAVES

MS. untraced.
William Archer Butler, Sermons Doctrinal and Practical, 1849, p. xxxv (—).

[Mar. 1849]

. . . I am very glad to learn that a volume of sermons from our lamented friend, Professor Butler,[1] is about to be published, with a sketch of his life. From what I have seen of him and his writings, I feel convinced that anything from his pen must be valued by the judicious, and I hope that this publication will soon be followed by his other theological and philosophical works, as well as by any poems that he may have left in manuscript. . . .

2099. W. W. to CHARLES GRAY[2]

Address: Capt Charles Gray RM.
MS. National Library of Scotland. Hitherto unpublished.

16th March 1849

Dear Sir,

Pray accept my thanks for your Tribute to the memory of Burns.[3]

Your verses are animated by a right feeling of the subject, and in my judgement they do their author no little credit.

I am old enough, had accidents favored, to have known Burns; but it was not my fortune ever to have seen him, which I cannot but regret, as I was old enough some years before he died, to have had a lively sympathy with his extraordinary genius.

[1] See L. 1816 above.

[2] Charles Gray (1782–1851), Captain in the Royal Marines, Scottish poet and song-writer: at this time living in retirement in Edinburgh.

[3] 'Sketches of Scottish Poets: Burns', *Lays and Lyrics*, 1841, p. 98.

Believe me to be with good wishes for your health and happiness,

your obliged
Wm Wordsworth

PS. I write from my Son's House Carlisle.

2100. M. W. to H. C. R.

Endorsed: *28 March. 49. Mrs Wordsworth.*
MS. Dr. Williams's Library.
Morley, ii. 692.

28 March [1849] Rydal.

My dear Friend

Before attending to the number of calls from my pen, I must write a line to you to say that on our return home[1] *last evening* we found among other things a Copy of Nineveh,[2] presented to my Husband by that kind Lady Mrs Austin in the name of her Nephew.—This she modestly tells us she is *encouraged* to do, from the manner in which you mentioned to her our wish to see the Book. Thanks for this great attention must be given by my Husband himself—but I must lose no time in making known to you that we have received this valuable gift, to prevent your forwarding the copy you had kindly *provided* for us—and for which nevertheless, we are at the same time as grateful to you as if we have received it Tired and cold stri[c]ken as I was in coming over Kirkstone on such a bitter day in our open carriage I could not refrain from beginning to read the book, and got thro' the preceding pages and the first Chapter with much interest—reading aloud to my husband—who was more oppressed than myself *with cold*—after my Sister[3] had taken *hers* to bed:—and, after more pressing duties are gone thro' we shall all return to the book with impatience today.

We left Willie and his Wife on Monday morn^g^—she remarkably well—he poor fellow, neither quite well in health or spirits. He is more cast down by the prospects before him than a less anxious temper would be—but truly his case is a hard one—and

[1] W. W. and M. W. had been on a round of family visits at Carlisle and Brigham (see *MW*, pp. 308–9).

[2] Layard's *Nineveh and its Remains* (see L. 2096 above).

[3] Mary Hutchinson.

I think he feels the '*indignity*', as he calls it, with which the higher powers are treating their faithful S^{t} than the loss of income which if the change is to take place must entirely alter his arrangements—The notion of the Office to be placed under the supervision of the 'Ganger'[1] galls him. Without any official notice the head Office has already *advertised* in the newspapers some part of what has been the Stamp-distributors duty to be removed to the Excise department.[2]—After 20 years devotion to the Service—and that the prime of his life W^{m} feels this to be unjust—If no remunerating plan lurks behind of which he has no hope. But why should I write this to you—merely because I feel you are interested in what concerns him

And now I must not begin with any other subject—or I shall be belated.

We have found our dear Sister as well as usual—but have not seen the Qs nor any one else since our arrival.

God bless you my dear friend, believe me with kindest remembrances and regards for all ever

Your obliged and affec.
M. Wordsworth

We passed Monday night with some relatives at *Penrith*[3]—and had an opportunity of renewing our notices, and haunts of the days of our Youth.

[1] An overseer in charge of a gang of workers, a term first recorded in *O.E.D.* this year.

[2] Willy W.'s prospects in the Stamp Office were again giving cause for concern, as W. W.'s letters to Peel later this year testify (see Ls. 2104, 2106 and 2108 below).

[3] M. W. spent the first eighteen years of her life at Penrith before moving to Sockburn in 1788 (see *EY* p. 31). The relatives she refers to in this letter cannot be identified with any certainty, but they were perhaps the descendants of Elizabeth Robinson, M. W.'s great aunt on the 'Monkhouse' side, who were in business in Penrith in 1850. See also L. 2114 below.

2101. W. W. to THE EIGHTH DUKE OF ARGYLL[1]

MS. The Duke of Argyll. Hitherto unpublished.

Rydal Mount
5th April 1849.

My dear Lord Duke,

I have transcribed with much pleasure the Sonnet according to your Grace's wishes,[2] and feel myself not a little honored by the Duchess requesting such a memorial of me, which perhaps her Grace may value more, as having been composed, extempore, and upon being told that the Transcriber was on the point of entering the eightieth year of his age.

Mrs Wordsworth and I are gratified by the expression of your wish, that we should visit you, a pleasure which at our age we dare scarcely calculate upon.

Begging you and the Duchess to accept our best wish. I have the honor to be

my dear Duke
faithfully yours
William Wordsworth

[1] George Douglas Campbell, 8th Duke of Argyll (1823–1900), of Inveraray Castle, politician and scientist: Lord Privy Seal under Aberdeen and Palmerston, and Secretary for India under Gladstone (1868): author of *Presbytery Examined: An Essay, critical and historical, on the Ecclesiastical History of Scotland since the Reformation*, 1848. He married (1844) Lady Elizabeth Leveson-Gower (d. 1878), eldest daughter of the 2nd Duke of Sutherland (see pt. iii, L. 1131), whom W. W. already knew from his visits to Stafford House in London, and the couple visited Rydal Mount in Sept. 1848. 'We have long wished for this pleasure, and it will be a great one . . .', the Duchess of Argyll had written from Trentham on 1 Sept.; and a week later the Duke sent his old tutor J. S. Howson, afterwards Dean of Chester, an account of their meeting with W. W. and D. W. and the poet's moving recitation of *Tintern Abbey*. The Duke had now written to W. W. on 2 Apr., 1849, recalling their previous visit, and asking for the poet's autograph. (*WL MSS.*). See also his *Autobiography and Memoirs*, 2 vols., 1906, edited by his second wife.

[2] See next letter.

2102. W. W. to THE EIGHTH DUKE OF ARGYLL

MS. The Duke of Argyll. Hitherto unpublished.

Rydal Mount
6th April 1849.

My dear Duke

On referring to your Grace's Letter I find that I made a mistake in not transcribing the Sonnet that you made choice of; which I now beg to enclose.[1]

I have the honor to be
faithfully
Your Grace's
much obliged Servnt
William Wordsworth

[*Enclosed, in W. W.'s hand, is* Scorn not the Sonnet. . . , *as in PW iii. 20.*]

2103. W.W. to ISABELLA FENWICK

MS. WL.
LY iii. 1323.

7th April 1849

I was sitting down to write to you, my beloved Friend, a few lines upon my entering, this day, my eightieth year, when your affectionate Letter was brought me. Pray accept my heart-felt thanks for the good wishes which it breathes. I wish I could add that I was more at ease in the recesses of my own nature, but God's will be done.

It will be a great comfort to us to have you again under our roof.

We are all deeply impressed by Baron Rolfe's[2] conduct in the course of his trial of that audacious Criminal, Rush.[3] What a

[1] The Duke replied on 7 Apr.: 'You have lived to see the birth and growth of a generation whose mind has been widely and deeply influenced by yr own. This is given to few: But it is given to fewer still to feel, as assuredly you may feel that this influence has been as *good* as it has been powerful.' (*WL MSS.*)

[2] The judge (see pt. i, L. 279).

[3] Isaac Jermy (1789–1848), Recorder of Norwich, had inherited the disputed property of Stanfield Hall, nr. Wymondham. On 28 Nov. 1848 John Blomfield

miserable Man must he be, if he has a grain of human feeling in his composition.

The Inmates of this House, Mrs Hutchinson, Wm and Fanny included, are all well.

I now give up my pen, with overflowing Love, to dear Mary,

most affectionately
yours
Wm Wordsworth

2104. W. W. to SIR ROBERT PEEL

MS. British Library. Hitherto unpublished.

Rydal Mount
7th April 1849

Dear Sir Robert,

Allow me to return my sincere thanks for your prompt and very friendly reply to my Letter.[1] I have taken the liberty of acting upon your suggestion, and have written to Sir Charles Wood,[2] though I have not the Honor of being known to Him.—

To you, dear Sir Robert, I may say that my Son, for his long service, has a perfect Knowledge of the duties of the Stamp Office; yet, should no vacancy occur, that might be offered to Him in *that* Department He would not object to any other, for which he might feel himself qualified, or to be employed in a more private capacity.

I cannot conclude without expressing how much I am gratified by your favorable opinion of the tendency of my

Rush, a tenant farmer on the estate, who had sided with the rival claimants, shot Jermy in the porch of the Hall, then entered the house, shot Jermy's son Isaac, and wounded the latter's wife and maid. Rush was tried at the Shire Hall, Norwich, on 29 Mar. 1849, convicted, and publicly hanged in front of the Castle on 14 Apr. The trial lasted six days, and excited considerable public interest.

[1] About Willy W.'s prospects (see L. 2100 above).

[2] Sir Charles Wood, 3rd Bart., 1st Viscount Halifax (1800–85), Chancellor of the Exchequer from 1846: President of the Board of Control under Aberdeen, First Lord of the Admiralty, and later Secretary for India, under Palmerston. He replied on 8 Apr.: 'In all the arrangements however advantageous they may ultimately be to the public, care has been taken of the existing holders of office, and I am not aware of any contemplated change, not conceived in the same spirit.' (*WL MSS.*)

writings.[1] Language to this effect from such a quarter cannot but be a comfort to one who this day enters upon his eightieth year—

I have the honor to be, dear Sir Robert
faithfully your much obliged
Wm Wordsworth

2105. W. W. to THE SECRETARY OF THE WINDERMERE LODGE SOCIETY

MS. Cornell. Hitherto unpublished.

Rydal Mount
12th April 1849

Mr Wordsworth returns thanks to the Members of the Windermere Lodge Society, and as he is not in the habit of attending public Dinners He begs to be excused accepting their kind invitation.

2106. W. W. to SIR ROBERT PEEL

MS. British Library. Hitherto unpublished.

Rydal Mount Ambleside
13th April 1849

Dear Sir Robert,

Many thanks for your last kind Letter enclosing a communication from Sir Charles Wood[2] which I beg leave to return.

Sir Charles thinks that the apprehensions of my Son in regard to the changes about to take place in the Stamp-office are without sufficient foundation.—His authority was a report from a Brother-distributor who had waited upon one of the Commis-

[1] Peel had written on 5 Apr. to explain that the nomination of W. W. jnr. to succeed his father in the Distributorship had not been influenced by 'ordinary' motives, but was 'a public Recognition of your own Services to the State in having employed the highest intellectual Powers in inculcating the Truths—and encouraging the Practices, which give Stability to Christian Communities.' (*WL MSS.*)

[2] Chancellor of the Exchequer. See L. 2104 above.

sioners and was told by Him that the Article in the Times was correct.

I have the honor to be, dear Sir Robert

faithfully your very much obliged

Wm Wordsworth

2107. W. W. to JOHN ADAMSON[1]

Address: To John Adamson, Newcastle-on-Tyne.
MS. Cornell transcript. Hitherto unpublished.

Rydal Mount
Ambleside.
15th May 1849.

Dear Sir,

Allow me to assure you of my great regret at the calamity which has befallen you in the destruction of your rare and choice library by fire.[2] The Sonnet which you have done me the favour to send me on the subject is expressive of a resignation which does you much honour under so grievous a trial.

Believe me dear Sir, yours faithfully

William Wordsworth

[1] John Adamson, F.S.A. (1787–1855), bibliophile: author of *Memoirs of Camoens*, 2 vols., 1820, and co-author, with Richard Charles Coxe (see L. 1869 above), of *Ballads from the Portuguese*, 1846. He was a friend of E. Q.'s, and provided notes for his translation of *The Lusiads*, Bks. i–v, published posthumously in 1853. W. W. had presumably met Adamson during one of his visits to Newcastle, and possessed several of his volumes (see *R.M.Cat.*, nos. 514, 531). For Adamson's relations with Southey, see Curry, i. 481.

[2] On 16 Apr.

2108. W. W. to SIR ROBERT PEEL

MS. Alan G. Hill. Hitherto unpublished.

7th June [1849]
St James's Mathon[1]
near Great Malvern.

Dear Sir Robert,

My Son, not taking the liberty to intrude upon you without my intervention has forwarded to me a memorial which, by the advice of the Chancellor of the Exr[2] (as shewn in the printed Letter enclosed) to his Brother Distributors He has prepared to be presented to the Lords of the Treasury.—But my Son having through me in the first instance communicated with you, and received your friendly advice is unwilling to act in any manner without your approbation,—I therefore, though very unwilling to trouble you, feel obliged once more to solicit your opinion whether the enclosed memorial should be presented, and if so, in what manner.

The accompanying notes from Sir Charles Wood to myself I had the pleasure to receive in consequence of the interest you had kindly expressed to him in this matter.

Thanking you, once more, sincerely for your good offices upon this occasion, I have the honor to remain, dear Sir Robert,

faithfully your much obliged
William Wordsworth

[1] W. W. and M. W. were spending the month with the Hutchinsons at Mathon. H. C. R. and Moxon joined them at Malvern, 21–26 June, where I. F. was also staying. See *HCR* ii. 690–1; *MW*, pp. 310–11, and Morley, ii. 698.

[2] Sir Charles Wood (see L. 2104 above).

2109. W. W. to JAMES CUMMING

Address: James E. Cumming, Esq., Sec^ry Cons. Club, Margaret Street, Greenock.
Stamp: (1) Birmingham (2) Greenock.
MS. National Library of Scotland. Hitherto unpublished.

St. James's Mathon
Near Great Malvern
18 June 1849

Sir,

The Letter which you have honoured me with has followed me from Rydal to this Place. In reply to the proposal which it communicates of the University of Glasgow electing me an honorary Member of their Body, I have to say that it will give me much pleasure to be so distinguished.

I have the honor to be
dear Sir
Your much obliged
William Wordsworth

2110. W. W. to EDWARD MOXON

MS. Cornell. Hitherto unpublished.

[*In M. W.'s hand*]

[Mathon]
19th June [1849]

Dear Mr Moxon,

As you kindly ask if there is "any thing else you can bring for us," I have ventured to put the Question to our dear friend Miss Fenwick who will be much obliged to you to procure for her at trade price a little book lately published by Seeley *A Commentary of the readings of the New Testament etc* by Lady Wake.[1] Also Archdeacon Wilberforce on the Atonement[2] and if there is, in

[1] Charlotte Murdoch, Lady Wake, *A Simple Commentary of the New Testament . . . in a Harmony of the Four Gospels*, 1849.

[2] R. I. Wilberforce (see L. 1633 above) did not write on the Atonement as such. The reference is presumably to his *Doctrine of Holy Baptism*, 1849.

print, an *Abridgement* of Calamy[1]—these two latter works Miss F. intends as a present to my Nephew, the Young Clergyman, with whom his Parents and sisters live—and where we are now staying, and where we shall be glad to see you: The little book is for the use of my Nieces[2] in their little School. I mention these particulars to shew you I do not trouble you in an idle cause.

With all good wishes believe me to be sincerely

yours — [*signed*] Wm Wordsworth

My Sister will wish to discharge her debt which *thro' me* is due to You—for Manning's Sermons[3] and Southey's Poems in double Column[4]—So please be prepared to tell her the costs as also that of the books I have *now* mentioned. The book on the Apocalipse[5] is for *ourselves*

2111. W. W. to FREDERICK WESTLEY

MS. Pierpont Morgan Library.
LY iii. 1326.

[? Summer 1849][6]

Dear Mr Westley,

We are glad to learn that you are coming among us;—and thank you for your offers of bringing down any parcel for us. I did order lately a few copies of my Vol: to be sent from Mr Moxon's; but I believe it will be already on its way; nevertheless

[1] Edmund Calamy (1671–1732), historian of Nonconformity, particularly in his *Abridgement of Baxter's History*, in which he listed the ministers ejected from the Church of England by the Act of Uniformity (1662), including his own grandfather Edmund Calamy, 'the Elder' (1600–66).

[2] Ebba and Sarah Hutchinson.

[3] 4 vols., 1842–50. Henry Edward Manning (1808–92), later Cardinal Archbishop of Westminster (1865), was Archdeacon of Chichester from 1841, a Tractarian sympathiser, and acknowledged leader of the high-church party after Newman's secession. He left the Anglican Church in 1851 after the Gorham Judgement, becoming an ardent ultramontane Catholic and advocate of Papal Infallibility and the Temporal Power at the time of the Vatican Council (1869–70).

[4] The one-volume edition of 1845.

[5] C. W. jnr.'s Hulsean Lectures at Cambridge *On the Apocalypse* (1848).

[6] Dated 1849 in a later hand.

I should be obliged if you would call, and take charge of any thing that might happen to be waiting for us.

Believe me,
my dear Sir
faithfully yours
Wm Wordsworth

Mrs W desires her kind remembrances.

2112. W. W. to JOHN KENYON

MS. Mr. W. Hugh Peal. Hitherto unpublished.

Rydal Mount
July 1st 1849—

Dear Mr Kenyon,

Through the hands of our common Friend Mr Robinson I had the pleasure of receiving your very acceptable present—the Volume of your Poems,[1] which is got up in a manner that does credit to the Publisher. We arrived here late on Saturday evening after an absence of six weeks among our Relatives and Friends in Herefordshire. A mournful return it is to this place, but upon that sorrow I must not dwell. May God give us strength to support our grievous and irreparable loss with resignation to his Will. It is not long that Persons in their 80th year can have to bear these trials.—

With every good wish, I remain dear Mr Kenyon

faithfully yours
Wm Wordsworth

2113. W. W. to C. W. JNR.

MS. British Library. Hitherto unpublished.

[early July 1849]

My dear Nephew,

Your letter with its enclosure has been forwarded to me from Mathon, as we do not leave Rydal 'till the 21st.[2] Your Friend is

[1] *A Day at Tivoli: with other verses*, 1849, dedicated to Elizabeth and Robert Browning, and published by Longmans.

[2] To visit the Stangers at Keswick (see Morley, ii. 703).

quite at liberty to make use of my Poems, only it will be proper to apprise Mr Moxon that he has my consent to do so, and to request *his* as He has an interest in the book—

We have now received your Lectures upon the Apocalypse,[1] and have commenced reading them, doubting not that we shall be both interested and pleased.

We have no intention to visit London and therefore cannot profit by your kind invitation. Miss Fenwick . . .

[*cetera desunt*]

2114. W. W. to EDWARD MOXON

MS. untraced.
Bookseller's Catalogue. LY iii. 1324.

July 7th, 1849

Dear Mr Moxon,

I have to acknowledge the receipt of the Laureate's Salary, for which I thank you.

We arrived safely at home and found all well on Sat. even^g^, leaving all well at Mathon, but alas my Nephew Thos. (who with his wife and babe[2] had arrived there on the day you left) reached Rydal on the Monday even^g^ with the sorrowful intelligence of the sudden death of my much beloved Brother, his Father, who having attended Church twice and received from the hands of his two Sons the holy Communion the previous day, went to bed in his usual spirits (his last act being to pat his little grandson) and fell asleep—waked at 2 o'clock and feeling unwell rang his bell which of course brought his family instantly to him. Before or about 3 o'clock he was no more!

This brief detail to you who so lately saw my Brother[3] cannot but be interesting, and you will be able to judge of our feelings on the astounding announcement, to me especially who for many years before our several marriages was his sole companion —we two out of a large family left by our parents, lived

[1] See L. 2110 above.

[2] Thomas Hutchinson, jnr. (see pt. ii, L. 670) had married Sarah Gill (1820–1905), and their first child, also Thomas (1848–1916), had been born the previous August.

[3] At Malvern.

together.[1] Mrs Wordsworth joins in best regards. Your parcel arrived before it was expected at Mathon. Will you please discharge the enclosed bill.

Ever yours sincerely
W. Wordsworth.

2115. W. W. to CHARLES CALLAHAN PERKINS[2]

Address: Charles C. Perkins Esq[re], care of Mess[rs] Greeve and Co, 20, Place St George, Paris—
Postmark: 17 July 1849.
Stamp: (1) Ambleside (2) Boulogne.
MS. Yale University Library. Hitherto unpublished.

Rydal Mount, near Ambleside.
17th July 1849.

Dear Sir,

You are quite at liberty to publish the little Poem which you name, or any other of my smaller pieces which you may think suitable to your purpose. I shall be happy to receive the Collection from your hands—

Bishop Doane[3] I greatly respect, and have been always truly glad to see him.—I have the satisfaction of receiving frequent communications from him.—

Your Work if forwarded to Mr Moxon 44 Dover Street will be duly received by me.—

I have the honor to be Dear Sir
your much obliged
William Wordsworth

[1] A puzzling statement as it stands, and not strictly speaking correct. If written by M. W., however, it would accurately reflect *her* early relations with Thomas Hutchinson, parallelling similar remarks elsewhere (see *MW*, p. 154). In the continuing absence of the MS., certainty is impossible; but it seems likely that this sentence was written in by her *in propria persona* (as was occasionally her practice), and that the interpolation was not recognised when the transcription was made.

[2] Charles Callahan Perkins (1823–86), Boston art critic and musician, studied in Rome, Paris, and Leipzig, and founded the Massachusetts School of Art and Boston Museum of Fine Arts: author of *Tuscan Sculptors*, 1864, *Italian Sculptors*, 1868, and numerous other works. The projected volume, mentioned below, is unidentified.

[3] See L. 1536 above.

Two of my Poems are addressed to the Sky-lark.[1] The one ending,

'True to the kindred points of heaven and home'

is very much the best.—

2116. W. W. to UNKNOWN CORRESPONDENT

MS. Cornell. Hitherto unpublished.

Rydal Mount
4th Augst 1849

Dear Sir

Absence from home prevented my receiving your Letter as soon as I should otherwise have done. I now write to assure you that you are quite at Liberty to take such Extracts from my Poems as may best suit your purpose; only as Mr Moxon 4 Dover Street my Publishers has a joint pecuniary interest in the Works it will be proper to ask his consent, informing Him that I have given mine.

I have the honor to be
dear Sir
sincerely yours
William Wordsworth[2]

[1] See *PW* ii. 141, 266.

[2] Shortly after this Elizabeth Sewell (1815–1906), sister of William Sewell (see L. 1458 above), and author of *Amy Herbert* (1844), visited Rydal Mount with an introduction from I. F. She was accompanied by Captain and Lady Jane Swinburne with their son Algernon, then aged 12. See *Autobiography of Elizabeth M. Sewell*, ed. Eleanor L. Sewell, 1907, pp. 106–10.

2117. W. W. to [?] EARL GREY[1]

Endorsed: 7 Sept 1849. Mr. Wordsworth. To defer Grandson's Exam. Ans 13.
Stamp: Master General-Ordinance. Received Sep. 8 1849.
MS. Cornell.
LY iii. 1324.

Rydal Mount
Ambleside
7th Septr 1849

My Lord

I much regret being obliged once again to throw myself upon your good offices by requesting you, if it be possible, to gain for my Grandson[2] the indulgence of the Master-general of the ordinance to allow his examination to be deferred untill May next. For his not being sufficiently prepared to present himself in November, I blame, as much as his own slackness, his Father, whose objection to the 'cramming' system has prevented the Youth from going to Woolwich; but now as the time of trial approaches, we find, unless the indulgence I solicit be granted that He has forfeited the hope of being admitted a Member of the College, which we shall much regret, He being a fine spirited Youth, and I doubt not would make a good Soldier. My Grandson will not have completed his sixteenth year untill the end of next July. If his appearance can be dispensed with till May next, without forfeiting his chance of admission, He will be sent without delay to one of the Woolwich Schools, and I trust that He may do himself credit at the following examination.

Begging You to excuse this long Letter I remain my Lord, very sincerely your Lordship's

obliged Servt
Wm Wordsworth[3]

[1] Sir Henry George Grey, 3rd Earl Grey (1802–94), Secretary for War and the Colonies, 1846–52.

[2] Henry.

[3] *The letter is further endorsed in pencil*: Mr Wordsworth was called up for the Examination in May last, and allowed to defer. He now asks for a second postponement; the rule is to grant only one, except in the case of proved Sickness: the Writer is Wordsworth the Poet. *And in another hand*: If the precedent is not absolutely inadmissible, let the request be complied with. [*This is initialled* R.]

2118. W. W. to ISABELLA FENWICK

MS. WL. Hitherto unpublished.

[Autumn 1849]

It seems a long time, my beloved Friend, since I wrote to you, and I now sit down with little or nothing to say but what your own heart and mind would suggest. Our grandson Henry is about to start for Woolwich, [*M. W. adds*: or rather to an establishment to *prepare* for his examination at Woolwich which has kindly be[en] suspended till next May.[1] Shooters Hill is the place to which he goes meanwhile, I believe] and though He is not very bookish we trust He will do well. His Sister goes to Edinburgh [*M. W. adds*: on the 29—they are both here at present] and we have good hopes of Her. Of Wm who is at Sedbergh we hear now and then, and nothing amiss. We have seen more of Mr Quillinan lately. As Mr Moxon desires to strike off another thousand copies of the double column edition of my Poems[2] [*M. W. adds*: Poems in a small Ed^n as you know was proposed to us at Mathon] Mr Q. is kindly engaged in correcting any mistakes (they are almost exclusively of Punctuation) which exist in the present.

We have had a very kind congratulatory letter from Lady Rolfe upon the birth of our Grand-daughter[3] at Carlisle. Will you be so good as to thank [her] for it when you write to Her. We have also had a similar from Mrs Wren Hoskyns[4] upon the same event. We are looking for Mrs Arnold's return with her Daughters. It will be some time before they are quiet at Foxhow as she expects a large influx of visitors on her arrival. Mrs. Fletcher offers her House to be let again for the Winter, and Mrs. Preston's much improved Cottage and grounds under Loughrigg may be had for any length of time; as she is foolish enough to be married tomorrow to Mr Hudson, Bookseller at Kendal. He is a respectable man, but has two children not overwise, we hear; therefore her Mother, good Mrs Nicholson, and I think she might have passed her widowhood with more satisfaction in her pleasant Habitation under Loughrigg—We should very much like to hear something of your Brother and your Niece and the

[1] See previous letter.

[2] This was a reissue of the one-volume edition of 1845.

[3] i.e. W. W. jnr.'s first child, Mary Louisa (1849–1906).

[4] See L. 2016 above.

rest of your dear Friends. W^{m} and Fanny mean to call their Daughter, Mary Louisa, after the two Grandmothers; but we don't like the combination of names. As the Child is a Daughter we think the maternal grandmother's name the most proper.

Farewell my beloved Friend
ever faithfully yours
Wm Wordsworth

[*M. W. adds*]

Dearest Friend our hearts would say much more than this sheet contains—but you feel with us—I am just prevailing upon my Husband to go to look at Mr Johnstone's[1] new house, on the other side of Grasmere Lake—the family have been 3 months there and he has not had the courage to look at these old friends yet—and they depart on Sat: next. Henry will travel with them. You remember whom I mean—Mr J. long ago curate of Grasmere.

2119. W. W. to EDWARD MOXON

MS. Henry E. Huntington Library.
LY iii. 1325.

8th Octr 1849

Dear Mr Moxon

Your communications were regularly received, and I thank you for them. When you see Dr Wordsworth or any of his family pray give my love to them.

ever with very kind regards to yourself Mrs Moxon and your Sister

I remain
faithfully yours
Wm Wordsworth

We should be very glad to see you here whenever it happens to suit you.

[1] The Revd. William Johnson (see pt. i, L. 1, and Morley, ii. 702–4). W. W. also saw Francis Merewether again this summer, and met Elizabeth Gaskell the novelist.

2120. W. W. to UNKNOWN CORRESPONDENT[1]

MS. University Library, Davis, California. Hitherto unpublished.

[*In John Carter's hand*]

Rydal Mount
25 Octr 1849

Dear Sir,

I beg to acknowledge the receipt of your letter of yesterday enclosing a Div^{d} Warrant for Seven Pounds 16/7 on the life of Mr. Wright[2] for Annuity due on the 5 July last.

I am, dear Sir,
Yours very truly,
[*signed*] William Wordsworth

[*W. W. adds*]

I am very much obliged by your long-continued kind attention to my little concerns. Hoping that yourself and family are in good health I remain

faithfully yours
W. W—

2121. M. W. to EDWARD MOXON

MS. untraced.
K.

Rydal Mount, Oct. 29, 1849

Dear Mr Moxon,

Will you thank Mrs. Moxon for her kind note?

I write to you, having seen that the first volume of Mr. Southey's letters will be published on the 1st (and also having seen that your new edition of Mr. W's poems[3] will be out on that day, which will cause you to be sending a parcel)—I write to beg that you will procure us a copy of that work, and likewise a copy of the "Notes" from Mr Southey's Place book,[4] which I

[1] Perhaps William Bell (see L. 2036 above).

[2] Unidentified.

[3] 6 vols., 1849–50, the last edition to appear under W. W.'s personal supervision.

[4] *Common-Place Book*, ed. J. W. Warter, 4 vols., 1849–51.

suppose has been published some time. And by the same parcel send us half a dozen copies of the selections from Mr. W's poems.[1]

The time is drawing on for our good friend Mr Robinson's annual visit to us,[2] which we always look forward to with much pleasure.

Cannot you make a Christmas holiday also and accompany him? You know we should be glad to see you, and a little of your company would be salutary to my husband. He is, thank God, quite well, and joins me in best regards to you and yours.

Believe me always, dear Mr Moxon, to be

Sincerely yours,
M. Wordsworth.

2122. W. W. to EDWARD MOXON

MS. Henry E. Huntington Library. Hitherto unpublished.

[*In John Carter's hand*]

Rydal Mount
31 Octr 1849.

Dear Mr Moxon,

Thank you for the two Books received yesterday. We are all pleased with their appearance, and presume that they are correctly printed.

Pray send us down a dozen copies of each, and also a dozen Copies of the *Excursion*,[3] in addition to the Books named by Mrs Wordsworth on Monday.[4]

With kind remembrances from Mrs Wordsworth and myself to Mrs Moxon and your Sister,

I am Dear Mr Moxon
v^y faithfully y^rs
[*signed*] William Wordsworth

[*W. W. adds*]

We should be very glad to see you here whenever it might suit you.—

[1] Burns's Selection (1843), reissued by Moxon (see L. 1760 above).

[2] Owing to a carbuncle, H. C. R. had to cancel his visit this year.

[3] The reissue (1847) of the 1836 stereotype edition.

[4] See previous letter.

2123. W. W. to WILLIAM PEARSON[1]

MS. Lancashire Record Office.
Pearson. LY iii. 1326.

Rydal Mount
1st Decr 1849.

Dear Mr Pearson,

Pray accept my cordial thanks for your kind remembrance of Mrs Wordsworth and myself, and for your acceptable Presents of the Print from that interesting object in Switzerland, and for the basket of apples, an article in which we were very poor. The Swill shall be returned according to your directions. You would have been thanked sooner but we did not receive the Basket of Apples Untill this morning. My Sister joins Mrs W. and me in the best good wishes of the approaching season. I need not say how happy we should be in seeing you and Mrs Pearson at any time. We are all in good health, and very sorry to hear that it has not been so with you, and the more so because winter has yet a long course to run. With every kind and good wish I remain,

my dear Friend
faithfully yours
William Wordsworth

2124. W. W. to WILLIAM CHARLES LAKE[2]

MS. untraced.
Memorials of William Charles Lake, ed. Katharine Lake, 1901, p. 174.

Rydal Mount, December 3,
1849.

My dear Mr Lake,

It gives me much pleasure to learn that you have such encouragement to become a candidate for the important office of

[1] Of Borderside. This letter is among the family papers of the late Sir Cuthbert Grundy. Attached to it is a note by Sir Cuthbert: 'It was through his wife Anne Greenhow (my mother's sister) whose mother (*née* Ralph) was a schoolfriend of Wordsworth's sister Dorothy, that uncle became acquainted with Wordsworth.'

[2] William Charles Lake (1817–97), educated at Rugby under Arnold (see L. 1657 above), and lifelong friend of A. P. Stanley: Fellow of Balliol (1838), unsuccessful candidate for the headmastership of Rugby (1849), rector of Huntspill, Somerset (1859), and Dean of Durham, 1869–94.

the Mastership of Rugby, and I heartily wish that you may succeed, both for the sake of the school and on your own account. I am induced to express this wish from the opinions I have had frequent opportunities of gathering, and the knowledge of your qualities both intellectual and moral, which appear to me *eminently* to fit you for such an office. It gave me pleasure to learn that you consider yourself so much indebted to my writings. I saw Mrs Arnold and her daughters at our chapel yesterday, all in good health. Mrs Wordsworth joins with me in best wishes for your health and welfare. Believe me, ever faithfully yours,

William Wordsworth

2125. W. W. to UNKNOWN CORRESPONDENT

MS. Historical Society of Pennsylvania.
David Bonnell Green, 'Two Wordsworth Letters', NQ cc (Nov. 1955), 489–90.

24th Decr 1849
Rydal Mount
Ambleside

My Dear Sir,

Pray accept my thanks for your remembrance of me at this season. The celery seed which you kindly sent has been put into the hands of my man-servant who will have it sown and will take care of it.

I am glad to have the account which you give of Mr Justice Talfourd. He will I am sure do credit to himself in his high office.

With much pleasure I return your good wishes—As to my own family you will be sorry to hear that some time ago we lost our only surviving Daughter—a most severe affliction to us. She was the third of our five children that have been taken from us by death. But we all are born to feel in some way or other that this is a world of trials. Believe me my dear Sir faithfully your much obliged

Wm Wordsworth

2126. W. W. to ISABELLA FENWICK

MS. WL. Hitherto unpublished.

Rydal Mount
2 Jan. 1850

Pray accept my thanks, beloved Friend for your Christmas Box which I could not but receive with a sad heart.

Today we are to dine at Mr Quillinans;[1] a trial which I feel that I am unable to bear as with due submission to God's Will I ought to do. May He have mercy upon me, and upon the Mother of Her whom we have lost. Our son John is with us for the Week; his three Sons being at Workington Hall. We hear from the Master[2] of William and Charles that they are making progress in their learning. As John is not likely to turn out a Scholar we wish to find some *un*classical School whither he may be sent, in order to prepare Him for any other way of life which may be open to us for Him.

Mr Robinson, as you probably may have heard, has been prevented by indisposition from paying us his customary Christmas visit; this is a great disappointment to us. We look for a visit from W^m^ shortly. Mr Carter is at present with him. Hannah Cookson has been so kind as to be our Inmate for some time. She is a very amiable Person, and endeared to me on Dora's account. My poor Sister is as well as usual[3] and thanks you for kind remembrance of us. She comes down-stairs to us almost every evening. We are thankful for any tidings which you give us of all your Relatives and Friends. And with the best wishes of the holy season I remain ever most faithfully yours

William Wordsworth

[1] See Morley, ii. 715. The party at E. Q.'s included Matthew Arnold and his wife.

[2] Of Sedbergh.

[3] Mrs. Arnold had reported to Lady Richardson on 13 Oct. 1849: 'I went to the Mount and there was poor Miss W. the sole representative. She was better than usual, and able to go back a little to old times, and said how good her brother had been to her, and how William had been the especial favourite. She talked too of his "Tintern Abbey" and said how fond Coleridge had been of it, and then she gave a tribute to *him* as I have heard her do before, showing how strong an impression his greatness and attaching qualities had left even on her enfeebled mind.' (*WL MSS.*)

2127. W. W. to UNKNOWN CORRESPONDENT[1]

MS. untraced.
LY iii. 1327.

Rydal Mount 18th Jan^ry 1850

Dear Madam,

Your kind Present, the Print of her Majesty, was received at Rydal this morning, and Mrs Wordsworth unites with me in returning thanks for this Memorial, such it will be to us, of your Visit; which we hope may be repeated; and that you will approve of the position which her Majesty occupies under our humble roof—Will your Ladyship be so kind as to inform the Gentleman who forwarded the Print (we have unfortunately mislaid his address) of the safe arrival. He was anxious to hear about it; and will you take the trouble to let him know that all of us in the family are much pleased with the Work.

I have the honor to be your Ladyship's much obliged

Wm Wordsworth

2128. W. W. to ROBERT PERCEVAL GRAVES

Address: The Revd R. P. Graves, Bowness.
Endorsed: Feb. 9/50. Condolence on my mother's death.
MS. Lilly Library, Indiana University.
London Mercury, vi (1922), 401.

Rydal Mount
Saturday morning. [9 Feb. 1850]

My dear Mr Graves,

Mrs Wordsworth unite[s] with me in sincere condolence upon the loss which you and Mrs Graves have sustained in the decease of your good and affectionate Mother. Her lively manner seemed to me to promise a protracted earthly existence, but it has pleased God to ordain it otherwise; and resignation to his will is never wanting when true Faith is vouchsafed. And this through the divine mercy, you, I doubt not, will be permitted to feel.

[1] Probably one of Queen Victoria's ladies-in-waiting.

Believe me to remain my dear Mr Graves with the best of good wishes faithfully

Yours
Wm Wordsworth

Turn over

We were thankful to receive from your own hand an assurance that both yourself and Mrs Graves were in the way of amendment.

2129. W. W. to ROBERT WESTALL[1]

MS. Alan G Hill. Hitherto unpublished.

[*In M. W.'s hand*]

Rydal Mount
Mar: 6 1850

Dear Sir,

I return (with a few inaccuracies corrected) the Memoir which I have found very interesting.

Many of the notices I have heard your late dear Father relate by this Fire-side in his modest manner; with us he was always a welcome visitant: and I have often had the pleasure of meeting him at the house of Mr Southey, who, like myself, esteemed him highly.

His Delineations of this Country must always be valued by those who visit it and wish to carry away faithful Portraitures of its beautiful Scenery.

I should have been glad if my recollection had permitted me with ability to be of further service to you in this work of filial love.

With kind remembrances from Mrs W. and myself to your dear Mother

I remain sincerely your's
[*signed*] William Wordsworth

[1] Son of William Westall the artist (see *MY* ii. 362, 510, 522; pt. ii, L. 636; pt. iii, L. 1048), who had died at St. John's Wood on 22 Jan. His son's *Memoir* was published in the *Art Journal* (1850), p. 104.

2130. W. W. to ROBERT PERCEVAL GRAVES

Endorsed: Mr Wordsworth March 8/50.
MS. Harvard University Library.
LY ii. 1327.

Rydal Mount, 8th March 1850

My dear Mr Graves,

I have just received your Letter. It gives me great pleasure to hear that your health is improving; but we much regret that you do not give the same favorable Report of Mrs Graves. Though I am not versed in music, I can have no possible objection to receive the honor intended to be conferred upon me by your Friend.

Mrs W. and I are glad to hear of the well doing of Madame Ranke.[1]

With kind remembrances to Mrs Graves in which Mrs W. unites, I remain my dear Sir, faithfully yours

William Wordsworth

2131. W. W. to JOHN PRINGLE NICHOL[2]

MS. Cornell. Hitherto unpublished.

Rydal Mount
15th March 1850

Mr Wordsworth feels himself much obliged to Professor Nichol for this valuable Book, upon the Architecture of the Heavenly Bodies—a subject that cannot but be interesting to every one.

Should Profr. Nichol come into this neighbourhood, it would give Mr Wordsworth much pleasure to see him at Rydal Mount.[3]

[1] Graves's sister.

[2] See L. 2081 above. *The Architecture of the Heavens*, 1838, the first of Nichol's popular manuals of astronomy, went through seven editions in seven years.

[3] This is W. W.'s last known letter. He had been taken ill the previous day and pleurisy supervened by the 20th, but the family remained hopeful until the end of the month. '. . . Having just left Mr. W.'s bedside,' E. Q. wrote to I. F. on the 26th, 'I can give you the very best report we have had yet to give. Mr. Green, who is not hasty to give an opinion told me he had no longer any fear of him. . . .Mr. W. was very cheerful, and would (contrary to his wont) have talked more than might be good for him—asked about politics, talked of the Gorham case. . .' (*MS. Bookseller's Catalogue*). But W. W. took a turn for the worse in the

first week of April (see *MW*, pp. 317–8), and thereafter all hope of recovery was lost. He died on the 23rd. 'We had known for two or three days, at least, that there was no hope,' E. Q. wrote to Sara Coleridge, 'but we were led to believe that the end was not as yet. At twelve o'clock this day, however, he passed away, very very quietly. Mrs. Wordsworth is quite resigned; there is always some sweetening of the bitterest cup; it was expected that he would linger, perhaps for some weeks, and that his sufferings would be extreme. But the mercy of God has shortened the agony, and we fondly hope that he did not suffer much pain . . . He remained to the last in the same quiet state, never moving; yet as this had been the case so long . . . it was by no means supposed that the last hour was so near.' (*WL MSS.*). See also Morley, ii. 724–6; *HCR* ii. 696–7, and Mrs. Humphry Ward, *A Writer's Recollections*, 1918, p. 80. The course of W. W.'s last illness may be followed in Jemima Q.'s Diary (*WL MSS.*), extracts from which are published in *Mem.* ii. 504 ff.

2132. D. W. to M. W.[1]

MS. WL. Hitherto unpublished.

October 22nd 1853

My dearest Sister,

I have had a good night so I think I will write. The weather was rough. I was in bed all day. I am well today. My love to Miss Fenwick and Miss Jane[2]—love to Hanna.[3]

Dorothy Wordsworth.

Mrs Pearson is very poorly and the Doctors say she cannot live. We have got a cow and very good milk she gives. I only wish you were here to have some of it.

Thomas Flick is a little better and we are all quite fit. Mary Fisher's Sister is just dead.[4]

[1] M. W. was staying with C. W. jnr. in London, and visiting the now infirm I. F. at Henry Taylor's, before going on with H. C. R. to see Mrs. Clarkson at Playford.

[2] M. W.'s granddaughter, soon to become Mrs. Kennedy.

[3] M. W.'s maid.

[4] This is D. W.'s last recorded letter. Under M. W.'s care she outlived her brother by five years, dying on 25 Jan. 1855. '. . .Notwithstanding the void that must henceforth remain at my heart,' M. W. wrote to C. W. jnr. and his wife soon afterwards, 'I shall ever feel thankful for the Almighty's goodness for having spared me to be the Solitary Lingerer, rather than the beloved Sufferer now laid to rest, and whose restless Spirit I humbly trust is now among the Blessed . . .' (*MW*, p. 353). M. W., almost blind but alert to the end, survived four years more, dying on 17 Jan. 1859 (see Morley, ii. 827).

INDEX